Salesforce Lightning Platform Enterprise Architecture

Third Edition

Architect and deliver packaged applications that cater to enterprise business needs

Andrew Fawcett

BIRMINGHAM - MUMBAI

Salesforce Lightning Platform Enterprise Architecture
Third Edition

Copyright © 2019 Packt Publishing

All rights reserved. No part of this book may be reproduced, stored in a retrieval system, or transmitted in any form or by any means, without the prior written permission of the publisher, except in the case of brief quotations embedded in critical articles or reviews.

Every effort has been made in the preparation of this book to ensure the accuracy of the information presented. However, the information contained in this book is sold without warranty, either express or implied. Neither the author, nor Packt Publishing or its dealers and distributors, will be held liable for any damages caused or alleged to have been caused directly or indirectly by this book.

Packt Publishing has endeavored to provide trademark information about all of the companies and products mentioned in this book by the appropriate use of capitals. However, Packt Publishing cannot guarantee the accuracy of this information.

Commissioning Editor: Richa Tripathi
Acquisition Editor: Alok Dhuri
Content Development Editor: Ruvika Rao
Technical Editor: Romy Dias
Copy Editor: Safis Editing
Project Coordinator: Francy Puthiry
Proofreader: Safis Editing
Indexer: Priyanka Dhadke
Senior Editor: Storm Mann
Production Designer: Joshua Misquitta

First published: September 2014
Second edition: March 2017
Third edition: November 2019

Production reference: 2230120

Published by Packt Publishing Ltd.
Livery Place
35 Livery Street
Birmingham
B3 2PB, UK.

ISBN 978-1-78995-671-9

www.packtpub.com

Packt.com

Subscribe to our online digital library for full access to over 7,000 books and videos, as well as industry leading tools to help you plan your personal development and advance your career. For more information, please visit our website.

Why subscribe?

- Spend less time learning and more time coding with practical eBooks and Videos from over 4,000 industry professionals

- Improve your learning with Skill Plans built especially for you

- Get a free eBook or video every month

- Fully searchable for easy access to vital information

- Copy and paste, print, and bookmark content

Did you know that Packt offers eBook versions of every book published, with PDF and ePub files available? You can upgrade to the eBook version at www.packt.com and as a print book customer, you are entitled to a discount on the eBook copy. Get in touch with us at customercare@packtpub.com for more details.

At www.packt.com, you can also read a collection of free technical articles, sign up for a range of free newsletters, and receive exclusive discounts and offers on Packt books and eBooks.

Foreword

At Dreamforce 2016, I was delighted to introduce a new, modern approach to developing apps on the Salesforce Lightning Platform that we call Salesforce DX (DX is short for Developer Experience). At its core, Salesforce DX has a number of core principles that we stay committed to today. Developers can:

- Drive all development from source code. Although you're not required to use version control for all your activities, we fully support it and even encourage it.
- Easily create (and delete) the environments you use for development and testing. Advances with scratch orgs, and some of the recent work that allows you to create sandboxes through the command-line interface, give you more control as a developer over the environments you use to build apps.
- Work better together as a team. Let's face it, having a bunch of people working together in one Sandbox or Developer Edition org can be difficult. We've focused on tooling and services to make it easier to let everyone work together in ways that don't impact your productivity and, in fact, improve it.
- Modularize your code (and even deploy it as a package, should you choose). This book goes into great detail regarding the many reasons why you might want to modularize your code.
- Use open standards and familiar tools for your development. We shifted away from using proprietary standards and tooling to make it easier for you to use tools and approaches you already know and use today.
- Easily implement continuous delivery. We know that there's a direct correlation between how often developers ship their code on the Lightning Platform and the long-term success they have. Salesforce DX makes it easier for developers to continually ship their code.

All of these principles come together to significantly change and improve the way developers can come together and build applications on the Lightning Platform.

Shortly before the launch of Salesforce DX, I bought a book called *Force.com Enterprise Architecture* by Andrew Fawcett. I hadn't yet met Andrew, but I knew of him through his reputation in the community. I planned to go through it from cover to cover, and apply everything Andrew wrote about in the context of the new tools and new approach to building applications on what was then the Force.com (now Lightning) Platform. Not only did I find it to be an excellent book, I learned a few things about the platform I didn't already know. I also found a bunch of issues with our tooling that I filed as bugs to be resolved before launch. Those who've built products know that one of the best gifts you can get is reproducible bugs. Finding and squashing bugs is a delightful process! (Incidentally, I use Trailhead today the same way, using new trails as opportunities to test our tooling and continually looking for ways to improve.)

I first met Andrew during a panel for analysts at the TrailheaDX Conference in June 2017. Adrian Kunzle (EVP of Platform at the time) and I spoke to analysts about the transformative nature of Salesforce DX. Some of our key pilot and launch partners joined us to share their own stories and insights. At the time, Andrew was the CTO for FinancialForce, a great partner that provides ERP and other products on Salesforce as well as an active participant in our early previews and pilots. I gained several insights from that panel that I believe are worth sharing.

First, there is no question that Andrew is the author of the definitive book on how to approach enterprise architecture with Salesforce. His depth of expertise and familiarity with building on the platform are unequaled. All the analysts and Salesforce employees were impressed by Andrew's ability to walk through the implications of Salesforce DX in the context of building apps.

Second, there's no one more passionate about the power of app development using the Lightning Platform. Having known Andrew now for several years, I've found there are two things that get him incredibly excited. The first is Lego, particularly if there is any kind of robotics or automation involved. The second is building apps on the Lightning Platform. Andrew literally gets giddy when it comes to explaining, teaching, and coaching people on how to build apps on the Lightning Platform. This passion and excitement comes through in this book and will inspire you with what you can build.

And finally, when I met Andrew, I knew I wanted to work with him. While you can't choose your family, you can often choose the people you work with. Andrew not only had the experience needed to continue to evolve and modernize the Lightning Platform in the years to come, but I knew he had the passion and commitment to be an amazing champion of our customers and partners along the way. And I have to say that it's been one of the great pleasures of my career to work with Andrew for the last couple of years.

What you have in your hands is an amazing learning resource that has evolved over the years. With its recent updates and improvements, it's become an essential tool to successfully build enterprise apps on the Lightning Platform. I'm confident that you'll be building amazing applications in no time by learning from Andrew's experience, and the recent updates that incorporate the tools and approaches made available by advances in Salesforce developer tooling.

Wade Wegner

SVP of Product at Salesforce

Contributors

About the author

Andrew Fawcett has over 25 years of experience holding several software development-related roles with a focus around enterprise-level product architecture. He is experienced in managing all aspects of the software development life cycle across various technology platforms, frameworks, industry design patterns, and methodologies.

He is currently a VP, Product Management, and a Salesforce Certified Platform Developer II at Salesforce.com. He is responsible for several key platform features and emergent products for Salesforce.com. He is an avid blogger, open source contributor and project owner, and an experienced speaker. He loves watching movies, Formula 1 motor racing, and building Lego! You can find him on Twitter at `@andyinthecloud`.

> *I would like to thank my wife, Sarah, for supporting me in writing this book, giving up our weekends, and encouraging me. Also, thank you for the endless supply of tea and biscuits when needed. When I needed to stretch my legs and take a break, our faithful French Bulldog, Lilo, was always happy to take me for a walk or play ball as well!*

About the reviewers

Jan Vandevelde is a Salesforce MVP, speaker, trainer, and blogger, and a Senior Salesforce Consultant at Salesforce Platinum Partner 4C. He is based in Belgium. He has been working on the Force.com platform since 2009. Currently, he is working as a Salesforce Consultant and is a regular contributor to the Trailblazer Community.

He has 15 certifications in Salesforce. He works on all aspects of Salesforce and is an expert in data migration, configuration, customization, and development, with his main expertise being in Sales Cloud, Service Cloud, Community Cloud, and Salesforce Quote-to-Cash. He is the leader of the Belgium User Group of Salesforce. He is one of the board members of Europe's community-led event, YeurDreamin.

John M. Daniel has been working in the technology sector for over 20 years. During that time, he has worked in a variety of technologies and project roles. Currently, he serves as the Director of Platform Architecture at Rootstock Cloud ERP, a leading cloud-based ERP solution that is native to the Salesforce Platform. He is a Salesforce MVP and holds multiple Salesforce certifications. He is currently working toward becoming a Certified Technical Architect. He loves to work on open source projects such as Force-DI, AT4DX, and the DomainBuilder framework. He has been a technical reviewer for *Mastering Salesforce DevOps*, *Learning Apex Programming*, and *Apex Design Patterns*. He co-leads his local Salesforce Developers User Group and can be found on Twitter at `@ImJohnMDaniel`.

> *I would like to thank my wife, Allison, for always giving me the freedom to pursue my interests.*

Michael Salem is a member of the emerging technologies team at Salesforce. They're a group of architects who are focused on emerging areas of cloud computing such as big data (and data architecture patterns at scale), computer vision, natural language processing, IoT, and blockchain. They help senior technology leaders understand where emerging technology can fit within their enterprise architecture and roadmap.

Before this, Michael held technology-focused roles working with Salesforce technology at a start-up, as well as working as a lead solution architect for client implementations with Model Metrics (acquired by Salesforce).

Michael holds an MBA with a focus on technology and has been working in technology for a decade.

> *I'd like to thank my wife, Leah, for being my best friend, for always making me laugh, for going on adventures with me, for celebrating the little things, and for always supporting my goals.*

Mohith Shrivastava has been building and architecting Salesforce applications since 2011, after he graduated from the National Institute of Engineering, Mysore.

He is currently a Salesforce MVP and holds multiple Salesforce certifications. He is an active contributor to the Salesforce Stack Exchange community.

Mohith has authored *Learning Salesforce Einstein* and *Salesforce Essentials for Administrators* for Packt. In his leisure time, he loves exploring the latest technologies and spending time with his family.

> *I would like to thank my parents for nurturing and helping me in all possible ways and allowing me to be where I am today. I'd like to thank my wife, Nisha, for her never-ending love and support.*

Searching for authors like you

If you're interested in becoming an author for Packt, please visit `authors.packtpub.com` and apply today. We have worked with thousands of developers and tech professionals, just like you, to help them share their insight with the global tech community. You can make a general application, apply for a specific hot topic that we are recruiting an author for, or submit your own idea.

Table of Contents

Preface   1
Chapter 1: Building and Publishing Your Application   7
  Introducing Salesforce DX   8
  Required organizations   9
  Introducing the book's sample application   11
  Package types and benefits   13
    The features and benefits of managed packages   14
  Creating your first managed package   15
    Setting and registering your package namespace   16
    Creating the package and assigning it to the namespace   17
    Adding components to the package   19
    Extension packages   21
  Package platform feature dependencies   23
    Release and beta packages   24
    Optional package dependencies   25
      Dynamic bindings   25
      Extension packages   26
  Supporting package upgradability   26
    Managing package ancestry   26
    Developing in scratch orgs containing ancestry information   28
  Becoming a Salesforce partner and the benefits of doing so   29
    Security review and benefits   30
    Getting the best out of the Partner Community   32
    Creating test and demo orgs via the Environment Hub   34
  Introduction to AppExchange and listings   34
  Installing and testing your package   36
    Automating package installation   38
  Understanding how to license your package   40
    The Licenses tab and managing customer licenses   42
    The Feature Parameters tab and managing features   43
    The Subscribers tab   44
    The Subscriber Overview page   45
    How licensing is enforced in the subscriber org   46
  Providing support   46
  Customer metrics   48
  Trialforce and Test Drive   48
    Distributing Salesforce Connected Apps   49
  Summary   50

Chapter 2: Leveraging Platform Features — 51
Packaging and upgradable components — 52
- Custom Fields – picklist values — 53
- Global picklists — 53
- Automating upgrade tasks with the Metadata API — 54

Understanding Custom Field features — 56
- Default field values — 56
- Encrypted fields — 58
  - Special considerations for Platform Encryption — 59
- Lookup options, filters, and layouts — 60
- Rollup summaries and limits — 66

Understanding the available security features — 68
- Functional security — 69
  - Your code and security review considerations — 73
- Data security — 74
  - Your code and security review considerations — 77

Platform APIs — 77
- Considerations for working well with the platform's APIs — 79

Localization and translation — 80
- Localization — 81
- Translation — 81

Building customizable user interfaces — 82
- Layouts — 83
- Customizing Lightning Components and Visualforce pages — 84
- Lightning App Builder and Components — 84

Email customization with email templates — 84
Process Builder, Workflow, and Flow — 85
Social features and mobile — 86
Creating and testing a new package version — 92
Summary — 93

Chapter 3: Application Storage — 95
Mapping out end user storage requirements — 96
Understanding the different storage types — 96
- Data storage — 98
  - Columns versus rows — 98
  - Visualizing your object model — 99
  - Considerations for configuration data — 101
    - Custom Metadata Type storage — 103
    - Custom Settings storage — 107
    - Big Objects storage — 108
- File storage — 109
- Record identification, uniqueness, and auto numbering — 109
  - Unique and external ID fields — 110
  - Auto Number fields — 110
    - Subscribers customizing the Auto Number Display Format — 113

Record relationships	113
Reusing the existing Standard Objects	115
Importing and exporting data	116
Salesforce DX CLI Data Import and Export	116
Salesforce Data Import Wizard	120
Options for replicating data	122
External data sources	123
Creating a new FormulaForce package version	124
Summary	126
Chapter 4: Apex Execution and Separation of Concerns	127
Execution contexts	128
Exploring execution contexts	128
Execution context and state	130
Platform Cache	131
Execution context and security	134
Execution context transaction management	135
Apex governors and namespaces	135
Namespaces and governor scope	136
Deterministic and non-deterministic governors	138
Key governors for Apex package developers	139
Where is Apex used?	140
Separation of concerns	144
Apex code evolution	145
Separating concerns in Apex	145
Separation of concerns in Lightning Components	146
Separation of concerns in an LWC	147
Separation of concerns in a Lightning Aura Component	148
Execution context logic versus application logic concerns	149
Improving incremental code reuse	151
Patterns of Enterprise Application Architecture	153
The Service layer	154
The domain model layer	154
The Data Mapper (selector) layer	155
Introducing the FinancialForce.com Apex Commons library	155
Unit testing versus system testing	155
Packaging the code	156
Summary	158
Chapter 5: Application Service Layer	159
Introducing the Service layer pattern	160
Implementation of design guidelines	161
Naming conventions	162
Bulkification	165
Sharing rules enforcement	166

Defining and passing data	168
Considerations when using SObject in the Service layer interface	170
Transaction management	170
Compound services	171
A quick guideline checklist	172
Handling DML with the Unit Of Work pattern	**173**
Without a Unit Of Work	176
With Unit Of Work	177
The Unit Of Work scope	180
Unit Of Work special considerations	181
Services calling services	**182**
Contract-Driven Development	**186**
Testing the Service layer	**192**
Mocking the Service layer	192
Calling the Service layer	**193**
From Lightning Component Apex Controllers	193
From Visualforce Apex Controllers	194
From the Apex Scheduler	195
Updating the FormulaForce package	196
Summary	**196**
Chapter 6: Application Domain Layer	**197**
Introducing the Domain layer pattern	**198**
Encapsulating an object's behavior in code	198
Interpreting the Domain layer	199
Domain classes in Apex compared to other platforms	200
Implementing design guidelines	**201**
Naming conventions	202
Bulkification	204
Defining and passing data	204
Transaction management	204
Domain class template	**205**
Implementing Domain Trigger logic	**207**
Routing trigger events to Domain class methods	207
Enforcing object security	209
Default behavior	209
Overriding the default behavior	210
Apex Trigger event handling	210
Defaulting field values on insert	211
Validation on insert	211
Validation on update	212
Implementing custom Domain logic	**213**
Object-oriented programming	**214**
Creating a compliance application framework	214
An Apex Interface example	215
Step 5 – Defining a generic service	216

Step 6 – Implementing the Domain class interface	217
Step 7 – The Domain class Factory pattern	218
Step 8 – Implementing a generic service	219
Step 9 – Using the generic service from a generic controller	221
Generic Compliance Verification UI with a Lightning Component	221
Generic Compliance Verification UI with Visualforce	224
Summarizing the implementation of the compliance framework	225

Testing the Domain layer — 229
Unit testing — 229
Test methods using DML and SOQL — 230
Test methods using the Domain class methods — 231
Calling the Domain layer — 233
Service layer interactions — 234
Domain layer interactions — 235
Updating the FormulaForce package — 237
Summary — 238

Chapter 7: Application Selector Layer — 239
Introducing the Selector layer pattern — 240
Implementing design guidelines — 241
Sharing conventions — 241
Naming conventions — 242
Bulkification — 243
Record order consistency — 243
Querying fields consistently — 244
The Selector class template — 246
Implementing the standard query logic — 248
Standard features of the Selector base class — 249
Enforcing object and field-level security — 250
Default behavior — 250
Overriding the default behavior — 250
Ordering — 252
Field Sets — 253
Multi-Currency — 254
Implementing the custom query logic — 255
A basic custom Selector method — 256
A custom Selector method with subselect — 256
A custom Selector method with related fields — 258
A custom Selector method with a custom dataset — 260
Combining Apex data types with SObject types — 263
SOSL and aggregate SOQL queries — 264
Introducing the Selector factory — 264
SelectorFactory methods — 265
Writing tests and the Selector layer — 266
Updating the FormulaForce package — 267
Summary — 267

Chapter 8: Building User Interfaces — 269
What devices should you target? — 269
Leveraging standard UIs and custom UIs — 270
Why consider Visualforce over Lightning Framework? — 273
Lightning Component programming frameworks — 273
Leveraging the Salesforce standard UIs and tools — 274
Overriding standard Salesforce UI actions — 275
Combining standard UIs with custom UIs — 277
Embedding a custom UI in a standard UI — 277
Embedding a standard UI in a custom UI — 280
Extending the Salesforce standard UIs — 281
Lightning Components — 281
Visualforce pages — 281
Generating downloadable content — 282
Generating printable content — 284
Overriding the page language — 285
Client-server communication — 286
Client communication options — 286
API governors and availability — 288
Database transaction scope and client calls — 289
Offline support — 290
Managing limits — 290
Object- and field-level security — 291
Enforcing security in Lightning Web Components — 292
Enforcing security in Visualforce — 295
Managing performance and response times — 300
Lightning Tools to monitor size and response times — 300
Lightning Tools to monitor locker service performance — 302
Visualforce view state size — 303
Considerations for managing large component trees — 303
Using the Service layer and database access — 304
Considerations for client-side logic and Service layer logic — 305
When should I use JavaScript for database access? — 306
Considerations for using JavaScript libraries — 307
Custom Publisher Actions — 308
Creating websites and communities — 309
Mobile application strategy — 309
Custom reporting and the Analytics API — 310
Updating the FormulaForce package — 311
Summary — 311

Chapter 9: User Interfaces with Lightning Framework — 313
Building a basic Lightning UI — 314
Introduction to the Lightning Design System — 316
Building your first component — 317

How does Lightning differ from other UI frameworks?	319
Lightning architecture	**320**
Containers	320
Introducing the Racing Overview Lightning app	322
Lightning Experience and Salesforce Mobile	323
Components	325
Separation of concerns	325
Encapsulation during development	326
Component markup (.html)	327
Component controller (.js)	328
Component CSS (.css)	329
Component metadata (.js-meta.xml) and component SVG (.svg) files	330
Component documentation (.auradoc)	331
Component tests (test subfolder)	332
Sharing JavaScript Code between components	332
Enforcing encapsulation and security at runtime	333
Expressing behavior	334
Access control	334
Methods	335
Child component events	336
Inter-component events	338
Platform namespaces	340
Base components	342
Data Service	342
Object-oriented programming	343
Object-level and field-level security	344
FormulaForce Lightning components	**344**
RaceStandings component	346
RaceCalendar component	349
RaceResults component	351
RaceSetup component	354
Making components customizable	**359**
Integrating with Lightning Experience	**362**
Using components on Lightning pages and tabs	366
Integrating with Lightning Flow	**366**
Integrating with Lightning Communities	**369**
Exposing components with Lightning Out	**370**
Updating the FormulaForce package	**371**
Summary	**371**
Chapter 10: Providing Integration and Extensibility	**373**
Reviewing your integration and extensibility needs	**374**
Defining the Developer X persona	374
Understanding and managing versioning	375
Versioning the API definition	375
Versioning the API definition of the Salesforce APIs	376
Versioning the API functionality	377
Translation and localization	378

[vii]

Terminology and platform alignment	380
What are your integration use cases?	380
Developer X calling your APIs on-platform	381
Developer X calling your APIs off-platform	382
SOAP versus REST	382
The OpenAPI Specification and Swagger	382
Developer X calling your APIs asynchronously through platform events	383
What are your application's extensibility use cases?	386
Standard platform APIs for integration	**387**
Apex Callable interface API	388
Application integration APIs	**389**
Providing Apex application APIs	389
Calling an application API from Apex	392
Modifying and depreciating the application API	394
Versioning Apex API definitions	394
Versioning Apex API behavior	397
Providing RESTful application APIs	398
Key aspects of being RESTful	399
What are your application resources?	399
Mapping HTTP methods	401
Providing Apex REST application APIs	402
Calling your Apex REST application APIs	404
Versioning Apex REST application APIs	405
Behavior versioning	405
Definition versioning	405
Exposing platform events	**407**
Exposing Lightning Components	**409**
Extending Process Builder and Flow	**410**
Versioning invocable methods	413
Alignment with platform extensibility features	**413**
Extending application logic with Apex interfaces	**414**
The MuleSoft platform	**418**
Summary	**418**
Chapter 11: Asynchronous Processing and Big Data Volumes	**421**
Creating a RaceData object with data	**422**
Using Apex to generate synthetic Race Data	424
Indexes, being selective, and query optimization	**425**
Standard and custom indexes	426
Ensuring queries leverage indexes	428
Factors affecting the use of indexes	428
Profiling queries	430
Skinny tables	435
Handling large result sets	436
Processing 50k maximum result sets in Apex	436
Processing unlimited result sets in Apex	437
Generating more Race Data	439

Leveraging Visualforce and Apex read-only mode	440
Processing unlimited result sets using the Salesforce APIs	441

Handling billions of records with big objects — 441
- Salesforce and NoSQL stores — 442
- Using a big object for race lap history — 443
- Importing big object data — 445
  - Using Data Loader to import data into a big object — 446
- Options to query big object data — 448
  - Synchronous big object SOQL queries — 448
  - Asynchronous big object SOQL queries — 451

Asynchronous processing — 454
- Asynchronous user experience design considerations — 455
- Asynchronous processing with workers and jobs — 458
  - Implementing a worker with @future — 458
  - Implementing a worker with Queueables — 459
  - Implementing a job with Batch Apex — 460
    - Performance of Batch Apex jobs — 465
    - Using external references in Apex DML — 466
- Asynchronous processing with platform events — 467
  - Using high-scale platform events to stream data ingestion — 469
  - Using Change Data Capture platform events to compute data — 471
  - Sending race data telemetry events through the Salesforce DX CLI — 472

Volume testing — 473
Summary — 474

Chapter 12: Unit Testing — 477
Comparing unit testing and integration testing — 478
- The testing pyramid on the Lightning Platform — 480
- Introducing unit testing — 481

Introduction to unit testing with Apex — 483
- Deciding what to test for and what not to test for in a unit test — 486
- Constructor dependency injection — 487
- Implementing unit tests with CDI and mocking — 489
- Other dependency injection approaches — 492
- Benefits of dependency injection frameworks — 494

Writing unit tests with the Apex Stub API — 495
- Implementing mock classes using Test.StubProvider — 495
- Creating dynamic stubs for mocking classes — 496
- Mocking examples with the Apex Stub API — 497
- Considerations when using the Apex Stub API — 499
- Using the Apex Stub API with mocking frameworks — 499
  - Understanding how ApexMocks works — 501
  - ApexMocks Matchers — 504

ApexMocks and Apex Enterprise Patterns — 504
- Unit testing a controller method — 504
- Unit testing a Service method — 505
- Unit testing a Domain method — 507

[ix]

Table of Contents

      Unit testing a Selector method   508
  Unit testing with Lightning Web Components   508
    Introduction to unit testing with Lightning Web Components   510
      Validating that the driver list is correctly bound to the table   512
      Validating that the selected drivers are sent to the server   514
  Summary   519

Chapter 13: Source Control and Continuous Integration   521
  Development workflow and infrastructure   522
    Creating and preparing your scratch orgs   523
    Understanding the developer workflow   525
  Developing with source control   528
    Populating your source control repository   529
    Deploying the code from source control   533
      Developing in scratch orgs with a namespace   534
      Leveraging the Salesforce REST APIs from the SFDX CLI and custom plugins   534
    Updating your source control repository   537
      Controlling what gets pulled down locally from your org   538
      Managing local files and committing to source control   538
  Hooking up continuous integration   541
    Using continuous integration to maintain code health   541
    Introducing the Jenkinsfile for CI   542
      Installing, configuring, and testing a Jenkins CI server   546
      Exploring Jenkins and CI further   550
  Releasing from source control   552
  Automated regression testing   553
  Summary   554

Chapter 14: Integrating with External Services   555
  Understanding inbound and outbound integrations   556
  Managing inbound integrations   558
    Introducing Salesforce Connected Apps   559
      Node.js application using a Connected App   565
  Understanding options for outbound integrations   568
    Managing outbound connections with Named Credentials   569
      Calling outbound connections from Apex   573
      Using per-user Named Credentials   574
    Accessing external services via External Services   575
    Accessing external data seamlessly via External Objects   580
  Summary   585

Chapter 15: Adding AI with Einstein   587
  Understanding Salesforce Einstein services and products   588
  Understanding Einstein Prediction Builder   590
  Understanding Einstein Discovery   591
    Discovering insights from Formula 1 race results   592
  Understanding Einstein Platform Services   599

Summary	600
Further reading	601

Other Books You May Enjoy — 603

Index — 607

Preface

Enterprise organizations have complex processes and integration requirements that typically span multiple locations around the world. They seek out the best-in-class applications that support not only their current needs, but also those of the future. The ability to adapt an application to their practices, terminology, and integrations with other existing applications or processes is key for them. They invest as much in your application as they do in you, as the vendor capable of delivering an application strategy that will grow with them.

Throughout this book, you will be shown how to architect and support enduring applications for enterprise clients with Salesforce by exploring how to identify architecture needs and design solutions based on industry-standard patterns.

Large-scale applications require careful coding practices to keep the code base scalable. You'll learn advanced coding patterns based on industry-standard enterprise patterns and reconceive them for Lightning Platform, allowing you to get the most out of the platform and incorporate best practices from the start of your project.

As your development team grows, managing the development cycle with more robust application life cycle tools, and using approaches such as Continuous Integration, become increasingly important. There are many ways to build solutions on the Lightning Platform; this book cuts a logical path through the steps and considerations for building packaged solutions from start to finish, covering all aspects from engineering to getting it into the hands of your customers and beyond, ensuring that they get the best value possible from your Lightning Platform application.

Who this book is for

This book is aimed at Lightning Platform developers who are looking to push past Lightning Platform basics and learn how to truly discover its potential. You will find this book handy if you are looking to expand your knowledge of developing packaged ISV software and complex, scalable applications for use in enterprise businesses with the Salesforce platform. This book will enable you to know your way around Lightning Platform's non-programmatic functionality as well as Apex, and aid you in learning how to architect powerful solutions for enterprise-scale demands. If you have a background in developing inside other enterprise software ecosystems, you will find this book an invaluable resource for adopting the Lightning Platform.

Preface

What this book covers

Chapter 1, *Building and Publishing Your Application*, gets your application out to your prospects and customers using packages, AppExchange, and subscriber's support.

Chapter 2, *Leveraging Platform Features*, ensures that your application is aligned with the platform features and uses them whenever possible, which is great for productivity when building your application, but—perhaps more importantly—it ensures that your customers are also able to extend and integrate with your application further.

Chapter 3, *Application Storage*, teaches you how to model your application's data to make effective use of storage space, which can make a big difference to your customer's ongoing costs and initial decision making when choosing your application.

Chapter 4, *Apex Execution and Separation of Concerns*, explains how the platform handles requests and at what point Apex code is invoked. It is important to understand how to design your code for maximum reuse and durability.

Chapter 5, *Application Service Layer*, focuses on understanding the real heart of your application: how to design it, make it durable, and future proof it around a rapidly evolving platform using Martin Fowler's Service pattern as a template.

Chapter 6, *Application Domain Layer*, aligns Apex code typically locked away in Apex Triggers into classes more aligned with the functional purpose and behavior of your objects, using object-orientated programming (OOP) to increase reuse and streamline code and leverage Martin Fowler's Domain pattern as a template.

Chapter 7, *Application Selector Layer*, leverages SOQL to make the most out of the query engine, which can make queries complex. Using Martin Fowler's Mapping pattern as a template, this chapter illustrates a means to encapsulate queries, making them more accessible and reusable, and making their results more predictable and robust across your code base.

Chapter 8, *Building User Interfaces*, covers the concerns of an enterprise application user interface with respect to translation, localization, and customization, as well as the pros and cons of the various UI options available in the platform.

Chapter 9, *Using Interfaces with Lightning Framework*, explains the architecture of this modern framework for delivering rich client-device agnostic user experiences, from a basic application through to using component methodology to extend Lightning Experience and Salesforce1 Mobile.

Preface

Chapter 10, *Providing Integration and Extensibility*, explains how enterprise-scale applications require you to carefully consider integration with existing applications and business needs while looking to the future by designing the application with extensibility in mind.

Chapter 11, *Asynchronous Processing and Big Data Volumes*, shows that designing an application that processes massive volumes of data, either interactively or asynchronously, requires consideration in understanding your customer's volume requirements and leverages the latest platform tools and features, such as understanding the query optimizer and when to create indexes.

Chapter 12, *Unit Testing*, explores the differences and benefits of unit testing versus system testing. This aims to help you understand how to apply dependency injection and mocking techniques to write unit tests that cover more code scenarios and run faster. You will also look at leveraging practical examples of using the Apex Stub API with the ApexMocks open source library and testing client logic with the Jest open source library.

Chapter 13, *Source Control and Continuous Integration*, shows that maintaining a consistent code base across applications of scale requires careful consideration of source control and a planned approach to integration as the application is developed and implemented.

Chapter 14, *Integrating with External Services*, explores how you and your customers can extend your application securely with services and data hosted outside of the Lightning Platform, using both code and configuration tools such as Flow.

Chapter 15, *Adding AI with Einstein*, explores services and features provided by Salesforce in order for you and your customers to add AI and machine learning capabilities to your application and its data.

To get the most out of this book

In order to follow the practical examples in this book, you will need to install the Salesforce DX CLI and Salesforce Extensions for Visual Studio Code. You will also require access to a Salesforce Developer Edition Org via https://developer.salesforce.com/ and a temporary Salesforce DevHub org via https://developer.salesforce.com/promotions/orgs/dx-signup.

The following is the list of the software requirements for this book:

- Salesforce DevHub Org Trial
- Salesforce Developer Edition Org (to register your test package namespace)
- Salesforce DX CLI

- Salesforce Extensions for Visual Studio
- Salesforce Developer Console (partial usage as needed)
- GitHub Desktop client

Author disclosure

At the time of publication, Andrew Fawcett works as a VP, Product Management, within Salesforce. The statements and opinions in this book are his own and not those of Salesforce.

Download the example code files

You can download the example code files for this book from your account at `www.packt.com`. If you purchased this book elsewhere, you can visit `www.packt.com/support` and register to have the files emailed directly to you.

You can download the code files by following these steps:

1. Log in or register at `www.packt.com`.
2. Select the **SUPPORT** tab.
3. Click on **Code Downloads & Errata**.
4. Enter the name of the book in the **Search** box and follow the onscreen instructions.

Once the file is downloaded, please make sure that you unzip or extract the folder using the latest version of:

- WinRAR/7-Zip for Windows
- Zipeg/iZip/UnRarX for Mac
- 7-Zip/PeaZip for Linux

The code bundle for the book is also hosted on GitHub at `https://github.com/PacktPublishing/Salesforce-Lightning-Platform-Enterprise-Architecture-Third-Edition`. In case there's an update to the code, it will be updated on the existing GitHub repository.

We also have other code bundles from our rich catalog of books and videos available at `https://github.com/PacktPublishing/`. Check them out!

Download the color images

We also provide a PDF file that has color images of the screenshots/diagrams used in this book. You can download it here:
`https://static.packt-cdn.com/downloads/9781789956719_ColorImages.pdf`.

Conventions used

There are a number of text conventions used throughout this book.

`CodeInText`: Indicates code words in text, database table names, folder names, filenames, file extensions, pathnames, dummy URLs, user input, and Twitter handles. Here is an example: "The `--package` parameter uses the package alias as defined in the `sfdx-project.json` file to identify the package we are creating this version against."

A block of code is set as follows:

```
{
  "packageDirectories": [
  {
  "path": "force-app",
  "package": "FormulaForce App",
  "default": true
  }
```

When we wish to draw your attention to a particular part of a code block, the relevant lines or items are set in bold:

```
],
"namespace": "fforce",
"sfdcLoginUrl": "https://login.salesforce.com",
"sourceApiVersion": "45.0",
"packageAliases": {
    "FormulaForce App": "0Ho6A000000CaVxSAK"
}
```

Any command-line input or output is written as follows:

```
sfdx force:org:open
```

Bold: Indicates a new term, an important word, or words that you see on screen. For example, words in menus or dialog boxes appear in the text like this. Here is an example: "Select **System info** from the **Administration** panel."

Warnings or important notes appear like this.

Tips and tricks appear like this.

Get in touch

Feedback from our readers is always welcome.

General feedback: If you have questions about any aspect of this book, mention the book title in the subject of your message and email us at customercare@packtpub.com.

Errata: Although we have taken every care to ensure the accuracy of our content, mistakes do happen. If you have found a mistake in this book, we would be grateful if you would report this to us. Please visit www.packt.com/submit-errata, selecting your book, clicking on the Errata Submission Form link, and entering the details.

Piracy: If you come across any illegal copies of our works in any form on the internet, we would be grateful if you would provide us with the location address or website name. Please contact us at copyright@packt.com with a link to the material.

If you are interested in becoming an author: If there is a topic that you have expertise in, and you are interested in either writing or contributing to a book, please visit authors.packtpub.com.

Reviews

Please leave a review. Once you have read and used this book, why not leave a review on the site that you purchased it from? Potential readers can then see and use your unbiased opinion to make purchase decisions, we at Packt can understand what you think about our products, and our authors can see your feedback on their book. Thank you!

For more information about Packt, please visit packt.com.

Building and Publishing Your Application

The key to turning an idea into reality lies in the execution. Having the inception of an idea and getting it implemented as an application and into the hands of users is an exciting journey and one that constantly develops and evolves between you and your users. One of the great things about developing on the **Lightning Platform** is the support you get from the platform beyond the core engineering phase of the production process.

In this first chapter, we will use the declarative and **Salesforce DX** aspects of the platform to quickly build an initial version of an application that we will use throughout this book. This will give you an opportunity to get some hands-on experience with some of the packaging and installation features that are needed to *release applications* to subscribers. We will also take a look at the facilities available to *publish* your application through **Salesforce AppExchange** (equivalent to Apple's App Store), and finally, provide end user support.

We will then use this application as a basis for incrementally releasing new versions of the application throughout the chapters of this book, building on our understanding of enterprise application development. The following topics outline what we will achieve in this chapter:

- Introducing Salesforce DX
- Required organizations
- Introducing the book's sample application
- Package types and benefits
- Creating your first managed package
- Package dependencies and uploading
- Supporting package upgradability
- Introduction to AppExchange and creating listings
- Installing and testing your package

- Becoming a Salesforce partner and the benefits of doing so
- Licensing
- Supporting your application
- Customer metrics
- Trialforce and Test Drive features

Introducing Salesforce DX

Throughout this book, we will be using the **Salesforce DX** tool. Salesforce provides this tool for developers to perform many development and time-saving tasks, such as creating developer environments (known as **Scratch Orgs**), creating projects, synchronizing code with source control, creating and managing packages, and much more. In fact, it optimizes and helps you automate the entire **Application Life Cycle** (**ALM**) process for your application and package. Throughout this book, you will learn key aspects of this process, starting in this chapter.

We will dive straight into using this tool's **Command Line Interface** (**CLI**) along with an **Integrated Development Environment** (**IDE**), **Microsoft Visual Studio Code** (**VSCode**), for which Salesforce has also created many useful extensions. You do not need to be an expert in Salesforce DX to complete this book but I do recommend you take the time to complete the basic Trailhead trails: `https://trailhead.salesforce.com/en/content/learn/trails/sfdx_get_started`.

Salesforce DX brings with it the second generation of packaging technology for ISVs building on the Lightning Platform; this is known as 2GP for short. Previous editions of this book used the first generation technology (1GP). If you were to compare the experience between the two technologies, you would see that the package creation process using 2GPs is now fully automated through the CLI and requires no UI interaction. This is also very advantageous in respect of building further automation around your release pipeline, which will be covered in Chapter 13, *Source Control and Continuous Integration*. This book focuses on creating new ISV packages and not migrating between 1GP and 2GP for existing packages. You can read more about 1GP and 2GP at `https://developer.salesforce.com/docs/atlas.en-us.sfdx_dev.meta/sfdx_dev/sfdx_dev_build_and_release_your_app.htm`.

Chapter 1

Required organizations

Several Salesforce organizations are required to develop and test your application. Salesforce DX allows you to manage many of these organizations, though, in due course, as your relationship with Salesforce becomes more formal, you will have the option of accessing their **Partner Portal** website to create organizations of different types and capabilities. We will discuss this in more detail later.

It's a good idea to have some kind of naming convention to keep track of the different organizations and logins. As stated earlier, these organizations will be used only for the purposes of learning and exploring in this book:

Username	Usage	Purpose
myapp@namespace.my.com	Namespace	In this org, we will define a unique identifier for our application, called a namespace. You can think of this as a web domain as it is also unique to your application across the Salesforce service. Create this org at https://developer.salesforce.com/.
myapp@devhub.my.com	Salesforce DX	Salesforce DX requires you to first connect to an org known as the Dev Hub. This org helps Salesforce and you to co-ordinate all the orgs you need for development and testing purposes. I recommend that, for this book, you use the free 30-day trial available at https://developer.salesforce.com/promotions/orgs/dx-signup.

You will have to substitute myapp and my.com (perhaps by reusing your company domain name to avoid naming conflicts) with your own values. You should take the time to familiarize yourself with andyapp@namespace.andyinthecloud.com.

[9]

Building and Publishing Your Application

The following are other organization types that you will eventually need in order to manage the publication and licensing of your application. However, they are not needed to complete the chapters in this book:

Usage	Purpose
Production/CRM Org	Your organization may already be using this org to manage contacts, leads, opportunities, cases, and other CRM objects. Make sure that you have the complete authority to make changes, if any, to this org since this is where you run your business. If you do not have such an org, you can request one via the Partner Program website described later in this chapter by requesting (via a case) a CRM ISV org. Even if you choose to not fully adopt Salesforce for this part of your business, this type of org is still required when it comes to utilizing the licensing aspects of the platform. Eventually, when you are ready to develop your package for real, this org will also become your Salesforce DX Dev Hub. For this book, we will use a temporary Dev Hub org as described earlier.
AppExchange Publishing Org (APO)	This org is used to manage your use of AppExchange. We will discuss this in the **Introduction to AppExchange and listings** section later in this chapter. This org is actually the same Salesforce org you designate as your production org and is where you conduct your sales and support activities from.
License Management Org (LMO)	Within this organization, you can track who installs your application (as leads), the licenses you grant them, and for how long. It is recommended that this is the same org as the APO described earlier.
Trialforce Management Org (TMO) and Trialforce Source Org (TSO)	Trialforce is a way to provide orgs with your preconfigured application data so that prospective customers can try out your application before buying it. It will be discussed later in this chapter.

> Typically, the LMO and APO can be the same as your primary Salesforce production org, which allows you to track all your leads and future opportunities in the same place. This leads to the rule of *APO = LMO = production org*. Though neither of them should be your actual developer or test org, you can work with Salesforce support and your Salesforce account manager to plan and assign these orgs.

Introducing the book's sample application

For this book, we will use the world of **Formula 1** motor car racing as the basis for a packaged application that we will build together. Formula 1 is, for me, the motor sport that is equivalent to enterprise application software, due to its scale and complexity. It is also a sport that I follow. My knowledge of both of these fields helped me when building the examples that we will use.

We will refer to our application as **FormulaForce** throughout this book, though please keep in mind Salesforce's branding policies when naming your own application, as they prevent the use of the word "Force" in company or product titles.

This application will focus on the data collection aspects of races, drivers, and their many statistics, utilizing platform features to structure, visualize, and process this data in both historic and current contexts.

Run the following commands to create a Salesforce DX project for your application and create a special org known as a **scratch org** for you to perform your development work in. This org is given the alias "dev" and set as the project default. These orgs only last 7 days (by default, the maximum is 30 days) so be sure to synchronize regularly, as described later in this chapter:

```
sfdx force:project:create --projectname formulaforce
cd formulaforce
sfdx force:org:create
 --definitionfile config/project-scratch-def.json
   --setalias dev
   --setdefaultusername
code .
```

> The preceding **code** command is used as a convenience to quickly open VSCode in the current directory. From here, you can open the **Integrated Terminal** and continue to execute Salesforce DX CLI commands from within the IDE.

Building and Publishing Your Application

The `.forceIgnore` file allows you to control which aspects of the scratch org and your local files are synchronized. Later in this book, in Chapter 2, *Leveraging Platform Features*, we will cover permission sets as a means to configure security rather than using the less flexible profiles feature. In preparation for this, enter the following into the `.forceIgnore` file and save it. This stops any unwanted profile changes that you might directly or indirectly make from being synchronized with your project:

```
# Profiles
**/profiles/**
```

For this chapter, we will create some initial **Custom Objects** and Fields, as detailed in the following table. Do not worry about creating any custom tabs just yet. You can use your preferred approach for creating these initial objects. Ensure that you have opened your project's current scratch org by running the following command:

sfdx force:org:open

From within Visual Studio Code and with your project open, you can use the shortcut key combination *Cmd + Shift + P* on a Mac or *Ctrl + Shift + P* on Windows to open the Command Palette. Start typing `SFDX Open` and you will see the `SFDX: Open Default Org` command to quickly open your scratch org without typing the preceding command. You can also run other Salesforce DX commands this way, such as creating scratch orgs.

Here is a list of objects along with their field names and types:

Object	Field name and type
`Season__c`	Name (text)
`Race__c`	Name (text) Season (Master Detail Lookup to `Season`)
`Driver__c`	Name (text)
`Contestant__c`	Name (Auto Number CONTEST-{00000000}) Race (Master Detail Lookup to `Race`) Driver (Lookup to `Driver`)

The following screenshot shows the preceding objects within the **Schema Builder** tool, available under the **Setup** menu:

Chapter 1

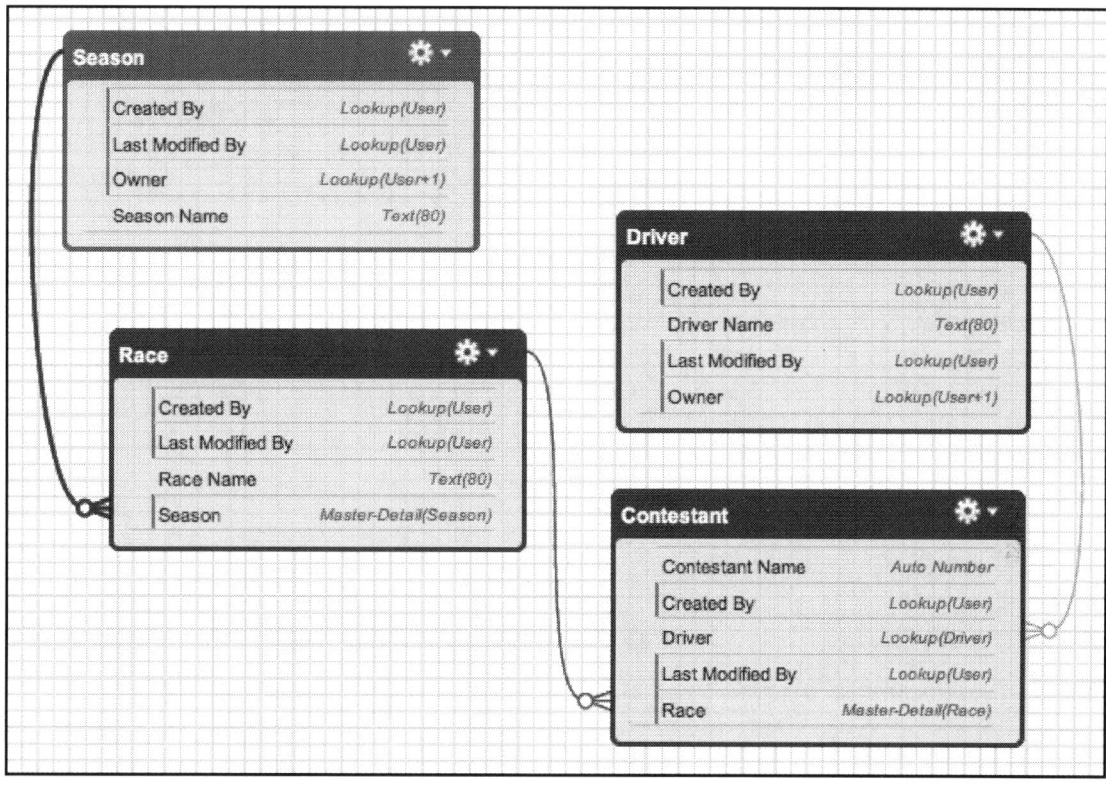

Once you have completed creating the preceding objects, you should synchronize them with your project:

```
sfdx force:source:pull
```

This is an important command when using Salesforce DX to ensure you always have the latest changes as a permanent record in file form. The entire project and the files representing your application can then be stored in source control from this point onward if desired. We will review these files further later.

Package types and benefits

A **package** is a container that holds your application components, such as Custom Objects, Apex code, Apex Triggers, Visualforce pages, Lightning Components, and so on. This makes up your application. While there are other ways to move components between Salesforce orgs, a package provides a container that you can use for your entire application or to deliver optional features by leveraging so-called **extension packages**.

Building and Publishing Your Application

Salesforce has evolved its packaging technology and now refers to its legacy packaging technology as **1GP (1st Generation Packaging)** and its latest technology as **2GP (2nd Generation Packaging)**. This book uses 2GP exclusively – keep this in mind when reviewing Salesforce documentation on the packaging.

There are two types of packages—**managed** and **unlocked**. Unlocked packages also result in the installation of components into another org; however, they can be readily modified or even deleted by the administrator of that org. While they can be used for upgrades, changes made in an installation org will be overwritten. Given these attributes, they are not particularly ideal from a support perspective. Moreover, the Apex code that you write is also visible for all to see, so your intellectual property is at risk.

Unlocked packages can be used for sharing template components that are intended to be changed by the subscriber. If you are not using GitHub or the GitHub Salesforce Deployment Tool (`https://github.com/afawcett/githubsfdeploy`), they can also provide a means to share open source libraries with developers.

The features and benefits of managed packages

This book focuses solely on managed packages. Managed packages have the following features, which are ideal for distributing your application. The org where your application package is installed is referred to as a **subscriber org** since users of this org subscribe to the services your application provides:

- **Intellectual Property (IP) protection**: Users in the subscriber org cannot see your Apex source code, although they can see your Visualforce pages code and static resources. While the Apex code is hidden, JavaScript code is not, so you may want to consider using a minify process to partially obscure such code.
- **The naming scope**: Your component names are unique to your package throughout the utilization of a namespace. This means that, even if you have object *X* in your application, and the subscriber has an object of the same name, they remain distinct. You will define a namespace later in this chapter.
- **The governor scope**: The code in your application executes within its own governor limit scope (such as DML and SOQL governors, which are subject to passing a Salesforce security review) and is not affected by other applications or code within the subscriber org. Note that some governors, such as the CPU time governor, are shared by the whole execution context (discussed in *Chapter 4, Apex Execution and Separation of Concerns*), regardless of the namespace.

- **Upgrades and versioning**: Once subscribers have started using your application, creating data, making configurations, and so on, you will want to provide upgrades and patches with new versions of your application.
- **Feature management:** Allows you to enable, disable, and track the use of features you create in your application.
- **Analytics:** Allows you to receive anonymous data from Salesforce relating to the use of components such as pages and objects in your application. You can use this information, for example, to monitor the adoption of new features you release.

There are other benefits to managed packages, but these are only accessible after becoming a Salesforce partner and completing the security review process; these benefits are described later in this chapter. Salesforce provides *ISVforce Guide* (otherwise known as the **Packaging Guide**) in which these topics are discussed in depth – bookmark it now! The *ISVforce Guide* can be found at `http://login.salesforce.com/help/pdfs/en/salesforce_packaging_guide.pdf`.

Creating your first managed package

Packages and subsequent versions are created using Salesforce DX CLI commands. The steps to be performed are:

1. Setting your package namespace
2. Creating the package and assigning it to the namespace
3. Adding components to the package

> **TIP**
> Not all aspects of the Lightning Platform can be packaged. To help ensure you are fully aware of what is supported and what is not, Salesforce has created an interactive report known as the **Salesforce Metadata Coverage** report. This can be found here: `https://developer.salesforce.com/docs/metadata-coverage`.

These steps will be discussed in the following sections.

Setting and registering your package namespace

An important decision when creating a managed package is the namespace; this is a prefix applied to all your components (Custom Objects, Visualforce pages, Lightning Components, and so on) and is used by developers in subscriber orgs to uniquely distinguish between your packaged components and others, even those from other packages. The namespace prefix is an important part of the branding of the application since it is implicitly attached to any Apex code or other components that you include in your package.

The namespace can be up to 15 characters, though I personally recommend that you keep it to less than this, as it becomes hard to remember and leads to frustrating typos if you make it too complicated. I would also avoid the underscore character as well. It is a good idea to have a naming convention if you are likely to create more managed packages in the future. The following is the format of an example naming convention:

```
[company acronym - 1 to 4 characters][package prefix 1 to 4 characters]
```

For example, the *ACME Corporation's Road Runner* application might be named `acmerr`.

Log in to the namespace org discussed earlier in this chapter. Navigate to the **Packages** page (accessed under the **Setup** menu, under the **Create** submenu). Click on the **Edit** button to begin a short wizard to enter your desired namespace. This can only be done once and must be globally unique (meaning it cannot be set in any other org), much like a website domain name.

> **Assigning namespaces**
>
> For the purposes of following along with this book, please feel free to make up any namespace you desire; for example, `fforce{yourinitials}`. Do not use one that you may plan to use in the future, since once it has been assigned, it cannot be changed or reused.

The following screenshot shows the **Packages** page:

Packages

Developer Settings [Edit]

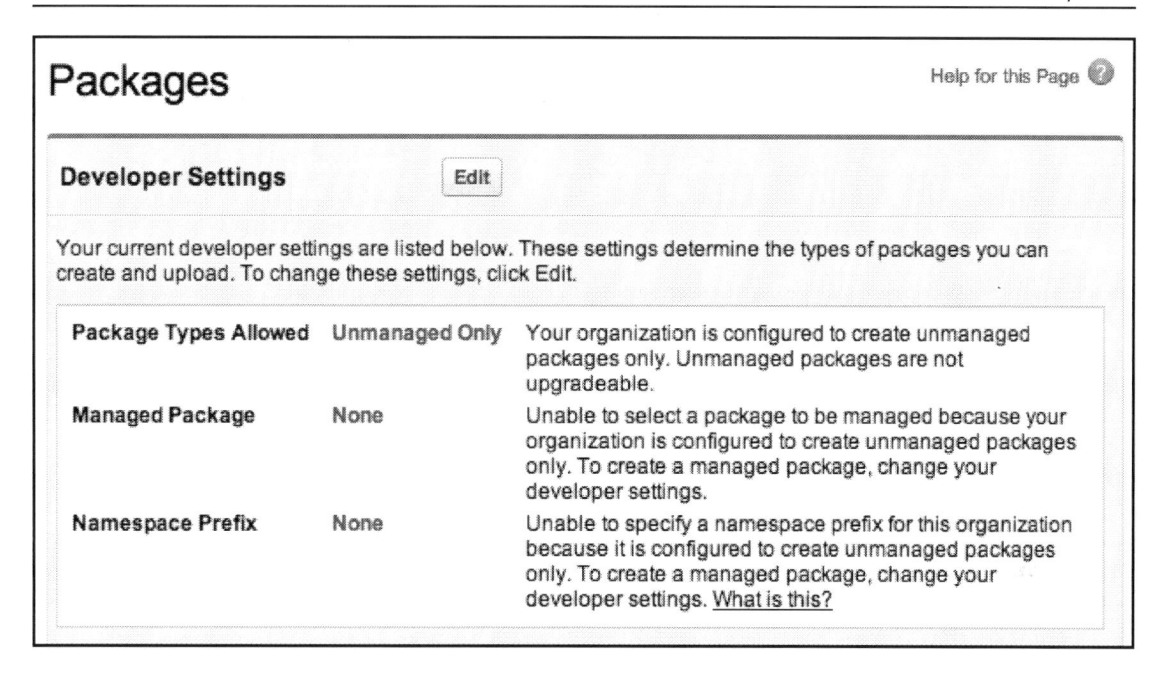

Your current developer settings are listed below. These settings determine the types of packages you can create and upload. To change these settings, click Edit.

Package Types Allowed	Unmanaged Only	Your organization is configured to create unmanaged packages only. Unmanaged packages are not upgradeable.
Managed Package	None	Unable to select a package to be managed because your organization is configured to create unmanaged packages only. To create a managed package, change your developer settings.
Namespace Prefix	None	Unable to specify a namespace prefix for this organization because it is configured to create unmanaged packages only. To create a managed package, change your developer settings. What is this?

Once you have set the namespace, the preceding page should look like the following screenshot, with the difference being that it is now showing the namespace prefix that you have used and that managed packages can now also be created. You are now ready to create a managed package and assign it to the namespace:

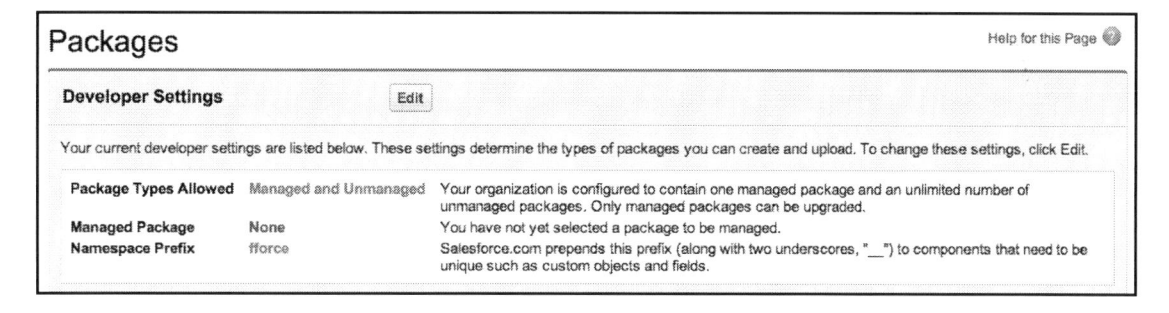

Packages

Developer Settings [Edit]

Your current developer settings are listed below. These settings determine the types of packages you can create and upload. To change these settings, click Edit.

Package Types Allowed	Managed and Unmanaged	Your organization is configured to contain one managed package and an unlimited number of unmanaged packages. Only managed packages can be upgraded.
Managed Package	None	You have not yet selected a package to be managed.
Namespace Prefix	fforce	Salesforce.com prepends this prefix (along with two underscores, "__") to components that need to be unique such as custom objects and fields.

You can now log out from the namespace org – it is no longer needed from this point on. Log in to your Dev Hub org and register your namespace with Salesforce DX. This allows you to create scratch orgs that use that namespace, allowing you to develop your application in a way that more closely represents its final form. Salesforce provides an excellent guide on registering your namespace at https://developer.salesforce.com/docs/atlas.en-us.sfdx_dev.meta/sfdx_dev/sfdx_dev_reg_namespace.htm.

Creating the package and assigning it to the namespace

Return to VSCode and edit your `sfdx-project.json` file to reference the namespace:

```
{
    "packageDirectories": [
        {
            "path": "force-app",
            "default": true
        }
    ],
    "namespace": "fforce",
    "sfdcLoginUrl": "https://login.salesforce.com",
    "sourceApiVersion": "45.0"
}
```

> The sample code associated with each chapter of this book *does not reference any namespace* in the `sfdx-project.json` file. If you want to continue using your namespace after you have refreshed your project for a given chapter, you must repeat the preceding edit with your own namespace. It is generally good practice to develop using the namespace of your package as it is closer to the final installed state of your code and thus will ensure any bugs related to namespace handling are identified earlier.

To create your package and register it with your DevHub, run the following command:

```
sfdx force:package:create
  --name "FormulaForce App"
  --description "FormulaForce App"
  --packagetype Managed
  --path force-app
```

Once the command completes, review your `sfdx-project.json` file again; it should look like the example that follows. In the following example, the ID starting with **0Ho** will vary:

```
{
    "packageDirectories": [
        {
            "path": "force-app",
            "package": "FormulaForce App",
            "default": true
        }
    ],
```

```
"namespace": "fforce",
"sfdcLoginUrl": "https://login.salesforce.com",
"sourceApiVersion": "45.0",
"packageAliases": {
"FormulaForce App": "0Ho6A000000CaVxSAK"
}
}
```

> **TIP**: Salesforce DX records your package and package version IDs here with aliases that you can edit or leave as the defaults. These aliases are easier to recall and understand at a glance when using other Salesforce DX CLI commands relating to packages. For example, the `sfdx force:package:install CLI` command supports an ID or an alias.

Adding components to the package

In this book, the contents of your project's `/force-app` package directory folder will become the source of truth for the components that are included in each release of your package. The following layout shows what your application should look like in source file form so far:

```
├── LICENSE
├── README.md
├── config
│   └── project-scratch-def.json
├── force-app
│   └── main
│       └── default
│           ├── layouts
│           │   ├── Contestant__c-Contestant\ Layout.layout-meta.xml
│           │   ├── Driver__c-Driver\ Layout.layout-meta.xml
│           │   ├── Race__c-Race\ Layout.layout-meta.xml
│           │   └── Season__c-Season\ Layout.layout-meta.xml
│           └── objects
│               ├── Contestant__c
│               │   ├── Contestant__c.object-meta.xml
│               │   └── fields
│               │       ├── Driver__c.field-meta.xml
│               │       └── Race__c.field-meta.xml
│               ├── Driver__c
│               │   └── Driver__c.object-meta.xml
│               ├── Race__c
│               │   ├── Race__c.object-meta.xml
│               │   └── fields
│               │       └── Season__c.field-meta.xml
```

Building and Publishing Your Application

```
|           └──  Season__c
|                    └──  Season__c.object-meta.xml
└── sfdx-project.json
```

> **TIP:** You can consider creating multiple dependent packages from within one project by using different package directory folders for each package. Each package can share the same namespace or choose another. By default, code is not visible between packages unless you explicitly mark it as `global`, a concept discussed later in this book. To make code accessible only between your own packages (sharing the same namespace) and not your customers, use the `@namespaceAccessible` annotation rather than the `global` keyword. We will discuss Extension Packages later in this chapter.

To create the first release of your package, run the following command (all on one line):

```
sfdx force:package:version:create
  --package "FormulaForce App"
  --definitionfile config/project-scratch-def.json
  --wait 10 --installationkeybypass
```

Some things to note about the previous command line parameters are as follows:

- The `--package` parameter uses the package alias as defined in the `sfdx-project.json` file to identify the package we are creating this version against.
- The `--wait` parameter ensures that you take advantage of the ability of the command to update your `sfdx-project.json` file with the ID of the package version.
- `--installationkeypass` is needed to ensure you agree to the fact that the package can be installed by anyone that has the ID. For your real applications, you may want to include a password if you feel there is a risk of this information being exposed.

At this stage in the book, we have simply added some Custom Objects, so the process of creating the package should complete reasonably quickly. Note that what you're actually uploading to is a central application store known as AppExchange (covered later), but don't worry – only those that know the package version ID (or password if you have one) can see and use it at this stage.

Once the preceding command completes, your `sfdx-project.json` file should look like the following. Again, the IDs will vary based on the ones shown here – each time you create a new version of your package, it will be recorded here:

```
{
    "packageDirectories": [
        {
            "path": "force-app",
            "package": "FormulaForce App",
            "versionName": "ver 0.1",
            "versionNumber": "0.1.0.NEXT",
            "default": true
        }
    ],
    "namespace": "fforce",
    "sfdcLoginUrl": "https://login.salesforce.com",
    "sourceApiVersion": "45.0",
    "packageAliases": {
        "FormulaForce App": "0Ho6A000000CaVxSAK",
        "FormulaForce App@0.1.0-1": "04t6A0000038K3GQAU"
    }
}
```

The `NEXT` keyword is used in the preceding `versionNumber` configuration to automatically assign a new version number each time a new package version is created.

Extension packages

As their name suggests, **extension packages** extend or add to the functionality delivered by the existing packages they are based on, though they cannot change the base package contents. They can extend one or more base packages, and you can even have several layers of extension packages, though you may want to keep an eye on how extensively you use this feature, as managing inter-package dependency can get quite complex, especially during development and deployment when using features such as **Push Upgrade**.

> If you want to use extension packages to control access to features of your application you want to sell as add-ons, for example, then you might want to consider the **Feature Management** feature. In this case, you would still package all of your application in one package but selectively hide parts of it through **Feature Parameters**.

Building and Publishing Your Application

Extension packages are created in much the same way as the process you've just completed, except that you must define the dependent package in the `sfdx-project.json` file (shown as follows) and ensure the Scratch Org has those base packages installed in it before use. The following is an example `sfdx-project.json` file showing a package dependency for a new extension package that is currently in development:

```
{
    "packageDirectories": [
        {
            "path": "force-app",
            "package": "FormulaForce - Advanced Analytics Addon",
            "default": true,
            "dependencies": [
                {
                    "package": "FormulaForce App@0.1.0-1"
                }
            ]
        }
    ],
    "namespace": "bookns1",
    "sfdcLoginUrl": "https://login.salesforce.com",
    "sourceApiVersion": "45.0",
    "packageAliases": {
        "FormulaForce App@0.1.0-1": "04t6A012003AB3GQAU"
    }
}
```

The project containing the preceding example configuration only contains the extension package components, since there is only one `packageDirectories` entry. In this case, the base package is developed in a separate project. However, as noted earlier, you can have multiple packages within a single SFDX project. This does have the benefit of being able to work on both base and extension packages together in one scratch org. However, it requires more careful management of the default package directory setting when performing synchronization operations. Personally, I find that having separate projects enforces a better mindset when managing how packages are coupled.

> **TIP**
> As shown later in this chapter, you can manually install any package in a scratch org, either via the browser with the package install URL or via the SFDX CLI. If a package takes a long time to install and configure, you may want to consider using the **Scratch Org Snapshots** feature, especially if you are building a CI/CD pipeline, as described later in this book, in `Chapter 13`, *Source Control and Continuous Integration*. Typically, a scratch org is empty when you create it; however, with this feature, you can have it include pre-installed base packages and related configuration or data.

As the code contained within extension packages makes reference to other Custom Objects, Custom Fields, Apex code, and so on that are present in base packages, the platform tracks these dependencies and the version of the base package present at the time the reference was made. When an extension package is installed, this dependency information ensures that the subscriber (customer) org has the correct version (minimum) of the base packages installed before permitting the installation of the extension package to complete.

> **TIP**
> You can also manage the dependencies between extension packages and base packages yourself through the **Versions** tab (when viewing an Apex class via the **Setup** menu) or **XML metadata** for applicable components (we will revisit versioning in Apex in `Chapter 10`, *Providing Integration and Extensibility*, while discussing API integration).

The preceding sections have described the package creation process, including the ability to create other extension packages to allow you to deploy parts of your application that are applicable to only a subset of your customers, for example, for a given market. The following sections introduce concepts that require more understanding before you release your package to your target customers. Some of these things cannot be reverted.

Package platform feature dependencies

Packages can have dependencies on platform features and/or other packages (as previously described). While some features of Salesforce are common, customers can purchase different editions and features according to their needs. Scratch orgs have access to most of these features for free. This means that, as you develop your application, it is important to understand when and when not to use those features (this is done in order to avoid unwanted dependencies that might block or inhibit the adoption of your application).

When referencing a certain Standard Object, field, or component type, you will make a prerequisite dependency on your package, which your customers will need to have before they can complete the installation. Some Salesforce features, for example, Multi-Currency or Chatter, have either a configuration or, in some cases, a cost impact on your users (different org editions). Carefully consider which features your package is dependent on.

As a best practice, to ensure you are targeting the intended features, update your scratch org configuration file and configure it to enable only the desired edition and platform features you wish to be dependent on. You may also want to have multiple scratch org configuration files for different testing purposes, especially if your application code has different code paths depending on a platform feature being enabled or not (as described later in this chapter).

The following example scratch org configuration file enables features relating to **Enterprise Edition** and, in addition, enables the **Multi-Currency** feature:

```
{
    "orgName": "FormulaForce App Testing with Multi Currency",
    "edition": "Enterprise",
    "features": ["MultiCurrency"]
}
```

> **TIP**
>
> You can also configure various settings through scratch org configuration files, such as the Case and Account settings found under the Setup menu. This can help further emulate your customers' own org configurations and thus improve the accuracy of your testing. For more information, see the Salesforce Help topic at https://developer.salesforce.com/docs/atlas.en-us.sfdx_dev.meta/sfdx_dev/sfdx_dev_scratch_orgs_def_file_config_values.htm.

Later in this book, we will be discussing Lightning Components. If you are packaging these, you will be implicitly imposing the need for your customers to utilize the Salesforce **My Domain** feature. This is not enforced at installation time, so it is an optional dependency. However, users will not be able to use your packaged Lightning Components without first enabling and configuring My Domain.

Release and beta packages

Once you have created your package, it's good practice to do further testing (sometimes called regression and/or acceptance testing) internally and/or with a selection of customers. This testing may result in the need to make changes that would normally be blocked if the package version had been installed in production. To give you the ability to do further testing and still make changes, packages are either in **Beta** or **Release** state, as described here:

- **Release**: Release packages can be installed in subscriber production orgs, and can also provide an upgrade path from previous releases. The downside is that you cannot delete the previously released components, or change certain things, such as a field's type. Changes to components that are marked **global,** such as Apex code methods and Lightning Component attributes, are also restricted. While Salesforce is enhancing the platform to provide the ability to modify certain released aspects, you need to be certain that your application release is stable before selecting this option.

- **Beta**: Beta packages cannot be installed in subscriber production orgs; you can install them only into other scratch orgs, **sandbox**, or Partner Portal created orgs. Also, Beta packages cannot be upgraded once installed; this is the reason why Salesforce does not permit their installation in production orgs. The key benefit is in the ability to continue to change new components of the release, to address bugs and features relating to user feedback, after which, you can create another Beta version.

Package versions are, by default, in Beta state. In order to promote them to Release, you need to run the following SFDX CLI command:

```
sfdx force:package:version:promote
  --package "FormulaForce App@0.1.0-1"
```

> **TIP**: The ability to delete previously published components (uploaded within a release package) is enabled by raising a support case with Salesforce Support. Once you have understood the full implications, they will enable it.

Optional package dependencies

It is possible to make some Salesforce features and/or base package component references (Custom Objects and Fields) optional aspects of your application. There are two approaches to this, depending on the type of feature.

Dynamic bindings

For example, the Multi-Currency feature adds a **CurrencyIsoCode** field to standard and Custom Objects. If you explicitly reference this field, for example, in your Apex code, Lightning pages or components, you will incur a hard dependency on your package. If you want to avoid this and make it a configuration option (for example) in your application, you can utilize dynamic Apex and Visualforce. Lightning value bindings are dynamic in nature, though the `aura:attribute` element type references will form a compile-time reference to the specified objects.

Extension packages

If you wish to package component types that are only available in subscriber orgs of certain editions, you can choose to include these in extension packages. For example, you may wish to support the Professional Edition, which does not support record types. In this case, create an Enterprise Edition extension package (as outlined above) for your application's functionality, which leverages the functionality from this edition.

> **TIP**: Note that you will need multiple scratch org configurations and partner testing orgs for each combination of features that you utilize in this way to effectively test the configuration options or installation options that your application requires.

Supporting package upgradability

Having just created and released your package, you can start to share it with your customers. Later in this chapter, we will discuss ways to list your package and install it. Before we get too far ahead though, let's first consider a very important aspect of managing your package – upgradability. As customers embrace your application, they will customize its features and APIs and expect them to continue working even after upgrades to the latest version.

Upgrading a package is as simple as installing the new version over an existing version (we will do this in the next chapter). The Lightning Platform manages package upgrades for you, without asking users to log out of the system or experience any interruption.

Salesforce DX managed packages have built-in support for upgradability and also help remove a lot of the traditional pain of ensuring you do not accidentally make breaking changes to your application or even, in most cases, worrying about writing upgrade scripts. For example, it will prevent you from deleting a Custom Object or Field that has previously been included in a released package or modifying an Apex global class or method.

Managing package ancestry

A package version ancestry is the lineage a valid upgrade path takes; in a simple case, this might be v1.0 to v1.1 to v1.2 and so on. In this case, the ancestor of v1.2 is v1.1 and the ancestor of v1.1 is v1.0, meaning that customers can upgrade from v1.0 to v1.1 or even from v1.0 straight to v1.2. We will follow this simple serial ancestry lineage as we build out the package throughout this book. That way, you will see the value of package upgradability.

> **TIP**
> In a more complex scenario, you may decide to split your upgrade paths if you decide to take a radically different direction with the product for new customers, in which case, you might start a new upgrade path like so: v1.1 | v1.2 | v2.0. This obviously needs very careful consideration but does allow you more freedom should you need it.

The `ancestorId` or `ancestorVersion` configurations within the `sfdx-project.json` file define the ancestry for the package version you are currently developing in your scratch orgs. We will explore what effect this has on developing in a scratch org later. This configuration also denotes the desired upgrade path during package creation, as described previously.

You can only define an ancestor of your next version based on an already released version of your package. In this chapter, we will use `ancestorId`. The ID to be used is actually the **05i** ID of your desired released package version. To retrieve this, run the following command:

```
sfdx force:package:version:report
  --package "FormulaForce App@0.1.0-1"
  --verbose
```

An example output from the preceding command is shown here:

```
=== Package Version
Name                             Value

Name                             ver 0.1
Subscriber Package Version Id    04t6A0000038K3GQAU
Id                               05i6A000000XZLyQAO
Package Id                       0Ho6A000000CaVxSAK
Version                          0.1.0.1
Description
Branch
Tag
Released                         true
```

Next, add the `ancestorId` configuration to the `sfdx-package.json` file as shown here:

```
{
  "packageDirectories": [
  {
  "path": "force-app",
  "package": "FormulaForce App",
  "versionName": "ver 0.1",
  "versionNumber": "0.1.0.NEXT",
  "ancestorId": "05i6A000000XZLyQAO",
```

Building and Publishing Your Application

```
        "default": true
        }
    ],
    "namespace": "fforce",
    "sfdcLoginUrl": "https://login.salesforce.com",
    "sourceApiVersion": "45.0",
    "packageAliases": {
    "FormulaForce App": "0Ho6A000000CaVxSAK",
    "FormulaForce App@0.1.0-1": "04t6A0000038K3GQAU"
    }
}
```

Each time you release a version of your package, you must repeat the preceding process. This is a significant part of your release process so be sure to document it carefully along with your other release management tasks.

Don't worry if you forget to manage ancestry throughout the rest of this book as you are only building a sample application and aren't sharing it with users who will care about upgrades.

> **TIP**
> For package versions created without ancestry, you will have to either use a new test scratch org to install the new release or uninstall a previous version from an existing test org. This is because the platform will not permit an upgrade to a package already installed in an org if the package being installed does have valid ancestry information, even if it shares the same namespace.

Developing in scratch orgs containing ancestry information

Next time you create a scratch org, you will notice that aspects of the **Setup** menu are now aware that certain components have been previously released to your customers and will block certain operations that would break upgradability, such as changing the API name or deletion. The following screenshot shows an example of such a notification:

Edit Custom Object
Team (Managed)

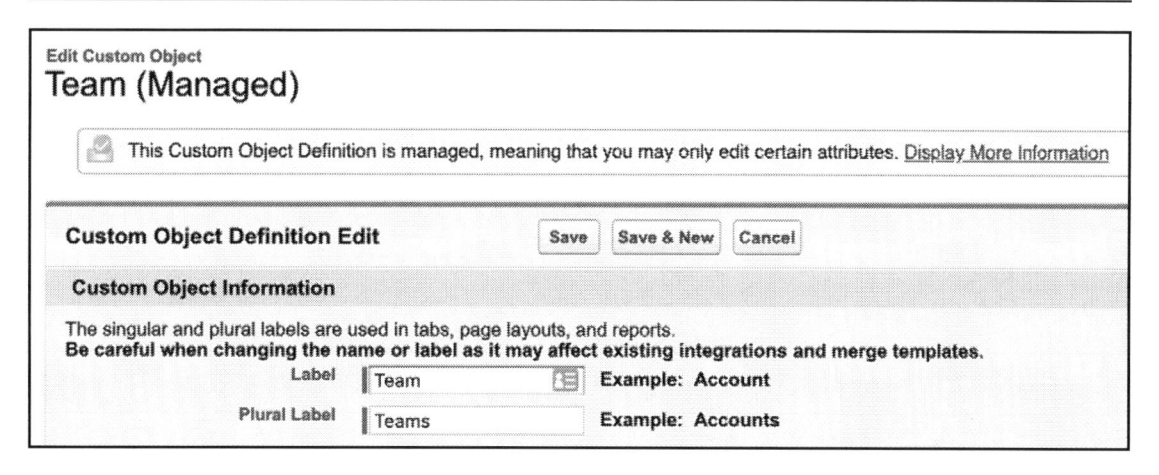

This Custom Object Definition is managed, meaning that you may only edit certain attributes. Display More Information

Custom Object Definition Edit — Save | Save & New | Cancel

Custom Object Information

The singular and plural labels are used in tabs, page layouts, and reports.
Be careful when changing the name or label as it may affect existing integrations and merge templates.

Label	Team	Example: Account
Plural Label	Teams	Example: Accounts

Of course, there is nothing stopping you from deleting a source file in your local copy of the package that is representing a previously released component, for example, the `Team__c` folder. If you try this, however, you will get an error during package creation. Either way, when you maintain ancestry information in your `sfdx-package.json` file, the system protects you from accidental or intentional breaking changes being made to your upgrade path.

> If you want to create a scratch org without ancestry information, you can use the `--noancestors` parameter on the `sfdx force:org:create` command. This can be useful when creating test orgs (which cannot have the same namespace as installed packages). Finally, keep in mind that the preceding enforcement, when developing in a scratch org with ancestry defined, is advantageous to identify upgrade breaking changes early in the release cycle. You may want to skip managing ancestry for this book, though it should be considered a good practice when developing for real.

Becoming a Salesforce partner and the benefits of doing so

The Salesforce Partner Program has many advantages. The first place to visit is `https://partners.salesforce.com/`. You will want to focus on the areas of the site relating to being an **Independent Software Vendor** (**ISV**) partner. From there, you can click on **Join Now**. It is free to join, though you will want to read through the various agreements carefully, of course.

Once you wish to start listing a package and charging users for it, you will need to arrange billing details for Salesforce to take the various fees involved. While this book is not equipped to go into the details, do pay careful attention to the Standard Objects used in your package, as this will determine the license type required by your users and the overall cost to them, in addition to your charges.

For example, integrating with CRM objects that existing Saleforce customers are already using, such as Account, Contact, and Opportunity can be beneficial to you as a feature of your application, since it's an appealing, immediate, and seamless integration not found on other platforms without further configuration or even, in some cases, coding effort.

If you're planning on using Standard Objects, and are in doubt about the costs (as they do vary depending on the type), you can request a conversation with Salesforce to discuss this; this is something to keep in mind in the early stages.

Make sure, when you associate a Salesforce user with the **Partner Community**, you utilize a user that you use daily (known as your **Partner Business Org** user) and not one from a development or test org. Once you have completed the signup process, you will gain access to the Partner Community. The following screenshot shows what the current Partner Community home page looks like. From here, you can access many useful services:

This is your primary place to communicate with Salesforce and access additional materials and announcements relevant to ISVs, so do keep checking it often. You can raise cases and provide additional logins to other users in your organization, such as other developers who may wish to report issues or ask questions.

Security review and benefits

The features described in this section are only available once your package has gone through a Salesforce-driven process known as a **security review**, which is initiated via your listing when logged into AppExchange. Unless you plan to give your package away for free, there is a charge involved in putting your package through this process.

While the review is optional and there is nothing stopping you from distributing your package installation URL directly, keep in mind that Salesforce displays a banner during installation and, once installed, it informs admins that the package has not gone through a security review. Furthermore, you will not be able to benefit from the ability to list your new application on AppExchange for others to see and review. More importantly, you will also not have access to the following features to help you deploy, license, and support your application. The following is a list of the benefits you get once your package has passed the security review:

- **Bypass subscriber org setup limits**: Limits such as the number of tabs and Custom Objects are bypassed. This means that if the subscriber org has reached its maximum number of Custom Objects, your package will still install. This feature is sometimes referred to as **Aloha**. Without this, your package installation may fail. You can determine whether Aloha has been enabled via the **Subscriber Overview** page that comes with the LMA application, which is discussed in the next section.
- **Licensing**: You are able to utilize the Salesforce-provided **License Management Application (LMA)** and **Feature Management Application (LFM)** in your LMO.
- **Subscriber support**: With this feature, users in the subscriber org can enable, for a specific period, a means for you to log in to their org (without exchanging passwords), reproduce issues, and enable much more detailed debug information, such as Apex stack traces. In this mode, you can also see custom settings that you have declared as protected in your package, which is useful for enabling additional debug or advanced features.
- **Push upgrade**: Using this feature, you can automatically apply upgrades to your subscribers without their manual intervention, either directly through the Push UI, on a scheduled basis, or via the Push API. You may use this for applying either smaller bug fixes that don't affect Custom Objects or APIs, or for deploying full upgrades. The latter requires careful coordination and planning with your subscribers to ensure that changes and new features are adopted properly.
- **Usage Metrics:** This feature provides additional analytics on how customers are using your application, such as the objects they are using and the parts of the user interface they are accessing. Your Product Management team can use this to drive roadmap priorities and track the adoption of new features.

> **TIP**
> Salesforce asks you to perform an automated security scan of your software via a web page (http://security.force.com/security/tools/forcecom/scanner). This service can be quite slow depending on how many scans are in the queue. Another option is to obtain the Eclipse plugin from the actual vendor, **CheckMarx**, at http://www.checkmarx.com, which runs the same scan but allows you to control it locally or via your **Continuous Integration** (**CI**) build system. There are a number of code analysis tools now available for Apex, such as the open source project **PMD**, which includes rules for security and other code quality checks: https://pmd.github.io/latest/pmd_rules_apex.html.

This book focuses on building a fully native application; as such, additional work involved in so-called "hybrid" applications (where parts of your application have been implemented on your own servers, for example) are not considered here. However, keep in mind that if you make any callouts to external services, Salesforce will also most likely ask you and/or the service provider to run a BURP scanner, to check for security flaws.

Make sure you plan a reasonable amount of time to go through the security review process; it is essential that you initially list your package, though if it becomes an issue, you have the option of issuing your package install URL directly to initial customers and early adopters.

Getting the best out of the Partner Community

It's worth taking some time to review the content and facilities in the Partner Community. Some of the key areas to take a look at are listed as follows:

- **Education and Trailhead**: This allows you to monitor the progress of other users in your organization on Trailhead. Trailhead is Salesforce's way of learning while doing. Users read about new technologies or development approaches and are then asked to perform some challenges to validate their understanding. They are awarded badges, as part of a gamification system. Using this tab, you can see who has the most badges!
- **Featured Groups**: This page, under **More**, allows you quick access to a number of Salesforce-managed Chatter groups. A key group is the Partner Alerts group. I would strongly recommend you set up an email digest for this group. Only Salesforce posts to this group, so a per-post digest level is tolerable and keeps you informed without having to log in to the community.

- **Support**: This is, of course, the place you go to raise cases with Salesforce. As you raise cases, the UI automatically attempts to search for known issues or support articles that might help answer your questions. You can also report and filter on open cases here.
- **Publishing**: This page allows you to list your creations on the Salesforce AppExchange site. Later sections in this chapter cover this in more detail.
- **Partner Alerts**: Partner Alerts are critical to keeping on top of changes to the service that could affect your development process and/or your customers. These might range from critical fixes, security improvements, to changes in behavior you need to be prepared for. Although rare, you may be asked to make changes to your solution by a certain deadline to ensure your users are not impacted:

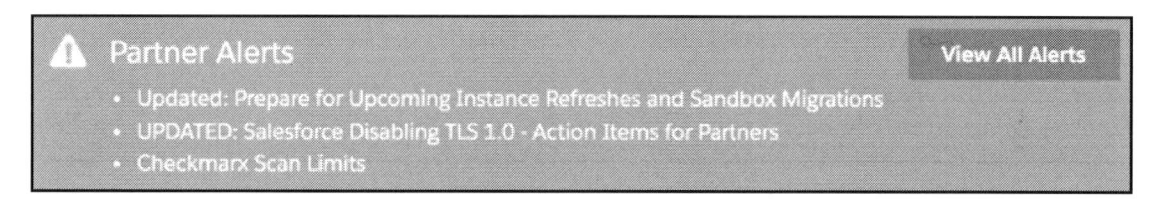

⚠ **Partner Alerts**   **View All Alerts**
- Updated: Prepare for Upcoming Instance Refreshes and Sandbox Migrations
- UPDATED: Salesforce Disabling TLS 1.0 - Action Items for Partners
- Checkmarx Scan Limits

There are many Chatter groups shown on the **Featured Groups** page in the Partner Community, shown as follows. Review them all and set up email digests to help keep you informed without having to manually log in and check through this page each time:

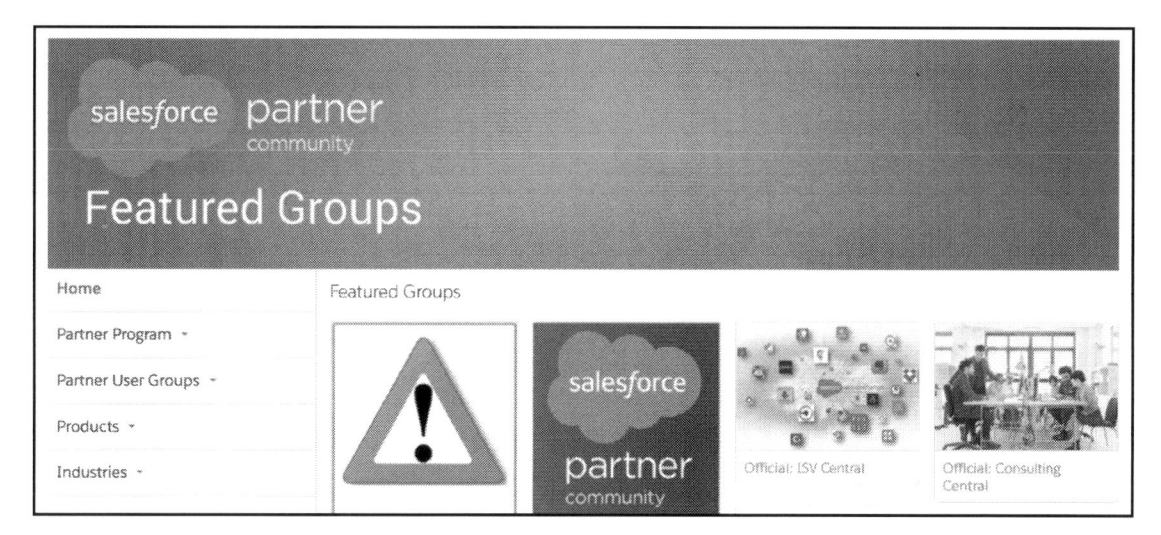

Creating test and demo orgs via the Environment Hub

Partners can use the Environment Hub to create orgs for further testing or demo purposes. Orgs can be linked and logins can be managed here as well. Unlike scratch orgs you can get from the Dev Hub, these orgs have additional user licenses. It is also possible to link your **Trailforce Source Org (TSO)** and create orgs based on templates you define, allowing you to further optimize the base org configuration for your own further testing and demo needs. For more information, review the Partner Community page detailing the Environment Hub (`https://partners.salesforce.com/s/education/general/Environment_Hub`).

Introduction to AppExchange and listings

Salesforce provides a website referred to as **AppExchange**, which lets prospective customers find, try out, and install applications built using the Lightning Platform. Applications listed here can also receive ratings and feedback. You can also list your mobile applications on this site as well.

> In this section, I will be using an AppExchange package that I already own. The package has already gone through the process to help illustrate the steps that are involved. For this reason, you do not need to perform these steps at this stage in the book; they can be revisited at a later phase in your development, once you're happy to start promoting your application.

Once your package is known to AppExchange, each time you release your package (as described previously), you effectively create a private listing. Private listings are not visible to the public until you decide to make them so. This gives you the chance to prepare any relevant marketing details and pricing information while final testing is completed. Note that you can still distribute your package to other Salesforce users or even early beta or pilot customers without having to make your listing public.

In order to start building a listing, you need to log in to the Partner Community and click the **Publishing** tab in the header. This will present you with your **Publishing Console**. Here, you can link and manage **Organizations** that contain your **Packages**, create **Listings**, and review **Analytics** regarding how often your listings are visited:

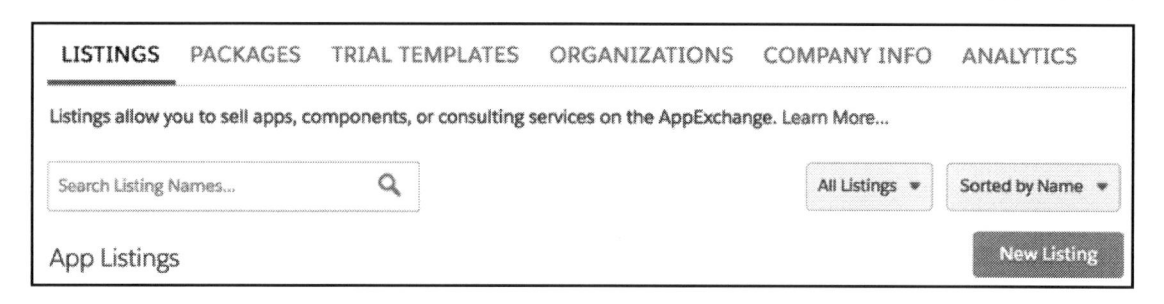

Select the **Publishing Console** option from the menu, then click on the **Create New Listing** button and complete the steps shown in the wizard to associate the packaging org with AppExchange; once completed, you should see it listed.

It's really important that you consistently log in to AppExchange using your APO user credentials. Salesforce will let you log in with other users. To make it easy to confirm, consider changing the user's display name to something like `MyCompany Packaging`:

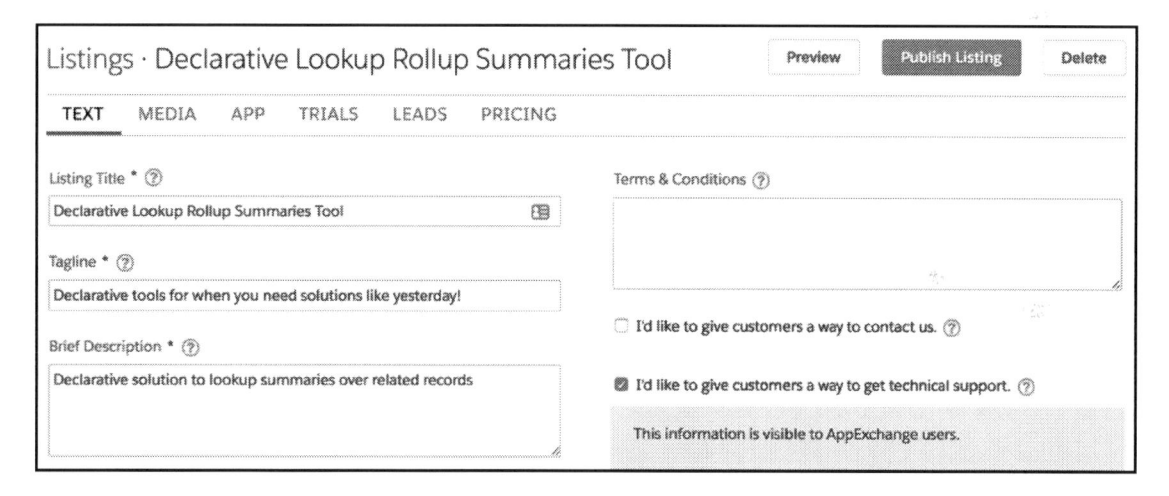

Though it is not a requirement to complete the listing steps, unless you want to try out the process yourself to see the type of information required, you can delete any private listings that you have created after you complete this book.

Installing and testing your package

There are two ways to install your package: through the browser's user interface with clicks or through the SFDX CLI—a more automated experience. For this chapter, we will use the browser user interface to get a better impression of what your end users will see (assuming you permit them to do the install themselves). In the next section, the SFDX CLI path will be discussed.

When you created your package version earlier in this chapter, you should have received an email with a link to install the package. If not, take the **04t** ID from your `sfdx-project.json` file and apply it to the end of the following URL:

```
https://login.salesforce.com/packaging/installPackage.apexp?p0=
```

Do not attempt to install your package in your project's current default scratch org where you developed the package. Instead, let's create a new scratch org for test purposes and open it to perform the install via the browser. Note that we are reusing the same scratch org configuration but you may want to have different configurations for testing:

```
sfdx force:org:create
  --definitionfile project-scratch-def.json
  --setalias test
  --noancestors
  --nonamespace
sfdx force:org:open -u test
```

Here are some things to note about the preceding command line parameters:

- The `--setalias` parameter defines an alias for this org as "test"; conversely, we used "dev" for the alias for the scratch org used to develop the package. This now means that you can easily open either org directly by just using the alias, without having to remember any user name or password. Note that the `-s` / `--setdefaultuser` parameter is not used here so the "dev" scratch org remains the default for synchronization.
- The `--noancestors` and `--nonamespace` parameters disable the standard behavior to have the scratch org inherit the namespace and ancestry behavior we discussed earlier. These are not needed to create scratch orgs for testing package installs.

Once the test scratch org opens, paste the preceding installation link into your browser. The installation process will start. A compact view of the initial installation page is shown in the following screenshot; click on the **Continue** button and follow the default installation prompts to complete the installation:

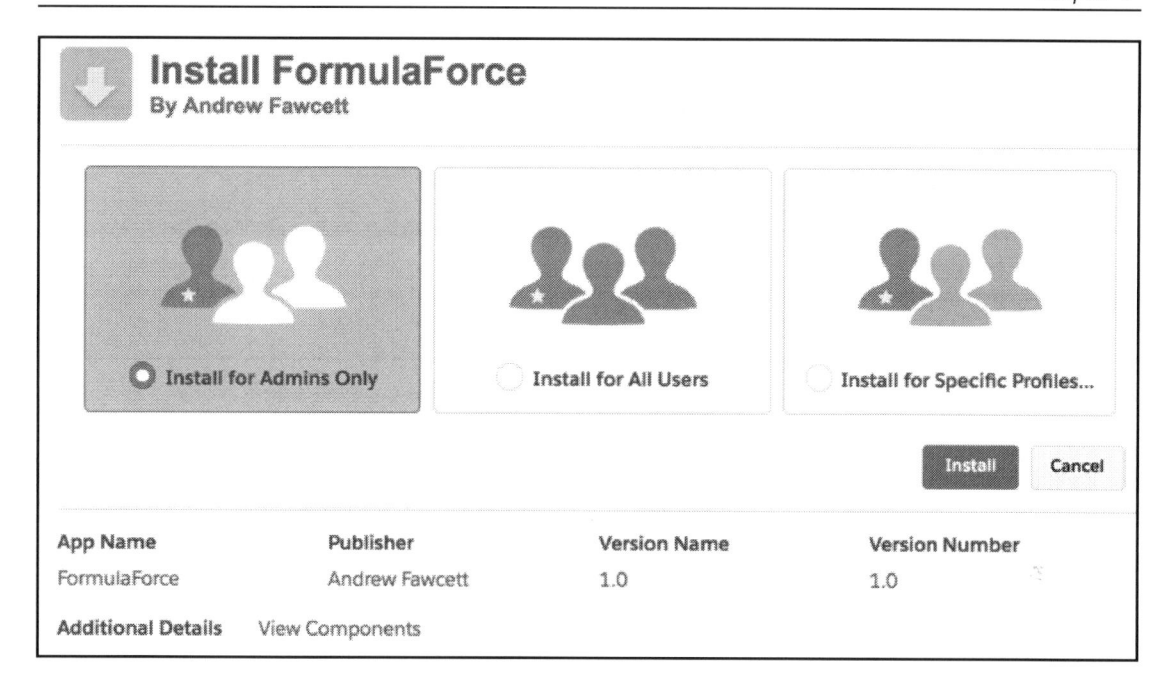

App Name	Publisher	Version Name	Version Number
FormulaForce	Andrew Fawcett	1.0	1.0

Additional Details View Components

> If your package has not gone through a **Salesforce Security Review**, as described earlier in this chapter, you will see a banner informing the user of this fact. This banner is also visible when users review installed packages under the **Setup** menu.

Package installation covers the following aspects (once the user has entered the package password, if one was set):

- **Package overview**: The platform provides an overview of the components that will be added or updated (if this is an upgrade) to the user. Note that, due to the namespace assigned to your package, these will not overwrite existing components in the subscriber org created by the subscriber.
- **Connected App and Remote Access**: If the package contains components that represent connections to the services outside of the Salesforce services, the user is prompted to approve these.

- **Approve Package API Access**: If the package contains components that make use of the client API (such as JavaScript code), the user is prompted to confirm and/or configure these. Such components will generally not be called much; features such as **JavaScript Remoting** are preferred, and they leverage the Apex runtime security configured post-installation.
- **Security configuration**: In this step, you can determine the initial visibility of the components being installed (objects, pages, and so on), selecting admin only or the ability to select the profiles to be updated. This option predates the introduction of **permission sets**, which permit post-installation configuration.

> **TIP**
> If you package profiles in your application, the user will need to remember to map these to the existing profiles in the subscriber org, as per step 2. This is a one-time option, as the profiles in the package are not actually installed, only merged. I recommend that you utilize permission sets to provide security configurations for your application. These are installed and are much more granular in nature.

When the installation is complete, navigate to the **Installed Packages** menu option under the **Setup** menu. Here, you can see confirmation of some of your package details, such as the namespace and version, as well as licensing details, which will be discussed later in this chapter.

> **TIP**
> It is also possible to provide a **Configure** link for your package, which will be displayed next to the package when installed and listed on the **Installed Packages** page in the subscriber org. Here, you can provide a Visualforce page to access configuration options and processes, for example. If you have enabled **Seat based licensing**, there will also be a **Manage Licenses** link to determine which users in the subscriber org have access to your package components, such as tabs, objects, and Visualforce pages. Licensing, in general, is discussed in more detail later in this chapter.

Automating package installation

It is possible to automate package installation using the Salesforce DX CLI. This can be useful if you want to automate the deployment of your packages to scratch orgs and/or other test orgs created as part of a **Continuous Integration** (**CI**) pipeline (as discussed in `Chapter 13`, *Source Control and Continuous Integration*). Run the following commands within the project directory (or VSCode Terminal pane).

The first command will first create a new scratch org, as described in the previous section; the next command will run the install command; and finally, the third command will open the test scratch org, where you can confirm via the **Setup** | **Installed Packages** menu item that the package has been installed:

```
sfdx force:org:create
   --definitionfile project-scratch-def.json
   --setalias test
   --noancestors
   --nonamespace
sfdx force:package:install
   --package "FormulaForce App@0.1.0-1"
   --publishwait 10
   --wait 10
   --targetusername test
sfdx force:org:open -u test
```

Note that the installation will also upgrade a package if the package is already installed. A few things to note about the preceding `sfdx force:package:install` parameters are as follows:

- The `--publishwait` parameter ensures that the command waits for any final background processing to complete before your package can be installed.
- The `--package` parameter uses the package alias defined in the `sfdx-project.json` file. This parameter can also take the **04t** ID as well (this is useful if the command is not run within the project directory).
- The `--targetusername` parameter uses the `test` scratch org alias to explicitly define which scratch org to install the package in, since the creation of the scratch org (via the preceding command) did not overwrite the default scratch org.

> **TIP**: The Salesforce DX CLI can also list packages installed in an org, for example, if you wanted to determine whether a dependent package needs to be installed or upgraded before running the preceding CLI. Finally, you can also uninstall packages if you wish.

Understanding how to license your package

Once you have completed the security review, you are able to request access to the LMA by raising support cases via the Partner Portal. Once this access is provided by Salesforce, use the installation URL to install it like any other package in your LMO.

> **TIP**: If you have requested a CRM for ISV's org (by raising a case in the Partner Portal), you may find the LMA already installed.

The following screenshot shows the **License Management Application** once installed:

Since it is not possible to execute this process for the sample package you have created, I will use a package that I already own and have already taken through the process, to help illustrate the steps that are involved. For this reason, you do not need to perform these steps.

After completing the installation, return to AppExchange and log in. Then, locate your listing in **Publisher Console** under **Uploaded Packages**. Next to your package, there will be a **Manage Licenses** link. After clicking on this link for the first time, you will be asked to connect your package to your LMO org. Once this is done, you will be able to define the license requirements for your package.

The following example shows the license for a free package, with an immediately active license for all users in the subscriber org:

Default License Settings

What organization do you use to manage your licenses (LMO)?
andyinthecloud.com (00D70000000JlxzEAG)

What type of default license does your application have?
○ Default license is a free trial
◉ Default license is active

What is the length of your default license?
◉ License does not expire
○ License length:

How many seats are available with your default license?
◉ License is site-wide
○ Default number of seats:

In most cases regarding packages that you intend to charge for, you would offer a free trial, rather than setting the license default to active immediately. For paid packages, select a license length, unless perhaps it's a one-off charge, and then select the license that does not expire. Finally, if you're providing a trial license, you need to carefully consider the default number of seats (users); users may need to be able to assign themselves different roles in your application to get the full experience.

> **TIP**
> While licensing is currently expressed at a package level, it is very likely that more granular licensing around the modules or features in your package will be provided by Salesforce in the future. This will likely be driven by the permission sets feature. As such, keep in mind a functional orientation to your permission set design.

Building and Publishing Your Application

If you configure a number of seats against the license, then the **Manage Licenses** link will be shown on the **Installed Packages** page next to your package. The administrator in the subscriber org can use this page to assign applicable users to your package. The following screenshot shows how your installed package looks to the administrator when the package has licensing enabled:

Installed Packages							
Action		Package Name	Publisher	Version Number	Namespace Prefix	Status	Allowed Licenses
Uninstall | Manage Licenses		Declarative Lookup Rollup Summaries Tool	Home	1.4	dlrs	Active	3

Note that you do not need to keep reapplying the license requirements for each version you upload; the last details you defined will be carried forward to new versions of your package until you change them. Either way, these details can also be completely overridden on the **License** page of the LMA application.

> **TIP**: You may want to apply a site-wide (org-wide) active license to extensions or add-on packages. This allows you to at least track who has installed such packages, even though you don't intend to manage any licenses around them since you are addressing licensing on the main package.

The Licenses tab and managing customer licenses

The **Licenses** tab provides a list of individual license records that are automatically generated when users install your package in their orgs. Salesforce captures this action and creates the relevant details, including **Lead** information. This also contains the contact details of the organization and the person who performed the installation, as shown in the following screenshot:

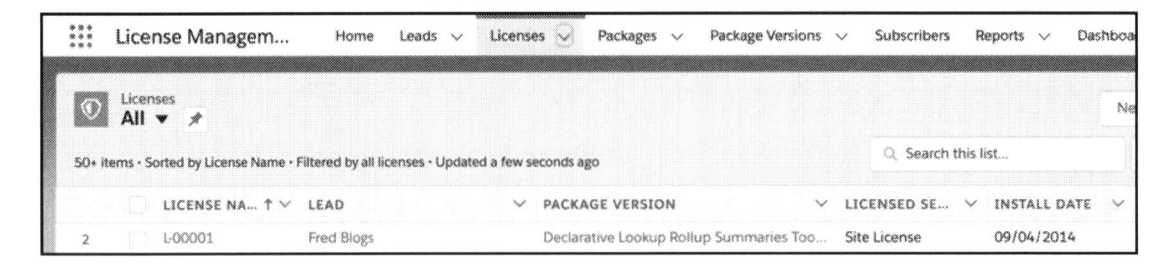

	License Managem...	Home	Leads	Licenses	Packages	Package Versions	Subscribers	Reports	Dashboa

	LICENSE NA... ↑	LEAD	PACKAGE VERSION	LICENSED SE...	INSTALL DATE
2	L-00001	Fred Blogs	Declarative Lookup Rollup Summaries Too...	Site License	09/04/2014

From each of these records, you can modify the current license details to extend the expiry period or disable the application completely. If you do this, the package will remain installed with all of its data. However, none of the users will be able to access the objects, Apex code, or pages, not even the administrator. You can also re-enable the license at any time. The following screenshot shows the **Details** section:

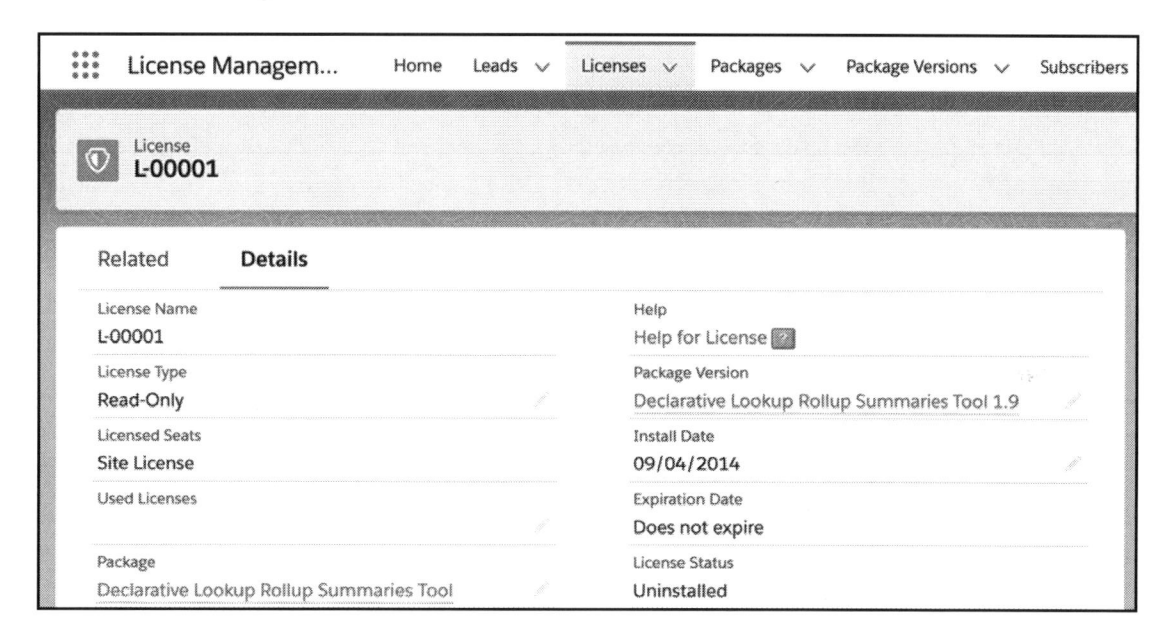

The Feature Parameters tab and managing features

Feature Management allows you to hide your application features (programmatically) and/or objects contained in your package until the user wants to use them or you have elected to enable them after purchase. Additionally, it allows you to embed tracking into your application logic to gather statistics such as when the user first used a feature or how often it was used. In order to use this feature, you need to install the **Feature Management Application (FMA)** (also available via a Salesforce Support Case) in your LMO. Once installed, the **Feature Parameters** tab allows you to view and manage the values of feature parameters embedded in your package.

Building and Publishing Your Application

The following example from one of my own test packages shows three parameters of varying data types that help track feature usage (Subscriber to LMO). You can read more about this use case at `https://github.com/afawcett/fmfc`. You can also create feature parameters that allow you to push values to subscriber orgs and thus remotely enable features (LMO to Subscriber) via code paths in your UI and Apex code that reference the same feature parameter:

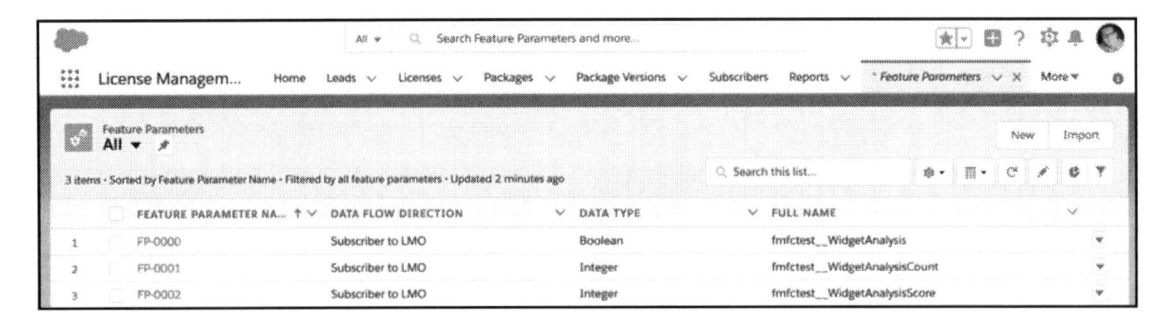

> There is extensive information on how to use Feature Management in the **ISVForce Guide**, which you can refer to at `https://developer.salesforce.com/docs/atlas.en-us.packagingGuide.meta/packagingGuide/fma_manage_features.htm`.

The Subscribers tab

The **Subscribers** tab lists all your customers or subscribers (it shows their **Organization Name** from the company profile) that have your packages installed (only those linked via AppExchange). This includes their **Organization ID**, **Edition** (Developer, Enterprise, or others), and also the type of instance (sandbox or production). You can view this here:

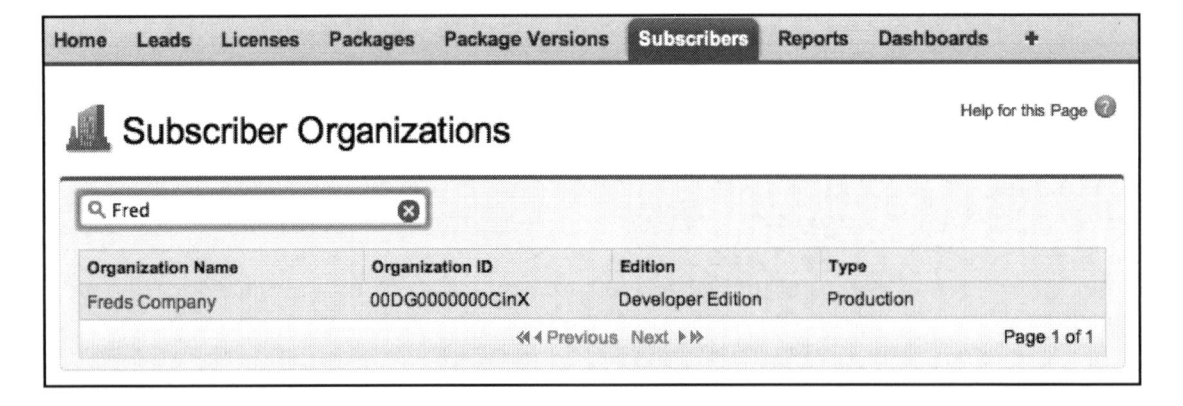

[44]

The Subscriber Overview page

When you click on **Organization Name** from the list in this tab, you are taken to the **Subscriber Overview** page. This page is sometimes known as the **Partner Black Tab**. This page is packed with useful information, such as the contact details (also seen via the **Leads** tab) and the login access that may have been granted (we will discuss this in more detail in the next section), as well as which of your packages they have installed, their current license status, and when they were installed. The following is a screenshot of the **Subscriber Overview** page:

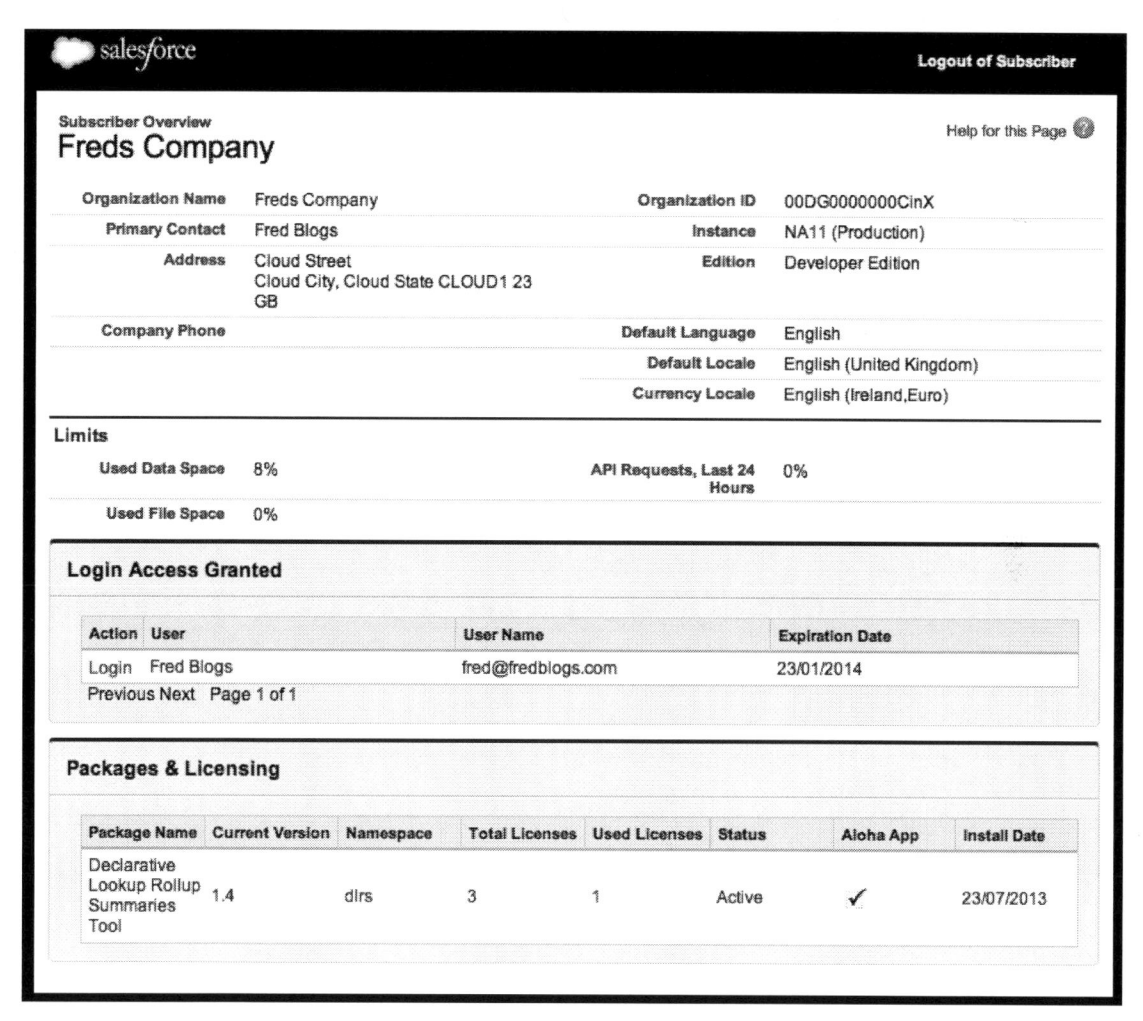

How licensing is enforced in the subscriber org

Licensing is enforced in one of two ways, depending on the execution context in which your packaged Custom Objects, Fields, and Apex code are being accessed from.

The first context is where a user is interacting directly with your objects, fields, tabs, and pages via the user interface or via the Salesforce APIs (Partner and Enterprise). If the user or the organization is not licensed for your package, these will simply be hidden from view, and, in the case of the API, will return an error. Note that administrators can still see packaged components under the **Setup** menu.

The second context is the type of access made from Apex code, such as an Apex Trigger or controller, written by the customers themselves or from within another package. This indirect way of accessing your package components is permitted if the license is site-wide (or org-wide) or there is at least one user in the organization that is allocated a seat.

This condition means that, even if the current user has not been assigned a seat (via the **Manage Licenses** link), they are still accessing your application's objects and code, although indirectly, for example, via a customer-specific utility page or Apex Trigger, which automates the creation of some records or the defaulting of fields in your package.

> Your application's Apex Triggers (for example, the ones you might add to Standard Objects) will always execute, even if the user does not have a seat license, as long as there is just one user seat license assigned to your package in the subscriber org. However, if that license expires, the Apex Trigger will no longer be executed by the platform, until the license expiry is extended.

Providing support

Once your package has completed the security review, additional functionality for supporting your customers is enabled. Specifically, this includes the ability to log in securely (without exchanging passwords) to their environments and debug your application. When logged in in this way, you can see everything the user sees, in addition to extended debug logs that contain the same level of detail as they would in a developer org.

First, your customer enables access via the **Grant Account Login** page. This time, however, your organization (note that this is the **Company Name** as defined in the packaging org under **Company Profile**) will be listed as one of those available in addition to Salesforce Support. The following screenshot shows the **Grant Account Login Access** page:

Grant Account Login Access

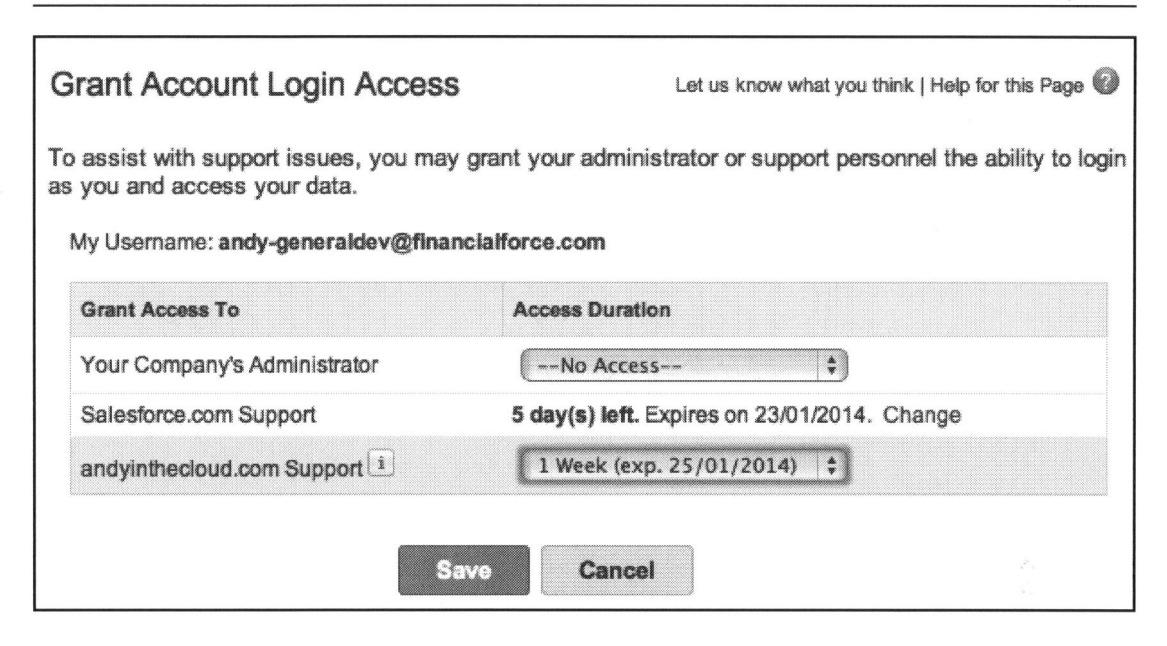

To assist with support issues, you may grant your administrator or support personnel the ability to login as you and access your data.

My Username: **andy-generaldev@financialforce.com**

Grant Access To	Access Duration
Your Company's Administrator	--No Access--
Salesforce.com Support	**5 day(s) left.** Expires on 23/01/2014. Change
andyinthecloud.com Support	1 Week (exp. 25/01/2014)

[Save] [Cancel]

Next, you log in to your LMO and navigate to the **Subscribers** tab as described. Open **Subscriber Overview** for the customer, and you should now see the link to **Login** as that user. From this point on, you can follow the steps given to you by your customer and utilize the standard **Debug Logs** and **Developer Console** tools to capture the debug information you need. The following screenshot shows a user who has been granted login access via your package to their org:

Login Access Granted

Action	User	User Name	Expiration Date
Login	Fred Blogs	fred@fredblogs.com	23/01/2014

Previous Next   Page 1 of 1

This mode of access also permits you to see protected custom settings and Custom Metadata, if you have included any of those in your package. If you have not encountered these before, it's well worth researching them as they provide an ideal way to enable and disable debug, diagnostic, or advanced configurations that you normally don't want your customers to see.

Customer metrics

Salesforce exposes information relating to the use of your package components in subscriber orgs. This enables you to report what Custom Objects and Visualforce pages your customers are using and, more importantly, those they are not. This information is provided by Salesforce and cannot be opted out of by the customer.

This facility needs to be enabled by Salesforce Support. Once enabled, the `MetricsDataFile` object is available in your production org and will receive a data file periodically that contains the metric's records. The **Usage Metrics Visualization** application can be found by searching on AppExchange, and can help with visualizing this information.

Trialforce and Test Drive

Large enterprise applications often require some consultation with customers to tune and customize them to their needs after the initial package installation. If you wish to provide trial versions of your application, Salesforce provides a means to take snapshots of the results of this installation and setup process, including sample data.

You can then allow prospective users who visit your AppExchange listing or your website to sign up to receive a personalized instance of a Salesforce org based on the snapshot you made. Potential customers can then use this to fully explore the application for a limited time until they sign up to be a paying customer. Such orgs will eventually expire when the Salesforce trial period ends for the org created (typically after 14 days). Thus, you should keep this in mind when setting the default expiry on your package licensing.

The standard approach is to offer a web form for the prospective user to complete in order to obtain the trial. Review the *Providing a Free Trial on your Website* and *Providing a Free Trial on AppExchange* sections of the *ISVforce Guide* for more on this.

You can also consider utilizing the Signup Request API, which gives you more control over how the process is started and the ability to monitor it, such that you can create the lead records yourself. You can find out more about this in the *Creating Signups Using the API* section in the *ISVforce Guide*. As a more advanced option, if you are an ISV with an existing application and wish to utilize Salesforce.com as a backend service, you can use this API to completely create and manage orgs on their behalf. Review the *Creating Proxy Signups for OAuth* and the *API Access* section in the *ISVforce Guide* for more information on this.

Alternatively, if the prospective user wishes to try your package in their sandbox environment, for example, you can permit them to install the package directly, either from AppExchange or from your website. In this case, ensure that you have defined a default expiry on your package license, as described earlier. In this scenario, you or the prospective user will have to perform the setup steps after installation.

Finally, there is a third option called **Test Drive**, which does not create a new org for the prospective user on request but does require you to set up an org with your application, preconfigure it, and then link it to your listing via AppExchange. Instead of the users completing a signup page, they click on the **Test Drive** button on your AppExchange listing. This logs them into your test drive org as read-only users. Because this is a shared org, the user experience and features you can offer to users is limited to those that mainly read information. I recommend that you consider Trialforce over this option unless there is some really compelling reason to use it.

> **TIP**
> When defining your listing in AppExchange, the **Leads** tab can be used to configure the creation of lead records for trials, test drives, and other activities on your listing. Enabling this will result in a form being presented to the user before accessing these features on your listing. If you provide access to trials through signup forms on your website, for example, lead information will not be captured.

Distributing Salesforce Connected Apps

If you plan to build any kind of platform integration, including a dedicated mobile application, for example, using Salesforce APIs or any you build using Apex, you will need to create and package what's known as a Connected App. This allows you, as the ISV, to set up the OAuth configuration that allows users of these integrations to connect to Salesforce, and thus, your logic and objects running on the platform. You don't actually need to package this configuration, but you are encouraged to do so since it will allow your customers to control and monitor how they utilize your solution.

Summary

This chapter has given you a practical overview of the initial package creation process, from using Salesforce DX through to installing it into another Salesforce org. While some of the features discussed cannot be fully exercised until you're close to your first release phase, you can head to development with a good understanding of how early decisions, such as references to Standard Objects, are critical to your licensing and cost decisions.

It is also important to keep in mind that, while tools such as Trialforce help automate the setup, this does not apply to installing and configuring your customer environments. Thus, when making choices regarding configurations and defaults in your design, keep in mind the costs to the customer during the implementation cycle.

Make sure you plan for the security review process in your release cycle (the free online version has a limited bandwidth) and, ideally, integrate a static analysis tool that supports security scanning into your CI build system as early as possible, since such tools not only monitor security flaws but also help report breaches in best practices, such as a lack of test asserts and SOQL or DML statements in loops.

In the following chapters, we will start exploring the engineering aspects of building an enterprise application as we build upgrades on the package created in this chapter, allowing us to better explore how the platform supports the incremental growth of your application.

> **TIP**
> As you revisit the tools covered in this chapter, be sure to reference the excellent *ISVforce Guide* at `http://www.salesforce.com/us/developer/docs/packagingGuide/index.htm` for the latest detailed steps and instructions on how to access, configure, and use these features.

2
Leveraging Platform Features

In this chapter, we will explore some key features of the Lightning platform that not only enable developers to build an application more rapidly but also provide key features to the end users of the application. Using these features in a balanced way is the key to ensuring that you and your users not only get the best out of the platform today but continue to do so in the future as the platform evolves.

A key requirement for an enterprise application is the ability to customize and extend its functionality, as enterprise customers have varied and complex businesses. You should also keep in mind that, as your ecosystem grows, you should ensure that your partner relationships are empowered with the correct level of integration options and that partners need to interface their solutions with yours; the platform also plays a key role here.

As we expand our FormulaForce package, we will explore the following to better understand some of the decision-making regarding platform alignment:

- Packaging and upgradable components
- Custom Field features
- Security features
- The platform APIs and platform events
- Localization and translation
- Building customizable user interfaces
- Email customization with email templates
- Workflow and Flow
- Social features and mobile

Packaging and upgradable components

The amount of time taken to install your application and then get it configured for live use by your customers is a critical part of your customer relationship. They are obviously keen to get their hands on your new and improved releases as quickly as possible. Careful planning and awareness of the components you are using support packaging, and are upgradeable, are important, as these things impact the effort involved in going live with your application.

When exploring the various platform features available to you, it is important to check whether the related component types can be packaged or not. For a full list of components that can be packaged, you can use the *Metadata Coverage* report at `https://developer.salesforce.com/docs/metadata-coverage`.

> **TIP**: If a component type relating to a feature you wish to use cannot be packaged, it does not necessarily mean it is of no use to you or your users, as it may well be something you can promote in your consulting team and to your end user admins to take advantage of after installation. Keep in mind how often you recommend this, though—especially if it starts to become a required post-installation task; this will increase the time it takes for your users to go live on your application.

Another aspect to consider is whether the component type is upgradeable; that is, if you define and include one release of your package, then modify it in a subsequent release, it will be updated in the subscriber (customer) organization. The table in the *Available Components* section of *ISVforce Guide* will also give you the latest information on this. Some component types that are not upgradeable are as follows:

- Layouts
- Email templates
- Reports
- List views

These features are key to your application design and are covered in more detail later in this chapter. It is also important that end users can customize these; hence, Salesforce allows them to be edited. Unfortunately, this means they are not upgradable; that is, in the case of layouts, for example, any new fields you add to your Custom Objects do not appear by default after an upgrade is made available to your users. However, new installations of your package will include the latest versions of those components of your package.

This also applies to some attributes of components that are flagged as upgradeable in the table referenced previously but have certain attributes that are then not upgradeable. Refer to the *Editing Components and Attributes After Installation* section of *ISVforce Guide* for the latest details on this. Some common attributes that are packable but not upgradable, hence are not end-user-modifiable either, are as follows:

- **Custom Field**: Picklist values
- **Validation Rule**: Active
- **Custom Object**: Action overrides

> **TIP**
> The active status of the Validation Rule is quite a surprising one; while the user cannot modify your packaged Validation Rule, they can disable it. For most purposes, this means that this platform feature becomes a post-install optional activity left to the end user, should they wish to implement rules unique to them. For validations you wish to implement in **Apex**, you can utilize a protected Custom Setting to control activation if desired (such settings are only visible to your support teams via subscriber support).

Custom Fields – picklist values

Probably the most surprising of the non-upgradable attributes of Custom Fields is the list of picklist values. These are completely modifiable by end users; they can be added, modified, or deleted. This means that you need to be very careful about how you reference these in your Apex code, and consequently, you should provide guidelines for your end users about editing and applying changes post-upgrade.

> **TIP**
> The Salesforce **Translation Workbench** tool, under the **Setup** menu, can be used to effectively re-label a picklist value by editing the user's current language without having to rename its value on the field definition. This can be done after the installation of the tool by the end user admin.

Also, remember that the platform treats picklist fields mostly as if they were text fields; as such, you can query and even update a picklist field with any value you like. Keep in mind that you can upgrade customer data (if you change or delete a picklist value) through an Apex post-install script.

Global picklists

An alternative to defining picklists at the field level is Global Picklists. Available under the **Setup** menu, they allow you to define and package picklists independent of fields and thus can be shared across multiple fields.

There are two significant differences to picklists defined in this way:

- They cannot be modified in the subscriber org by the end user
- They are validated by the platform if the user or code attempts to update a field with an invalid picklist value

If you require picklists on your fields to be customized or don't have any issues with them being modified, then you can define picklists at the field level. Otherwise, Global Picklists are the more natural—and the safest—default to use in cases where your data model requires fields with fixed values, even if there is no reuse between fields. Keep in mind that users can still modify the labels of global picklist entries through Salesforce's **Translation Workbench**, regardless of the route you choose.

Automating upgrade tasks with the Metadata API

Salesforce, as ever, is great at providing APIs; the **Metadata API** is no exception, as it provides pretty broad coverage of most things that can be done under the **Setup** menu. This means that it is feasible to consider the development of upgrade tools to assist in upgrading components such as layouts or picklist values. Such tools will have to handle the logic of merging changes and confirming them with the user, for example, providing a means to merge new fields into layouts, which the user selects from a UI prompt.

> Salesforce requires you to declare to your users that you are modifying metadata in their org via a notification message in the applicable UI. The security review process will look to ensure that this is present.

Currently, there are two flavors of the Metadata API that can be used from Apex code:

- **Option 1**: Through Apex HTTP callouts using the Metadata SOAP or REST APIs. For more information, head to `https://developer.salesforce.com/docs/atlas.en-us.api_meta.meta/api_meta/meta_intro.htm`. Using this API from Apex code running in Lightning Experience requires a Named Credential setup to set up the required authentication. Visualforce pages do not require this and can use `UserInfo.getSessionId`.

- **Option 2**: The Apex Metadata API has the benefit of being more direct (no HTTP callout restrictions need to be considered), and, for managed packages that have passed the security review process, fewer user permissions are required by the user executing the code. However, it only supports a small subset of Metadata Types, Layout, and Custom Metadata at the time of writing. Review the **Metadata Coverage Report** to get the latest coverage: `https://developer.salesforce.com/docs/metadata-coverage`. For more information on this API, look at the Apex Developers Guide: `https://developer.salesforce.com/docs/atlas.en-us.apexcode.meta/apexcode/apex_metadata.htm`.

> **TIP**
> With respect to Option 1, making callouts to SOAP HTTP APIs can be tricky to form and interpret the XML payloads required. To make this easier, there is an open source project that has provided an Apex wrapper around the Metadata SOAP API at `https://github.com/financialforcedev/apex-mdapi`. There are samples included in this library that show how to manipulate layouts and other Metadata types.

The following Apex code shows how the Apex Metadata API can be used to programmatically update a layout to add a new custom button (not included in this chapter). This code can be used as part of a tool you provide with your application or separately by your consultants:

```
// Read the layout
List<Metadata.Metadata> layouts =
    Metadata.Operations.retrieve(Metadata.MetadataType.Layout,
    new List<String> {'Driver__c-Driver Layout'});
Metadata.Layout layout = (Metadata.Layout) layouts.get(0);

// Add a button to the layout
if(layout.customButtons==null) {
    layout.customButtons = new List<String>();
}
layout.customButtons.add('anewbutton');

// Update the layout
Metadata.DeployContainer container = new Metadata.DeployContainer();
container.addMetadata(layout);
Id asyncResultId = Metadata.Operations.enqueueDeployment(container, new DeployCallback());

public class DeployCallback implements Metadata.DeployCallback {
    public void handleResult(Metadata.DeployResult result,
        Metadata.DeployCallbackContext context) {
        if (result.status == Metadata.DeployStatus.Succeeded) {
```

```
            // Deployment was successful, take appropriate action.
            System.debug('Deployment Succeeded!');
        } else {
            // Deployment wasn't successful, take action.
            System.debug('Deployment Failed!');
        }
    }
}
```

The previous code uses the Apex Metadata API as defined by Salesforce, which is designed to be quite generic. If you want to manipulate Custom Metadata records, you might want to check out my Custom Metadata Service library. You can find out more about this library here: https://github.com/afawcett/custommetadataapi. This library also provides support for using the API from Visualforce and Lightning Component contexts.

> You might be tempted to consider using these APIs from package post-install scripts. There are several limitations to calling either flavor of the Metadata API from such execution contexts, such as the lack of a real user context and the lack of a UI to prompt the user or report errors. For this reason, my advice is to include a separate post-install setup UI experience you can offer to your customers' admins. As discussed in the previous chapter, you can provide a link via your package configuration link.

Understanding Custom Field features

Custom Fields carry many more features than you might think; they are much more than the simple field definitions you find on other platforms. Having a good understanding of a Custom Field is key to reducing the amount of code you write and improving the user experience and reporting of your application's data.

Default field values

Adding default values to your fields improves the usability of your application and can reduce the number of fields needed on the screen, as users can remove fields with acceptable defaults from the layouts.

Default values defined on Custom Fields apply in the native user interfaces and Visualforce UIs (providing the `apex:inputField` component is used), and in some cases, through the APIs. You can define a default value based on a formula using either literal values and/or variables such as `$User`, `$Organization`, and `$Setup`.

Let's try this out. Create a **Year** text field on the **Season** object, as per the following screenshot. Make sure that you select the **External ID** checkbox as this cannot be changed on the field once the package is uploaded at the end of this chapter. This will become important in the next chapter:

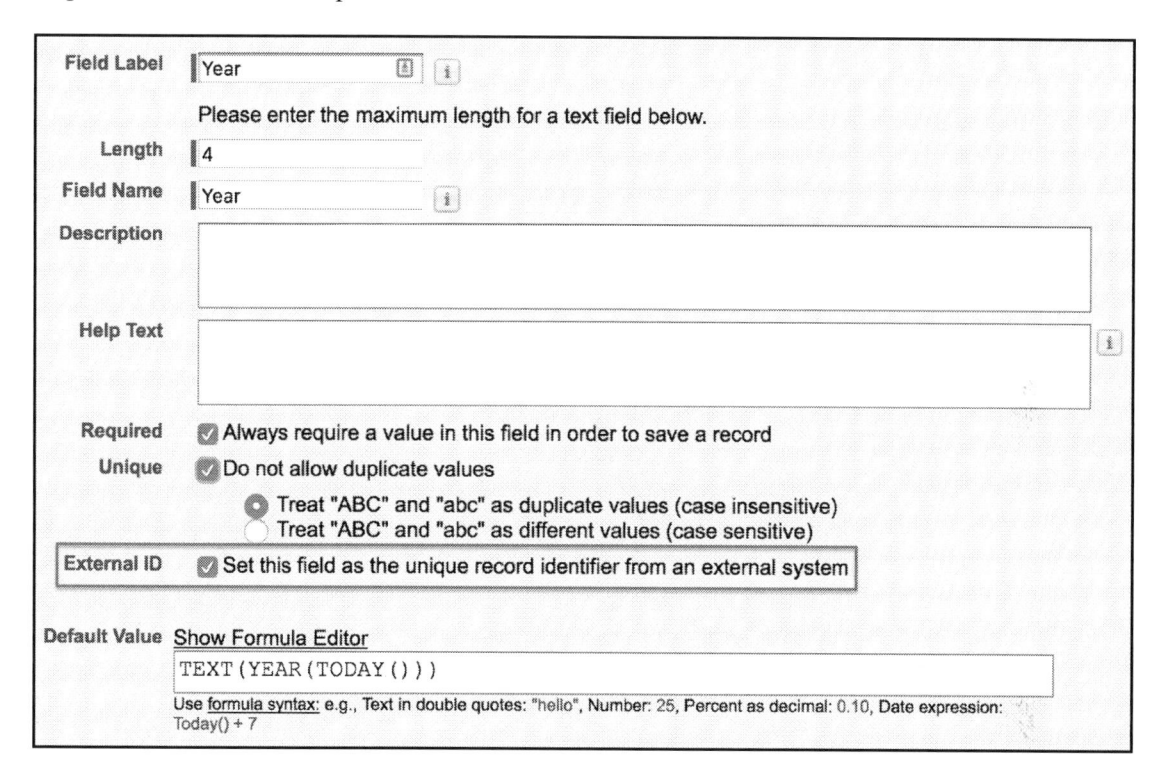

Field Label	Year
	Please enter the maximum length for a text field below.
Length	4
Field Name	Year
Description	
Help Text	
Required	☑ Always require a value in this field in order to save a record
Unique	☑ Do not allow duplicate values
	⦿ Treat "ABC" and "abc" as duplicate values (case insensitive)
	○ Treat "ABC" and "abc" as different values (case sensitive)
External ID	☑ Set this field as the unique record identifier from an external system
Default Value	Show Formula Editor
	`TEXT(YEAR(TODAY()))`
	Use formula syntax: e.g., Text in double quotes: "hello", Number: 25, Percent as decimal: 0.10, Date expression: Today() + 7

> **TIP**: The default value you define cannot be overridden through customization in the subscriber org; however, you can reference a Custom Setting (hierarchy type only) in a default value formula using a `$Setup` reference. This allows some customization by editing the Custom Setting at an organization, profile, or individual user level.

To create a record in the **Season** object, we need to first create a tab for it. Perform the following steps in the package org to try out this process:

1. Create a tab for the **Season** object.
2. Go to the **Season** tab and click on **New**.

3. This results in the current year being displayed in the **Year** field, as shown in the following screenshot:

Unfortunately, by default, the Apex code does not apply default values when you construct an `SObject` in a direct manner via new `Season()`; however, if you utilize the `SObjectType.newSObject` method, you can request that defaults are applied as follows:

```
Season__c season = (Season__c)
    Season__c.SObjectType.newSObject(null, true);
System.assertEquals('2019', season.Year__c);
```

Encrypted fields

However unlikely you feel data theft might occur, there are some markets and government regulations that require data encryption. Salesforce offers two ways to help ensure your application data is stored in data centers in an encrypted form. There are two options to consider for encrypting field values at rest, that is, records physically stored on permanent storage:

- **Classic Encryption**: Encrypted fields leverage 128-bit master keys and use the **Advanced Encryption Standard** (**AES**) algorithm to store values; they are displayed using a character mask (currently not developer-definable). Such fields are packageable, though this only applies to text fields.
- **Platform Encryption**: Customers that have purchased the Salesforce Shield add-on can enable 256-bit AES encryption for certain standard fields and Custom Fields of their choosing. It can be applied to email, phone, text, text area, URL, and date and date/time fields. While the encryption level is higher, this facility does come with some significant restrictions – these are covered in the next section.

Encrypted field values are visible to those who have the **View Encrypted Data** permission, which is a facility that may not be something your requirements tolerate. This also includes users whom you grant login access to, such as through subscriber support. Apex, Visualforce Page, Lightning Components, and Validation Rule logic you package can see unencrypted values, so extra care is needed by developers if you want to mask field values. If your only concern is compliance with encryption at rest, this may not be such an issue for you.

Special considerations for Platform Encryption

Salesforce recommends that you only consider this feature if government regulations for your market require it. When developing a packaged solution, your main consideration is what happens if a subscriber wishes to enable it on a standard field you reference in your solution or in one of your packaged fields.

> **TIP**
> For those that do want to promote support for this feature through their AppExchange listing, there is an indicator that can be applied to your listing by Salesforce to show prospective customers you support Platform Encryption.

When implementing the 256-bit encryption used by Platform Encryption, by default, Salesforce opted for probabilistic encryption over deterministic encryption. Since the encryption is not deterministic (an encrypted value is the same each time), it is not possible to index fields that have this level of encryption applied. This results in the most significant restrictions for developers and platform functionality regarding querying a field.

Without an index, the platform cannot provide a performant way to allow code to filter, group, or order by encrypted fields in queries. If code attempts to do so at runtime, an exception will occur. Your package installation may be blocked if it detects queries inside Apex code that would not be compatible with these restrictions. Conversely, once your package is installed and the user attempts to enable encryption, this action may fail. Salesforce provides a report in both cases to inform the user which fields are problematic.

It is possible to work around these restrictions in one of two ways, depending on the chosen encryption type for a given field:

- **Using Deterministic Encryption** will enable some basic filtering but not all. For example, you can run reports or SOQL that compares encrypted fields with a given literal value for equality (case sensitive and case insensitive is a configuration). However, other filter operations, such as greater than or like, are not supported.

- **Using Probabilistic Encryption** with conditional code, by using Dynamic SOQL to allow runtime formation and the execution of effected queries where encryption is not enabled. In cases where encryption is enabled, you can perform filtering, grouping, and ordering in Apex and/or via **Salesforce Object Search Language** (**SOSL**). However, both these options should be considered carefully as they have their own restrictions and may not be the most performant.

Ultimately, you may need to accept that you have to selectively hide functionality in your solution in cases where neither of the above workarounds is acceptable to maintain a good user experience. This decision is one you have to make in conjunction with your users as to how acceptable a trade-off this would be.

> Note that deterministic encryption is not as strong as probabilistic encryption. For more information, see the Salesforce Help topic here: https://help.salesforce.com/articleView?id=security_pe_deterministic.htm.

I highly recommend that you leverage the **Education** section in the Partner Success Community. Under the **MORE RESOURCES** section, you will find a page with videos and other resources dedicated to ISVs.

> Regardless of whether or not you plan to support Platform Encryption, it may still be an important requirement for your enterprise customers when your application must co-exist with other Salesforce products and other Partner solutions. I recommend that you prepare a statement to set expectations early on what level of support you provide, such as which standard fields and package fields are supported. Make sure your prospects can make informed decisions; otherwise, they may dismiss your application from their shortlists unnecessarily.

Lookup options, filters, and layouts

The standard lookup UI from Salesforce can be configured to make it easier for users to recognize the correct record to select and filter out those that are not relevant, and, if necessary, prevent them from deleting records that are in use elsewhere in your application, all without writing any code.

Perform the following steps in the package org to try out this process:

1. Create **Tabs** for the `Driver` and `Race` objects.
2. Add an **Active** checkbox field to the `Driver` Custom Object; ensure that the default is **checked**.

3. Create a driver record; for example, `LewisHamilton`.
4. From the **Season** record created in the previous section, create a **Race** record; for example, `Spa`.
5. Associate `LewisHamilton` with the `Spa` race via the **Contestants** relationship.

First, let's ensure that drivers cannot be deleted if they are associated with a `Contestant` record (meaning they have or are taking part in a race). Edit the **Driver** field on the **Contestant** object and enable **Don't allow deletion of the lookup record that's part of a lookup relationship**. This is similar to expressing a **referential integrity** rule in other database platforms:

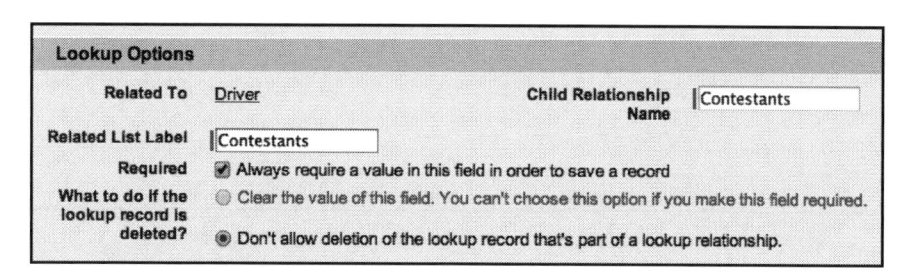

Lookup Options

Related To	Driver	Child Relationship Name	Contestants
Related List Label	Contestants		
Required	☑ Always require a value in this field in order to save a record		
What to do if the lookup record is deleted?	○ Clear the value of this field. You can't choose this option if you make this field required.		
	● Don't allow deletion of the lookup record that's part of a lookup relationship.		

Now, if you try to delete **Lewis Hamilton**, you should receive a message as shown in the following screenshot. This also applies if you attempt to delete the record via Apex DML or the Salesforce API:

> Your attempt to delete Lewis Hamilton could not be completed because it is associated with the following contestants.: CONTESTANT-00000000

You've just saved yourself some Apex trigger code and used a platform feature.

Let's take a look at another lookup feature, known as **lookup filters**. Formula 1 drivers come and go all the time; let's ensure when selecting drivers to be in races, via the `Driver` lookup on the `Contestant` record, that only active drivers are shown and are permitted when entered directly.

Perform the following steps in the packaging org to try out this feature:

1. Create a **Driver** record, for example, `Rubens Barrichello` and ensure that the **Active** field is unchecked.

Leveraging Platform Features

2. Edit the **Driver** field on the **Contestant** object and complete the **Lookup Filter** section, as shown in the following screenshot, entering the suggested messages in the **If it doesn't, display this error message on save** and **Add this informational message to the lookup window** fields, and click on **Save**:

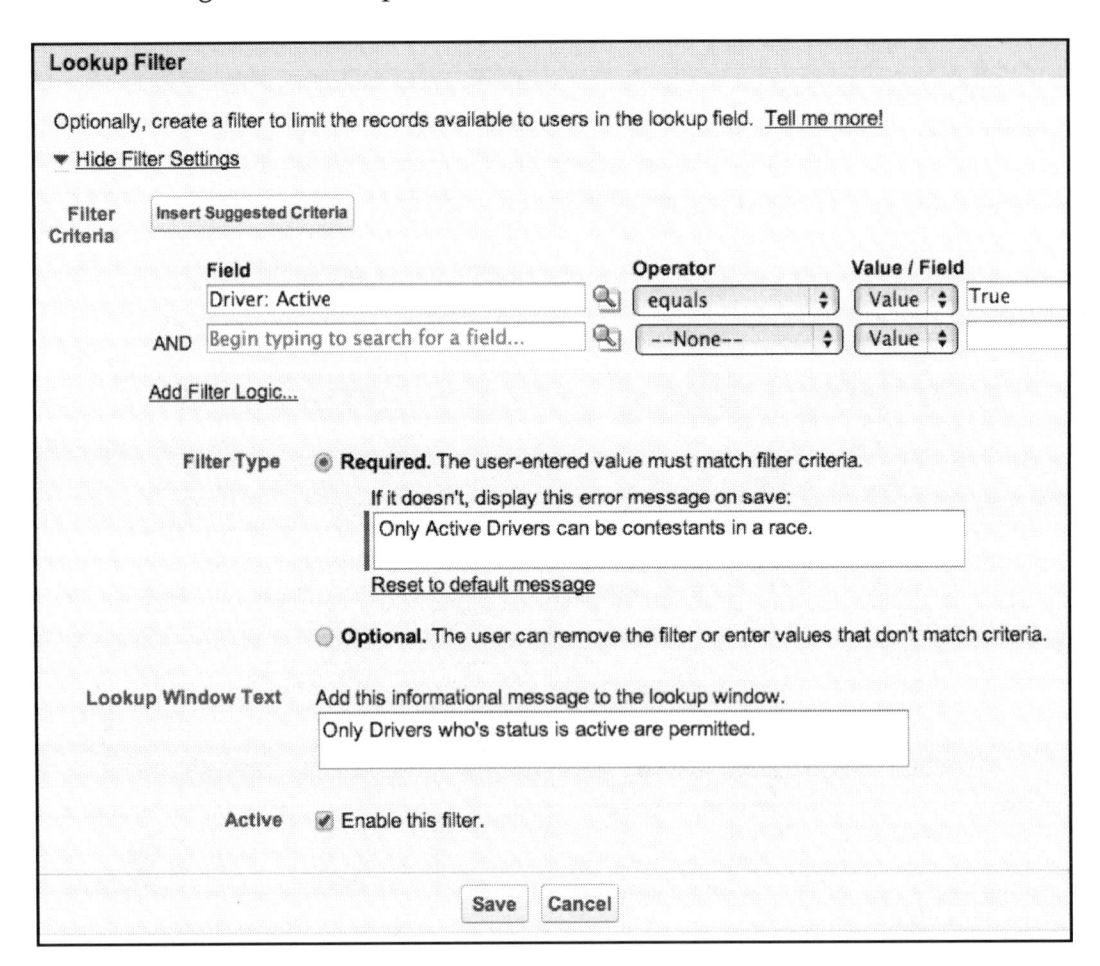

Lookup Filter

Optionally, create a filter to limit the records available to users in the lookup field. Tell me more!

▼ Hide Filter Settings

Filter Criteria [Insert Suggested Criteria]

	Field	Operator	Value / Field
	Driver: Active	equals	Value — True
AND	Begin typing to search for a field...	--None--	Value —

Add Filter Logic...

Filter Type ● **Required.** The user-entered value must match filter criteria.

If it doesn't, display this error message on save:

> Only Active Drivers can be contestants in a race.

Reset to default message

○ **Optional.** The user can remove the filter or enter values that don't match criteria.

Lookup Window Text Add this informational message to the lookup window.

> Only Drivers who's status is active are permitted.

Active ☑ Enable this filter.

[Save] [Cancel]

[62]

You can have up to five active lookup filters per object. This is not a limit that is set by your package namespace. Use them sparingly to give your end users room to create their own lookup filters. If you don't have a strong need for filtering, consider implementing it as an Apex trigger validation.

Test the filter by attempting to create a `Contestant` child record for the `Spa` record. First, by using the lookup dialog, you will see the informational message entered previously and will be unable to select `Rubens Barrichello`, as shown in the following screenshot:

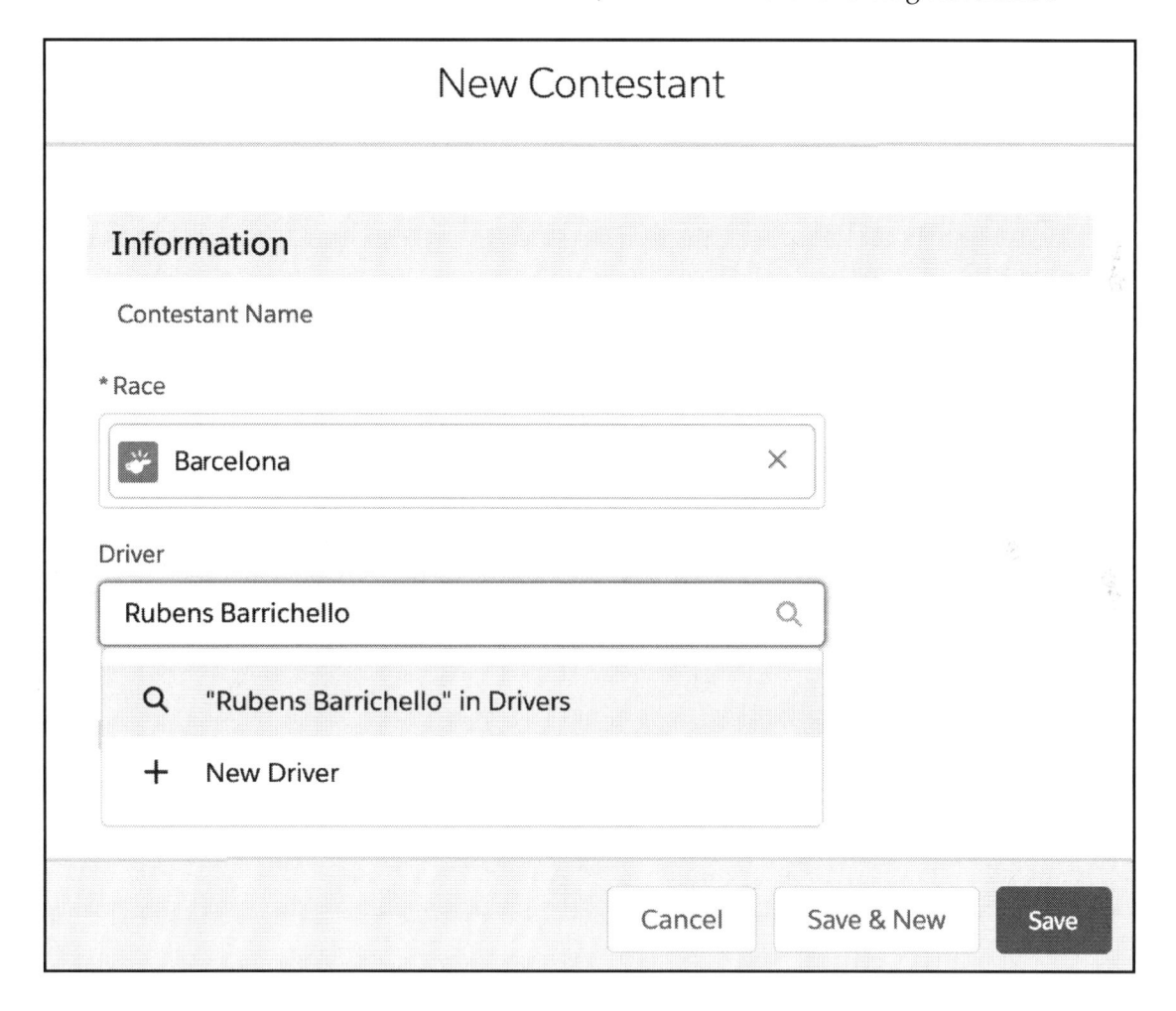

If you attempt to enter an inactive driver's name directly, this is also blocked, as shown in the following screenshot:

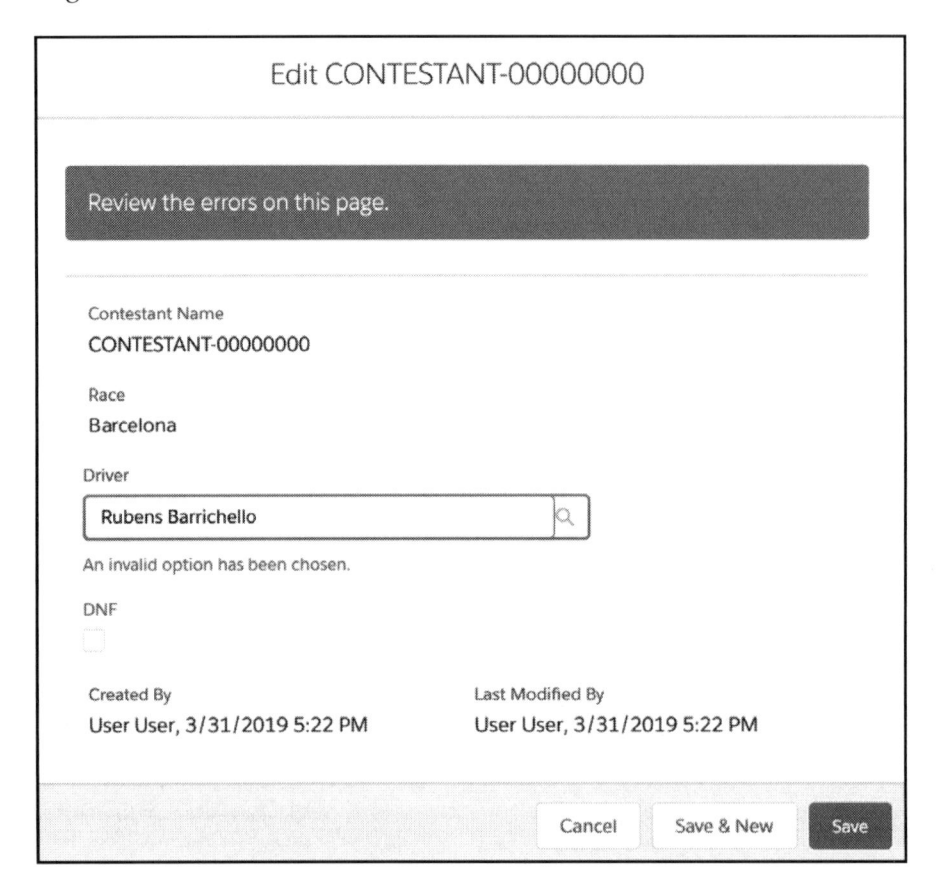

Edit CONTESTANT-00000000

Review the errors on this page.

Contestant Name
CONTESTANT-00000000

Race
Barcelona

Driver
Rubens Barrichello
An invalid option has been chosen.

DNF

Created By
User User, 3/31/2019 5:22 PM

Last Modified By
User User, 3/31/2019 5:22 PM

Cancel | Save & New | Save

> At the time of writing, Lightning Experience does not show the error message configured and, instead, shows a generic error message as shown in the preceding screenshot. The message is correctly displayed when users are using Salesforce Classic.

This validation is also enforced through Apex DML and Salesforce APIs. Unlike Validation Rules, it cannot be disabled by the end user. However, changes related to records, such as making the driver subsequently inactive, are permitted by the platform. In this case, the next time the `Contestant` record is edited, the error given in the preceding screenshot will occur.

Finally, you are also able to display additional columns on lookup dialogs, which help the user identify the correct record based on other fields. The following steps describe how to do this:

1. Add a **Nationality** field to the **Driver** object of the **Picklist** type, and enter the following values: `British`, `Spanish`, `Brazilian`, `Finnish`, and `Mexican`.
2. Edit the existing **Driver** records and set an appropriate value in the **Nationality** field.
3. Locate the **Search Layouts** section of the **Driver** object, edit the **Lookup Dialogs** layout, add the **Nationality** field created in step 1, and save the layout. When selecting a driver, the lookup should now show this additional field, as follows:

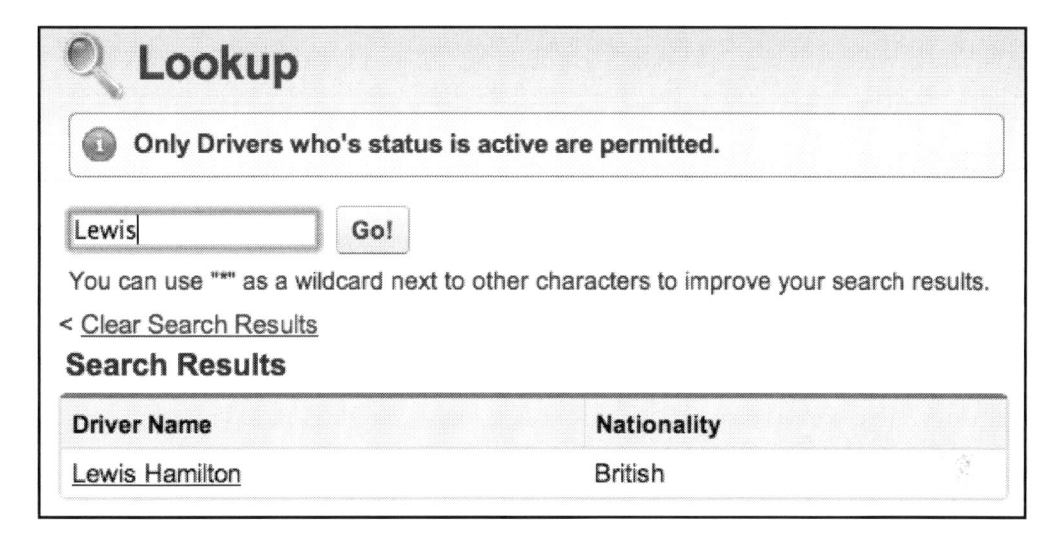

> The previous screenshot is using Salesforce Classic, the older UI technology. Currently, at the time of publishing, while it is possible to customize the fields shown when searching for records within Lightning Experience, picklist field types such as the **Nationality** field are not supported. You can read more about adding additional fields to search results in Lightning Experience here: `https://help.salesforce.com/articleView?id=search_lookup_config_lex.htmtype=5`.

Lookups are a hugely powerful declarative feature of the platform; they are not just used to express application data model relationships, but they actually enforce the integrity of data as well, thereby making the user's job of entering data much easier.

Rollup summaries and limits

When it comes to performing calculations on your data, the platform provides a number of options: reports, the Analytics API, dashboards, Apex Triggers, Visualforce, and Rollup Summaries. The Rollup summary option provides a code-free solution with the ability to apply some condition filtering. Rollup summary fields can then also be referenced and combined with other features such as formula fields and Validation Rules.

The key requirement is that there is a Master-Detail relationship between the detail records being summarized on the field being added to the master records, such as that between **Race** and **Contestant**. The following example will total the number of competitors that did not finish a given race (or DNF in Formula 1 terms).

Perform the following steps in the package org to try out this process:

1. Create a **DNF** field on the **Contestant** object using the **Checkbox** field type.
2. Create a **Driver** record for `Charles Pic` and add him to the `Spa` race via the **Contestant** object, checking the **DNF** field.
3. Create a **Total DNFs** field on the **Race** object using a **Rollup Summary** field type. Select the **Contestants** object from the **Summarized Object** dropdown and **COUNT** as **Rollup-Up Type** and apply the **Filter Criteria** field, as shown in the following screenshot, to select only **Contestant** records with the **DNF** field checked:

Chapter 2

Step 3. Define the summary calculation — Step 3 of 5

Select Object to Summarize

- Master Object: Race
- Summarized Object: Contestants

Select Roll-Up Type

- ● COUNT
- ○ SUM
- ○ MIN
- ○ MAX

Field to Aggregate: --None--

Filter Criteria

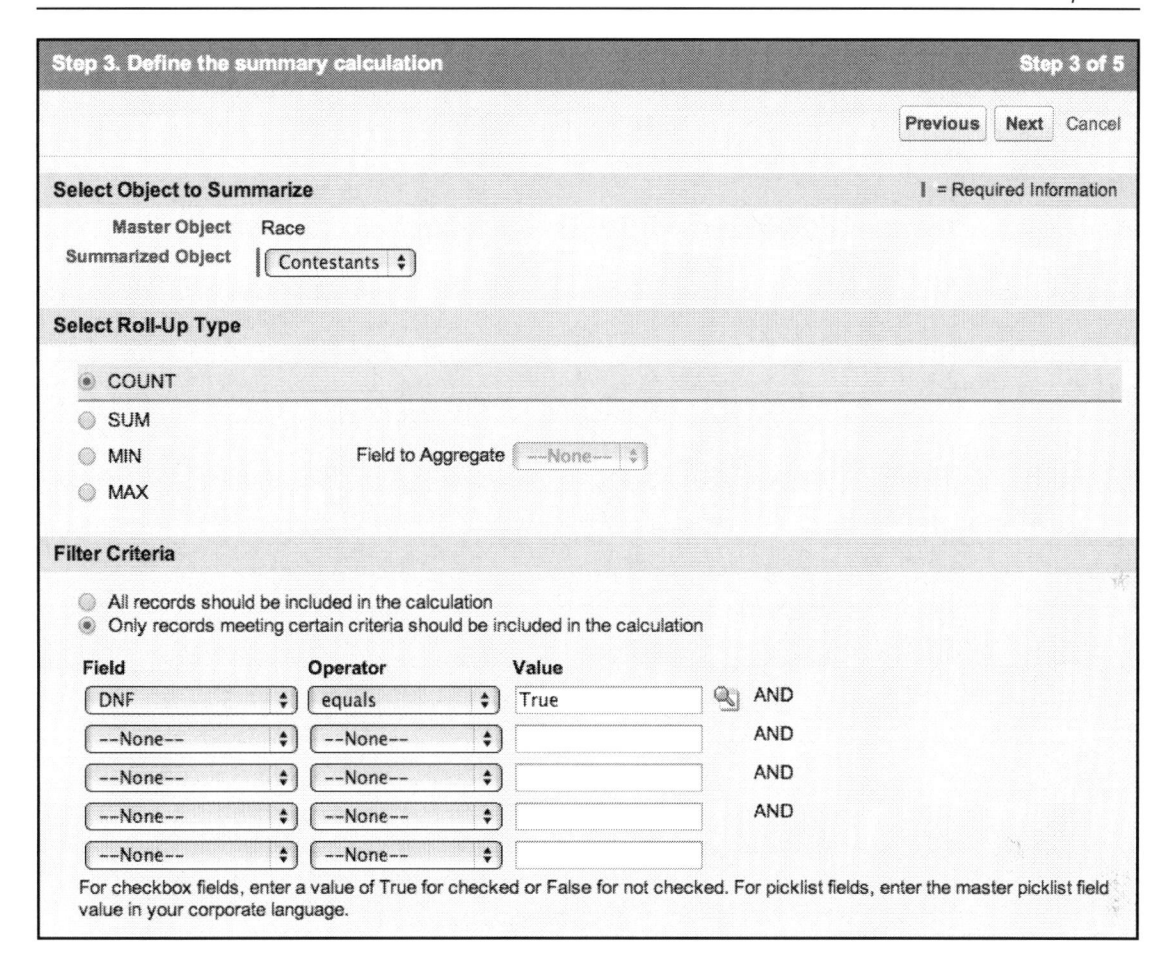

- ○ All records should be included in the calculation
- ● Only records meeting certain criteria should be included in the calculation

Field	Operator	Value	
DNF	equals	True	AND
--None--	--None--		AND
--None--	--None--		AND
--None--	--None--		AND
--None--	--None--		

For checkbox fields, enter a value of True for checked or False for not checked. For picklist fields, enter the master picklist field value in your corporate language.

Navigate to the `Spa` record and note that **Total DNFs** shows the value **1**. Experiment by changing the status of the **DNF** field on the **Driver** records to see the value recalculate.

Rollup summaries provide a real-time calculation once configured. However, when creating or changing rollups, Salesforce states that it can take up to 30 minutes. You can read more about them by searching for *About Roll-Up Summary Fields* in the documentation and by reviewing the *Roll-Up Summary Field* technology overview knowledge base article at `http://help.salesforce.com/apex/HTViewSolution?id=000004281`.

> **TIP:** You can combine the use of Rollup summary fields in your Apex trigger logic; for example, you can add the Apex logic to check the number of DNFs in the `after` phase of the trigger on the **Race** object. Your users can also apply Validation Rules on the **Race** object that references its Rollup summary fields. Any changes to **Contestant** detail records that cause this Validation Rule to be invalid will prevent updates to the related **Contestant** record.

As you can imagine, calculating Rollup summaries can be quite an intensive job for the Salesforce servers. As such, Salesforce limits the total number of Rollup summaries to 25 per object, though this can be increased to 40 by contacting Salesforce Support with a valid business case. Keep in mind that, as a packaged application provider, this limit is not scoped by your namespace, unlike other limits. This means that if you use all 10, your end users will not be able to add their own post-installation. Similarly, if they have created their own post-installation and an upgrade causes the limit to be breached, the install will fail.

> **TIP:** While this can be a powerful feature, carefully consider other summarization options listed in the previous paragraph and whether your users really need this information in real time or to be accessible from formulas and Validation Rules. If not, a good compromise is a Visualforce page, which can be added inline into the **Page Layout** objects. The Visualforce page can utilize the `readonly=true` attribute in which the Apex controller logic can utilize aggregate SOQL queries to aggregate up to 5 million records (subject to appropriate indexes and within standard timeout tolerance). This page can then display when the user reviews the record in the UI and is thus calculated on demand. Enhancing standard Salesforce pages with Visualforce is discussed in more detail later in this chapter.

Understanding the available security features

The platform provides security controls to manage the accessibility of functionalities in your application and also the visibility of the individual records it creates. As an application provider, your code has a responsibility to enforce security rules as well as provided integrations that help administrators configure security easily. This section is not aimed at taking a deep dive into the security features of the platform but is more to aid in understanding the options, best practices, and packaging implications.

One of the key checks the security review process described in the previous chapter makes is to scan the code to ensure it is using the appropriate Apex conventions to enforce the security rules administrators of your application configure, as not all security checks are enforced automatically for you.

This chapter discusses the following two categories of security as provided by the platform:

- **Functional security**: Security that applies to application objects and some code entry points (providing APIs), and also Visualforce pages that deliver the features of the application, is referred to here as functional security.
- **Data security**: In contrast to security applied to individual record data created and maintained by the application, this type of security is referred to as data security.

Functional security

Both **Profiles** and **Permission Sets** can be created and packaged in your application to help administrators of your application control access to your objects, fields, tabs, and pages. Fundamentally, profiles have been historically used to prepackage roles, such as *team principle,* that you envisage the user having when using your application. In contrast, Permission Sets can be used to express the functionality in your application, such as *the ability to assign a driver to a race*.

By now, most people are familiar with configuring profiles to control security. The issue is that they can eventually lead to a proliferation of profiles; as small differences in needs between users arise, profiles are then cloned and this increases the administration overhead when performing common changes. To manage this, Salesforce created Permission Sets, which are a much more granular way of expressing security controls.

From an application perspective, you can package Permission Sets and even have them upgraded automatically as they change in accordance with the new or updated functionality in your application. They can also assign them after installation, in contrast to profiles, which can only be done during installation. Also, unlike profiles, administrators cannot edit them, though they can clone them if there is a need (this is not possible in Professional and Group Editions of Salesforce). Because of these benefits, it is recommended that Permission Sets be used over profiles when packaging security information about your application.

It is important to plan your use of Permission Sets from the start so that your development team keeps them updated and their usage remains consistent throughout. Consider the following when designing your Permission Set strategy:

- **Think features, not roles**: Do not be tempted to fall back to expressing the roles you envisage your application's users being assigned. Enterprise organizations are large and complex; rarely does one size fit all. For example, a **team principle** can have many different responsibilities across your application from one installation to another. If you get this wrong, the administrator will be forced to clone the Permission Set, resulting in the start of the proliferation of unmanaged Permission Sets that do not track with the new or changed functionality as your package is upgraded.
- **Granularity**: As you design the functionality of your application, modules are defined (you can use **Application** under **Setup** to indicate these), and, within these objects, tabs, or pages, each has distinct operations. For example, the **Contestant** object might describe the ability to indicate that a driver has crashed out of the race and update the appropriate **DNF** field, which is **Update DNF Status**. For example, this permission might be assigned to the race controller user. In contrast, you might have a less granular Permission Set called **Race Management**, which encompasses the **Update DNF Status** permission plus others. Considering this approach to design your Permission Sets means that administrators have less work to assign to users, while, at the same time, they have the power to be more selective should they wish to.
- **Naming convention**: When the administrator is viewing your Permission Sets in the Salesforce UI, ensure they are grouped according to the functional aspects of your application by considering a naming convention, for example, `FormulaForce - Race Management` and `FormulaForce - Race Management - Update DNF Status`.

At the time of writing, **Permission Set Groups** are available as a pilot feature to eligible customers. Assuming this feature will eventually be made generally available (GA), it will allow you to include them in your package groupings of Permission Sets. Such groupings, as described in the granularity discussion above, can then be physically aligned with your actual product features, thus simplifying the assignment of permissions by feature even further. You can read more about this feature here: https://help.salesforce.com/articleView?id=perm_set_groups.htm.

One of the limitations of the **License Management Application (LMA)** described in the previous chapter is that it is not very granular; you can only effectively grant user licenses to the whole package and not modules or key features within it. With the introduction of Permission Set licenses, Salesforce looks to be heading down the path of providing a means to define your licensing requirements with respect to Permission Sets. At the time of writing, there is no support for developers to create their own; this looks like the next obvious step. This is something to consider when designing your Permission Sets for use as license control; for example, one day, you may be able to use this to enforce a pricing model for high-priced licenses associated with the **Race Management** permission.

Perform the following steps in the package org to try out this process:

1. Create a `Race Management` custom application (under **Setup | Create**) and add the **Driver**, **Season**, and **Race** tabs created earlier to it; make the **Race** tab the default and check the **Visible in Lightning Experience** checkbox.
2. Create a `Race Analytics` custom application and add the **Race** and **Reports** tabs to it; make the **Reports** tab the default and check the **Visible in Lightning Experience** checkbox.
3. Create the Permission Sets for the FormulaForce application, as shown in the following table. Leave the **User License** field set to **None**.

4. Finally, add the following Permission Sets to the FormulaForce package:

Permission Set	Permissions
Label: FormulaForce - Race Management **Name:** FormulaForceRaceManagement	**Race Management** (Custom Application) **Race Analytics** (Custom Application) The **Season** tab (Custom Tab) The **Race** tab (Custom Tab) The **Driver** tab (Custom Tab) **Object** (Custom Object, Full Access) The **Race** object (Custom Object, Full Access) The **Driver** object (Custom Object, Full Access) The **Contestant** object (Custom Object, Full Access)
Label: FormulaForce - Race Management - Update DNF Status **Name:** FormulaForceRaceManagementUpdateDNFStatus	The **Contestant** object (Custom Object, Read, Edit) **DNF** (Custom Field, Read, Edit)
Label: FormulaForce - Race Analytics **Name:** FormulaForceRaceAnalytics	**Race Analytics** (Custom Application) The **Race** object (Custom Object, Read Only, Read DNF)

Here, Full Access means it gives access to read, create, edit, and delete all Custom Fields. Also, at the time of writing, the Custom Application and Custom Tab components within Permission Sets are not packable. Until they become packable, it is recommended that you still maintain this information in Permission Sets.

The Salesforce DX CLI has commands that allow you to easily assign permission sets, for example, when you have just deployed your application to a new scratch org. The following commands will assign the above permission sets to the current user:

```
sfdx force:user:permset:assign
  --permsetnam FormulaForceRaceManagementUpdateDNFStatus
sfdx force:user:permset:assign
  --permsetnam FormulaForceRaceManagement
sfdx force:user:permset:assign
  --permsetnam FormulaForceRaceAnalytics
```

Your code and security review considerations

Not all of the code you write will automatically be subjected to enforcement by the platform through the object- and field-level security defined by the Permission Sets or profiles assigned to users. While certain Visualforce and Lightning components such as `apex:inputField`, `apex:outputField`, `lightning:recordEdit`, and `lightning:recordView` enforce security, other ways in which you obtain or display information to users will not enforce security, such as `apex:inputText`, `apex:outputText`, `ui:outputText`, and `ui:inputText`. The differences will be discussed in more detail in a later chapter.

When your code is performing calculations or transformations on fields in the controller, expose this data indirectly via Apex bindings or remote action methods on your controller; for this, you need to add additional checks yourself. This also applies to any customer-facing Apex code such as `global` methods or Apex REST APIs you build.

In these cases, you can use the **Apex Describe** facility to specifically check the user's profile or Permission Set assignment for access and prevent further execution by returning errors or throwing exceptions. The formal reference information for implementing this can be found in the following two Salesforce articles:

- **Enforcing CRUD and FLS**: https://developer.salesforce.com/page/Enforcing_CRUD_and_FLS
- **Testing CRUD and FLS Enforcement**: https://developer.salesforce.com/page/Testing_CRUD_and_FLS_Enforcement

> **TIP:** Currently in pilot at the time of writing is an enhancement to the SOQL syntax that performs object and field read access checks without the need to write this code to perform these checks yourself. This is enabled by adding `WITH SECURITY_ENFORCED` to the end of the SOQL. For more information, refer to the Apex Developers Guide (https://developer.salesforce.com/docs/atlas.en-us.apexcode.meta/apexcode/apex_classes_perms_enforcing.htm).

The Salesforce security review scanner and team insist that you check Custom Object-level security (CRUD security for short) and include checking for every field that is accessed (**field-level security (FLS)**).

Implementing code to check both needs careful consideration, planning, and monitoring. Implementing FLS is especially complex with multiple use cases and contexts applying different usage patterns within your code base. For some functionalities, you may wish the application to access certain objects and/or fields on the user's behalf without checking security; document these cases well, as you might need to present them to Salesforce.

Implementing CRUD security is something we will revisit in later chapters on the Domain and Selector layers of your Apex code, where some automated support within the library used to support these patterns has been provided.

> **TIP:** It's best to review and document your approach and use CRUD and FLS checking as a part of defining your coding conventions, and, if in doubt, discuss it with your Salesforce **Technical Account Manager** (**TAM**) or by raising a support case in Partner Portal. This way, you will also have some reference decisions and conversations to use when providing input and background to the security review team.

Note that it is a common misconception that applying the `with sharing` or `inherit sharing` keywords to your Apex classes will automatically enforce CRUD or FLS security, but it does not. These keywords solely control the records returned when querying objects, so are in fact related only to data security.

Data security

Regardless of which Custom Objects or Fields are accessible to the end user through their profile or Permission Set assignments, there may still be a requirement to filter which records certain users can see; for example, certain race data during and after the race can only be visible to the owning teams.

Salesforce allows this level of security to be controlled through the **Owner** field on each record and, optionally, a facility known as sharing. This is defined via the **Sharing Settings** page (under **Security Controls | Setup**), in the packaging org for the FormulaForce application. This page is shown in the following screenshot:

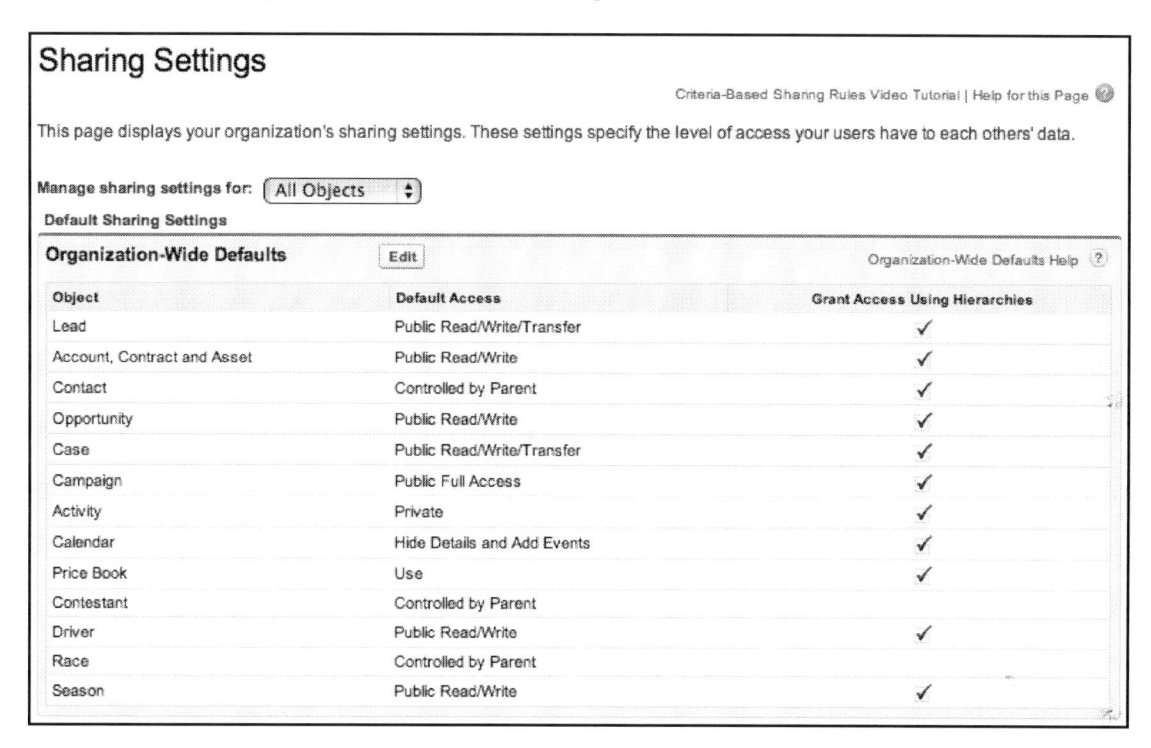

Sharing Settings

This page displays your organization's sharing settings. These settings specify the level of access your users have to each others' data.

Manage sharing settings for: All Objects

Default Sharing Settings

Organization-Wide Defaults

Object	Default Access	Grant Access Using Hierarchies
Lead	Public Read/Write/Transfer	✓
Account, Contract and Asset	Public Read/Write	✓
Contact	Controlled by Parent	✓
Opportunity	Public Read/Write	✓
Case	Public Read/Write/Transfer	✓
Campaign	Public Full Access	✓
Activity	Private	✓
Calendar	Hide Details and Add Events	✓
Price Book	Use	✓
Contestant	Controlled by Parent	
Driver	Public Read/Write	✓
Race	Controlled by Parent	
Season	Public Read/Write	✓

You can see the Standard Objects and also the Custom Objects we have created so far listed here. When you click on **Edit**, **Default Access** shows that the access options vary based on whether the object is a standard or Custom Object, as Salesforce has some special access modes for certain Standard Objects such as **Price Book**.

> **TIP**: Notice that where an object is in a child relationship with a parent record, in the case of **Race** and **Session**, there is no facility to control the security of this object. Thus, when you are designing your application object schema, make sure that you consider whether you or your users will need to utilize sharing on this object; if so, it might be better to consider a standard lookup relationship.

Leveraging Platform Features

For the Custom Objects that exist as a part of the FormulaForce application, you can define **Public Read/Write**, **Public Read Only**, and **Private**. The default value is always **Public Read/Write**.

The default access defines the starting position for the platform to determine the visibility of a given record using the **Owner** field and the object's **sharing rules**. In other words, you cannot use these features to hide records from a given user if the object has **Public Read** or **Public Read/Write** default access.

> **TIP:** Although this setting is packaged with Custom Objects, it is editable in the subscriber org and is thus not upgradable. If you decide to change this in a later release, this will need to be done manually as a post-install task.

If you set the **Private** default access and do nothing, the **Owner** field determines the visibility of the records. By default, the owner is the user that created the record. Thus, users can only see records they create or records created by other users below them in the **role hierarchy** (if enabled). A record owner can be a user or a group (known as **Queue** within the API), for example, members of a specific racing team. Users can choose to manually share a record they own with other users or groups also.

Sometimes, a more sophisticated and dynamic logic is required; in these cases, sharing rules can be added and they can be created either declaratively (from the **Sharing Settings** page) or programmatically. Regardless of the approach used, the platform creates a `Share` object (for example, for a `RaceData__c` object, this would be `RaceData__Share`) that contains records resulting from the evaluation of sharing rules; these records can be queried like any other object, which is useful for debugging.

> **TIP:** For the ultimate in flexibility, you can write logic within an Apex trigger or scheduled job to directly create, update, or delete sharing records, for example, in the `RaceData__Share` object. In this case, the criteria for sharing records can be practically anything you can express in code. You first define a sharing reason against the applicable Custom Object, which will be automatically included in your package. This is used as a kind of tag for the sharing records your application code creates versus sharing records created through sharing rules defined in the subscriber org. Also note that, if the platform detects references to the `Share` object for a given object listed on the **Sharing Settings** page, it will prevent the subscriber org administrator from changing the default access from **Private** to **Public**.

Your code and security review considerations

The platform will enforce record visibility in cases where the user attempts to navigate to a record directly in the Salesforce UI, including reports they run and the access provided via Salesforce APIs when they use third-party applications.

However, keep in mind that your Apex code runs at the system level by default; thus, it's important to pay attention to the use of the `inherit sharing`, `without sharing`, and `with sharing` keywords for all classes. This is also something the security review scanner will look for. You might as well ask when using the `without sharing` keyword makes sense; such a use case might be when you explicitly want system-level logic to see all records on behalf of an operation or validation the user is performing.

Platform APIs

Salesforce provides a number of APIs to access and manipulate records in its own objects that belong to applications such as CRM; these APIs are also extended to support Custom Objects created by admins or provided by packages installed in the subscriber org. Salesforce dedicates a huge amount of its own and community-driven documentation resources you can reference when educating partners and customer developers on the use of these APIs. Thus, it is important that your application works well with these APIs.

Platform APIs are enabled for Enterprise Edition orgs and above, though if you have a need to consume them in Professional or Group Edition orgs, Salesforce can provide a Partner API token (following the completion of a security review) to enable their use; this is unique to your application and so does not provide access for code other than yours.

Typically, unless you are developing an off-platform utility or integration to accompany your application, you may not find your application consuming these APIs at all, though there are some you might want to consider, highlighted in the following bullets. Keep in mind, however, that if you do, in addition to the Partner API token, the subscriber org's daily API limit will also be consumed; hence, ensure that your usage is as network-optimal as possible.

Enterprise-level customers often have complex integration requirements both on- and off-platform; typically, Salesforce utilizes the SOAP and REST technologies to make these APIs available to any number of platforms and languages such as Java and Microsoft .NET. In `Chapter 9`, *User Interfaces with Lightning Framework*, we will discuss how you can extend the features of the platform's data-orientated APIs with your own more application-process-orientated APIs.

Leveraging Platform Features

> **TIP**: Note that not all platform APIs have an Apex variant that can be called directly, though this does not necessarily mean that they cannot be used. Apex supports making outbound HTTP callouts either via a WSDL or by directly creating and parsing the required requests and responses.

The following list details some of the main APIs that may be of use to your Enterprise-level customers wishing to develop solutions around your application:

- **Enterprise API**: This SOAP API is dynamically generated based on the objects present at the time in the subscriber org, meaning that any tool (such as data-mapping tools) or developer consuming it will find the information it exposes familiar and easy to access. One downside, however, is that this can end up being quite a large API to work with, as Enterprise customer orgs often have hundreds of objects and fields in them.
- **Partner API**: This is also a SOAP API; unlike the Enterprise API, it provides a more generic CRUD-based API to access the record in the subscriber org. Its name can be a bit misleading, as there is no restriction on non-partners using it, and, as it is lighter than the Enterprise API, it's often the first choice.
- **REST API**: This provides another CRUD style API, similar to the Partner API, but, in this case, it is based on the more popular REST technology standard. It's often preferred when building mobile applications and is also fast becoming popular as the default API for Java and .NET.
- **User Interface API**: This provides a singular API that provides mobile applications or custom UIs not built on the Salesforce platform with a response that not only contains record data pre-filtered by the user's security access but also metadata such as layouts and applicable actions for the requesting device type.
- **Metadata API and Tooling API**: These SOAP APIs provide a means to automate many of the tasks performed under the **Setup** menu and those performed by developers when editing code. While these might not be of direct interest to those integrating with your application, as many of these tasks are performed initially and then only rarely, it might be something to consider using in tools you want to provide to keep the implementation times of your application low.
- **Streaming API**: This API utilizes an HTTP long polling protocol known as the Bayeux protocol to allow callers to monitor in near real time and record activity in Salesforce. This API can be used on a page to monitor race data as it arrives and display it to the user in near real time. A number of platform features support streaming, Push Topics, Platform Events, and Change Data Capture.
    - **Push Topics** allow you to configure criteria on standard and Custom Objects that, when met, will send an event to a specific channel.

- **Platform Events** allow you to create an event, much like a Custom Object, that has specific fields describing the event payload. Using various platform features, such as Apex, Process Builder, Flow, and Lightning, you can publish events yourself and subscribe to those created by others. I will be covering Platform Events in more detail in a later chapter.
- **Change Data Capture (CDC)** sends events to the stream whenever users create, update, or delete data. It can be enabled for Custom Objects and some Standard objects.

- **Replication API**: Sometimes it is not possible or desirable to migrate all data into Salesforce through Custom Objects. In some cases, this migration is too complex or cost-prohibitive. This REST and Apex API allows replication solutions to determine for a given period of time which records for a given object have been created, updated, or deleted.
- **Bulk API**: This REST-based API allows the import and export of large numbers of records in CSV or XML format up to 10 MB in size per batch job.
- **Async SOQL**: This REST-based API allows you to process billions of records stored in Big Objects, Field Audit Trail, or Event Monitoring objects and extract aggregated subsets of that data into Custom Objects for more direct processing and filtering. For more information, see this Salesforce help topic: `https://developer.salesforce.com/docs/atlas.en-us.bigobjects.meta/bigobjects/async_query_examples.htm`.

Considerations for working well with the platform's APIs

The following are some considerations to ensure that your application objects are well placed to work well with the platform's APIs:

- **Naming Custom Objects and Fields**: When naming your Custom Objects and Fields, pay attention to **API Name** (or **Developer Name**, as it is sometimes referred to as). This is the name used when referencing the object or field in the APIs and Apex code mentioned in the previous section. Personally, I prefer to remove the underscore characters that the Salesforce Setup UIs automatically place in the default API names when you tap out of the **Label** field, as doing so makes the API name shorter and is easier to type with fewer underscore characters. It then ends up reflecting the camel case used by most APIs; for example, `RaceData__c` instead of `Race_Data__c`.

- **Label and API name consistency**: While it is possible to rename the label of a Custom Field between releases of your application, you cannot rename the API name. Try to avoid doing so, as causing inconsistency between the field label and API name makes it harder for business users and developers to work together and locate the correct fields.
- **Naming Relationships**: Whenever you define **Master-Detail** or **Lookup Relationship**, the platform uses the plural label value of the object to form a relationship API name. This API name is used when querying related records as part of a subquery, for example, `select Id, Name, (select Id, Name from Races) from Season__c`. When creating relationship fields, pay attention to the default value entered into the **Child Relationship Name** field, removing underscores if desired and checking whether the names make sense. For example, if you create a lookup field to the `Driver__c` object called **Fastest Lap By** on the `Race__c` object, the default relationship API name will be **Races**. When using this in a subquery context, it will look like `select Id, Name, (select Id, Name from Races) from Race__c`. However, by naming the relationship `FastestLaps`, this results in a more self-describing query: `select Id, Name, (select Id, Name from FastestLaps) from Race__c`.
- **Apex Triggers bulkification and performance**: When testing Apex Triggers, ensure that you accommodate up to 200 records; this is the default chunk size that Salesforce recommends when utilizing its bulk APIs. This tests the standard guidelines around bulkification best practices; although smaller chunk sizes can be configured, it will typically reduce the execution time of the overall process. Also related to execution time is the time spent within the Apex trigger code, when users solely update fields that have been added in the subscriber org. In these cases, executing the Apex trigger logic is mostly redundant, as none of the fields this logic is interested in will have changed. Therefore, encourage the optimization of the Apex trigger logic to execute expensive operations (such as the execution of SOQL) only if fields that have been packaged have changed.

Localization and translation

It is important to take localization and translation into consideration from the beginning as it can become difficult and costly to apply it later. Fortunately, the platform can do a lot of work for you.

Localization

When using the native user interface, it automatically formats the values of numeric and date fields according to the **Locale** field on the user profile. **Visualforce** pages using the `apex:outputField` and `apex:inputField` components will automatically format values, and outputting local sensitive values in any other way will need to be handled manually in your Apex controller code or in your JavaScript code. **Lightning components** using `lightning:outputField` and `lightning:inputField` also honor localization.

> **TIP**: It's not always possible to use Visualforce or Lightning tags as described above. For example, if the information you are displaying is not contained within a Custom Object field but in some calculated Viewstate in your Apex controller. The format methods on various type classes, such as `Date`, `DateTime`, and `Decimal`, can be used to generate a formatted string value that you can bind to your pages. You can also determine the user's ISO locale code via `UserInfo.getLocale()`.

Translation

Literal text entered when defining components such as Custom Objects, Fields, and layouts is automatically available to the Salesforce **Translation Workbench** tool. However, literal text used in the Apex code, Visualforce pages, and Lightning Components needs special attention from the developer through the use of Custom Labels.

It is important to avoid the concatenation of Custom Label values when forming messages to the end user, as it makes it harder for translators to understand the context of the messages and, if needed, resequence the context of the message for other languages. For example, take the `The driver XYZ was disqualified` message. The following is bad practice:

```
String message = 
    Label.TheDriver + driverName + Label.WasDisqualified;
```

This is good practice:

```
String message = String.format(
    Label.DriverDisqualified, new String[] { driverName});
```

The `DriverDisqualified` Custom Label will be defined as follows:

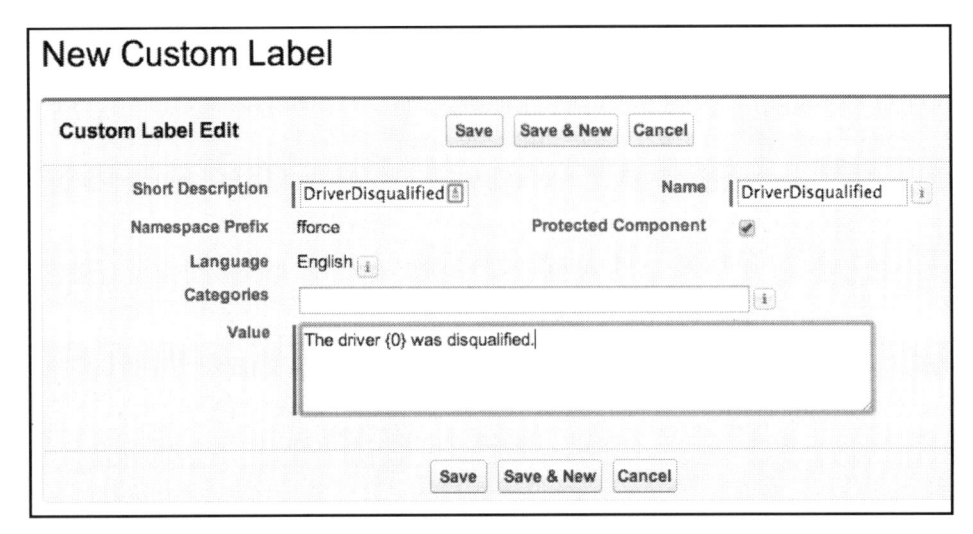

New Custom Label

Short Description	DriverDisqualified
Namespace Prefix	fforce
Language	English
Categories	
Value	The driver {0} was disqualified.
Name	DriverDisqualified
Protected Component	✓

> **TIP**: When creating Custom Labels, be sure to pay attention to the **Protected** checkbox. If you uncheck it, end users can reference your labels, which you might want to consider if you wish them to reuse your messages, for example, in custom **Email Templates** or **Visualforce** pages. However, the downside is that such labels cannot ever (currently) be deleted from your package as your functionality changes.

Finally, remember that, in Visualforce or Lightning, you can utilize the `apex:outputField` or `lightning:outputField` components to render the field labels so long as they are contained in `apex:pageBlockSection` or `lightning:recordView`.

Building customizable user interfaces

The most customizable aspect of the user interface your application delivers is the one provided by Salesforce through its highly customizable layout editor, which provides the ability to customize standard user interface pages (including those now delivered via the Salesforce1 mobile client) used to list, create, edit, and delete records.

Lightning Experience is the latest user interface experience available for your desktop users. Salesforce Classic or Aloha is the name given to the existing user interface. It's radically different both in appearance and technology. Fortunately, your existing investments in layouts and Visualforce are still compatible. Lightning, however, does bring with it a more component-driven aspect, and, with it, new tools that allow even greater customization of the overall user experience.

Keep in mind that any user experience you deliver that does not leverage the standard user interface will take added effort on behalf of the developer, typically utilizing Custom Settings and Fieldsets to provide customization facilities. Visualforce pages or Lightning components can be used to customize parts of or completely replace the standard user interface. This will be covered in more detail in Chapter 8, *Building User Interfaces*.

> It is worth noting that subscriber org administrators can modify the page overrides defined and packaged on your Custom Objects to re-enable the Salesforce standard user interface, instead of using your packaged Visualforce or Lightning page. As such, it's worth thinking about paying some aesthetic attention to all your Custom Object layouts. Also, note that action overrides and layout components do not get upgraded.

Layouts

The following is a brief summary of the customization features available beyond the standard sections and field order. These allow you to add graphs and custom UIs that help combine the layout customization with the flexibility and power of Visualforce:

- **Visualforce**: Layout sections allow you to embed a Visualforce page using Standard Controllers. While this is only supported on standard view pages, you are able to do whatever you wish on the Visualforce page itself.
- **Report charts**: Recently, the ability to embed a report chart into a layout has been added to the platform. This is a powerful feature to enhance the information provided to the user using a parameterized report.
- **Actions**: These allow you to describe, either declaratively or programmatically, additional actions beyond the standard platform actions. They are only applicable if you have enabled Chatter for the object.
- **Custom buttons**: Much like actions, these allow additional buttons on the detail and list view pages to invoke application-specific functionality. Creating Custom Buttons and hooking them up to your Apex code is covered in Chapter 8, *Building User Interfaces*.

Customizing Lightning Components and Visualforce pages

When you are considering building Visualforce pages or Lightning Components, always give consideration to end users who want to extend the layout and/or tables you define with their own Custom Fields. Fieldsets and Custom Metadata offer a means to customize your UIs; later chapters will go into this in more detail. For Lightning Components, you can also expose attributes (parameters) that are accessible to users using visual builders such as Lightning App Builder, Lightning Flow, and Lightning Community Builder.

Lightning App Builder and Components

Lightning App Builder (available under the **Setup** menu) can be used by users in a subscriber org to customize the user experience of Salesforce Mobile and Lightning Experience. This tool allows users to build brand-new pages using a drag and drop tool as well as to customize existing Lightning Experience pages provided by Salesforce such as the Home Page and Record Detail pages.

> The Record Detail component leverages the existing layouts defined via the existing layout editor to determine the layout of fields when displaying records.

Lightning Components are the fundamental building blocks that determine what information and functionality are available in Salesforce Mobile and Lightning Experience user experiences. Some standard components are provided by Salesforce and can also be built by other developers, as well as being included in your package to expose your functionality. In `Chapter 8`, *Building User Interfaces*, we will be taking a deeper look at the architecture of Lightning and how it affects how you deliver functionality in your application.

Email customization with email templates

Using Apex, you can write code to send emails using the Messaging API. This allows you to dynamically generate all attributes of the emails you wish to send: the from and to address, subject title, and body. However, keep in mind that end users will more than likely want to add their own logo and messaging to these emails, even if such emails are simply notifications aimed at their internal users.

Instead of hardcoding the structure of emails in your code, consider using email templates (under the **Setup** menu). This feature allows administrators in the subscriber org to create their own emails using replacement parameters to inject dynamic values from records your objects define. Using a Custom Setting, for example, you can ask them to configure `DeveloperName` of the email template to reference in your code. You can package email templates as starting points for further customization, though keep in mind that they are not upgradable.

> **TIP**
> If data included in the email is not stored as a field on a Custom Object record or formula field, consider providing some Visualforce custom components in your package that can be used in Visualforce email templates. These components can be used to invoke the Apex code from the email template to query information and/or perform calculations or reformat information.

Process Builder, Workflow, and Flow

Salesforce provides several declarative tools to implement business processes and custom user experience Flows. End user operations such as creating, updating, or starting an approval process for a record can be customized through two tools, known as **Workflow** and **Lightning Process Builder**. When you need to implement a UI Flow that provides a wizard or interview-style user experience, you can use the **Lightning Flow** tool. This tool can be used to define more complex conditional business processes that need to read and update records. Automation Flows, or sometimes "headless Flows," are Flows that do not interact with the user and can be referenced within Apex code as well as Process Builder.

> **TIP**
> Lightning Flow lets you build engaging UIs but has its limits since it is not a programming language in a traditional sense. This does not mean, however, if you or your users hit a roadblock you have to abandon it. Lightning Components can now be embedded into Lightning Flow UIs to fill this gap when needed. This is just one of many areas in which including Lightning Components in your package can add value to the platform tools your customers have access to.

Process Builder is the successor to Workflow. It provides the same functionality plus additional features for updating child records, for example, and extensibility for developers. It is also easier for end users to build and visualize more complex processes with its more modern graphical layout. Though you can use both interchangeably, its best to focus on one or the other, making it easier to locate and maintain customizations.

As an application developer, these can be created and packaged as part of your application. Such components are upgradable (provided that they are marked as **Protected**). Typically, however, package developers tend to leave the utilization of these features to consultants and subscriber org admins in preference to Apex and/or Visualforce, where more complex logic and user experiences can be created.

> **TIP**
> Just as these tools can be used by administrators to customize their orgs, you may want to consider exposing your Apex-driven application business processes through Invocable Methods, to effectively extended the functionality available to admins through these tools. Put another way, this allows users of the Lightning Process Builder and Lightning Flow tools to invoke your application's functionality through clicks not code. We will be revisiting this in `Chapter 10`, *Providing Integration and Extensibility*.

Social features and mobile

Chatter is a key social feature of the platform; it can enable users of your application to collaborate and communicate contextually around the records in your application as well as optionally inviting their customers to do so, using the Chatter Communities feature. It is a powerful aspect of the platform but covering its details is outside the scope of this book.

You can enable Chatter under the **Chatter Settings** page under **Setup**, after which you can enable **Feed Tracking** (also under **Setup**) for your Custom Objects. This setting can be packaged, though it is not upgradable and can be disabled by the subscriber org administrator. Be careful when packaging references to Chatter such as this, as well as including references to the various Chatter-related objects, since this will place a packaging install dependency on your package, requiring all your customers to also have this feature enabled.

By creating actions on your Custom Objects, you can provide a quick way for users to perform common activities on records, for example, updating a contestant's status to DNF. These actions are also visible through the Salesforce1 mobile application, so they enhance the productivity of the mobile user further, compared to standard record editing.

Perform the following steps in the packaging org to try this out:

1. Enable **Feed Tracking** for the `Race`, `Driver`, and `Contest` Custom Objects, as described earlier; the fields being tracked are not important for the following steps, but you may want to select them all to get a better feel for the type of notifications Chatter generates. Also enable **Publisher Actions** from the **Chatter Settings** page.
2. Navigate to the `Contestant` object definition and locate the **Buttons, Links and Actions** section. Create a new action and complete the screen as follows:

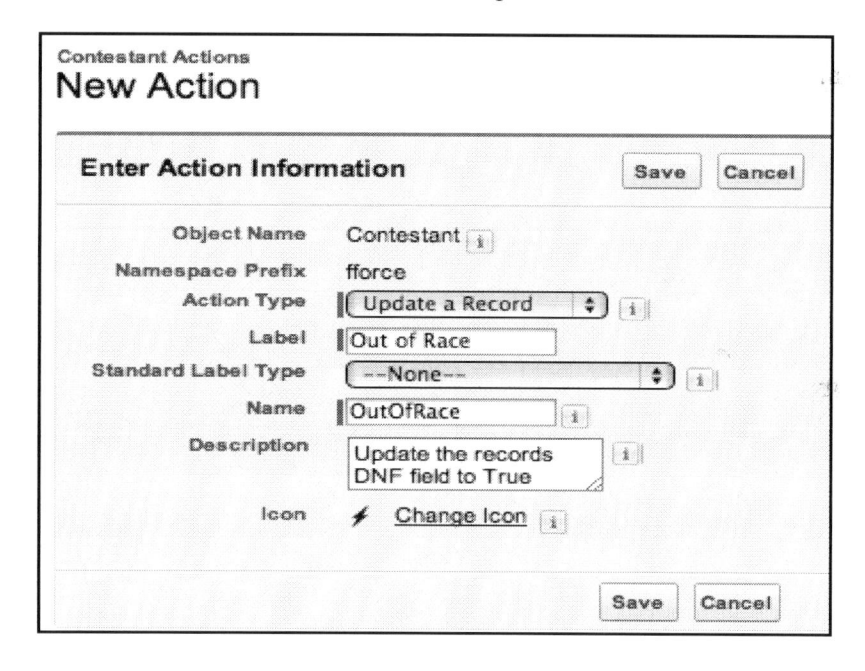

Contestant Actions
New Action

Enter Action Information   Save   Cancel

Object Name	Contestant
Namespace Prefix	fforce
Action Type	Update a Record
Label	Out of Race
Standard Label Type	--None--
Name	OutOfRace
Description	Update the records DNF field to True
Icon	⚡ Change Icon

Save   Cancel

Leveraging Platform Features

3. When prompted to design the layout of the action, accept the default layout shown and click on **Save**. On the **Contestant Action** page shown, click on **New** to add a new **Predefined Field Value** option to assign TRUE to the DNF field as part of the action to update the record:

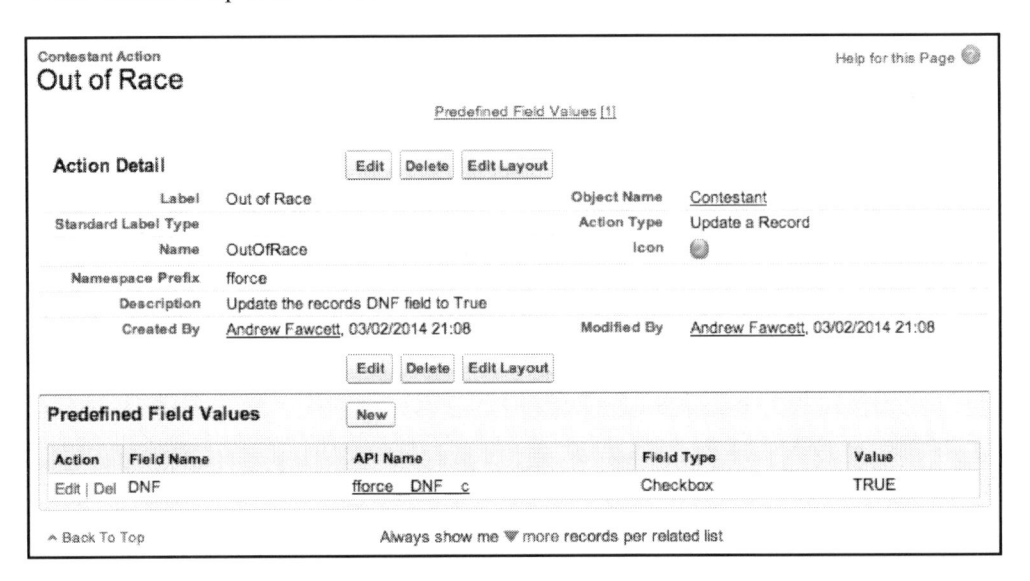

Contestant Action		Help for this Page
Out of Race		

Predefined Field Values [1]

Action Detail   Edit   Delete   Edit Layout

Label	Out of Race		Object Name	Contestant
Standard Label Type			Action Type	Update a Record
Name	OutOfRace		Icon	
Namespace Prefix	fforce			
Description	Update the records DNF field to True			
Created By	Andrew Fawcett, 03/02/2014 21:08		Modified By	Andrew Fawcett, 03/02/2014 21:08

Edit   Delete   Edit Layout

Predefined Field Values   New

Action	Field Name	API Name	Field Type	Value
Edit | Del	DNF	fforce__DNF__c	Checkbox	TRUE

▲ Back To Top   Always show me ▼ more records per related list

4. Finally, edit the **Contestant** layout and drag the **Out of Race** action onto the layout (you may need to click on the **override the global publisher layout** link in the layout editor before you can do this).

5. After performing these steps, you will see the **Out of Race** action being displayed in the UI, as shown in the following screenshots. If you're viewing a **Contestant** record in the Salesforce Classic UI, the action is accessed from a drop-down menu in the Chatter UI region of the page and will look like this:

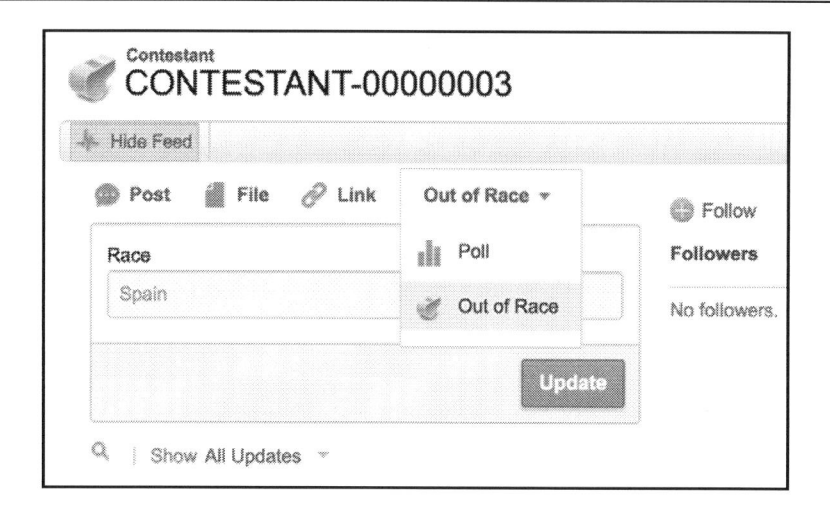

If you're viewing the **Contestant** record in the Lighting Experience UI, it will look like this:

Notice how Lightning Experience relocates the Action **Out of Race** button from the Chatter UI in Salesforce Classic to include it alongside other buttons (top right) that are relevant to the record. A modal pop-up style is also used. This is one of many examples where Salesforce has adopted a different UX design for the existing functionality you define.

Leveraging Platform Features

If you're viewing the record via the Salesforce1 mobile application, it will look like this:

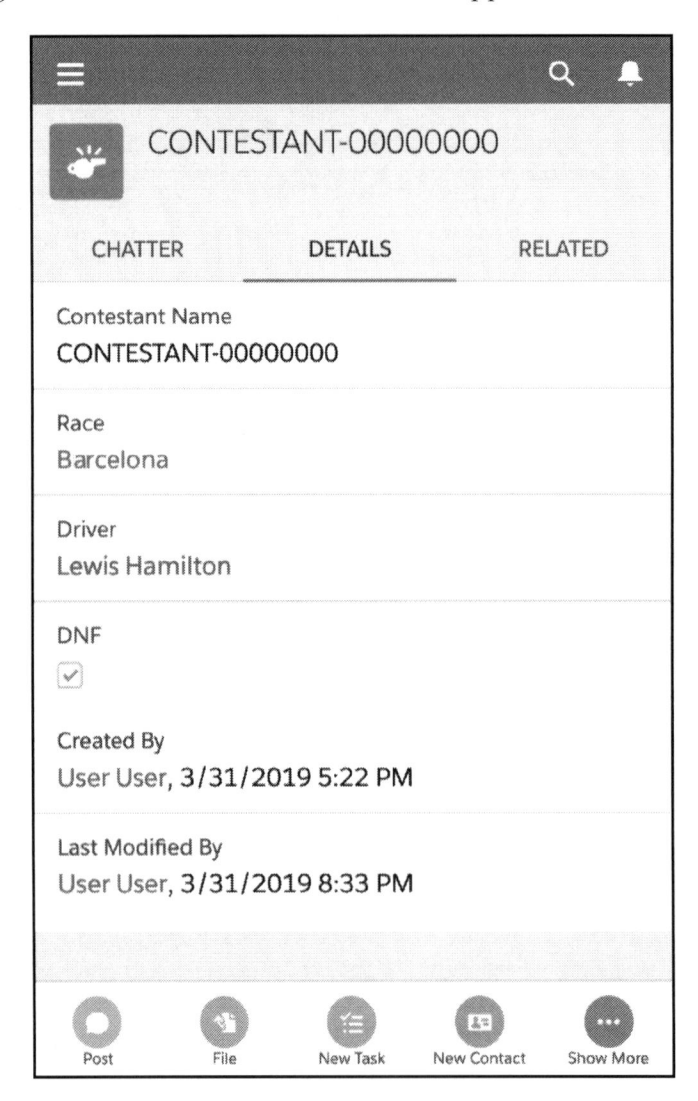

When the user taps the **Show More** icon, the following screen is displayed:

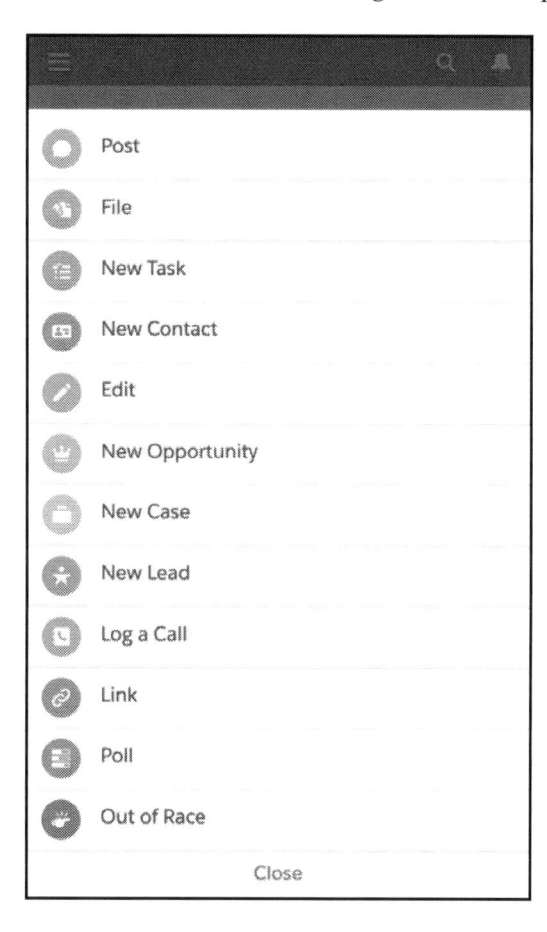

- Post
- File
- New Task
- New Contact
- Edit
- New Opportunity
- New Case
- New Lead
- Log a Call
- Link
- Poll
- Out of Race

As you can see from the preceding screenshot, the Salesforce Mobile application lists all the standard actions and the new **Out of Race** action. As we complete this chapter, you may want to update your test package with a new version.

Creating and testing a new package version

If you are following along instead of using the source code provided for this chapter, be sure to run `sfdx force:source:pull` to synchronize the changes made in this chapter. Take the time to review your project file contents after completing the steps in this chapter and then perform another package creation and test an install of the new package in a separate testing scratch org. If you need a reminder of these steps, refer to `Chapter 1`, *Building and Publishing Your Application*.

> **TIP**
> Do not forget to update your ancestry configuration in your `sfdx-project.json` file as per the instructions in `Chapter 1`, *Building and Publishing Your Application*, to reference the package version created in that chapter; otherwise, your new package will not be eligible to upgrade from a previous version install.

If you choose to perform the install through the browser in the same test scratch org used you used in `Chapter 1`, *Building and Publishing Your Application*, then you will effectively be performing an upgrade. If you do not have that scratch org anymore, simply install the `Chapter 1`, *Building and Publishing Your Application*, package version first. All being well, you should see a confirmation page like the one shown in the following screenshot, showing new or changed components being installed:

Package Components

▼ Apps (2)

Action	Component Name	Parent Object	Component Type	Installation Notes
Create	Race Analytics		App	This is a brand new component.
Create	Race Management		App	This is a brand new component.

▼ Resources (3)

Action	Component Name	Parent Object	Component Type	Installation Notes
Create	Out of Race	Contestant	Action	This is a brand new component.
Create	All	Driver	List View	This is a brand new component.
Create	All	Season	List View	This is a brand new component.

▼ Permission Sets (3)

Action	Component Name	Parent Object	Component Type	Installation Notes
Create	FormulaForce - Race Analytics		Permission Set	This is a brand new component.
Create	FormulaForce - Race Management - Update DNF Status		Permission Set	This is a brand new component.
Create	FormulaForce - Race Management		Permission Set	This is a brand new component.

Only a part of the screenshot is shown, though you can see that it shows the custom application, action, and Permission Set components added in this chapter. Further down, the upgraded confirmation page shows the updated Custom Object, and new Custom Fields are shown in the following screenshot:

Action	Component Name	Parent Object	Component Type	Installation Notes
▼ Objects (2)				
Update	Contestant		Custom Object	This is an upgraded component. It will be updated to the new version.
Update	Driver		Custom Object	This is an upgraded component. It will be updated to the new version.
▼ Fields (8)				
Create	Active	Driver	Custom Field	This is a brand new component.
Create	DNF	Contestant	Custom Field	This is a brand new component.
Create	Nationality	Driver	Custom Field	This is a brand new component.
Update	Driver	Contestant	Custom Field	This is an upgraded component. It will be updated to the new version.
Create	Total DNFs	Race	Custom Field	This is a brand new component.
Create	Fastest Lap By	Race	Custom Field	This is a brand new component.
Create	Driver and Race	Contestant	Custom Field	This is a brand new component.
Create	Year	Season	Custom Field	This is a brand new component.

Notice that once you have upgraded the package in your testing org, the layouts for **Season**, **Driver**, and **Race** do not feature the new fields added in this release of the package. This is due to the fact that layouts are not upgraded.

Summary

In this chapter, you have seen a number of platform features that directly help you build key structural and functional aspects of your application without writing a line of code, in turn, further enabling your customers to extend and customize their application. The chapter also focused on optimizing the tasks performed by consultants and administrators to install and configure an application. Finally, you were made aware of limits imposed within the subscriber org and ways to avoid them, and now have an awareness of them when packaging your application.

Continue to review and evolve your application by first looking for opportunities to embrace these and other platform features and you will ensure that you and your customers' strong alignment with the current and future platform features continues to grow. In the next chapter, we will dive deeper into options and features related to the storage of data on the platform.

> **TIP**
> Make sure to refer to the *Salesforce Limits Quick Reference Guide* PDF describing the latest limits of the features discussed in this chapter and others at http://login.salesforce.com/help/pdfs/en/salesforce_app_limits_cheatsheet.pdf.

3
Application Storage

It is important to consider your customer's storage needs and use cases with regard to their data creation and consumption patterns early in the application design phase. This ensures that your object schema is the most optimal one with respect to large data volumes, data migration processes (inbound and outbound), and storage cost. In this chapter, we will extend the Custom Objects in the **FormulaForce** application as we explore how the platform stores and manages data. We will also explore the difference between your application's operational data, configuration data, and the benefits of using **Custom Metadata Types** for configuration management and deployment.

You will gain a good understanding of the types of storage provided and how the costs associated with each are calculated. It is also important to understand the options that are available when it comes to reusing or attempting to mirror Standard Objects such as **Account**, **Opportunity**, or **Product**, which extend the discussion further into license cost considerations. You will also become aware of the options for standard and custom indexes over your application data and big data, which will prepare you for the topic of handling large data volumes, covered in `Chapter 11`, *Asynchronous Programming and Big Data Volumes*, later in this book. Finally, we will have some insight into platform features for *consuming external data storage* from within the platform.

In this chapter, we will cover the following topics:

- Mapping out end user storage requirements
- Understanding the different storage types
- Record identification, uniqueness, and auto numbering
- Record relationships
- Reusing existing Standard Objects
- Applying external IDs and unique fields
- Importing and exporting application data
- Options for replicating and archiving data
- External data sources

Mapping out end user storage requirements

During the initial requirements and design phase of your application, the best practice is to create user categorizations known as personas. Personas consider a user's typical skills, needs, and objectives. Using this information, you should also start to extrapolate their data requirements, such as the data they are responsible for creating (either directly or indirectly, by running processes), and what data they need to consume (reporting). Once you have done this, try to provide an estimate of the number of records that they will create and/or consume per month.

> **TIP**: Share these personas and their data requirements with your executive sponsors, your market researchers, early adopters, and, finally, the whole development team so that they can keep them in mind and test against them as the application is developed.

For example, in our FormulaForce application, it is likely that **managers** will create and consume data, whereas **race strategists** will mostly consume a lot of data. **Administrators** will also want to manage your application's configuration data. Finally, there will likely be a background process in the application, generating a lot of data, such as the process that records race data from the cars and drivers during the qualification stages and the race itself, such as sector (a designated portion of the track) times.

You may want to capture your conclusions regarding personas and data requirements in a spreadsheet along with some formulas that help predict data storage requirements (which will be discussed later in this chapter). This will help in the future as you discuss your application with Salesforce during the AppExchange listing process, and will be a useful tool during the sales cycle as prospective customers wish to know how to budget their storage costs with your application installed.

Understanding the different storage types

The storage used by your application records contributes to the most important part of the overall data storage allocation on the platform. There is also storage used by the files uploaded by users and that used by so-called **Big Objects**. Big Objects are a type of object, allowing you to store billions of records of data in the platform (we will discuss them later in this chapter). By default, in a Scratch org, you can store up to 1 million records in your Big Objects.

Chapter 3

From the **Storage Usage** page under the **Setup** menu, you can see a summary of the storage used, including those that reside in the Salesforce Standard Objects.

> Later in this chapter, we will be creating a Custom Metadata Type object to store configuration data. Storage consumed by this type of object is not reflected on the **Storage Usage** page and is managed and limited in a different way.

The following screenshot shows the **Storage Usage** page:

Storage Usage

Help for this Page

Your organization's storage usage is listed below.

Storage Type	Limit	Used	Percent Used
Data Storage	200.0 MB	68 KB	0%
File Storage	50.0 MB	0 B	0%
Big Object Storage	1,000,000	0	0%

Current Data Storage Usage

Record Type	Record Count	Storage	Percent
Badges	12	24 KB	35%
Access	12	24 KB	35%
Races	5	10 KB	15%
System Streaming Channels	2	4 KB	6%
Last Used App	1	2 KB	3%
Seasons	1	2 KB	3%
Drivers	1	2 KB	3%

The preceding screenshot shows some sample **Race**, **Season**, and **Driver** record counts.

> **TIP**
> The preceding screenshot also shows which users are using the most amount of storage. In addition to the individual's **UserDetails** page, you can also locate the **Used Data Space** and **Used File Space** fields; next to these are the links to view the user's data and file storage usage.

Application Storage

The limit shown for each is based on a calculation between the minimum allocated data storage, depending on the type of organization or the number of users, and multiplied by a certain amount of MB, which also depends on the organization type; whichever is greater becomes the limit. For more details of this, click on the **Help for this Page** link shown on the page.

Data storage

Unlike other database platforms, Salesforce typically uses a fixed 2 KB per record size as part of its storage usage calculations, regardless of the actual number of fields or the size of the data within them on each record—this is true for all Custom Objects and Big Objects. Note that this record size also applies even if the Custom Object uses large text area fields. There are some exceptions to this rule, such as **Campaigns**, which take up 8 KB, and stored **Email Messages**, which use up the size of the contained email. In this part of the chapter, we will be reviewing what influences data storage and the types of data storage that you can choose from.

Columns versus rows

Given the calculation in the preceding section, you may want to consider whether your data model has multiple occurrences of data that have a known maximum value. In these cases, consider the option of creating multiple columns (or multiple sets of columns) instead of a new object that will use up additional storage. Enterprise Edition orgs currently support up to 500 fields per object. For example, in Formula 1 racing, it is well established that there are only three rounds of qualification before the race in order to determine the starting positions, where each driver competes for the fastest lap.

This could be modeled as a **Qualification Lap** child object to the Contestant object; however, in this case, it will only ever have a maximum of three records per contestant in it. A more optimal data storage design is a set of new fields in the Contestant object.

Perform the following steps in the packaging org to try out this process:

1. Create three fields of type Number(6,3), for example, **Qualification 1 Lap Time** (Qualification1LapTime__c), on the Contestant object. Ensure that the **Required** checkbox is unchecked when creating these fields since not all drivers make it through to the final qualification rounds. Note that, here, we have used numerals instead of words, for example, QualificaitonOneLapTime__c, as this can help in situations where dynamic Apex is iterating over the fields.

[98]

2. Create a roll-up summary field on the **Race** object, `Poll Position Lap Time`, utilize the **MIN** option when selecting the roll-up type, and select the `Qualification 1 Lap Time` field in **Field to Aggregate**, as shown in the following screenshot:

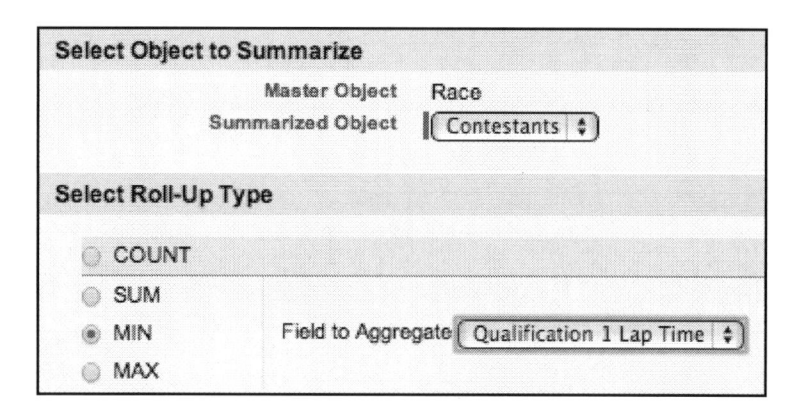

![Roll-up summary field configuration showing Master Object: Race, Summarized Object: Contestants, Roll-Up Type: MIN selected, Field to Aggregate: Qualification 1 Lap Time]

3. Finally, update the permission sets to grant read and write access to the new fields that you have just added to the **Race Management** permission set, and read access within the **Race Analytics** permission set.

Keep in mind that you can also use formula fields to add or apply further logic to data stored in columns, emulating what would have been filtered or aggregating queries over equivalent rows. There is also a benefit to reducing the number of SOQL and DML operations that your code needs to perform when taking this approach.

Visualizing your object model

It is an essential idea to build an **Entity Relationship Diagram** (**ERD**) of your object model; not only is this a good resource for you and your team, but it can also help your customers understand where the data that they are creating resides, and help them build reports and integration solutions. Salesforce provides an interactive tool known as **Schema Builder** (accessed via the button from the **Objects** page under **Setup**) that can help with this; it can also be used to create new objects and fields.

Application Storage

At this stage in the book, the FormulaForce application data model should look something like this:

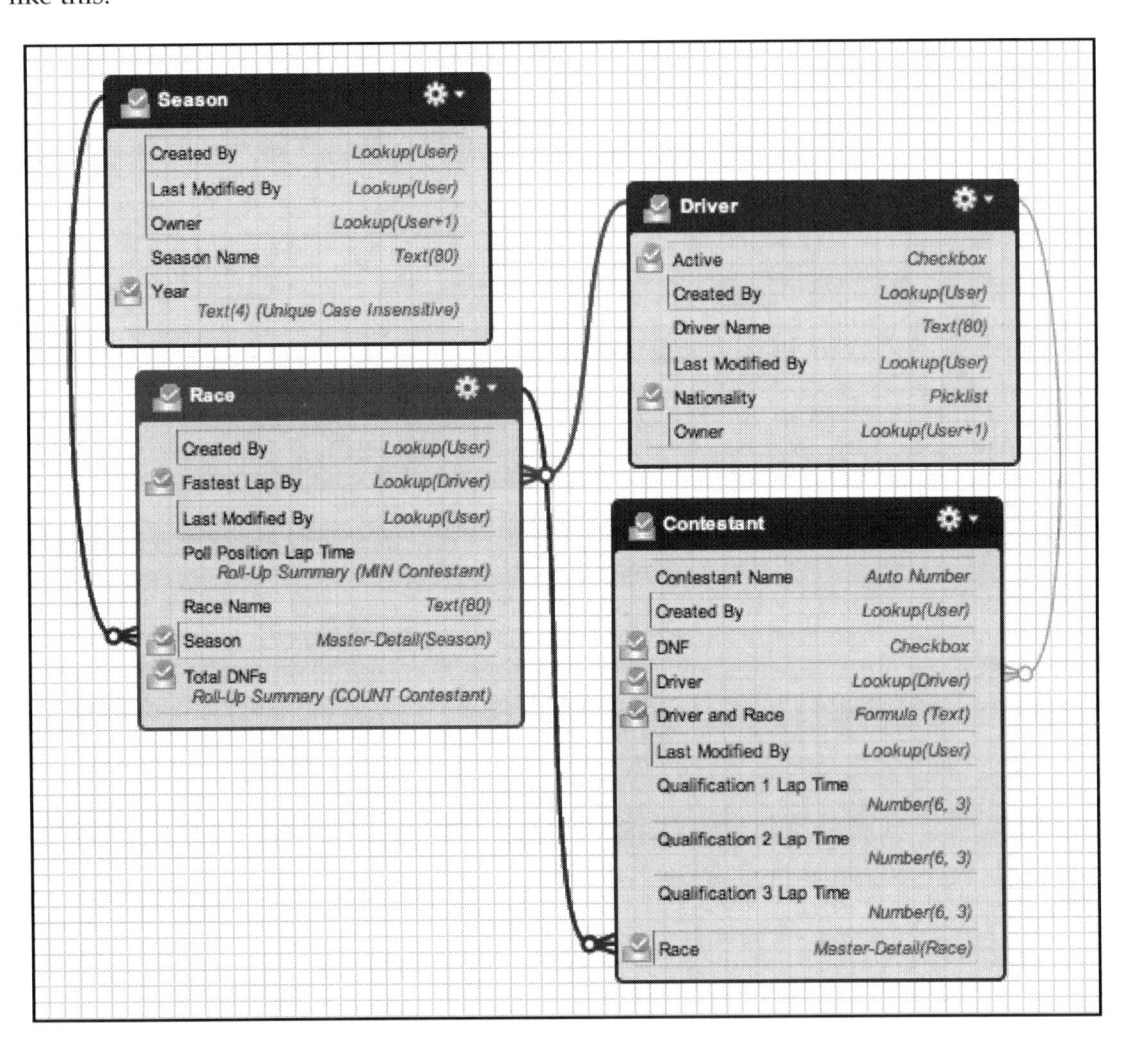

Season
Created By	Lookup(User)
Last Modified By	Lookup(User)
Owner	Lookup(User+1)
Season Name	Text(80)
Year	Text(4) (Unique Case Insensitive)

Driver
Active	Checkbox
Created By	Lookup(User)
Driver Name	Text(80)
Last Modified By	Lookup(User)
Nationality	Picklist
Owner	Lookup(User+1)

Race
Created By	Lookup(User)
Fastest Lap By	Lookup(Driver)
Last Modified By	Lookup(User)
Poll Position Lap Time	Roll-Up Summary (MIN Contestant)
Race Name	Text(80)
Season	Master-Detail(Season)
Total DNFs	Roll-Up Summary (COUNT Contestant)

Contestant
Contestant Name	Auto Number
Created By	Lookup(User)
DNF	Checkbox
Driver	Lookup(Driver)
Driver and Race	Formula (Text)
Last Modified By	Lookup(User)
Qualification 1 Lap Time	Number(6, 3)
Qualification 2 Lap Time	Number(6, 3)
Qualification 3 Lap Time	Number(6, 3)
Race	Master-Detail(Race)

> If you are creating **logging** solutions in your application, keep in mind the storage that is used for this type of data. For example, how does the user perform bulk deletion of the records? Should this be scheduled? Also, how do you communicate this information to them? A log object can be configured with workflow rules by the subscriber to perhaps email users as critical log entries are inserted. If your users are using Chatter, you may want to consider providing the facility (perhaps as an option through dynamic Apex, in order to avoid a package dependency) of using a Chatter post to notify the user. Chatter posts, comments, and track changes are not counted by Salesforce under storage usage. However, any files and photos you upload are counted against file storage.

Considerations for configuration data

Most applications need to provide some way to configure their functionality to allow administrators and users to tailor it to their needs. As we have seen in `Chapter 2`, *Leveraging Platform Features*, Salesforce provides many facilities for this for you and your users. However, what if the part of your application you want to provide configuration for is unique to your application domain? For example, perhaps a list of the official fastest lap times for each track.

In our case, imagine we want to provide our customers with the current approved list of fastest lap times for each track as part of the package so that they don't have to look this up themselves and enter these manually. However, you still want to allow users to manage the fastest laps for tracks not known to your application.

Custom Settings and Custom Metadata Types are two platform features to consider for storing and managing configuration for your application before considering Custom Objects. Custom Metadata, in many ways, is a successor to both alternatives, though, at this time, there are still some features that may cause you to consider using other options.

Application Storage

The following table can help you decide which object type to use based on your configuration requirements:

Configuration Object Requirement	Custom Object	Custom Setting Object	Custom Metadata Type Object
Objects can be hidden from org administrators.	No	Yes	Yes
Records can be included in your package.	No	No	Yes
Packaged records can be protected from user edits and upgraded.	N/A	N/A	Yes
The ability to edit fields on packaged records can be controlled.	N/A	N/A	Yes
The layout of the standard Salesforce UI can be defined and packaged.	Yes	No	Yes
Object relationships are supported for more complex configuration.	Yes	No	Yes
Apex access.	CRUD	CRUD	CRU
Records can be defined at an org, user, or profile level.	No	Yes	No
Records can have custom validation applied via Validation Rules and/or Apex Triggers.	Yes	No	No
Reduction in configuration management overhead.	Rekey or use Data Loaders	Rekey or use Data Loaders	Installed by default; also use native Change Sets and Packages to manage customer-specific configuration
Ability for partners and other developers to build extension packages that package specific forms of your configuration.	No	No	Records can also be included in extension packages

Use the preceding table to carefully choose the best object type that suits your application's needs for each feature. You can use a mixture of object types within your package if desired; although, keep in mind, that it is not possible to change the type of object once your package is released.

> When reading Custom Metadata Type records, SOQL can be used and queries do not count toward the maximum number allowed, though the 50,000 row limit still applies. Custom Metadata Type records can be manipulated using either the Apex Metadata API (create and update only) and the Salesforce SOAP Metadata API operations (full CRUD). As we discussed in Chapter 2, *Leveraging Platform Features*, I would recommend, when writing Apex code, to use the Apex Metadata API. I created this open source library to make this process easier: https://github.com/afawcett/custommetadataapi.

In our case, the desire to package track lap time configuration records, and thus allow them to be upgraded, fits well with Custom Metadata Types. There is also no need to update this configuration information programmatically from Apex, but simply read it instead.

The current inability to update Custom Metadata Type records is something that might be an issue for you if you wish to build a custom UI for your configuration—in our case, the standard Salesforce UI is sufficient.

Custom Metadata Type storage

From the **Custom Metadata Type** page under **Setup**, you can both create Custom Metadata Type objects and manage the records they contain. Any records you create can be included in your package and are thus available to your Apex logic immediately after the installation of your package.

Perform the following steps to create the **Track Lap Records** MDT object:

1. Create a **Track Lap Records** Custom Metadata Type by clicking on **New**, and enter TrackLapRecords as the API name.
2. From the **Visibility** field, select **All Apex code and APIs can use the type, and it is visible in Setup.** This is done since we want to allow the administrator to record their own fastest lap times in addition to those we include. You can choose the **Only Apex code in the same managed package can see the type** option if all records in this object are to be used only by your application logic, for example, for internal configuration.

Application Storage

3. The page for describing your new Custom Metadata Type object looks very similar to that used by the Custom Object. As noted in the preceding table, you cannot define some features, such as Custom Buttons, though, in comparison to Custom Settings, you can define your own layout. There are also more field types available. The following screenshot shows what a Custom Metadata Type definition looks like:

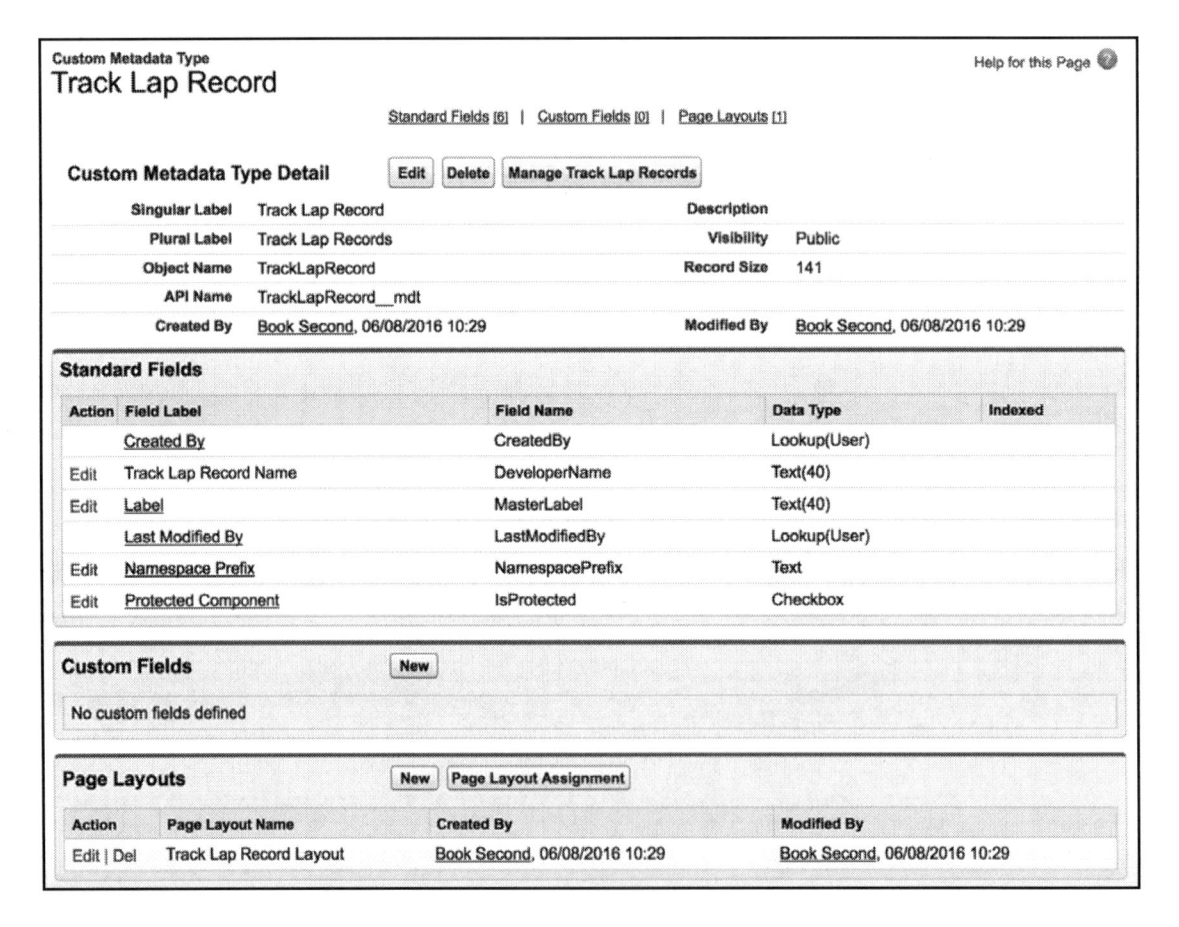

Custom Metadata Type Detail			
Singular Label	Track Lap Record	Description	
Plural Label	Track Lap Records	Visibility	Public
Object Name	TrackLapRecord	Record Size	141
API Name	TrackLapRecord__mdt		
Created By	Book Second, 06/08/2016 10:29	Modified By	Book Second, 06/08/2016 10:29

Standard Fields

Action	Field Label	Field Name	Data Type	Indexed
	Created By	CreatedBy	Lookup(User)	
Edit	Track Lap Record Name	DeveloperName	Text(40)	
Edit	Label	MasterLabel	Text(40)	
	Last Modified By	LastModifiedBy	Lookup(User)	
Edit	Namespace Prefix	NamespacePrefix	Text	
Edit	Protected Component	IsProtected	Checkbox	

Custom Fields

No custom fields defined

Page Layouts

Action	Page Layout Name	Created By	Modified By
Edit | Del	Track Lap Record Layout	Book Second, 06/08/2016 10:29	Book Second, 06/08/2016 10:29

You can see, in the preceding screenshot, that the API name for Custom Metadata Type objects ends with `_mdt` and has different standard fields. We will use the `DeveloperName` field as a unique name for the race track on which the lap record was achieved. Later, we will include records from this object in the package. The `isProtected` field is used to determine whether the recorded data can be edited by the administrator of the package.

Create fields on the `TrackLapRecord_mdt` object, as described in the following table, accepting the default shown for the **Field Manageability** field when you add each field. The following table lists the fields to create with their API name and field data type:

Object	Field name and type
`TrackLapRecords__mdt`	`DriverName__c Text(60)`
	`Time__c Number(5,3)`
	`Year__c Text(4)`

You may have noticed the following option when creating the preceding fields:

Field Manageability	Who can change field values after records are installed via managed package? ● Only the package developer (via package upgrade) ○ Any user with the Customize Application permission (package upgrades won't overwrite the value) ○ No one

This option only applies with respect to records included in the package. It determines which fields the package administrator can change for those records. For example, you might want to add a **Notes** text field to the object that the administrator can edit, but protect all other fields. For the fields that we added here, the default setting is important because we want our package updates to update changes in new lap records on tracks known to the application. The following screenshot shows the fields that you previously created along with the **Field Manageability** status:

Custom Fields [New]

Action	Field Label	API Name	Data Type	Field Manageability	Indexed	Controlling Field	Modified By
Edit | Del	Driver Name	DriverName__c	Text(60)	Upgradable			App Developer, 06/08/2016 13:26
Edit | Del	Time	Time__c	Number(5, 3)	Upgradable			App Developer, 06/08/2016 13:27
Edit | Del	Year	Year__c	Text(4)	Upgradable			App Developer, 06/08/2016 13:28

Using the information shown in the following screenshot, enter some sample data. To do this from the object definition page, click on **Manage Track Lap Records** to begin entering the configuration data. Deselect the **Protected** checkbox when adding records.

> The **Protected** checkbox, displayed when creating records, determines whether the record is visible in the customer org. Protected records are hidden from the user, but your own packaged Apex code can still query them. It is a good idea to use protected records for internal configuration.

Application Storage

The following screenshot shows the sample data you should create:

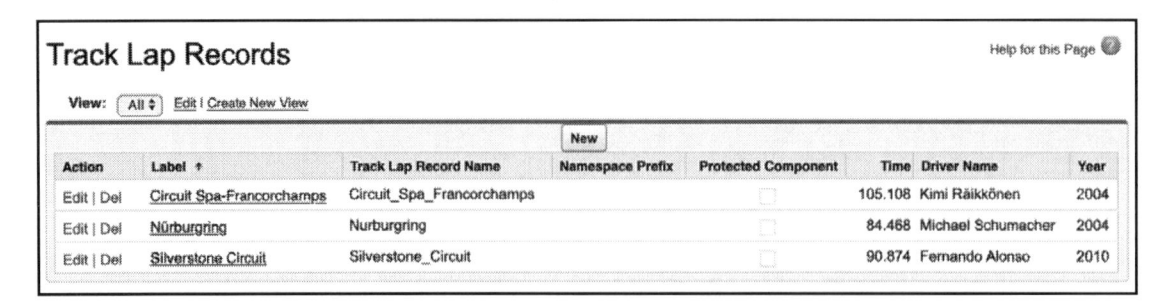

Action	Label ↑	Track Lap Record Name	Namespace Prefix	Protected Component	Time	Driver Name	Year
Edit | Del	Circuit Spa-Francorchamps	Circuit_Spa_Francorchamps			105.108	Kimi Räikkönen	2004
Edit | Del	Nürburgring	Nurburgring			84.468	Michael Schumacher	2004
Edit | Del	Silverstone Circuit	Silverstone_Circuit			90.874	Fernando Alonso	2010

Once you have created the sample data, you should see something similar to the preceding screenshot.

> **TIP**
> You can also define a **List View** to make it easier for you to manage Custom Metadata Type records in the Scratch org. You cannot initially edit the default **All** view, although you can create one with the same name; click on **Create New View**. This **List View** is not packaged.

Storage used by Custom Metadata Type records is not shown on the **Storage Usage** page. The calculation used is based on the maximum record size, which is based on the field size and not the standard 2 KB used on Custom Objects. Records created by users can total up to 10 MB. Your packaged records also get their own 10 MB limit. You can calculate the storage used by reviewing the record size shown on the **Custom Metadata Types** page. The following screenshot shows a summary of all Custom Metadata Type objects:

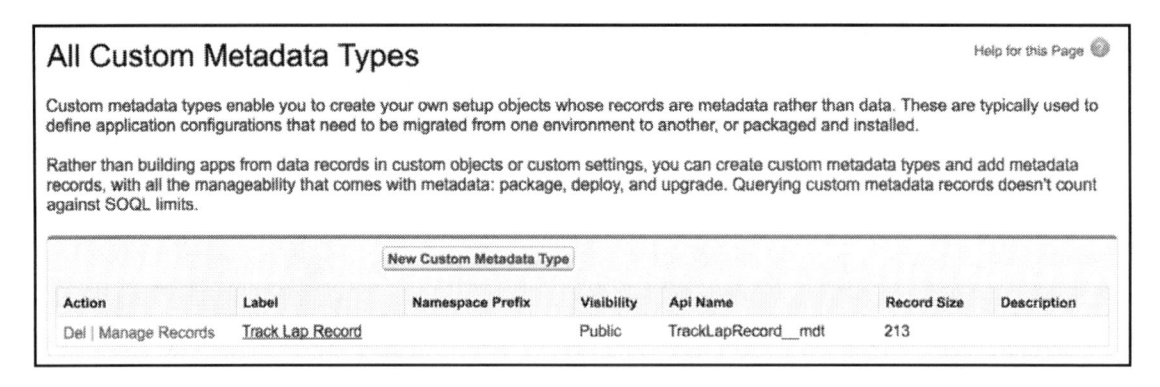

All Custom Metadata Types

Custom metadata types enable you to create your own setup objects whose records are metadata rather than data. These are typically used to define application configurations that need to be migrated from one environment to another, or packaged and installed.

Rather than building apps from data records in custom objects or custom settings, you can create custom metadata types and add metadata records, with all the manageability that comes with metadata: package, deploy, and upgrade. Querying custom metadata records doesn't count against SOQL limits.

Action	Label	Namespace Prefix	Visibility	Api Name	Record Size	Description
Del | Manage Records	Track Lap Record		Public	TrackLapRecord__mdt	213	

The preceding screenshot is a good way of determine the visibility and amount of data storage used by Custom Metadata Types. To add these records to the package, perform an `sfdx force:source:pull` command. This should download the following files to your `/force-app/customMetadata` folder:

```
└── force-app
    └── main
        └── default
            └── customMetadata
                ├── TrackLapRecord.Circuit_Spa_Francorchamps.md-meta.xml
                ├── TrackLapRecord.Nurburgring.md-meta.xml
                └── TrackLapRecord.Silverstone_Circuit.md-meta.xml
```

If you wish, you can now perform the commands discussed in Chapter 1, *Building and Publishing Your Application*, to build a new version of the package—this will now include the preceding Custom Metadata Type and records. When you install the package in your test org, you will see the records under the **Setup** menu option, **Custom Metadata Types**.

> The Custom Metadata Type feature has an interesting history. In its pilot phase, the Custom Metadata Type feature was known as Platform on Platform. The branding later changed; however, at the time, Salesforce felt that this described the potential of this technology to start building your own platform packages that added new metadata types to the platform. As stated in the table in the **Considerations for configuration data** section, the ability for others to package your Custom Metadata Type records is a realization of this vision.

In this section, we created an object of **Custom Metadata Type** and created some records within it. Since track lap records are a form of predefined data, they are an ideal choice for **Custom Metadata Types** because records in such objects can be included in your package. The next section will explore a different type of configuration object type, **Custom Settings**.

Custom Settings storage

Custom Settings are slightly different from Custom Objects with respect to data storage limits in that they do not exist in the same storage area. Custom Settings are ideal for data that is read often, but written infrequently. Salesforce caches data in these objects in something it calls the **Application Cache** and provides a means to query it quickly without query governor limits being applied. However, unlike Custom Objects, they do not support Apex Triggers or Validation Rules.

Application Storage

There are limits on the storage they can consume, per organization and per namespace. This means that if you create a Custom Setting and add it to your managed package, it gets its own storage limit. The storage limit for Custom Settings starts with 1 MB for a fully licensed user and can go up to a maximum of 10 MB. If you need to determine how much storage is being used, you can view the current storage utilization from the **Custom Settings** page under **Setup**.

Big Objects storage

Salesforce's **Big Objects** offer a different kind of storage solution. These objects are designed to store **billions of records**, such as those receiving device input, either in an **Internet of Things** (**IoT**) scenario or data archive. Every Salesforce org has 1 million records' worth of Big Object storage for free; after that, you can contact your Salesforce account manager to purchase further increments. For size calculation purposes, each record is considered 2 KB in size regardless of the field data size.

Record data is typically written on mass using bulk loading and later read frequently, or, put another way, it is "written less and read often." In contrast, Custom Objects are designed for millions of records, not billions. As such, older race data stored in the **Race Data** Custom Object, introduced later in this chapter, could be considered a good candidate to place in a **Race Data History** object. We will explore this use case for Big Objects further in `Chapter 11`, *Asynchronous Processing and Big Data Volumes*.

> **TIP**
> Big Objects support synchronous SOQL just like Custom Objects; however, due to the nature of accessing billions of records, filtering is restricted. Asynchronous SOQL (or Async SOQL for short) allows you to perform a wider subset of SOQL over the records, including complex aggregations. The output of such queries can be placed in Custom Objects to enable you to perform further reporting and analysis. For more information, refer to the *Big Objects Implementation Guide* at `https://developer.salesforce.com/docs/atlas.en-us.bigobjects.meta/bigobjects/`.

File storage

Salesforce has many ways to store file-based data, ranging from the historic **Document** tab, to the more sophisticated **Content** tab, to using the **Files** tab, not to mention **Attachments**, which can be applied to your Custom Object records if enabled. Each has its own pros and cons for end users, with size limits that are well defined in the Salesforce documentation. Going forward, only **Files** will be supported by Salesforce, and so the use of **Files** is recommended over other file storage options. For example, only the **Files** tab is supported in Lightning Experience.

From the perspective of application development, as with data storage, be aware of how much your application is generating on behalf of the user and give them the means to control and delete that information. In some cases, consider whether the end user would be happy to have the option to recreate the file on demand (perhaps as a PDF) rather than always having the application store it.

Record identification, uniqueness, and auto numbering

Every record in Salesforce has an **Id** field and, with a few exceptions, a **Name** field or **DeveloperName** field for Custom Metadata Type objects. The **Id** field is unique, but is not human readable, meaning it cannot be entered or, for most of us on this planet, easily remembered!

The Standard and Custom Objects default value for the **Name** field is to provide a means for the user to enter their own textual description for the record, such as the race name or the driver name. The **Name** field is not enforced as being unique. Being the primary means by which the user identifies records, this can be a problem, and is something that the end user needs to avoid. This aspect of the platform can be particularly problematic with accounts and contacts, hence, AppExchange has a number of so-called "deduplication" applications you can try.

> **TIP**
> The `Database.merge` and `merge` DML statements support the merging of accounts, leads, and contact records. Salesforce also provides its own functionality to manage duplicate records. You can read more about this here: `https://help.salesforce.com/articleView?id=managing_duplicates_overview.htmtype=5`.

Carefully considering how you want your users to identify records can avoid additional work for them that might detract from their enjoyment of your application. The following sections provide information on ways in which you can help avoid duplicate records.

Unique and external ID fields

When adding fields, you can indicate whether the values stored within them are **unique** and/or **external identifiers**. For unique fields, the platform will automatically enforce this rule regardless of how records are created or updated, rejecting records with no unique values. By utilizing fields designated as external ID fields, you can simplify the data loading process for users; this will be discussed later in this chapter in more detail. Both of these field modifiers result in a custom index being created, which can help optimize query performance.

> **TIP**: You can help users avoid creating duplicate records with the same name by ensuring that other identifying fields such as these are also added to the **lookup layout**, as described in the previous chapter.

Let's add **Unique** and **External Id** fields to record the driver's Twitter handle. Perform the following steps in the packaging org to try this out:

1. Create a new **Text** field, **Twitter Handle** (`TwitterHandle__c`), with a length of 15 on the **Driver** object, and check the **Unique** and **External Id** checkboxes.
2. Utilize the **Driver** records entered in the previous chapters to update the fields and confirm that the system prevents duplicate Twitter handles. Lewis Hamilton's Twitter handle is `LewisHamilton`, and Ruben's is `rubarrichello`.
3. Update the permission sets that have read and write permissions for the new field to **Race Management**, and read-only permissions to **Race Analytics**.

By following the preceding steps, you have ensured that there can be no duplicate records that have the same value in the **Twitter Handle** field. In the next section, you can see how using **Auto Number** fields can provide a unique numbering system for records.

Auto Number fields

The Lightning Platform supports an automatic sequence field type, which can be applied to the **Name** field during and after object creation (as long as the object has not been previously included as part of a prior package release upload). It can also be applied to a brand new field. The platform handles incrementing the sequence and ensures that there are no duplicates.

Apply **Auto Number** within the FormulaForce application in order to give a unique auto-incrementing identifier to the **Race Data** records as they are inserted. Perform the following steps in the packaging org to try this out:

1. Create a new **Race Data** (`RaceData__c`) object; for **Record Name**, enter `Race Data Id`, and select **Auto Number** from the **Data Type** field.
2. In the **Display Format** field, enter `RDID-{000000000}` and `1` in the **Starting Number**. Finally, check the **Allow Reports** field.
3. Add a **Lookup** field called `Race` (`Race__c`) to relate records in this object to the existing `Race` object. Select the **Don't allow deletion of the lookup record that's part of a lookup relationship** option to prevent the deletion of race records if race data exists. We will add further fields to this object in a later chapter.
4. Create a tab for the **Race Data** object that we just created and add the tab to the **Race Management** and **Race Analytics** applications. By doing this, the tab and object will automatically be added to the package ready for the next upload.
5. Create a test record to observe the **Race Data Name** field value. The following screenshot shows how the record looks once you have created it:

6. Update the permission sets with the new object and fields, giving read and write permission to **Race Management**, and read-only permission to **Race Analytics**.

While it is possible to add new Custom Fields to objects that have already been packaged and released to your customers, you cannot currently add new **Auto Number** fields to an object that has already been packaged, for example, the **Driver** object.

Apex tests creating test records that utilize **Auto Number** fields can be configured by an org setting to not increment the sequence number outside of the test, which would create gaps in the sequence from the end user's perspective. Access this setting in the subscriber org via the **Options...** button on the **Apex Test Execution** page under **Setup**, as follows:

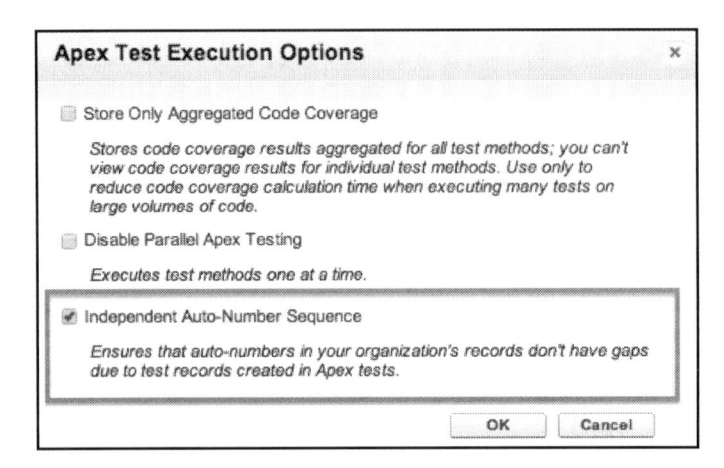

Apex Test Execution Options

- Store Only Aggregated Code Coverage
  Stores code coverage results aggregated for all test methods; you can't view code coverage results for individual test methods. Use only to reduce code coverage calculation time when executing many tests on large volumes of code.
- Disable Parallel Apex Testing
  Executes test methods one at a time.
- ☑ Independent Auto-Number Sequence
  Ensures that auto-numbers in your organization's records don't have gaps due to test records created in Apex tests.

[OK] [Cancel]

The **Display Format** determines the formatting but not the maximum sequence number. For example, if a format of `SEQ{0000}` is used, and the next sequence number created is 10,000, the platform will display it as `SEQ10000`, ignoring the format digits. The maximum of an **Auto Number** field is stated in the Salesforce documentation as being a maximum length of 30 characters, of which 10 are reserved for the prefix characters. It also states that the maximum starting number must be less than 1,000,000,000.

The platform does not guarantee that there will be no gaps in an **Auto Number** sequence field. Errors in creating records can create gaps as the number assigned during the insert process is not reused. Thus, set expectations accordingly with your users when using this feature.

> **TIP**
> One workaround to creating an unbroken sequence would be to create a Custom Object with the **Name** field that utilizes the **Auto Number** field type; for example, `Job References`. Then, create a relationship between this object and the object records to which you require the sequence to be applied; for example, `Jobs`. Then, write an **Apex Scheduled** job that inserts records on a daily basis into the `Job References` object for each `Jobs` record that is currently without a `Job Reference` relationship. Then, run reports over the `Job References` object. To ensure that no `Job` records are deleted, thus creating gaps, you can also enable the lookup referential integrity feature described in the following sections.

Auto Number fields are a great way to ensure that users can uniquely identify records. The next section explains an approach you can recommend to your customers who want to use a different prefix for the numbering sequence.

Subscribers customizing the Auto Number Display Format

Be aware that **Display Format** cannot be customized once it is packaged and installed in the subscriber org. However, it is possible to create a custom formula field in the subscriber org to remove the prefix from the **Name** field value and reapply whatever prefix is needed. For example, the following formula will isolate the numeric portion of the **Name** field value and apply a new prefix specified in the formula (this could also be driven by a Custom Setting or conditional logic in the formula):

```
'MYID-' + MID(Name, 4, LEN(Name) + 4)
```

When this formula field is applied for a record whose **Auto Number** is `RD-000000001`, the formula would display as follows:

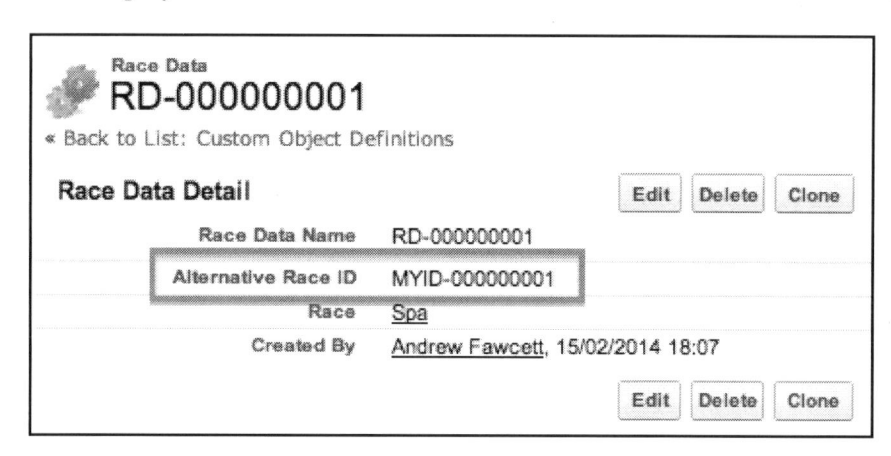

```
Race Data
RD-000000001
« Back to List: Custom Object Definitions

Race Data Detail                              Edit   Delete   Clone

         Race Data Name    RD-000000001
       Alternative Race ID  MYID-000000001
                    Race   Spa
              Created By   Andrew Fawcett, 15/02/2014 18:07

                                              Edit   Delete   Clone
```

The preceding use case shows the flexibility of formula fields to display record data in different forms. This is a very powerful feature that both you and your customers can leverage.

Record relationships

A relationship is formed by a **Lookup** field being created from one object to another, often referred to as a parent and child relationship. There are two types of relationships in Salesforce: **Master-Detail** and **Lookup**.

Application Storage

> Custom Metadata Type objects only support lookup relationships to other Custom Metadata Type objects or other Custom Object or Custom Field metadata. Some features described in this section only apply to Custom Objects, such as lookup filters and referential integrity. Custom Setting objects do not support any form of record relationships.

In some aspects, these types of relationships share similarities in how they are referenced when using SOQL and Apex and how they are input through the user interface (such as **lookup filters** described in the previous chapter). However, there are different **limits** depending on the **referential integrity** features that you use. You should keep these in mind when defining your own object model within your package, as well as considering what your customers may also add as part of their customizations, since the limits are shared. These considerations are as follows:

- Utilizing the **Master-Detail** form of relationship provides a powerful way to model containment, where one parent object record acts as a container for other child records; in our example, a race contains **Contestants**:
  - The platform will automatically cascade delete the child records when the parent is deleted, and it will also enforce the need for a parent reference when the child records are created.
  - By default, the platform prevents users from moving the child records to another parent by editing the relationship field. However, you can disable this validation and permit this by selecting the **Child records can be reparented to other parent records after they are created** option.
  - With the use of **Rollup Summary** fields, it also becomes possible to build calculated fields based on values of the child record fields.
  - Salesforce, however, does recommend that this kind of parent-child relationship does not exceed 10,000 child records; otherwise, the platform will not support the cascade delete of child records.
  - You can define up to three levels of Master-Detail relationships.
- Utilizing the **Lookup** type of relationship allows you to model connections between related records that are optional and may also have other relationships not necessarily in an ownership or containment relationship to their parents. Keep in mind the following points when using **Lookup** fields to define relationships:
  - Deletion of parent records will not result in a cascade delete of related child records; this can be enabled via **Salesforce Support**, though this setting will not be packaged.

[114]

- Unlike with Master-Detail, you can elect for the platform to enforce referential integrity during the creation of the field by utilizing the **Don't allow deletion of the lookup record that's part of a lookup relationship** option.
- Currently, the **Rollup Summary** fields are not supported when using a lookup relationship.

Lookup fields of either kind are automatically indexed by the platform, making queries, in some cases, faster. We will focus more on indexes in `Chapter 11`, *Asynchronous Processing and Big Data Volumes*. The maximum number of relationship fields per object is 40.

> **TIP**: While it is possible to add new Custom Fields to objects that have already been packaged and released to your customers, you cannot add a new Master-Detail relationship to an object that has already been packaged.

Record relationships are a key feature of defining your application's object model. This section has highlighted some areas you should consider carefully, as some may have future restrictions on your application and your customer's ability to customize it. A key aspect of the Lightning Platform is the existing objects it contains. The following section shares some considerations to keep in mind when leveraging Salesforce Standard Objects.

Reusing the existing Standard Objects

When designing your object model, a good knowledge of the existing **Standard Objects** and their features is key to knowing when and when not to reference them. Keep in mind the following points when considering the use of Standard Objects:

- **From a data storage perspective**: Ignoring Standard Objects creates a potential data duplication and integration effort for your end users if they are already using similar Standard Objects as pre-existing Salesforce customers. Remember that adding additional Custom Fields to the Standard Objects via your package will not increase the data storage consumption for those objects.

Application Storage

- **From a license cost perspective**: Conversely, referencing some Standard Objects might cause additional license costs for your users, since not all are available to the users without additional licenses from Salesforce. Make sure that you understand the differences between **Salesforce (CRM)** and **Salesforce Platform** licenses with respect to the Standard Objects available. Currently, the Salesforce Platform license provides **Accounts** and **Contacts**; however, to use **Opportunity** or **Product** objects, a Salesforce (CRM) license is needed by the user. Refer to the Salesforce documentation for the latest details on this.

Use your user personas to define what Standard Objects your users use and reference them via lookups, Apex code, and Visualforce accordingly. You may wish to use **extension packages** and/or **dynamic Apex** and SOQL to make these kinds of references optional. Since **Developer Edition** orgs have all these licenses and objects available (although in a limited quantity), make sure you review your package dependencies before clicking on the **Upload** button each time to check for unintentional references.

Importing and exporting data

Salesforce provides a number of its own tools for **importing** and **exporting** data, as well as a number of third-party options based on the Salesforce APIs; these are listed on AppExchange. This section will focus on a more complex scenario when importing records with other record relationships, as it is not possible to predict and include the IDs of related records, such as the **Season** record ID when importing **Race** records; this section will present two solutions to this:

- Salesforce DX CLI Data Import and Export
- Salesforce Data Import Wizard

The following subsections will go into the preceding tools in more detail.

Salesforce DX CLI Data Import and Export

When developing and testing your solution, it is useful to have sample data that you can easily import into your objects. Salesforce DX provides some useful CLI commands that help in this regard. We are starting to develop a complex object model that contains multiple objects and various relationships. The **JSON** files in the /data folder included in the sample code for this chapter contain sample data for the **Season**, **Driver**, and **Race** objects.

> This section highlights the more advanced tree import and export commands. For a full list of commands, you can refer to the CLI reference here: https://developer.salesforce.com/docs/atlas.en-us.sfdx_cli_reference.meta/sfdx_cli_reference/cli_reference_force_data.htm#cli_reference_force_data.

This simple example illustrates how a single record for the `Season` object is represented in the `/data/Season_c.json` file. Take note of the `referenceId` attribute – this is an important detail in understanding how other files reference this record, since it does not yet have the usual Salesforce ID (since it has not been inserted into the database):

```
{
    "records": [
        {
            "attributes": {
                "type": "Season__c",
                "referenceId": "Season__cRef1"
            },
            "Name": "2019",
            "Year__c": "2019"
        }
    ]
}
```

Now, let's look at the `/data/Race__c.json` file, where you can see references to the preceding record using the `Season__cRef1` value in the following code block. In addition, you can see references to records from the `/data/Driver__c.json` file (not shown):

```
{
    "records": [
        {
            "attributes": {
                "type": "Race__c",
                "referenceId": "Race__cRef1"
            },
            "Name": "Spa",
            "Season__c" : "@Season__cRef1",
            "FastestLapBy__c": "@Driver__cRef1"
        },
        {
            "attributes": {
                "type": "Race__c",
                "referenceId": "Race__cRef2"
            },
            "Name": "Melbourne",
            "Season__c" : "@Season__cRef1",
```

Application Storage

```
                    "FastestLapBy__c": "@Driver__cRef1"
                },
                {
                    "attributes": {
                        "type": "Race__c",
                        "referenceId": "Race__cRef3"
                    },
                    "Name": "Shanghai",
                    "Season__c" : "@Season__cRef1",
                    "FastestLapBy__c": "@Driver__cRef1"
                },
                {
                    "attributes": {
                        "type": "Race__c",
                        "referenceId": "Race__cRef4"
                    },
                    "Name": "Monte Carlo",
                    "Season__c" : "@Season__cRef1",
                    "FastestLapBy__c": "@Driver__cRef1"
                },
                {
                    "attributes": {
                        "type": "Race__c",
                        "referenceId": "Race__cRef5"
                    },
                    "Name": "Budapest",
                    "Season__c" : "@Season__cRef1",
                    "FastestLapBy__c": "@Driver__cRef1"
                }
        ]
    }
```

The preceding JSON shows the contents of the `Race__c.json` file.

> **TIP**
>
> Each data file can contain up to 200 records. In order to insert more records than this, you can split records over multiple data files and reference them from the plan file described later in this section. For significant volume imports, you should consider using the **Salesforce DX** `data:bulk:upsert` command. For more flexibility with respect to field mapping and external IDs, the **Salesforce Data Loader tool** also has its CLI and configuration. Finally, another option to consider is creating programmatic scripts to generate data. This approach will be discussed further in `Chapter 11`, *Asynchronous Processing and Big Data Volumes*.

[118]

The /data folder contains four JSON files, three JSON data files, one file for each object we are importing data into, and a plan JSON file. The plan file connects all three data files together and allows Salesforce DX to insert the correct Salesforce ID values as they become known. As such, the order in which the data import files are listed is also important.

The following is the /data/Data-plan.json file included in the code for this chapter. The ability to manage references, as described earlier, is enabled by setting the saveRefs and resolveRefs attributes to true, as follows:

```
[
    {
        "sobject": "Driver__c",
        "saveRefs": true,
        "resolveRefs": true,
        "files": [
            "Driver__c.json"
        ]
    },
    {
        "sobject": "Season__c",
        "saveRefs": true,
        "resolveRefs": true,
        "files": [
            "Season__c.json"
        ]
    },
    {
        "sobject": "Race__c",
        "saveRefs": true,
        "resolveRefs": true,
        "files": [
            "Race__c.json"
        ]
    }
]
```

Finally, run the following SFDX CLI command to import the preceding records:

```
sfdx force:data:tree:import --plan ./data/Data-plan.json
```

The following is an example of a CLI used to export the preceding data files for each object, in this case, the **Driver** object. It uses SOQL to define what fields to export:

```
sfdx force:data:tree:export -q "SELECT Name, TwitterHandle__c, Nationality__c FROM Driver__c"
```

Application Storage

While the preceding command does not support lookup relationship field values, it does support Master-Detail relationship data, allowing you to export child records by using an inner sub-select in the SOQL query supplied. For lookup relationship fields, relationship fields must be added manually, as demonstrated in the examples in this section.

Salesforce Data Import Wizard

In the preceding example, an entire set of records across multiple objects was being imported. For your end users, they may have more targeted requirements since they have already entered records in other objects. Also, given their skills may not be as technical, it is important to offer them a more graphical experience that requires no knowledge of JSON. For this requirement, Salesforce provides **Data Import Wizard**, which is available under the **Setup** menu.

> **TIP**: This tool supports Custom Objects, Custom Settings, and some standard objects such as **Leads**, **Contacts**, **Accounts**, **Campaign Members**, and **Solutions**. Custom Metadata Type records are essentially considered metadata by the platform and, as such, you can use packages, developer tools, and Change Sets to migrate these records between orgs. There is an open source CSV data loader for Custom Metadata Types at `https://github.com/haripriyamurthy/CustomMetadataLoader`.

It is straightforward to import a CSV file with a list of race **Seasons** since this is a top-level object and has no other object dependencies. However, to import **Race** information (which is a related child object to **Season**), the **Season** and **Fastest Lap By** record IDs are required, which will typically not be present in a **Race** import CSV file by default. Note that IDs are unique across the platform and cannot be shared between orgs.

> **TIP**: If you need a reminder of the structure of these objects, refer to the Schema Builder screenshot shown in `Chapter 2`, *Leveraging Platform Features*.

External ID fields help address this problem by allowing Salesforce to use the existing values of such fields as a secondary means to associate records being imported that need to reference parent or related records. All that is required is that the related record **Name** or, ideally, a unique external ID, be included in the import data file.

The `Races.csv` file includes three columns: `Year`, `Name`, and `Fastest Lap By` (of the driver who performed the fastest lap of that race). The following shows the content of the `Races.csv` file included in the sample code for this chapter:

```
Year,Name,Fasted Lap By
2019,Spa,LewisHamilton
2019,Melbourne,LewisHamilton
2019,Shanghai,LewisHamilton
2019,Monte Carlo,LewisHamilton
2019,Budapest,LewisHamilton
```

The driver in the preceding CSV file is indicated by their Twitter handle. You may remember that a **Driver** record can also be identified by this since the field has been defined as an **External ID** field. To perform the following steps, the 2019 season record and the Lewis Hamilton driver record should already be present in your Scratch org. If not, refer to the previous chapter to create these. Now, run the **Data Import Wizard** and complete the settings, as shown in the following screenshot:

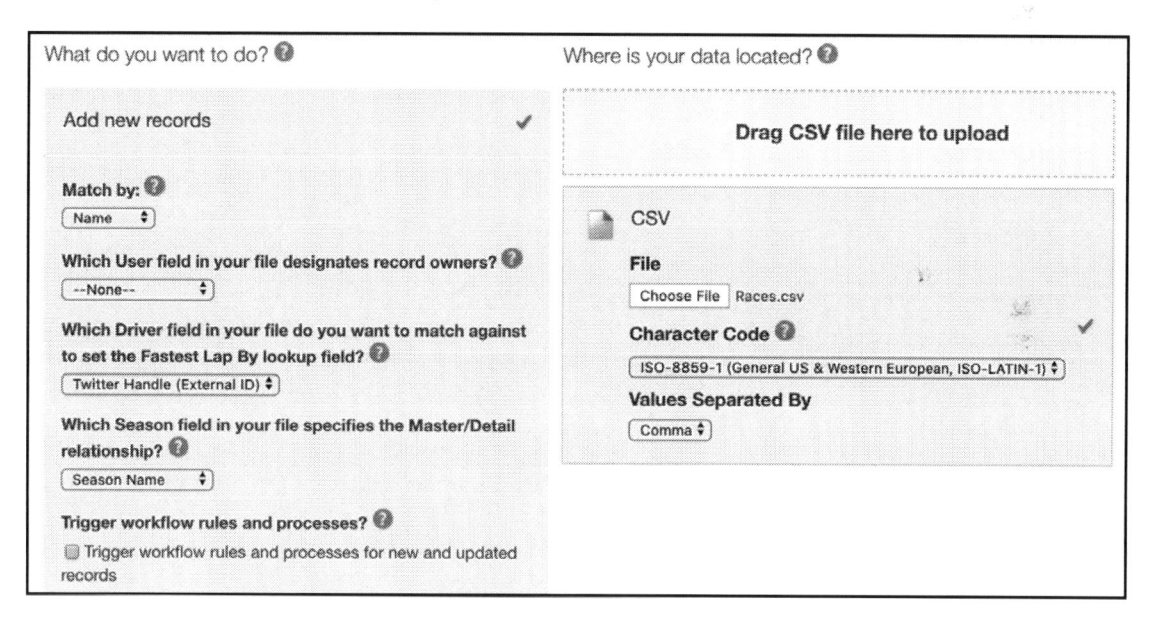

Next, complete the field mappings, as shown in the following screenshot:

Edit Field Mapping: Races

Your file has been auto-mapped to existing Salesforce fields, but you can edit the mappings if you wish. Unmapped fields will not be imported.

Edit	Mapped Salesforce Object	CSV Header	Example	Example	Example
Change	Season	Year	2019	2019	2019
Change	Race Name	Name	Spa	Melbourne	Shanghai
Change	Fastest Lap By	Fasted Lap By	LewisHamilton	LewisHamilton	LewisHamilton

Click on **Start Import** and then review the results once the data import has completed. You should find that four new **Race** records have been created under 2019 **Season**, with the **Fastest Lap By** field correctly associated with the Lewis Hamilton **Driver** record.

Note that these tools will also stress your Apex Trigger code for volumes, as they typically have the bulk mode enabled and insert records in chunks of 200 records. Thus, it is recommended that you test your triggers to at least this level of record volumes. Later chapters will present coding patterns to help ensure that your code supports the bulk mode.

Options for replicating data

Enterprise customers often have legacy and/or external systems that are still being used or that they wish to phase out in the future. As such, they may have requirements to replicate aspects of the data stored in the Salesforce platform to another platform.

The following lists some platform and API facilities that can help you and/or your customers build solutions to replicate data:

- **Replication API**: This API exists in both the web service SOAP and Apex form. It allows you to develop a scheduled process to query the platform for any new, updated, or deleted records within a given time period for a specific object. The getUpdated and getDeleted API methods return only the IDs of the records, requiring you to use the conventional Salesforce APIs to query the remaining data for the replication. The frequency at which this API is called is important in order to avoid gaps. Refer to the Salesforce documentation for more details.

- **Outbound Messaging**: This feature offers a more real-time alternative to the replication API. An outbound message event can be configured using the standard workflow feature of the platform. This event, once configured against a given object, provides a **Web Service Definition Language** (**WSDL**) file that describes a web service endpoint to be called when records are created and updated. It is the responsibility of a web service developer to create the endpoint based on this definition. Note that there is no provision for deletion with this option.
- **Bulk API**: This API provides a means to manage up to 5,000 chunks of Salesforce data (up to 10 MB or 10,000 records per chunk) per rolling 24-hour period. Salesforce and third-party data loader tools, including the Salesforce Data Loader tool, offer this as an option. It can also be used to delete records without them going into the recycle bin. This API is ideal for building solutions to archive data.

> **Heroku Connect** is a seamless data replication and synchronization solution between Salesforce and Heroku Postgres. For further information, refer to `https://www.heroku.com/connect`.

There are, of course, a number of AppExchange solutions listed that provide applications that use these APIs already. Another option for importing data into the Lightning Platform is integration with external data sources. This is described in more detail in the next section.

External data sources

One of the downsides of having data not stored on the platform is that the end users have to move between applications and logins to view data; this causes an overhead, as the process and data are not connected.

Salesforce Connect (previously known as Lightning Connect) is a chargeable add-on feature of the platform. It has the ability to surface external data within the Salesforce user interface via the so-called **External Objects** and **External Data Sources** configurations under **Setup**. They offer similar functionality to Custom Objects, such as List View, Layouts, Custom Buttons, and also Reports.

External Data Sources can be connected to existing OData-based endpoints and secured through OAuth or Basic Authentication. Alternatively, Apex provides a Connector API, whereby developers can implement adapters to connect to other HTTP-based APIs. Depending on the capabilities of the associated External Data Source users accessing External Objects, using the data source can read and even update records through the standard Salesforce UIs, such as Salesforce Mobile and desktop interfaces.

Application Storage

Creating a new FormulaForce package version

If you wish, you can create a new version of the `FormulaForce` package and install it in your test Scratch org, as described in `Chapter 1`, *Building and Publishing Your Application*. The summary page during the installation of new and upgraded components should look like the following screenshot:

▼ Tabs (1)				
Action	Component Name	Parent Object	Component Type	Installation Notes
Create	Race Data		Tab	This is a brand new component.

▼ Resources (3)				
Action	Component Name	Parent Object	Component Type	Installation Notes
Create	All	RaceData__c	List View	This is a brand new component.
Create	Race Data Layout	RaceData__c	Page Layout	This is a brand new component.
Create	Track Lap Record Layout	TrackLapRecord__mdt	Page Layout	This is a brand new component.

▼ Objects (2)				
Action	Component Name	Parent Object	Component Type	Installation Notes
Create	Race Data		Custom Object	This is a brand new component.
Create	Track Lap Record		Custom Metadata Type	This is a brand new component.

▶ Permission Sets (3)				

▼ Fields (9)				
Action	Component Name	Parent Object	Component Type	Installation Notes
Create	Twitter Handle	Driver	Custom Field	This is a brand new component.
Create	Race	RaceData__c	Custom Field	This is a brand new component.
Create	Qualification 3 Lap Time	Contestant	Custom Field	This is a brand new component.
Create	Driver Name	TrackLapRecord__mdt	Custom Field	This is a brand new component.
Create	Qualification 1 Lap Time	Contestant	Custom Field	This is a brand new component.
Create	Year	TrackLapRecord__mdt	Custom Field	This is a brand new component.
Create	Time	TrackLapRecord__mdt	Custom Field	This is a brand new component.
Create	Qualification 2 Lap Time	Contestant	Custom Field	This is a brand new component.
Create	Poll Position Lap Time	Race	Custom Field	This is a brand new component.

The preceding screenshot shows a portion of the components that will be installed. The following screenshot shows further information from the package's install page:

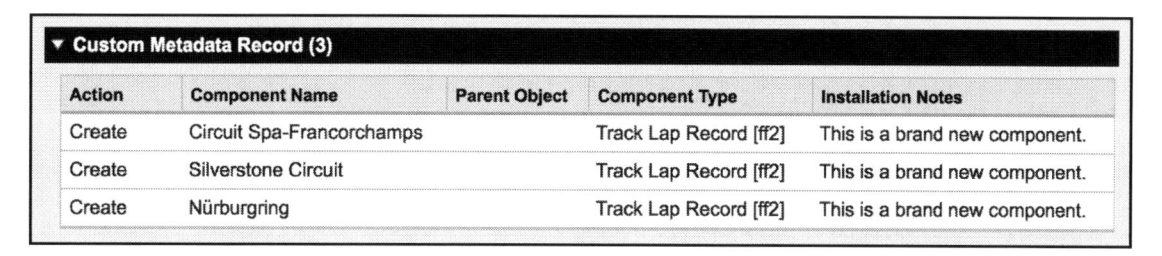

Action	Component Name	Parent Object	Component Type	Installation Notes
Create	Circuit Spa-Francorchamps		Track Lap Record [ff2]	This is a brand new component.
Create	Silverstone Circuit		Track Lap Record [ff2]	This is a brand new component.
Create	Nürburgring		Track Lap Record [ff2]	This is a brand new component.

▼ Custom Metadata Record (3)

The preceding screenshot shows the Custom Metadata Type records that will be installed during the package installation. Once you have installed the package in your test Scratch org, visit the **Custom Metadata Types** page under **Setup** and click on **Manage Records** next to the object. You will see that the records are shown as **Managed** and cannot be deleted. Click on one of the records to see that the field values themselves also cannot be edited. This is the effect of the **Field Manageability** checkbox when defining the fields. The following screenshot shows how a packaged Custom Metadata Type record is displayed in your test org:

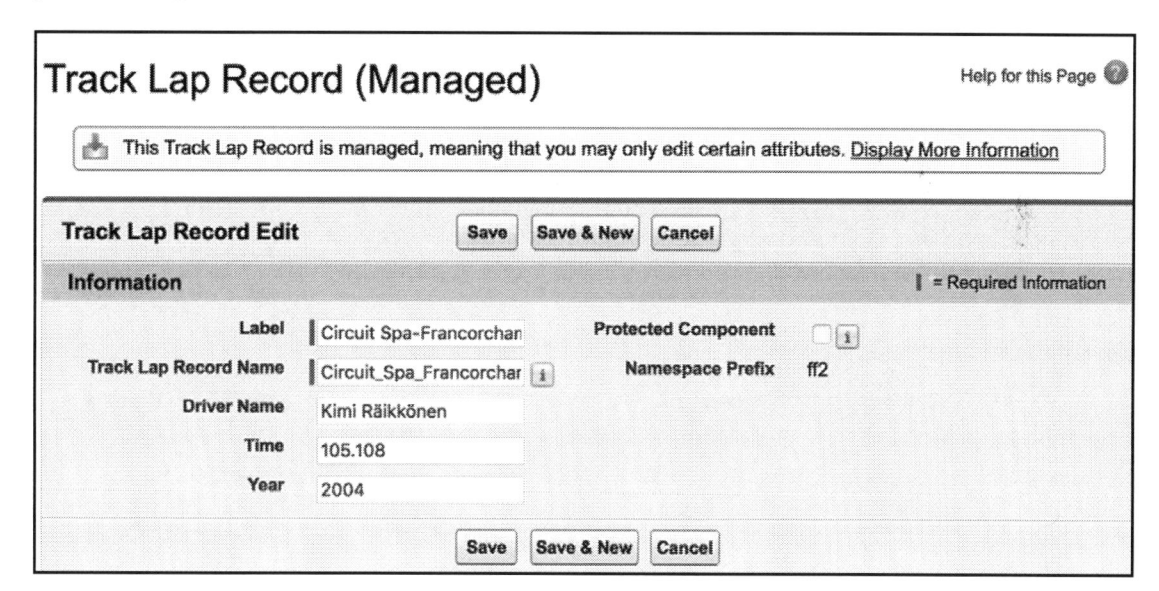

Track Lap Record (Managed)

This Track Lap Record is managed, meaning that you may only edit certain attributes. Display More Information

Track Lap Record Edit

Information

| = Required Information

- Label: Circuit Spa-Francorchan
- Track Lap Record Name: Circuit_Spa_Francorchar
- Driver Name: Kimi Räikkönen
- Time: 105.108
- Year: 2004
- Protected Component: ☐
- Namespace Prefix: ff2

[125]

Application Storage

In the preceding screenshot, you can see the confirmation message, indicating that it is a packaged record and that editing is restricted. Also, note that the **Namespace Prefix** value is `ff2`; this will differ from yours; this is expected. As a further way to explore Custom Metadata Type features during a package upgrade, try changing or adding **Track Lap Time** records, for example, update a track time on an existing record. Create a new version of the package, and then upgrade your test Scratch org. You will see that the records are updated automatically. Conversely, any records you created in your test Scratch org will be retained between upgrades.

This section highlighted some advanced features of packaging Custom Metadata Types that allow you to control what record data is updated in your customer's org and what is not.

Summary

In this chapter, you have learned about the declarative aspects of developing an application on the platform that applies to how an application is stored and how relational data integrity is enforced through the use of the **Lookup** field deletion constraints and defining unique fields. The Master-Detail relationships allowed you to model containment concepts in your data model to allow you to represent clear ownership concepts for your user's data. We also learned how to consider the data storage implications of extending your schema across columns instead of rows, and the benefits of the cost of storage for your end users. Finally, you also learned about a new type of object known as the Big Object, for storing billions of records in Salesforce.

In this chapter, we have now covered some major aspects of the platform with respect to packaging, platform alignment, and how your application data is stored, as well as the key aspects of your application's architecture. Custom Metadata has been used in this chapter to illustrate a use case for configuration data. This book will explain further use cases for this flexible platform feature in the upcoming chapters.

In the next few chapters of this book, we will start to look at **Enterprise coding patterns**, effectively engineering your application code to work in harmony with the platform features, and grow with your needs and the platform. This is important because enterprise applications do not consist solely of declaratively build features, such as the ones used in this chapter, but they also frequently require a great deal of code. It is really important for the ongoing pace of development that your coding standards are well-defined and understood by your developers.

4
Apex Execution and Separation of Concerns

When starting to write Apex, it is tempting to start with an Apex Trigger or Apex Controller class and to start placing the required logic in those classes to implement the desired functionality. This chapter will explore a different starting point; one that allows the developer to focus on writing application business logic (the core logic of your application) in a way that is independent of the calling context. It will also explain the benefits that it brings in terms of reuse, code maintainability, and flexibility, especially when applying code to different areas of the platform.

We will explore the ways in which Apex code can be invoked, the requirements and benefits of those contexts, their commonalities, their differences, and the best practices that are shared. We will distill these into a layered way of writing code that teaches and embeds **separation of concerns** (SOC) in the code base from the very beginning. We will also introduce a naming convention to help with code navigation and enforce an SOC further.

At the end of the chapter, we will have written some initial code, setting out the framework to support SOC and the foundation for the next three chapters to explore some well-known **Enterprise Application Architecture** patterns in more detail. Finally, we will package this code and install it in the test org.

This chapter will cover the following topics:

- Apex execution contexts
- Apex governors and namespaces
- Where Apex is used
- Separation of concerns
- Patterns of Enterprise Application Architecture
- Unit testing versus system testing
- Packaging the code

Execution contexts

An execution context on the platform has a beginning and an end; it starts with a user or system action or event, such as a button click or part of a scheduled background job, and is typically short-lived, with seconds or minutes instead of hours before it ends. It is especially important in multitenant architecture because each context receives its own set of limits around queries, database operations, logs, and the duration of the execution.

In the case of background jobs (**Batch Apex**), instead of having one execution context for the whole job, the platform splits the information being processed and hands it back through several execution contexts in a serial fashion. For example, if a job was asked by the user to process 1,000 records and the batch size (or scope size in Batch Apex terms) was 200 (which is the default), this would result in five distinct execution contexts, one after another. This is done so that the platform can throttle the execution of jobs up or down, or if needed, pause them between scopes.

You might think that an execution context starts and ends with your Apex code, but you would be wrong. Using some Apex code is introduced later in this chapter; we will use the debug logs to learn how the platform invokes Apex code.

Exploring execution contexts

For the next two examples, imagine that an Apex trigger has been created for the **Contestant** object and an Apex class has been written to implement some logic to update the contestants' championship points depending on their position when the race ends.

In the first example, the **Contestant** record is updated directly from the UI and the **Apex Debug** log shown in the next screenshot is captured.

Notice the **EXECUTION_STARTED** and **EXECUTION_FINISHED** lines; these show the actual start and end of the request on the Salesforce server. The **CODE_UNIT_STARTED** lines show where the platform invokes Apex code. Also, note that the line number shows **EXTERNAL**, indicating the platform's internal code called the Apex code. For the sake of brevity, the rest of the execution of the code is collapsed in the screenshot:

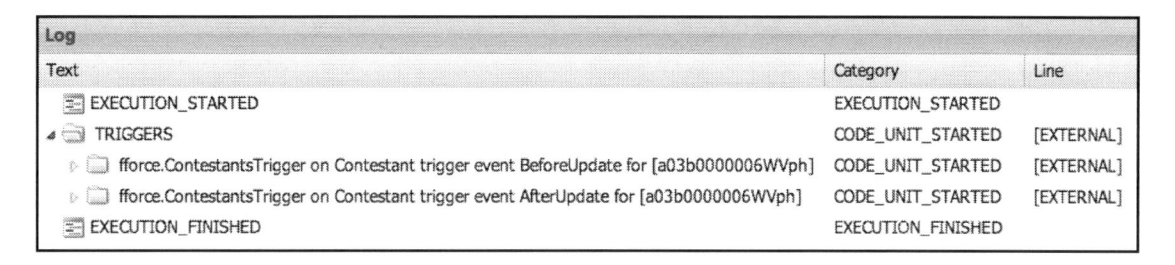

Log			
Text		Category	Line
EXECUTION_STARTED		EXECUTION_STARTED	
▸ TRIGGERS		CODE_UNIT_STARTED	[EXTERNAL]
▸ fforce.ContestantsTrigger on Contestant trigger event BeforeUpdate for [a03b0000006WVph]		CODE_UNIT_STARTED	[EXTERNAL]
▸ fforce.ContestantsTrigger on Contestant trigger event AfterUpdate for [a03b0000006WVph]		CODE_UNIT_STARTED	[EXTERNAL]
EXECUTION_FINISHED		EXECUTION_FINISHED	

In this second example, imagine that some Apex code was executed to calculate the contestants' championship points once the race ends. In this case, the code was executed from an **Execute Anonymous** prompt (though in the application, this would be a button); again, the Apex Debug log was captured and is shown in the next screenshot.

Again, you can see the **EXECUTION_STARTED** and **EXECUTION_FINISHED** entries, along with the three **CODE_UNIT_STARTED** entries—one for the `RaceService.awardChampionshipPoints` Apex method called from the **Execute Anonymous** prompt and two others for the Apex Trigger code:

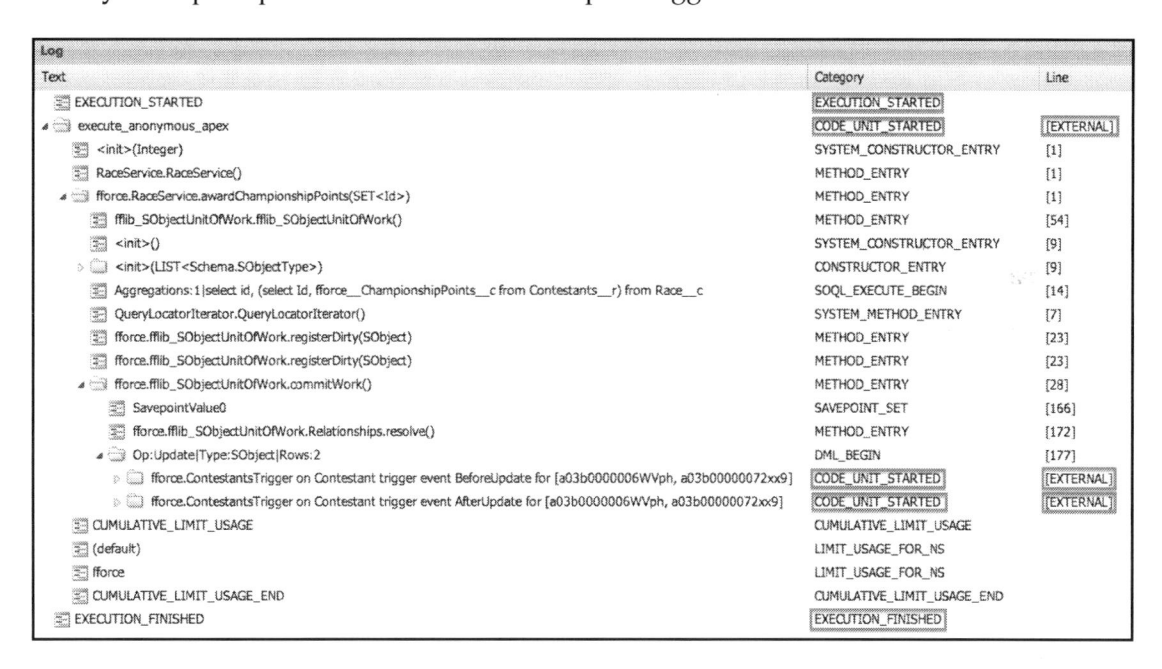

Log		
Text	Category	Line
EXECUTION_STARTED	EXECUTION_STARTED	
execute_anonymous_apex	CODE_UNIT_STARTED	[EXTERNAL]
<init>(Integer)	SYSTEM_CONSTRUCTOR_ENTRY	[1]
RaceService.RaceService()	METHOD_ENTRY	[1]
▸ fforce.RaceService.awardChampionshipPoints(SET<Id>)	METHOD_ENTRY	[1]
fflib_SObjectUnitOfWork.fflib_SObjectUnitOfWork()	METHOD_ENTRY	[54]
<init>()	SYSTEM_CONSTRUCTOR_ENTRY	[9]
▸ <init>(LIST<Schema.SObjectType>)	CONSTRUCTOR_ENTRY	[9]
Aggregations:1|select id, (select Id, fforce__ChampionshipPoints__c from Contestants__r) from Race__c	SOQL_EXECUTE_BEGIN	[14]
QueryLocatorIterator.QueryLocatorIterator()	SYSTEM_METHOD_ENTRY	[7]
fforce.fflib_SObjectUnitOfWork.registerDirty(SObject)	METHOD_ENTRY	[23]
fforce.fflib_SObjectUnitOfWork.registerDirty(SObject)	METHOD_ENTRY	[23]
▸ fforce.fflib_SObjectUnitOfWork.commitWork()	METHOD_ENTRY	[28]
SavepointValue0	SAVEPOINT_SET	[166]
fforce.fflib_SObjectUnitOfWork.Relationships.resolve()	METHOD_ENTRY	[172]
▸ Op:Update|Type:SObject|Rows:2	DML_BEGIN	[177]
▸ fforce.ContestantsTrigger on Contestant trigger event BeforeUpdate for [a03b0000006WVph, a03b00000072xx9]	CODE_UNIT_STARTED	[EXTERNAL]
▸ fforce.ContestantsTrigger on Contestant trigger event AfterUpdate for [a03b0000006WVph, a03b00000072xx9]	CODE_UNIT_STARTED	[EXTERNAL]
CUMULATIVE_LIMIT_USAGE	CUMULATIVE_LIMIT_USAGE	
(default)	LIMIT_USAGE_FOR_NS	
fforce	LIMIT_USAGE_FOR_NS	
CUMULATIVE_LIMIT_USAGE_END	CUMULATIVE_LIMIT_USAGE_END	
EXECUTION_FINISHED	EXECUTION_FINISHED	

What is different from the first example is, which you can see by looking at the **Line** column, that the execution transitions show the lines of the Apex code being executed and **EXTERNAL**. When DML statements are executed in Apex to update the **Contestants** records, the Apex code execution pauses while the platform code takes over to update the records. During this process, the platform eventually then invokes Apex Triggers and once again, the execution flows back into Apex code.

Essentially, the execution context is used to wrap a request to the Salesforce server; it can be a mix of the execution of the Apex code, Validation Rules, workflow rules, trigger code, and other logic executions. The platform handles the overall orchestration of this for you. The Salesforce **Developer Console** tool offers some excellent additional insight into the time spent on each of these areas. The following screenshot shows an example of this view:

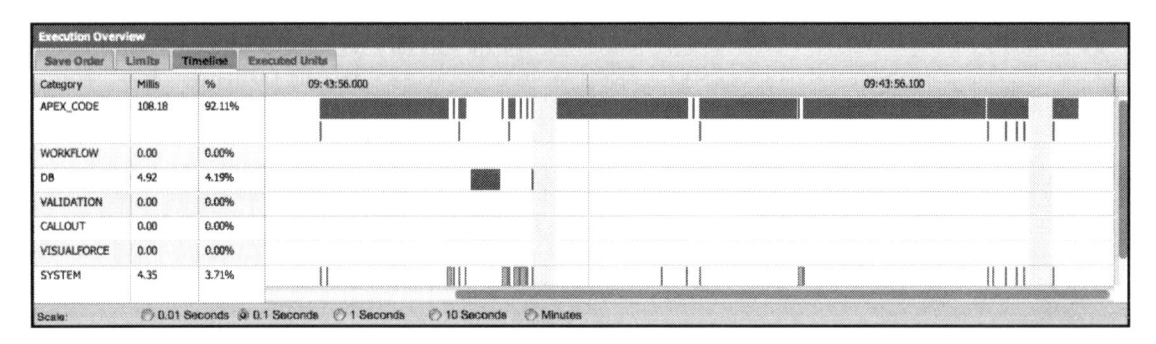

Category	Millis	%	09:43:56.000	09:43:56.100
APEX_CODE	108.18	92.11%		
WORKFLOW	0.00	0.00%		
DB	4.92	4.19%		
VALIDATION	0.00	0.00%		
CALLOUT	0.00	0.00%		
VISUALFORCE	0.00	0.00%		
SYSTEM	4.35	3.71%		

If the subscriber org has added Apex Triggers to your objects, these are executed in the same execution context. If any of these Apex code units throw unhandled exceptions, the entire execution context is stopped and all database updates performed are rolled back, which is discussed in more detail later in this chapter.

Execution context and state

The server memory storage used by the Apex variables created in an execution context can be considered the state of the execution context; in Apex, this is known as the **heap**. On the whole, the server memory resources used to maintain an execution context state are returned at the end; thus, in a system with short-lived execution contexts, resources can be better managed. By using the CPU and heap governors, the platform enforces the maximum duration of an execution context and Apex heap size to ensure the smooth running of the service; these are described in more detail later in this chapter.

State management is the programming practice of managing the information that the user or job needs between separate execution contexts (requests to the server) invoked as the user or job goes about performing the work, such as a wizard-based UI or a job aggregating information. Users, of course, do not really understand execution contexts and state; they see tasks via the user interface or jobs they start based on field inputs and criteria they provide. It is not always necessary to consider state management as some user tasks can be completed in one execution context; this is often preferable from an architecture perspective as there are overheads in state management. Although the platform provides some features to help with state management, using them requires careful consideration and planning, especially from a data-volume perspective.

On other programming platforms, such as Java or Microsoft .NET, static variables are used to maintain the state across execution contexts, often caching information to reduce the processing of subsequent execution contexts or to store common application configurations. The implementation of the `static` keyword in Apex is different; its scope applies only to the current execution context and no further. Thus, an Apex static variable value will not be retained between execution contexts, though they are preserved between multiple Apex code units (as illustrated in the previous section). Thus, in recursive Apex Trigger scenarios, allow the sharing of the static variable to control recursion.

> Custom Settings may offer a potential parallel in Apex where other programming languages use static variables to store or cache certain application information. Such information can be configured to be org, user, or profile scope and is low-cost to read from Apex. However, if you need to cache information that may have a certain life span or expiry, such as the user session or across a number of users, you might want to consider Platform Cache. Platform Cache also provides greater flexibility for your customers in terms of purchasing additional storage (Custom Settings are limited to 10 MB per package).

Platform Cache

Caching information is not a new concept and is available on many other platforms, for example, **MemCache** is a popular open source framework for providing a cache facility. The main motivation for considering caching is performance.

As mentioned earlier, state is not retained between requests. You may find that common information needs to be constantly queried or calculated. If the chances of such information changing are low, caches can be considered to gain a performance benefit. The cost, in terms of Apex execution (CPU Governor) and/or database queries (SOQL and Row Governors) has to be less than retrieving it from the cache.

> **TIP:** Salesforce recommends the use of the `System.currentTimeMillis` method to output debug statements around code and/or queries to determine the potential benefit. Do not depend on the debug log timestamps.

Platform Cache allows you to retain state beyond the scope of the request, up to 48 hours for the org-level cache and 8 hours for the session-level cache. A session-level cache only applies to the interactive context, and it is not available in async Apex. Your code can clear cached information ahead of the expiry times if users change information that the cached information is dependent on. Apex provides APIs under the `Cache` namespace for storing (putting), retrieving (getting), and clearing information from either of the caches. There is also a `$Cache` variable to retrieve information from the session cache within a Visualforce page. Unfortunately, there is currently no `$Cache` access for Lightning Component markup at the time of writing. As such, Apex Controllers must be used.

> **TIP:** You can enable **Cache Diagnostics** on the **User Detail** page. Once enabled, you can click the **Diagnostics** link next to a cache partition (more on this later in this section). This provides useful information on the size of entries in the cache and how often they are being used. This can be useful during testing. Salesforce recommends using this page sparingly, as generating the information is expensive.

Think carefully about the lifespan of what you put in the cache—once it goes in, the whole point is that it stays in the cache as long as possible and thus the performance benefit is obtained more often than not. If you are constantly changing it or clearing the cache out, the benefit will be reduced. Equally, information can become stale and out of date if you do not correctly consider places in your application where you need to invalidate (clear) the cache. This consideration can get quite complex depending on what you are storing in the cache, for example, if the information is a result of a calculation involving a number of records and objects.

> Stale-cached information can impact your validations and user experience and thus potentially cause data integrity issues if not considered carefully. If you are storing information in the org-level cache for multiple users, ensure that you are not indirectly exposing information other users would not have access to via their sharing rules, object, or field-level security.

The amount of cache available depends on the customer org type. Enterprise edition orgs currently get 10 MB by default, whereas Unlimited and Performance edition orgs get 30 MB. You cannot package storage, though more can be purchased by customers. To test the benefits of Platform Cache in a Developer edition org, you can request a trial allocation from Salesforce from the **Platform Cache** page, under **Setup**. Salesforce uses a **Least Recently Used** (**LRU**) algorithm to manage cache items.

The amount of cache available can be partitioned (split), much like storage partitions on a hard disk. This allows the administrator to guarantee a portion of the allocation is used for a specific application only, and, if needed, adjust it depending on performance needs. As the package developer, you can reference local partitions (created by the administrator) by name dynamically. You can also package a partition name for use exclusively by your application and reference it in your code. This ensures any allocation assigned after the installation of your package by the administrator to your partition is guaranteed to be used by your application. If your code was to share a partition, you may not want other applications constantly pushing out your cached entries, for example.

> Packaged partitions cannot be accessed by other code in the customer org or other packages; only by code in the corresponding package namespace. You may want to provide the option (via Custom Settings) for administrators to configure your application to reference local partitions, perhaps allowing administrators to pool usage between applications. Consider using the `Cache.Visibility.NAMESPACE` enumeration when adding entries to the cache, to avoid code outside your package accessing entries. This could be an important security consideration, depending on what you are caching. Salesforce itself uses MemCache internally to manage the platform. Platform Cache is likely a wrapper exposing part of the internals to Apex developers. Refer to the blogpost *Salesforce Architecture - How They Handle 1.3 Billion Transactions A Day* at `http://highscalability.com/blog/2013/9/23/salesforce-architecture-how-they-handle-13-billion-transacti.html`.

The Salesforce *Apex Developers Guide* contains a *Platform Cache* subsection that goes into further detail on the topics I have covered in this section, including further best practices and usage guidelines. You can refer to this guide at `https://developer.salesforce.com/docs/atlas.en-us.apexcode.meta/apexcode/apex_cache_namespace_overview.htm`.

Execution context and security

As discussed in the last chapter, the platform provides security features to allow subscribers or administrators to manage CRUD operations on your objects as well as individual **field-level security** (**FLS**), ideally through the assignment of some carefully considered permission sets that you have included in your package, in addition to providing the ability to define sharing rules to control record visibility and editing.

Within an Apex execution context, it is important to understand whose responsibility it is (the platform's or developer's) to provide enforcement of those security features. With respect to sharing rules, there is a default security context, which is either set by the platform or can be specified using specific keywords within the Apex code. These two types of security are described in further detail in the following bullets:

- **Sharing security**: Through the use of the `with sharing` keyword when applied to an Apex class declaration, the Apex runtime provides support to filter out records returned by SOQL queries automatically that do not meet the sharing rules for the current user context. If it is not specified, then this is inherited from the outermost Apex class that controls the execution; however, it is good practice to apply the `inherit sharing` keyword to indicate to future developers and the Salesforce security review process that this is indeed your intent. Conversely, the `without sharing` keyword can be used to explicitly enable the return of all records meeting the query, regardless of the sharing rules. This is useful when implementing referential integrity, for example, where the code needs to see all the available records, regardless of the current user's sharing rules.
- **CRUD and FLS security**: As discussed in the previous chapter, it is the Apex developer's responsibility to use appropriate programming approaches to enforce this type of security. When building user interfaces on the platform, CRUD and FLS are only enforced through the use of the appropriate Visualforce or Lightning components, such as `apex:inputField`, `apex:outputField`, `lightning:inputField`, or `lightning:outputField` (when used within `lightning:recordViewForm` or `lightning:recordEditForm`). The Apex code within an execution context runs within the system mode with respect to CRUD and FLS accessibility, which means that, unless your code checks for permitted access, the platform will always permit access. Note that this is regardless of the use of the `with sharing` keyword, which only affects the records that are visible to your code.

In summary, both are controlled and implemented separately as follows:

- Row-level security applies only to `with sharing` usage.
- CRUD security and FLS need separate coding considerations.

In later chapters of this book, we will look at some places to position this logic to make it easier to manage and less intrusive for the rest of the code.

Execution context transaction management

Handling database transactions in Apex is simpler than other platforms. By default, the scope of the transaction wraps the entire execution context. This means that if the execution context completes successfully, any record data is committed. If an unhandled exception or error occurs, the execution context is aborted and all record data is rolled back.

Unhandled Apex exceptions, governor exceptions, or Validation Rules can cause an execution context to abort. In some cases, however, it can be desirable to perform only a partial rollback. For these cases, the platform provides **Savepoints** that can be used to place markers in the execution context to record the data written at the point the Savepoint was created. Later, a Savepoint can be used in the execution as the rollback position to resume further processing in response to error handling or a condition that causes an alternative code path resulting in different updates to the database.

> It is important to realize that catching exceptions using the Apex `try` and `catch` keywords, for example, in Visualforce Controller methods, results in the platform committing any data written up until the exception occurs. This can lead to partially updated data across the objects being updated in the execution context, giving rise to data integrity issues in your application. Savepoints can be used to avoid this, by using a rollback in the `catch` code block. This does, however, present quite a boilerplate overhead for the developer each time. Later in this book, we will review this practice in more detail and introduce a pattern known as **Unit of Work** to help automate this.

Apex governors and namespaces

Platform governors prevent any one execution context from consuming excessive resources on the service, which could be detrimental to its users. Overall, an execution context cannot exceed 10 minutes, though within an execution context, in practice, other limits would likely be reached before this.

Apex Execution and Separation of Concerns

For example, Apex code units executing within an execution context can only collectively execute for a maximum of 10 or 60 seconds depending on the context. Over the years, Salesforce has worked hard to consolidate what was once a confusing array of governors, which also varied based on a number of Apex code contexts. Thankfully, these days, governors are much easier to follow, and vary only based on the context, being interactive or batch (asynchronous).

Namespaces and governor scope

An important consideration for a packaged solution is the scope of a governor. In other words, does it apply only to the packaged code or to all code executing in the execution context? Remember that an execution context can contain code from other developers within the subscriber org or other packaged solutions installed.

Your package namespace acts as a container for some governors, which protects your code from limits being consumed by other packaged code (triggers, for example) running in the execution context. The platform supports an unlimited number of namespace scopes within one execution context. For code that has not been deployed as part of a managed package, such as code developed directly in the subscriber org, there is a default namespace.

Code running in a namespace cannot exceed governors that are scoped by the namespace (as highlighted later in this chapter). Although an execution context can run code from unlimited namespaces, a cross-namespace cumulative limit is enforced. This is 11 times the specific per namespace limit. For example, a maximum of 1,650 DML statements (150 per namespace) would be allowed across any number of namespaces. For more examples, refer to the *Execution Governors and Limits* page in the *Apex Developer Guide*, in the subsection entitled *Per-Transaction Certified Manage Package Limits*.

> In reality, 150, in my view, is quite a lot of DML for a single namespace to be performing. If you're observing **bulkification**, this would require you to be updating 150 distinct objects in one request! If that is the case and you are following DML bulkification, you may want to review your object model design to see if you can denormalize it a bit further.

You can see evidence of namespaces in play when you observe the debug logs within your packaging org. Just before each Apex code unit completes, notice how the `LIMIT_USAGE_FOR_NS` section of the debug log is repeated for the `default` and `fforce` namespaces (your namespace will be different) as follows, allowing you to review the incremental usage of governors throughout the execution context:

```
13:47:43.712 (412396000)|CUMULATIVE_LIMIT_USAGE
13:47:43.712|LIMIT_USAGE_FOR_NS|(default)|
  Number of SOQL queries: 0 out of 100
  Number of query rows: 0 out of 50000
  Number of SOSL queries: 0 out of 20
  Number of DML statements: 0 out of 150
  Number of DML rows: 0 out of 10000
  Number of code statements: 0 out of 200000
  Maximum CPU time: 0 out of 10000
  Maximum heap size: 0 out of 6000000
  Number of callouts: 0 out of 10
  Number of Email Invocations: 0 out of 10
  Number of fields describes: 0 out of 100
  Number of record type describes: 0 out of 100
  Number of child relationships describes: 0 out of 100
  Number of picklist describes: 0 out of 100
  Number of future calls: 0 out of 10

13:47:43.712|LIMIT_USAGE_FOR_NS|fforce|
  Number of SOQL queries: 1 out of 100
  Number of query rows: 1 out of 50000
  Number of SOSL queries: 0 out of 20
  Number of DML statements: 2 out of 150
  Number of DML rows: 3 out of 10000
  Number of code statements: 85 out of 200000
  Maximum CPU time: 0 out of 10000
  Maximum heap size: 0 out of 6000000
  Number of callouts: 0 out of 10
  Number of Email Invocations: 0 out of 10
  Number of fields describes: 0 out of 100
  Number of record type describes: 0 out of 100
  Number of child relationships describes: 0 out of 100
  Number of picklist describes: 0 out of 100
  Number of future calls: 0 out of 10
13:47:43.712|CUMULATIVE_LIMIT_USAGE_END
13:47:43.412|CODE_UNIT_FINISHED|execute_anonymous_apex
```

Note that all governors are shown in the summary regardless of their scope; for example, the CPU time governor is an execution scope governor. This allows you to follow the consumption of the Apex CPU time across Apex code units from all namespaces. The **Developer Console** option provides some excellent tools to profile the consumption of governors.

Deterministic and non-deterministic governors

When considering governors from a testing and support perspective, you should be aware of which governors are deterministic and which are not. For example, when profiling your application, this is being able to obtain the exact same results (such as the preceding results) from the debug logs from repeated running of the exact same test. The following outlines examples of both types of governors:

- Examples of deterministic governors are the SOQL and DML governors. If you repeat the same test scenario (within your development or packaging orgs), you will always get the same utilization of queries and updates to the database; thus, you can determine reliably whether any changes in these need to be investigated.
- An example of a non-deterministic governor is the CPU time governor. The amount of time used between executions will vary based on the load at any given time on the Salesforce servers. Thus, it is hard to determine accurately whether changes in your application are truly affecting this or not. That said, it can be a useful indicator, depending on the variance you're seeing between builds of your software. However, keep in mind that the baseline information you capture will become increasingly less accurate as time goes by, for example, between platform releases.

In the CPU governor, the platform limits the length of time the execution context is allowed to spend executing the Apex code to 10 seconds for interactive context, and 60 seconds for asynchronous context (for example, Batch Apex), though in practice the platform appears to exercise some tolerance. In contrast, the number of SOQL queries or DML statements is always constant when applied to a consistent test scenario.

As the CPU governor is non-deterministic, it should only be used as a guideline when testing. My recommendation is not to use the `Limits.getCPULimit()` method as a branching mechanism between interactive and batch processing in your application. If you require this type of branching, focus on using aspects of your application such as selection criteria, the number of rows selected, or some other configurable setting in the subscriber org, perhaps via a Custom Setting.

You may want to consider testing certain governors within an Apex test context to monitor for changes in how many queries or DML are being consumed. Such tests can give you an early warning sign that inefficiency has crept into your code. Use the `Limits` class methods to capture the before and after state of the SOQL and/or DML governors. Then, apply either a strict comparison of the expected usage (for example, 10 queries expected after the execution of the test) or a plus or minus tolerance to allow for code evolution.

Key governors for Apex package developers

The following table is a summary of key governors, their scope, and whether they are deterministic. Note that Salesforce is constantly monitoring the use of its service and adapting its governors. Always check for the latest information on governors in the *Apex Developer Guide*.

Governor	Scope	Deterministic
Execution context timeout	Execution context	No
Apex CPU governor	Execution context	No
SOQL queries	Namespace	Yes
DML statements	Namespace	Yes
Query rows	Namespace	Yes

Where is Apex used?

The following table lists the types of execution contexts that Apex code can be run from and considerations with respect to security and state management. While a description of how to implement each of these is outside the scope of this book, some aspects, such as Batch Apex, are discussed in more detail in a later chapter when considering data volumes:

Execution context	User	Security	State management
Anonymous Apex	Current user	Sharing is enforced by default, unless disabled by applying the `without sharing` keyword to the enclosing class. CRUD and FLS are enforced by default, but only against the code entered directly into the **Execute Anonymous** window. The code will fail to compile if the user does not have access to the objects or fields referenced. Note that checking is only performed by the platform at compilation time; if the code calls a pre-existing Apex class, there is no enforcement within that class and any other class it calls.	See Note 2.

[140]

Execution context	User	Security	State management
Apex Controller Action Method **Note:** Used only by Visualforce pages	Current user	Sharing is not enforced by default; the developer needs to apply the `with sharing` keyword to the enclosing class. CRUD and FLS are not enforced by default; the developer needs to enforce this in code.	Any member variable declared on the Apex Controller that is not static or marked with the `transient` keyword will be included in **View State**. Visualforce automatically maintains this between interactions on the page. Use it carefully, as large View State sizes can cause performance degradation for the page. **Developer Console** has an excellent View State browser tool.
Apex Controller Remote and Aura Actions **Note:** Remote Action methods are used by Visualforce and Aura Action methods are used by Lightning Components	Current user	Sharing is not enforced by default; the developer needs to apply the `with sharing` keyword to the enclosing class. It is required for Salesforce security review. CRUD and FLS are not enforced by default; the developer needs to check this in code.	Remote Action and Aura Action Apex methods are already static, as stated previously; any static data is not retained in Apex. Thus, there is no state retained between remote action calls made by the client JavaScript. Typically, in these cases, the state of the task the user is performing is maintained on the page itself via the client-side state. As a result of not having to manage the state for the developer, these types of methods are much faster than the action methods described in the preceding section.

Execution context	User	Security	State management
Apex Trigger and Apex Async Trigger	Current user	Sharing is not enforced by default; the developer needs to apply the `with sharing` keyword in the outermost Apex class (if present, for example, Apex Controller). Triggers invoked through the Salesforce UIs or APIs run without sharing implicitly; if you need to apply with sharing, move your trigger code into an Apex class and call that from the trigger code. CRUD and FLS are not enforced by default; the developer needs to enforce this in the code.	Static variables are shared between Apex Trigger invocations within an execution context. This allows some caching of commonly used information and/or recursive trigger protection to be implemented if needed.

Execution context	User	Security	State management
Batch Apex	User who submitted the job.	Sharing is not enforced by default; the developer needs to apply the `with sharing` keyword to the enclosing class. CRUD and FLS are not enforced by default; the developer needs to enforce this in the code.	Batch Apex splits work into distinct execution contexts, driven by splitting up the data into scopes (typically, 200). If the `Database.Stateful` interface is implemented, the class member variable values of the implementing Apex class are retained between each invocation. The `transient` keyword also applies here. The `final` keyword can be used to retain the initial member variable values throughout the job's execution.
Platform event subscription	System user (See Note 3)	See Note 1.	See Note 2.
Package post install script	System user (See Note 3)	See Note 1.	See Note 2.
Queueable	User who submitted the work	See Note 1.	See Note 2.
Apex scheduler	User who scheduled the job	See Note 1.	See Note 2.
Inbound messaging	Based on inbound message configuration	See Note 1.	See Note 2.
Invocable method	Current user	See Note 1.	See Note 2.
Apex REST API	Current user	See Note 1.	See Note 2.
Apex Web Service	Current user	See Note 1.	See Note 2.

The following notes apply to the rows in the preceding table:

- **Note 1**: Unless otherwise stated in the preceding table, the default position is as follows regarding security:
    - Sharing is not enforced by default; the developer needs to apply the `with sharing` keyword to the enclosing class.
    - CRUD and FLS are not enforced by default; the developer needs to check this in the code.
- **Note 2**: For state management, unless stated otherwise in the previous table, the default position is as follows:
    - No static or member variable values are retained between invocations of the Apex class methods between execution contexts.
- **Note 3**: The system user is not a physical user in the system. Be sure you understand this implication when performing database operations in this context, for example when updating and inserting records. In the case of platform event subscriptions (discussed in a later chapter), the `UserId` field contains the ID of the user who generated the event.

Separation of concerns

As you can see, there are a number of places Apex code is invoked by various platform features. Such places represent areas for valuable code to potentially hide. It is hidden because it is typically not easy or appropriate to reuse such logic as each of the areas mentioned in the previous table has its own subtle concerns with respect to security, state management, transactions, and other aspects such as error handling (for example, catching and communicating errors) as well as varying needs for bulkification.

Throughout the rest of this chapter, we will review these requirements and distill them into SOC that allows a demarcation of responsibilities between the Apex code used to integrate with these platform features versus the code implementing your application business logic, such that the code can be shared between platform features today and in the future more readily. Speaking more generally, SOC, regardless of the platform you are developing on, helps simplify your code base, allowing others to work on it more easily and independently. A key value is the ability to isolate changes and minimize the risk of wide, sweeping changes to your application.

Apex code evolution

Apex Triggers can lead to a more traditional pattern of `if`/`then`/`else` style coding, resulting in a procedural logic that is hard to maintain and follow. This is partly because they are classes and, as such, they don't naturally encourage breaking up the code into methods and separate classes. As we saw in the previous table, Apex Triggers are not the only execution context for Apex; others do support Apex classes and the **object-orientated programming** (OOP) style, often leveraging system-defined Apex interfaces to allow the developer to integrate with the platform, such as Batch Apex.

Apex has come a long way since its early introduction as a means of writing more complex Validation Rules in Apex Triggers. These days, the general consensus in the community is to write as little code as possible directly in an Apex Trigger, instead of delegating the logic to separate Apex classes. For a packaged application, there is no compelling reason to have more than one Apex Trigger per object. Indeed, the Salesforce security review has been known to flag this even if the code is conditioned to run independently.

A key motivation to move the Apex Trigger code into an Apex class is to gain access to the more powerful language semantics of the Apex language, such as OOP, allowing the developer to structure the code more closely to the functions of the application and gain better code reuse and visibility.

Separating concerns in Apex

Each execution context has its own requirements for your code, such as implementing system interfaces, annotations, or controller bindings. Within this code are further coding requirements relating to how you engineer your application code, which leads to a set of common architecture layers of concern, such as loading records, applying validations, and executing business logic.

Understanding these layers allows us to discover a different way to write application code than simply writing all our code in a single Apex class, which becomes tightly coupled to the execution context and thus less flexible in the future.

To manage these layers of concern in the code, create separate classes—those that are bound to the specific execution context (such as Batch Apex, Scheduler, Apex REST, and Inbound Messaging) and those that contain the application business logic that implements the actual task for the user.

The following UML diagram shows the Apex classes that implement the requirements (or concerns) of the execution context and Apex classes to execute the application's business logic. The dotted line indicates SOC between the UI controller (these could be Visualforce or Lightning Component Controllers) classes and the classes implementing the application's business logic:

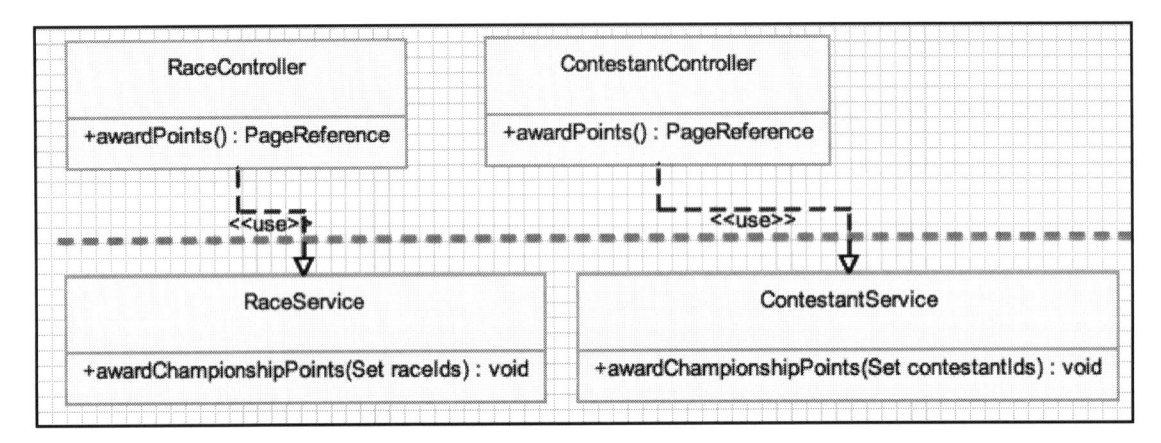

```
┌─────────────────────────────────┐      ┌─────────────────────────────────────┐
│         RaceController          │      │        ContestantController         │
├─────────────────────────────────┤      ├─────────────────────────────────────┤
│ +awardPoints() : PageReference  │      │ +awardPoints() : PageReference      │
└─────────────────────────────────┘      └─────────────────────────────────────┘
              │ <<use>>                                │ <<use>>
- - - - - - - │ - - - - - - - - - - - - - - - - - - - │ - - - - - - - - - - - - -
              ▼                                        ▼
┌─────────────────────────────────────┐  ┌─────────────────────────────────────────────┐
│            RaceService              │  │              ContestantService              │
├─────────────────────────────────────┤  ├─────────────────────────────────────────────┤
│ +awardChampionshipPoints(Set raceIds) : void │ +awardChampionshipPoints(Set contestantIds) : void │
└─────────────────────────────────────┘  └─────────────────────────────────────────────┘
```

Separation of concerns in Lightning Components

Like the Visualforce use of the **Model View Controller** (**MVC**), **Lightning Components** also support SOC by splitting up the implementation of the component into several distinct source files that each have their own concerns. As Lightning Components are implemented on the client side, a component's various source files represent a way to implement separation of concerns within the HTML, CSS, and JavaScript code you write.

Lightning Components can be developed using two frameworks, the original Aura-based framework and the latest HTML5 web standard base framework. These are known as **Lightning Web Components** (**LWC**) and **Lightning Aura Components**.

LWCs offer greater alignment with the modern web programming standards that have emerged since the Aura-based framework was first created by Salesforce. They are recommended as they provide broader access to existing skills and thus existing knowledge. The following sections include a summary of both in terms of SOC, though further samples throughout the book will focus on the latest LWC framework.

In either framework, the Lightning Components client-side controllers can communicate with an Apex Controller class via the `@AuraMethod` annotation, and thus access classes implementing your share application business logic, as shown in the preceding diagram.

> **TIP:** LWC have better rendering performance than those based on the Aura framework, since they leverage more of the browser's technology, which is more optimized as it works closer to the hosting operating system. Salesforce does allow you to build with both frameworks and combine components (with some restrictions) on the same page. I recommend you review carefully which components you want to port over to the new framework and do so incrementally in a prioritized way, based on performance and the likelihood of changes going forward.

Separation of concerns in an LWC

When creating an **LWC** in **Visual Studio Code**, it creates a folder for your component with the following files in it:

```
├── force-app
│   └── main
│       └── default
│           ├── lwc
│           │   ├── driverStats
│           │   │   ├── driverStats.html
│           │   │   ├── driverStats.js
│           │   │   └── driverStats.js-meta.xml
```

In comparison to Aura-based components, LWC-based components are much simpler. The preceding `.js` file contains client-side JavaScript logic, including bindings to references made in the `.html` file. It uses the JavaScript `import` statement to import other components, libraries, or resources. Because LWC is more standards-based, you can create ES6 modules to share common logic between your components. In addition, you can also use OOP with your components, such as base classes.

> Later in this book, in `Chapter 9`, *User Interfaces with Lightning Framework*, we will be building some LWCs to package within our FormulaForce application.

Separation of concerns in a Lightning Aura Component

When creating a **Lightning Aura Component** in **Visual Studio Code**, it creates a folder for your component with the following files in it:

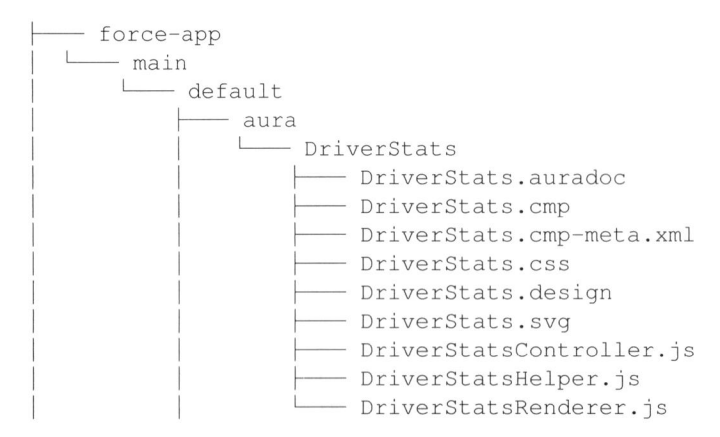

```
├── force-app
│   └── main
│       └── default
│           ├── aura
│           │   └── DriverStats
│           │       ├── DriverStats.auradoc
│           │       ├── DriverStats.cmp
│           │       ├── DriverStats.cmp-meta.xml
│           │       ├── DriverStats.css
│           │       ├── DriverStats.design
│           │       ├── DriverStats.svg
│           │       ├── DriverStatsController.js
│           │       ├── DriverStatsHelper.js
│           │       └── DriverStatsRenderer.js
```

The following describes the recommended concern for each of these files:

1. `...Controller.js`: Code in this file is responsible for implementing bindings to the visual aspects of the component, defined via the markup defined in the `.cmp` file. Unlike a Visualforce Controller, it only contains logic providing bindings to the UI. The client-side state of your component is accessed via the Controller.
2. `...Helper.js`: Code in this file is responsible for the logic behind your component's behavior, button presses, and other interactions, which lead to accessing the backend Apex Controller, combining inputs and outputs to interface with the user and the backend. Methods on the helper take an instance of the Controller to manipulate the state and UI.
3. `..Renderer.js`: Code in this file is only needed in more advanced scenarios where you want to override or modify the HTML DOM created by the Lightning framework itself using markup expressed in your `.cmp` file. It is focused on the presentation of your component in the browser.

Execution context logic versus application logic concerns

In this section, we will review the needs/concerns of the execution context and how each can lead to a common requirement of the application business logic. This helps define the guidelines around writing the application business logic, thus making it logical and more reusable throughout the platform and application:

- **Error handling**: When it comes to communicating errors, traditionally, a developer has two options: let the error be caught by the execution context or catch the exception to display it in some form. In the Visualforce Apex Controller context, it's typical to catch exceptions and route these through the `ApexPage.addMessage` method to display messages to the user via the `apex:pageMessages` tag. In the Lightning Component Apex Controller context, it's recommended to catch exceptions and re-throw them as `AuraHandledException`. In the Batch Apex context, letting the platform know that the job has failed involves allowing the platform to catch and handle the exception instead of your code. If you want to track these errors yourself, you can subscribe to the platform event called `BatchApexErrorEvent`. For Apex REST classes, unhandled exceptions will automatically output exceptions in the REST response:
    - **Application business code implication**: The point here is that there are different concerns with regard to error handling within each execution context. Thus, it is important for application business logic not to dictate how errors should be handled by calling the code.
- **Transaction management**: As we saw earlier in this chapter, the platform manages a single default transaction around the execution context. This is important to consider with the error-handling concern, particularly if errors are caught, as the platform will commit any records written to the database prior to the exception occurring, which may not be desirable and may be hard to track down:
    - **Application business code implication**: Understanding the scope of the transaction is important, especially when it comes to writing application business logic that throws exceptions. Callers, especially those catching exceptions, should not have to worry about creating `Database.Savepoint` to rollback the state of the database if an exception is thrown.

- **Number of records**: Some contexts deal with a single database record, such as a Visualforce standard controller, and others deal with multiple records, such as Visualforce standard set controllers or Batch Apex. Regardless of the type of execution context, the platform itself imposes governors around the database operations that are linked with the number of records being processed. Every execution context expects code to be bulkified (minimal queries and DML statements).
    - **Application business code implication**: Though some execution contexts appear to only deal with a single record at a time in reality because database-related governors apply to all execution context types, it is good practice to assume that the application code should consider bulkification regardless. This also helps make the application code more reusable in future from different contexts.
- **State management**: Execution contexts on the Lightning Platform are generally stateless; although, as described earlier in this chapter, there are some platform facilities to store state across execution contexts:
    - **Application business code implications**: As state management solutions are not always available and are also implemented in different ways, the application code should not attempt to deal directly with this concern and should make itself stateless in nature (the use of Platform Cache in order to improve performance is the exception to this rule). If needed, provide custom Apex types that can be used to exchange the state with the calling execution context code, for example, a controller class.
- **Security**: It could be said that the execution context should be the one concerned with enforcing this, as it is the closest to the end user. This is certainly the case with a controller execution context where Salesforce recommends the `with sharing` keyword is placed. However, when it comes to CRUD and FLS security, the practicality of placing enforcement at the execution context entry point will become harder from a maintenance perspective, as the code checking the user permissions will have to be continually maintained (and potentially repeated) along with the needs of the underlying application business code:
    - **Application business code implication**: The implication here is that it is the concern of both the execution context and the application business logic to enforce the user permissions. However, in the case of sharing, it is mainly that the initial Apex caller should be respected. As we dive deeper into the engineering application business logic in later chapters, we will revisit security several times.

> **TIP**
>
> A traditional approach to logging errors for later review is to use a **log table**. While on the Lightning Platform this can be implemented to some degree, keep in mind that some execution contexts work more effectively with the platform features if you don't catch exceptions and let the platform handle it. For example, the **Apex Jobs** page will correctly report failed batches along with a summary of the last exception. If you implement a logging solution to catch these exceptions, the visibility of failed batch jobs will be hidden from administrators. Make sure that you determine which approach suits your users best. My recommendation for **Batch Apex** would be to implement your own subscriber to `BatchApexErrorEvent`. You can see an open source library I created to illustrate this here: `https://github.com/afawcett/force-brf`.

Improving incremental code reuse

There is SOC between code invoked directly through an execution context and the application business logic code within an application. This knowledge is important to ensure that you can effectively reuse application logic easily, incrementally, and with minimal effort. It is the developer's responsibility to maintain this SOC by following patterns and guidelines set out in the chapters of this book and those you devise yourself as part of your own coding guidelines.

Reuse needs may not always be initially obvious. However, by following SOC and the design patterns in this book, when they do arise as your application evolves and new platform features are added, the process is more organic without refactoring, or, worse, copy and pasting the code!

To illustrate a reuse scenario, imagine that in the first iteration of the FormulaForce application, awarding points to a race contestant was accomplished by the user through an **Award Points** button on the **Contestant** detail page for each contestant. Also, the newsletter functionality was accessed by manually clicking the **Send News Letter** button on the **Season** detail page each month.

Apex Execution and Separation of Concerns

The class for the first iteration is shown in the next diagram. Note that you can already see the beginning of SOC between the Apex Controller logic and application business logic, which is contained in the classes ending in `Service`. The Service layer is discussed in more detail later in this chapter:

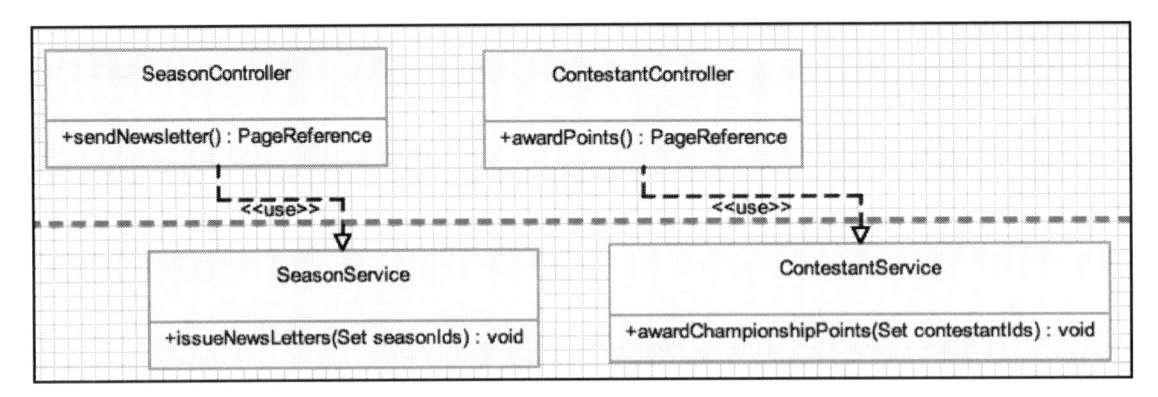

```
┌─────────────────────────────────────┐   ┌─────────────────────────────────────────┐
│         SeasonController            │   │          ContestantController           │
├─────────────────────────────────────┤   ├─────────────────────────────────────────┤
│ +sendNewsletter() : PageReference   │   │ +awardPoints() : PageReference          │
└─────────────────────────────────────┘   └─────────────────────────────────────────┘
              │ <<use>>                                │ <<use>>
              ▼                                        ▼
┌─────────────────────────────────────┐   ┌─────────────────────────────────────────────┐
│           SeasonService             │   │             ContestantService               │
├─────────────────────────────────────┤   ├─────────────────────────────────────────────┤
│ +issueNewsLetters(Set seasonIds):void│   │ +awardChampionshipPoints(Set contestantIds):void│
└─────────────────────────────────────┘   └─────────────────────────────────────────────┘
```

Now, imagine that in the second iteration of the application, user feedback requested that the awarding of points should also be available at the race level and applied in one operation for all contestants through a button on the **Race** detail page. In the following class diagram, you can see that the `ContestService` class is now reused by the `RaceService` class in order to implement the `RaceController.awardPoints` service method:

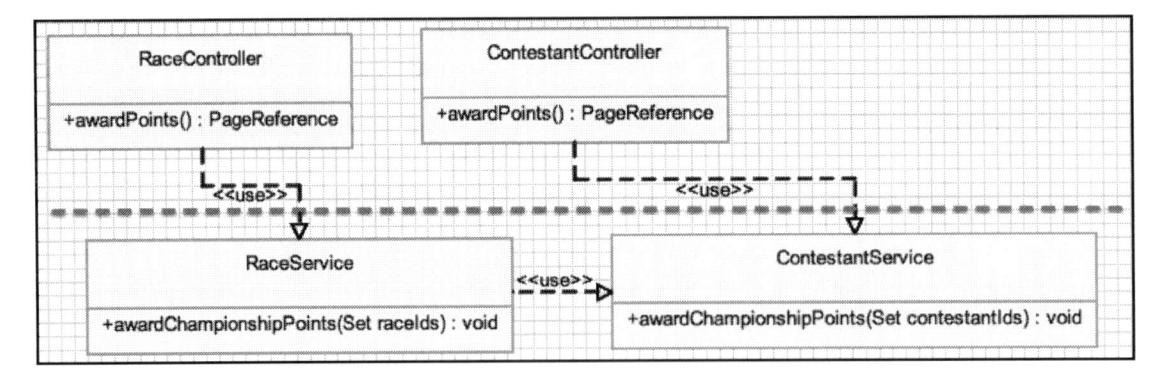

```
┌─────────────────────────────────────┐   ┌─────────────────────────────────────────┐
│          RaceController             │   │          ContestantController           │
├─────────────────────────────────────┤   ├─────────────────────────────────────────┤
│ +awardPoints() : PageReference      │   │ +awardPoints() : PageReference          │
└─────────────────────────────────────┘   └─────────────────────────────────────────┘
              │ <<use>>                                │ <<use>>
              ▼                                        ▼
┌─────────────────────────────────────┐   ┌─────────────────────────────────────────────┐
│           RaceService               │──▶│             ContestantService               │
├─────────────────────────────────────┤<<use>>├─────────────────────────────────────────┤
│ +awardChampionshipPoints(Set raceIds):void│   │ +awardChampionshipPoints(Set contestantIds):void│
└─────────────────────────────────────┘   └─────────────────────────────────────────────┘
```

An additional enhancement was also requested to permit the newsletter functionality to use the platform scheduler to automatically issue the newsletter. The following diagram shows that the `SeasonService` class is now reused by both the `SeasonNewsLetterSchedule` class as well as the `SeasonController` class:

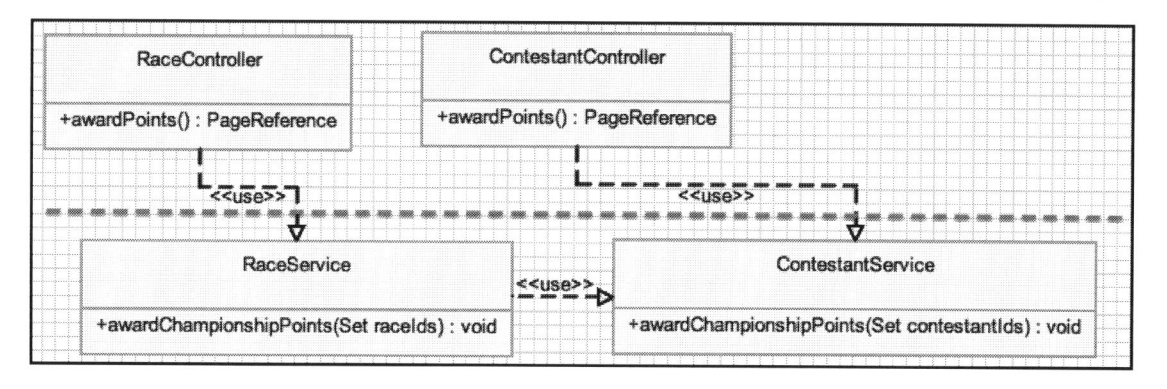

```
┌─────────────────────────────────────────────────────────────────────────┐
│   ┌──────────────────────────┐        ┌──────────────────────────────┐  │
│   │     RaceController       │        │    ContestantController      │  │
│   ├──────────────────────────┤        ├──────────────────────────────┤  │
│   │ +awardPoints() : PageReference │  │ +awardPoints() : PageReference │ │
│   └──────────────────────────┘        └──────────────────────────────┘  │
│              │                                      │                    │
│              └──<<use>>──┐              └──<<use>>──┐                   │
│  ─ ─ ─ ─ ─ ─ ─ ─ ─ ─ ─ ─▽─ ─ ─ ─ ─ ─ ─ ─ ─ ─ ─ ─ ─ ─▽─ ─ ─ ─ ─ ─ ─    │
│   ┌──────────────────────────┐        ┌──────────────────────────────┐  │
│   │      RaceService         │ <<use>>│      ContestantService       │  │
│   ├──────────────────────────┤───────▷├──────────────────────────────┤  │
│   │+awardChampionshipPoints(Set raceIds) : void │ │+awardChampionshipPoints(Set contestantIds) : void│
│   └──────────────────────────┘        └──────────────────────────────┘  │
└─────────────────────────────────────────────────────────────────────────┘
```

The preceding examples have shown that code from the first iteration can be reused either from the new application business logic or from a new execution context in the case of the scheduler. In the next chapter, we will take a further look at the Service layer, including its design guidelines that make this kind of reuse possible.

Patterns of Enterprise Application Architecture

So far, we have only discussed SOC between the Apex code invoked from an execution context (Apex Controller, Scheduler, Batch Apex, and so on) and reusable application business logic code placed in the `Service` classes. However, there are further levels of granularity and patterns that help focus and encapsulate application logic further, known as Enterprise Application Architecture patterns.

The general definitions of the patterns used in the next three chapters of this book are not inherently new, but are a new implementation for this platform. They have been and continue to be incredibly popular on other platforms. The original author of these patterns is Martin Fowler, who describes the other patterns in his book, *Patterns of Enterprise Application Architecture* (http://www.martinfowler.com/books/eaa.html).

This book takes some of the patterns in Martin Fowler's book and applies them to the platform, while also taking the opportunity to bake in a few best practices on the Force.com platform. The next section is a short summary of those we will be taking a closer look at.

The Service layer

The following is Martin Fowler's definition of the Service layer (http://martinfowler.com/eaaCatalog/serviceLayer.html):

> "Defines an application's boundary with a layer of services that establishes a set of available operations and coordinates the application's response in each operation."

You have had a little preview of this pattern in action in this chapter. You can see that for the business application logic, it forms an initial entry point, encapsulating operations and tasks the end users perform.

Its methods and behavior are designed so that it is agnostic of the caller, making it adaptable to multiple execution contexts easily, as shown in the earlier examples. It also has a role to play in your application's API strategy.

The domain model layer

The following is Martin Fowler's definition of the domain layer (http://martinfowler.com/eaaCatalog/domainModel.html):

> "An object model of the domain that incorporates both behavior and data. At its worst, business logic can be very complex. Rules and logic describe many different cases and slants of behavior, and it's this complexity that objects were designed to work with."

If you think of the Service layer as the band conductor, the Apex classes that make up the Domain layer are the instruments it conducts, each with its own role and responsibility in making the music!

The Domain layer in a Force.com context helps group and encapsulate logic specific to each physical Custom Object in the application. Also, while utilizing object-oriented concepts such as interfaces and inheritance to apply common behavioral aspects between your Custom Objects in your application, such as security, it is responsible for applying validations and processing historically done in the Apex Triggers code directly. Note that the Service layer can leverage these classes to form high-level business application logic that spans multiple objects and thus can access and reuse domain object-specific logic.

The Data Mapper (selector) layer

The following is Martin Fowler's definition of the Data Mapper layer (http://martinfowler.com/eaaCatalog/dataMapper.html):

> "A layer of Mappers (473) that moves data between objects and a database while keeping them independent of each other and the mapper itself."

Making effective use of database queries to fetch data is as important on Force.com as any other platform. For complex object models, having SOQL do some of the heavy lifting can lead to some fairly sophisticated queries. Encapsulating how data from the database is mapped into memory is the role of the Data Mapper layer.

In Martin Fowler's world, this usually involves mapping database result set records returned in Java classes (known as **Plain Old Java Objects** (POJO) or **Data Transformation Objects** (DTO)). However, Apex provides us with these data structures for each of our Custom Objects in the form of SObject. Thus, the role of this pattern is slightly different, as the SOQL query itself explicitly selects SObject fields representing the data. Hence, this pattern has been renamed to reflect its key responsibility more accurately.

Introducing the FinancialForce.com Apex Commons library

There is an Apex class library used to support these patterns, which is also used in this book. The Apex Commons library is from an open source project started by FinancialForce.com and launched in the community at the Dreamforce 2012 event.

Since then, the patterns have been adopted by other developers on the platform and have been extended with additional features such as fieldsets and security. We will be using this library in the next three chapters as we explore the enterprise patterns they support in more detail. The GitHub repository can be found at https://github.com/financialforcedev/fflib-apex-common.

Unit testing versus system testing

When it comes to testing the Apex code, we know the drill: write good tests to cover your code, assert its behavior, and obtain at least 75 percent coverage. Force.com will not allow you to upload packaged code unless you obtain this amount or higher. You also have to cover your Apex Trigger code, even if it's only a single line, as you will soon see is the case with the implementation of the Apex Triggers in this book.

However, when it comes to unit testing, what Force.com currently lacks, however, is a mocking framework to permit more focused and isolated testing of the layers, mentioned in the previous sections, without having to set up all the records needed to execute the code you want to test. This starts to make your Apex tests feel more like system-level tests, having to execute the full functional stack each time.

While conventions such as **test-driven development** (**TDD**) are possible, they certainly help you think about developing true unit tests on the platform. Doing so can also be quite time-consuming to develop and then wait for these tests to run due to growing data setup complexity. Such tests end up feeling more like system- or integration-level tests because they end up testing the whole stack of code in your application.

The good news is that the layering described in this book does give you opportunities to isolate smaller tests to specific aspects, such as validation, or insert logic. As we progress through each layer in the upcoming chapters, we'll finish with an entire chapter focusing on implementing a true unit testing approach using an open source mocking framework known as Apex Mocks; it has been shared with the community by FinancialForce.com and is heavily based on the Java Mockito framework: `https://github.com/financialforcedev/fflib-apex-mocks`.

Packaging the code

The source code provided with this chapter contains skeleton Apex classes shown in the UML diagrams used earlier in the chapter. In the upcoming chapters, we will flesh out the methods and logic in them. The following is a list of the Apex classes added in this chapter and the application architecture layer they apply to:

Apex class	Layer
`SeasonController.cls`	Visualforce Controller
`SeasonControllerTest.cls`	Apex test
`ContestantController.cls`	Visualforce Controller
`ContestantControllerTest.cls`	Apex test
`RaceController.cls`	Visualforce Controller
`RaceControllerTest.cls`	Apex test
`SeasonNewsletterScheduler.cls`	Apex Scheduler
`SeasonNewsletterSchedulerTest.cls`	Apex test
`RaceService.cls`	Race Service
`RaceServiceTest.cls`	Apex test

`SeasonService.cls`	Season Service
`SeasonServiceTest.cls`	Apex test
`ContestantService.cls`	Contestant Service
`ContestantServiceTest.cls`	Apex test

> **TIP**
> Note that there is one class, `SeasonNewsLetterScheduler`, that requires the use of the `global` access modifier. This ensures that the class cannot be deleted or renamed in future releases. This might feel restrictive, but it is the key to supporting the **Apex Scheduler** feature in this case. It is important when users upgrade to new versions of your package that the schedules they have defined continue to reference the code in your package.

If you create a new version of the package and install it in your test org, you should see a confirmation installation summary page that looks something like the following:

▼ Code (14)

Action	Component Name	Parent Object	Component Type	Installation Notes
Create	SeasonNewsletterScheduler		Apex Class	This is a brand new component.
Create	SeasonController		Apex Class	This is a brand new component.
Create	SeasonService		Apex Class	This is a brand new component.
Create	RaceService		Apex Class	This is a brand new component.
Create	RaceServiceTest		Apex Class	This is a brand new component.
Create	SeasonNewsletterSchedulerTest		Apex Class	This is a brand new component.
Create	RaceController		Apex Class	This is a brand new component.
Create	ContestantServiceTest		Apex Class	This is a brand new component.
Create	SeasonControllerTest		Apex Class	This is a brand new component.
Create	ContestantControllerTest		Apex Class	This is a brand new component.
Create	ContestantController		Apex Class	This is a brand new component.
Create	RaceControllerTest		Apex Class	This is a brand new component.
Create	SeasonServiceTest		Apex Class	This is a brand new component.
Create	ContestantService		Apex Class	This is a brand new component.

Summary

In this chapter, we have taken an in-depth look at how the platform executes Apex code and the different contexts from which it does so. We have also taken the time to understand how key concepts such as state and security are managed, in addition to highlighting some Apex governors and their respective scopes.

This has enabled us to identify some common needs, and using the principles of separation of concerns we can develop guidelines to be applied to layers in our business application code, making the Apex logic more reusable and accessible from different contexts as your application functionality and, indeed, the platform itself evolve.

As we progress further into practicing SOC, the Domain, Service, and Selector layer patterns will become a further layer of separation within our application business logic. We will continue to define the naming and coding guidelines as we progress through the next three chapters so that it becomes easier to maintain a good SOC for the existing developers and those just starting to work on the code.

> If you have an existing code base and are wondering where to start with refactoring its code into the layers described in this chapter, my advice is to concentrate initially on forming your Service layer contract and refactoring as much true business logic code into it as possible. Make your execution context classes, such as controllers and Batch Apex classes (but not triggers initially), as thin as possible, leaving them to focus solely on their responsibilities, such as error handling. This will get some of your true business application logic, at least, contained below the Service layer, even if it might not be factored precisely how you would want it had you written it from scratch. After this, you can focus on expanding this to refactoring the trigger logic into Domain, then the query logic into separate selector classes, perhaps incrementally, as you revise areas of the application for enhancements.

5
Application Service Layer

If your application was considered a living organism, the Service layer would be its beating heart. Regardless of how the environment and the things that interact with it change over time, it must remain strong and be able to adapt. In this chapter, we begin our journey with the three coding patterns: Service, Domain, and Selector, which were introduced in Chapter 4, *Apex Execution and Separation of Concerns*.

In this chapter, we will review the pattern as set out by Martin Fowler and then review how this has been applied to the Lightning Platform in Apex, describing design guidelines born from the *separation of concerns* we defined in the previous chapter.

One concern of this layer is interacting with the database; a later chapter will cover querying this in more detail. This chapter will focus on updating the database and introducing a new pattern, **Unit Of Work**, which helps make your code more streamlined and bulkified.

At the end of this chapter, we will extend the FormulaForce application to provide a means to calculate driver championship points and issue a newsletter. The code developed in the Service layer will be invoked from Custom Buttons and the Apex Scheduler. Later chapters will also cover further uses of the Service layer.

The following aspects of the Service layer will be covered in this chapter:

- Introducing the Service layer pattern
- Implementation design guidelines
- Handling DML with the Unit Of Work
- Services calling services
- Contract-Driven Development
- Testing the services
- Calling the services

Introducing the Service layer pattern

The following is Martin Fowler's definition of the Service layer (`http://martinfowler.com/eaaCatalog/serviceLayer.html`):

> *"Defines an application's boundary with a layer of services that establishes a set of available operations and coordinates the application's response in each operation."*

The use of the word *boundary* in Martin's definition is interesting, as this literally represents the point of separation or boundary between the concerns of the application's business logic in the Service layer and execution contexts caller. This might be a Visualforce or Lightning Component Controller class or a Batch Apex class, as illustrated in the UML diagrams shown in the previous chapter.

The following illustration shows just some of the types of callers that an Apex Service layer is designed to support. By following the design guidelines given in the next diagram, you can ensure that your Service layer code can be called from any one of these features and others in the future:

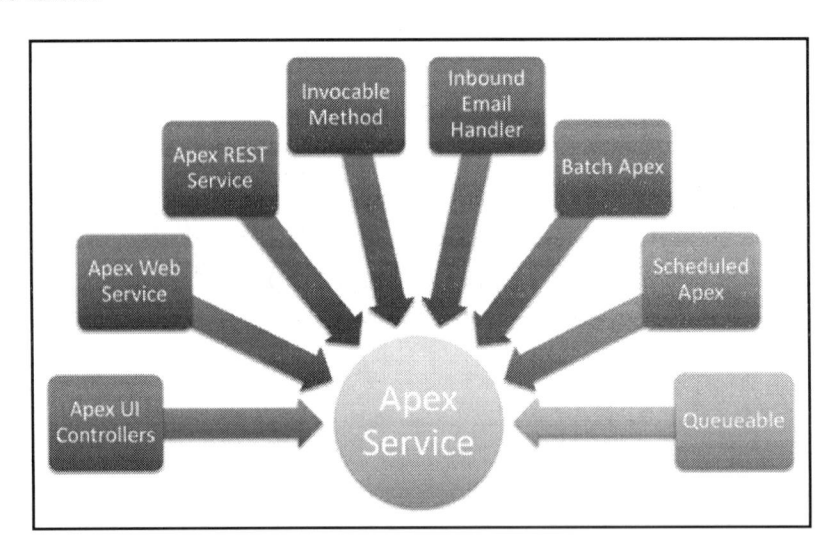

This book will illustrate the use of the Service layer in a number of these areas.

The reference to boundaries in Martin's definition is also an important point with respect to the encapsulation of the application's true business logic. You must be diligent about this encapsulation since the Service layer cannot coordinate the behavior of the application without it. The patterns in this book help to promote better thinking about encapsulation. However, there are no ways to express dependencies between Apex code in the way other languages such as Java might use the `package` and `protected` keywords, for example. As such, it is down to us to make sure that there is a solid awareness and desire to honor them.

> **TIP**
> Code reviews are an integral part of any development process. One easy indicator that your application business logic may be leaking outside of your Service layer is the increasing amount of code in the calling classes, such as Visualforce or Lightning Component Controllers or Batch Apex classes. Remember that these classes have their own concerns as well, such as handling and reporting errors and presenting information that the Service layer or your Custom Objects need. Though, generally, if the code looks to be doing more than this, it could be a sign that there is some code that should have been factored into a Service method. The hard part is often failing a code review based on this observation, particularly if the author claims there is no current reuse case. While that may be true, ignoring it in the beginning and letting it remain increases technical debt, limits reuse (that is, whether the next developer will have time to refactor), and increases the risk of inconsistent behavior across your application.

Finally, keep in mind that the information exchanged with the Service layer is not necessarily targeted to a specific use case or caller requirement. It is the responsibility of the calling code, such as a Visualforce or Lightning Component Controller or even code written by a subscriber org developer, to translate between the chosen client user interface and the Service layer interface.

In `Chapter 10`, *Providing Integration and Extensibility*, we will also explore exposing your Service layer as an API for external consumption. For these reasons, the Service layer has to be agnostic or unbiased toward any particular caller.

Implementation of design guidelines

Having studied the *Separation of Concerns* in the previous chapter and reflected on the previous illustration, the following design guidelines help to ensure that the Service layer is agnostic of the caller, easy to locate, and encourages some Lightning Platform best practices, such as bulkification. Note that bulkification is not just a concept for Apex Triggers; all the logic in your application must make efficient use of governed resources.

Naming conventions

A colleague of mine used to reference the following when talking about naming:

> "There are only two hard things in Computer Science: cache invalidation and naming things."
>
> – Phil Karlton

In my career so far, I have come to realize that there is some truth in this statement. Naming conventions have never been as important on the Lightning Platform as it is currently without a means to group or structure code files, using a directory structure, for example. Instead, all classes are effectively in one root folder called `/classes`.

Thus, it comes down to the use of naming conventions to help clarify purpose (for developers, both new and old, working on the code base) and to which layer in your architecture a class belongs. Naming does not, however, stop at the class name level; the enums, methods, and even parameter names all matter.

> **TIP**
>
> It is a good idea to work with those designing and documenting your application in order to establish and agree on an **application vocabulary of terms**. This is not only a useful reference for your end users to get to know your application, but also helps in maintaining consistency throughout your user interface and can also be used in the implementation of it, right down to the method and class names used. This comes in handy, especially if you are planning on exposing your Service layer as a public API (I'm a big fan of clear, self-documenting APIs).

The following points break down some specific guidelines for the Service layer, though some are also applicable throughout your application code:

- **Avoid acronyms**: In general, try to avoid using acronyms (as far as possible); while these might be meaningful to those experienced in working on the application, newcomers will find it harder to navigate the code as they learn the application functionality and code base. This applies more so if you're using your Service layer as an API. Though it can be tempting from a typing perspective, a good editor with autocompletion should resolve this concern pretty well. Widely used and understood acronyms such as ID are reasonable.

- **Class names**: Ending your class name with the `Service` suffix allows developers to filter easily in order to find these critical classes in your application code base. The actual name of the service can be pretty much anything you like, typically a major module or a significant object in your application. Make sure, however, that it is something from your application's vocabulary. If you've structured your application design well, your service class names should roughly fall into the groupings of your application's modules; that is, the naming of your Service layer should be a by-product of your application's architecture and not a thing you think up when creating the class:
    - Some bad examples are `UtilService`, `RaceHelper`, `BatchApexService`, and `CalcRacePointsService`. These examples either use acronyms that are platform feature bias or potentially to contextualized. Classes with the name `Helper` in them are often an indication that there is a lack of true understanding of where the code should be located; watch out for such classes.
    - Some good examples are `CommonService`, `RaceService`, and `SeasonService`. These examples clearly outline some major aspects of the application and are general enough to permit future encapsulation of related operations as the application grows.
- **Method names**: The `public` or `global` method names are essentially the business operations exposed by the service. These should also ideally relate or use terms expressed in your application's end user vocabulary, giving the same thought to these as you would give to a label or button for the end user, for example. Avoid naming them in a way that ties them to their caller; remember that the Service layer doesn't know or care about the caller type:
    - Some bad examples are `RaceService.recalcPointsOnSave`, `SeasonService.handleScheduler`, and `SeasonService.issueWarnings`. These examples are biased either toward the initial caller use case or toward the calling context; nor does the `handleScheduler` method name really express enough about what the method is actually going to perform.
    - Some good examples are `RaceService.awardChampionshipPoints`, `SeasonService.issueNewsLetter`, and `DriverService.issueWarnings`. These examples are named according to what they do, correctly located, and unbiased to the caller.

Application Service Layer

- **Parameter names and types**: As with method and class names, keep them focused on the data they represent, and ideally use consistent terms. Keep in mind that the type of your parameter can also form a part of the meaning of the parameter, and may help in some cases with the implementation of the Service method. For example, if the parameter is intended to receive a list of IDs, consider using `Set` instead of `List`, as typically, duplicate IDs in the list are unwanted. For the `Map` parameters, I always try to use the `somethingABySomethingB` convention in my naming so it's at least clear what the map is keyed by. In general, I actually try to apply these conventions to all variables, regardless of them being method parameters:
    - Some bad examples are `List<String>driverList` and `Map<String, DriverPerformance>mapOfPerformance`. These examples are either not using the correct data type and/or are using unclear data types as to the list or map contents; there is also some naming redundancy.
    - Some good examples are `Set<Id>driverIds` and `Map<String,DrivePerformance>drivePerformanceByName`. These examples use the correct types and help in documenting how to use the `Map` parameter correctly; the reader now knows that the `String` key is a name. Another naming approach is `somethingsToName`, for example. Also, the `Map` parameter name no longer refers to the fact that it is a map because the type of parameter communicates this well enough.
- **Inner class names**: While there is no formal structure to Apex classes in the form of a typical directory facility (or package structure, in Java terms), Apex does support the concept of inner classes to one level. These can sometimes be used to define classes that represent parameter data that is only relevant to the service methods. Because inner classes are always qualified by the name of the parent class, you do not need to repeat it:
    - Some bad examples are `SeasonService.SeasonSummary` and `DriverService.DriverRaceData`. These examples repeat the parent class name.
    - Some good examples are `SeasonService.Summary` and `DriverService.RaceDetails`. These examples are shorter as they are qualified by the outer class.

These guidelines should not only help to ensure whether your Service layer remains more neutral to its callers and thus more consumable now and in the future, but also follow some best practices around the platform. Finally, as we will discuss in Chapter 10, *Providing Integration and Extensibility*, following these guidelines leaves things in good shape to expose as an actual API, if desired.

> **TIP**
> If you're having trouble agreeing on the naming, you can try a couple of things. Firstly, try presenting the name and/or method signatures to someone not as close to the application or functionality to see what they interpret from it. This approach could be considered as parallel to a popular user experience acceptance testing approach, fly-by reviews. Obviously, they may not tell you precisely what the actual intent is, but how close or not they get can be quite useful when deciding on the naming. Secondly, try writing out pseudocode for how calling code might look; this can be useful to spot redundancy in your naming. For example, SeasonService.issueSeasonNewsLetter(Set<Id>seasonIdList) could be reduced to SeasonService.issueNewsLetter(Set<Id>seasonIds), since the scope of the method within the SeasonService method need not include Season again, and the parameter name can also be shortened since its type infers a list.

Bulkification

It's well known that the best practice of Apex is to implement bulkification within Apex Triggers, mainly because they can receive and process many records of the same type. This is also true for the use of StandardSetController classes or Batch Apex, for example.

As we identified in the previous chapter, handling bulk sets of records is a common requirement. In fact, it's one that exists throughout your code paths, since DML or SOQL in a loop at any level in your code will risk hitting governor limits.

For this reason, when designing methods on the Service layer, it is appropriate that you consider list parameters by default. This encourages the development of bulkified code within the method and avoids the caller having to call the Service method in a loop.

The following is an example of non-bulkified code:

```
RaceService.awardChampionShipPoints(Id raceId)
```

Application Service Layer

The following is an example of bulkified code:

```
RaceService.awardChampionShipPoints(Set<Id>raceIds)
```

A non-bulkified method with several parameters might look like this, for example:

```
RaceService.retireFromRace(Id raceId, String reason)
```

A bulkified version of the preceding method signature can utilize an Apex inner class, as described earlier and shown in the following example, in the *Defining and passing data* subsection.

> Sometimes, implementing bulkified versions of Service methods are more costly and complex than what the callers will realistically require, so this should not be seen as a fixed guideline, but should at least always be considered.

Sharing rules enforcement

As discussed in the previous chapter, by default, Apex code runs in system mode, meaning no sharing rules are enforced. However, business logic behavior should, in general, honor sharing rules. To avoid sharing information to which the user does not have access, sharing rule enforcement must be a concern of the Service layer.

The Salesforce security review requires Apex controller class entry points to honor this, although your Service layer will be called by these classes and thus could inherit this context. Keep in mind that your Service layer is effectively an entry point for other points of access and integrations (as we will explore in a later chapter and throughout the book).

Thus, the default concern of the Service layer should be to enforce sharing rules. Code implemented within the Service layer or called by it should inherit this using the `inherited sharing` keyword. Code should only be elevated to running in a context where sharing rules are ignored when required, otherwise known as the `without sharing` context. This would be in cases where the service is working on records on behalf of the user. For example, a service might calculate or summarize some race data but some of the raw race data records (from other races) may not be visible to the user.

To enforce sharing rules by default within a Service layer, the `with sharing` keyword is used on the `class` definition, as follows:

```
public with sharing class RaceService
```

Other Apex classes you create, including those we will go on to discuss around Selector and Domain patterns, should use the `inherited sharing` modifier such that they inherit the context—this allows them to be reused in either context more easily.

> **TIP**
> You should aim to use one of the three sharing keywords in each class you create. This declares the intent of the code within the class with respect to security. The absence of this can give rise to ambiguity or cause delays in your Salesforce security review process as the source code scanner or the person reviewing your code has to raise failures to be resolved. This chapter and the next will offer further guidelines on this as well.

If a `without sharing` context is needed, a private inner class approach, as shown in the following example, can be used to temporarily elevate the execution context to process queries or DML operations in this mode:

```
// Class used by the Service layer
public inherited sharing class SomeOtherClass {

  // This method inherits sharing context from Service
  public static void someMethod {
    // Do some work in inherited context
    // ...

    // Need to do some queries or updates in elevated context
    new ElevatedContext().restOfTheWork(workToDo);
  }

  private void restOfTheWork(List<SomeWork>workToDo) {
    // Additional work performed by this class
    // ...
  }

  private without sharing class ElevatedContext {
    public void restOfTheWork(List<SomeWork>workToDo) {
      // Do some work in a elevated (without sharing) context
      SomeOtherClass.restOfWork(workToDo);
    }
  }
}
```

Note that you can consider making the ability to run logic a parameter of your Service layer if you feel certain callers will want to disable this enforcement. The preceding code sample could be adapted to conditionally execute the `restOfWork` method directly or via the `ElevatedContext` inner class in this case.

Application Service Layer

> Object- and field-level security are also important considerations when deciding when to enforce and when not. Later chapters that focus more on the Domain and Selector patterns will discuss this topic further.

Defining and passing data

While defining data to be exchanged between the Service layer and its callers, keep in mind that the responsibility of the Service layer is to be caller-agnostic. Unless you're explicitly developing functionalities for such data formats, avoid returning information through JSON or XML strings; allow the caller (for example, a JavaScript remoting controller) to deal with these kinds of data-marshaling requirements.

As per the guidelines, using inner classes is a good way to express and scope data structures used by the Service methods; the following code also illustrates a bulkified version of the multi-parameter non-bulkified method shown in the previous section.

> **TIP**: Thinking about using inner classes in this way can also be a good way to address the symptom of primitive obsession (http://c2.com/cgi/wiki?PrimitiveObsession).

Take a look at the following code:

```
public with sharing class ContestantService {

  public class RaceRetirement{
  public Id contestantId;
    public String reason;
  }

  public static void retireFromRace(
      List<RaceRetirement> retirements) {
    // Process race retirements...
  }
}
```

> **TIP**: Try to avoid too much service coupling by reusing inner classes between services. If this is starting to happen, it may be an indication that you perhaps need a new shared or common service.

Always keep in mind that the Service method really only needs the minimum information to do its job, and express this through the method signature and related types so that callers can clearly see that only that information is required or returned. This avoids doubt and confusion in the calling code, which can result in it passing too little or redundant information.

The preceding example utilizes read and write member variables in the `RaceRetirement` class, indicating both are required. The inner class of the `RaceRetirement` class is only used as an input parameter to this method. Give some consideration before using an inner class, such as both input and output types, since it is not always clear which member variables in such classes should be populated for the input use case or which will be populated in the output case.

However, if you find such a need for the same Apex type to be used as both an output and input parameter, and some information is not required on the input, you can consider indicating this via the **Apex property** syntax by making the property read-only. This prevents the caller from populating the value of a member field unnecessarily; for example, consider the following Service methods in the `RaceService` method:

```
public static Map<Id, List<ProvisionalResult>>
  calculateProvisionalResults(Set<Id>raceIds)
{
  // Implementation
}

public static void applyRaceResults(
   Map<Id, List<ProvisionalResult>> provisionalResultsByRaceId)
{
  //Implementation
}

public class ProvisionalResult{
  public Integer racePosition {get; set;}
  public Id contestantId {get; set;}
  public String contestantName {get; private set;}
}
```

While calling the `calculateProvisionalResults` method, the `contestantName` field is returned as a convenience but is marked as read-only since it is not needed when applied in the context of the `applyRaceResults` method.

Considerations when using SObject in the Service layer interface

In the following example, the Service method appears to add the `Race` records as the input, requiring the caller to query the object and also decide which fields have to be queried. This is a loose contract definition between the Service method and the caller:

```
RaceService.awardChampionShipPoints(List<Race__c> races)
```

A better contract to the caller is to just ask for what is needed, in the case of the following example, the IDs:

```
RaceService.awardChampionShipPoints(Set<Id>raceIds)
```

Even though IDs that relate to records from different object types could be passed (you might consider performing some parameter validation to reject such lists), this is a more expressive contract, focusing on what the service really needs. The caller now knows that only the ID is going to be used.

In the first example, when using the `Race__c` SObject type as a parameter type, it is not clear which fields callers need to populate, which can make the code fragile, as it is not something that can be expressed in the interface definition. Additionally, the fields required within the service code could change and require caller logic to be refactored. This could also be an example of failing in the encapsulation concern of the business logic within the Service layer.

It can be said that this design approach incurs additional overhead, especially if the caller has already queried the `Race` record for presentation purposes and the service must then re-query the information. However, in such cases, maintaining encapsulation and reuse concerns can be more compelling reasons. Careful monitoring of this consideration makes the service interface clearer, better encapsulated, and, ultimately, more robust.

Transaction management

A simple expectation of the caller when calling the Service layer methods is that if there is a failure via an exception, any work done within the Service layer up until that point is rolled back. This is important as it allows the caller to handle the exception without fear of any partial data being written to the database. If there is no exception, then the data modified by the Service method can still be rolled back, but only if the entire execution context itself fails; otherwise, the data is committed.

This can be implemented using a `try/catch` block in combination with `Database.Savepoint` and the `rollback` method, as follows:

```
public static void awardChampionshipPoints(Set<Id>raceIds){
  // Mark the state of the database
  System.SavepointserviceSavePoint = Database.setSavePoint();
  try {
    // Do some work
  } catch (Exception e){
    // Rollback any data written before the exception
    Database.rollback(serviceSavePoint);
    // Pass the exception on for the caller to handle
    throw e;
  }
}
```

Later in this chapter, we will look at the Unit Of Work pattern, which helps manage the Service layer transaction management in a more elegant way than having to repeat the preceding boilerplate code in each Service method.

Compound services

As your Service layer evolves, your callers may find themselves needing to call multiple Service methods at a time, which should be avoided.

To explain this, consider that a new application requirement has arisen for a single Custom Button to update the *Drivers* standings (the position in the overall season) in the championship with the feature to issue a new season newsletter.

The code behind the Apex controller action method might look like the following code:

```
try {
  Set<Id> seasons = new Set<Id> { seasonId };
  SeasonService.updateStandings(seasons);
  SeasonService.issueNewsLetters(seasons);
}
catch (Exception e) {
  // Handle exception...
}
```

The problem with the preceding code is that it erodes the encapsulation and thus reuses the application Service layer by putting functionality in the controller, and also breaks the transactional encapsulation.

[171]

For example, if an error occurs while issuing the newsletter, the standings are still updated (since the controller handles exceptions), and thus, if the user presses the button again, the driver standings in the championship will get updated twice!

The best way to address this type of scenario, when it occurs, is to create a new compound service, which combines the functionality into one new Service method call. The following example also uses an inner class to pass the season ID and provide the issue newsletter option:

```
try {
  SeasonService.UpdateStandingsupdateStandings =
    new SeasonService.UpdateStandings();
  updateStandings.seasonId = seasonId;
  updateStandings.issueNewsletter = true;
  SeasonService.updateStandings(
    new List <SeasonService.UpdateStandings> { updateStandings })
}
catch (Exception e) {
  // Handle exception...
}
```

It may be desirable to retain the original Service methods used in the first example in cases where this combined behavior is not always required.

Later in this chapter, we will see how the implementation of the preceding new Service method will reuse the original methods and thus introduce the ability for existing Service methods to be linked to each other.

A quick guideline checklist

Here is a useful table that summarizes the earlier guidelines:

When thinking about...	The guidelines are...
Naming conventions	• Suffix class names with service. • Stick to application vocabulary. • Avoid acronyms. • Class, method, and parameter names matter. • Avoid redundancy in names. • Utilize inner classes to scope by service.
Sharing rules	• Use the `with sharing` keyword on Service classes. • Elevate to `without sharing` only when needed and only for as short a time as possible. • By default, the best practice is to use the `inherited sharing` keyword on all other classes consumed by the service class logic.

Bulkification	• On Service methods, utilize list parameters over single parameters to encourage optimized service code for bulk callers. • Single instance parameters can be used where it's overly expensive to engineer bulkified implementations and there is little functional benefit.
Defining and passing data	• Keep data neutral to the caller. • Leverage inner classes to scope data. • Pass only what is needed.
Transaction management	• Callers can assume that work is rolled back if exceptions are raised by the Service methods, so they can safely handle exceptions themselves. • Wrap the Service method code in `SavePoint`.
Compound services	• Maintain the Service layer's functional encapsulation by monitoring for multiple Service method calls in one execution context. • Create new Service methods to wrap existing ones or merge existing methods as needed.

Handling DML with the Unit Of Work pattern

The database maintains relationships between records using record IDs. Record IDs are only available after the record is inserted. This means that the related records, such as child object records, need to be inserted in a specific dependency order. Parent records should be inserted before child records, and the parent record IDs are used to populate the relationship (lookup) fields on the child record objects before they can be inserted.

The common pattern for this is to use the `List` or `Map` keyword to manage records inserted at a parent level, in order to provide a means to look up parent IDs, as child records are built prior to being inserted. The other reasoning for this is bulkification; minimizing the number of DML statements being used across a complex code path is vital to avoid hitting governor limits on the number of DML statements required, as such lists are favored over executing individual DML statements per record.

The focus on these two aspects of inserting data into objects can often detract from the actual business logic required, making code hard to maintain and difficult to read. The following section introduces another of Martin Fowler's patterns, the Unit Of Work, which helps address this, as well as providing an alternative to the boilerplate transaction management using `SavePoint`, as illustrated earlier in this chapter.

The following is Martin Fowler's definition of Unit Of Work (`http://martinfowler.com/eaaCatalog/unitOfWork.html`):

> *"Maintains a list of objects affected by a business transaction and coordinates the writing out of changes and the resolution of concurrency problems."*

Application Service Layer

In an extract from the web page, he also goes on to make these further points:

> *"You can change the database with each change to your object model, but this can lead to lots of very small database calls, which ends up being very slow.*
>
> *A Unit Of Work keeps track of everything you do during a business transaction that can affect the database. When you're done, it figures out everything that needs to be done to alter the database as a result of your work."*

Although these statements don't appear to relate to the Lightning Platform, there are parallels with respect to the cost of making multiple DML statements, both in terms of governors and general performance. There is also a statement about transaction management at a business (or service) level, which applies to the responsibility of the Service layer.

In order to best illustrate these benefits, let's review the implementation of a service to load some historic data into the `Season`, `Race`, `Driver`, and `Contest` objects. Each of these objects has several relationships, as illustrated in the following screenshot:

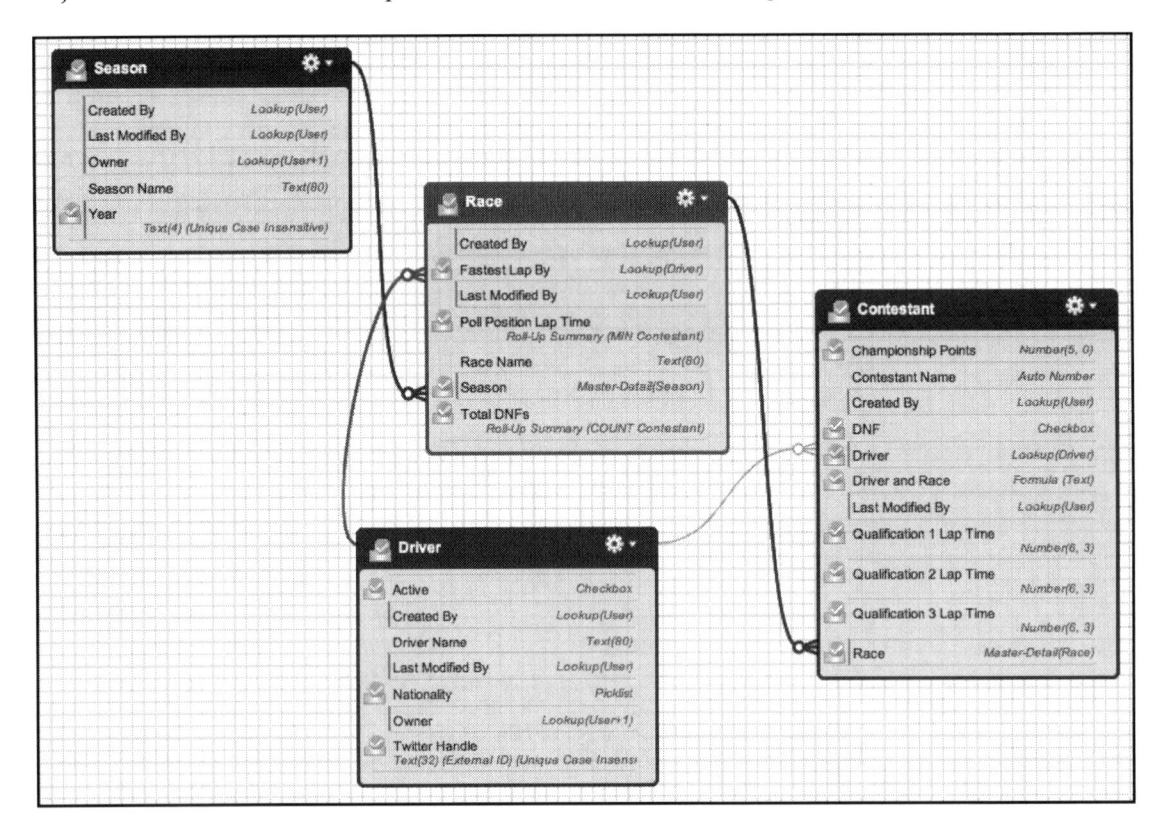

Consider the following sample JSON format to import data into the application:

```
{
  "drivers": [
  {
    "name": "Lewis Hamilton",
    "nationality": "British",
    "driverId": "44",
    "twitterHandle": "lewistwitter"
  }],
  "seasons": [
  {
    "year": "2013",
    "races": [
    {
      "round": 1,
      "name": "Spain",
      "contestants": [
      {
        "driverId": "44",
        "championshipPoints": 44,
        "dnf": false,
        "qualification1LapTime": 123,
        "qualification2LapTime": 124,
        "qualification3LapTime": 125
      }]
    }]
  }]
}
```

The preceding JSON code is an example of a structure is used by the sample code to effectively load records into multiple objects, as shown in the earlier screenshot. Parsing this JSON and persisting it into the objects is made easier by using the Unit Of Work since the developer does not need to think about the relationship order or performing separate DMLs for each. In order to understand this benefit better, we first take a look at how this looks without the Unit Of Work.

Without a Unit Of Work

This first example shows a traditional approach using `Map` and `List` to import the data, obeying bulkification, and inserting a dependency order. The important logic highlighted in the following code copies data from the imported data structures into the objects; everything else is purely managing transaction scope and inserting dependencies:

```
public static void importSeasons(String jsonData) {

  System.Savepoint serviceSavePoint = Database.setSavePoint();
  try{
    // Parse JSON data
    SeasonsData seasonsData =
        (SeasonsData) JSON.deserializeStrict(
          jsonData, SeasonService.SeasonsData.class);

    // Insert Drivers
    Map<String, Driver__c>driversById =
      new Map<String, Driver__c>();
    for(DriverData driverData : seasonsData.drivers)
      driversById.put(driverData.driverId, new Driver__c(
      Name = driverData.name,
      DriverId__c = driverData.driverId,
      Nationality__c = driverData.nationality,
      TwitterHandle__c = driverData.twitterHandle));
      insert driversById.values();

    // Insert Seasons
    Map<String, Season__c>seasonsByYear =
      new Map<String, Season__c>();
    for(SeasonData seasonData : seasonsData.seasons)
      seasonsByYear.put(seasonData.year,
        new Season__c(
          Name = seasonData.year, Year__c = seasonData.year));
      insert seasonsByYear.values();

    // Insert Races
    Map<String, Race__c>racesByYearAndRound =
      new Map<String, Race__c>();
    for(SeasonData seasonData : seasonsData.seasons)
      for(RaceData raceData : seasonData.races)
        racesByYearAndRound.put(seasonData.Year + raceData.round,
          new Race__c(
            Season__c = seasonsByYear.get(seasonData.year).Id,
            Name = raceData.name));
        insert racesByYearAndRound.values();
```

```
        // Insert Contestants
        List<Contestant__c> contestants =
          new List<Contestant__c>();
        for(SeasonDataseasonData : seasonsData.seasons)
        for(RaceDataraceData : seasonData.races)
            for(ContestantDatacontestantData
                    : raceData.contestants)
    contestants.add(
        new Contestant__c(
            Race__c = racesByYearAndRound.get(
                seasonData.Year + raceData.round).Id,
            Driver__c = driversById.get(
                contestantData.driverId).Id,
            ChampionshipPoints__c =
                contestantData.championshipPoints,
            DNF__c = contestantData.dnf,
            Qualification1LapTime__c =
                contestantData.qualification1LapTime,
            Qualification2LapTime__c =
                contestantData.qualification2LapTime,
            Qualification3LapTime__c =
                contestantData.qualification3LapTime
        ));
      insert contestants;
    } catch (Exception e) {
      // Rollback any data written before the exception
      Database.rollback(serviceSavePoint);
      // Pass the exception on
      throw e;
    }
  }
```

> This data import requirement could have been implemented by using the data loading tools, as described in the earlier chapter. One reason you may decide to take this approach is to offer an easier option from your own UIs that can be made available to general users without administrator access.

With Unit Of Work

Before we take a closer look at how the **FinancialForce Apex Enterprise Pattern** library has helped us implement this pattern, let's first take a look at the following revised example of the code shown earlier. This code utilizes a new Apex class called `Application`. This class exposes a static property and method to create an instance of a Unit Of Work.

Application Service Layer

> The source code for this chapter includes the FinancialForce Apex Enterprise Pattern library, as well as the FinancialForce Apex Mocks library it depends on. We will explore the Apex Mocks library in a later chapter, where we will focus on writing unit tests for each of the patterns introduced in this book.

The `fflib_ISObjectUnitOfWork` Apex Interface is used to expose the features of the Unit Of Work pattern to capture the database work as records are created, thus the remaining logic is more focused and avoids `Map` and `List` and repeated iterations over the imported data shown in the previous example. It also internally bulkifies the work (DML) for the caller. Finally, the `commitWork` method call performs the actual DML work in the correct dependency order while applying transaction management.

Consider the following code:

```
// Construct a Unit Of Work to capture the following working
fflib_ISObjectUnitOfWork uow =
   Application.UnitOfWork.newInstance();

// Create Driver__c records
Map<String, Driver__c>driversById =
new Map<String, Driver__c>();

for(DriverDatadriverData : seasonsData.drivers){
  Driver__c driver = new Driver__c(
    Name = driverData.name,
    DriverId__c = driverData.driverId,
    Nationality__c = driverData.nationality,
    TwitterHandle__c = driverData.twitterHandle);
  uow.registerNew(driver);
  driversById.put(driver.DriverId__c, driver);
}

for(SeasonDataseasonData : seasonsData.seasons){
  // Create Season__c record
  Season__c season = new Season__c(
    Name = seasonData.year,
    Year__c = seasonData.year);
  uow.registerNew(season);
  for(RaceDataraceData : seasonData.races){
    // Create Race__c record
    Race__c race = new Race__c(Name = raceData.name);
    uow.registerNew(race, Race__c.Season__c, season);
    for(ContestantDatacontestantData : raceData.contestants){
      // Create Contestant__c record
      Contestant__c contestant = new Contestant__c(
```

```
            ChampionshipPoints__c = contestantData.championshipPoints,
            DNF__c = contestantData.dnf,
            Qualification1LapTime__c =
                contestantData.qualification1LapTime,
    Qualification2LapTime__c =
                contestantData.qualification2LapTime,
    Qualification3LapTime__c =
                contestantData.qualification3LapTime);
          uow.registerNew (contestant, Contestant__c.Race__c, race);
          uow.registerRelationship(contestant,
              Contestant__c.Driver__c,
              driversById.get(contestantData.driverId));
        }
      }
    }
    // Insert records registered with uow above
    uow.commitWork();
```

The following is the implementation of the `Application` class and the `UnitOfWork` static property. It leverages a simple factory class that dynamically creates instances of the `fflib_SObjectUnitOfWork` class through the `newInstance` method:

```
public class Application
{
  // Configure and create the UnitOfWorkFactory for
  //   this Application
  public static final fflib_Application.UnitOfWorkFactory UnitOfWork =
      new fflib_Application.UnitOfWorkFactory(
          new List<SObjectType> {
              Driver__c.SObjectType,
              Season__c.SObjectType,
              Race__c.SObjectType,
              Contestant__c.SObjectType});
}
```

The `fflib_Application.UnitOfWorkFactory` class exposes the `newInstance` method that internally creates a new `fflib_SObjectUnitOfWork` instance. This is not directly exposed to the caller; instead, the `fflib_ISObjectUnitOfWork` interface is returned (this design aids the mocking support we will discuss in a later chapter). The purpose of this interface is to provide the methods used in the preceding code to register records for insert, update, or delete, and implement the `commitWork` method.

I recommend that you create a single application Apex class like the one shown previously, where you can maintain the full list of objects used in the application and their dependency order; as your application's objects grow, it will be easier to maintain.

Application Service Layer

The `fflib_ISObjectUnitOfWork` interface has the following methods in it. The preceding example uses the `registerNew` and `registerRelationship` methods to insert records and ensure that the appropriate relationship fields are populated. Review the documentation of these methods in the code for more details. The following screenshot shows a summary of the methods:

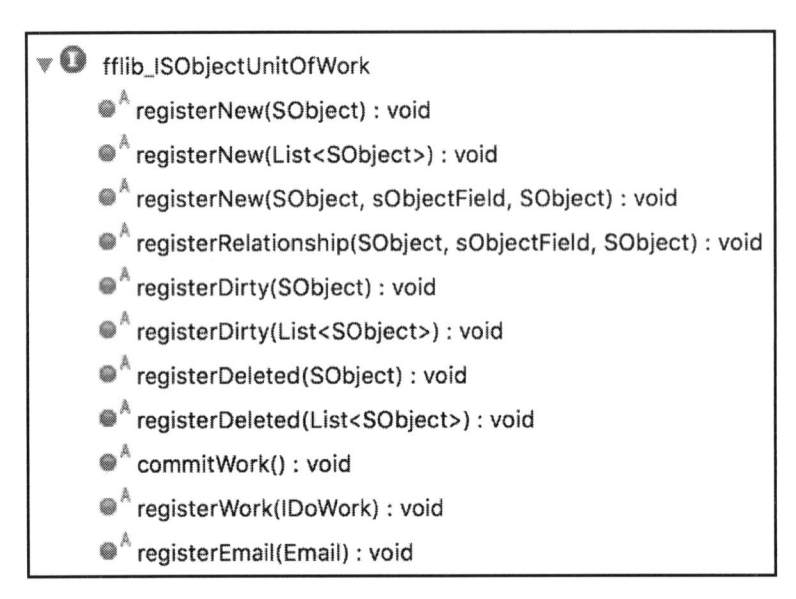

```
fflib_ISObjectUnitOfWork
    registerNew(SObject) : void
    registerNew(List<SObject>) : void
    registerNew(SObject, sObjectField, SObject) : void
    registerRelationship(SObject, sObjectField, SObject) : void
    registerDirty(SObject) : void
    registerDirty(List<SObject>) : void
    registerDeleted(SObject) : void
    registerDeleted(List<SObject>) : void
    commitWork() : void
    registerWork(IDoWork) : void
    registerEmail(Email) : void
```

Call the `registerDirty` method with a `SObject` record you want to update and the `registerDeleted` method to delete a given `SObject` record. You can also call a combination of the `registerNew`, `registerDirty`, and `registerDeleted` methods.

> **TIP**
> The previous diagram only shows a selection of the full methods available. Consult the source code and comments for further information. For example, recent contributions from the community have included support for including sending platform events (we will cover these in more detail later in the book). There is also more extensibility through virtual methods that can be overridden to listen to or modify its behavior.

The Unit Of Work scope

To make the most effective use of the Unit Of Work's ability to coordinate database updates and transaction management, maintain a single instance of the Unit Of Work within the scope of the Service method, as illustrated in the previous section.

If you need to call other classes that also perform database work, be sure to pass the same Unit Of Work instance to them, rather than allowing them to create their own instance. We will explore this a little later in this chapter.

> **TIP**
> It may be tempting to maintain a `static` instance of a Unit Of Work so that you can refer to it easily without having to pass it around. The downside of this approach is that the access to becomes broader than a given Service method execution scope, since Apex can be invoked from many different places its hard to guarantee it will always be from within a Service method. Even if a static is used, code registering records with a static Unit Of Work must still depend on an outer Apex code unit committing the work. Finally, it also gives a false impression that the Unit Of Work is useable after a commit has been performed.

Unit Of Work special considerations

Depending on your requirements and use cases, the standard methods of Unit Of Work may not be appropriate. The following is a list of some use cases that are not handled by default and may require a custom work callback to be registered:

- **Self and recursive referencing**: Records within the same object that have lookups to each other are not currently supported, for example, account hierarchies.
- **More granular DML operations**: The `Database` class methods allow the ability to permit some records to be processed when others fail. The DML statements executed in the Unit Of Work are defaulted to all or nothing.
- **Sending emails**: Sending emails is considered a part of the current transaction; if you want to register this kind of work with the Unit Of Work, you can do so via the `registerEmail` method. Multiple registrations will be automatically bulkified.

The following is a template for registering a customer work callback handler with Unit Of Work. This will be called during the `commitWork` method within the transaction scope it creates. This means that if work fails in this work callback, it will also call other work registered with the same Unit Of Work to rollback.

Application Service Layer

Take a look at the following code:

```
public inherited sharing class CustomAccountWork implements
    fflib_SObjectUnitOfWork.IDoWork {

  private List<Account> accounts;

  public CustomAccountWork (List<Account> accounts) {
     this.accounts = accounts;
  }

  public void doWork(){
     // Do some custom account work e.g. hierarchies
  }
}
```

Then, register the custom work as per the following example:

```
uow.registerNew...
uow.registerDirty...
uow.registerDeleted...
uow.registerWork(new CustomAccountWork(accounts));
uow.commitWork();
```

The Unit Of Work pattern described in the proceeding sections helps you focus your coding efforts on implementing business logic and not on how records are persisted. In the next section, we will look at some more advanced service-related concepts.

Services calling services

In the previous chapter, I described a reuse use case around a FormulaForce application feature that awards championship points to contestants. We imagined the first release of the application providing a Custom Button only on the **Contestant** detail page and then the second release also providing the same button but on the **Race** detail page.

In this part of the chapter, we are going to implement the respective Service methods, emulating this development cycle and, in turn, demonstrating an approach to call between Service layer methods, passing the Unit Of Work correctly.

First, let's look at the initial requirement for a button on the **Contestant** detail page; the method in the `ContestantService` class looks like the following:

```
public static void awardChampionshipPoints(Set<Id>contestantIds) {

   fflib_SObjectUnitOfWorkuow =
```

[182]

```
      Application.UnitOfWork.newInstance();

  // Apply championship points to given contestants
  Map<Integer, ChampionshipPoint__mdt>pointsByTrackPosition =
     new ChampionshipPointsSelector().selectAllByTrackPosition();
  for(Contestant__c contestant :
     new ContestantsSelector().selectById(contestantIds)) {
    // Determine points to award for the given position
    ChampionshipPoint__mdtpointsForPosition =
       pointsByTrackPosition.get(
          Integer.valueOf(contestant.RacePosition__c));
    if(pointsForPosition!=null) {
      // Apply points and register for update with uow
      contestant.ChampionshipPoints__c =
      pointsForPosition.PointsAwarded__c;
      uow.registerDirty(contestant);
    }
  }
}
```

This method utilizes the **Selector** pattern to query the database; this will be described in its own chapter later in this book. The method also uses a protected Custom Metadata Type object, **Championship Points**, to look up the official championship points awarded for each position the contestants finished in the race. This Custom Metadata Type object and its records are provided with the source code for this chapter:

Action	Label	Championship Point Name	Points Awarded ↓
Edit | Del	1st	TrackPosition1	25
Edit | Del	2nd	TrackPosition2	18
Edit | Del	3rd	TrackPosition3	15
Edit | Del	4th	TrackPosition4	12
Edit | Del	5th	TrackPosition5	10
Edit | Del	6th	TrackPosition6	8
Edit | Del	7th	TrackPosition7	6
Edit | Del	8th	TrackPosition8	4
Edit | Del	9th	TrackPosition9	2
Edit | Del	10th	TrackPosition10	1

Application Service Layer

> **TIP**
> Custom Metadata Type records can be packaged and installed with the FormulaForce application without any further configuration by the customer. Since they belong to a protected Custom Metadata Type object, they will not be visible or editable to the user. Indeed, this information is tightly controlled by the **Federation Internationale de l'Automobile (FIA)** and is updated a minimum of once a year. In this form, they can easily be edited using the **Manage Records** link on the **Custom Metadata Type** page under **Setup**, and then upgraded when the customers install the latest version of the package or when you push the package to them. While this information could have been hardcoded in Apex code, it is easier to manage and update in this form and demonstrates how internal configuration can be encoded using Custom Metadata Types and records.

The service is called from the `ContestantController` action method, which is bound to the button on the **Contestant** detail page (via a **Lightning Action Component**), as follows:

```
@AuraEnabled
public void awardPoints(Id contestantId){
  try {
    ContestantService.awardChampionshipPoints(
       new Set<Id> { contestantId });
  } catch (Exception e) {
    Application.throwAuraHandledException(e);
  }
  return null;
}
```

> **TIP**
> The previous code uses the `throwAuraHandledException` utility method on the `Application` class to simplify throwing the type of exceptions Lightning Components require through the `AuraHandledException` exception class. Later in this chapter, we will revisit this utility method in more detail.

In the next release, the same behavior is required from the `RaceController` method to apply the logic to all contestants in the *Race* page. The controller method looks like the following:

```
public void awardPoints(Id raceId){
  try {
    RaceService.awardChampionshipPoints(new Set<Id> { raceId });
  }
  catch (Exception e){
    Application.throwAuraHandledException(e);
  }
}
```

In order to provide backward compatibility, the original Custom Button on the Contestant detail page and thus the Service method used by the controller are to be retained. Because the original method was written with bulkification in mind to begin with, reusing the ContestantService logic from the new RaceService method is made possible.

The following code is what the RaceService.awardChampionshipPoints method looks like. Again, a Selector class is used to query the *Race* records and the *Contestant* child records in a single query such that the child records are also available:

```
public static void awardChampionshipPoints(Set<Id>raceIds){
   fflib_SObjectUnitOfWork uow =
      Application.UnitOfWork.newInstance();

   // Query Races and contestants, bulkify contestants
   List<Contestant__c> contestants = new List<Contestant__c>();
   For(Race__c race :
         new RacesSelector().selectByIdWithContestants(raceIds)) {
      contestants.addAll(race.Contestants__r);
   }

   // Delegate to contestant service
   ContestantService.awardChampionshipPoints(uow, contestants);
   // Commit work
   uow.commitWork();
}
```

By using method overloading, a new version of the existing ContestantService.awardChampionshipPoints method was added to implement the preceding code without impacting other callers. The overloaded method takes, as its first parameter, the Unit Of Work (created in RaceService) and then the *Contestant* list.

> The problem with this additional method is that it inadvertently exposes an implementation detail of the service to potential non-service calling code. It would be ideal if Apex supported the concept of the protected keyword found in other languages, which would hide this method from code outside of the Service layer. The solution is to simply ensure that developers understand that such method overrides are only for use by other Service layer callers.

Application Service Layer

The following resultant code shows that the `ContestantService` methods now support both the new `RaceService` caller and the original `ContestantController` caller. Also, there is only one instance of Unit Of Work in either code path, and the `commitWork` method is called once all the work is done:

```
public static void awardChampionshipPoints(Set<Id>contestantIds)
{
  fflib_ISObjectUnitOfWorkuow =
     Application.UnitOfWork.newInstance();

  // Apply championship points to selected contestants
  awardChampionshipPoints(uow,
     new ContestantsSelector().selectById(contestantIds));

  uow.commitWork();
}

public static void awardChampionshipPoints(
  fflib_ISObjectUnitOfWork uow, List<Contestant__c> contestants)
{
  // Apply championship points to given contestants
  Map<Integer, ChampionshipPoint__mdt>pointsByTrackPosition =
     new ChampionshipPointsSelector().selectAllByTrackPosition();
  for(Contestant__c contestant : contestants) {
    // Determine points to award for the given position
    ChampionshipPoint__mdtpointsForPosition =
       pointsByTrackPosition.get(
          Integer.valueOf(contestant.RacePosition__c));
    if(pointsForPosition!=null) {
      // Apply points and register for udpate with uow
      contestant.ChampionshipPoints__c =
         pointsForPosition.PointsAwarded__c;
      uow.registerDirty(contestant);
    }
  }
}
```

Contract-Driven Development

If you have a large piece of functionality to develop, with a complex Service layer and user interface client logic, it can be an advantage to decouple these two streams of development activity so that developers can continue in parallel, meeting up sometime in the future to combine efforts.

An approach to this is sometimes referred to as **Contract-Driven Development**. This is where there is an agreement on a contract (or service definition) between the two development streams before they start their respective developments. Naturally, the contract can be adjusted over time, but having a solid starting point will lead to smoother parallel development activity.

This type of development can be applied by implementing a small factory pattern within the Service layer class. The main methods on the service class are defined as normal, but their internal implementation can be routed to respective inner classes to provide an initial **dummy implementation** of the service, which is active for the client developers, for example, and another **production implementation**, which can be worked on independently by the service developers.

> Because the static Service methods actually exposed to callers don't expose this factory implementation, it can easily be removed later in the development cycle.

Take, for example, a requirement in the FormulaForce application to provide a user interface to preview the final finishing positions of the drivers once the race is complete (known as the provisional positions). Development needs to start on the user interface for this feature as soon as possible, but the Service layer code has not been written yet. The client and Service layer developers sit down and agree on what is needed, and then define the skeleton methods in the Service layer together.

The first thing they do within the service class is create an Apex Interface that describes the Service methods, which is the contract. The methods on this interface follow the same design guidelines as described earlier in this chapter.

The following code shows the definition of the `IRaceService` Apex Interface:

```
public interface IRaceService {
  Map<Id, List<RaceService.ProvisionalResult>>
      calculateProvisionResults(Set<Id>raceIds);
  void applyRaceResults(Map<Id,
      List<RaceService.ProvisionalResult>>
          provisionalResultsByRaceId);
  void awardChampionshipPoints(Set<Id>raceIds);
}
```

Next, an implementation of this interface for the dummy (or sometimes known as a **Stub**) client implementation of this service is created, `RaceServiceImplStub`, along with another class for the service developers to continue to develop independently as the client developer goes about their work, `RaceServiceImpl`.

Application Service Layer

Consider the following code:

```
public class RaceServiceImplStub implements IRaceService {

  public Map<Id, List<RaceService.ProvisionalResult>>
      calculateProvisionResults(Set<Id>raceIds) {

    // Dummy behavior to allow callers of the service be developed
    // independent of the main service implementation
    Id raceId = new List<Id>(raceIds)[0];
    RaceService.ProvisionalResulthamilton =
        new RaceService.ProvisionalResult();
    hamilton.racePosition = 1;
    hamilton.contestantName = 'Lewis Hamilton';
    hamilton.contestantId = 'a03b0000006WVph';
    RaceService.ProvisionalResultrubens =
        new RaceService.ProvisionalResult();
    rubens.racePosition = 2;
    rubens.contestantName = 'Rubens Barrichello';
    rubens.contestantId = 'a03b00000072xx9';
    return new Map<Id, List<RaceService.ProvisionalResult>> {
      new List<Id>(raceIds)[0] =>
      new List<RaceService.ProvisionalResult>
      { hamilton, rubens } };
  }

  public void applyRaceResults(
      Map<Id,List<RaceService.ProvisionalResult>>
        provisionalResultsByRaceId) {
    throw new RaceService.RaceServiceException(
      'Not implemented');
  }

  public void awardChampionshipPoints(Set<Id>raceIds) {
    throw new RaceService.RaceServiceException(
      'Not implemented');
  }
}

public class RaceServiceImpl implements IRaceService {
  public Map<Id, List<RaceService.ProvisionalResult>>
      calculateProvisionResults(Set<Id>raceIds) {
    throw new RaceService.RaceServiceException(
      'Not implemented');
  }

  public void applyRaceResults(
    Map<Id,List<RaceService.ProvisionalResult>>
```

[188]

```
            provisionalResultsByRaceId) {
      throw new RaceService.RaceServiceException(
        'Not implemented');
    }

    public void awardChampionshipPoints(Set<Id>raceIds) {

      fflib_ISObjectUnitOfWorkuow =
           Application.UnitOfWork.newInstance();

      // Query Races and contestants
      List<Contestant__c> contestants = new List<Contestant__c>();
      for(Race__c race :
          new RacesSelector().selectByIdWithContestants(raceIds))
      {
         contestants.addAll(race.Contestants__r);
      }

      // Delegate to contestant service
      ContestantService.awardChampionshipPoints(uow, contestants);

      // Commit work
      uow.commitWork();
    }
}
```

Finally, the standard Service methods are added, but are implemented via the `service` method, which is used to resolve the correct implementation of the Service methods to use. The following Service methods leverage the appropriate implementation of the preceding interface:

```
public with sharing class RaceService {

  public static Map<Id, List<ProvisionalResult>>
      calculateProvisionResults(Set<Id>raceIds) {
    return service().calculateProvisionResults(raceIds);
  }

  public static void applyRaceResults(
      Map<Id, List<ProvisionalResult>>
          provisionalResultsByRaceId) {
    service().applyRaceResults(provisionalResultsByRaceId);
  }

  public static void awardChampionshipPoints(Set<Id>raceIds) {
    service().awardChampionshipPoints(raceIds);
  }
```

Application Service Layer

```
    private static IRaceService service() {
      return (IRaceService)
          Application.Service.newInstance(IRaceService.class);
    }

    public class RaceServiceException extends Exception {}

    public class ProvisionalResult {
      public Integer racePosition {get; set;}
      public Id contestantId {get; set;}
      public String contestantName {get; set;}
    }
  }
```

The `service` method utilizes the `Application` class once more; this time a `Service` factory has been used to allow the actual implementation of the `IRaceService` interface to vary at runtime. This allows developers to control which of the two preceding implementations shown they want the application to use based on their needs. The default is to use the `RaceServiceImpl` class; however, by inserting a record in the **Services** Custom Metadata Type object this can be overridden—more on this to follow.

The factory exposed via the `Service` field in the `Application` class extends the `fflib_Application.ServiceFactory` class, which instantiates the configured class provided in `Map` passed to the factory. This factory also supports mocking the service implementation, something that will be discussed in more detail in a later chapter.

The factory has been extended to look for configured alternative service implementation classes via a protected (and thus hidden to end users) Custom Metadata object called **Services**, which is included in the source code for this chapter.

You can see this being queried as follows:

```
  public class Application {
    // Configure and create the ServiceFactory for this Application
    public static final fflib_Application.ServiceFactory Service =
        new Application.ServiceFactory (
          new Map<Type, Type> {
            IRaceService.class => RaceServiceImpl.class });

    // Customized Service factory overrides via Custom Metadata
    private class ServiceFactory extends
        fflib_Application.ServiceFactory {

      private Map<String, String> servicesByClassName =
          new Map<String, String>();
```

[190]

```
public ServiceFactory(
    Map<Type,Type> serviceInterfaceTypeByServiceImplType) {

  super(serviceInterfaceTypeByServiceImplType);

  // Map of overridden services defined by the developer
  for(Service__mdt serviceOverride :
     [select DeveloperName, NamespacePrefix, ApexClass__c
      from Service__mdt]) {
    servicesByClassName.put(
    serviceOverride.NamespacePrefix + '.'
    serviceOverride.DeveloperName,
    serviceOverride.ApexClass__c);
  }
}

public override Object newInstance(
    Type serviceInterfaceType) {

  // Has the developer overridden the Service impl?
  if(!Test.isRunningTest() &&
       servicesByClassName.containsKey(
          serviceInterfaceType.getName())) {
    String overridenServiceImpl =
       servicesByClassName.get( serviceInterfaceType.getName());
    return Type.forName(overridenServiceImpl).newInstance();
  }

  // Base factory returns mocked or registered impl
  return super.newInstance(serviceInterfaceType);
  }
 }
}
```

> Querying Custom Metadata records does not count against the SOQL governor; however, the records returned do count against the maximum 50k record limit.

Application Service Layer

By creating the following Custom Metadata record, the client developers can configure the application to use the stub implementation without making any code changes:

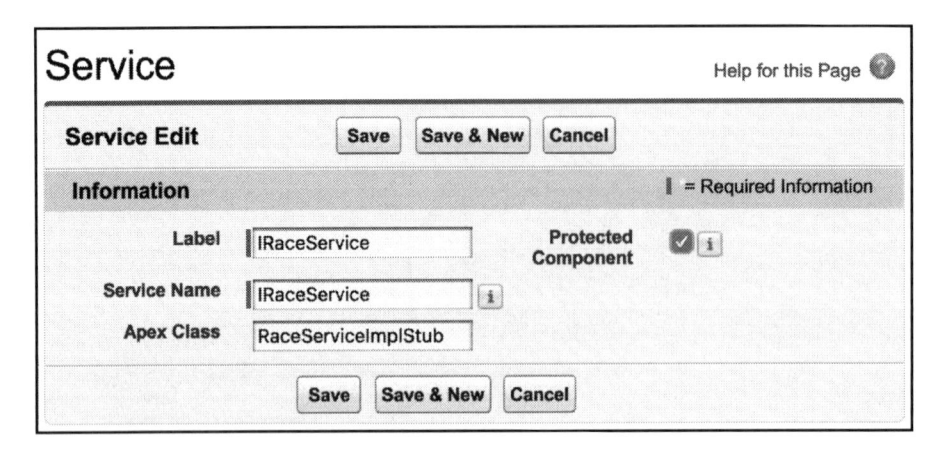

Service

Service Edit — Save | Save & New | Cancel

Information — = Required Information

- Label: IRaceService
- Service Name: IRaceService
- Apex Class: RaceServiceImplStub
- Protected Component: ✓

> **TIP:** This approach could be used to provide a custom extensibility feature in your application by making the Custom Metadata Type object **Public** and allowing customers or partners to override packaged implementations of your services. Use this approach with care, however, and only when it adds value to your customers or partners.

Testing the Service layer

It is tempting to allow the testing of the Service layer to be done via tests around the calling code, such as Apex controller tests. However, depending solely on this type of testing leaves the Service layer logic open to other use cases that may not strictly be covered by the controller logic. For example, a certain Apex controller will only pass in a single record and not multiple ones. Make sure to develop specific Apex tests against the Service layer as the functionality is developed.

Mocking the Service layer

Sometimes, the data setup requirements of the Service layer are such that it makes writing Apex tests for controllers or other callers, such as Batch Apex, quite complex and thus expensive, not only in server time for the test to run (due to data setup for each test method) but also in developer time, while preparing a full set of test data.

Chapter 5

While you still need to test the full stack of your code, there is an approach called **mocking**, which can be used in conjunction with the previously mentioned factory pattern, which will allow the test context for the given service caller to implement its own test implementation of the service that mimics (with hardcoded test responses) different behaviors that the controller is expecting from the Service method. This allows the controller tests to be more varied and focused when devising tests. Again, this mocking approach has to be used in combination with full stack tests that truly execute all the code required. `Chapter 12`, *Unit Testing*, will cover mocking the Service layer in more detail.

Calling the Service layer

The preceding examples have shown the use of the service class methods from Lightning Component Apex controller methods. Let's take a closer look at what is happening here, the assumptions being made, and also at two other callers, an Apex Scheduler and a Visualforce Apex Controller. Throughout the rest of the book, you will also see other examples such as Batch Apex and Platform Event Subscriptions.

Keep the following in mind when reviewing the following use cases:

- There is no need for the calling code shown in the following sections to concern itself with rolling back changes made within the service that may have been made to object records up to the exception being thrown, since the caller is safe in the assumption that the Service method has already ensured this is the case.
- Error handling in each of the following sections is unique, yet the way in which errors are received from the service layer is consistent.

These aspects between the service and its callers are essentially *Separation Of Concerns* at work, ensuring each part of your code is doing exactly what it needs to do.

From Lightning Component Apex Controllers

The following code revisits a Lightning Apex Controller example shown earlier in this chapter. The error handling approach used here is worthy of further elaboration. Lightning Components require that all Apex exceptions to wrapped in an `AuraHandledException`. In the following example, this is done by calling a utility method:

```
@AuraEnabled
public static void awardPoints(Id raceId) {
   try {
      RaceService.awardChampionshipPoints(new Set<Id> { raceId });
```

Application Service Layer

```
    }
    catch (Exception e) {
      Application.throwAuraHandledException(e);
    }
}
```

The utility method looks like this:

```
public static void throwAuraHandledException(Exception e) {
    String message = e.getMessage();
    AuraHandledException error =
      new AuraHandledException(message);
    error.setMessage(message);
    throw error;
}
```

This method also takes care of converting a regular exception into an Aura exception and ensuring the error message contained within the exception thrown is visible from your Apex tests, as can be seen by studying the `SeasonControllerTest` that has been included in the source code related to this chapter.

From Visualforce Apex Controllers

> **Visualforce** is an old user interface technology that has now been superseded by Lightning Components. The following information is provided if you are working with a pre-existing code base that is still using Visualforce.

The following code represents code from a Visualforce Apex controller class utilizing `StandardController` that provides support for the Visualforce page associated with a Custom Button on the `Race` object. Notice how it wraps the record ID in `Set`, honoring the bulkified method signature:

```
public PageReference awardPoints(){
  try{
    RaceService.awardChampionshipPoints(
       new Set<Id> {standardController.getId() });
  }
  catch (Exception e){
    ApexPages.addMessages(e);
  }
  return null;
}
```

> The constructor of these controllers is not shown, but it essentially stores `StandardController` or `StandardSetController` in a member variable for later reference by the controller methods.

The following code outlines a similar version that can be used when `StandardSetController` is being used, in the case where a Custom Button is required on the object's list view:

```
public PageReference awardPointsToRaces(){
  try {
    RaceService.awardChampionshipPoints(
      new Map<Id, SObject>(
        standardSetController.getRecords()).keySet() );
  }
  catch (Exception e){
    ApexPages.addMessages(e);
  }
  return null;
}
```

> **TIP**: The `Map` constructor in Apex will take a list of SObjects and automatically build a map based on the IDs of the SObjects passed in. Combining this with the `keySet` method provides a quick way to convert the list of records contained in `StandardSetController` into a list of IDs required by the Service method.

In both cases, any exceptions are routed to the `apex:pageMessages` component on the page (which should be one of the first things you should consider adding to a page) by calling the `ApexPages.addMessages` method that is passing in the exception.

From the Apex Scheduler

Finally, let's look at an example from the `SeasonNewsletterScheduler` class. As with the controller example, it handles the exceptions itself, in this case, by emailing the user with any failures. Consider the following code:

```
global void execute(SchedulableContext sc) {
  try {
    SeasonService.issueNewsLetterCurrentSeason();
  } catch (Exception e) {
    Messaging.SingleEmailMessage mail =
        new Messaging.SingleEmailMessage();
    mail.setTargetObjectId(UserInfo.getUserId());
```

[195]

```
    mail.setSenderDisplayName(UserInfo.getUserName());
    mail.setSubject('Failed to send Season Newsletter');
    mail.setHtmlBody(e.getMessage());
    mail.setSaveAsActivity(false);
    Messaging.sendEmail(
       new Messaging.SingleEmailMessage[] { mail });
  }
}
```

Updating the FormulaForce package

Finally, deploy the code included in this chapter and ensure any new Apex classes (especially test classes) are added to the package and perform a release. You may want to take some time to further review the code provided with this chapter, as not all of the code has been featured in this chapter. Some new fields have been added to the *Contestant* and *Season* objects as well, which will automatically be added to the package. Two new metadata objects, *Championship Points* and *Services*, have been added. *Championship Point* records must also be added to the package. Do not package any *Service* records.

Summary

In this chapter, we have taken the first step in developing a robust coding convention to manage and structure the coding complexities of an enterprise application. This first layer encapsulates your application's business process logic in an agnostic way that allows it to be consumed easily across multiple Apex entry points, both those required today by your application and those that will arise in the future as the platform evolves.

We have also seen how the Unit Of Work pattern can be used to help bulkify DML statements, manage record relationships and implement a database transaction, and allow your Service layer logic to focus more on the key responsibility of implementing business logic. In the upcoming chapters, we will see how it quickly becomes the backbone of your application. Careful adherence to the guidelines around your Service layer will ensure it remains strong and easy to extend.

In the next chapter, we will look at the Domain layer, a pattern that blends the data from a Custom Object alongside applicable logic related to a Custom Object's behavior that relates to that data. This includes logic traditionally placed in Apex Triggers, but it is also optional to further distribute and layer code executed in the Service layer.

6
Application Domain Layer

The objects used by your application represent its domain. Unlike other database platforms where the record data is, by default, hidden from end users, the Lightning Platform displays your record data through the standard Salesforce UI, reports, dashboards, and Salesforce Mobile application. Field and relationship labels that you give your objects and fields are also used by these UI experiences. From the moment you create your first object, you start to define your application's domain, just as Salesforce Standard Objects represent the CRM application domain.

Martin Fowler's *Patterns of Enterprise Application Architecture* also recognizes this concept as a means of code encapsulation to combine the data expressed by each object with behaviors written in code that affect or interact with that data. This could be Apex Trigger code, providing defaulting and validation, or code awarding championship points to contestant records or checking racing rules compliance.

This chapter will extend the functionality of the FormulaForce application using the Domain layer pattern, as well as highlight specific concerns, guidelines, best practices, and demonstrate how the Domain layer integrates with both Apex Triggers and the application's Service layer code.

The following topics will be covered in this chapter:

- Introducing the Domain layer pattern
- Implementing design guidelines
- The Domain class template
- Implementing the Domain Trigger logic
- Implementing the custom Domain logic
- Object-orientated programming
- Testing the Domain layer
- Calling the Domain layer
- Updating the FormulaForce package

Introducing the Domain layer pattern

The following is Martin Fowler's definition of the Domain layer (http://martinfowler.com/eaaCatalog/domainModel.html):

> "An object model of the domain that incorporates both behavior and data."

Like the Service layer, this pattern adds a further layer of separation of concerns and factoring of the application code, which helps to manage and scale a code base as it grows.

> "At its worst business logic can be very complex. Rules and logic describe many different cases and slants of behavior, and it's this complexity that objects were designed to work with. A Domain Model creates a web of interconnected objects, where each object represents some meaningful individual, whether as large as a corporation or as small as a single line on an order form."

Martin's reference to objects in the preceding quote is mainly aimed at objects created from instantiating classes that are coded in an OOP language such as Java or .NET. In these platforms, such classes act as a logical representation of the underlying database-table relationships. This approach is typically referred to as **Object Relational Mapping (ORM)**.

In contrast, a Lightning developer reading the term "object" will tend to first think about Standard or Custom Objects rather than something resulting from a class instantiation. This is because Salesforce has done a great job of binding the data with behavior through their declarative definition of an object, which, as we know, is much more than just fields. It has formulas, filters, referential integrity, and many other features that we have discussed in earlier chapters available without writing any code.

Taking into consideration these declarative features, they are essentially a means to enable certain behaviors. Hence, a Lightning Custom or Standard Object does already meet some of the encapsulation concerns of the Domain layer pattern.

Encapsulating an object's behavior in code

Apex Triggers present a way to write code to implement additional behavior for Custom Objects (or Standard Objects for that matter). They provide a place to implement more complex behavior associated with database events such as **create**, **update**, and **delete**.

However, as an Apex Trigger cannot have `public` methods, it does not provide a means to write code that logically belongs to the object but is not necessarily linked with a database event. An example of this would be logic to calculate **Contestants** championship points or checking for compliance against the many Formula 1 rules and regulations, which we will look at later in this chapter. Furthermore, Apex Triggers do not present the opportunity to leverage OOP approaches, also discussed later in this chapter.

As a result, developers often end up putting this logic elsewhere, sometimes in a controller or helper class of some kind. Thus, the code implementing the behavior for a given object becomes fragmented and there is a breakdown of separation of concerns.

Lifting your Apex Trigger code out of the body of the trigger and into an **Apex Class**, perhaps named by some convention based on the object name, is a good start to mitigating this fragmentation; for example, `RaceTriggerManager` or `RaceTriggerHandler`. Using such approaches, it then becomes possible to create other methods and break up the code further. These approaches are only the beginning when seeking a more complete interpretation of the Domain Model concept described in this chapter.

Using the `Manager` or `Handler` approach tends to attract logic relating to the Apex Trigger event model and nothing else, leaving other object-related logic to find less obvious locations in the code base.

Interpreting the Domain layer

In this chapter, we look at the platform's interpretation of the Domain layer pattern, one which ensures that behavior invoked both through Apex Trigger events and through direct Apex method calls (from the Service layer and other Domain classes) is considered.

> **Platform Event Subscriptions** (via Apex Triggers) and **Async Apex Triggers** are specialized forms of Apex Triggers that do not directly apply to the Domain layer pattern described in this chapter. They will be covered in `Chapter 11`, *Asynchronous Processing and Big Data Volumes*.

A single Domain class can be created to encapsulate all of the behavior and will begin to leverage OOP principles, such as interfaces, to further enrich the code for reuse and *Separation of Concerns*, which we will explore later in this chapter.

Application Domain Layer

The following diagram illustrates two consumers of the Domain layer classes—the code from the **Service layer**, and also direct interactions with objects resulting in **Apex Trigger** events, which will also be routed to the same Domain layer class:

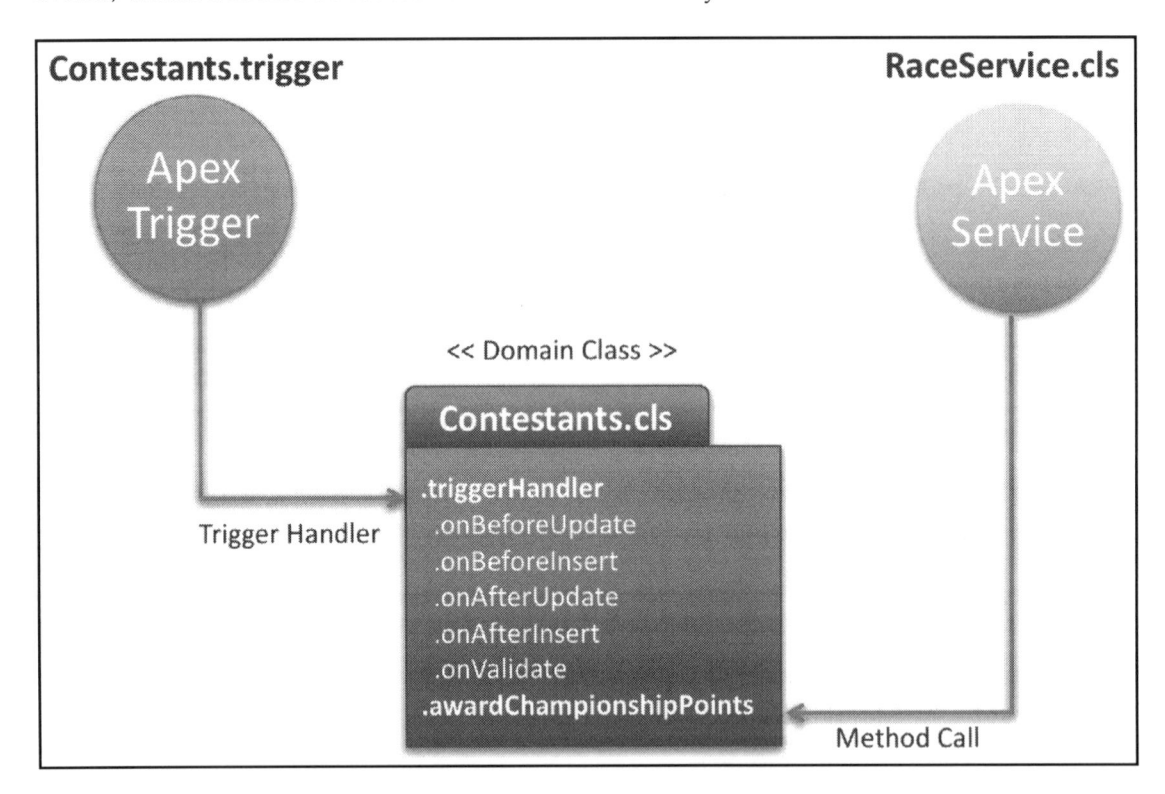

Contestants.trigger — Apex Trigger — Trigger Handler

RaceService.cls — Apex Service — Method Call

<< Domain Class >>
Contestants.cls
- .triggerHandler
- .onBeforeUpdate
- .onBeforeInsert
- .onAfterUpdate
- .onAfterInsert
- .onValidate
- .awardChampionshipPoints

Application development in Lightning Platform focuses heavily on objects; these objects store your application's data and protect its integrity. In this section, you can see how they are critical parts of your application regardless of whether the user is manipulating records directly or through your applications service code. This combination of managing data and behavior is something that will be explored in the next section.

Domain classes in Apex compared to other platforms

As we have seen in earlier chapters, a Standard or Custom Object is exposed within the Apex runtime as a **concrete type** that can be instantiated to populate record fields for insertions in the database or to determine which types are used to return records queried from it.

When considering the Domain pattern, the first inclination is perhaps to extend the applicable SObject, such as `Account` or `Race__c` through **Apex inheritance** with the `extends` keyword. Unfortunately, the **Apex compiler** does not support this approach. Even if it were to support this, given the best practices of bulkification, writing code that deals with a single record instance at a time will quickly lead to governor issues.

Instead, the Domain class implementation covered here uses the **composition** approach to combine record data and behavior. This is sometimes known as the **wrapper class** approach; it is so named because it wraps the data that it relates to as a class member variable.

The Apex implementation of the wrapper class is no different, except that we choose to wrap a list of records to enforce **bulkified implementations** of the logic within. The following pseudocode illustrates the instantiation of an **Apex Domain class**:

```
List<Race__c> raceRecords =
    [select Id, Name from Races__c where Id in :raceIds];

Races races = new Races(raceRecords);
```

Another implementation difference compared to other platforms, such as Java and .NET, is the creation of accessor methods to obtain related parent and child records. Though it is possible to write such methods, they are not recommended; for example, `Contestants.getRaces` or `Races.getContestants`.

This implementation avoids coding these types of accessors, as the `SObject` objects in Apex already provide a means to traverse relationships (if queried) as needed. The bulk nature of Apex Domain classes also makes these types of methods less useful and it is more appropriate for the caller to use the Selector classes to query the required records as and when needed, rather than as a result of invoking an accessor method.

To summarize, the Apex Domain classes described in this chapter focus on wrapping lists of records and methods that encapsulate the object's behavior and avoid providing accessor methods for query-related records.

Implementing design guidelines

As with the previous chapter, this section provides some general design and best practice guidelines for designing a **Domain layer class** for a given object. Note that some of these conventions are shared by the **Service layer**, which also calls the Domain layer because conventions such as bulkification apply to the logic written here as well.

Application Domain Layer

Naming conventions

The key principle of the Domain layer pattern is to lay out the code in such a way that it maps to the business domain of the application. In a Lightning application, this is typically supported by Custom Objects. As such, it's important to clearly indicate which Domain layer class relates to which Standard or Custom Object:

- **Avoid acronyms**: As per the previous chapter, try to avoid these unless it makes your class names unworkably long.
- **Class names**: Use the plural name of your Custom Object for the name of your Domain class. This sets the tone for the scope of the record that the class deals with as clearly being bulkified, as described in the following subsection:
  - Some bad examples are `Race.cls` and `RaceDomain.cls`.
  - Some good examples are `Races.cls` and `Teams.cls`.
- **Method names**: Methods that relate to the logic associated with database operations or events should follow the `onEventName` convention. Other method names should be descriptive and avoid repeating the name of the class as part of the name:
  - Some bad examples are `Races.checkInserts` and `Races.startRace`.
  - Some good examples are `Races.onBeforeInsert` and `Races.start`.
- **Parameter names and types**: Much of what was described in the previous chapter applies here. Though passing in a list of records to the Domain class methods is not required, this is available as a class member variable to all the Domain class methods, as you will see later in this chapter:
  - Some bad examples are as follows:

    ```
    Races.onBeforeInsert(
      List<Race__c>racesBeingInserted)
    Races.start(
      List<Id>raceIds)
    ```

  - Some good examples are as follows:

    ```
    Races.onBeforeInsert()
    Races.start()
    ```

- **Inner classes and interfaces**: Much of what was described in the previous chapter also applies here. As the data being managed is expressed in terms of the actual Custom Objects themselves and that information is available as a class member variable, there is typically less of a need for inner classes representing data to be passed in and out of a Domain class.

The following diagram shows how the Domain classes that are used in this chapter map to their respective **Custom Objects**:

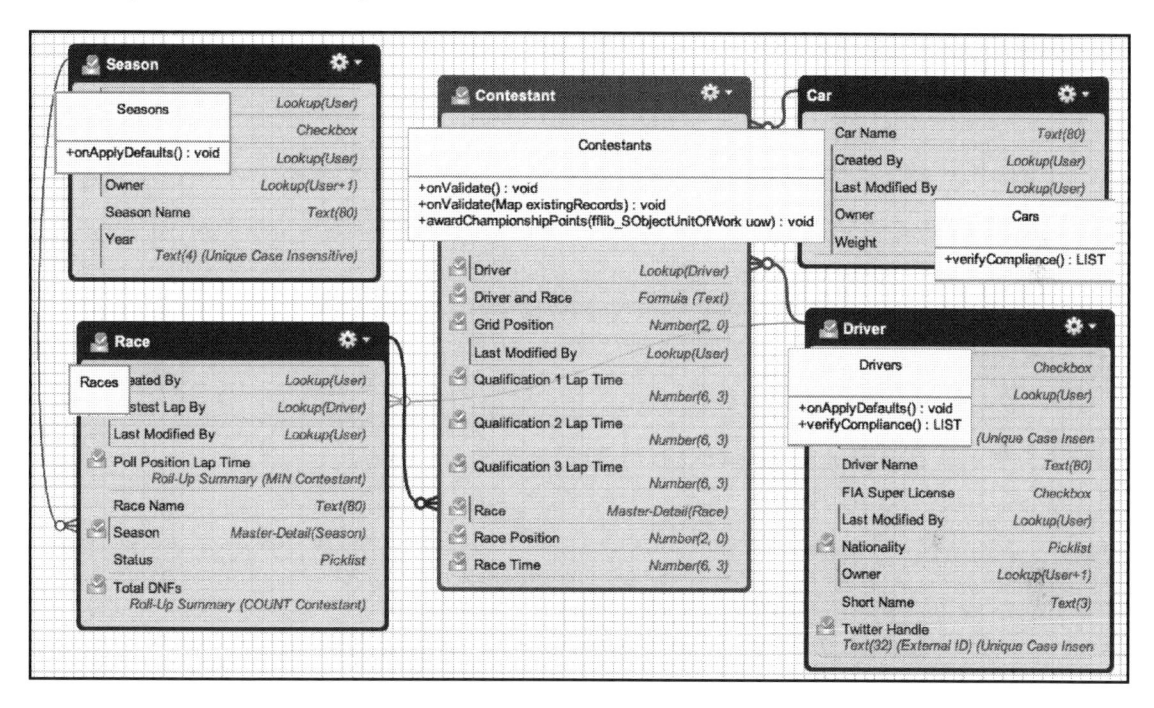

Each Domain class receives the records that its methods act on in its constructor. The methods shown in the Domain classes are described in more detail as we progress through this chapter.

Bulkification

As with the Service layer, code written in the Domain layer is encouraged to think about records in a bulk context. This is important when Domain class methods are being called from an Apex Trigger context and the Service layer code, both of which carry the same bulkification requirement.

Instead of enforcing bulkification through passing parameters and ensuring that parameter types are bulkified, as with the Service layer, the information in the Domain class logic acts on, and is driven by, its member variables, which are then bulkified. In this case, the `Records` class property returns a `List<SObject>` object:

```
public override void onValidate() {
   for(Contestant__c race : (List<Contestant__c>) Records) {
   }
}
```

In addition to overriding methods from the base class, as shown in the preceding example, you can also write your own methods. The next section discusses this approach and how you should think about the information you pass to such methods.

Defining and passing data

Most methods in Domain classes already have the information they need through the `Records` property (the state the Domain class was constructed with). As such, there is little need to pass data information on the methods themselves. However, for some custom behavior methods (those not reflecting the Apex Trigger logic), you might want to pass other domain objects and/or a **Unit Of Work** as additional parameters. Examples later in this chapter help illustrate this.

Transaction management

For Domain class methods that perform database operations, there are two design guidelines: utilize a transaction context (Unit Of Work) passed as a parameter to the method or create one for the scope of the Domain class method execution.

Domain class template

The implementation of the Domain class in this chapter utilizes the **Financial Lightning Apex Enterprise Patterns** library, which is open source and is included in the sample code of this chapter. In this library, the Apex base class, `fflib_SObjectDomain`, is provided to help implement the Domain layer pattern.

A basic template for a Domain class utilizing this base class is shown in the following code snippet:

```
public inherited sharing class Races extends fflib_SObjectDomain {
  public Races(List<Race__c> races) {
    super(races);
  }

  public class Constructor
    implements fflib_SObjectDomain.IConstructable {
    public fflib_SObjectDomain construct(
        List<SObject>sObjectList) {
      return new Races(sObjectList);
    }
  }
}
```

The first thing to note is that the **constructor** for this class takes a list of `Race__c` records, as per the guidelines described previously. The code implemented in a domain class is written with bulkification in mind. The base class constructor initializes the `Records` base class property.

> The inner class, `Constructor`, is present to permit the dynamic creation of the Domain class in an Apex Trigger context. This is actually working around the lack of full reflection (the ability to reference the class constructor dynamically) in the Apex language. The name of this inner class must always be `Constructor`.

Application Domain Layer

By extending the `fflib_SObjectDomain` class, the Domain class inherits properties and methods it can override to implement its own methods, such as the `Records` property, which provides access to the actual record data. There are `virtual` methods provided to make the implementation of the **Apex Trigger** easier, as well as some specialized events such as `onValidate` and `onApplyDefaults`. The following class overview illustrates some of the key methods in the base class that the Domain classes can override:

- fflib_SObjectDomain(List<SObject>, SObjectType)
- onApplyDefaults() : void
- onValidate() : void
- onValidate(Map<Id, SObject>) : void
- onBeforeInsert() : void
- onBeforeUpdate(Map<Id, SObject>) : void
- onBeforeDelete() : void
- onAfterInsert() : void
- onAfterUpdate(Map<Id, SObject>) : void
- onAfterDelete() : void
- onAfterUndelete() : void
- handleBeforeInsert() : void
- handleBeforeUpdate(Map<Id, SObject>) : void
- handleBeforeDelete() : void
- handleAfterInsert() : void
- handleAfterUpdate(Map<Id, SObject>) : void
- handleAfterDelete() : void
- handleAfterUndelete() : void

The `fflib_SObjectDomain` class is part of an open source library. As such, it is always receiving great contributions from the community. Be sure to check the latest version of this class for new methods and features!

Implementing Domain Trigger logic

The most common initial use case for a Domain class is to encapsulate the Apex Trigger logic. In order to enable this, a small Apex Trigger is required to invoke the `triggerHandler` method. This will route the various Trigger events to the appropriate methods in the Domain class (as shown in the preceding screenshot), avoiding the need for the usual `if/else` logic around `Trigger.isXXXX` variables.

The name of this trigger can be anything, though it makes sense to match it with that of the corresponding Domain class. Once this is in place, you can ignore it and focus on implementing the Domain class methods as follows:

```
trigger Seasons on Season__c (
  after delete, after insert, after update,
  before delete, before insert, before update) {
    fflib_SObjectDomain.triggerHandler(Seasons.class);
}
```

In the next section, we will explore how Apex Trigger events are routed to specific methods that you can implement in the Domain class.

Routing trigger events to Domain class methods

The following diagram illustrates the flow of execution from the Apex Trigger to the Domain class, `triggerHandler`, and then to the individual methods:

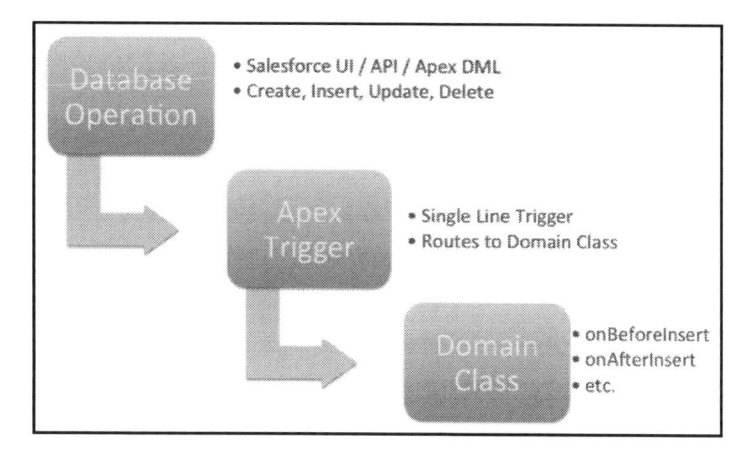

Application Domain Layer

To help you understand how traditional Apex Trigger events are mapped to the various virtual methods in the base class, the following table describes the code path taken from when the base class's `fflib_SObjectDOmai.triggerHandler` method is invoked, through to the specific event-based methods that can be overridden by a Domain class:

Trigger context	Base class records property value	Base class handle method called (refer to the following note)	Base class event method(s) called (refer to the following note)
Trigger.isBefore			
`Trigger.isInsert`	`Trigger.new`	`handleBeforeInsert()`	`onApplyDefaults()` `onBeforeInsert()`
`Trigger.isUpdate`	`Trigger.new`	`handleBeforeUpdate(Map<Id,SObject> existingRecords)`	`onBeforeUpdate(Map<Id,SObject> existingRecords)`
`Trigger.isDelete`	`Trigger.oldMap`	`handleBeforeDelete()`	`onBeforeDelete()`
Trigger.isAfter			
`Trigger.isInsert`	`Trigger.new`	`handleAfterInsert()`	`onValidate()` `onAfterInsert()`
`Trigger.isUpdate`	`Trigger.new`	`handleAfterUpdate(Map<Id,SObject> existingRecords)`	`onValidate(Map<Id,SObject> existingRecords)` `onAfterUpdate(Map<Id,SObject> existingRecords)`
`Trigger.isDelete`	`Trigger.oldMap`	`handleAfterDelete()`	`onAfterDelete()`

Note that handle methods can also be overridden if you wish to implement your own handling. The `existingRecords` parameter represents the value of `Trigger.oldMap`.

The base class uses the template method pattern (http://en.wikipedia.org/wiki/Template_method_pattern). This ensures that when overriding the `onXXX` methods from the base class, you do not need to worry about calling the base class version of the method, as is the typical developer requirement when overriding methods in OOP.

Enforcing object security

Salesforce requires developers to implement the **Object CRUD (Create, Read, Update, and Delete) security** and **Field Level security** checks using the methods on the `SObjectDescribe` and `SObjectFieldDescribe` Apex runtime types.

By default, the preceding handle methods in the `fflib_SObjectDomain` base class used in this chapter automatically perform the Object CRUD security on behalf of the developer's Domain class logic.

> Note that, currently, the base class still leaves implementation of Field Level security to the developer to implement.

A developer-controlled configuration option provided by the base class allows each Domain class to control whether this default behavior is enabled. For example, objects that are typically maintained by the application code on behalf of the user may not wish to have this check enforced, such as the awarding of championship points. This type of access is sometimes referred to as *system-level* access, as the system performs an operation on behalf of the user. Thus, by accepting the default to enforce this check, it would require users to be granted access that would not be appropriate elsewhere in the application. Another motivation for not leveraging the default enforcement would be a preference to code these checks in your controller logic more explicitly. Consider carefully whether the default enforcement is what you need in each case.

Default behavior

The handler method checks the required security before calling the preceding event methods and throws a `DomainException` exception if the user does not have the required access (forcing the entire Trigger context to stop). For example, when the `handleAfterInsert` method is invoked, the `SObjectDescribe.isCreatable` method is used.

Overriding the default behavior

To make it easier to configure the `fflib_SObjectDomain` class throughout the application, as well as provide a means to establish shared or common Domain logic code, a new base class is created as follows:

```
/**
 * Application specific Domain base class,
 *   customize fflib_SObjectDomain and add common behavior
 **/
public inherited sharing abstract class ApplicationDomain extends
      fflib_SObjectDomain {
  public ApplicationDomain(List<SObject> records) {
    super(records);
    // Disable CRUD security enforcement at the Domain class level
    Configuration.disableTriggerCRUDSecurity();
  }
}
```

Thus, Domain classes in this application extend the preceding `ApplicationDomain` class instead:

```
public inherited sharing class Contestants
    extends ApplicationDomain {
  public Contestants(List<Contestant__c> contestants) {
    super(contestants);
  }
}
```

Note that this approach requires that the developer takes over exclusive responsibility for implementing Object CRUD security checking them.

Apex Trigger event handling

The upcoming sections illustrate some Apex Trigger examples with respect to the FormulaForce application. They utilize the `Drivers` and `Contestants` Domain classes included in the sample code for this chapter, along with the following new fields:

- In the `Driver__c` object, a new field called `ShortName__c` as a **Text** type, with a maximum size of three characters, has been created.
- In the `Race__c` object, there is a new field called `Status__c` as a **Picklist** type, with the **Scheduled**, **In Progress**, **Red Flagged**, and **Finished** values. The default value is scheduled by ticking the **Use first value as default value** checkbox.

Defaulting field values on insert

Although the `onInsertBefore` method can be overridden to implement logic to set default values on record insert, the following code, added to the `Contestants` Domain class, has chosen to override the `onApplyDefaults` method instead. This was used as it is more explicit and permits a *Separation of Concerns* between the defaulting code and the record insert code, although both are fired during the insert phase:

```
public override void onApplyDefaults() {
  for(Driver__c driver : (List<Driver__c>) Records) {
    if(driver.ShortName__c == null) {
      // Upper case first three letters of drivers last name
      String lastName = driver.Name.substringAfterLast(' ');
      driver.ShortName__c = lastName.left(3).toUpperCase();
    }
  }
}
```

The preceding code attempts to populate the driver short name, which is typically made up of the first three characters of their second name in uppercase, so **Lewis Hamilton** will become **HAM**.

Validation on insert

The following validation logic applies during record creation. It has been added to the `Contestants` Domain class and ensures that contestants are only added when the race is in the **Scheduled** state.

It also demonstrates the use of a **Selector** pattern class to bulk load records from the `Race__c` Custom Object, and this pattern will be covered in detail in the next chapter:

```
public override void onValidate() {
  // Bulk load the associated races
  Set<Id>raceIds = new Set<Id>();
  for(Contestant__c contestant : (List<Contestant__c>) Records) {
    raceIds.add(contestant.Race__c);
  }
  Map<Id, Race__c>associatedRaces =
    new Map<Id, Race__c>(
      new RacesSelector().selectById(raceIds));
  // Only new contestants to be added to Scheduled races
  for(Contestant__c contestant :
    (List<Contestant__c>) Records) {
    Race__c race = associatedRaces.get(contestant.Race__c);
    if(race.Status__c != 'Scheduled') {
```

```
            contestant.addError(
                'Contestants can only be added to scheduled races');
        }
    }
}
```

By overriding the `onValidate` method, the logic always invokes the after phase of the Apex Trigger. As no further edits can be made to the record fields, this is the safest place to perform the logic. Always keep in mind that your Apex Trigger might not be the only one assigned to the object. For example, once your package is installed in a subscriber org, a subscriber-created custom trigger on your object might fire before yours (the order of trigger invocation is non-deterministic) and will attempt to modify fields. Thus, for managed package triggers, it is highly recommended that validation be performed in the after phase to ensure complete confidence and security, as the data will not be modified further after validation.

Validation on update

An alternative method, `override`, is provided to implement the validation logic applicable to record updates. This is an overload of the `onValidate` method shown in the preceding example, used to pass in the current records on the database for comparison if needed:

```
    public override void onValidate(Map<Id,SObject> existingRecords) {
        // Only validate records where the Driver has been changed
        List<Contestant__c> changedDrivers =
          getChangedRecords(
            new Set<SObjectField> { Contestant__c.Driver__c });
        // Bulk load the associated races
        Map<Id, Race__c> associatedRaces =
          queryAssociatedRaces(changedDrivers);
        // Can only change drivers in scheduled races
        for(Contestant__c contestant : changedDrivers) {
          Race__c contestantRace =
             associatedRaces.get(contestant.Race__c);
          if(contestantRace.Status__c != 'Scheduled') {
             contestant.Driver__c.addError(
                'You can only change drivers for scheduled races' );
          }
        }
    }
```

> **TIP**
> The previous code also highlights a way to optimize validation logic compute time by focusing only on applicable changes to records. In this case, the `getChangedRecords` base class method is used to return only records where the `Driver__c` field has been changed.

The preceding code leverages a new custom Domain class method to share the code responsible for loading associated Race records for Contestants across the `onValidate` method shown in the previous example. This method also uses the `Records` property to determine Contestants in scope:

```
private Map<Id, Race__c> queryAssociatedRaces() {
  // Bulk load the associated races
  Set<Id>raceIds = new Set<Id>();
  for(Contestant__c contestant : (List<Contestant__c>) Records) {
    raceIds.add(contestant.Race__c);
  }
  return new Map<Id, Race__c>(
     new RacesSelector().selectById(raceIds));
}
```

The preceding method is marked as `private`, as there is currently no need to expose this functionality to other classes. Initially, restricting methods in this way is often considered best practice and permits easier internal refactoring or improvements in the future. If a need arises that requires access to this functionality, the method can be made `public`.

Implementing custom Domain logic

A Domain class should not restrict itself to containing logic purely related to Apex Triggers. In the following example, the code introduced in the previous chapter to calculate championship points has been refactored into the `Contestants` Domain class. This is a more appropriate place for it, as it directly applies to the Contestant record data and can be readily shared between other Domain and Service layer code (which we will look at later in this chapter):

```
public void awardChampionshipPoints(fflib_ISObjectUnitOfWorkuow) {
   // Apply championship points to given contestants
   Map<Integer, ChampionshipPoint__mdt> pointsByTrackPosition =
      new ChampionshipPointsSelector().selectAllByTrackPosition();
   for(Contestant__c contestant : (List<Contestant__c>) Records) {
     // Determine points to award for the given position
     ChampionshipPoint__mdt pointsForPosition =
        pointsByTrackPosition.get(
        Integer.valueOf(contestant.RacePosition__c));
```

Application Domain Layer

```
            if(pointsForPosition!=null) {
               // Apply points and register for udpate with uow
               contestant.ChampionshipPoints__c =
                  pointsForPosition.PointsAwarded__c;
                  uow.registerDirty(contestant);
            }
         }
      }
```

Note that the **Unit Of Work** is passed as a parameter here so that the method can register work (record updates) with the calling Service layer method responsible for committing the work. Once again, as with the previous Domain class methods, the `Records` property is used to access the Contestant records to process.

Object-oriented programming

One of the big advantages of using Apex classes is the ability to leverage the power of **object-oriented programming (OOP)**. OOP allows you to observe commonalities in data or behavior across your objects to share code or apply common processing across different objects.

An example of such a commonality in the Formula 1 world are rules; every aspect of the sport has a set of rules and regulations to comply with, such as **drivers** owning an **FIA Super License**, the weight of the car they drive should be at least above a defined minimum, and ensuring that a **team** has not exceeded the maximum distance while testing their cars. Such compliances are checked regularly, both before and after a race.

Creating a compliance application framework

In our FormulaForce application, we want to create a compliance framework that will check these regulations across the different objects while also providing a consistent user interface experience for the end user to verify compliance. The initial requirement is to place a **Verify Compliance** button on the **Detail Pages** on all applicable objects.

The UI **Controller** and **Service code** that perform the verification process should be generic and reusable across these objects, while the actual compliance-checking logic associated with each object will be specific. By using an **Apex Interface**, we can define this common requirement for the applicable Domain classes to implement.

In this section, we will implement this requirement using an Apex Interface and a generic service that can be passed record IDs for different Domain objects across the application. Creating such a service avoids code duplication by having to repeat the logic of handling the results within the code of each Domain class and provides a centralized service for the controller to consume regardless of the object type in scope.

By using an Apex Interface and a generic service, we separate the functional concerns of implementing compliance functionality as follows:

- The Service layer code is concerned solely with executing the compliance-checking process through the interface.
- The Controller code is concerned with calling the service class method to execute the compliance check and then presenting the results to the user consistently.
- The Domain layer classes that implement the interface focus solely on validating the record data against the applicable rules according to the type of the object.

Having this *Separation of Concerns* makes it easy to significantly modify or extend the ways in which the checking is invoked and presented to the user without having to revisit each of the Domain layer classes, or, conversely, modify the compliance logic of one object without impacting the overall implementation across the application.

An Apex Interface example

Interfaces help express common attributes or behaviors across different domain classes. In this section, we will use an Apex Interface to help expose the compliance-checking logic encapsulated in each of the applicable Domain classes.

In order to exercise and implement the compliance framework, the FormulaForce application has gained a few extra fields and objects. These objects, additional classes, and Visualforce pages are all included in the code samples of this chapter.

To summarize, the following steps have been taken to implement the compliance framework requirement. You can follow along with these or simply refer to the sample code of this chapter:

1. Create a new **Car** object and tab.
2. Create a new **Weight** field of type **Number** and length **6** on the **Car** object.
3. Create a new **FIA Super License** field to the **Driver** object.
4. Create a new `Cars` Domain class and `CarsSelector` Selector class.
5. Create a new `ComplianceService` class and `ICompliant` interface.

Application Domain Layer

6. Create new `Cars` and `Drivers` Domain classes and implement the `ICompliant` interface.
7. Update the `Application` class to implement a Domain class factory.
8. Create a new `ComplianceService.verify` method that utilizes the Domain factory.
9. Create a user interface to access the service from the various objects that implement the interface.

> The last step will create two user interfaces: one for Salesforce Classic and one for Lightning Experience. The `ComplianceController` class provides a generic controller class for each specific Visualforce page per object. In addition, the `ComplianceChecker` bundle provides a generic Lightning Component called **Compliance Checker**, which can be dropped on any object page.

The following sections describe, in further detail, the Apex coding from *step 5* onward.

Step 5 – Defining a generic service

The aim is to develop a common service to handle all compliance verifications across the application. So, a new `ComplianceService` class has been created with a `verify` method on it that is capable of receiving IDs from various objects. If there are any verification errors, they will be thrown as part of an exception. If the method returns without throwing an exception, the given records are compliant. The following code snippet shows the creation of a new `ComplianceService` class with a `verify` method:

```
public with sharing class ComplianceService {
  /**
   * Provides general support to verify compliance in the
   * application
   * @throws ComplianceException for any failures
   **/
  public static void verify(Set<Id>recordIds) {
    // Query the given records and delegate to the
    //   corresponding Domain class to check compliance
    //   and report failures via ComplianceException
  }
```

Before we look further into how this service method can be implemented, take a look at the new `ICompliant` interface and the `verifyCompliance` method that will be implemented by the `Drivers` and `Cars` Domain classes:

```
public with sharing class ComplianceService {
  /**
   * Interface used to execute compliance checking logic
   * in each domain class
   **/
  public interface ICompliant {
    List<VerifyResult>verifyCompliance();
  }

  /**
   * Results of a compliance verification for a given record
   **/
  public class VerifyResult {
    public Id recordId;
    public String complianceCode;
    public Boolean passed;
    public String failureReason;
  }
}
```

In the next step, we will implement the `ICompliant` interface on a Domain class.

Step 6 – Implementing the Domain class interface

The `Drivers` Domain class implements the interface as follows (note that only a portion of the class is shown). It checks whether the **FIA Super License** field is checked and reports an appropriate compliance code and failure message if not:

```
public inherited sharing class Drivers extends ApplicationDomain
  implements ComplianceService.ICompliant {
  public List<ComplianceService.VerifyResult> verifyCompliance() {
    List<ComplianceService.VerifyResult> compliances =
      new List<ComplianceService.VerifyResult>();
    for(Driver__c driver : (List<Driver__c>) Records) {
      ComplianceService.VerifyResult license =
        new ComplianceService.VerifyResult();
      license.ComplianceCode = '4.1';
      license.RecordId = driver.Id;
      license.passed = driver.FIASuperLicense__c;
      license.failureReason =
      license.passed ? null :
          'Driver must have a FIA Super License.';
```

Application Domain Layer

```
        compliances.add(license);
      }
      return compliances;
   }
}
```

The `Cars` Domain class (of which only a portion of the class is shown) implements the `verifyCompliance` method as follows, checking whether the car is over the specified weight:

```
public inherited sharing class Cars extends ApplicationDomain
   implements ComplianceService.ICompliant {
   public List<ComplianceService.VerifyResult> verifyCompliance() {
      List<ComplianceService.VerifyResult> compliances =
         new List<ComplianceService.VerifyResult>();
      for(Car__c car : (List<Car__c>) Records) {
         // Check weight compliance
         ComplianceService.VerifyResult license =
            new ComplianceService.VerifyResult();
         license.ComplianceCode = '4.1';
         license.RecordId = car.Id;
         license.passed =
            car.Weight__c !=null && car.Weight__c>= 691;
         license.failureReason = license.passed ? null :
            'Car must not be less than 691kg.';
         compliances.add(license);
      }
      return compliances;
   }
}
```

In this step, we specifically implemented the `IComplaint` interface for the `Cars` Domain class. In the next step, we will see how the Factory pattern can be used to construct not just this Domain class, but also other Domain classes that are implementing this interface.

Step 7 – The Domain class Factory pattern

The next step is to dynamically construct the associated Domain class based on the record IDs passed into the `ComplianceService.verify` method. This part of the implementation makes use of a **Factory pattern** implementation for Domain classes.

> A Wikipedia reference to the Factory pattern can be found at http://en.wikipedia.org/wiki/Factory_method_pattern.

The implementation uses the Apex runtime `Id.getSObjectType` method to establish `SObjectType`, and then, via `Maps` (shown in the following code), it determines the applicable Domain and Selector classes to use (to query the records).

The Apex runtime `Type.newInstance` method is then used to construct an instance of the Domain and Selector classes. The factory functionality is invoked by calling the `Application.Domain.newInstance` method. The `Domain` field on the `Application` class is implemented using the `fflib_Application.DomainFactory` class as follows:

```
public class Application {
  public static final fflib_Application.DomainFactory Domain =
    new fflib_Application.DomainFactory(
      Application.Selector,
      // Map SObjectType to Domain Class Constructors
      new Map<SObjectType, Type> {
        Race__c.SObjectType =>Races.Constructor.class,
        Car__c.SObjectType =>Cars.Constructor.class,
        Driver__c.SObjectType =>Drivers.Constructor.class });
}
```

As a developer, you can, of course, instantiate a specific Domain class directly. However, this Domain factory approach allows for the specific Domain class to be chosen at runtime based on `SObjectType` associated with the ID passed to the `newInstance` method. This is key to implementing the generic service entry point as shown in the next step. The preceding initialization of the Domain factory also passes in `Application.Selector`; this is another factory pattern relating to classes that are able to query the database. The next chapter will cover the Selector pattern and the Selector factory in more detail.

Step 8 – Implementing a generic service

The `Application.Domain.newInstance` method used in the following code is used to access the Domain instance factory defined in the last step.

Application Domain Layer

This method returns `fflib_ISObjectDomain`, as this is a common base interface for all Domain classes. Then, using the `instanceof` operator, it determines whether it implements the `ICompliant` interface, and, if so, it calls the `verifyCompliance` method. The following code shows the implementation of a generic service:

```
public with sharing class ComplianceService {
  public static void verify(Set<Id>recordIds) {
    // Dynamically create Domain instance for these records
    fflib_ISObjectDomain domain =
       Application.Domain.newInstance(recordIds);
    if(domain instanceof ICompliant) {
      // Ask the domain class to verify its compliance
      ICompliantcompliantDomain = (ICompliant) domain;
      List<VerifyResult>verifyResults =
         compliantDomain.verifyCompliance();
      if(verifyResults!=null) {
        // Check for failed compliances
        List<VerifyResult> failedCompliances =
          new List<VerifyResult>();
        for(VerifyResultverifyResult : verifyResults) {
          if(!verifyResult.passed) {
              failedCompliances.add(verifyResult);
          }
        }
        if(failedCompliances.size()>0) {
          throw new ComplianceException(
            'Compliance failures found.', failedCompliances);
          return;
        }
      }
    }
    throw new ComplianceException(
      'Unable to verify compliance.', null);
  }
}
```

Note that if the `verify` method is passed IDs for an object that does not have a corresponding Domain class, an exception is thrown from the factory. However, if a domain class is found, but does not implement the interface, the preceding code simply returns without an error, although what the developer will do in this case is up to them.

Step 9 – Using the generic service from a generic controller

In this step, we will utilize the same `ComplianceService.verify` method from a Lightning Component controller and also discuss a summary of the same approach using Visualforce. These user interfaces are also highly generic and thus easier to apply to new objects in future releases.

Generic Compliance Verification UI with a Lightning Component

The component described in this section can be placed on a Lightning Experience or Salesforce Mobile record page for any object without any further configuration. The component utilizes `ComplianceService` to dynamically invoke the appropriate Domain class and apply the applicable verification process.

> Lightning Components will be covered in more detail in a later chapter. This component demonstrates one of the many places where components can be used to extend Lightning Experience and other aspects of the platform.

The following code shows the Apex Controller for the component:

```
public with sharing class ComplianceCheckerComponent {

@AuraEnabled
public static List<String> verify(Id recordId) {
  try {
    // Verify the given record for compliance
    ComplianceService.verify(newSet<Id> { recordId });
    // Success, all good!
    Return null;
  } catch (Exception e) {
    // Report message as normal via apex:pageMessages
    List<String> messages = new List<String> { e.getMessage() };
    // Display additional compliance failure messages?
    If(e instanceofComplianceService.ComplianceException) {
      ComplianceService.ComplianceExceptionce =
        (ComplianceService.ComplianceException) e;
      for(ComplianceService.VerifyResultverifyResult :
          ce.failures) {
        messages.add(String.format('{0} ({1})',
          new List<String> {
            verifyResult.failureReason,
            verifyResult.complianceCode }));
      }
```

```
        }
        return messages;
    }
}
```

The following code shows the component markup, JavaScript controller, and helper—`ComplianceChecker.cmp`:

```
<aura:component
implements="force:hasRecordId,flexipage:availableForRecordHome"
controller="ComplianceCheckerComponent" access="global">
    <aura:dependency resource="markup://force:editRecord"
        type="EVENT" />   <aura:attribute name="category" type="String"
        default="success" />
    <aura:attribute name="messages" type="String[]"/>
    <aura:handler name="init" value="{!this}"
        action="{!c.onInit}"/>
    <aura:handler event="force:refreshView"
        action="{!c.onRefreshView}"/>
    <div class="{!'slds-box slds-theme-' + v.category}">
      <aura:iteration items="{!v.messages}" var="message">
        <p><ui:outputText value="{!message}"/></p>
      </aura:iteration>
    </div>
</aura:component>
```

The preceding code handles the `force:refreshView` event sent by the Lightning Experience framework when the user edits records. Because the `flexipage:availableForRecordHome` interface is specified, this component can only be placed on record pages. The `ComplianceCheckerControler.js` file is as follows:

```
({
  onInit : function(component, event, helper) {
    helper.verifyCompliance(component, event, helper);
  },
  onRefreshView : function(component, event, helper) {
    helper.verifyCompliance(component, event, helper);
  }
})
```

The `ComplianceCheckerHelper.js` file is as follows:

```
({
    verifyCompliance : function(component) {
        var action = component.get("c.verify");
        action.setParams({ "recordId" :
           component.get("v.recordId") });
        action.setCallback(this, function(response) {
          .if(response.getState() === 'SUCCESS') {
            var messages = response.getReturnValue();
            if(messages!=null) {
               component.set("v.category", "error");
               component.set("v.messages", messages);
            } else {
               component.set("v.category", "success");
               component.set("v.messages", ["Verified compliance" ]);
            }
          }
        });
        $A.enqueueAction(action);
    }
})
```

Unlike the Visualforce page, no specific reference to an object is made, allowing the component to be used on any page.

If you wanted to restrict the visibility of the component within the Lightning App Builder tool, where users customize Lightning Experience and Salesforce1 Mobile, you can utilize the `sfdc:objects` tag in your `.design` file. The following shows an example of this:

```
<sfdc:objects>
 <sfdc:object>Driver__c</sfdc:object>
 <sfdc:object>Car__c</sfdc:object>
</sfdc:objects>
```

The component in this section does not use the latest **Lightning Web Component** framework from Salesforce in this case. This is because, at the time of writing, handling the `force:refreshView` event was not supported; therefore, the preceding component uses the **Aura framework**. Fortunately, Salesforce allows you to mix components developed in either framework – we will be exploring this further in a later chapter.

Application Domain Layer

Generic Compliance Verification UI with Visualforce

Visualforce is an older user interface technology that has now been superseded by Lightning Components. The following information is provided if you are working with a pre-existing code base that is still using Visualforce.

A generic Visualforce Controller, `ComplianceController`, has been created with a `verify` action method that calls the service. Note that at no time have we yet referred to a specific Custom Object or Domain class, ensuring that this controller and service are generic and able to handle objects of different types. The following code shows how the generic `ComplianceService.verify` method is being called from the `ComplianceController.verify` method:

```
public PageReference verify() {
  try {
    // Pass the record to the compliance service
    ComplianceService.verify(
      new Set<Id> { standardController.getId() });
    // Passed!
    ApexPages.addMessage(
      new ApexPages.Message(
        ApexPages.Severity.Info, 'Compliance passed'));
  }
  catch (Exception e) {
    // Report message as normal via apex:pageMessages
    ApexPages.addMessages(e);
    // Display additional compliance failure messages?
    if(e instanceofComplianceService.ComplianceException)
    {
      ComplianceService.ComplianceExceptionce
        (ComplianceService.ComplianceException) e;
      for(ComplianceService.VerifyResultverifyResult :
          ce.failures) {
        ApexPages.addMessage(new ApexPages.Message(
          ApexPages.Severity.Error,
          String.format('{0} ({1})',
            new List<String> {
              verifyResult.failureReason,
              verifyResult.complianceCode })));
      }
    }
  }
  return null;
}
```

A Visualforce page for each object is then created to bind this generic controller to Custom Buttons on the **Driver** and **Car** detail pages. This is the only specific reference made to objects that implement the ComplianceService.ICompliant interface and is only needed in order to create the Custom Buttons in Salesforce Classic. The following page for the Driver object defines a button that uses the generic ComplianceController.verify method:

```
<apex:page standardController="Driver__c"
    extensions="ComplianceController" action="{!verify}">
  <apex:pageMessages/>
  <apex:form>
    <apex:commandButton value="Cancel" action="{!cancel}"/>
  </apex:form>
</apex:page>
```

Now that we have seen how the compliance framework can be referenced throughout the rest of the application code, in the next section, we will summarize this implementation and understand the benefits this approach has had on how the user experience is delivered.

Summarizing the implementation of the compliance framework

Using an Apex Interface and the Factory pattern, a framework has been put into place within the application to ensure that the compliance logic is implemented consistently, and this is a simple matter of implementing the Domain class interface and placing the generic Lightning component on each Lightning page in order to enable the feature for other objects in the future.

> As this has been implemented as a service, it can easily be reused from a Batch Apex or Scheduled context as well.

Application Domain Layer

The following screenshot shows the **Compliance Checker** Lightning Component within the **Lightning App Builder** tool being placed on the **Driver** page:

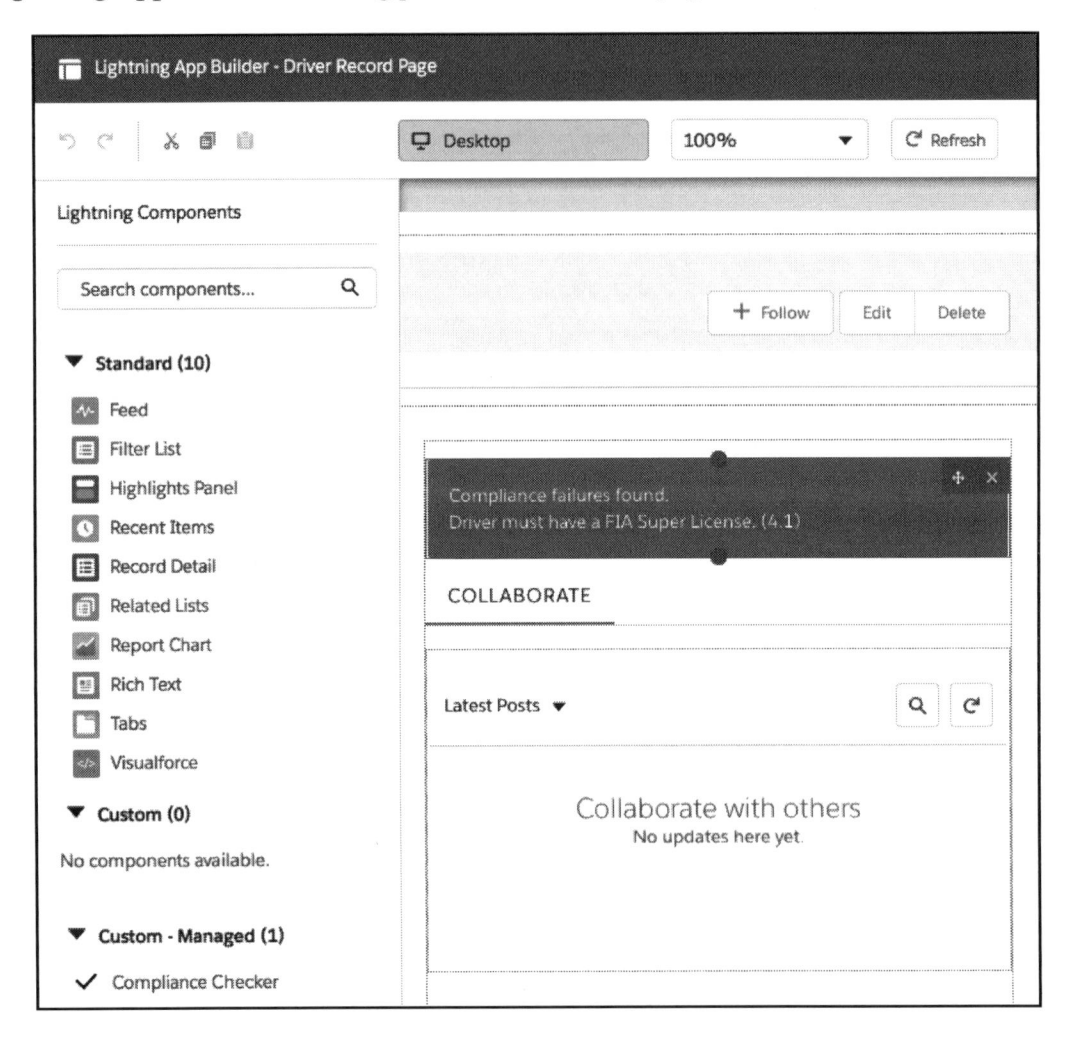

The following screenshot shows the **Compliance Checker** component on the **Driver** page. In Lightning Experience, there is no button; the component is embedded in the page and reacts to the field updates the user makes. So, the verification is performed immediately:

Chapter 6

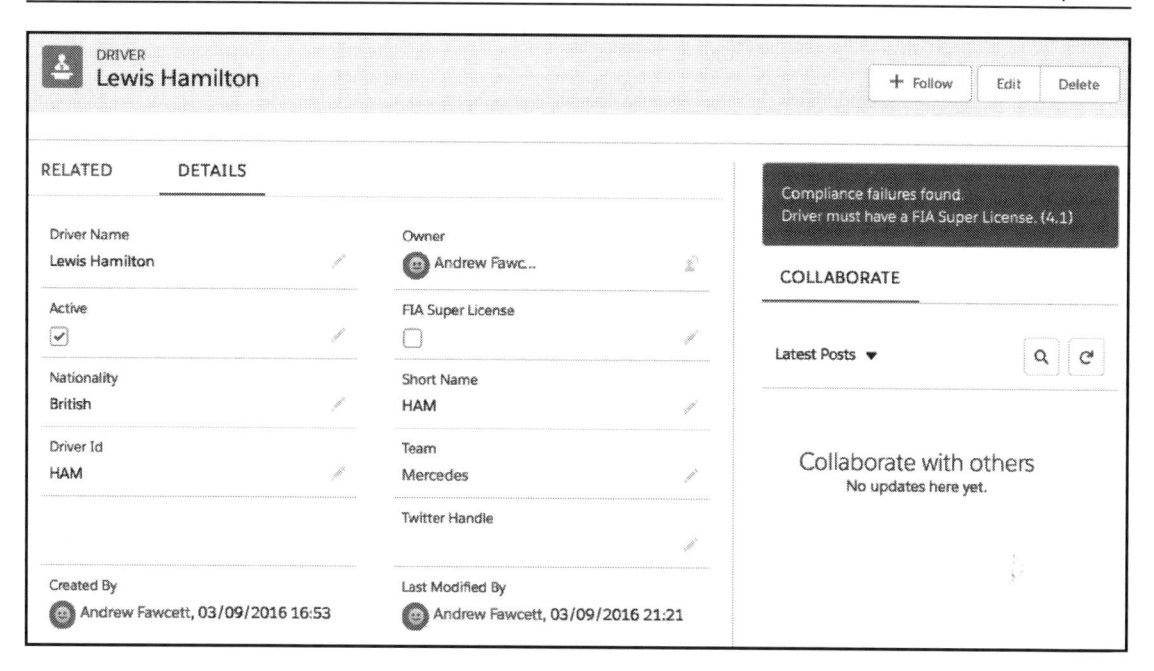

Salesforce Classic is an older user interface technology that has now been superseded by **Lightning** (as shown in the preceding screenshot). The following screenshots are useful if you are still working with Salesforce Classic with some of your customers and/or in your own organization. The following illustrates the **Verify Compliance** button on the **Driver** object. Ensure that the **FIA Super License** field is unchecked before clicking on the button:

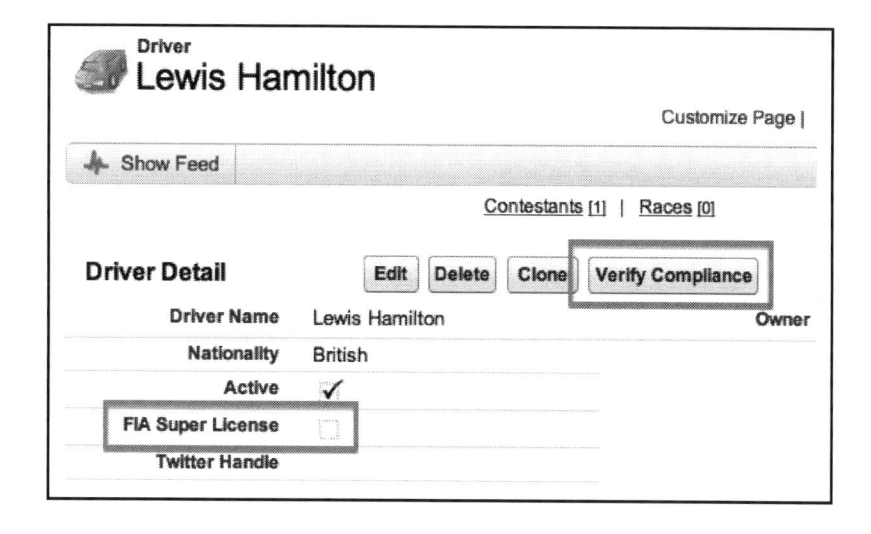

[227]

Application Domain Layer

The following errors should be displayed:

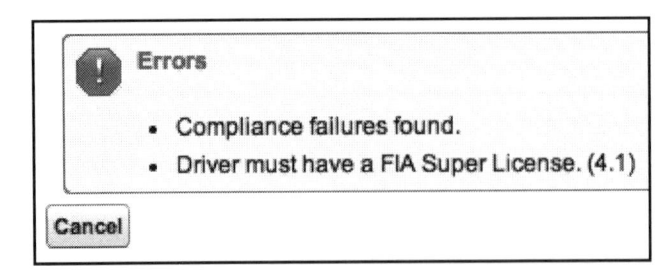

> **Errors**
> - Compliance failures found.
> - Driver must have a FIA Super License. (4.1)
>
> [Cancel]

The following screenshot shows the **Verify Compliance** button on the **Car** object:

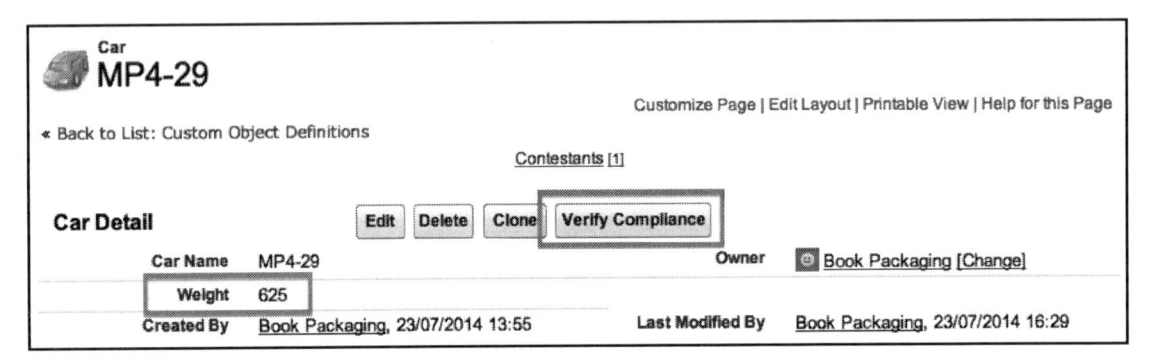

> **Car**
> **MP4-29**
>
> Customize Page | Edit Layout | Printable View | Help for this Page
>
> « Back to List: Custom Object Definitions
>
> Contestants [1]
>
> **Car Detail** [Edit] [Delete] [Clone] [Verify Compliance]
>
> Car Name: MP4-29
> Weight: 625
> Created By: Book Packaging, 23/07/2014 13:55
> Owner: Book Packaging [Change]
> Last Modified By: Book Packaging, 23/07/2014 16:29

The following errors are shown by the generic controller defined/created previously:

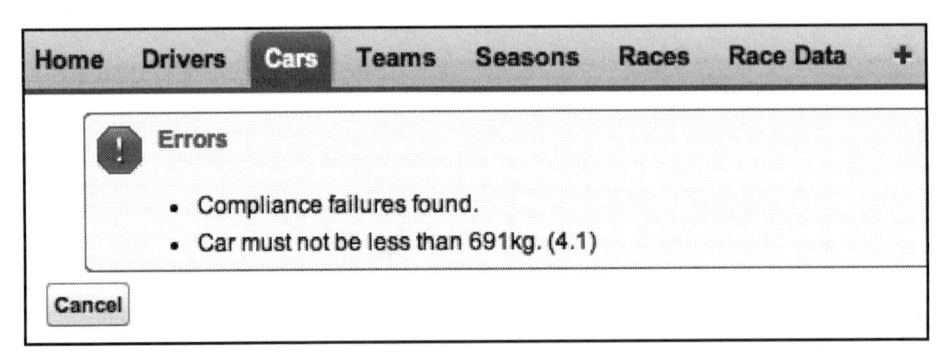

> Home | Drivers | **Cars** | Teams | Seasons | Races | Race Data | +
>
> **Errors**
> - Compliance failures found.
> - Car must not be less than 691kg. (4.1)
>
> [Cancel]

Now that we have seen how the Domain layer is applied to an application, in the next section, we will understand how to write tests for the Domain layer.

Testing the Domain layer

Testing your Domain code can be accomplished in the standard Lightning manner. Typically, test classes are named by suffixing `Test` to the end of the Domain class name, for example, `RacesTest`. Test methods have the option to test the Domain class code functionality either directly or indirectly.

Indirect testing is accomplished using only the DML and SOQL logic against the applicable Custom Objects and asserting the data and field errors arising from these operations. Here, there is no reference to your Domain class at all in the test code.

However, this only tests the Apex Trigger Domain class methods. For test methods that represent custom domain behaviors, you must create an instance of the Domain class. This section will illustrate examples of both indirect and direct testing approaches.

Unit testing

Although developing tests around the Service layer and related callers (controllers, batch, and so on) will also invoke the Domain layer logic, it is important to test as many scenarios specifically against the Domain layer as possible, passing in different configurations of record data to test both success and failure code paths and making sure that your Domain layer logic is as robust as possible. The principles of unit testing, in general, can be described as follows:

- The term **unit** refers to a small portion of application code that has inputs and outputs (including exceptions) that you want to ensure quality for as a developer. In OOP languages such as Apex, this could be an interface or public methods on a class or just a specific method.
- The unit **test code** for such a method focuses on invoking the method or interface in as many different combinations of inputs and expected outputs (including exceptions) as possible.
- It's **good practice** to write test code that uses as many inputs as possible and not just those you imagine the current callers may use. This ensures the unit of code being tested is robust enough for future scenarios. This can be quite important for Domain class code testing as this class's code protects the integrity of the customer's data.
- `Chapter 12`, *Unit Testing*, will go deeper into the principles of unit testing, including the ability to avoid the scope of your unit tests growing through dependencies.

Application Domain Layer

The testing of the Domain layer falls into the preceding definitions. The following sections illustrate the traditional and still very much valid approach to testing your Domain class code through setting up test data using DML and executing the code. In a later chapter, we will review an Apex Mocking framework (similar to **Mockito** in Java), which provides a much leaner and more targeted means to test your Domain code.

Test methods using DML and SOQL

To test the Apex Trigger methods of the Domain class, the traditional use of DML and SOQL can be applied alongside the use of the Apex runtime `DMLException` methods to assert not only the error message but also other details. The following Apex test method illustrates how to do this:

```
@IsTest
private static void testAddContestantNoneScheduled() {
  // Test data
  Season__c season =
    new Season__c(Name = '2014', Year__c = '2014');
  insert season;
  Driver__c driver =
    new Driver__c(
      Name = 'Lewis Hamilton', DriverId__c = '42');
  insert driver;
  Race__c race =
   new Race__c(Name = 'Spa',
      Status__c = 'In Progress',
      Season__c = season.Id);
  insert race;

  Test.startTest();
  try {
    // Insert Contestant to In Progress race
    Contestant__c contestant =
        new Contestant__c(
          Driver__c = driver.Id,
          Race__c = race.Id);
    insert contestant;
    System.assert(false, 'Expected exception');
  }
  catch (DMLException e) {
    System.assertEquals(1, e.getNumDml());
    System.assertEquals(
      'Contestants can only be added to Scheduled Races.',
      e.getDmlMessage(0));
    System.assertEquals(
```

```
      StatusCode.FIELD_CUSTOM_VALIDATION_EXCEPTION,
      e.getDmlType(0));
  }
  Test.stopTest();
}
```

The preceding error is a record-level error; the DMLException class also allows you to assert field-level information for field-level errors. The following code shows such a test assertion; note that the data setup code is not shown:

```
Test.startTest();
Try {
  contestant.Driver__c = anotherDriver.Id;
  update contestant;
  System.assert(false, 'Expected exception');
}
catch (DmlException e) {
  System.assertEquals(1, e.getNumDml());
  System.assertEquals(
    'You can only change drivers for scheduled races',
    e.getDmlMessage(0));
  System.assertEquals(Contestant__c.Driver__c,
    e.getDmlFields(0)[0]);
  System.assertEquals(
    StatusCode.FIELD_CUSTOM_VALIDATION_EXCEPTION,
    e.getDmlType(0));
}
Test.stopTest();
```

In this section, the Domain class logic was tested indirectly by observing the outcome of inserting and updating records into the database. This will only test methods associated with those operations. In the next section, we will see how to test custom Domain class methods.

Test methods using the Domain class methods

In order to test custom Domain class methods, an instance of the Domain class should be created in the test method, using test records created in memory or queried from the database having been inserted, as shown in the previous tests.

Application Domain Layer

The following example shows the `Contestants.awardChampionship` method being tested. Note that the test creates a temporary Unit Of Work, but does not commit the work. This is not strictly needed to assert the changes to the records, as the `Records` property can be used to access the changes and assert the correct value that has been assigned:

```
@IsTest
private static void testAddChampionshipPoints() {
  // Test data
  ChampionshipPoints__c championShipPoints =
    new ChampionshipPoints__c(
      Name = '1', PointsAwarded__c = 25);
  insert championShipPoints;
  Season__c season =
    new Season__c(Name = '2014', Year__c = '2014');
  insert season;
  Driver__c driver =
    new Driver__c(
      Name = 'Lewis Hamilton', DriverId__c = '42');
  insert driver;
  Race__c race =
    new Race__c(
      Name = 'Spa', Status__c  = 'Scheduled',
      Season__c = season.Id);
  insert race;
  Contestant__c contestant =
    new Contestant__c(
      Driver__c = driver.Id, Race__c = race.Id);
  insert contestant;
  race.Status__c = 'Finished';
  update race;
  contestant.RacePosition__c = 1;
  update contestant;

  Test.startTest();
    Contestants contestants =
      new Contestants(new List<Contestant__c> { contestant });
  contestants.awardChampionshipPoints(
    Application.UnitOfWork.newInstance());
  System.assertEquals(25, ((Contestant__c)
      contestants.Records[0]).ChampionshipPoints__c);
  Test.stopTest();
}
```

Chapter 6

Performing SOQL and DML in tests is expensive in terms of CPU time and adds to the overall time it takes to execute all application tests, which becomes important once you start to consider **Continuous Integration** (covered in a later chapter); for example, whether it is always necessary to commit data updates from the Domain layer, as Service layer tests might also be performing these types of operations and asserting the results.

Calling the Domain layer

The Domain layer is positioned with respect to visibility and dependency below the Service layer. This, in practice, means that Domain classes should not be called directly from the execution context code, such as Visualforce Controllers, Lightning Component Controllers, or Batch Apex, as it is the Service layer's responsibility to be the sole entry point for business process application logic.

That being said, we saw that the Domain layer also encapsulates an object's behavior as records are manipulated by binding Apex Trigger events to methods on the Domain class. As such, Apex Triggers technically form another point of invocation.

Finally, there is a third caller type for the Domain layer, and this is another Domain class. Restrict your Domain class callers to the following contexts only:

- **Apex Triggers**: This calls via the `fflib_SObjectDomain.handleTrigger` method.
- **Service layer**: This layer directly creates an instance of a Domain class via the new operator or through the Domain factory approach discussed earlier in this chapter. Typically, the Domain class custom methods are called in this context.
- **Domain layer**: Other Domain classes can call other Domain classes; for example, the `Races` Domain class can have some functionality it implements that also requires the use of a method on the `Contestants` Domain class.

> Note that it is entirely acceptable to have a Domain class with no Service class code referencing it at all, such as in the case where the Domain class solely implements the code for use in an Apex Trigger context and doesn't contain any custom Domain methods. Then, the only invocation of the Domain class will be indirect via the trigger context.

Application Domain Layer

Service layer interactions

While implementing the compliance framework earlier in this chapter, we saw how a Domain class can be dynamically created within a generic service method. Typically, Domain classes are created directly. In this section, we will see a couple of examples of these.

The following code shows the Domain class constructor being passed records from a Selector class, which returns `List<Contestant__c>` for the purposes of this chapter. Notice that the Unit Of Work is created and passed to the Domain class custom method so that this method can also register work of its own to be subsequently committed to the database:

```
public class ContestantService {
  public static void awardChampionshipPoints(
    Set<Id>contestantIds) {
      fflib_SObjectUnitOfWork uow =
         Application.UnitOfWork.newInstance();

      // Apply championship points to given contestants
      Contestants contestants =
          new Contestants(
             new ContestantsSelector().selectById(contestantIds));
      contestants.awardChampionshipPoints(uow);

      uow.commitWork();
   }
}
```

You might have noticed that this example reworks the Service example from the previous chapter by refactoring the code and calculating the points closer to the object for which the code directly applies by basically moving the original code to the Domain class.

This second example also reworks the code from the previous chapter to leverage the Domain layer. In this case, the `RaceService` class also implements an `awardChampionshipPoints` method. This can also benefit from the `Contestants` Domain class method. Note how easy it is to reuse methods between the Service and Domain layers, as both ensure that their methods and interactions are bulkified:

```
public class RaceService {

   public void awardChampionshipPoints(Set<Id>raceIds) {
      fflib_SObjectUnitOfWork uow =
         Application.UnitOfWork.newInstance();

      List<Contestant__c> contestants =
```

```
            new List<Contestant__c>();    for(Race__c race :
            new RacesSelector().selectByIdWithContestants(raceIds)) {
            contestants.addAll(race.Contestants__r);
        }
        // Delegate to Contestant Domain class
        new Contestants(contestants).awardChampionshipPoints(uow);

        // Commit work
        uow.commitWork();
    }
}
```

The Service layer is not the only layer that interacts with the Domain layer. In the next section, we will see how classes within the Domain Layer can interact with each other.

Domain layer interactions

In the following example (also included in the sample code for this chapter), a new Custom Object is created to represent the teams that participate in the races. The **Driver** object has gained a new **Lookup** field called **Team** to associate the drivers with their teams.

Leveraging the compliance framework built earlier, a **Verify Compliance** button for the **Team** records is also added to provide a means to check certain aspects of the team that are compliant (such as the maximum distance cars can cover during testing), as well as whether all the drivers in this team are still compliant (reusing the existing code).

> This will be done by adding the compliance verification code in the new `Teams` Domain class call and by delegating logic to the `Drivers` Domain class method to implement the same logic for drivers within the team.

The following components have been added to the application to support this example:

- A new **Team** object and tab
- A new **Testing Distance** number field with a length of **6** on the **Team** object
- A new **Team** lookup field on the **Driver** object
- A new `Teams` Domain class

Application Domain Layer

> **TIP:** You don't always have to create an Apex Trigger that calls the `fflib_SObjectDomain.triggerHandler` method if you don't plan on overriding any of the Apex Trigger event handler methods.

Being able to call between the Domain layer classes permits the driver compliance-checking code to continue to be reused at the **Driver** level as well as from the **Team** level. This Domain class example shows the `Teams` Domain class calling the `Drivers` Domain class:

```
public class Teams extends fflib_SObjectDomain
  implements ComplianceService.ICompliant {
  public List<ComplianceService.VerifyResult> verifyCompliance() {
    // Verify Team compliance
    List<ComplianceService.VerifyResult>teamVerifyResults =
      new List<ComplianceService.VerifyResult>();
    for(Team__c team : (List<Team__c>) Records) {
      ComplianceService.VerifyResulttestingDistance =
        new ComplianceService.VerifyResult();
      testingDistance.ComplianceCode = '22.5';
      testingDistance.RecordId = team.Id;
      testingDistance.passed = team.TestingDistance__c!=null ?
        team.TestingDistance__c <= 15000 : true;
      testingDistance.failureReason = testingDistance.passed ?
        null : 'Testing exceeded 15,000km';
      teamVerifyResults.add(testingDistance);
    }

    // Verify associated Drivers compliance
    teamVerifyResults.addAll(
      new Drivers(
        new DriversSelector().selectDriversByTeam(
          new Map<Id, SObject(Records).keySet()))
            .verifyCompliance());

    return teamVerifyResults;
  }
}
```

> The bulkification guideline applied to the Domain layer is being leveraged in the preceding code, as the `Drivers` Domain class logic was reused directly, with no changes, from the `Teams` Domain class. Also, note that the implementation of the `Drivers` Domain class was, and is, still unaware of the split of drivers by team.

Chapter 6

The following screenshot shows the new **Team** object and **Compliance Checker** component added to the **Team** page using **Lightning App Builder**. The team record and related driver records have compliance issues. For the team record, there is an invalid **Testing Distance** value greater than **15,000 km**. The **FIA Super License** field on the **Driver** record for **Lewis Hamilton**, which is unchecked, is not shown:

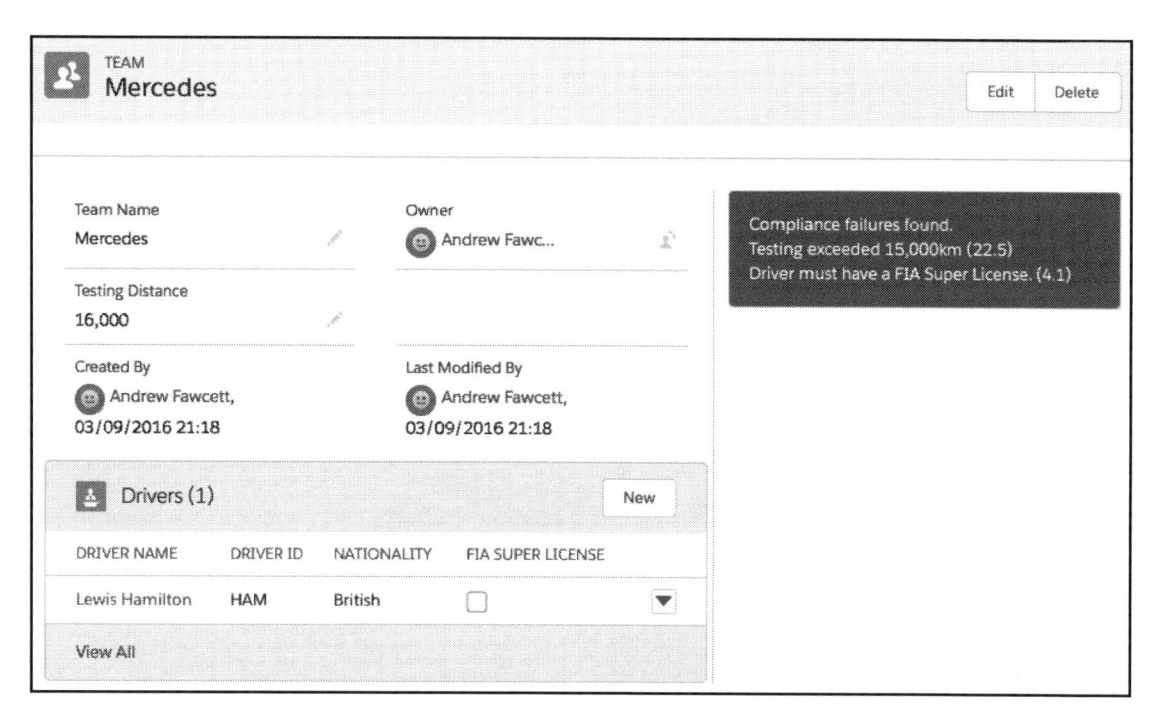

As we conclude this chapter, the final step is to package the changes in a new version of the FormulaForce package, as described in the next section.

Updating the FormulaForce package

As described in `Chapter 1`, *Building and Publishing Your Application*, utilize the source code provided with this chapter to create a new version of your package and install it in a test org. Keep in mind that the new **Verify Compliance** button added in this chapter has been added to the **Driver** layout since the last release of the package. Since layouts are non-upgradable components, this will need to be added manually after installation in the test org when upgrading, as will any new Custom Fields added throughout this chapter.

Application Domain Layer

You would typically notify users of post installation steps through your upgrade and installation guide. You will also have to ensure that users are made aware of any Lightning Components as part of your solution. As previously noted, packaging Lightning pages creates a dependency on the My Domain feature having been enabled by the customer.

> **TIP**: If you package Lightning pages with your components on them, this will require your users to have the My Domain feature enabled and thus potentially limit the number of customers your package can be installed with. This is true, especially for those who have not yet fully adopted Lightning Experience.

Summary

In this chapter, you've learned a new way to factor business logic beyond encapsulating it in the Service layer—one that aligns the logic—implementing the validation changes and interpretation of an object's data through a Domain class named accordingly. As with the Service layer, this approach makes such code easy to find for new and experienced developers working on the code base.

A Domain class combines the traditional Apex Trigger logic and custom Domain logic, such as the calculation of championship points for a contestant or the verification of compliance rules against the cars, drivers, and teams.

By utilizing Apex classes, the ability to start leveraging OOP practices emerges, using interfaces and factory methods to implement functional subsystems within the application to deliver not only implementation speed, consistency, and reuse, but also help support a common user experience. Domain classes can call between each other when required to encompass the behavior of related child components, such as drivers within a team.

Finally, when testing the Domain layer, keep in mind the best practice used for unit testing to test as much of the code in isolation with varied use cases and data combinations despite the fact that other tests, such as those from the Service layer and other callers, will also exercise the code paths, though this is likely to be with less variation.

In the next chapter, we will complete the trio of patterns from Martin Fowler by taking a deeper look at the Selector pattern. This has already been utilized a few times in this chapter when reading data from the various Custom Objects used in the application.

Application Selector Layer

Apex is a very expressive language that is used to perform calculations and transformations of data entered by the user or records read from your Custom Objects. However, **SOQL** also holds within it a great deal of expressiveness to select, filter, and aggregate information without having to resort to Apex. SOQL is also a powerful way to traverse relationships (up to five levels) in one statement, which would otherwise leave developers in other platforms performing several queries.

Quite often, the same or similar SOQL statements are required in different execution contexts and business logic scenarios throughout an application. Performing these queries inline, as and when needed, can rapidly become a maintenance problem as you extend and adapt your object schema, fields, and relationships.

This chapter introduces a new type of Apex class, the **Selector**, based on **Martin Fowler's Mapper pattern**, which aims to **encapsulate** the SOQL query logic, making it easy to access, maintain, and reuse such logic throughout the application.

The following aspects will be covered in this chapter:

- Introducing the Selector layer pattern
- Implementation design guidelines
- The Selector class template
- Implementing the standard query logic
- Implementing the custom query logic
- Introducing the Selector factory

Application Selector Layer

Introducing the Selector layer pattern

The following is Martin Fowler's definition of the **Data Mapper layer** on which the **Selector layer** pattern is based (http://martinfowler.com/eaaCatalog/dataMapper.html):

> *"A layer of Mappers (473) that moves data between objects and a database while keeping them independent of each other and the Mapper itself."*

In Martin's definition, he is referring to objects as those resulting from the instantiation of classes within an OO language such as Java or Apex. Of course, in the Force.com world, this has a slightly ambiguous meaning, but is more commonly thought of as the Standard or Custom Object holding the record data.

One of the great features of the Apex language is that it automatically injects object types in the language that mirror the definition of the Custom Objects you define. These so-called **SObjects** create a type-safe bond between the code and the database schema, though you can also leverage **Dynamic Apex** and **Dynamic SOQL** to change these references at runtime if needed.

Essentially, SObjects are the native in-memory representation of the data read from the database. Thus, a traditional **Plain Old Java Object** (**POJO**) approach in Apex is not strictly required to expose the record field data. Additionally, through relationship fields such as `Race__c.Drivers__r`, related records can be accessed without the need for the usual POJO relationship accessor methods or properties.

For this reason, the role of **Apex classes** that represent the Selector layer code described in this chapter is much more focused on encapsulating the application's SOQL queries, promoting **reuse** and **data consistency** rather than mapping information from the database into memory.

> You might consider the Domain classes as data wrappers around `SObject`, as they contain a list of SObjects. However, this is not the intent; the Domain class methods purely expose behavioral methods. The `Records` property exposes the `SObject` list so that callers can access the field data in the usual manner.

The following diagram illustrates where Apex classes implementing the Selector layer fit in terms of its interaction and reuse within the Service and Domain layers, as well as other execution contexts such as **Batch Apex**:

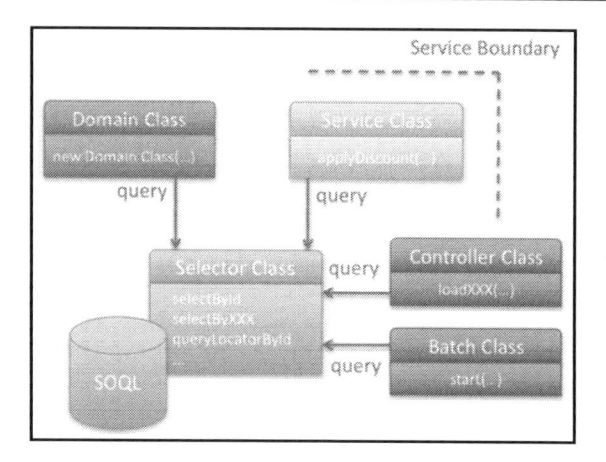

As you can see, for the most part, the Selector is a layer that exists conceptually below the Service layer (under the Service boundary), though it can be reused from execution contexts that perform database queries, such as Batch Apex and Controllers.

Implementing design guidelines

The methods in the Selector classes encapsulate common SOQL queries made by the application, such as `selectById`, as well as more business-related methods, such as `selectByTeam`. This helps the developers who consume the Selector classes to identify the correct methods to use for the business requirement and avoids replication of SOQL queries throughout the application.

Each method also has some standard characteristics, such as the `SObject` fields selected by the queries executed, regardless of the method called. The overall aim is to allow the caller to focus on the record data returned and not how it was read from the database.

Sharing conventions

As stated in the previous chapter, it is good practice to explicitly indicate which sharing mode you want your query logic to run in by default. Thus, every Selector class should use the `inherited sharing` keyword, as shown in the following example. If you follow the convention outlined for your Service class, the `with sharing` context will be inherited. The following example shows the best practice to always define `inherited sharing`:

```
public inherited sharing class RacesSelector
```

By using inherited sharing, this does allow for all the queries in the Selector class to be called within a `without sharing` context when this is enabled by the calling class. However, if you consider sharing as a form of record filtering, much like the logic expressed in the `WHERE` clause, then the encapsulation of this type of filter criteria also truly belongs as an internal implementation concern within the Selector class. So, if you require that some SOQL queries are executed within the Selector code using the `without sharing` context and others the inherited context, then I recommend using the Elevate pattern within the Selector class, as described in the *Sharing rules enforcement* section of `Chapter 5`, *Application Service Layer*. One example of the elevate pattern is a query that summarizes race data when some of the race data may not be visible to the current user, but the result must still represent all race data.

Naming conventions

By now, you're starting to get the idea about naming conventions. The Selector classes and methods borrow guidelines from other layers with a few tweaks. Consider the following naming conventions when writing the Selector code:

- **Class names**: In naming a Selector class, you typically follow the same convention as a Domain class, taking the plural name of the object it is associated with and appending the word `Selector` at the end. However, you can group common cross-object queries into a single module scoped class, for example, `InvoicingSelector`. The following lists some good and bad examples of this convention:
    - Some bad examples are `RaceSOQLHelper` and `SOQLHelper`.
    - Some good examples are `RacesSelector`, `DriversSelector`, and `RacingAnalyticsSelector`.
- **Method names**: The `select` prefix is a good way to express the shared purpose of the Selector methods, followed by a description of the primary criteria and/or relationships used. As with the Service and Domain methods, avoid repeating terms already used in the class name:
    - Some bad examples are `getRecords`, `getDrivers`, `loadDrivers`, `selectDriversById`, and `selectRacesAndContestants`.
    - Some good examples are `selectById`, `selectByTeam`, `selectByIdWithContestants`, and `selectByIdWithContestantsAndDrivers`.

- **Method signatures**: Selector methods typically return a `Map`, `List`, or `QueryLocator` method exposing the resulting SObjects, thereby supporting the bulkification needs of the platform and other layers such as the Domain class constructors and Batch Apex. Method parameters reflect the parameterized aspects of the `WHERE` clause; again, these should also be bulkified whenever it is applicable to do so:
    - These examples are bad because they either do not accept lists or their method names are not descriptive enough:

    ```
    selectById(Id recordId)
    DriverSelector.select(Set<Id>teamIds)
    Database.QueryLocatorqueryForBatch(Set<Id> ids)
    ```

    - These examples are good because they take lists that support bulkification:

    ```
    selectById(Set<Id> raceIds)
    selectByTeam(Set<Id> teamIds)
    ```

In this section, we covered some subtle, but important, naming conventions in how you name your methods and define the parameters they take. Paying attention to these details is important to how other developers understand and consume the features of a given selector class. In the following section, we will discuss how this applies to bulkifcaiton, which is a common best practice on the Lightning Platform.

Bulkification

As you can see, based on the method naming and signature convention examples, as with the Service and Domain layers, it's important to consider that, in most cases, the caller will want to honor the bulkification best practices. Make sure that the method return types and parameter types are list types—those such as `Set`, `List`, `Map`, `QueryLocator`, or `Iterator` can be used.

Record order consistency

Quite often, the `order by` clause is overlooked when writing SOQL queries, and this can lead to client/controller developers implementing this themselves. The default ordering of the platform is non-deterministic, though it sometimes appears to reflect the insert order, so the absence of an `order by` clause can often go unnoticed in testing. By using a Selector, you can apply a default order sequence to all Selector methods.

Returning `Map<Id, SObject>` instead of `List<SObject>` might seem like a good way to help callers process the information. Maps in Apex have a predictable iterator order; however, it is not clear from the documentation whether this is the order in which items are added to the map. If you're concerned about this, keep in mind that the result of using the `order by` clause in the Selector might be affected if `Map` is used. Given the ease with which maps by SObject ID are created by passing the list into the `Map` constructor, it's often best to leave this option to wrap or not wrap the list returned up to the calling code.

Querying fields consistently

It is a good practice to avoid re-querying the same record(s) more than once within the same Apex execution if this can be avoided. Rather than repeating queries for the same record solely to query different fields, it is desirable to factor code such that it can pass the queried data as parameters from one method to another, for example, from a Service method to a Domain method.

However, this practice can become problematic because, when using SOQL, the developer must explicitly list the fields needed at the time the statement is executed, typically stating only those fields needed by the most immediate code path ahead.

Later, as the code evolves, the `SObject` data is passed between methods, particularly shared code. Runtime exceptions can occur if an attempt is made to read from a field that was not originally included in the initial SOQL. This results in the same code executing successfully in one scenario, but failing in another, due to SOQL statements for the same data being inconsistently expressed by the developers in separate locations of the application.

For example, consider the fact that the `Contestants.awardChampionshipPoint` Domain class method is updated to utilize the `RaceTime__c` field as well as the `RacePosition__c` field. This method is called from the `ContestantService` and `RaceService` classes. Ignoring the Selector concept for a moment, the following change to `ContestantService` will work just fine to meet this new requirement:

```
Contestants contestants =
    new Contestants(
 [select Id, RacePosition__c, RaceTime__c
     from Contestant__c order by RacePosition__c]);
contestants.awardChampionshipPoints(uow);
```

However, if left unchanged, the following code from the `RaceService` class will cause the same method to fail with an `SObject row was retrieved via SOQL without querying the requested field: Contestant__c.RaceTime__c` exception:

```
List<Contestant__c> contestants = new List<Contestant__c>();
for(Race__c race :
    [select Id,
        (Select RacePosition__c from Contestants__r)
     from Race__c where Id in :ids])
contestants.addAll(race.Contestants__r);
new Contestants(contestants).awardChampionshipPoints(uow);
```

Also, note that the `order by` clause is missing from this example, but specified in the previous one; therefore, in this case, the order of the records returned is non-deterministic. These last two examples illustrate that the records passed to the shared `Contestants` Domain class have the potential to vary in order by caller. This could give rise to unexpected behavior if the Domain class logic is dependent on the order.

These are the two possible ways to fix these inconsistencies, though neither is ideal:

- Update the `awardChampionshipPoints` method to have it perform its own SOQL query, and ensure that it always gets the information it needs regardless of what was initially passed into the Domain class constructor. While this is arguably more contained, it is wasteful in regard to SOQL queries and performance.
- Search for SOQL statements across the application code and update the corresponding SOQL logic in each area (including relationship sub-selects).

Of course, ensuring that both areas have adequate unit and integration testing also reduces the risk somewhat, but neither really helps increase the performance or encourage SOQL reuse. One of the benefits of the Selector pattern is to encapsulate a list of commonly used fields such that all the methods on the Selector return SObjects populated with a consistent set of fields that can be relied on throughout the application code, as long as the Selector is used to query the records.

> Querying more fields can generally be at odds with the desire to maintain a low **heap** and/or **client response size** when querying a large number of records in a single execution context, particularly if the Selector is returning queried data for display in the client. In a later section of this chapter, we will see how it is possible to use an Apex data class to represent only the field data queried.

Application Selector Layer

In this section, we understood the implications of being inconsistent in the way in which your code makes queries to the same object with respect to the fields included in the query. This leads us into the next part of this chapter, which introduces a base type that can be used to ensure your code avoids this pitfall and also reduces the amount of SOQL logic you need to write.

The Selector class template

A Selector class, like the Domain class, utilizes inheritance to gain some standard functionality. In this case, the base class, delivered through the **FinancialForce.com Enterprise Apex Patterns** library, `fflib_SObjectSelector`, is used to reduce the coding overhead in performing queries, adding some standard behaviors, and supporting best practices. These will be discussed in further detail throughout this chapter.

A basic example of a Selector class for querying **Races** is as follows:

```
public inherited sharing class RacesSelector
   extends fflib_SObjectSelector {

   public List<Schema.SObjectField> getSObjectFieldList() {
      return new List<Schema.SObjectField> {
         Race__c.Id,
         Race__c.Name,
         Race__c.Status__c,
         Race__c.Season__c,
         Race__c.FastestLapBy__c,
         Race__c.PollPositionLapTime__c,
         Race__c.TotalDNFs__c };
   }

   public Schema.SObjectTypegetSObjectType() {
      return Race__c.sObjectType;
   }
}
```

The preceding code uses a base class that uses Dynamic SOQL to implement the features described in this chapter. In some cases, one potential disadvantage this can bring is that references to the fields are made without the Apex compiler knowing about them, and, as such, when you attempt to delete or rename fields, no warning is given that the given field is already referenced. To avoid this in the preceding case, the `SObjectField` reference to the field is used, which is obtained by stating the `SObject` name followed by the field name separated by a period. This is somewhat like a static property on the `SObject` type. This approach ensures that the platform knows the class is referencing the fields, even though they are being used in a dynamic SOQL context.

With this minimal example, the following standard query can be made by leveraging the `selectSObjectsById` base class method. This method takes the information provided by the preceding methods and constructs a SOQL query dynamically and executes it via `Database.executeQuery`:

```
List<Race__c> races = (List<Race__c>)
    new RacesSelector().selectSObjectsById(raceIds);
```

> **TIP**
> Note that the `fflib_SObjectSelector.selectSObjectsById` base class method performs a number of features, described later in this chapter. Also, note that an instance of the Selector was created but was not actually stored. Using an instance of this class permits the use of base classes to inherit behavior. Additional benefits of using instances of Selectors are covered later in this chapter when we discuss **Selector factories** and testing.

The preceding Selector method example dynamically creates the following SOQL:

```
SELECT
    Name, TotalDNFs__c, Status__c, Season__c, Id,
    PollPositionLapTime__c, FastestLapBy__c
    FROM Race__c
WHERE id in :idSet ORDER BY Name
```

Application Selector Layer

As we progress through this chapter, you will see how the preceding SOQL is generated by using the features of the `fflib_SObjectSelector` base class. The following table shows some of the key base class methods of the `fflib_SObjectSelector` class that are available to your Selector methods and also those that can be overridden:

Method	Modifier	Purpose
`getSObjectType`	Abstract	Tells the base class which SObject is being described.
`getSObjectFieldList`	Abstract	Returns a list of common fields used when build queries are used in this selector class.
`selectSObjectsById`	Public	Executes a dynamically generated SOQL query that selects the fields specified by the `getSObjectFieldList` method.
`getOrderBy`	Virtual	Optionally override this to change the default order by applying to queries generated or executed by the base class.
`getSObjectFieldSetList`	Virtual	Optionally provide a list of Field Sets for the base class query generator to consider when generating a list of fields to query.
`newQueryFactory`	Public	Provides an object-oriented means to further customize the queries generated by the base class before executing them.

Note that the `getSObjectType` and `getSObjectFieldList` methods are abstract and therefore must be implemented as minimum, as per the previous example. The following sections describe these methods in further detail. Do also take some further time to explore further methods and associated code comments in the base class code.

Implementing the standard query logic

The previous Selector usage example required a cast of the list to be returned to a list of `Race__c` objects, which is not ideal. To improve this, you can easily add a new method to the class to provide a more specific version of the base class method, as follows:

```
public List<Race__c> selectById(Set<Id>raceIds){
  return (List<Race__c>) selectSObjectsById(raceIds);
}
```

Therefore, the usage code now looks like this:

```
List<Race__c> races =
   new RacesSelector().selectById(raceIds);
```

By using a selector for querying races, the preceding code is much smaller and therefore easier to read by other developers. In the next section, we will discover what other standard features are provided by the `fflib_SObjectSelector` class.

Standard features of the Selector base class

The `fflib_SObjectSelector` base class contains additional functionality to provide more query consistency and integration with the platform. This applies to the preceding `selectSObjectsById` method as well as your own. The following sections highlight each of these features.

You can, of course, extend the standard features of this base class further. Perhaps there is something you want all your queries to consider, a common field or aspect to your schema design, or a feature that is common to most of your selectors. In this case, create your own base class and have your selectors extend that, as follows:

```
public inherited sharing abstract class ApplicationSelector
    extends fflib_SObjectSelector
{
  // Add your common methods here
}
public class RacesSelector
    extends ApplicationSelector
{
  // Methods using methods from both base classes
}
```

The preceding code samples illustrate how and where to place code that is both common (in the `ApplicationSelector` class) and specific (in the `RaceSelector` class) to your query logic throughout your application. In the following sections, we will use the `ApplicationSelector` class to customize the behavior of all Selector classes.

Enforcing object and field-level security

Salesforce requires developers to implement the **object read security** and **field-level read security** checks when querying. This typically uses the methods on the `SObjectDescribe` and `SObjectFieldDescribe` Apex runtime types. The following sections describe the `fflib_SObjectSelector` base class support with respect to this.

Default behavior

By default, the base class methods in the `fflib_SObjectSelector` base class automatically perform object read security. The ability of the base class to enforce field-level read security is also available but is not enforced by default.

In both cases, if enforcement is enabled and user object or field-level read permissions have not been granted for the object or fields referenced in the `getSObjectType` and `getSObjectFieldSetList` methods, an exception will be thrown.

> The `WITH SECURITY_ENFORCED` keyword has recently been added to the SOQL syntax. At the time of writing, it is in Beta status. Including this keyword in queries essentially performs the same security checks as described previously, but is implemented by the platform for you when the query is executed. In theory, the `fflib_SObjectSelector` and `fflib_QueryFactory` classes could be updated to utilize this feature once it is generally available without changes to their caller's assumptions with respect to object and Field-level security. The benefit of this would be less complexity in these classes and the calling code will leverage the natural optimization this brings over these classes having to make such checks themselves. As this feature is still in Beta, the community supporting these base classes has yet to make this change at the time of writing. Regardless of the base class support, if you are writing entirely manual queries in your Selector and wish to easily support checking object and field-level security, this is something to keep in mind.

Overriding the default behavior

You may wish to disable the aforementioned default enforcement in cases where objects are read by the application code on behalf of the user; for example, reading the race data to update other areas of the application on behalf of the user. Such access is often referred to as *system-level* access. In these cases, you may not wish to have this check enforced.

Allowing this enforcement check to be executed in some cases may not be desirable since, as demonstrated in the preceding example, it then requires users to be granted access to the underlying race data object in order to use aspects of the application that read but do not display race data to the user. Another motivation for disabling the selector default behavior would be a preference to code these checks in your controller logic more explicitly.

Constructor parameters provided by the fflib_SObjectSelector class allow each Selector class to control whether security enforcement is enabled. This is also available to any code instantiating a Selector class, allowing this decision to be made on a per use case basis; for example, when the selector is used within a Controller class.

To make it easier to configure the fflib_SObjectSelector class throughout the application, as well as to provide a means to establish a place for shared or common Selector logic code, a new base class can be created as follows:

```
public inherited sharing abstract class ApplicationSelector
   extends fflib_SObjectSelector {

    public ApplicationSelector() {
        this(false);
    }

    public ApplicationSelector(Boolean includeFieldSetFields) {
        // Disable the default base class read security checking
        //   in preference to explicit checking elsewhere
        this(includeFieldSetFields, false, false);
    }

    public ApplicationSelector(
        Boolean includeFieldSetFields,
        Boolean enforceCRUD,
        Boolean enforceFLS) {
        // Disable sorting of selected fields to aid debugging
        //   (performance optimization)
        super(
           includeFieldSetFields, enforceCRUD, enforceFLS, false);
    }
}
```

Application Selector Layer

The preceding sample also leverages another configuration parameter of the `fflib_SObjectSelector` base class, the `sortSelectFields` parameter. This has been added to allow disablement of the sorting of the field names while building the SOQL queries. While this can aid debugging, it does have a performance overhead. For backward compatibility, the base class retains this behavior but allows for it to be disabled optionally. The Selector classes in this book extended the `ApplicationSelector` class instead of the standard `fflib_SObjectSelector` class:

```
public inherited sharing class RacesSelector
    extends ApplicationSelector {
```

> Note that the approach described in this section essentially requires that the developer takes over exclusive responsibility for implementing object and field-level security checking themselves. In advanced use cases, this may be preferable when a query contains a mixture of fields that you want to perform field-level security on and some you do not (that is, those the code needs to read, but are never required by the user). This will be discussed in further detail in a later chapter.

When using base types in any programming language, it is important to understand what behavior they are providing and accept or reject it for your needs. In this section, we were able to adjust the base behavior to suit our needs with respect to security.

Ordering

As mentioned in the Naming conventions section, having a default order to records is important so as to avoid the random non-deterministic behavior of the platform SOQL engine. The `selectSObjectById` base class method calls the `getOrderBy` method to determine which field(s) to use in order to order the records returned from the Selector.

The default behavior is to use the `Name` field (if available, otherwise `CreatedByDate` is used). As such, the previous usage is already ordering by `Name` without further coding. If you wish to change this, override the method as follows. This example is used by the `ContestantsSelector` class to ensure that contestants are always queried in the order of season, race, and their race position:

```
public override String getOrderBy() {
    return 'Race__r.Season__r.Name, Race__r.Name, RacePosition__c';
}
```

Later in this chapter, you will see how custom Selector methods can be constructed; these have the option of using the `getOrderBy` method. This allows some methods to use a different `order by` clause other than the default if you wish to do so.

Field Sets

As discussed in `Chapter 2`, *Leveraging Platform Features,* utilization of the Field Sets platform feature is key to ensuring that your application is strongly aligned with the customization capabilities that your application's users expect. However, you might be wondering what this has to do with querying data. Well, even though most of our discussions around this feature will focus on the use of it in a UI context, the additional Custom Fields added to the subscriber org still need to be queried in order for them to be displayed; otherwise, an exception will occur just the same as if you had failed to query a packaged field.

To use this feature, you need to override the `getSObjectFieldSetList` method and construct the Selector with the `includeFieldSetFields` parameter. The default constructor sets this parameter to false so that, in general, the **Field Sets** fields are not included. The following example assumes a field set on the **Race** object called `SeasonOverview` (included in the source code of this chapter):

Field Sets			
Action	Field Label	API Name	Where is this used?
Edit | Del	Season Overview	fforce__SeasonOverview	Used when displaying Race details on the Season overview page.

The following code illustrates the configuration of this feature (note that the logic in the base class also ensures that if the subscriber adds your own packaged fields to the Field Set, such fields are only added to the SOQL statement field list once):

```
public RacesSelector() {
  super();
}

public RacesSelector(Boolean includeFieldSetFields) {
  super(includeFieldSetFields);
}

public override List<Schema.FieldSet>getSObjectFieldSetList() {
  return new List<Schema.FieldSet>
    { SObjectType.Race__c.FieldSets.SeasonOverview };
}
```

Field Sets are a key feature for your customers to enable extensibility within your logic and user interfaces. This allows them to have your application understand Custom Fields they add to objects in order to extend your application's data storage needs for their own purposes. In the next section, we will take a look at another key platform feature that extends the data model in order to support Multi-Currency use cases that some of your customers may have.

Multi-Currency

As discussed in Chapter 2, *Leveraging Platform Features*, enabling and referencing certain platform features can create dependencies on your package, which require your customers to also enable those features prior to installation, and this might not always be desirable. One such feature is **Multi-Currency**. Once this is enabled, every object gains a CurrencyISOCode field; it then also appears on layouts, reports, and so on. Salesforce ensures that subscribers are fully aware of the implications before enabling it.

If you want to leverage it in your application (but do not think it will be something that all your customers will require), you have the option to reference this field using Dynamic Apex and Dynamic SOQL. It is in this latter area that the fflib_SObjectSelector base class provides some assistance.

> **TIP**
> You might want to consider the approach described here when working with Personal Accounts, as certain fields on the **Account** object are only present if this feature is enabled.

If you explicitly listed the CurrencyISOCode field in your getSObjectFieldList method, you will, therefore, bind your code and the package that contains it to this platform feature. Instead, what the base class does is use the UserInfo.isMultiCurrencyOrganization method to dynamically include this field in the SOQL query that it executes. Note that you still need to utilize **Dynamic Apex** to retrieve the field value, as shown in the following code:

```
List<Team__c> teams = (List<Team__c>)
    new TeamsSelector().selectSObjectsById(teamIds);
for(Team__c team : teams) {
    String teamCurrency =
        UserInfo.isMultiCurrencyOrganization() ?
          (String) team.get('CurrencyIsoCode') :
          UserInfo.getDefaultCurrency();
}
```

For Domain logic, you might want to put a common method in your own Domain base class (such as the `ApplicationDomain` class described in the last chapter). This way, you can encapsulate the preceding turnery operation into a single method. The sample code for this chapter contains the `ApplicationDomain.getCurrencyCodes` method, which can be used as follows:

```
public override onBeforeInsert() {
  Map<Id, String> currencies = getCurrencyCodes();
  for(Team__c team : (List<Team__c>) Records) {
    String teamCurrency = currencies.get(team.Id);
  }
}
```

Implementing the custom query logic

Take a look at the implementation of the `selectSObjectById` base class method we have been using so far in this chapter. The following `buildQuerySObjectById` method code gives us an indication of how we implement custom Selector methods; it also highlights the `newQueryFactory` base class method usage:

```
public List<SObject> selectSObjectsById(Set<Id>idSet) {
  return Database.query(buildQuerySObjectById());
}
private String buildQuerySObjectById() {
  return newQueryFactory().
          setCondition('id in :idSet').
          toSOQL();
}
```

The `newQueryFactory` method exposes an alternative object-orientated way to express a SOQL query. It follows the **fluent** design model with its methods, making code less verbose. For more information on this approach, see https://en.wikipedia.org/wiki/Fluent_interface.

The instance of `fflib_QueryFactory` returned by this method is preconfigured with the object, fields, order by, and any field set fields expressed through the selector methods discussed previously. As described earlier, it will also enforce security enabled. So, in general, all you need to do is provide a SOQL where clause via the `setCondition` method, as shown in the preceding code. Finally, the `toSOQL` method returns the actual SOQL query string that is passed to the standard `Database.query` method.

Application Selector Layer

The `fflib_QueryFactory` class methods provide an alternative to using the standard string concatenation or `String.format` approach when building dynamic SOQL queries. The original author of the `fflib_QueryFactory` class, **Chris Peterson**, was motivated in creating it to avoid the fragility that string-based methods can give, as well as to provide a more readable means to understand what such code was doing. In addition to this, because the class supports using `SObjectField` references as opposed to field name references in strings, such code is less prone to **SOQL injection vulnerabilities**.

A basic custom Selector method

Let's first look at a basic example, which queries `Driver__c` based on the team they are assigned to. As per the guidelines, the parameters are bulkified and allow you to query for drivers across multiple teams if needed:

```
public List<Driver__c> selectByTeam(Set<Id>teamIds) {
  return (List<Driver__c>)
    Database.query(
      newQueryFactory().
        setCondition('Team__c in :teamIds').
        toSOQL());
}
```

By using the `newQueryFactory` method, the `fflib_QueryFactory` instance is already populated with knowledge of the field list, object name, and `order by` clause specified in the selector. Therefore, this Selector method behaves consistently in terms of the fields populated and the order of the records returned.

A custom Selector method with subselect

In the following example, the querying being made uses a **sub-select** to also include child records (in this case, Contestants within Race). The key thing here is that the `RacesSelector` method (shown in the following code) reuses an instance of the `ContestantsSelector` class to access its field list and perform the security checking:

```
public List<Race__c>selectByIdWithContestants(Set<Id>raceIds) {
  fflib_QueryFactoryracesQueryFactory = newQueryFactory();
  fflib_QueryFactorycontestantsSubQueryFactory =
    new ContestantsSelector().
      addQueryFactorySubselect(racesQueryFactory);
  return (List<Race__c>) Database.query(
    racesQueryFactory.setCondition('Id in :raceIds').toSOQL());
}
```

[256]

The preceding code uses the `fflib_SObjectSelector` class's `addQueryFactorySubselect` method. This method creates a new `fflib_QueryFactory` instance and passes it on to the query factory passed into the method, in this case, `racesQueryFactory`. When the `toSOQL` method is called on the outer query factory, it automatically generates sub-queries for any contained query factories.

By reusing an instance of the `ContestantsSelector`, it is ensured that no matter how a list of `Contestant__c` records is queried (directly or as part of a sub-select query), the fields are populated consistently. The `getOrderBy` method on `ContestantSelector` is also used to ensure that even though the records are being returned as part of a sub-select, the default ordering of Contestant records is also maintained.

Let's take another look at the example used earlier to illustrate how this pattern has avoided the dangers of inconsistent querying. Although the `Contestant__c` records are queried from two different selectors, `RacesSelector` and `ContestantsSelector`, the result in terms of fields populated is the same due to the reuse of the `ContestantsSelector` class in the preceding implementation.

The following example shows the standard `selectById` method being used to query **Contestants** to pass to the `Contestants` Domain class constructor, as part of the Service layer implementation to award championship points:

```
List<Contestant__c> contestants =
    new ContestantsSelector().selectById(contestantIds);
new Contestants(contestants).awardChampionshipPoints(uow);
```

The following alternative example shows the custom `selectByIdWithContestants` method on `RaceSelector` being used to query **Races** and **Contestants** to pass to the `Contestants` Domain class constructor to achieve the same result:

```
List<Contestant__c> contestants = new List<Contestant__c>();
for(Race__c race :
  new RacesSelector().selectByIdWithContestants(raceIds)) {
    contestants.addAll(race.Contestants__r);
}
new Contestants(contestants).awardChampionshipPoints(uow);
```

In either of these two examples, the fields and ordering of the records are consistent, despite the way in which they have been queried, either as a direct query or sub-select. This gives the developer more confidence in using the most optimal approach to query the records needed at the time.

Application Selector Layer

The `selectByIdWithContestants` method generates the following SOQL:

```
select
  Name, TotalDNFs__c, Status__c, Season__c, Id,
  PollPositionLapTime__c, FastestLapBy__c,
  (select    Qualification1LapTime__c, ChampionshipPoints__c,
    Driver__c, GridPosition__c, Qualification3LapTime__c,
  RacePosition__c, Name, DNF__c, RaceTime__c,
  Id, DriverRace__c, Qualification2LapTime__c, Race__c
  from Contestants__r
  order by Race__r.Season__r.Name, Race__r.Name,
    RacePosition__c)
  from Race__c where id in :raceIds order by Name
```

In this section, we discussed how to use the Selector pattern to query child records. The following section will cover how to include fields from related records.

A custom Selector method with related fields

In addition to querying child records, related records can also be queried using the SOQL field dot notation. This provides an additional way to optimize the querying of additional record information, along with having to make an additional query.

The following is an example of a custom Selector method for the `ContestantsSelector` class, where **Contestant** records are queried along with the related **Driver** record fields. The resulting `Contestant__c` objects expose the `Driver__r` field, which provides an instance of `Driver__c` populated with the `Driver__c` fields specified in `DriversSelector`:

```
public List<Contestant__c>selectByIdWithDriver(Set<Id>driverIds) {
  fflib_QueryFactorycontestantFactory = newQueryFactory();

  new DriversSelector().
    configureQueryFactoryFields(
    contestantFactory,
    Contestant__c.Driver__c.getDescribe().getRelationshipName());

  return Database.query(
    contestantFactory.setCondition('Id in :driverIds').toSOQL());
}
```

The `fflib_SObjectSelector.configureQueryFactoryFields` method adds the Selector fields to the query factory passed as the first parameter, utilizing the relationship prefix specified in the second parameter.

Due to the reuse of `DriversSelector` in the `ContestantsSelector` classes method in the preceding code, the examples in the next code block return consistently populated `Driver__c` records. This is important to the logic contained within the Domain class's `Drivers.verifyCompliance` method. This flexibility allows for the most optimal way of querying `Driver__c` records and safer reuse of the Domain class method regardless of how the records were queried.

This first example constructs the `Drivers` Domain class with results from the standard `selectById` method on the `DriversSelector` class:

```
List<Driver__c> drivers =
   new DriversSelector().selectById(driverIds);
List<ComplianceService.VerifyResult> results =
   new Drivers(drivers).verifyCompliance();
```

This second example achieves the same, but queries the **Drivers** records via the custom Selector method, `selectByIdWithDriver`, on the `ContestantsSelector` class:

```
List<Driver__c> drivers = new List<Driver__c>();
List<Contestant__c> contestants =
   new ContestantsSelector().selectByIdWithDriver(contIds);
for(Contestant__c contestant : contestants)
drivers.add(contestant.Driver__r);
List<ComplianceService.VerifyResult> results =
   new Drivers(drivers).verifyCompliance();
```

Again, both of these examples have shown that even when using related fields in SOQL, the resulting records can be kept in alignment with the desired fields as expressed by the selectors. The `selectByIdWithDriver` method generates the following SOQL:

```
SELECT
  Qualification1LapTime__c, ChampionshipPoints__c, Driver__c,
  GridPosition__c, Qualification3LapTime__c, RacePosition__c,
  Name, DNF__c, RaceTime__c, Id, DriverRace__c,
  Qualification2LapTime__c, Race__c,
  Driver__r.FIASuperLicense__c, Driver__r.Name,
  Driver__r.Id, Driver__r.Team__c
FROM Contestant__c
WHERE Id in :driverIds
ORDER BY Name
```

This section illustrated how you can include the driver-related fields when querying the contestants. If you require more granular control over specific fields from different related objects, you can use a custom dataset to express this information in a clear way.

A custom Selector method with a custom dataset

SOQL has a very rich dot notation to traverse relationship (lookup) fields in order to access other fields on related records within a single query. To obtain the following information in a tabular form, it needs to traverse up and down the relationships across many of the objects in the FormulaForce application object schema:

- The season name
- The race name
- The race position
- The driver's name
- The car name

First, let's consider the following SOQL and then look at how it and the data it returns can be encapsulated in a `ContestantsSelector` class method. Note that the common `order by` clause is also applied here, as was the case in the previous example:

```
select
   Race__r.Season__r.Name,
   Race__r.Name,RacePosition__c,
   Driver__r.Name,
   Driver__r.Team__r.Name,
   Car__r.Name
from
 Contestant__cwhere
 Race__c in :raceIdsorder by
    Race__r.Season__r.Name, Race__r.Name, RacePosition__c
```

This query will result in partially populated `Contestant__c` objects; not only that, but relationship fields will also expose partially populated `Season__c`, `Car__c`, and `Driver__c` records. Therefore, these are highly specialized instances of records to simply return into the calling code path.

The following code shows an alternative to the preceding query using a new `ContestantsSelector` method. The biggest difference from the previous ones is that it returns a **custom Apex data type** and not the `Contestant__c` object. You can also see that it's much easier to see what information is available and what is not:

```
List<ContestantsSelector.Summary> summaries =
  new ContestantsSelector().
    selectByRaceIdWithContestantSummary(raceIds).values();
for(ContestantsSelector.Summary summary : summaries) {
  System.debug(
    summary.Season + ' ' +
```

```
      summary.Race + ' ' +
      summary.Position + ' ' +
      summary.Driver + ' ' +
      summary.Team + ' ' +
      summary.Car);
}
```

Depending on your data, this would output something like the following debug:

```
USER_DEBUG|[26]|DEBUG|2016 Spa 1 Lewis Hamilton Mercedes MP4-29
USER_DEBUG|[26]|DEBUG|2016 Spa 2 Rubens Barrichello Williams FW36
```

The Selector method returns a new **Apex inner class** that uses Apex properties to explicitly expose only the field information queried, thus creating a clearer contract between the Selector method and the caller.

It is now not possible to reference the information that has not been queried and would result in runtime errors when code attempts to reference fields that are not queried. The following shows an Apex inner class that the Selector uses to explicitly expose only the information queried by a custom Selector method:

```
public class Summary {
  private Contestant__c contestant;
  public String Season {
    get { return contestant.Race__r.Season__r.Name; } }
  public String Race {
    get { return contestant.Race__r.Name; } }
  public Decimal Position {
    get { return contestant.RacePosition__c; } }
  public String Driver {
    get { return contestant.Driver__r.Name; } }
  public String Team {
    get { return contestant.Driver__r.Team__r.Name; } }
  public String Car {
    get { return contestant.Car__r.Name; } }
  @TestVisible
  private Summary(Contestant__c contestant)
    { this.contestant = contestant; }
}
```

The Summary class contains an instance of the query data privately, so no additional heap is used up. It exposes the information as read-only and makes the constructor private (though accessible from test code to support mocking), indicating that only instances of this class are available through the ContestantsSelector class.

Application Selector Layer

The following code shows the Selector method that performs the actual query:

```
public Map<Id, List<Summary>>
    selectByRaceIdWithContestantSummary(Set<Id>raceIds) {

    Map<Id, List<Summary>>summariesByRaceId =
      new Map<Id, List<Summary>>();for(Contestant__c contestant :
    Database.query(
     newQueryFactory(false).
        selectField(Contestant__c.RacePosition__c).
        selectField('Race__r.Name').
        selectField('Race__r.Season__r.Name').
        selectField('Driver__r.Name').
        selectField('Driver__r.Team__r.Name').
        selectField('Car__r.Name').
        setCondition('Race__c in :raceIds').
        toSOQL())){
      List<Summary> summaries =
        summariesByRaceId.get(contestant.Race__c);
      if(summaries==null) {
        summariesByRaceId.put(
        contestant.Race__c, summaries = new List<Summary>());
        summaries.add(new Summary(contestant));
      }
    }

    return summariesByRaceId;
}
```

You can utilize the Apex Describe API to add compile-time checking and referential integrity to the preceding relationship references. For example, instead of hardcoding `Race__r.Name`, you can use the following:

```
Contestant__c.Race__c.getDescribe().
  getRelationshipName() + '.' + Race__c.Name
```

The preceding code shows the `newQueryFactory` method being passed `false`. This instructs the base class not to configure the query factory returned with the selector fields. This allows the caller to use the `selectField` method to specify particular fields as required.

If you are implementing an Apex interface that references a custom Selectors method using custom datasets, as described in this section, you should consider creating the class as a top-level class. This avoids potential circular dependencies occurring between the interface and Selector class.

Combining Apex data types with SObject types

It is possible to combine Apex data types with SObject data types in a response from Selector methods. This is as long as when you return SObject data types, they are populated according to the fields indicated by the corresponding Selector.

For example, let's say we want to return an entire `Driver__c` record associated with the **Contestant** object, instead of just the **Driver** name. The change to the `Summary` Apex class will be to expose the queried `Driver__c` record, which is safe as it has been populated in accordance with `DriversSelector`. The following code shows how the `Summary` class can be modified to expose the `Driver__c` record, as queried in the custom Selector method:

```
public class Summary {
  public Driver__c Driver {
    get { return contestant.Driver__r; } }
    ...
}
```

In this example, a `DriversSelector` instance is used to obtain the field list, which is injected into the query factory along with other specific fields:

```
fflib_QueryFactory contestantQueryFactory =
  newQueryFactory(false).
    selectField(Contestant__c.RacePosition__c).
    selectField('Race__r.Name').
    selectField('Race__r.Season__r.Name').
    selectField('Car__r.Name').
    setCondition('Race__c in :raceIds');

new DriversSelector().
  configureQueryFactoryFields(
    contestantQueryFactory,
    Contestant__c.Driver__c.getDescribe().getRelationshipName());

Map<Id, List<Summary>> summariesByRaceId =
  new Map<Id, List<Summary>>();
for(Contestant__c contestant :
    Database.query(contestantQueryFactory.toSOQL())) {
```

The preceding code shows how you can combine Selector classes to reuse the fields defined by the `DriversSelector` class when performing a query for **Contestants** in the `ContestantSelector` class. This ensures that records from the **Driver** object are returned consistently regardless of whether they are queried directly or indirectly by querying **Contestants**.

SOSL and aggregate SOQL queries

SOQL is not the only way to query information from the database. Lightning Platform also provides a powerful **Salesforce Object Search Language (SOSL)** facility. Like SOQL, this returns SObjects. While this chapter has not covered this variation in depth, the use of Selector methods to encapsulate SOSL is appropriate and, in fact, provides a good abstraction from the caller, allowing the developer of the Selector to use either SOQL or SOSL in future without impacting the callers.

Likewise, **Aggregate SOQL** queries are also good candidates to encapsulate in Selector methods. However, in these cases, consider using Apex native data types (for example, a list of values) or lists of custom Apex data types to expose the aggregate information.

> The consolidated source code for this book, available in the `master` branch of the GitHub repository, contains a `RaceDataSelector` class. Within this class is a custom Selector method, `selectAnalysisGroupByRaceName`, that demonstrates the use of a SOQL aggregate query.

Introducing the Selector factory

Chapter 6, *Application Domain Layer*, introduced the concept of a **Domain factory**, which was used to dynamically construct Domain class instances implementing a **common Apex Interface** in order to implement the compliance framework.

The following code is used in the `ComplianceService.verify` method's implementation, making no reference at all to a Selector class to query the records needed to construct the applicable Domain class:

```
fflib_SObjectDomain domain =
  Application.Domain.newInstance(recordIds);
```

So, how did the Domain factory retrieve the records in order to pass them to the underlying Domain class constructor? The answer is that it internally used another factory implementation called the **Selector factory**.

As with the Domain factory, the Selector factory resides within the `Application` class as a static instance, exposed via the `Selector` static class member, as follows:

```
public class Application
{
  // Configure and create the SelectorFactory for this Application
  public static final fflib_Application.SelectorFactory Selector =
    new fflib_Application.SelectorFactory(
      new Map<SObjectType, Type> {
        Team__c.SObjectType =>TeamsSelector.class,
        Race__c.SObjectType =>RacesSelector.class,
        Car__c.SObjectType =>CarsSelector.class,
        Driver__c.SObjectType =>DriversSelector.class,
        Contestant__c.SObjectType => ContestantsSelector.class });

  // Configure and create the DomainFactory for this Application
  public static final fflib_Application.DomainFactory Domain =
    new fflib_Application.DomainFactory(
      Application.Selector,
      // Map SObjectType to Domain Class Constructors
      new Map<SObjectType, Type> {
        Team__c.SObjectType =>Teams.Constructor.class,
        Race__c.SObjectType =>Races.Constructor.class,
        Car__c.SObjectType =>Cars.Constructor.class,
        Driver__c.SObjectType =>Drivers.Constructor.class,
        Contestant__c.SObjectType =>
          Contestants.Constructor.class});
}
```

Notice that the Selector factory is passed to the Domain factory in the preceding example. The following sections outline the methods on the factory and relevant use cases.

SelectorFactory methods

The `SelectorFactory` class has two methods on it: `newInstance` and `selectById`. The following code illustrates both these methods by showing two equivalent usage examples to retrieve records given a set of IDs:

```
List<Contestant__c> contestants =
  Application.Selector.selectById(contestantIds);

List<Contestant__c> contestants =
  Application.Selector.newInstance(Contestant__c.SObjectType)
  .selectSObjectsById(contestantIds);
```

As you can see from the preceding code, the `selectById` method provides a shortcut to access the generic `selectSObjectById` method from the `fflib_ISObjectSelector` interface and, as saw earlier in this chapter, is implemented by the `fflib_SObjectSelector` base class. As such, all Selector classes are guaranteed to provide it. It offers a cleaner way of querying records in the standard way without having to know the Apex class name for the Selector. This effectively is how the Domain Factory can dynamically instantiate a Domain class instance loaded with records on behalf of the developer.

> The method internally uses `Id.getSObjectType` (on the first ID that is passed in) to look up the Selector class through the map defined previously and instantiate it (via `Type.newInstance`).

You would use the `newInstance` method instead of just instantiating directly via the `new` operator in the Selector class when you are writing generic code that handles different types of objects. In other cases, you can continue to instantiate Selector classes in the normal manner using the `new` operator.

Writing tests and the Selector layer

When writing tests specifically for a Selector class method, the process is almost as per the standard Apex testing guidelines; insert the data you need to support the queries, call the Selector methods, and assert the results returned. You can review some of the Selector tests included in this chapter.

> **TIP**
> If you have implemented Selector methods that return `QueryLocator` instances (for use by Batch Apex callers), you can still assert the results of these methods. Use the `iterator` method to obtain `QueryLocatorIterator`, and then call the `next` and `hasNext` methods to return the results to pass to your assert statements.

Of course, other Apex tests around the **Controllers**, **Batch Apex**, **Domain**, and **Service** layers may also invoke the Selector methods indirectly, thus providing code coverage, but not necessarily testing every aspect of the Selector classes.

> **TIP**: Try to ensure that your Apex tests test the layers and functional components of the application as much as possible in isolation to ensure that the existing and future callers don't run into issues.

As highlighted previously, often writing more isolated Apex tests can be made harder due to the fact that the code being tested often requires records to be set up in the database. By leveraging the Selector factory option described earlier, a **mocking** approach can be taken to the Selector methods, which can help make writing more isolated and varied component or class-level tests easier. We will revisit this topic in `Chapter 12`, *Unit Testing*.

Updating the FormulaForce package

Review the updated code supplied with this chapter and create a new **package version** so that you can test out the upgrade process of your package if desired. During the installation of the new package version, you should observe that the new Field Set component added in this chapter is shown as one of the new components included in the upgrade.

Summary

Through the Selector pattern covered in this chapter, you have learned about a powerful layer of encapsulation that is used for some critical logic in your application. This enforces the best practices surrounding security and provides a more consistent and reliable basis for code dealing with the `SObject` data.

You also learned that Selectors can also assume the responsibility and concern for platform features such as **Multi-Currency** and **Field Sets**. Ultimately, allowing the caller – be that the Service, Domain, Apex Controllers, or Batch Apex—to focus on their responsibilities and concerns leads to cleaner code that is easier to maintain and evolve.

With the introduction of the Selector factory, we discovered some common features provided by this layer in the form of the `Application.Selector.selectById` and `Application.Selector.newInstance` methods, opening up the potential for more dynamic scenarios, such as the compliance framework highlighted in the last chapter.

I'd like to summarize this chapter along with Chapter 5, *Application Service Layer*, and Chapter 6, *Application Domain Layer*, with a simple, but expressive, diagram that shows how the Service layer code turns with the help of the Domain and Selector layers. These three patterns on Lightning Platform help to add value to the developer through consistency, as well as support best practices pertaining to bulkification and code reuse:

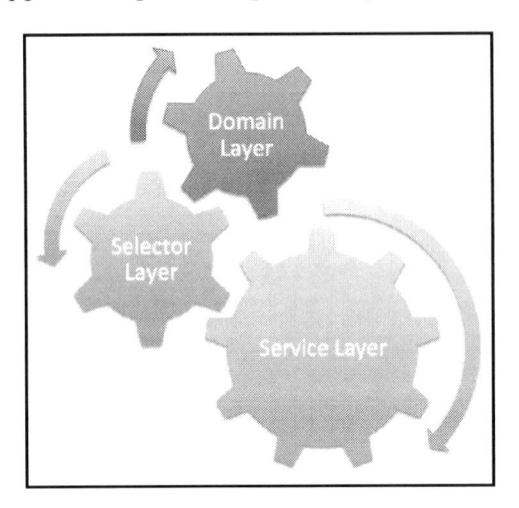

While this is the last chapter focusing on a Lightning Platform implementation of Martin Fowler's Enterprise Application Architecture patterns, we will revisit the role of the Selector in a later chapter and focus on Batch Apex, as well as continue to leverage our Service layer in later chapters that discuss application integration. In the next chapter, we will move to the user experience of your application and understand the tools and frameworks the platform provides to you and your users.

8
Building User Interfaces

If I was to list all the technologies that have come and gone most often in my career, I would say it has to be those that impact the user experience. Being a UI technology developer is a tough business; the shift from desktop to web to mobile to device agnostic has shaken things up, and this situation is still ongoing! This means that the investment in this part of your application architecture is important, as is the logic you put in it. Putting the wrong kind of logic in your client tier can result in inconsistent behavior and, at worst, expensive rework if you decide to shift client technology in the future.

This chapter will cover the aspects of delivering a user interface for Lightning-based applications, getting the most from the Salesforce standard UIs, and building custom UIs with Lightning versus Visualforce. We will also cover using third-party-rich client frameworks, contrasting their architecture's pros and cons with respect to platform features and performance. In addition, we will also explore how to use the **Service layer** and the **Domain layer** patterns to ensure that your users' interaction with your application is consistent, regardless of the user interface approach. We will cover the following topics in this chapter:

- Which devices should you target?
- Leveraging the Salesforce standard UIs
- Generating downloadable and printable content
- Client-server communication
- Managing limits
- Object- and field-level security
- Managing and monitoring UI response times
- Considerations for using third-party JavaScript libraries
- Creating websites and external-facing pages for communities
- Mobile applications
- Custom reporting and the Analytics API

Building User Interfaces

What devices should you target?

One of the first questions historically asked when developing a web-based application is *What desktop browsers and versions shall we support?* These days, you should not be thinking so much about the software installed on the laptops and desktops of your users, but rather the devices they own.

The answer might still include a laptop or desktop, though no longer is it a safe assumption that these are the main devices your users use to interact with your application. Mobile phones, tablets, watches, or skills for voice recognition devices such as **Alexa** or, depending on your target market, they might be larger devices, such as cars or vending machines! So, make sure that you think big and understand all the types of devices your customers and their customers might use to interact with your application.

> **TIP**
> For desktop and laptop users interacting with your Lightning application, delivering a user interface is a combination of using the standard Salesforce UI and any custom UIs you might have built with HTML and JavaScript. Given this fact, it is a good idea to base your supported browser matrix on that which is supported by Salesforce. You can find this by searching for `Salesforce supported browsers` in Google. At the time of writing, the PDF listing supported browsers can be found at `https://help.salesforce.com/apex/HTViewHelpDoc?id=getstart_browser_overview.htmlanguage=en`.

Developing against multiple devices can be expensive, not only to develop the solution, but also to perform testing across multiple devices. In this chapter, we will take a look at a range of options, ranging from those provided by Salesforce at no additional development cost, to building totally customized user interfaces using Lightning Components, Visualforce, and other technologies.

Leveraging standard UIs and custom UIs

Choice can be a good thing, but sometimes, the choices are not so clear, especially when new technologies are emerging and overlapping with existing ones. In this chapter and the next, we will be exploring features that help you make the choice between **standard UIs** automatically rendered by the platform, building your own **custom UIs** or, in fact, balancing the use of both. With the new **Lightning Component** technology from Salesforce, deciding what technology to use for a given custom UI requires some consideration.

Salesforce has historically provided **Visualforce** as the recommended technology for building custom UIs. To some developers, it resembles Java Server Pages or .NET Active Server Pages. They also provide a great number of ways to extend their standard UIs with custom UIs built with Visualforce, allowing you to make the choice at a more granular function-by-function level, depending on what works best for your particular user personas. This is also true when using the more recent and recommended **Lightning** technology.

Salesforce's user experience is delivered in different forms. There is the **Salesforce Mobile** application for mobiles, and now two options for desktop users. The two desktop UIs from Salesforce are now known as **Lightning Experience** (or **LEX** for short) and **Salesforce Classic**. Lightning Experience is the default user experience for new customers, whereas Salesforce Classic is the older UI and is still used by some customers that have not migrated.

The FormulaForce application in the Lightning Experience standard UI is shown as follows:

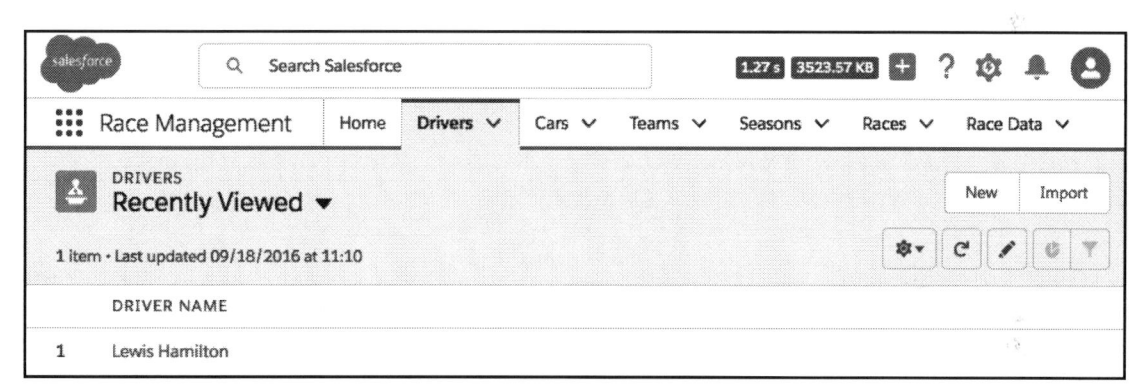

> There are more options to brand your application in Lightning Experience. We will cover this further in the next chapter. As stated earlier, Lightning Experience is now the default and Salesforce recommended user experience to target when building and customizing applications on the platform.

This is how it is shown in the Salesforce Classic standard UI:

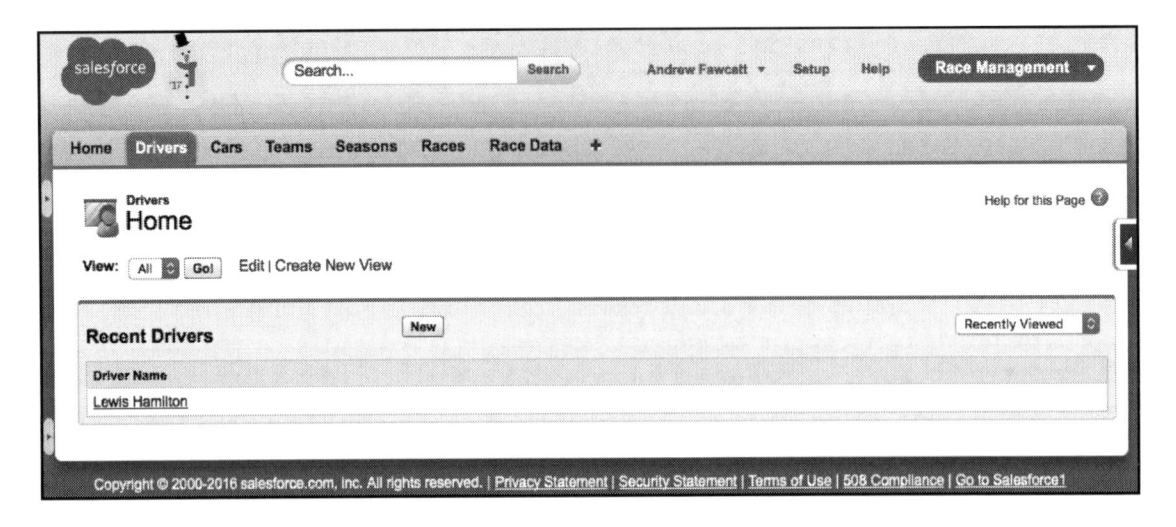

Lightning Experience brings with it an entirely new **client-side architecture**, which departs from the **server-side rendering** its predecessor (Salesforce Classic and Visualforce) provided. For backward compatibility, Visualforce UIs can still be used within Lightning Experience, although using Visualforce in LEX will not offer the same level of extensibility or visual appeal as custom UIs built using the Lightning framework.

> **TIP**
>
> Lightning Experience provides many more integration points for developers to extend the standard UI, reducing the need to build an entirely new replacement page from scratch. This chapter and the next will explore in more detail the ways in which Lightning Components can be used to extended Lightning Experience features with your own, thereby reducing the development costs for you and giving your customers even more value from the Salesforce standard UIs and customization tools.

For the first time, developers can now use the same programming framework and themes that Salesforce has used to build their own products. Its programming framework is known as **Lightning Framework**. Salesforce has chosen to open source their styling framework used by Lightning, which is known as the **Salesforce Lightning Design System (SLDS)**.

Why consider Visualforce over Lightning Framework?

So why is Visualforce still a consideration? Lightning Framework has, over the years, become a rich and rounded programming framework in terms of reusable components and developer tooling. In its latest incarnation, known as **Lightning Web Components**, it has aligned even more closely with ubiquitous programming skills and standards that you may already be familiar with, such as **W3C Web Components** (`https://github.com/w3c/webcomponents/`).

If you're reading this book having already developed a Lightning (or Force.com as it was previously known) application prior to the advent of the Lightning Framework programming model, you will still very much be interested in leveraging Visualforce until you can migrate. In this case, you will also no doubt be interested in ways to combine both technologies. So you can perhaps start to develop new features in Lightning Framework.

Lightning Component programming frameworks

In its initial incarnation, the Lightning Component framework used the **Aura** programming framework. This framework was created by Salesforce to handle many of the generic programming needs of web developers at the time. Since then, technologies and standards applied in modern web browsers have moved on and much of what Aura provided has now been effectively absorbed by the latest browser runtimes. Salesforce has taken a fresh look at modern web programming and has determined that a revised framework was required. The result, the **Lightning Web Component** (LWC) framework, is something that embraces more ubiquitous programming standards and tools (and thus more access to developer skills when hiring), while also resulting in a more performant rendering of components as the browser runtime is more optimized.

Salesforce uses the term **Lightning Component** when referring to a component's usage regardless of the programming framework used to develop it. This is useful when it comes to talking generally about how components fit into the general platform programming model and features since they have strived to ensure both types of components can co-exist to help developers incrementally adopt the new programming model. The terms Lightning Aura Component and LWC are used to refer to the old and new programming models, respectively. This book follows the same convention.

> Lightning Web Components will be the preference for this book where possible. However, in some cases (as already seen in the previous chapter with the Compliance Checker component), this programming framework still has some feature gaps at the time of writing compared to Aura-based components.

Leveraging the Salesforce standard UIs and tools

Salesforce puts a lot of effort into its desktop- and mobile-based UIs. These declarative UIs and related UI builder tools are the first to see advancements, such as the ability to dynamically display content based on expressions. These standard UIs and tools are also the primary method by which your subscribers will customize your application's appearance. Furthermore, the UI will evolve with Salesforce's frequent updates. In some cases, new features are available to your users even without you updating your application.

> **TIP**: In general, aspects of your application that had already leveraged the standard UI in Salesforce Classic will just work fine in Lightning Experience without change, and will also automatically adopt the new look and feel. However, if you have utilized Visualforce extensively and/or used unsupported features such as JavaScript Custom Buttons, you will have to make some changes. Carefully test and explore your application in Lightning Experience to understand what changes you need to make. In the next chapter, we will explore some key aspects of this transition and balancing the two technologies.

In general, you should ensure that for all the objects in your application, you make the best use of the standard UI by ensuring that your packaged layouts and **Lightning Pages** are highly polished and make use of every last drop of the declarative features. It is even worth considering this practice for those objects that might be typically accessed through Visualforce or Lightning-based custom UIs.

Considering the standard UI as a kind of primary or default UI also ensures that the validation in your Domain classes is complete, which ensures that it is not possible to enter invalid data regardless of how that data is entered – custom UI, standard UI, or API.

Ensure that you apply the same UI review processes you undertook on your custom UIs to the standard UI layouts. Take care to review field labels, sections, button names, and general layout, while also looking for options to add more related information through report charts or embedding custom UIs, as described later in this chapter. Also, consider making use of record types and different layouts to help reduce the number of fields that a user has to enter.

> **TIP**
> Keep in mind that Salesforce layouts packaged in your application are not upgradable, as they can be edited by the subscriber. So, no matter what improvements you make to your layouts in subsequent releases, these will only be available to new customers, and not to those who are upgrading to newer versions of the application. New aspects of layouts are typically expressed in your install/upgrade documentation.

Overriding standard Salesforce UI actions

You can override the Salesforce standard UI for the following actions: **Accept**, **Tab**, **Clone**, **Delete**, **Edit**, **List**, **New**, and **View** for an object with your own programmatic UI pages, completely replacing the standard UI pages.

The following screenshot shows the action override options for the **Edit** action. As you can see, you have the flexibility to target different overrides depending on the experience the user is using; **Salesforce Classic**, **Lightning Experience**, or **Salesforce Mobile**:

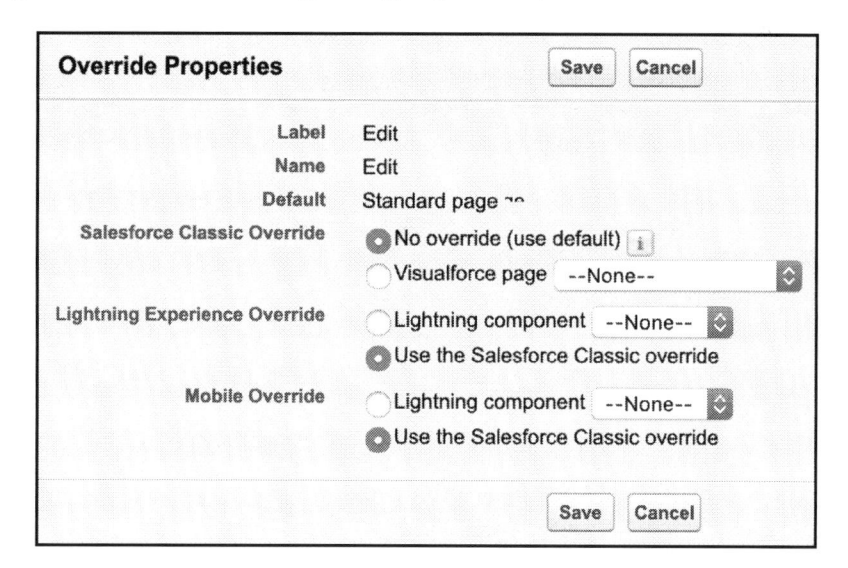

> Only the **Edit**, **New**, **View**, and **Tab** actions can be overridden, as shown in the preceding screenshot. All other actions can only be overridden with Visualforce pages and only apply in the Salesforce Classic user experience. Considering how significant the differences are between Salesforce Classic and Salesforce Lightning Experience, this is understandable.

Be aware that if you take this option, you're taking on the responsibility of not only ensuring that you provide a way for new fields added to your application's objects to be added to the UIs you build, but also that new platform features of the standard UI appear in your page as Salesforce evolves the platform. So, make sure to review the standard UI page functionality before making the decision to package and override the applicable action, and also consider a hybrid approach, which is described in the next subsection.

If you decide to build a custom UI, the best way to keep inline is to use the Salesforce-provided standard UI components. In Visualforce, these are available in the `apex` namespace. In Lightning, you can leverage the components in the `lightning` namespace. In either case, you can style custom UI HTML elements with the Lightning Design System.

Using Salesforce-provided components is not, however, a 100% solution; for example, **Chatter** does not automatically appear on pages unless a developer enables it. Another significant consideration is that Custom Fields or related lists that subscribers have added to your objects need special consideration in your page code to ensure that they are surfaced through the use of the **Field Sets** and the standard **Related List Lightning Component** or `apex:relatedList` component in Visualforce, for example.

Finally, note that although the **Action overrides** can be packaged, they are nonupgradable, so changes will not apply to existing subscribers. Also, the subscriber can remove them post-installation if they prefer to access the Custom Object through the standard UI, so this is another reason to make sure that you consider the standard UI for all of your objects as a standard practice.

> As an alternative to overriding an existing standard action, consider creating custom buttons, placing them on the object's **Detail page** and/or **List View layouts**, and naming the button something like **Enhanced Edit** or **Enhanced New**. Custom buttons are available in both Salesforce Classic and Lightning Experience standard UIs and allow you to invoke custom UIs built with Visualforce pages. If you are not interested in Salesforce Classic, you can invoke a Lightning Component from the standard UI in LEX by either embedding it in a **Lightning Page**, such as the **Lightning Record Page** layout (as shown in Chapter 6, *Application Domain Layer*), or utilizing **Lightning Component Actions** (discussed in Chapter 9, *User Interfaces with Lightning Framework*).

Combining standard UIs with custom UIs

Unless your user experience is such that it is entirely different from that offered by the standard UIs, always try to retain as much of the standard UIs as you can. The platform provides a number of ways to do this, which we will be exploring through this chapter and the next. In this section, we will explore ways to embed parts of a custom UI in specific regions of the standard UI, and vice versa.

Embedding a custom UI in a standard UI

In `Chapter 6`, *Application Domain Layer*, we looked at a Lightning Component that can be placed on the Lightning Record Page layout. This approach only applies to Lightning Experience and also provides some additional benefits, such as being able to listen to events Lightning Experience fires as users in-line edit the record details. This approach currently only applies when viewing the record details. The following screenshot is a reminder of what the **Compliance Verification** component looks like when placed on the standard UI:

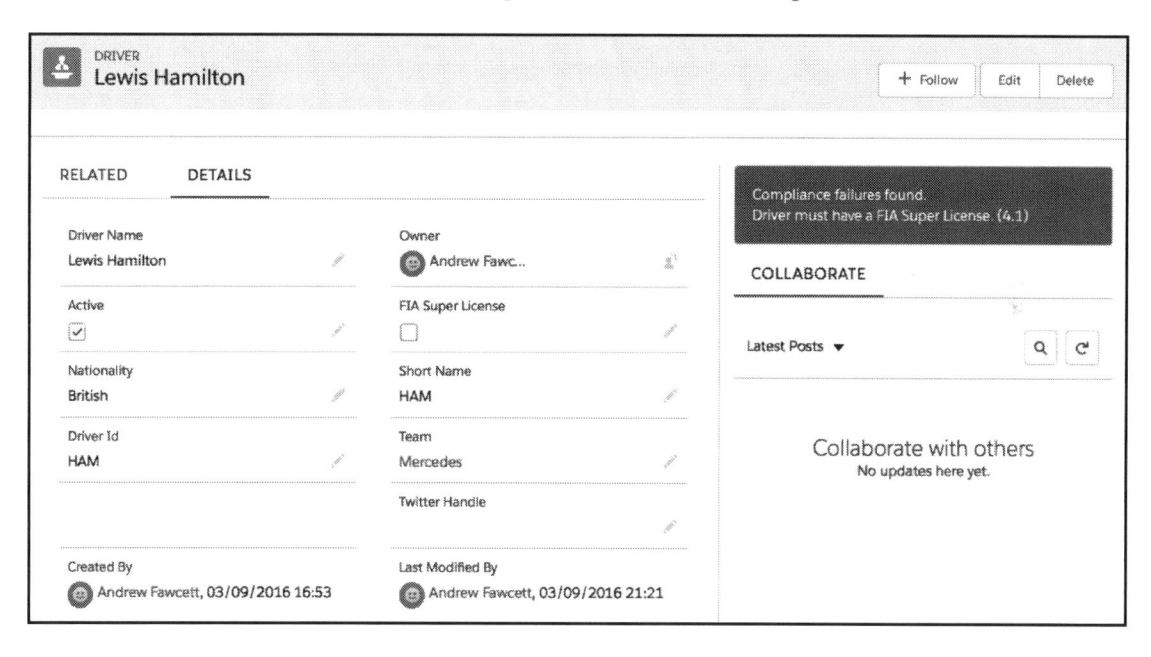

Let's now look at an example that shows how to customize the standard UI that applies both to Salesforce Classic and Lightning Experience by embedding a Visualforce page in a detailed **Page Layout**, as shown in the following screenshot for the `Race` object. Page Layouts are leveraged in both Salesforce Classic and Lightning Experience.

Building User Interfaces

The following Visualforce page uses the `lightningStylesheets` attribute to indicate that the page style should automatically reflect the container it is running in, as shown in the following screenshots. It reuses the **Extension Controller** from the previous chapter:

```
<apex:page standardController="Race__c"
    lightningStylesheets="true"
    extensions="RaceSummaryController"
    action="{!loadSummary}">
    <apex:outputPanel>
        <apex:pageBlock>
            <apex:pageBlockTable value="{!Summary}"
                 var="summaryRow">
                <apex:column value="{!summaryRow.Position}">
                    <apex:facet name="header">Position</apex:facet>
                </apex:column>
                <apex:column value="{!summaryRow.Driver}">
                    <apex:facet name="header">Driver</apex:facet>
                </apex:column>
                <apex:column value="{!summaryRow.Team}">
                    <apex:facet name="header">Team</apex:facet>
                </apex:column>
                <apex:column value="{!summaryRow.Car}">
                    <apex:facet name="header">Car</apex:facet>
                </apex:column>
            </apex:pageBlockTable>
        </apex:pageBlock>
    </apex:outputPanel>
</apex:page>
```

As the page uses `StandardController`, it appears in the layout editor and can be positioned on the layout:

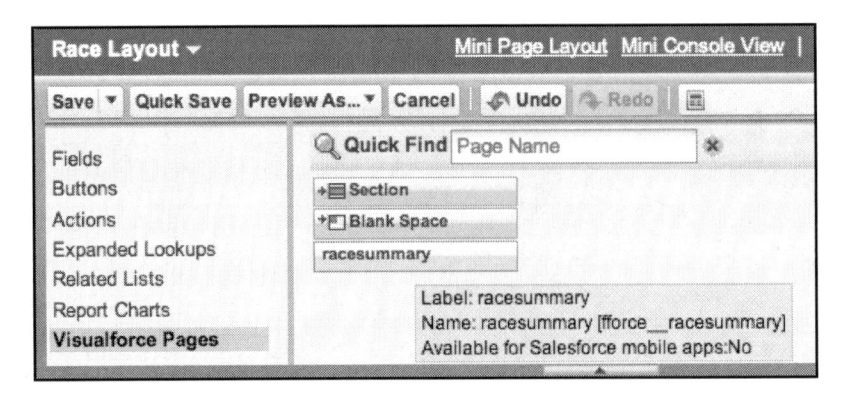

You can then drag and drop it into an existing or new section on the layout. In Lightning Experience, the page looks like the following screenshot:

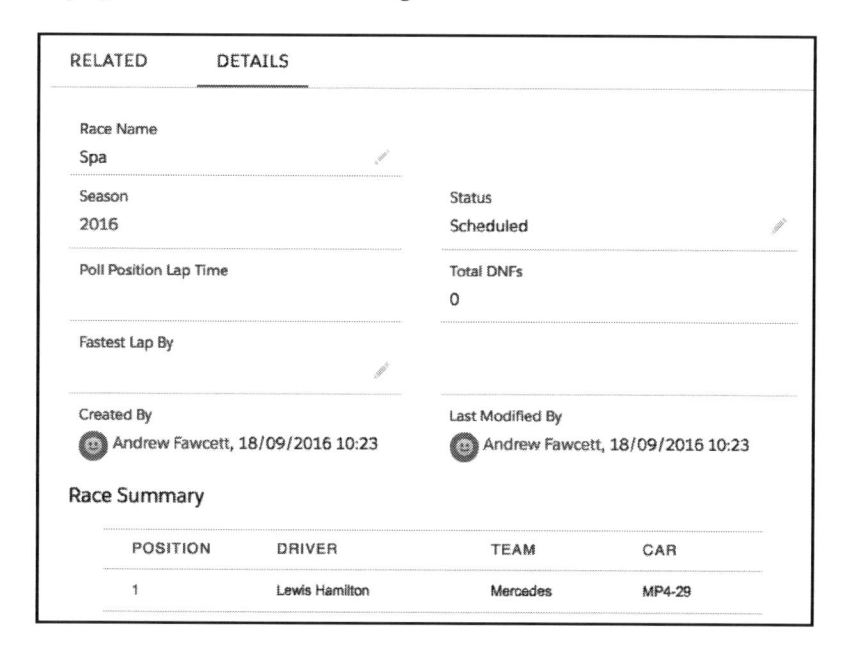

RELATED	DETAILS
Race Name	
Spa	
Season	**Status**
2016	Scheduled
Poll Position Lap Time	**Total DNFs**
	0
Fastest Lap By	
Created By	**Last Modified By**
Andrew Fawcett, 18/09/2016 10:23	Andrew Fawcett, 18/09/2016 10:23

Race Summary

POSITION	DRIVER	TEAM	CAR
1	Lewis Hamilton	Mercedes	MP4-29

The result will look something like the following screenshot in Salesforce Classic:

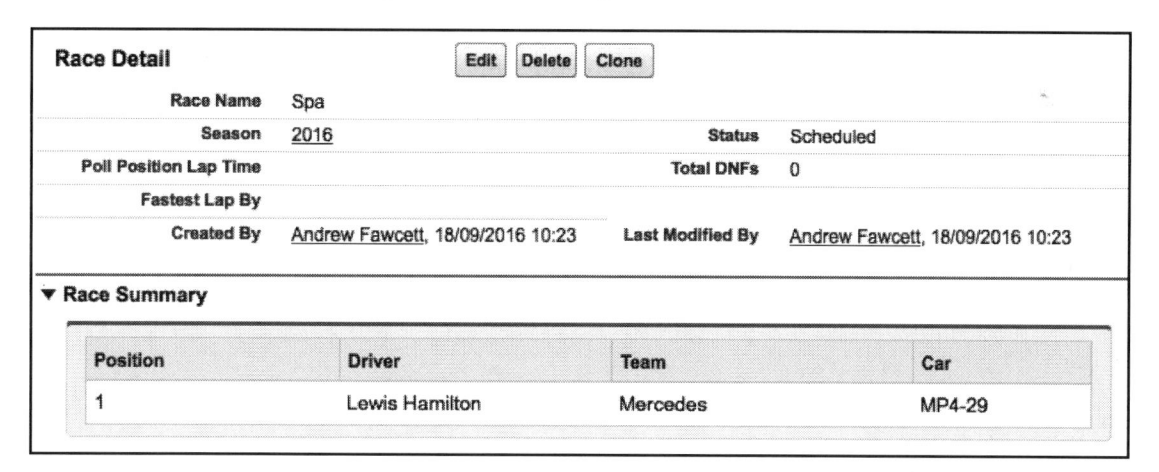

Race Detail   Edit Delete Clone

Race Name	Spa		
Season	2016	**Status**	Scheduled
Poll Position Lap Time		**Total DNFs**	0
Fastest Lap By			
Created By	Andrew Fawcett, 18/09/2016 10:23	**Last Modified By**	Andrew Fawcett, 18/09/2016 10:23

▼ **Race Summary**

Position	Driver	Team	Car
1	Lewis Hamilton	Mercedes	MP4-29

> **TIP**
> When in Salesforce Classic, this approach only applies to the layouts when users are viewing records. You can, however, provide a means for users to edit the information through such Visualforce pages, even though they are rendered on the view page for the record. There is, however, no way to refresh the main page when you do so. While the width of the Visualforce page will adjust automatically, the height is fixed, so be sure to set accordingly to common data volumes. Unlike Salesforce Classic, users in Salesforce LEX will see embedded Visualforce pages in layouts when creating and editing records as well as viewing them. Ensure that your pages expect these scenarios in LEX; for example, the `StandardController.getId` method will return `null` in a record create scenario, and your code should handle this accordingly.

Embedding a standard UI in a custom UI

Embedding the standard UI within your custom UI can, at first, seem like a good idea. However, some additional work, as outlined below, is still required if you want all of the functionality you see in the standard UI pages. For this reason, my personal preference in Lightning Experience is to extend the standard Lightning Page with custom Lightning Components. You can still provide your own editing experiences for certain fields or data and hook into the same client-side record data and notifications via the **Lightning Data Service API**.

Depending on the custom UI technology you use, there are different options to embed the standard UI page layout. These options also respect object- and field-level security and, as such, minimize the coding you need to do yourself:

- **For Lightning Experience**, the `lightning:lightning-record-form`, `lightning:lightning-record-edit-form`, and `lightning:lightning-record-view-form` components support both record editing and viewing within custom UIs built using Lightning Components. However, in contrast to the `apex:detail` component in Visualforce, custom action buttons are not rendered.
- **For Salesforce Classic**, the `apex:detail` tag can be used on a Visualforce page to render most of the look and feel of the standard UI; note that it is not automatically restyled when the page is shown in Lightning Experience. Also, this component is not very granular; for example, you cannot add your own buttons alongside the standard buttons it renders. This means that your page buttons need to be rendered elsewhere on the page, making the UI look inconsistent and confusing. In addition, this component only renders a read-only view of the record layout.

Extending the Salesforce standard UIs

The previous sections described a way to embed custom UIs within the standard UIs as a means of extending the Salesforce UIs with your own application's functionality. The following sections outline the further options available in Salesforce Classic and LEX, respectively. Some features exist in both, while others have been re-envisioned in LEX through the ability to embed and invoke Lightning Components from different areas.

Lightning Components

The following is a list of platform areas that accept Lightning Components:

- Record Pages
- Home Pages
- Lightning Tabs and Pages
- Lightning Component Actions
- Lightning Experience Utility Bar
- Lightning App Builder
- Lightning Community and Community Builder
- Lightning Out for Visualforce
- Lightning Out for Any App
- Lightning Flow

In `Chapter 6`, *Application Domain Layer*, we explored adding the **Verify Compliance** Lightning Component to Record Pages. In the next chapter, we will build some new Lightning Components to allow us to take a closer look at some of the other areas in the preceding list. You should also refer to the *Lightning Developer Guide* for full details.

Visualforce pages

Visualforce is not only a powerful way to create entirely new pages for your application, but also augments the Salesforce UI in multiple places. As we've seen so far, you can use it to extend the standard UI layouts and add custom buttons. Here is a list of platform areas that accept Visualforce pages:

- Layout sections
- Custom Buttons
- Custom Tabs

Building User Interfaces

- Custom Tab Splash page
- Chatter Custom Publisher Actions
- Sidebar component
- Dashboard component
- Lightning pages

Profiles and Permission Sets also reference Visualforce pages; users must be given access to a page before they can use it from these areas.

> **TIP**: Notice how the list of areas where Visualforce pages can be used differs from the list in the previous section. This is because Visualforce really relates to the Salesforce Classic user experience. Salesforce is focusing more and more on the Lightning Experience user experience and, thus, the aforementioned aspects are really only relevant if you plan to support both this and Salesforce Classic for your users. If you do, you may want to carefully consider if you need full parity between your features or if you want to leverage the fact that your application is more powerful when running within Lightning Experience to encourage your customers to adopt it.

Generating downloadable content

The `contentType` attribute allows you to control how the browser interprets the page output; with this attribute, you can, for example, output some CSV, JSON, or XML content. Using a controller binding, this can be dynamically generated output. This can be useful to generate content to download. The following changes have been made to the FormulaForce application and are included in the code for this chapter:

- Added a new method, `generateSummaryAsCSV`, to `RaceService`
- Added a new `getCSVContent` method to `RaceSummaryController`
- Added a new `racesummaryascsv` Visualforce page
- Added a new Custom Button, **Download Summary**, to the **Race** layout

The new method is added to the existing `RaceSummaryController` class, but is only used by the new page. Feel free to review the new `Service` method; note that it also uses the `ContestantsSelector.selectByRaceIdWithContestantSummary` method introduced in the previous chapter. Here is the new controller method calling it:

```
public String getCSVContent() {
  return RaceService.generateSummaryAsCSV(
    new Set<Id> { standardController.getId() });
}
```

> **TIP**: The `RaceService` class contains the logic to generate the CSV file and not the controller class. Although, at first, you might consider this controller logic, if you think about it from a general data export perspective, there could equally be an API requirement in the future for external developers wanting to automate the CSV export process; hence, placing this logic in the Service layer facilitates this.

The new Visualforce page utilizes the `contentType` attribute as follows:

```
<apex:page
  standardController="Race__c"
  extensions="RaceSummaryController"
  contentType="application/csv#{!Race__c.Name} Race
  Summary">{!CSVContent}
</apex:page>
```

As this page uses a Standard Controller, a Custom Button can be created; once it has been clicked, instead of the page opening, the browser prompts you to download the file:

| Race Detail | Edit | Delete | Clone | Download Summary |

Race Name Spa
Season   2014

Clicking the **Download Summary** button results in the following prompt to download the resulting CSV file:

[Spa Race Summary]

Building User Interfaces

> **TIP** You may have noticed in the preceding VisualForce code that the `apex:pagecontentType` attribute contained a # and some text. If you put a # symbol after the content type, you can specify a default filename to be presented to the user when the file downloads. Also note that the Visualforce formula can also be used in attribute values, and this is how the **Race** name appears in the filename. This also allows you to vary `contentType` dynamically if required. While this example works quite well to illustrate the `contentType` attribute, it should be noted that the platform-reporting engine also supports CSV exports. As such, if you are considering CSV export facilities, it is worth first considering asking users to leverage reports; thus, they have more freedom to control the output.

Generating printable content

Salesforce has a built-in PDF generation engine that can take your HTML markup and turn it into a PDF. This is a very useful feature for generating more formal documents such as invoices or purchase orders.

You can access it using the `renderAs` attribute of the `apex:page` element on a Visualforce page, setting it to `pdf`. Note that you would typically dedicate a specific Visualforce page for this purpose rather than attempt to use this attribute on one that's used for other purposes.

> **TIP** Make sure that you use as much vanilla HTML and CSS as possible; the Visualforce standard components do not always render well in this mode. For this reason, it is also useful to use the `standardStylesheets` attribute to disable Salesforce CSS as well.

You can also programmatically access this capability by using the `PageReference.getContentAsPDF` method and attach the PDF generated to records for the future. If you would rather generate PDF content without using a Visualforce page, you can generate the HTML programmatically and leverage the `Blob.toPDF` method. In *Chapter 2*, *Leveraging Platform Features*, we covered translation and localization, so we will not be revisiting it in further detail here. Just to reiterate, it is important to consider translation and localization requirements from the outset, as they can be expensive to retrofit afterward.

Also, note that in the preceding example, the `$ObjectType` global variable was used in the Visualforce page to access the **Custom Field** label for the column title. Ensuring that you leverage approaches like this will reduce the number of **Custom Labels** you need to create and, ultimately, your translation costs.

> **TIP:** Lightning Components do not currently support `$ObjectType`; as a workaround, you can use Apex Describe to expose this via your Apex Controller.

In Visualforce, you can use the `apex:inputField` and `apex:outputField` components to render and receive input from the user, which is locale sensitive. In Lightning, utilize the `lightning:formattedNumber` and `lightning:formattedDateTime` components.

Overriding the page language

By default, the Visualforce page looks up translated text for Custom Field labels and Custom Labels that you reference on your page or in your Apex code through the user's locale. However, if you wish to override this, you can specify the `<apex:page> language` attribute, for example, if you wish to use a Visualforce page to generate a newsletter in different languages and wish to preview them before sending them out.

> There is no equivalent functionality for Lightning Components; these always leverage the language of the user.

This does not apply to any descriptive field values such as `Name`, or any custom description fields that you add to your objects. In order to provide translation for the data entered by a user, you must develop such a feature yourself. There is no platform support for this.

Client-server communication

Fundamentally, any communication between the user's chosen device (client) and the data and logic available on the Salesforce server occurs using the **HTTP** protocol. As a Lightning developer, you rarely get involved with the low-level aspects of forming the correct HTTP `POST` or HTTP `GET` request to the server and parsing the responses:

- **For Lightning Aura Components**, the `$A.enqueueAction` JavaScript method can be called from a component's client-side controller method to access the Apex code.
- **For Lightning Web Components**, the `@wire` protocol can be used to bind properties in your client-side controller to methods in your Apex code.
- **For Visualforce**, the `apex:commandButton` and `apex:actionFunction` components can be used to invoke Apex code.

Salesforce also takes care of the security aspects for you, ensuring that the user is logged in and has a valid session to make the request to the server. There are also a number of options to perform **CRUD** operations on Standard or Custom Objects directly from your client-side JavaScript code without any need for Apex code.

It is important that you correctly place the logic in your Domain and Service layers to make sure that, regardless of the client communication options, the backend of your application behaves consistently and that each client has the same level of functionality available to it. The sections in this chapter will show how to ensure that, regardless of the communications approach utilized, these layers can be effectively reused and accessed consistently.

Client communication options

Although the upcoming sections discuss the various communications in further detail, a full walk-through of them is outside the scope of this book. The Salesforce documentation and developer site offer quite an extensive set of examples on their use.

The aim of this chapter is to explain the architecture decisions behind using them, the related limits, and how each interacts with the Apex code layers introduced in the previous chapters.

This table lists the various client communication options available, along with the types of UI they are typically utilized by. It also indicates whether the API calls are governed (refer to the following subsection on what this means):

Communication Option	Lightning Components	Visualforce Pages (1)	Websites	Native Device UIs (3)	API Limits Enforced?
Lightning Apex Action via `@AuraEnabled` Apex annotation and invoked via `$A.enqueAction` for Lightning Aura Components and the `@wire` annotation for Lightning Web Components. (Apex code)	Yes	No	No (5)	No	No
Lightning Data Services (Object record access)	Yes	No	No (5)	No	No
Visualforce AJAX Components (`apex:commandButton` or `apex:actionFunction`) (Apex code)	No	Yes	Yes (1)	No	No
Visualforce JavaScript Remoting (Apex code)	No	Yes	Yes (1)	No	No
Visualforce JavaScript Remote Objects (Object record access)	No	Yes	Yes (1)	No	No
Salesforce REST/SOAP APIs (Data and UI APIs and others)	Partial (4)	Yes	Yes (2)	Yes	Yes
Salesforce Streaming API (Various forms of events, such as custom platform events, change data capture events when records are updated)	Yes	Yes	Yes (2)	Yes	Yes

The following notes apply to the preceding table:

1. As Visualforce pages are essentially dynamically rendered HTML pages output by Salesforce servers, they can also be used to build public-facing websites and also pages that adapt to various devices, such as mobile phones and tablets (given the appropriate coding by the developer).
2. Websites built using traditional off-platform languages, such as .NET, Java, Ruby, or PHP, are required to access Salesforce via the REST/SOAP and Streaming APIs only.

3. A client is built using a device-specific platform and UI technology, such as a native mobile application using Xcode, Java, or a natively wrapped HTML5 application.
4. Lightning utilizes the `Content-Security-Policy` HTTP header as recommended by **W3C**. This controls how (use of HTTPS) and from where (Lightning domain only) resources are loaded from the server. Since the Salesforce APIs are served from a different domain, they cannot be called directly from JavaScript code inside a Lightning Component. Instead, you must call such APIs on the server side from the component's Apex controller. However, using **Lightning Data Services** and the **lightning/ui*Api Wire Adapters and Functions**, you can access a subset of these APIs more directly from within your Lightning Component controller code.
5. **Lightning Out** is a technology that allows Lightning Components to be hosted on external websites. Components running within Lightning Out are still able to use Lightning Server Side and Lightning Data Services to communicate with the backend.

> The AJAX Toolkit is a JavaScript library used to access the Salesforce SOAP API from a Visualforce or HTML page. It is the oldest way in which you can access Salesforce objects and also Apex Web Services from JavaScript. Though it is possible to utilize it from Custom Buttons and Visualforce pages, my recommendation is to utilize one of the more recent Visualforce communication options (by associating Visualforce pages to your Custom Buttons rather than JavaScript). Salesforce only supports the very latest version of this library, which is also quite telling in terms of their commitment to it.

API governors and availability

As shown in the preceding table, for some communication methods, Salesforce currently caps the number of API requests that can be made in a rolling 24-hour period (though this can be extended through Salesforce support). This can be seen on the **Company Information** page under **Setup** and the **API Requests, Last 24 Hours**, and **Streaming API Events, Last 24 Hours** fields.

Note that these are not scoped by your application's namespace, unlike other governors (such as the SOQL and DML ones). As such, other client applications accessing the subscriber org can consume, and thus compete with, your application for this resource. If possible, utilize a communication approach listed in the preceding table that does not consume the **API limits**. If you cannot avoid this, ensure that you are monitoring how many requests your client is making and where aggregating them using relationship queries and/or Apex calls is possible.

> If you are planning on targeting **Professional Edition**, be sure to discuss your API usage with your **Partner Account Manager**. Accessibility within this edition of Salesforce when using APIs such as the Salesforce SOAP/REST API, Streaming API, and AJAX Toolkit is different from other editions. For the latest information, you can also review the *API Access in Group and Professional Editions* section in the *ISVforce Guide*, available at `https://na1.salesforce.com/help/pdfs/en/salesforce_packaging_guide.pdf`.

Database transaction scope and client calls

As discussed in `Chapter 4`, *Apex Execution and Separation of Concerns*, the transaction context spans the execution context for a request made to the Salesforce server from a client. When writing the client code in JavaScript, be careful when using CRUD-based communication options such as **Lightning Data Service, JavaScript Remote Objects**, and the Salesforce API, as the execution scope in the client does not translate to a single execution scope on the server.

Each CRUD operation that the client makes is made in its own execution scope and, thus, its own transaction. This means that if your client code hits an error midway through a user interaction, prior changes to the database are not rolled back. To wrap several CRUD operations in a single database transaction, implement the logic in Apex and call it through one of the previous means, such as Visualforce JavaScript Remote Actions or a Lightning Server Side Action. Note that this is generally a good practice anyway from a service-orientated application design perspective.

> If your client code is able to utilize the Salesforce REST APIs (as per the preceding table), you can also consider using the **Salesforce Composite and Tree APIs**. These APIs allow you to group multiple records together in one operation, and thus they will be performed in a single transaction.

Offline support

The `manifest` attribute on the Visualforce `apex:page` element is part of the HTML5 standard to support offline web pages. While a full discussion on its use is outside the scope of this book, one thing to keep in mind is that any information you store in the browser's local offline storage is not secure. This attribute requires the use of the `docType` attribute to indicate that the page output is HTML5-compliant.

Salesforce, however, introduced this feature mainly to support **hybrid** mobile applications, wanting to utilize Visualforce pages within a native mobile application container that supports offline mode. It is not supported in any other context. In this case, the offline content is stored within the mobile application's own private store.

Hybrid mobile applications in the context of Salesforce Mobile SDKs are those that use a small application native to the mobile device that hosts a mobile browser that then utilizes the Salesforces login and Visualforce pages to deliver the application. In general, this would require a network connection; however, with the help of the `manifest` attribute, offline support can be achieved.

> Lightning components cannot control this attribute currently since they do not own the page. It is the responsibility of the Salesforce Mobile and Salesforce LEX standard UIs to implement this attribute. Salesforce Mobile does support some offline capabilities in terms of record editing; however, there is no support currently for Visualforce- or Lightning-based custom UIs.

Managing limits

Normally, the total number of records retrieved within a single controller execution context is 50,000 records (in total across all **SOQL** queries executed). In addition, Visualforce components such as `apex:dataTable` and `apex:repeat` can only iterate over 1,000 items before a runtime exception is thrown.

At the time of writing, the `readOnly` attribute (specified on the `apex:page` component) changes this to 1 million records and 10,000 iterations within Visualforce components on the page (refer to the Salesforce documentation for the latest update). As the name suggests, no updates to the database can occur, which basically means no DML at all. Note that queries are still governed by timeouts.

> If you require a more granular elevation of the SOQL query rows governor, you can apply the `@ReadOnly` Apex attribute to a JavaScript Remoting method in your controller, and not at the page level as described previously. Again, this method will not be able to use DML operations to update the database, but you will gain access to querying a higher number of query rows. Note that the iterator limit increase is not applicable in this context, as JavaScript Remoting and Visualforce iterator components cannot be used together. At the time of writing, Lightning Components do not provide access to this functionality. Apex Controller methods exposed via the `@AuraEnabled` method are subject to the standard Apex query limits.

Object- and field-level security

Ensuring that object- and field-level security configuration is respected in your custom UIs is a key part of your responsibility to your customers in providing a secure solution. The standard UIs do this automatically for you, but it requires further consideration for custom UIs. In this section, we will explore how to do this for both Lightning Web Components and Visualforce pages. Lightning Aura Components has more limited support for it.

The following custom UIs illustrate how object- and field-level security is applied (or not) depending on the binding approach and/or components used. This will help you understand when you need to add additional code or just rely on the standard components.

In the use case used in the next two sections, two users are used; one has full access, and the other has been given the following permissions via their profile:

- Read-only access to the `Status__c` field
- No access at all to the `FastestLapBy__c` field

> A common confusion point is the use of the `with sharing`, `without sharing`, and `inherited sharing` keywords on the associated Apex controllers. These keywords have no effect at all on the enforcement of field-level security; they purely determine record visibility and, hence, affect only SOQL queries made within the controller.

Enforcing security in Lightning Web Components

First, review the Lightning Web Component; each section shows the following use case:

- Use Case A shows the use of `lightning-input-field`.
- Use Case B shows the use of `lightning-output-field`.
- Use Case C shows the use of `lightning-input`.
- Use Case D shows the use of `lightning-formatted-text`.
- Use Case E shows the use of an SObject field expression.
- Use Case F shows the use of a controller property expression.

The following code fragments show the HTML used by the following Lightning Web Component (the controller code is also included in this chapter, but is not shown here for brevity). Each code fragment illustrates different ways to expose field values.

For **Use Case A**, the field references look like this:

```
<lightning-input-field
  field-name={statusField}></lightning-input-field>
<lightning-input-field
  field-name={fastestLapByField}></lightning-input-field>
```

For **Use Case B**, the field references look like this:

```
<lightning-output-field
  field-name={statusField}></lightning-output-field>
<lightning-output-field
  field-name={fastestLapByField}></lightning-output-field>
```

For **Use Case C**, the field references look like this:

```
<lightning-input
  type="text" value={race.Status__c} label='Status'>
</lightning-input>
<lightning-input
  type="text" value={race.FastestLapBy__c} label='Fastest Lap By'
</lightning-input>
```

For **Use Case D**, the field references look like this:

```
<p>Status <lightning-formatted-text value={race.Status__c}></lightning-formatted-text></p>
<p>Fastest Lap By <lightning-formatted-text value={race.FastestLapBy__c}></lightning-formatted-text></p>
```

For **Use Case E**, the field references look like this:

```
<p>The value of Status__c is '{race.Status__c}'</p>
<p>The value of FastestLapBy__c is '{race.FastestLapBy__c}'</p>
```

For **Use Case F**, the field references look like this:

```
<p>The value of Status__c is '{status}'</p>
<p>The value of FastestLapBy__c is '{fastestLapBy}'</p>
```

To make it easier to understand the effects of field-level security, the component outputs debug text at the top of the component to confirm the current field access configured for the user. As you can see, in each case, the visibility and editability for both of the fields aligns with the current user's field-level security, as they have full read and write access to the field values. The following screenshot shows how the UI reacts when the user has full access:

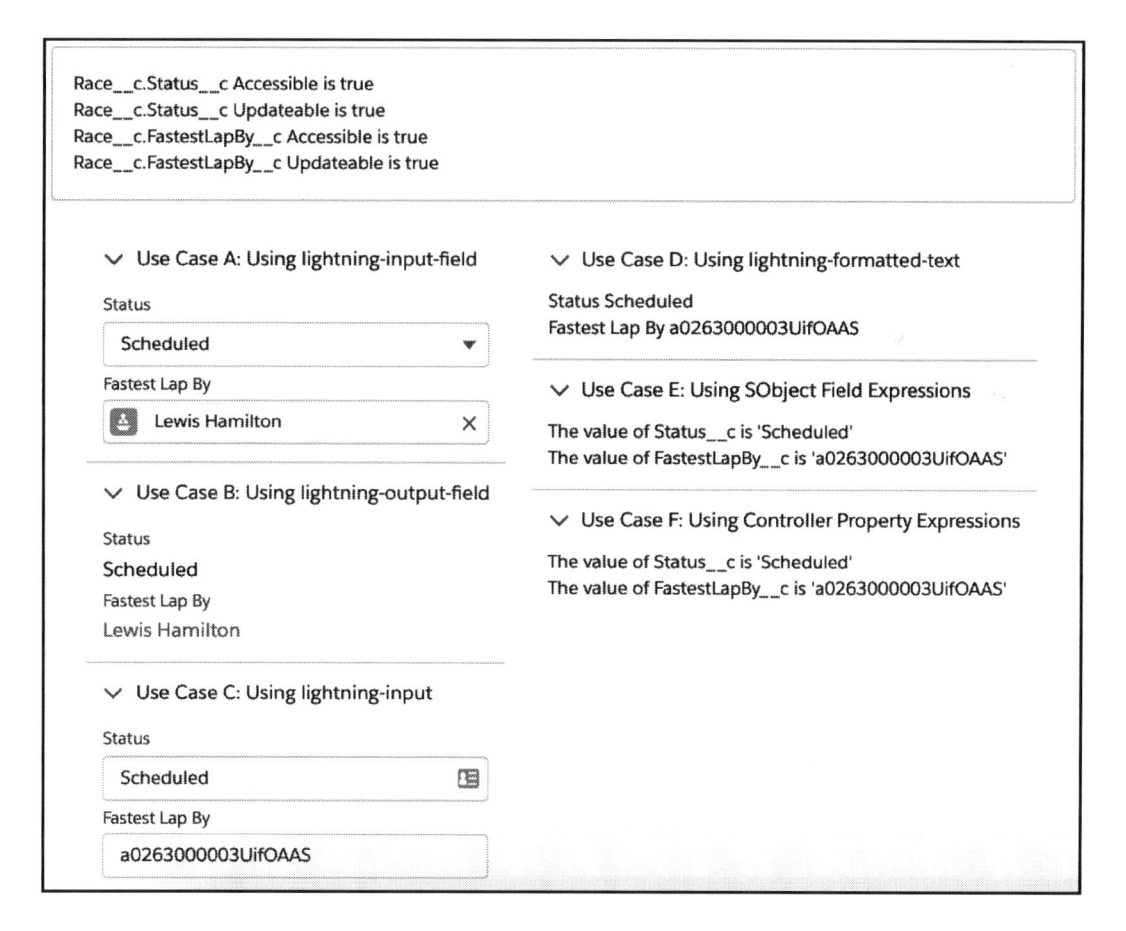

Race__c.Status__c Accessible is true
Race__c.Status__c Updateable is true
Race__c.FastestLapBy__c Accessible is true
Race__c.FastestLapBy__c Updateable is true

∨ Use Case A: Using lightning-input-field

Status
[Scheduled ▼]

Fastest Lap By
[🧑 Lewis Hamilton ✕]

∨ Use Case B: Using lightning-output-field

Status
Scheduled
Fastest Lap By
Lewis Hamilton

∨ Use Case C: Using lightning-input

Status
[Scheduled 🔲]
Fastest Lap By
[a0263000003UifOAAS]

∨ Use Case D: Using lightning-formatted-text

Status Scheduled
Fastest Lap By a0263000003UifOAAS

∨ Use Case E: Using SObject Field Expressions

The value of Status__c is 'Scheduled'
The value of FastestLapBy__c is 'a0263000003UifOAAS'

∨ Use Case F: Using Controller Property Expressions

The value of Status__c is 'Scheduled'
The value of FastestLapBy__c is 'a0263000003UifOAAS'

Building User Interfaces

> The Apex `FLSDemoController` is included in the sample code for this chapter; it simply reads a `Race__c` record in your org. The full component HTML code (not shown here) also uses the `lightning-record-edit` component to read Race record data. Finally, study the `flsDemo.js` component controller to see how it programmatically discovers a field level of access for the current user.

In contrast to the preceding scenario, the following screenshot and explanations confirm how the same component code reacts and displays to a user who has reduced field access; it shows that in some cases, the **Fastest Lap By** field has been hidden and that the **Status** field is read-only. Notice that this is not the case for all use cases shown:

- For **Use Case C**, the field is read only, so its value is accessible and placed in the input field. As it is a `lightning-input` field, it does not honor the field-level security status of the field and the field is editable when it should not be.
- For **Use Case E** and **Use Case F**, the `FastedLapBy__c` field value is shown because neither SObject field bindings or bindings to controller properties will enforce field-level security. In this case, the responsibility lies with the developer to check the field-level security in the controller code.

The following screenshot shows how the UI reacts for a user with reduced field access:

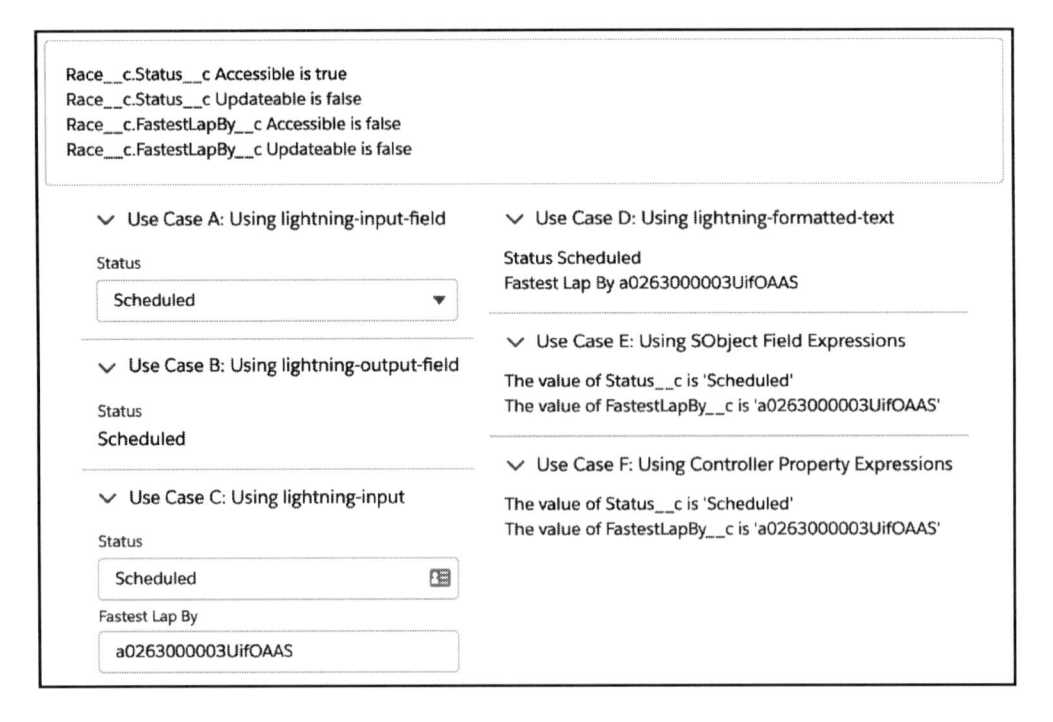

```
Race__c.Status__c Accessible is true
Race__c.Status__c Updateable is false
Race__c.FastestLapBy__c Accessible is false
Race__c.FastestLapBy__c Updateable is false
```

∨ Use Case A: Using lightning-input-field

Status

[Scheduled ▼]

∨ Use Case B: Using lightning-output-field

Status
Scheduled

∨ Use Case C: Using lightning-input

Status

[Scheduled]

Fastest Lap By

[a0263000003UifOAAS]

∨ Use Case D: Using lightning-formatted-text

Status Scheduled
Fastest Lap By a0263000003UifOAAS

∨ Use Case E: Using SObject Field Expressions

The value of Status__c is 'Scheduled'
The value of FastestLapBy__c is 'a0263000003UifOAAS'

∨ Use Case F: Using Controller Property Expressions

The value of Status__c is 'Scheduled'
The value of FastestLapBy__c is 'a0263000003UifOAAS'

Using the `lightning-input-field` and `lightning-output-field` components is not only the best way to ensure that field-level security is enforced without any code, but they also bring with them additional features, such as formatting field values such as currency values, translating record IDs to record names, and showing drop-down lists for picklist fields.

> **TIP**
> To use `lightning-input-field`, you have to use `lightning-record-edit`, which does not require an Apex controller to be written. However, if your requirements are advanced such that you need to invoke an Apex controller method to process field data, you can use the `value` property on the `lightning-input-field` component to access the current value.

Enforcing security in Visualforce

Visualforce pages exposing the SObject information (either via Standard, Custom, or Extension Controllers) can leverage built-in **object and field-level security enforcements** when using components or expressions that reference SObject fields directly; such usage will honor the user's field-level security. However, Visualforce expressions referencing SObject fields by way of a controller property are not affected, as the Visualforce engine cannot tell whether the controller property in turn refers to an SObject field.

When using the `apex:inputField` and `apex:outputField` components, fields (including the label, if present) will be hidden or made read-only accordingly. A less well-known fact is that direct SObject field expressions are also affected by field-level security; for example, `{!Race__c.Status__c}` will not be evaluated (no output emitted to the page) if the user has no read access to the `Status__c` field. This behavior is particularly subtle and is not well documented.

> The documentation states that when using components such as `apex:inputText` and `apex:outputText`, these will not enforce field security. While this is correct, security is always applied to **SObject field expressions**. So, if a field is not visible (as opposed to just read-only), even the `apex:outputText` component will not display a value. However, if a field is read-only and is used with `apex:inputText` (for example), it will render as an editable field. Thus, the general guideline here is that if you have an SObject field expression, use the recommended `apex:inputField` and `apex:outputField` components.

Building User Interfaces

First, review the Visualforce page; each section shows the following use case:

- Use Case A shows the use of `apex:inputField`.
- Use Case B shows the use of `apex:outputField`.
- Use Case C shows the use of `apex:inputText`.
- Use Case D shows the use of `apex:outputText`.
- Use Case E shows the use of an SObject field expression.
- Use Case F shows the use of a controller property expression.

To make it easier to compare, messages are shown on the page to confirm the level of field access. `FLSDemoController` is included in the sample code for this chapter; it simply reads the first `Race__c` record in your org. It exposes two string properties, indirectly exposing the `Status__c` and `FastestLapBy__c` field values. The following code shows the Visualforce page used to illustrate the effects of using different Visualforce bindings and components against the permissions of the current user:

```
<apex:pageMessage summary="Race__c.Status__c Accessible is
        {!$ObjectType.Race__c.fields.Status__c.Accessible}"
        severity="info"/>
<apex:pageMessage summary="Race__c.Status__c Updatable is
        {!$ObjectType.Race__c.fields.Status__c.Updateable}"
        severity="info"/>
<apex:pageMessage
        summary="Race__c.FastestLapBy__c Accessible is
         {!$ObjectType.Race__c.fields.FastestLapBy__c.Accessible}"
        severity="info"/>
<apex:pageMessage
        summary="Race__c.FastestLapBy__c Updatable is
         {!$ObjectType.Race__c.fields.FastestLapBy__c.Updateable}"
        severity="info"/><apex:pageBlock>

<apex:pageBlockSection title="Use Case A: Using apex:inputField">
  <apex:inputField value="{!Race.Status__c}"/>
  <apex:inputField value="{!Race.FastestLapBy__c}"/>
</apex:pageBlockSection>

<apex:pageBlockSection title="Use Case B: Using apex:outputField">
  <apex:outputField value="{!Race.Status__c}"/>
  <apex:outputField value="{!Race.FastestLapBy__c}"/>
</apex:pageBlockSection>

<apex:pageBlockSection title="Use Case C: Using apex:inputText">
  <apex:inputText value="{!Race.Status__c}"/>
  <apex:inputText value="{!Race.FastestLapBy__c}"/>
</apex:pageBlockSection>
```

```
<apex:pageBlockSection title="Use Case D: Using apex:outputText">
  <apex:outputText value="{!Race.Status__c}"/>
  <apex:outputText value="{!Race.FastestLapBy__c}"/>
</apex:pageBlockSection>

<apex:pageBlockSection
    title="Use Case E: Using SObject Field Expressions">
  <apex:pageBlockSection>
    The value of Status__c is '{!Race.Status__c}'
  </apex:pageBlockSection>
  <apex:pageBlockSection>
    The value of FastestLapBy__c is '{!Race.FastestLapBy__c}'
  </apex:pageBlockSection>
</apex:pageBlockSection>

<apex:pageBlockSection
    title="Use Case F: Using Controller Property Expressions">
  <apex:pageBlockSection>
    The value of Status__c is '{!Status}'
  </apex:pageBlockSection>
  <apex:pageBlockSection>
    The value of FastestLapBy__c is '{!FastestLapBy}'
  </apex:pageBlockSection>
</apex:pageBlockSection>
```

In addition to using Apex described within your Apex controller code, you can also directly determine a field's accessibility using the $ObjectType global variable within your binding expressions on the page. For example, you can use the following expression to hide an entire section based on a given field's security, {!$ObjectType.Race__c.fields.Status__c.Accessible}.

Building User Interfaces

For a user with full access, this page displays as follows:

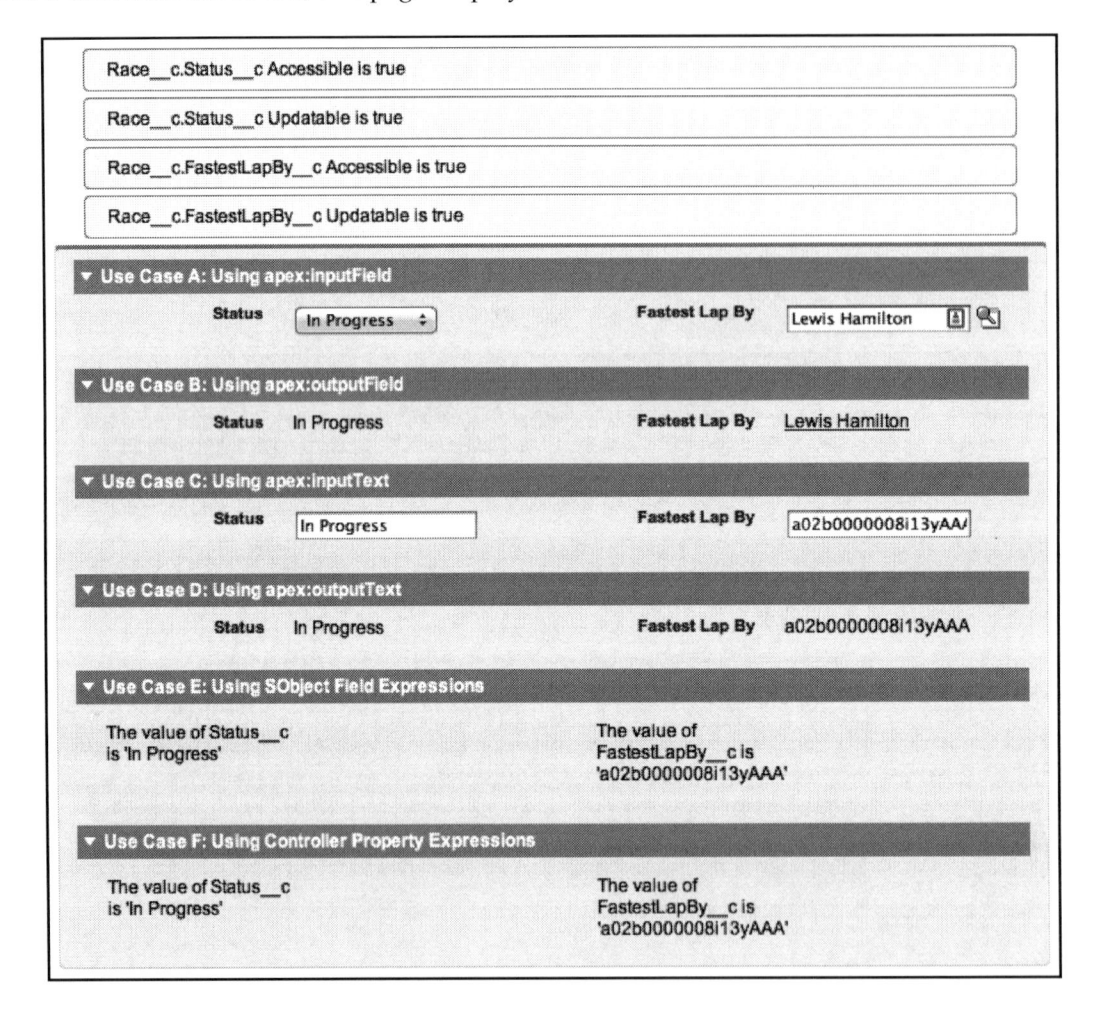

```
Race__c.Status__c Accessible is true
Race__c.Status__c Updatable is true
Race__c.FastestLapBy__c Accessible is true
Race__c.FastestLapBy__c Updatable is true
```

▼ Use Case A: Using apex:inputField

| Status | In Progress | Fastest Lap By | Lewis Hamilton |

▼ Use Case B: Using apex:outputField

| Status | In Progress | Fastest Lap By | Lewis Hamilton |

▼ Use Case C: Using apex:inputText

| Status | In Progress | Fastest Lap By | a02b0000008i13yAA/ |

▼ Use Case D: Using apex:outputText

| Status | In Progress | Fastest Lap By | a02b0000008i13yAAA |

▼ Use Case E: Using SObject Field Expressions

The value of Status__c is 'In Progress'

The value of FastestLapBy__c is 'a02b0000008i13yAAA'

▼ Use Case F: Using Controller Property Expressions

The value of Status__c is 'In Progress'

The value of FastestLapBy__c is 'a02b0000008i13yAAA'

In contrast, the following screenshot and explanations confirm how the same page reacts and displays to a user with reduced field access; this screenshot shows that the **Fastest Lap By** field has been hidden and that the **Status** field is read-only, as expected. Notice that this is not the case for all fields shown on the page, the exceptions being **Use Case C** and **Use Case F**:

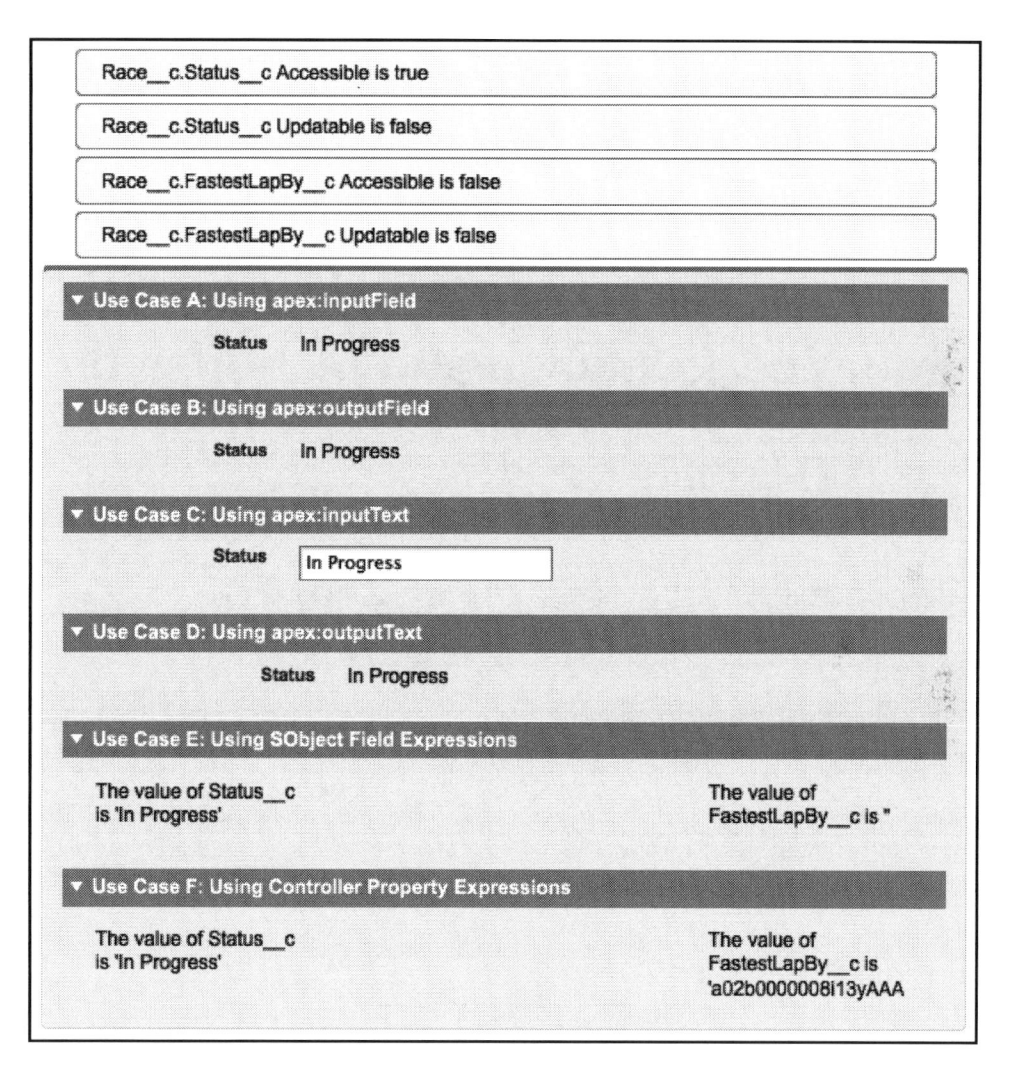

```
Race__c.Status__c Accessible is true
Race__c.Status__c Updatable is false
Race__c.FastestLapBy__c Accessible is false
Race__c.FastestLapBy__c Updatable is false
```

▼ **Use Case A: Using apex:inputField**

  Status   In Progress

▼ **Use Case B: Using apex:outputField**

  Status   In Progress

▼ **Use Case C: Using apex:inputText**

  Status   [In Progress]

▼ **Use Case D: Using apex:outputText**

  Status   In Progress

▼ **Use Case E: Using SObject Field Expressions**

  The value of Status__c   The value of
  is 'In Progress'   FastestLapBy__c is ''

▼ **Use Case F: Using Controller Property Expressions**

  The value of Status__c   The value of
  is 'In Progress'   FastestLapBy__c is
                                   'a02b0000008i13yAAA

We can also make the following observations with respect to the preceding screenshot:

- For Use Case C, the field is read-only, so its value is accessible and placed in the input field. As it is an `apex:inputText` field, it does not honor the field-level security status of the field, and the field is editable when it should not be.
- For Use Case F, the `FastedLapBy__c` field value is shown because it is not using a SObject field binding; it is using a binding to controller property, which is indirectly exposing the field value. In this case, the responsibility lies with the developer to check the field-level security in the controller code.

Now that we have reviewed security aspects in respect to building custom user experiences, the following section explores approaches to monitor and optimize performance.

Managing performance and response times

The response times in your solutions can make a big difference to the usability of the application. This section provides information on how to monitor and manage response times in Lightning and Visualforce.

Lightning Tools to monitor size and response times

In Lightning, it is important to monitor the complexity of your component hierarchy. While it is good to be componentized for reasons of separation of concerns, too much of it can result in a heavy component tree and result in poor performance. Salesforce provides an excellent tool known as **Lightning Inspector**, which provides insights into your component hierarchy and the rendering times for each component. You can download and install it from the Google Chrome web store.

The following shows an example screenshot for the FormulaForce application:

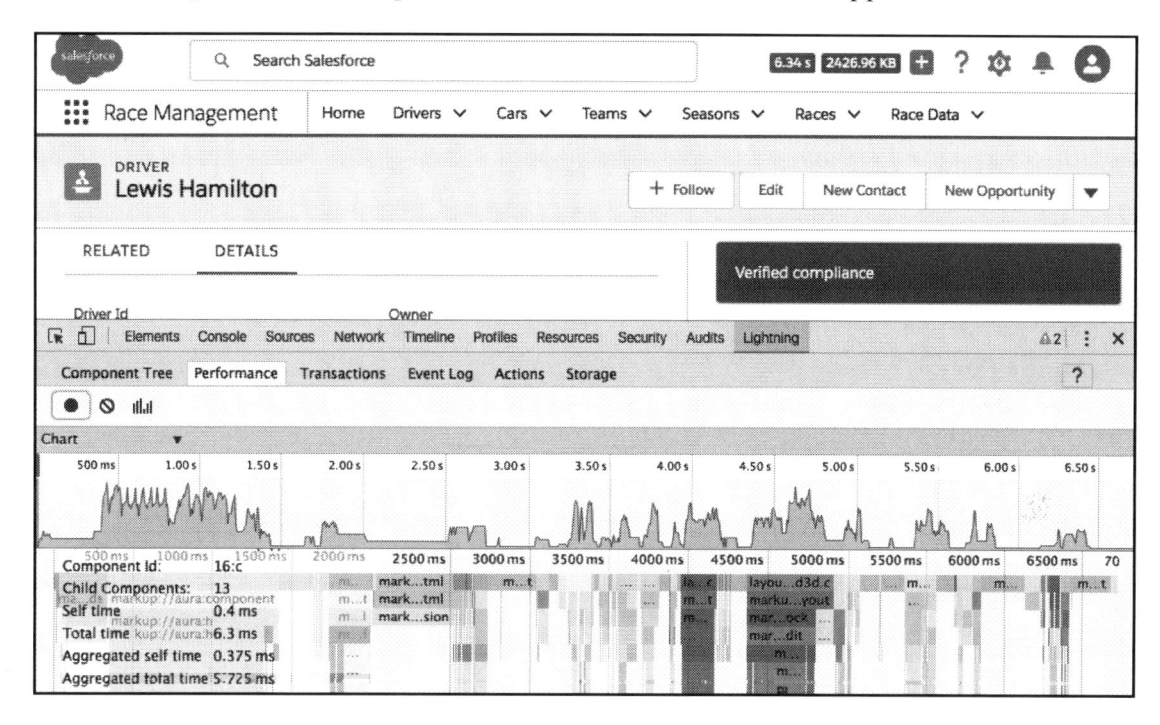

You may also have noticed that LEX displays page size and response time in the header:

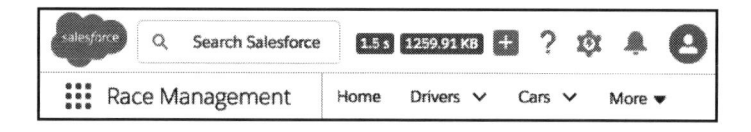

The preceding diagrams show additional performance information available to developers, showing the page load time and the size of the page. In the next section, we will review the tools used to understand the performance impact the locker service can have on your code.

Lightning Tools to monitor locker service performance

Locker service is a security layer automatically injected into your Lightning Component code by the platform to ensure that information the component can access stays within the scope of content on the page that only each component manages. This is important for users since they may configure a **Lightning Page** (via **Lightning App Builder**) with Lightning Components from multiple vendors and they need to be confident they are isolated from each other.

Salesforce provides the **Locker Console** as part of its **Lightning Web Component Developers Guide** website (`https://developer.salesforce.com/docs/component-library/documentation/lwc`). The following screenshot shows the output from the **Benchmark** button, which can be used to run performance tests on fragments of Lightning Web Component code:

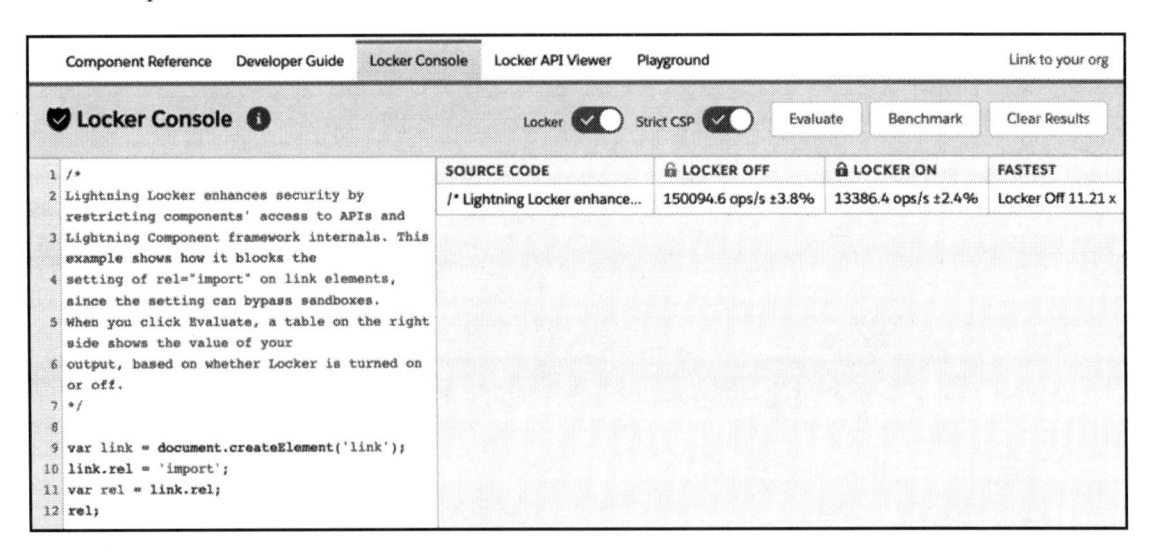

Take the time to review the rest of the features, such as the **Locker API Viewer**, **Playground**, and the **Component Reference**, which provides an interactive way to try out the base Lightning Components provided by Salesforce.

Visualforce view state size

Visualforce Developer's Guide has a section within it entitled *Best Practices for Improving Visualforce Performance* (`https://www.developerforce.com/guides/Visualforce_in_Practice.pdf`), which outlines some excellent ways to ensure that your pages remain responsive. I highly recommend that you take the time to read through it. There is, however, one point in that topic that I want to elaborate on further in this section:

> *"If your view state is affected by a large component tree, try reducing the number of components your page depends on."*

This symptom can result in poor response times, even for pages that are properly optimized in all other regards described in the documentation. The cause stems from the internal overhead of the Salesforce Visualforce components, known as **internal view state**, which increases when you have many such components on the page, typically in tabular or `apex:repeat` scenarios.

Depending on your Visualforce page design, it can often represent proportionally more than the data the developer explicitly places in the view state through controller properties and member variables. Together, they both contribute to reaching the 145 KB limit on view state size, though before this is reached, larger view states can affect response times.

Considerations for managing large component trees

Here are a few considerations when designing Visualforce pages utilizing tables or repeated sections that contain the native Visualforce components:

- View state is only generated if you have an `apex:form` tag on the page; if you don't need one, then you should remove it, for example, in view-only pages.
- Consider if you need to use Visualforce components such as `apex:outputField`, or if using HTML elements directly with a Visualforce expression would suffice. HTML elements consume no view state. However, be careful to consider localization features the standard components provide when doing this, such as formatting dates and numbers; you might need to perform this in the Apex code and bind to the formatted values.
- Avoid nested `apex:repeat` tags that contain Visualforce components. If possible, flatten a nested structure with the Apex logic in your controller and expose a single iterable list property that results in the same output.

Building User Interfaces

- Consider moving to a stateless controller mode, as described in the following section.
- Consider implementing pagination in your page.

> **TIP**
> For further analysis, search `http://salesforce.stackexchange.com/` for *How to reduce a large internal view state / what is in the internal view state?*

Using the Service layer and database access

To make Lightning Component controller server-side calls to Apex, use the `@AuraEnabled` annotation method and the applicable Lightning Aura Component or Lightning Web Component communication method (as outlined in the earlier table) to invoke the method:

```
public with sharing class RaceResultsController {
  @AuraEnabled
  public static List<RaceService.ProvisionalResult>
      loadProvisionalResults(Id raceId) {
    try {
        return RaceService.calculateProvisionResults(
          new Set<Id>{ raceId }).get(raceId);
    } catch (Exception e) {
        Application.throwAuraHandledException(e);
    }
  }
}
```

You will need to ensure that you throw an `AuraHandledException` exception from your controller code to allow the platform to pass the error to your client code. As previously discussed, we are using a utility function in the `Application` class for this. You will also need to apply the `@AuraEnabled` method to accessors for Apex types referenced by the Controller methods:

```
public class ProvisionalResult {
    @AuraEnabled
    public Integer racePosition {get; set;}
    @AuraEnabled
    public Id contestantId {get; set;}
    @AuraEnabled
    public String contestantName {get; set;}
}
```

As with the Visualforce standard controller action methods you've seen in the earlier chapters, the **Service** layer can also be called from **Visualforce JavaScript Remoting** methods, as follows:

```
public with sharing class RaceResultsController {
  @RemoteAction
  public static List<RaceService.ProvisionalResult>
     loadProvisionalResults(Id raceId) {
    return RaceService.calculateProvisionResults(
       new Set<Id>{ raceId }).get(raceId);
  }
}
```

In either case, when exceptions are thrown, the platform takes care of catching the exception and passing it back to the calling client-side JavaScript code for it to display accordingly. In short, there is no need to invent your own error message handling system; just let the platform handle passing it back to the client JavaScript code for you. Remember, though, that you still need to handle displaying the error message in your client-side JavaScript logic.

Considerations for client-side logic and Service layer logic

With the addition of more complex logic in the client via JavaScript, more attention needs to be given to the **separation of concerns**. The following points provide some guidelines for this:

- **Single service method per remoting method**: A single Service layer method invocation rule should still be observed when developing remoting methods on the controller. If multiple Service layer methods are being called, this becomes a sign that a new aggregate Service layer method should be created and called instead.
- **Avoid remoting client bias**: Do not be tempted to design your Service layer solely around your JavaScript Remoting controller method needs (the needs of your JavaScript client). Always consider the Service layer as client-agnostic; this becomes particularly important if you want to also later expose your Service layer as an API to your application.

- **Apex Enum types**: If you utilize Enum types in your Service layer design (to be honest, why would you not?), they are very expressive and self-documenting! However, they unfortunately, at this time, are not supported by the JavaScript Remoting JSON deserializer, which means that you can return Apex data structures containing them, but cannot receive them from the client (a platform exception occurs). The workarounds are to either not use Enums and drop back to using string data types, or to create Apex class data types within the controller class and perform your own marshaling between these types and service types (leveraging the `Enum.name()` method to map Enums to string values). The choice is between your desire to protect your Service layer's use of Enums (especially if it is your public-facing API) and the effort involved. Hopefully, at some point, Salesforce will fix this issue.

When should I use JavaScript for database access?

Lightning Data Service and **JavaScript Remote Objects** (Visualforce) are designed to expose a "SOQL- and DML-like API" for use by client JavaScript code. They provide a way to query and update the database without having to go through the legacy AJAX Toolkit or Salesforce REST APIs that incur charges to the daily API limit.

Visualforce Developer's Guide has an excellent topic that describes the best practices around using this feature, entitled *Best Practices for Using Remote Objects* (`https://developer.salesforce.com/docs/atlas.en-us.pages.meta/pages/pages_remote_objects_considerations.htm`), which I highly recommend that you read and digest fully. *The Lightning Aura Component Developer Guide* also has samples describing the Lightning Data Service (`https://developer.salesforce.com/docs/atlas.en-us.218.0.lightning.meta/lightning/data_service.htm`) and the *Lightning Web Component Developer Guide* (`https://developer.salesforce.com/docs/component-library/documentation/lwc/lwc.data_ui_api`).

The main aspect from the references that I would like to highlight is the one that relates to your awareness of transactional boundaries in close conjunction with maintaining a good Separation of Concerns. Resist the temptation to invoke multiple database operations within a single JavaScript code block, as each will be executed in its own Salesforce execution context and, thus, transaction. This means that if an error occurs in your JavaScript code, previous operations will not be rolled back.

If you find yourself in this situation, it is also likely that you should be positioning such code in your application's Service layer and using the applicable communication method to call an Apex controller method that can invoke your Service layer method. At this point, you can perform multiple database operations knowing that they will be wrapped by a transaction.

That said, if you have use cases that result in a single database operation, then you can, of course, consider using this feature, safely assured that your Apex Trigger and Domain layer code will continue to enforce your data validation and integrity.

Finally, note that querying records from JavaScript does not invoke your Selector code. So the fields queried and populated in the resulting SObject records on the client will not always be the same in all cases throughout your JavaScript code.

Considerations for using JavaScript libraries

As discussed, the more you move toward a stateless server-side controller and the rich client architecture of Lightning Components, the more options open up to you in leveraging client-side components not presently provided by Salesforce. The Lightning Component library, at the time of writing, is growing fast, so you should always check the *Lightning Component Reference* first (https://developer.salesforce.com/docs/component-library/overview/components)!

Consider the use of third-party UI libraries carefully on a per-case basis (not all of your application UI has to use the same approach) and make sure that you appreciate the value of the platform features that you are leaving behind. Expect to adjust your expectations around your client developer's skills, velocity, and tooling. Libraries such as AngularJS, React, View.js, and Ember.js (to name only a few) can provide additional convenience, flexibility, and components available in their respective communities over the Salesforce-based Lightning Components.

> **TIP**
> Lightning implements a security layer around your components, known as the locker service. This blocks eval, enforces the use of strict mode, and restricts access to the DOM outside your components own boundaries. Check that the third-party libraries you intend to use in Lightning Components are compatible with this type of security context.

All of these libraries require a good deal of JavaScript programming knowledge, including its OOP style of programming. Some provide the **Model View Controller** (**MVC**) frameworks as well, such as **AngularJS**. If you search on Google for Salesforce and, for example, AngularJS, you will find many examples and articles from the community and the Salesforce Developer Evangelists team.

Here are some aspects of developing with such libraries, which you should consider:

- **Developer flow**: Optimize the process from storing the JavaScript code in source control, pushing it into an org for testing, editing code, and debugging it, and then placing it back into Source Control. If you are using Lightning Components, this is optimized for you. You can import external JavaScript libraries using the `import` statement. If you use Static Resources, Visual Studio code will allow you to store the external libraries in uncompressed form and will automatically zip them up each time you push your code to the scratch org.

- **Security**: Salesforce takes a great deal of care with their Visualforce and Lightning components to ensure that the escape values are displayed by the components to prevent attacks such as HTML injection. Check your components' escape values to ensure that they inject into the DOM from your database records, or you could find yourself open to attack and delays getting through the Salesforce Security Review.

- **Testing frameworks**: There are a number of approaches when testing rich clients, ranging from unit testing frameworks that have the developer write a JavaScript code to testing commercial applications that actually drive the web browser and assert the state of the page. Make sure that you invest according to the amount of JavaScript code your application contains.

Custom Publisher Actions

In `Chapter 2`, *Leveraging Platform Features*, we created a **Publisher Action** to mark a **Contestant** as a **DNF** (Did Not Finish) object easily from a Chatter feed. This leveraged the declarative approach to creating Publisher Actions, based on creating or updating a related record. If your use case does not fit into this type of operation, you can use Lightning Component to develop a **Lightning Action**.

Creating websites and communities

Salesforce now recommends that **Lightning Communities** is used to create websites for your users, customers, and partners. This feature is based on **Lightning Components** and uses **Lightning Community Builder** to allow you to leverage templates that you can customize with standard Lightning Components or customer components you build.

Historically, Salesforce provided the following two ways to create public-facing web content, which are still available for existing customers, although Lightning Communities should be seen as the successor to these capabilities:

- **Force.com Sites**: This offers a means to create public-facing authenticated or public websites using Visualforce pages. Due to this, it can access Standard and Custom Objects using the approaches described in this chapter, reusing components and services from your application as needed. The Force.com site configuration cannot be packaged, though the pages and controllers you create to support them can be. This feature is available in the **Enterprise** and **Developer Edition** orgs. It is possible to use Lightning Components via Lightning Out for Visualforce pages.

- **Sites.com**: This is a declarative website product that is targeted at non-technical users. Visualforce pages cannot be used directly with Site.com, though components available with Site.com can access your application's Custom Objects and, as such, will invoke your Apex Trigger and thus Domain logic code. It is possible to use Lightning Components with Sites.com via Community Builder.

Mobile application strategy

Mobile application development using Salesforce has been a hot topic for the last few years, starting with the use of various well-known mobile frameworks, such as jQuery mobile, and AngularJS, along with Salesforce's own APIs, including **OAuth** for authentication, and the **Salesforce REST API** to access Standard and Custom Object records, leading up to the current development around the latest Salesforce Mobile application.

The interesting thing about this is that it has evolved in a different way to the browser UI, which started with the standard declarative-driven UI and could then be augmented with a more developer-driven solution, such as Visualforce. For a mobile UI, up until the release of Salesforce Mobile, we only had the option of building a custom UI with a developer.

Building User Interfaces

As things stand today, we now have both options available for building mobile UIs. As such, make sure that you understand first and foremost the capability of the Salesforce Mobile application and its ability to surface your objects through its standard UI. **Lightning Actions** provide an excellent way to enhance the **Chatter feed** presence of your application and also add the same actions to your users' Salesforce Mobile experience.

Salesforce Mobile's UI model is not for everyone; it is, like the browser UI, mostly data-centric if you wish to expose a more fine-tailored, process-driven user experience for a very specific mobile application. If this is something you feel you need, you can review the Salesforce Mobile website to choose the architecture and APIs that suit your needs the best (https://developer.salesforce.com/mobile).

> **TIP**
> For added company branding, Salesforce provides a service known as **Mobile Publisher** that allows its customers to publish their own application based on Lightning Platform and Salesforce Mobile in the **AppleApple VPP App Store** or **Google Play** store. Their employees can then access fully branded applications easily from their devices. As an application developer, you should at least be aware of this service and make sure your Lightning Components work well in Salesforce Mobile. You can learn more about this service via this Trailhead module: https://trailhead.salesforce.com/content/learn/modules/salesforce1_branded_apps.

Custom reporting and the Analytics API

Sometimes, the standard output from the **Salesforce Reporting** engine is just not what your users are looking for. They require formatting or a layout not supported by Salesforce, but the way in which they have defined the report is appealing to them.

The **Salesforce Analytics API** allows you to build a Visualforce page or mobile application that can execute a given **tabular**, **summary**, or **matrix report** and return its data into your client code to be rendered accordingly. The API is available directly to Apex developers and as a **REST API** for native mobile applications.

> **TIP**
> You might want to consider using a report to drive an alternative approach to selecting records for an additional process in your application by leveraging the flexibility of the **Report Designer** as a kind of record selection UI.

Updating the FormulaForce package

As in previous chapters, feel free to update your package and try out an installation of the package in your test org.

Summary

In this chapter, we learned that Salesforce provides a great standard UI experience that is highly customizable and adaptable to new features of the platform without you necessarily releasing new revisions of your application. We observed that at its core, it is a data-centric user experience, which means that most tasks come down to creating, editing, or deleting records of some kind. Having a strong focus on your Domain layer code ensures that it protects the data integrity of your application.

We learned that if you want to express a more complex process or a series of tasks, Lightning and Visualforce allow you to be more expressive, using components or other HTML libraries to create the user experience needed for the task at hand. While this is very powerful, it is important to always consider the standard UI and, wherever possible, augment or complement it with the standard Salesforce components rather than making this the only way of interacting with your application.

When we discussed custom user experiences, we learned that it is equally important to observe best practices around engineering for performance and security. Thus, I recommend you consider carefully and choose wisely the degree to which you depart from the standard UI and/or standard components because the further you move away from these, the more responsibility and complexity you have to deal with as a developer. Look for opportunities to create hybrid standard UI and custom UI combinations to get the best of both worlds.

We considered your application's data and the fact that, sometimes, viewing it can be something you want to carefully consider for your target users; we learned that the Salesforce Analytics API allows you to harness the power of the Salesforce Report Designer and engine with a more tailored rendering of the reporting data returned.

Building User Interfaces

As you have discovered, there are combinations of technologies and approaches to building a mobile user experience for your users. In summary, start with the standard UI in the browser; start with what Salesforce provides you and your users with as standard. The Salesforce Mobile mobile application is effectively a platform feature that users expect to be able to use with your application objects like any other. As we discussed, building custom UIs for use within Salesforce Mobile is best accomplished using Lightning Components. However, if you choose to build your own mobile application, you can choose to develop it using one of Salesforce's Mobile SDKs as a starting point; alternatively, if you have the skills and experience, use them as a guide on how to call the various Salesforce APIs.

In the next chapter, we will go into more detail on ways to balance both Lightning and Visualforce technologies, allowing you to start using Lightning Framework for new features while you consider options for migrating your existing Visualforce pages.

9
User Interfaces with Lightning Framework

Lightning is a rich client-side framework for developing device-agnostic and responsive **user experiences** (**UXs**) as well as for supporting mobile, tablet, and desktop. Unlike **Visualforce**, it was built from the ground up with today's multi-device rich client demands in mind. It is used by Salesforce themselves and is also available to developers to build their own standalone or platform-integrated UIs. Using **Lightning Out**, developers can also integrate UIs built with Lightning into **external sites** and applications. An emphasis on componentization is at the heart of its architecture and plays a key part in providing a means to implement reuse, separation of concerns, and extensibility.

This chapter provides an architectural overview of the Lightning Component architecture while contrasting it with its predecessor, Visualforce. New **Lightning Components** called **Race Calendar**, **Race Results**, **Race Standings**, and **Race Setup** will allow us to explore the development process and styling using the **Lightning Design System**.

Using the new components, we will explore the options for, and the benefits of, integrating components into **Lightning Experience**, **Salesforce Mobile**, and **Lightning Communities**, as well as existing Visualforce pages. **Lightning Out** and **Lightning Out for Visualforce** allow existing solutions to continue to support Salesforce Classic while moving toward Lightning. **Lightning Flow** integration allows you and/or your users to customize the UIs built with the clicks-not-code **Lightning Flow Builder** tool with your packaged components.

User Interfaces with Lightning Framework

We will cover the following topics in this chapter:

- Overview of the two Lightning component frameworks
- Understanding the various component containers
- Building components that your end users can customize
- Using components to extend Lightning UIs and tools
- Understanding how to write secure JavaScript code
- Styling your Lightning UIs

Building a basic Lightning UI

Before we dive into the more complex components included in the sample code for the FormulaForce application, let's first create a simple **Lightning application** to better understand the architecture of Lightning. Think of a Lightning application as a **container** for your UI, essentially your HTML markup. Containers are effectively things you can navigate to in the browser; they get their own URL based on the name that you give them.

> As we will explore later in the chapter, **Lightning Experience**, **Salesforce Mobile**, **Lightning Communities**, and **Lightning Flow** are also containers built by Salesforce in the same way as the example that follows.

If you want to follow along with the next few steps, ensure that you have installed Visual Studio Code and have the extension for **Lightning Web Components** installed. We will be taking a closer look at the features around Lightning later in this chapter.

Follow these steps to create your first Lightning application:

1. Open Visual Studio Code and create a **Salesforce DX** project by pressing *Cmd* + *Shift* + *P* and selecting **SFDX: Create Project**.
2. Locate the `/force-app/main/default/aura` folder in the **Explorer** pane and right-click on it, selecting the **SFDX: Create Lightning Application** menu option.
3. Give your application the name `myapp` and press *Enter* to accept the defaults.

4. A Lightning application in source form is a folder that contains one or more files depending on the type. In this case, you will have a `.app` file, a `.css` file, and three `.js` files. Open the `myapp.app` file and enter the following markup, and then save the file:

   ```
   <aura:application>
     <h2>Success your first Lightning App</h2>
   </aura:application>
   ```

5. Create a **scratch org** for your project and push the code to it. Containers are essentially pages that you can navigate to with your browser. These work outside of the standard UIs from Salesforce, but still require you to log in.

6. After the push operation completes, open the scratch org and take note of the URL in the browser. This might be something like the following for the default Lightning Experience container: `https://site-momentum-8333-dev-ed.lightning.force.com/lightning/page/home`.

7. To launch the Lightning application you just created, modify the URL as follows, substituting `site-momentum-8333-dev-ed` in the URL for your scratch org's domain, as here: `https://site-momentum-8333-dev-ed.lightning.force.com/c/myapp.app`.

> The `c` in the preceding URL represents the default namespace of your org. If your org has a namespace, or you're attempting to launch a Lightning application from an installed package with a namespace of `coolapps`, for example, exchange it with the `/coolapps/myapp.app` namespace.

You should see the following message in your browser:

```
Success your first Lightning App
```

This type of Lightning application is known formally as a **Standalone Lightning App** in the *Lightning Components Developer Guide* (for more information, you can refer to `https://developer.salesforce.com/docs/atlas.en-us.lightning.meta/lightning/intro_framework.htm`).

Introduction to the Lightning Design System

Lightning brings with it a rich and sophisticated CSS library for styling the look and feel of your HTML. This is **Salesforce's Lightning Design System (SLDS)**. While you can include its CSS as a static resource in your application, it is not required for native Lightning UIs, such as the ones featured in this chapter.

By using the `extends` attribute in the following code, we can ask the framework to always include the latest platform version and start using its CSS classes to brighten up our output:

```
<aura:application extends="force:slds">
 <div class="slds-notify_container">
   <div class="slds-notify slds-notify--alert slds-theme--success slds-theme--alert-texture" role="alert">
     <span class="slds-assistive-text">Success</span>
     <h2>Success! Your first Lightning App</h2>
   </div>
 </div>
</aura:application>
```

> **TIP**
> Note the use of the `role` attribute and the `slds-assistive-text` class in the preceding code. While these are not required technically, they are present to ensure compatibility with users who require assistance in reading the screen. Lightning includes, and encourages support for, HTML5 standards around **accessibility**. We will discuss this further later in the chapter.

If you refresh your browser, you will now see what is shown in the following screenshot. The preceding HTML code was based on that provided on the SLDS website:

Success your first Lightning App

The SLDS (`https://www.lightningdesignsystem.com`) website is full of great sample HTML markup allowing you to explore, design, and test statically what you want your UIs to look like. Using a simple Lightning application like the previous one, you can continue to copy and paste examples to try different combinations out and access the data in your scratch org through them.

Keep in mind, however, that in order to be productive as a developer, what you really need is a component library with components that encapsulate the preceding HTML code, so that you can define once and reuse, rather than copying and pasting HTML over and over. You can build your own components, as we will see later, and leverage the SLDS within them as well.

Fortunately, Salesforce provides a large (and growing) number of basic to advanced components already styled by the SLDS for you, known as **base Lightning components**. We will explore these later in the chapter. Additionally, the **Component Reference** contains a rich set of examples for each available component (https://developer.salesforce.com/docs/component-library/overview/components). Also included is the **Playground** facility, which can be used to further explore sample code directly in the browser:

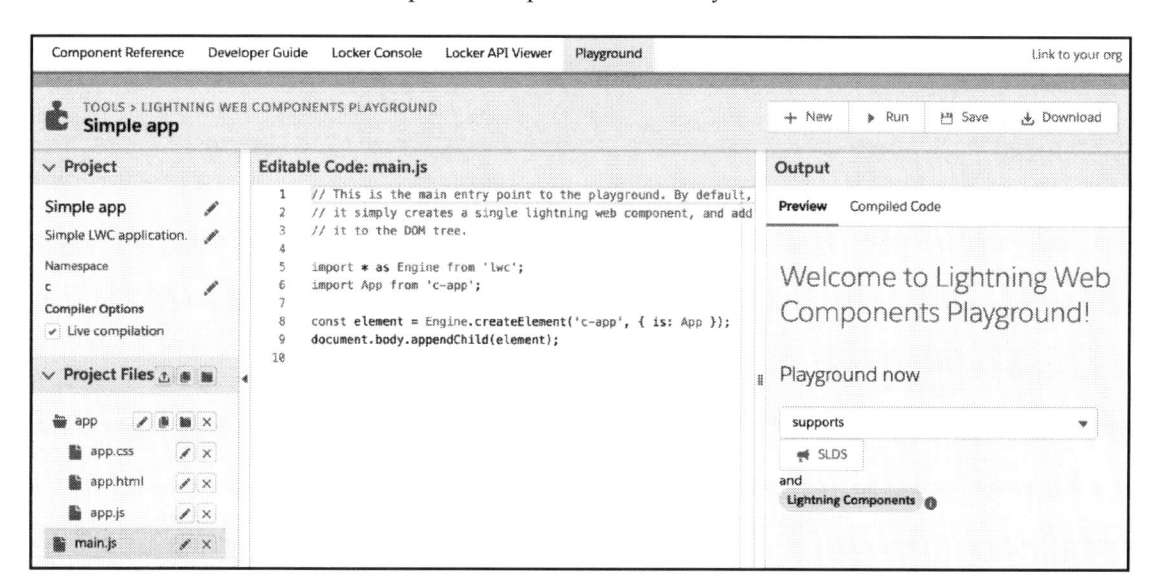

As you can see, this is a great way to try out fragments of code without having to use a scratch org. In the next section, we will create our first component within the Microsoft Visual Studio IDE tool, leveraging the Salesforce DX extensions.

Building your first component

Now, we will create a Lightning Web Component to encapsulate our success message – a component that could, for example, be the basis of a more reusable one for general informational messages:

1. Within the Visual Studio code project you created earlier, locate the /force-app/main/default/lwc folder in the **Explorer** pane and right-click on it, selecting the **SFDX: Create Lightning Web Component** menu option.
2. Give your component the name mycomponent and press *Enter* to accept the defaults.

3. Take the markup contained with the `aura:application` tag in the `myapp.app` file and paste the contents into your new `template` tag in the new `mycomponent.html` file, while also modifying the message, as shown here:

```
<template>
  <div class="slds-notify_container">
    <div class="slds-notify slds-notify--alert
                slds-theme--success
                slds-theme--alert-texture" role="alert">
      <span class="slds-assistive-text">Success</span>
      <h2>Success your first Lightning Component</h2>
    </div>
  </div>
</template>
```

4. Finally, modify the `myapp.app` file to use your new component:

```
<aura:applicationextends="force:slds">
  <c:mycomponent/>
</aura:application>
```

Refresh the browser and you will see the following:

> Success your first Lightning Component

The preceding code is the basic introduction to Lightning component development, intended to help you understand the high-level architecture of Lightning and how it fits into the standard HTML page model used by the internet. It is also providing an introduction to the styling and design framework that is the SLDS.

The Lightning component created here was created with the Lightning Web Component framework (the successor to the Lightning Aura Component framework). This means it uses the new modern browser standards, such **ECMAScript**, **web components**, **templates**, and **shadow DOM**. This means that you get a better return on the investment of your time when learning how to use Lightning Web Components, and if you are hiring, you get access to a broader set of already skilled applicants.

You can read more about these technologies at the following resources:

- `https://www.ecma-international.org/ecma-262/9.0/index.html`
- `https://developer.mozilla.org/en-US/docs/Web/Web_Components`
- `https://developer.mozilla.org/en-US/docs/Web/Web_Components/Using_custom_elements`

- `https://developer.mozilla.org/en-US/docs/Web/Web_Components/Using_templates_and_slots`
- `https://developer.mozilla.org/en-US/docs/Web/Web_Components/Using_shadow_DOM`

How does Lightning differ from other UI frameworks?

So far, things might feel quite familiar if you have developed in other UI frameworks, such as Salesforce's own Visualforce, or others, such as **Java Server Pages** (**JSP**) or ASP .NET. We have defined some markup, used CSS, and seen how we can encapsulate reusable portions of HTML. When the user navigates to the URL, the Lightning platform server-side code serves up the appropriate HTML to launch the specified application and render the referenced components. If you are a Visualforce developer, you might be thinking that this is not all that different from the use of Visualforce pages and Visualforce components.

While there are other similarities to other frameworks, such as the use of expressions, for example, the biggest departure from those technologies is the life cycle of the page itself. A server-side architecture often requires that the whole page be refreshed when the user performs an action. The information on the page, the *state* of the page, is transmitted back and forth between the client and the server each time the user performs an action. Server-side controller code controls validations, the loading of data, and the conditional display of the UI.

Increasingly, UI designs are catering for HTML pages that represent a single application or a workspace that users open and keep open. Users access different modules and perform various operations within them. This is typically known as the **Single-Page Application** (**SPA**) architecture. The traditional server-side page-refresh model is not responsive enough to meet these needs, especially in scenarios such as when only a portion of the page needs updating, for example. Even when the traditional **Asynchronous JavaScript and XML** (**AJAX**) approach is deployed, often the entire state of the page needs transmitting back to the server-side controller. Server-side UI frameworks are also not well suited for developing UXs that tolerate a lack of connectivity in temporary offline scenarios.

In contrast, Lightning applications are long-lived in the browser and depend on JavaScript code to manipulate the DOM of the page to load new content and functionality. The state of the operation the user is performing is stored in the browser and only transmitted when needed by the server to retrieve and update the database.

Lightning architecture

In this section, we will discuss key layers of the Lightning architecture, which will allow you to have a better framework of understanding as we go deeper.

A key aspect that took me by surprise at first is the need to write **client-side controllers** in JavaScript. This can be particularly puzzling at first if you are a Visualforce developer, but it is a vital part of being a Lightning developer and is a reflection of its client-side architecture. As we saw in the previous chapter, Apex server-side controllers still play a part, but are mainly used for accessing your backend Apex Services and Selectors.

In general, Lightning development is much more componentized. In terms of how the UI is designed and how the code is factored, the two are much more aligned, making it easier to maintain and navigate code. This also gives a much greater emphasis on the separation of concerns within the UI tier.

Containers

As we saw in the previous section, we created a basic container called `myapp` using a standalone Lightning app. It contained a single instance of our `mycomponent` component. It may not have looked like much, but `<aura:application>` provided a number of services for its components and for you as the developer. The following list details some of these services and how they are provided:

- It constructed the page `<HTML>` tag and loaded the appropriate JavaScript and CSS resources, such as the SLDS, and the Lightning JavaScript runtime, which allows your components to react to user interactions through client-side controller code.

> The `extends` attribute allows for inheritance from other `<aura:application>`-based applications. The preceding example extends the platform's `force:slds` application to inject the CSS for the SLDS.

- It loaded the components within its body, namely, the `mycomponent` component, but also any HTML markup that is present is also injected into the page. Each component started its own life cycle within the container. Much like an object in Apex, it was constructed, initialized, tracked, and can be destroyed.

> **Component management** is an important service since it helps avoid a common pitfall when developing rich client applications: poor resource management. Each HTML tag and its associated data takes up memory in the browser, and throughout the lifetime of the page, the amount of memory taken up can easily climb and cause issues if not properly managed.

- **URL parameters** are mapped automatically to `aura:attribute` components specified in the body of `aura:application`. See here, for example:

  ```
  /c/myapp.app?myparam=myvalue

  <aura:application extends="force:slds">
    <aura:attribute name="myparam" type="String"/>
    <h2>The value of myparam is '{!v.myparam}'</h2>
  </aura:application>
  ```

  This results in the following text being displayed in the browser:

  ```
  The value of myparam is 'myvalue'
  ```

- **URL-centric navigation** is an important aspect of the user experience and is an expectation when users are bookmarking or sharing links to records or certain pages in your web application. Since the application is designed to be long-lived, and changing the URL causes the entire page to reload, an alternative is needed. Modifying the bookmark portion of a URL does not reload the page. As such, Lightning applications leverage this to add more context to links stored by users, as well as using it during the application's own navigation. You can see this in action as you navigate through Lightning Experience. The framework provides the `aura:locationChange` event (Aura) or the standard `window.onhaschange` event (LWC) for your client-side logic to listen on to determine when changes are made.

You can see a simple example of the URL convention used at `/c/myapp.app#showraceresults-2016`.

You can read more about the attributes of `aura:application` in the *Lightning Aura Components Developer Guide*. Also, refer to the *Lightning Web Components Developer Guide* for more details on the navigation service, which is recommended when building more complex navigations that work within Salesforce containers. Not all the services may be relevant, depending on the container you're using. However, it is good to have a basic understanding of how things work even if you only ever leverage the Salesforce containers.

User Interfaces with Lightning Framework

Introducing the Racing Overview Lightning app

The **Racing Overview** Lightning standalone app is contained in the sample code for this chapter. It can be accessed through `/c/RacingOverviewLWC` for LWC, or via the **Lightning Experience** container through the **Race Overview** tab, as shown in the following screenshot.

> If you wish to review the same components written in Aura, use `/c/RacingOverviewAura`. Note that unless otherwise stated, this chapter focuses on building components using the Lightning Web Component framework. Aura versions are also included in the sample code for this book for you to compare.

The following screenshot shows what the app looks like and gives a first look at the Lightning components we will be covering in more detail throughout the rest of this chapter:

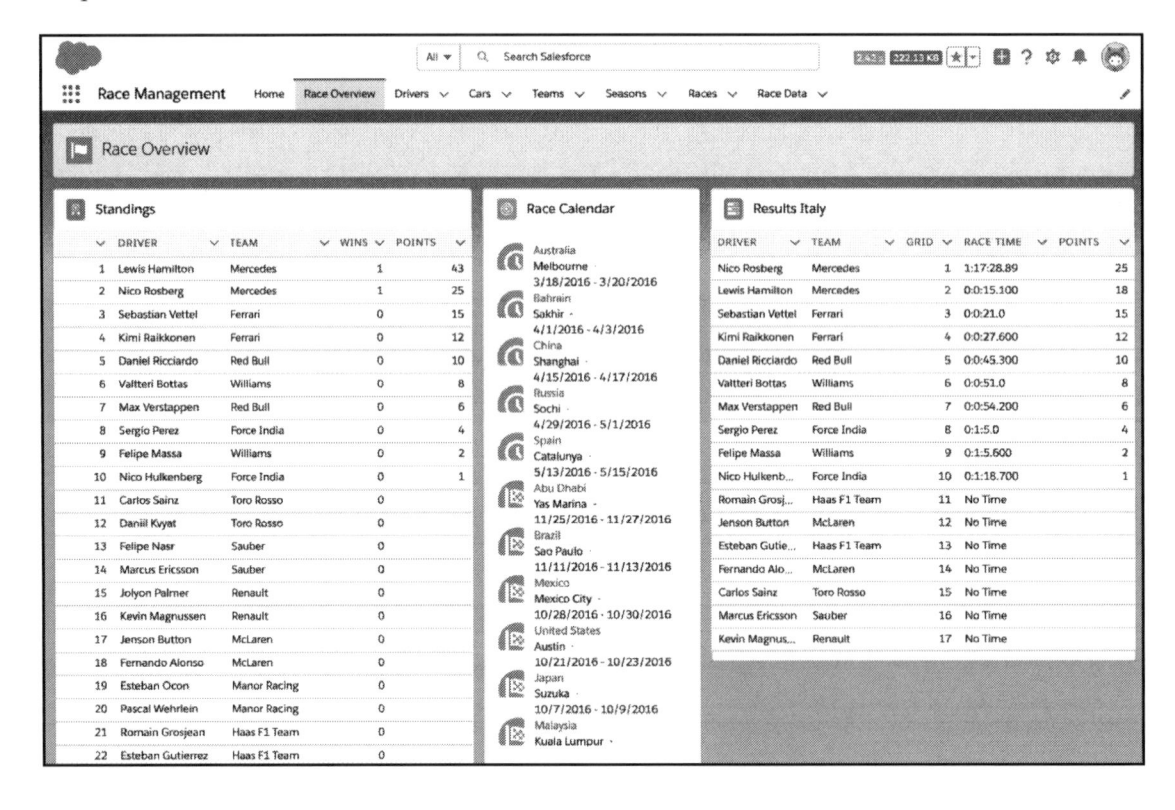

The sample record data shown in the preceding screenshot can be injected into your scratch org by running the `sfdx force:apex:execute` command (without any arguments) from the command line. When prompted, paste the following script and press *Ctrl + D* to execute it:

```
PageReference sampleData =
 new PageReference('/resource/sampledata');
String sampleDataJSON =
 sampleData.getContent().toString();
String orgNameSpace =
 SObjectDataLoader.class.toString().
 removeEnd('SObjectDataLoader').removeEnd('.');
SObjectDataLoader.deserialize(
 sampleDataJSON.replace('ns__',
 orgNameSpace.length()==0 ? '' : orgNameSpace+'__'));
```

Developing components with the Lightning component framework allows you to provide the same UI not only to users using desktop devices, but also mobile devices. In the next section, we will see how Salesforce Mobile can be used to render your components on a mobile device.

Lightning Experience and Salesforce Mobile

Salesforce has created its own standard UI containers for its own products and customer applications through Lightning application containers, known as **Lightning Experience** and **Salesforce Mobile**. Both are served up via the `/one/one.app` URL:

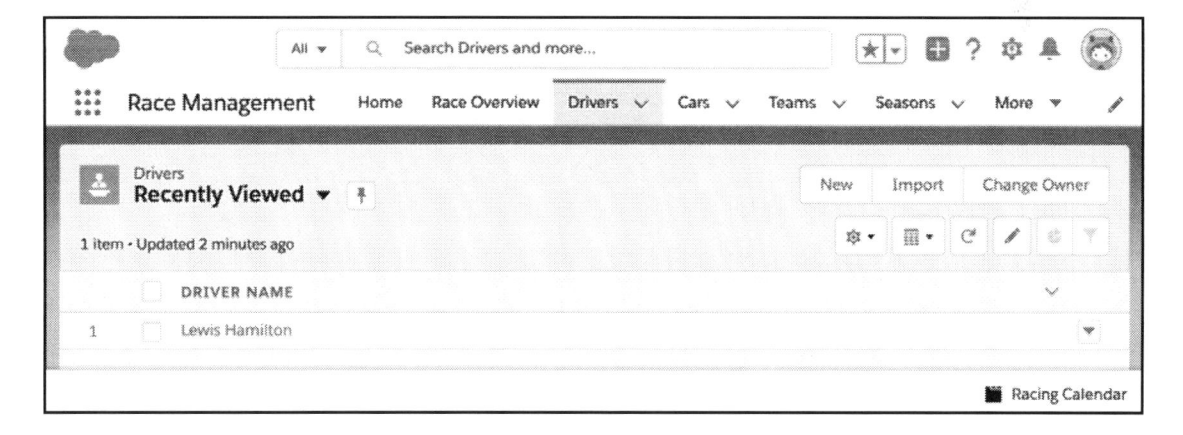

User Interfaces with Lightning Framework

> **TIP:** When testing your code for Salesforce Mobile, you can use your browser's tools to change the device type to mobile. Refresh the page and the Salesforce Mobile app will be displayed.

The Race Management app is configured, as shown in the following screenshot, within the sample code for this chapter to display in both Lightning Experience, as shown in the preceding screenshot, and Salesforce Mobile:

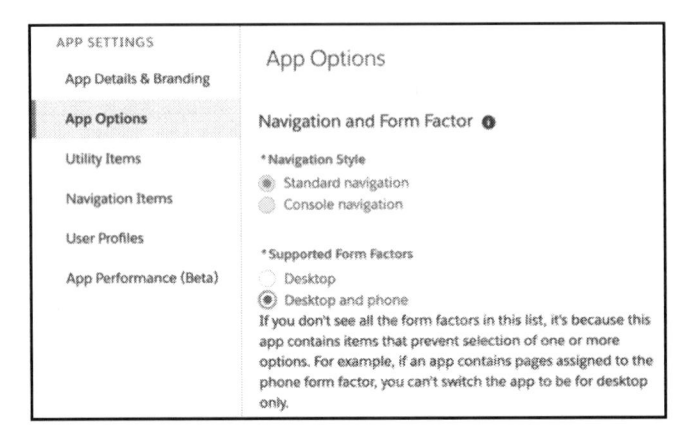

The following screenshot shows what the Race Management application looks like when running in Salesforce Mobile:

[324]

As we have seen in the previous chapters, Salesforce does not restrict loading to just its own components in these containers. Salesforce also provides various ways in which developers can load the components they write in order to integrate and extend the standard user experience with respect to their specific application objects and processes.

Salesforce allows developers to leverage the same components that they have built and tested for use in their applications as well. For example, as shown in Chapter 8, *Building User Interfaces*, the `lightning-record-edit-view` component is used to edit a record. The `lightning/platformShowToast` service can be used to display pop-up notifications. We will look later at the various ways in which both these components and Salesforce containers can be used and extended.

Components

Page-level design is no longer the focus in Lightning; a component-first mindset is the mindset you should have. This does not dismiss the need for good UX design, however. Rather, it involves a closer collaboration between the UX designer and the developer.

Creating one huge component to serve your needs is not recommended and will not make use of the Salesforce UI customization facilities in the way that your users will expect. From a coding perspective, it will be hard to maintain and not reusable, as it will likely not fit everyone's needs.

A better approach is to work with your UX designer on the mockups and think about how you can break up the UI into reusable or distinct elements. Later in this chapter, I will explain how I approached this thinking when devising the components for the FormulaForce application.

> **TIP**: Having a good knowledge of the extensibility points within Salesforce UIs is also important when designing your user experience. The standard UI may offer most of the user experience required, leaving the developer to focus on one or two single components that add the remainder.

Separation of concerns

Lightning components are built with separation of concerns in mind from the ground up. The contents of a **Lightning component** folder, and the contents as we know them thus far, are split into separate files for the **markup** (view) and **JavaScript** code (controller). They are all grouped under a single subfolder. This is a clever way that Salesforce uses to get us to really consider the way we engineer our Lightning code and how our components interact.

As with most things in engineering, separation of concerns is not a given by just using the technology alone. Some aspects are enforced for you; other things are subject to guidelines and good component design. If you get it right, you will not only get reusable, robust, and enduring UI components within your application UI, but also within the evolving Salesforce containers, as well as for the ever-increasing number of mobile devices, and even for integration with third-party websites if needed.

Keeping in mind the separation of concerns is as vital when developing a rich client application as it is when engineering your application's backend business logic.

Encapsulation during development

An important aspect of a component's implementation is encapsulation. Its ability to keep its implementation from impacting the operation of other components on the page is a critical aspect of what makes the container model work – especially since all components occupy the same HTML DOM for the page. In actual fact, Lightning leverages the shadow DOM (https://developer.mozilla.org/en-US/docs/Web/Web_Components/Using_shadow_DOM), which is a key part of ensuring that Lightning Web Components do not impact one another.

In Visual Studio Code, Lightning components use folders to collect together the source files needed to implement each of the specific aspects of the Lightning component that you are creating. The following screenshot shows a **Lightning Web Component** included in this book in Visual Studio Code:

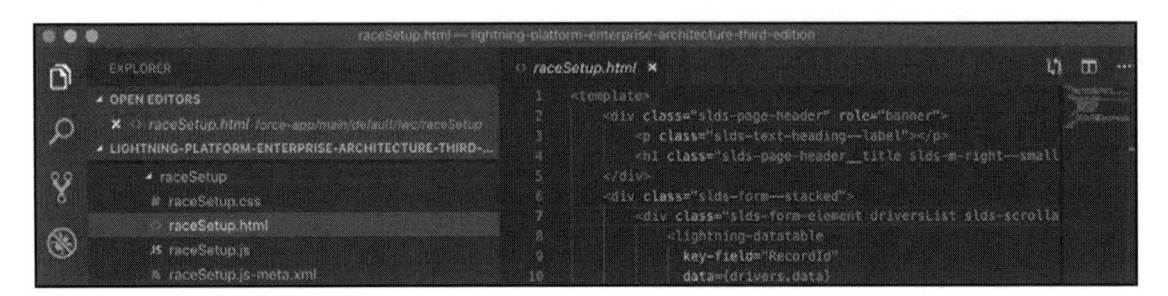

> Also, refer to the Lightning component bundle type in the *Metadata API Developers Guide* (https://developer.salesforce.com/docs/atlas.en-us.api_meta.meta/api_meta/meta_lightningcomponentbundle.htm).

The following screenshot shows a **Lightning Aura component** included in this book in Visual Studio Code:

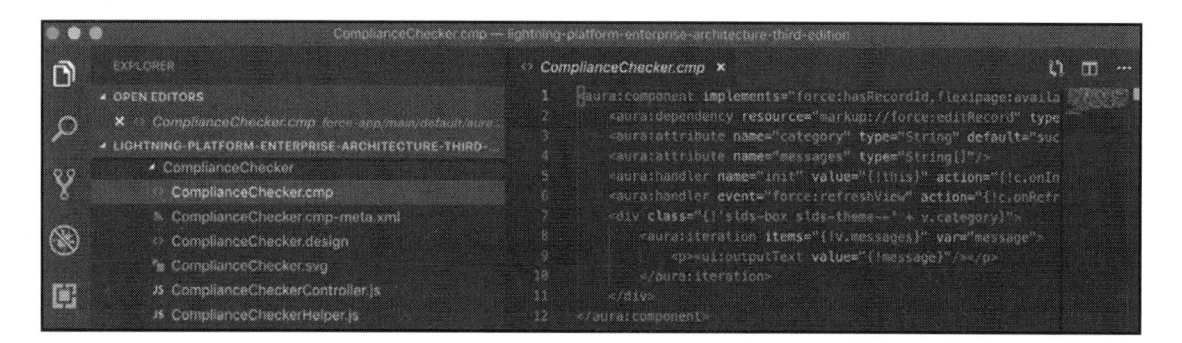

[Screenshot of ComplianceChecker.cmp in Visual Studio Code]

> Also, see the Aura definition bundle type in the *Metadata API Developers Guide* (https://developer.salesforce.com/docs/atlas.en-us.api_meta.meta/api_meta/meta_auradefinitionbundle.htm).

The following sections focus on the content of a **Lightning Web Component** folder.

Component markup (.html)

Component markup contains the **XHTML markup** for a component's appearance. Its root element is `template`. It can include references to valid HTML elements and/or other components, as we saw in the `mycomponent` example earlier.

Among the markup, you can also specify **bindings** for dynamic aspects of the component, such as a table or field values. Unlike with Visualforce, these are not bindings to Apex class properties. Bindings refer to properties and methods defined in the component's controller.

When **controller properties** are **annotated** accordingly, the framework ensures that when the value of an attribute changes (through controller code), any markup that references it via a binding expression is refreshed. This is a very powerful feature and helps you to avoid the need for extensive coding around the page DOM. In fact, this is generally discouraged in all but advanced scenarios, such as custom component rendering or the use of third-party libraries.

The following is a simple example of binding definition and usage. When the controller changes the attribute value, the `<b>` tag will be automatically refreshed. The following is a very basic example. The code to set the property value is not shown for reasons of brevity.

The `myComponent.js` file is as follows:

```
import { LightningElement, track } from 'lwc';

export default class MyComponent extends LightningElement {
  @track
  myProperty;
}
```

The `myComponent.html` file is as follows:

```
<template>
  <b>The value of myProperty is {myProperty}</b>
</template>
```

> The `import` statement can also be used in controller code to provide similar functionality to that of Visualforce for accessing Custom Fields and static resources. Consult the *@salesforce Modules* section in the *Lightning Web Components Developer Guide* for more information on these.

Component controller (.js)

The `.js` file contains the **client-side controller** code for the component. You must have one of these to define dynamic behavior in your component, including any dynamic initialization. The only way to call code in an **Apex controller** is from the client-side controller code; unlike Visualforce, there is no direct way to do so from the markup.

Properties and methods defined within the controller class relate to corresponding **binding** references in the `.html` file. Actions are events that occur in the browser, such as clicking a button, hovering over an element, scrolling, or an event from the container or another component. We will discuss **events** in a later section. The following is some simple button markup in a `.html` file using an expression to reference a client-side controller function.

The `myComponent.html` file is as follows:

```
<template>
  <lightning-button label="Add Drivers" onclick="{addDrivers}">
  </lightning-button>
</template>
```

The framework automatically handles the setup of the HTML event listeners for you and routes them to the specified controller method. The `component`, `event`, and `helper` parameters are always injected by the framework.

The `myComponent.js` file is as follows:

```
import { LightningElement } from 'lwc';

export default class RaceSetup extends LightningElement {
  addDrivers(event) {
  }
}
```

> The `import` statement can also be used to obtain a reference to an **Apex controller method** that the client code wishes to call. We will review an example of this scenario later in the chapter.

As you can see, Lightning Web Component controllers are using the latest ECMAScript standards relating to **class definitions in JavaScript**. As a result, the code is much cleaner and easier to understand than the traditional client JavaScript you might be used to. You can read more about this language feature at https://developer.mozilla.org/en-US/docs/Web/JavaScript/Reference/Classes.

Component CSS (.css)

When styling your component, you should leverage the designs and CSS provided by the SLDS, as shown in the `mycomponent` example earlier. This will ensure that your UI continues to stay in line with the Salesforce containers it resides in, as well as any further advances with respect to supporting new devices and layout types.

> **TIP**
> Using Salesforce base components from the `lightning` namespace, such as `lightning-button`, `lightning-input`, and `lightning-tabSet`, automatically ensures that you are using the SLDS.

However, if you do need to define your own styles, do so via custom CSS classes added to the components `.css` file. The framework will ensure that these will be encapsulated within the component and will not affect other components on the page.

> You should not attempt to modify the HTML `style` attribute of the element. Utilize the HTML `class` attribute to apply your own styles.

Any CSS you define is automatically scoped to your component. The following example is used in the **Race Calendar** component to highlight a race when the user clicks on it:

```
lightning-tile.active {
    background: rgb(255, 236, 149);
}
```

The corresponding component markup uses a binding to apply the `class` attribute value:

```
<lightning-tile label={name} href="/" type="media"
    class={raceStyle} onclick={raceClicked}>
```

The controller property calculates the correct value based on the value of the `selected` property (defined elsewhere in the controller):

```
get raceStyle() {
  return this.selected===true ?
     'slds-tile_board active' : 'slds-tile_board'
}
```

> **TIP:** The **token** is a feature of the Lightning framework that allows you to reuse colors and font values expressed by Salesforce in your own styles. The preceding example reuses a token from the SLDS that defines what color a selected item is. To include the standard SLDS tokens for use in your components, you must create an `aura:tokens` Lightning bundle, called `defaultTokens`. This has already been included in the sample code for this chapter. In this, you can also define your own tokens via the `aura:token` element. There is no direct support for tokens in Lightning Web Components. However, if you have an outer Lightning Aura component that imports them, the tokens are available to child Lightning Web Components.

Component metadata (.js-meta.xml) and component SVG (.svg) files

Component metadata and component SVG files are XML-based files that allow you to customize the appearance of your component when exposing it through the **Lightning App Builder** and **Lightning Community Builder** tools, such as when configuring the icon used to identify the component in the sidebar.

This allows your users to use drag and drop tools to configure Salesforce UIs with specific components contained within your package. Refer to the *Making components customizable* section later in this chapter for further discussion and examples of this capability.

The following is an example for the `raceCalendar.js-meta.xml` file and indicates that the component can be used by users on record, home, and custom Lightning pages that they create:

```xml
<?xml version="1.0" encoding="UTF-8"?>
<LightningComponentBundle xmlns="http://soap.sforce.com/2006/04/metadata"
fqn="raceCalendar">
    <apiVersion>45.0</apiVersion>
    <isExposed>true</isExposed>
    <masterLabel>Race Calendar</masterLabel>
    <targets>
        <target>lightning__RecordPage</target>
        <target>lightning__AppPage</target>
        <target>lightning__HomePage</target>
    </targets>
</LightningComponentBundle>
```

> For a full description of the configuration options for this file, consult the documentation at `https://developer.salesforce.com/docs/component-library/documentation/lwc/lwc.reference_configuration_tags`.

Component documentation (.auradoc)

When it comes to writing Lightning Aura components, the Aura documentation framework is built dynamically based on the components in the org, including those from Salesforce. If you plan to allow other developers to use your packaged components, you can use this file to place documentation that describes the purpose and features of the component.

> **TIP**: You should also leverage the `description` attribute available on `aura:component, aura:attribute, aura:method, aura:event, aura:interface,` and `aura:registerEvent`.

Developers can access documentation expressed this way at `https://<myDomain>.lightning.force.com/auradocs/reference.app`. See the *Making components customizable* section later in this chapter for an example and further discussion of how to expose your components for use outside your package.

> At the time of writing, this file type is not supported for **Lightning Web Components**, only **Lightning Aura components**. Meanwhile, you should continue to focus on ensuring that any exposed components and properties are labeled clearly via the metadata file described in the previous section. Check the documentation for the latest information on this here: `https://developer.salesforce.com/docs/component-library/documentation/lwc/migrate_bundles`.

Component tests (test subfolder)

The test code for your component resides in a subfolder named `__test__`. Salesforce have embraced the open source framework known as **Jest** (`https://jestjs.io/en/`). *Chapter 12, Unit Testing*, will go into more detail on writing tests for Lightning Web Components. Finally, note that these tests are not uploaded to Salesforce and, thus, should be stored in your source control system and run locally as part of your build pipeline. This will also be covered in more detail in `Chapter 13`, *Source Control and Continuous Integration*.

Sharing JavaScript Code between components

You may place other `.js` files in the component folder and reference them using the `import` keyword in your `controller.js` file. Additionally, you can also create Lightning Web Components without any `.html` files that are purely used to share JavaScript code between one or more components. Once again, an industry-standard convention is leveraged here in the form of **ES6 modules**. For more information, consult the Salesforce documentation on this topic at `https://developer.salesforce.com/docs/component-library/documentation/lwc/lwc.create_javascript_share_code`. The `pubsub` component included in the sample code contained within this chapter is an example of a shared utility library and will be utilized later in this chapter by the `racecalendar` and `raceresults` components.

> **TIP:** Remember to share only client-side logic this way; the sharing of business logic is still the concern of your Apex services.

Enforcing encapsulation and security at runtime

JavaScript code on a page can traverse the entire page content via the HTML DOM API and obtain information or modify other aspects of the page. This breaks encapsulation at runtime, and also breaks **security best practices** for container architectures such as Lightning. Imagine that, as an admin, you have installed a component that you placed on your home page and it obtained important data and transmitted it back to another server.

It is unlikely that such a component would pass through the **Salesforce security review** and on to **AppExchange**. There is another reason why, in Lightning, this type of component is not permitted. **Lightning Locker**, a service designed to block this type of logic from executing at runtime, either intentionally or unintentionally, has been created by Salesforce. You may unintentionally write code that is considered not secure by using features that do not comply with the industry-standard **Content Security Policy** (**CSP**). Features such as the use of `eval`, and certain properties and methods on the `window` object, are also not supported within the security context that the Locker service creates.

The following screenshot shows the Locker API viewer, which helps you determine which APIs are supported and what APIs are not:

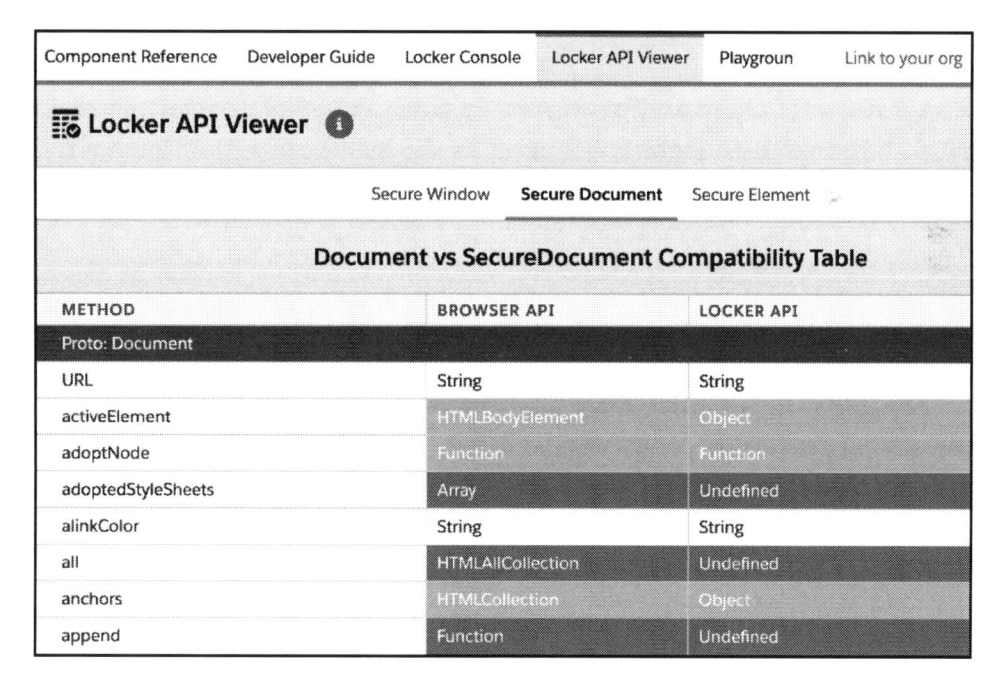

METHOD	BROWSER API	LOCKER API
Proto: Document		
URL	String	String
activeElement	HTMLBodyElement	Object
adoptNode	Function	Function
adoptedStyleSheets	Array	Undefined
alinkColor	String	String
all	HTMLAllCollection	Undefined
anchors	HTMLCollection	Object
append	Function	Undefined

> Locker is enabled for all Lightning Web Components. However, certain browsers may not support the required features to enable it. At the time of writing, this was only IE11. Consult the documentation at `https://developer.salesforce.com/docs/component-library/documentation/lwc/lwc.security_ls_unsupported` for the latest information.

Expressing behavior

Now we know how Lightning allows us to encapsulate our implementation. However, it is also important to keep in mind that the vision behind components is sharing and reusability—not just within your own application, but by other consumers of your application. As with an Apex class exposing an API, it is important to carefully manage the ways in which the consumers of your components are permitted to interact with priorities and methods.

Access control

Apex uses visibility keywords to control what classes, properties, and methods are visible within the scope of the class, within a package, and outside it. The same level of control is available for the Lightning components you place in your package.

JavaScript methods and properties within the controller are private by default. You can, however, add the `@api` annotation to enable access by other components in your package namespace. In the example shown here, the race component is used to display information about a given race and receives the information to display via properties:

```
import { LightningElement, api } from 'lwc';

export default class Race extends LightningElement {
    // Public properties
    @api
    raceId;
    @api
    name;
    @api
    raceDate;
    @api
    completed;
    // ...
```

These properties can be referenced programmatically or via HTML. The `raceCalendar` component references these properties in its markup as shown:

```
<template for:each={calendar.data} for:item="race">
    <ul class="slds-has-dividers_bottom-space" key={race.Id}>
        <c-race
            race-id={race.Id}
            name={race.Name}
            race-date={race.RaceDate}
            completed={race.Completed}
            location={race.Location}
            selected={race.Selected}
            onselect={handleSelect}>
        </c-race>
    </ul>
</template>
```

> **TIP**: As with Apex, it is actually best practice to mark something as having the lowest level of access unless you have good reason to increase it. As such, the samples in this book mostly utilize `private` attributes, as these represent the internal state of the component and should not be accessible even to any other components, including those within the package. As with general Apex coding, this best practice helps manage coupling and allows for greater factoring freedom.

The *Making components customizable* section will explain additional ways to expose your components to Lightning platform tools such as **Lightning App Builder**.

Methods

You can use the `@api` annotation to expose a method from a child component to the parent component's controller logic. Component method calls are basically a way to communicate downward through your component's structure, in contrast to events (described in the next section), which can be used to communicate upward.

Methods can return values and/or accept parameters as per normal JavaScript programming semantics. Note that `@api` only exposes methods to other components in your package and not to components defined by your customers. The following is a basic example:

```
@api
myMethod(myParameter) {
    return 'somevalue';
}
```

In this next example, the logic in a parent component controller is using the standard browser `querySelector` method to obtain a reference to a child component. Once an instance of the child component is returned, the code then calls the exposed method directly as usual. The following snippet searches for a child component with the HTML tag name of `lightning-datatable` and returns the first one found:

```
var selectedRows =
  this.template.querySelector(
    'lightning-datatable').getSelectedRows();
```

> **TIP**
> The `querySelector` method is a browser standard and is also quite advanced in terms of the selector queries it accepts. You might be tempted to try to match on ID; Salesforce does not recommend this, and instead recommends using the HTML tag name, CSS class, or a value assigned to one of the `data-*` attributes (https://developer.mozilla.org/en-US/docs/Web/HTML/Global_attributes/data-*).

Child component events

Your components can send an event just like the standard browser HTML elements. In fact, Lightning Web Components utilize the standard `CustomEvent` API, which you can find documented at https://developer.mozilla.org/en-US/docs/Web/API/CustomEvent. In the sample code included in this chapter, the `race` component (child) is contained by the `raceCalendar` component (parent). The `race` component sends an event to the `raceCalendar` component when the user clicks it. This type of event can only bubble up through components that are contained within the component's parent-child hierarchy.

The following example shows a fragment of HTML from the `raceCalendar` component that references the `race` component. Using the `onselect` attribute, it passes an event handler defined in its controller for the clicked event exposed by the race component.

The `raceCalendar.html` file is as follows:

```
...
<c-race
  race-id={race.Id}
  name={race.Name}
  race-date={race.RaceDate}
  completed={race.Completed}
  location={race.Location}
  selected={race.Selected}
  onselect={handleSelect}>
...
```

The following example shows the handler referenced in the preceding code block. The `event` parameter is based on the standard definition defined at https://developer.mozilla.org/en-US/docs/Web/API/CustomEvent. The `detail` property is set by the race component and, in this case, contains the ID of the **Race** record the user clicked. The `raceCalendar.js` file is as follows:

```
handleSelect(event) {
    const raceId = event.detail;
    ...
}
```

Let's now review how the `race` component exposed the select event used in the preceding code. This component has encapsulated the behavior of what the user clicks, so that the parent component does not have to concern itself with such details. In the following fragment, from the race component, you can see that it is using the `lightning-tile` component and setting its own event handler on the standard `click` event. Because events bubble upward, clicking on it and its children will be result in an event. The `race.html` file is as follows:

```
<lightning-tile label={name} href="/" type="media"
    class={raceStyle} onclick={raceClicked}>
    <lightning-avatar slot="media" fallback-icon-name={raceIcon}> .
</lightning-avatar>
    <ul class="slds-list_vertical slds-has-dividers_right">
        <li class="slds-item">{location}</li>
        <li class="slds-item">{raceDate}</li>
    </ul>
</lightning-tile>
```

The following `race.js` code shows how the internal click handler receives the event, uses state contained by the component (`raceId`), and then dispatches (sends) the event. The `race.js` file is as follows:

```
raceClicked() {
  this.dispatchEvent(
    new CustomEvent('select', { detail: this.raceId }));
}
```

Note that the `race` component did not have to explicitly declare that it sends the `select` event. The framework simply matches the parent component's use of the `onselect` attribute with the firing of the event by the name used, prefixing the attribute with `on` by convention.

> **TIP:** The standard documentation for fire events includes a very important security guideline I also want to emphasize here the fact that when you assign the `detail` property to `CustomEvent`, do not use an object reference – or at least use a cloned reference to an object if you do. The reason for this is due to JavaScript passing objects by reference. So, if you pass an instance of an internal object (for example, part of your component's internal state), you risk the handler for the event modifying that object via this reference. This would break best practices regarding encapsulation and potentially result in hard-to-find bugs in your code. You can read more about managing events at https://developer.salesforce.com/docs/component-library/documentation/lwc/lwc.events_create_dispatch.

Inter-component events

At the time of writing, Salesforce has not exposed a means by which Lightning Web Components that are not nested within one another or even known by one another can communicate. For **Lightning Aura components**, these are called **application events**. While Salesforce works on closing this feature gap, the sample code in this chapter is utilizing a small utility library.

The `pubsub` component contains a utility library provided by Salesforce within their own code samples (at the time of writing) to demonstrate how inter-component communication can be achieved between loosely coupled components that may not be in the same parent-child hierarchy.

When users of the **Race Overview** page click on races in the **Race Calendar**, the **Race Results** component is automatically updated to show the applicable race results (you can try this out for yourself by clicking on **Italy**). These two components are not contained within one another; they are simply placed on the same Lightning page together. The publication and subscribe event pattern is ideal for this communication requirement.

> **TIP:** You could create a **Race Overview** component that contains these two components and use the component event approach described in the previous section to communicate between them. However, if you do this, you reduce the flexibility of building with components and exposing them to your customers to reconfigure the layout of the page or use the components independently, as in the case of the utility bar discussed later in this chapter.

The `raceCalendar.js` controller imports the `pubsub` library `fireEvent` method and calls it when a race is clicked. The following lines of code highlight these two aspects. The `raceCalendar.js` file is as follows:

```
// Import the pubsub utility library
import { fireEvent } from 'c/pubsub';

// Code within the handleSelect method
fireEvent(
   this.pageRef, 'raceSelected',
     { raceId: raceId, raceName: raceName });
```

The `raceResults.js` controller imports the `pubsub` library `registerListener` and `unregisterAllListeners` methods. These methods are called by the following methods to subscribe and unsubscribe to the event during component creation and deletion.

Here is `raceResults.js`:

```
connectedCallback() {
   registerListener('raceSelected', this.handleRaceSelected, this);
}
disconnectedCallback() {
   unregisterAllListeners(this);
}
```

The `handleRaceSelected` method updates two properties that are tracked by the framework. When changes occur in those properties, this triggers calls to **Apex** and updates to the component's UI. We will discuss communication with Apex later in this chapter:

```
handleRaceSelected(race) {
   this.raceId = race.raceId;
   this.raceName = race.raceName;
}
```

> **TIP**
> Check out the latest information in this Salesforce help topic for sending events between components that are not in the same parent-child hierarchy: https://developer.salesforce.com/docs/component-library/documentation/lwc/lwc.events_pubsub.

Platform namespaces

Lightning leverages namespaces to segregate layers and functionality. Namespaces are used in the same way as other parts of the platform, with a prefix ahead of the artifact you wish to reference, such as a component. The following table lists some of the core namespaces provided with the platform and what framework can use them:

Namespace	Framework	Purpose
`lightning`	LWC and Aura	Also known as **base Lightning components**, these are discussed in further detail in the following section.
`aura`	Aura only	Based on the core framework used to build Lightning, **Aura**, this remains an **open source framework** managed by Salesforce. Core components and markup are defined in this namespace. Aspects of this namespace are designed to be agnostic of the hosting platform. You can run Aura on a Java stack if you want to!
`force`	Aura only	Contains aspects that relate to the **Force.com** platform, such as knowledge of **SObjects** and components that replicate the Custom Object layout UI in Lightning. The `force:inputField` and `force:ouptutField` components mimic those found in Visualforce under the `apex` namespace. It contains interfaces that are used when integrating into Lightning Experience and Salesforce Mobile containers.
`forceCommunity`	Aura only	Represents interfaces used to integrate components into the Lightning Community container.
`ui`	Aura only	Includes reusable UI components for basic form-based user experiences. These components predate the SLDS and, thus, are not styled with it by default. You can apply SLDS styles yourself. In terms of the roadmap, Salesforce is focusing on the `lightning` namespace going forward.

The following screenshot shows the **Lightning Web Component** documentation page:

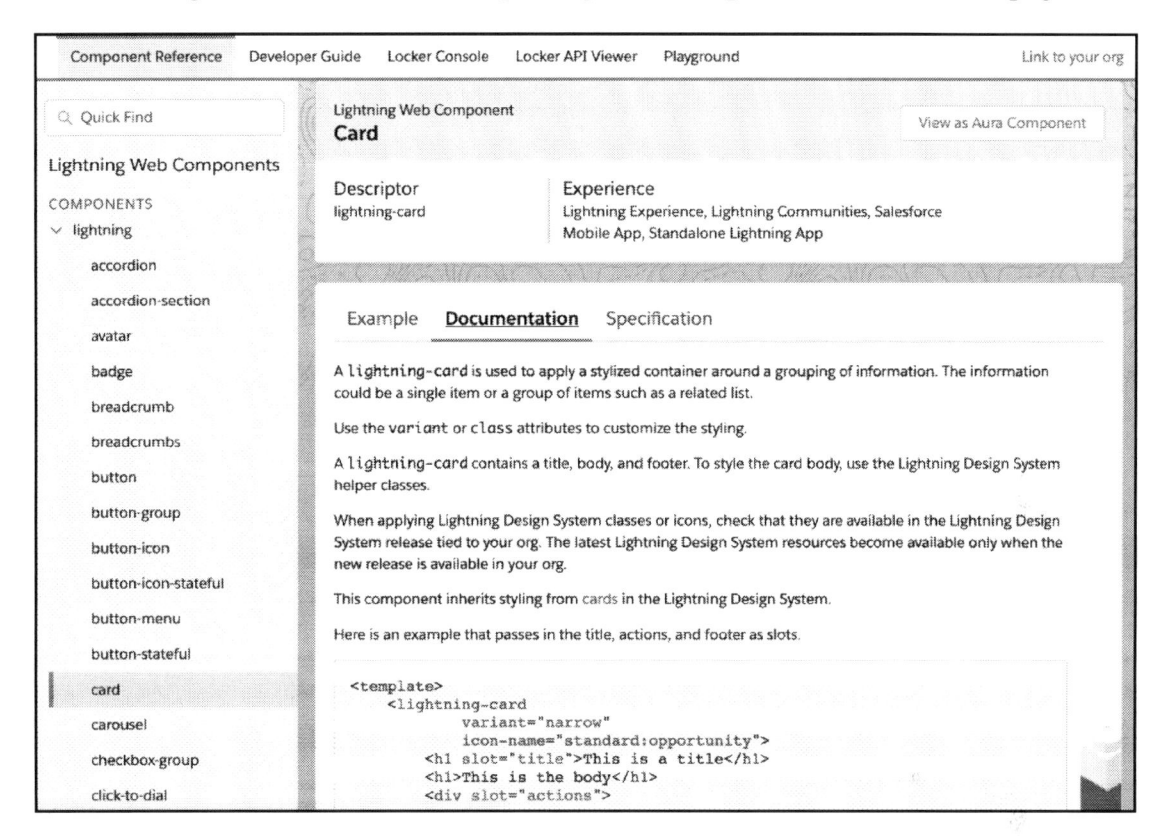

As you can see, going to this page is a good way to discover all of the supported namespaces and components within them, including those exposed from packages installed in the org.

Base components

The components in the `lightning` namespace are recommended by Salesforce as they provide functionally rich and styled UI components using the SLDS. They have stated that they will continue to receive updates as the SLDS evolves. As such, they are recommended to ensure that components stay in alignment with the look and feel of the rest of the platform. The following screenshot shows the Lightning component reference:

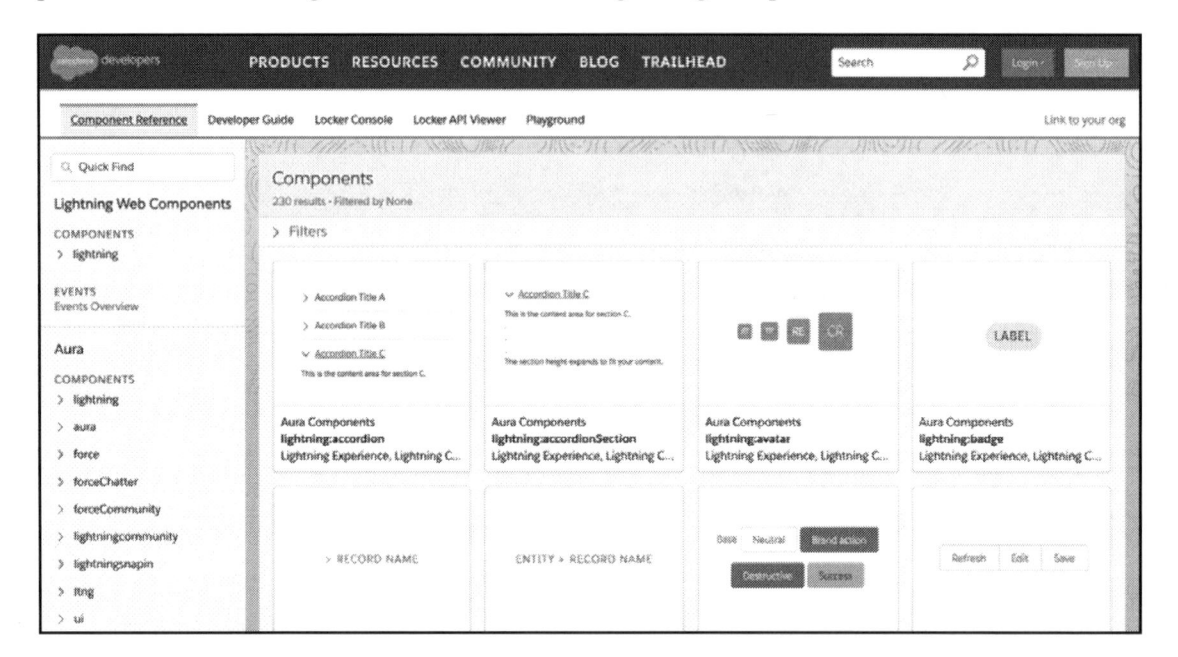

> Not all components are exposed to **Lightning Web Components** at the time of writing. Check this link for the latest updates from Salesforce: https://developer.salesforce.com/docs/component-library/documentation/lwc/lwc.migrate_map_aura_lwc_components.

Data Service

Lightning Data Service can be used as an alternative to writing an Apex controller in scenarios where you simply wish to create, read, update, or delete a record. You can consider Data Service's role much like the role of the **standard controller** in Visualforce, but instead, it exists in the client tier and is interacted with by code in the client controller.

Some of the benefits of using Lightning Data Service are listed here:

- **Data caching and optimization**: Data is cached on the client side, thus reducing network traffic, which improves performance and data usage for mobile applications.
- **Data consistency**: Data is shared by other components when making updates so that the user interface is always showing the correct information to the user, regardless of whether it was rendered using a Salesforce component or one of your own.
- **Security**: Record data is filtered automatically based on the user's record-sharing rules, object, and field access.
- **Advanced input forms**: When used in combination with `lightning-edit-form`, `lightning-view-form`, and `lightning-form`, you can create custom forms that are tightly bound to the field definition in order to render the correct field type and label.

> **TIP**
> Be careful not to allow such client-side facilities to allow business logic to leak into the client tier. In all but the simplest cases, you will likely still want to delegate to an Apex service to perform business logic. Also, keep in mind the transactional scope; multiple updates from the client will each have their own transaction.

Object-oriented programming

Through its use of the latest **ECMAScript**, **Lightning Web Component** controllers are able to leverage **Object-Oriented Programming** (**OOP**) principles using syntax that is recognizable by those more familiar with Apex. As you have seen through the code samples in this chapter, the use of **inheritance** is already used extensively when creating a component controller:

```
import { LightningElement, api } from 'lwc';

export default class Race extends LightningElement {
    // ...
}
```

This enables you to define your own base class for common functionality across all your components. This could be an alternative to explicitly asking each component to import a utility library, as shown earlier in this chapter. Much like with Apex, you can also override base class methods and leverage the `super` keyword to call base class methods as needed. Interfaces, however, are not yet implemented. You can read more about **ECMAScript classes** here: `https://developer.mozilla.org/en-US/docs/Web/JavaScript/Reference/Classes#Defining_classes`.

Object-level and field-level security

The `flsDemo` component included in the sample code for Chapter 8, *Building User Interface*, includes examples of using the `lightning-record-edit-form` component to render input and output fields relating to fields on your application's objects that observe the user's object- and field-level security without additional coding on your behalf. These components are very flexible, allowing you to produce either a **record layout** as defined by the administrator, or a more selective set of fields as defined by your component.

If you are not using the previously described approach, it is your responsibility as a developer to enforce object and field security within Lightning. This can be done with the traditional **Apex Describe** approaches within Apex controllers, or by using the `lightning/uiObjectInfoApi` service `getObjectInfo` method, which is callable from your component's controller. This latter approach is also highlighted within the sample `flsDemo` component controller.

Finally, keep in mind that the client cannot be trusted, and enforcement should also always be done at the server end; otherwise, unauthorized data can be transmitted to the client and the user could use browser debug tools to inspect the JSON payloads sent from the server.

It is up to the developer as to how the UI manifests to the user. This might simply result in a message indicating that the user requires more permission, or you may choose to dynamically hide (which should include omitting values from the server response) or disallow edits to certain fields or table rows, for example.

FormulaForce Lightning components

In designing the Lightning components for the FormulaForce sample application contained in this book, I wanted to try to demonstrate some key integration points within the Salesforce UIs, while also ensuring that the use cases fit with the application domain.

I focused on Lightning Experience and Salesforce Mobile. It is also good practice to think platform-first before embarking on any extensive development. I started with the following use cases and then devised a set of components to deliver the functionality:

- **Race Overview**: While the standalone Lightning application we looked at earlier was a good means to get started with the components, it's not a Salesforce-integrated solution. What I wanted to do was integrate the Lightning Experience home page, through the **Lightning App Builder** customization tool. I wanted to do this not only to show the overall standings (leaderboard) but to allow users to **filter information** through the race calendar to show the results from each completed race.
- **Race Calendar accessibility**: The race calendar is a key piece of information that users will likely want at hand when using other parts of the application. The **Lightning Experience utility bar** (or footer) is specific to your application and contains components that you want to always be accessible.
- **Race Setup assistance**: There is a junction object between Race Records and Drivers called Contestants. This can make setting up a race overly complex from a user experience perspective. As such, I wanted to leverage **Lightning component actions** to provide a custom UI to add drivers to a race.
- **Race Results overview**: Race results are the combined result of information from the Contestants, Driver, Team, and Car objects. I wanted to provide an easy and contextual way of viewing the race results from the **home page** and **Race Record page** through the **Lightning App Builder** customization tool.
- **Race Feedback Survey**: This feature displays a pop-up survey that reuses the Race Results component with an input field to capture comments about the race from the user and post them to the chatter feed.

Let's take a closer look at the components that I came up with.

RaceStandings component

The following screenshot shows the topmost portion of the `c-raceStandings` component:

	DRIVER	TEAM	WINS	POINTS	
1	Lewis Hamilt...	Mercedes	1	43	
2	Nico Rosberg	Mercedes	1	25	
3	Sebastian Ve...	Ferrari	0	15	
4	Kimi Raikkon...	Ferrari	0	12	
5	Daniel Ricciar...	Red Bull	0	10	
6	Valtteri Bottas	Williams	0	8	
7	Max Verstap...	Red Bull	0	6	
8	Sergio Perez	Force India	0	4	
9	Felipe Massa	Williams	0	2	
10	Nico Hulken...	Force India	0	1	
11	Carlos Sainz	Toro Rosso	0		
12	Daniil Kvyat	Toro Rosso	0		

The following component markup is a simplified HTML `<table>` styled using the SLDS:

```
<template>
    <lightning-card title="Standings" icon-name="standard:reward">
        <lightning-datatable
            key-field="Driver"
            data={standings.data}
            columns={columns}
            hide-checkbox-column="true">
        </lightning-datatable>
    </lightning-card>
</template>
```

Other notable aspects of the `RaceStandings` component are listed here:

- The corresponding `raceCalendar.js-meta.xml` file references the `lightning__RecordPage`, `lightning__AppPage`, and `lightning__HomePage` targets, which permit the component to be dropped on to the home-, record-, and application-level pages edited by Lightning App Builder.
- `template for-each` is similar to Aura's `aura:iteration` or Visualforce's `apex:repeat` components, in that it will iterate over a bound list and repeat the markup defined within.

- It uses two **Lightning base components**, `lightning-card` and `lightning-table`, as these both apply SLDS styling and, in the case of the table component, implement much of the formatting and rendering of complexity that would normally have to be implemented if only the standard HTML `TABLE` element was used.
- The controller uses an `@wire` annotation on the `standings` property that instructs the framework to make a call to the Apex controller `getStandings` method (imported via the `import` statement) to load the information from the server. The response updates the standings attribute, which, in turn, causes the framework to refresh the HTML table with the records:

    ```
    import { LightningElement, wire, track } from 'lwc';
    import getStandings from
    '@salesforce/apex/RaceStandingsComponentController.getStandings';

    const columns = [
        { label: '', fieldName: 'Position',
           type: 'number', fixedWidth: 70 },
        { label: 'Driver', fieldName: 'Driver' },
        { label: 'Team', fieldName: 'Team' },
        { label: 'Wins', fieldName: 'Wins',
          type: 'number', fixedWidth: 70 },
        { label: 'Points', fieldName: 'Points',
          type: 'number', fixedWidth: 100 }
    ];

    export default class RaceStandings extends LightningElement {
        @track
        columns = columns;
        @wire(getStandings)
        standings;
    }
    ```

- The **Apex controller** method uses the `ContestantsSelector` class. In the following example, the members of the selector class, `ContestantsSelector.Standing`, do not support the `@AuraEnabled` attribute (Apex enums are not supported), so this class was not used directly in the response. The alternative `RaceStanding` class allows the response to the client to be more focused on the needs of the client code:

    ```
    public with sharing class RaceStandingsComponentController {

        @AuraEnabled(cacheable=true)
        public static List<RaceStanding> getStandings() {
            try {
    ```

User Interfaces with Lightning Framework

```
            List<RaceStanding> raceStandings =
                new List<RaceStanding>();
            for(ContestantsSelector.Standing standing :
                new ContestantsSelector()
                    .selectStandingsForCurrentSeason()) {
                RaceStanding raceStanding = new RaceStanding();
                raceStanding.Position = standing.Position;
                raceStanding.Driver = standing.Driver;
                raceStanding.Team = standing.Team;
                raceStanding.Wins = standing.Wins;
                raceStanding.Points = standing.Points;
                raceStandings.add(raceStanding);
            }
            return raceStandings;
        } catch (Exception e) {
            Application.throwAuraHandledException(e);
        }
        return null;
    }
    public class RaceStanding {
        @AuraEnabled
        public Integer Position;
        @AuraEnabled
        public String Driver;
        @AuraEnabled
        public String Team;
        @AuraEnabled
        public Integer Wins;
        @AuraEnabled
        public Integer Points;
    }
}
```

The `@AuraEnabled` annotation is similar to the `@RemoteAction` annotation used with Visualforce. Both require the method to be static, and thus stateless. They can also be used together on the same method, thereby helping with migration from Visualforce to Lightning. In this case, it is used for both Lightning Aura components and Lightning Web Components communication with Apex. Finally, note that the `cacheable=true` attribute is used on the annotation. For `@wire` bindings such as the one used in this example, it is required to allow the framework to optimize communications by storing the response locally. After a time set by the framework, it will refresh this case by calling your Apex method. Apex methods are blocked from making DML changes, so as to enforce best practice around not changing data in such scenarios. For further information, consult the documentation at https://developer.salesforce.com/docs/component-library/documentation/lwc/apex.

RaceCalendar component

The following screenshot shows the topmost portion of the `c-raceCalendar` component:

When the user clicks on a race, the selected race is highlighted and a component event is fired. This event will later be received by the `c-raceResults` component (described in the next chapter). This event pattern was covered in an earlier section, *Inter-component events*.

The following component markup uses an HTML unordered list, `<ul>`. The list is styled using the SLDS, where each item uses the `c-race` component (highlighted in the *Child component events* section) to show each race as its own tile:

```
<template>
    <lightning-card title="Race Calendar"
        icon-name="standard:campaign">
        <template if:true={calendar.data}>
            <div class="slds-p-around_medium lgc-bg">
                <template for:each={calendar.data} for:item="race">
                    <ul class="slds-has-dividers_bottom-space"
                        key={race.Id}>
                        <c-race
                            race-id={race.Id}
```

```
                            name={race.Name}
                            race-date={race.RaceDate}
                            completed={race.Completed}
                            location={race.Location}
                            selected={race.Selected}
                            onselect={handleSelect}>
                    </c-race>
                </ul>
            </template>
        </div>
    </template>
</lightning-card>
</template>
```

Other new and notable aspects of this component are listed here:

- It uses another custom Lightning Web Component, c-race, included in this chapter's source code and highlighted in the *Child component events* section. It is responsible for displaying race details such as the name and date, highlighting a race, and sending a select event when the user clicks on it.
- The onselect attribute on the c-race component wires up an event handler that calls the handleSelect method:

```
import { LightningElement, wire } from 'lwc';
import { CurrentPageReference } from 'lightning/navigation';
import { fireEvent } from 'c/pubsub';
import getRaceCalendar from
'@salesforce/apex/RaceCalendarComponentController.getRaceCalendar';

export default class RaceCalendar extends LightningElement {

    @wire(CurrentPageReference)
    pageRef;
    @wire(getRaceCalendar)
    calendar;
    currentlySelectedRate;

    handleSelect(event) {
        // Determine selected Race details
        const raceId = event.detail;
        const selectedRace =
            this.calendar.data.find(race => race.Id === raceId);
        const raceName = selectedRace.Name;
        // Toggle selected Race
        if(this.currentlySelectedRate!=null) {
            this.currentlySelectedRate.selected = false;
        }
```

```
            this.currentlySelectedRate = event.currentTarget;
            this.currentlySelectedRate.selected = true;
            // Send raceSelected component event
            fireEvent(this.pageRef, 'raceSelected',
                { raceId: raceId, raceName: raceName });
        }
    }
```

- The Apex controller method (not shown) to load the race calendar splits and correctly orders the races into two lists (based on whether or not the race has been completed already), which are then sent to the component. This reduces the amount of JavaScript needed in the controller and helper files.

RaceResults component

The following screenshot shows the topmost portion of the `c-raceResults` component:

Driver	Team	Grid	Race Ti...	Points
Nico Rosbe...	Mercedes	1	1:17:28.89	25
Lewis Hami...	Mercedes	2	0:0:15.100	18
Sebastian ...	Ferrari	3	0:0:21.0	15
Kimi Raikk...	Ferrari	4	0:0:27.600	12
Daniel Ricc...	Red Bull	5	0:0:45.300	10
Valtteri Bot...	Williams	6	0:0:51.0	8
Max Versta...	Red Bull	7	0:0:54.200	6
Sergio Perez	Force India	8	0:1:5.0	4
Felipe Massa	Williams	9	0:1:5.600	2
Nico Hulke...	Force India	10	0:1:18.700	1
Romain Gr...	Haas F1 Te...	11	No Time	
Jenson But...	McLaren	12	No Time	
Esteban G...	Haas F1 Te...	13	No Time	
Fernando ...	McLaren	14	No Time	
Carlos Sainz	Toro Rosso	15	No Time	
Marcus Eric...	Sauber	16	No Time	
Kevin Mag...	Renault	17	No Time	

Results Italy

The `c-raceResults` component follows a similar implementation approach to the `c-raceStandings` component, but also includes some additional flexibility to support record pages in Lightning, which allows it to know which race record the user is viewing:

```
<template>
    <lightning-card title={raceTitle} icon-name="standard:poll">
        <lightning-datatable
            key-field="Driver"
            data={results.data}
            columns={columns}
            hide-checkbox-column="true">
        </lightning-datatable>
    </lightning-card>
</template>
```

The following code fragments from the component are notable:

- The corresponding `raceResults.js-meta.xml` file references the `lightning__RecordPage`, `lightning__AppPage`, and `lightning__HomePage` targets, which permit the component to be dropped on to the home, record, and application page types, which can be edited by **Lightning App Builder**.
- The following component controller code uses the event pattern described in the *Inter-component events* section to receive events sent by the `c-raceCalendar` component described in the previous section:

```
import { LightningElement, api, wire, track } from 'lwc';
import { CurrentPageReference } from 'lightning/navigation';
import { registerListener, unregisterAllListeners} from 'c/pubsub';
import getRaceResults from
'@salesforce/apex/RaceResultsComponentController.getRaceResults';

const columns = [
    { label: 'Driver', fieldName: 'Driver' },
    { label: 'Team', fieldName: 'Team' },
    { label: 'Grid', fieldName: 'Grid',
        type: 'number', fixedWidth: 70 },
    { label: 'Race Time', fieldName: 'RaceTime' },
    { label: 'Points', fieldName: 'Points',
        type: 'number', fixedWidth: 100 }
];

export default class RaceResults extends LightningElement {

    // Public properties
    @api
```

```
            recordId;

            // Internal properties
            @wire(CurrentPageReference)
            pageRef;
            @wire(getRaceResults, { raceId: '$recordId' })
            results;
            @track
            columns = columns;
            @track
            raceName = '';

            get raceTitle() {
                return 'Results ' + this.raceName;
            }

            /**
             * Listen to raceSelected component event to
             *    update the race results
             */
            connectedCallback() {
                registerListener('raceSelected',
                    this.handleRaceSelected, this);
            }
            disconnectedCallback() {
                unregisterAllListeners(this);
            }

            /**
             * Update the bound raceId to the @wire to refresh
             *    race details
             * @param {} race
             */
            handleRaceSelected(race) {
                this.recordId = race.raceId;
                this.raceName = race.raceName;
            }
        }
```

- The `connectedCallback` and `disconnectedCallback` methods can be used to place logic that needs to be executed when a component is created or destroyed. In this case, they are used to start and stop listening to the `raceSelected` event.
- The `@track` annotation is used to instruct the framework to update the UI whenever the value in the property changes. In this case, the name of the race is updated. Note that `@wire` properties inherit this behavior so you do not need to specify both attributes.

User Interfaces with Lightning Framework

- The `recordId` property is used as a parameter to an `@wire` binding in the controller that corresponds to a parameter on an associated Apex controller method. If it is not null, it will load the applicable race results and display them. Since the component can be dropped on the home page, this can be null in that context. The container will automatically set an `@api` annotated property specifically named `recordId` when the component is placed on record pages (refer to the *Integrating with Lightning Experience* section for a screenshot illustrating this mode).
- `handleRaceSelected` is called when the `raceSelected` event is received. The method extracts `raceId` and `raceName` from the event parameters and refreshes the race results by setting the `recordId` property, which, in turn, causes the framework to call the Apex controller method.
- The preceding pattern allows the component to exist on both the record and home pages and still be contextual.

RaceSetup component

RaceSetup is a UI that is linked with a **Lightning Action** button on the **Race** object. Lightning Actions are shown as modal popups on the display to the user. The container manages the popup, while the content of the popup is controlled by the developer.

At the time of writing, Lightning Web Components do not support Lightning Actions. However, this gives an ideal opportunity to illustrate the fact that **Lightning Aura components** can wrap (contain) **Lightning Web Components** very easily. This capability allows you to gradually migrate your components rather than migrate them all at once. In addition, this feature allows you to still leverage Lightning Web Components in places where they are not, as yet, fully supported by wrapping them in a Lightning Aura component.

In this section, we will use two components: `c:raceSetupAction`, which is a Lightning Aura component, and `c-raceSetup`, which has been developed as a Lightning Web Component. The former will fulfill the required API to expose a Lightning component as a Lightning Action, including receiving the record ID and closing the pop-up dialog that the container provides to display the component. The `c:raceSetupAction` Aura markup looks like this:

```
<aura:component
    implements="force:lightningQuickActionWithoutHeader,
                force:hasRecordId"
    access="global">
```

```
    <c:raceSetup
        raceId="{!v.recordId}"
        onclose="{!c.handleClose}"
        onadded="{!c.handleAdded}"></c:raceSetup>
</aura:component>
```

The following code fragments from the component are notable:

- The preceding component uses the `aura:component implements` attribute to indicate that it can be used as a Lightning Action, and also that it is able to receive the page's record ID. `force:lightningQuickActionWithoutHeader` is used to indicate that this component can be used when creating an **action** on an object definition. When the user invokes the action, the component will show in a popup without the default header and cancel button, which is the preference here since the component is rendering its own buttons. Otherwise, the component would have implemented `force:lightningQuickAction`.
- It references a Lightning Web Component via `c:raceSetup` (note that a colon is used in place of a dash in an Aura framework context).
- The `onclose` and `onadded` attributes are used to implement the child-eventing pattern described earlier in this chapter between the two components. This event pattern is used here to allow the parent Aura-based component to perform tasks on behalf of the child component that it cannot perform itself.
- The Aura component controller code that handles the preceding two events ensures that the required `force:closeQuickAction` and `force:refreshView` events are sent to the container to close the popup and/or refresh the page. These are only supported by Lightning Aura components at the time of writing, so this must be done on behalf of the Lightning Web Component contained by this component. For more information on these events, you can refer to the *Lightning Aura Developers Guide* at `https://developer.salesforce.com/docs/atlas.en-us.lightning.meta/lightning/lightning_component_actions.htm?search_text=actions`.
- When creating an action on the race object, it is the `c:raceSetupAction` Aura component that is configured in the Setup UI. Once Salesforce provides support for Lightning Web Components as Lightning Actions, this Aura component wrapper can be removed or simply retained and removed later when time permits.

The following screenshot shows the contents of the Lightning Action popup through the `c:raceSetupAction` (Lightning Aura component) component containing an instance of the `c-raceSetup` component (Lightning Web Component):

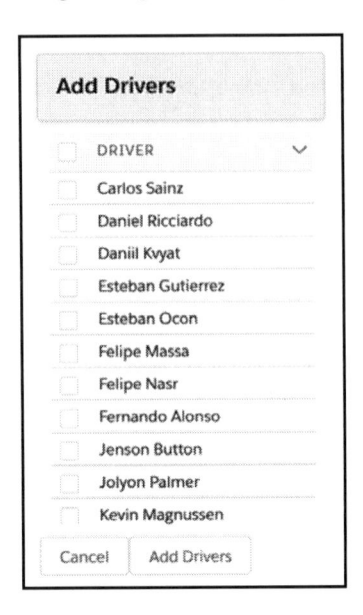

Add Drivers

	DRIVER	⌄
☐	Carlos Sainz	
☐	Daniel Ricciardo	
☐	Daniil Kvyat	
☐	Esteban Gutierrez	
☐	Esteban Ocon	
☐	Felipe Massa	
☐	Felipe Nasr	
☐	Fernando Alonso	
☐	Jenson Button	
☐	Jolyon Palmer	
☐	Kevin Magnussen	

Cancel   Add Drivers

The `c-raceSetup` Lightning Web Component leverages the `lightning-datatable` component to display a table with a list of drivers. This component is used to display checkboxes next to each row. The `lightning-button` component is used to display the **Cancel** and **Add Drivers** buttons:

```
<template>
    <div class="slds-page-header" role="banner">
        <p class="slds-text-heading--label"></p>
        <h1 class="slds-page-header__title slds-m-right--small
            slds-truncate slds-align-left">Add Drivers</h1>
    </div>
    <div class="slds-form--stacked">
      <div class="slds-form-element driversList slds-scrollable--y">
          <lightning-datatable
            key-field="RecordId"
            data={drivers.data}
            columns={columns}>
          </lightning-datatable>
      </div>
      <div class="slds-form-element">
          <lightning-button label="Cancel"
              onclick={handleCancel}></lightning-button>
```

```
            <lightning-button label="Add Drivers"
                onclick={handleAddDrivers}></lightning-button>
        </div>
      </div>
</template>
```

The following code fragments from the component are notable:

- The list of drivers is obtained by binding to the `drivers` property, which is using the `@wire` annotation to invoke an Apex controller method to retrieve the required data. This code is not shown, as this pattern has been shown earlier in this chapter when exploring other components.
- The `handleCancel` controller code sends the `close` component event to its parent, indicating that the user has clicked the **Cancel** button. As described previously, the parent component then sends the required container event to close the pop-up dialog. The `handleCancel` code looks like this:

    ```
    handleCancel() {
      // Notify the parent to send e.force:closeQuickAction
      this.dispatchEvent(new CustomEvent('close', { detail: null }));
    }
    ```

- The `handleAddDrivers` button controller code retrieves the selected table rows from the `lightning-datatable` component and calls an Apex controller method to add the selected **Drivers** to the **Race**. Depending on the success or failure of that operation, it will send an `added` event to the parent component or display an error using the `ShowToastEvent` event.

The following snippet shows the `handleAddDrivers` controller method:

```
handleAddDrivers() {
   // Construct list of selected drivers
   var selectedRows =
      this.template.querySelector(
         'lightning-datatable').getSelectedRows();
   var selectedDrivers = [];
   selectedRows.forEach(element => {
      selectedDrivers.push(element.RecordId); });
   // Call Apex controller methods to add drivers
   addDrivers(
         { raceId : this.raceId,
            driversToAdd : selectedDrivers })
      .then(result => {
         // Send toast confirmation to user
         this.dispatchEvent(
            new ShowToastEvent({
```

```
                    title: 'Add Drivers',
                    message: 'Add ' + result + ' drivers.',
                    variant: 'success',
                }));
                // Notify the parent to send force:closeQuickAction
                this.dispatchEvent(new CustomEvent('added',
                    { detail: result }));
            })
            .catch(error => {
                // Send toast confirmation to user
                this.dispatchEvent(
                    new ShowToastEvent({
                        title: 'Add Drivers',
                        message : error.body.message,
                        variant: 'error',
                    }));
            });
    }
```

The following code fragments from the component are notable:

- A reference to the `lightning-datatable` component is obtained, and the `getSelectedRows` method on this component is used to build a list of selected drivers and their record IDs.
- An `import` statement (not shown in the preceding code) is used to import the Apex controller method, `addDrivers`. Rather than using the `@wire` protocol here, the method is called directly, with the response or error handled within the controller method. Note that this code is using **JavaScript Promises**, which is an internet standard for streamlining how async processing is handled effectively within the browser. You can read more about this at https://developer.mozilla.org/en-US/docs/Web/JavaScript/Guide/Using_promises.
- The `CustomEvent` type is also imported through the import statement and is used to send an event that the container receives before displaying the associated message.

The following screenshot shows the resulting toast message when the user clicks **Add Drivers**:

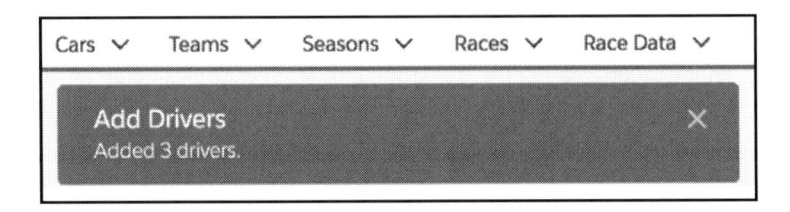

> **TIP**
> In the preceding example, literal text is used. Best practice is to use a **Custom Label**. You can import Custom Labels into Lightning Web Components through the `import` statement. For more information, see https://developer.salesforce.com/docs/component-library/documentation/lwc/create_labels.

Making components customizable

The components included in this chapter will appear in **Lightning App Builder** and are thus available for the developer and consumers of the package to drag and drop onto pages. The following screenshot shows how the components in this chapter appear in Lightning App Builder:

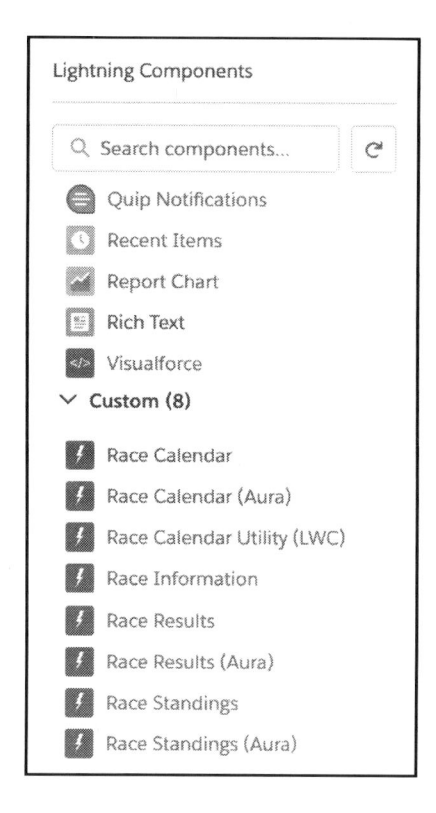

```
Lightning Components

🔍 Search components...        ↻

  ⊖  Quip Notifications
  🕒 Recent Items
  📊 Report Chart
  📝 Rich Text
  </> Visualforce

∨ Custom (8)

  ⚡ Race Calendar
  ⚡ Race Calendar (Aura)
  ⚡ Race Calendar Utility (LWC)
  ⚡ Race Information
  ⚡ Race Results
  ⚡ Race Results (Aura)
  ⚡ Race Standings
  ⚡ Race Standings (Aura)
```

User Interfaces with Lightning Framework

Although only Lightning Web Components are featured in this chapter, this book's sample code contains example components built using both Lightning Aura components and Lightning Web Components, hence both being shown in the previous screenshot. Unless otherwise stated in the component's description, components are Lightning Web Components.

To further expose components and properties to Lightning tools such as **Lightning App Builder**, **Lightning Community Builder**, and **Lightning Flow**, you must reference them and their properties in your component metadata file.

Exposing parts of your application's user interface as components in these tools is very powerful as it lets your customers effectively build their own pages and experiences using the platform's tools if needed. An example of configuring this type of access is shown in the following code. This example is from `race.js-meta.xml`, which exposes the `c-race` component:

```xml
<?xml version="1.0" encoding="UTF-8"?>
<LightningComponentBundle xmlns="http://soap.sforce.com/2006/04/metadata">
    <apiVersion>45.0</apiVersion>
    <isExposed>true</isExposed>
    <masterLabel>Race Information</masterLabel>
    <description>Displays ... Race</description>
    <targets>
        <target>lightning__RecordPage</target>
        <target>lightning__AppPage</target>
        <target>lightning__HomePage</target>
    </targets>
    <targetConfigs>
      <targetConfig targets="lightning__RecordPage,
            lightning__AppPage,lightning__HomePage">
        <property name="raceId" type="String" label="Rade Id" />
        <property name="name" type="String" label="Name" />
        <property name="location" type="String" label="Location"/>
        <property name="raceDate" type="String"
            label="Race Date" />
        <property name="selected" type="Boolean"
            label="Show as Selected"/>
        <property name="completed" type="Boolean"
            label="Show as Completed"/>
        </targetConfig>
    </targetConfigs>
</LightningComponentBundle>
```

If you drag and drop the **Race Information** component into **Lightning App Builder**, its properties are displayed as shown in the following screenshot:

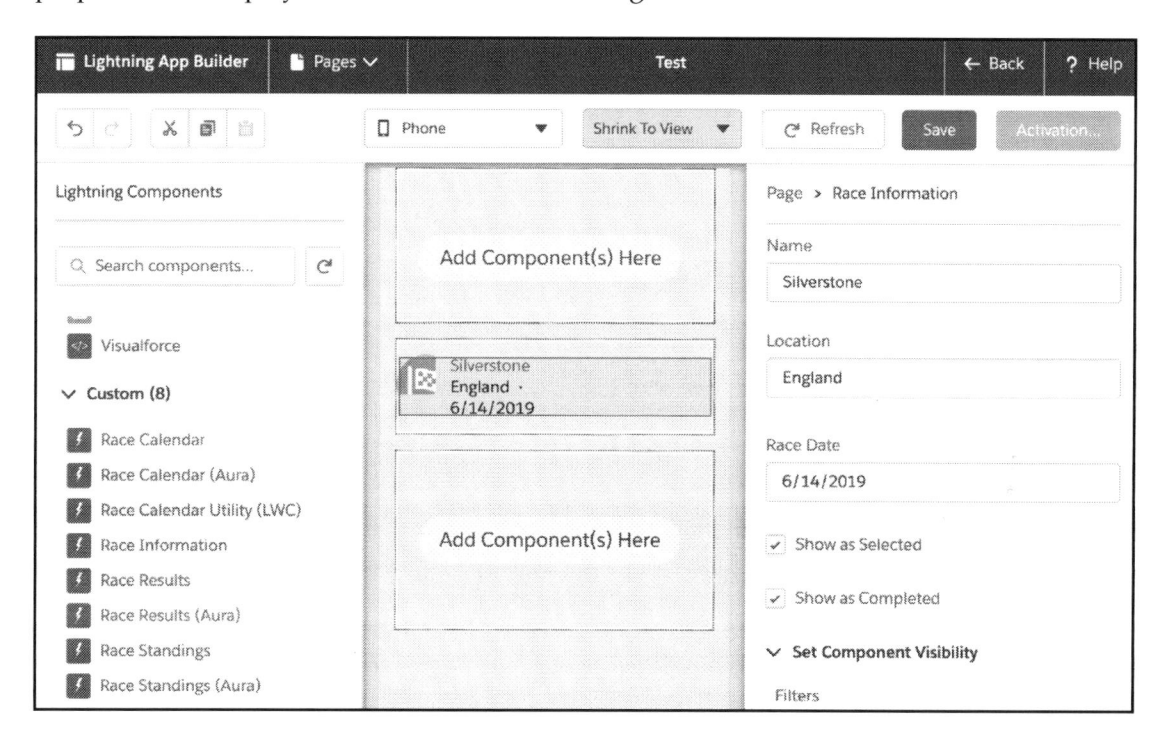

As with Apex classes, consider carefully the implications on your components' evolution between package releases when exposing components and properties to consumers of your package. To support backward compatibility between upgrades, changes are limited to artifacts that have this access control applied.

The **Race Result** component metadata file includes additional markup to indicate to Lightning App Builder that the component is only relevant to the `Race__c` Custom Object, so it does not show up as an option to end users when editing **Team** record pages, for example:

```xml
<?xml version="1.0" encoding="UTF-8"?>
<LightningComponentBundle xmlns="http://soap.sforce.com/2006/04/metadata" fqn="raceResults">
    <apiVersion>45.0</apiVersion>
    <isExposed>true</isExposed>
    <masterLabel>Race Results</masterLabel>
    <targets>
        <target>lightning__RecordPage</target>
```

```
            <target>lightning__AppPage</target>
            <target>lightning__HomePage</target>
        </targets>
        <targetConfigs>
            <targetConfig targets="lightning__RecordPage">
                <objects>
                    <object>Race__c</object>
                </objects>
            </targetConfig>
        </targetConfigs>
    </LightningComponentBundle>
```

Now that you have learned about how to create a Lightning Web Component, it's time to learn how to use one within a container so that your users can interact with it.

Integrating with Lightning Experience

The screenshots in this section highlight the various points at which the components have now been integrated with Lightning Experience. These components are still available to the Race Overview standalone app we started this chapter with. Through additional metadata configurations, they now support more advanced container features.

This screenshot shows the **Race Results** and **Race Standing** components on the **home page**, with the **Race Calendar** component accessible via the **utility bar**. The race results are updated as the user selects races from the **Race Calendar**:

Chapter 9

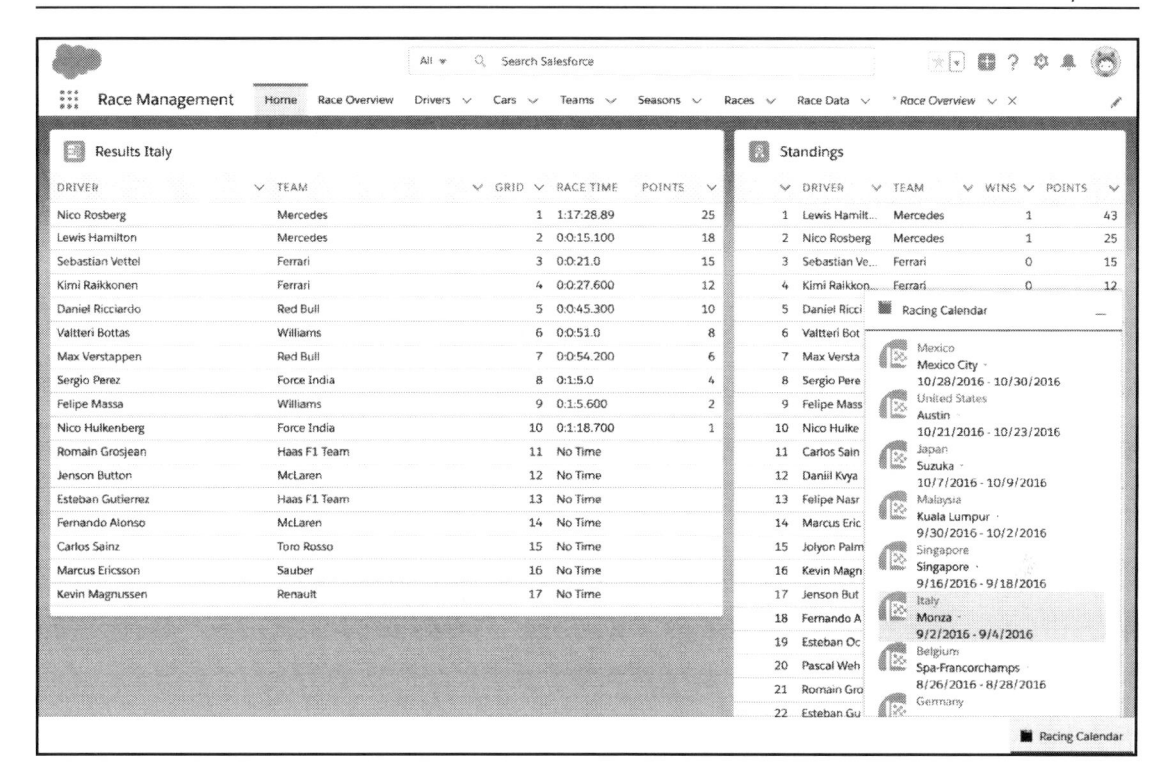

> **TIP**: Lightning Web Components do not currently support the utility bar at the time of writing. As with the Race Setup approach described in an earlier section, an Aura wrapper was used to expose the **Race Calendar** component.

This screenshot shows the **Race Setup** component appearing as a result of the user clicking the **Add Drivers** action on the race record page. Lightning component actions are configured under **Actions** from the **Race** object definition page under **Setup**:

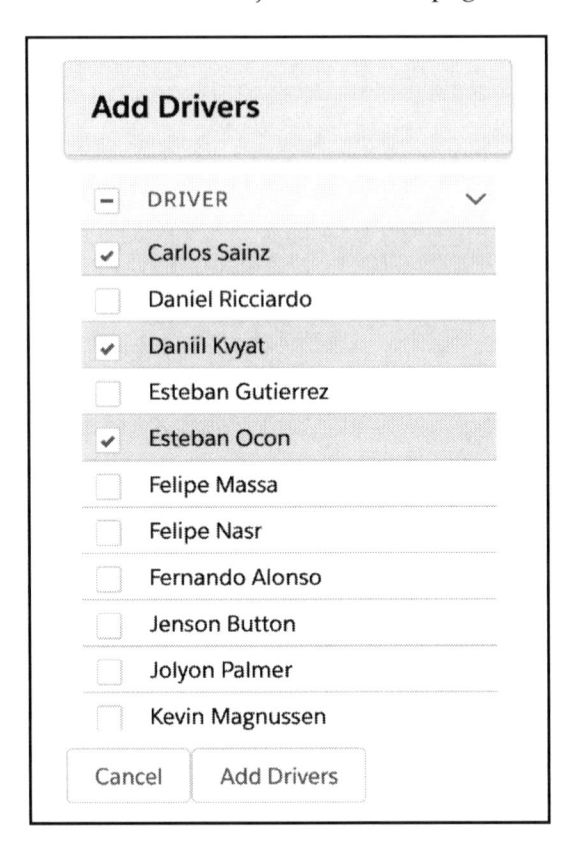

This final screenshot shows the **Race Results** component again, but this time on the race record page. **Lightning App Builder** was used to add a new tab, **Results**, and the **Race Results** component was dragged and dropped on it. This illustrates that components can support multiple locations within Lightning Experience:

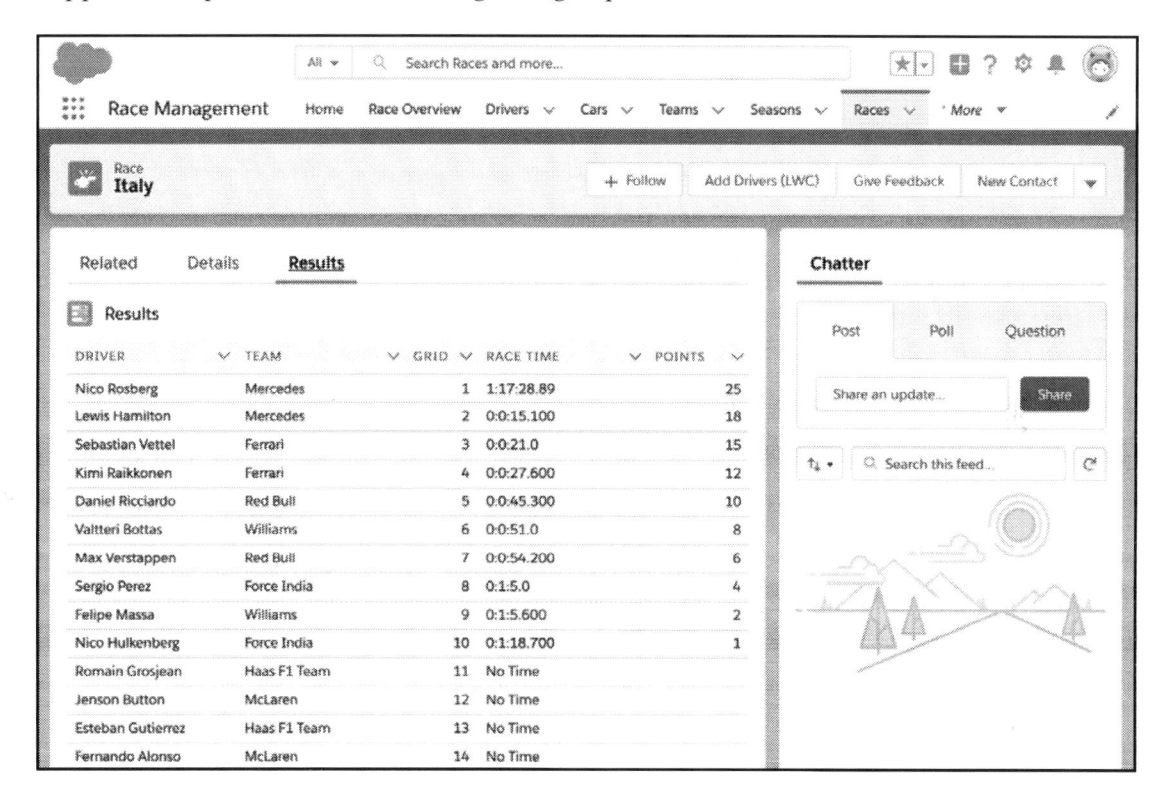

DRIVER	TEAM	GRID	RACE TIME	POINTS
Nico Rosberg	Mercedes	1	1:17:28.89	25
Lewis Hamilton	Mercedes	2	0:0:15.100	18
Sebastian Vettel	Ferrari	3	0:0:21.0	15
Kimi Raikkonen	Ferrari	4	0:0:27.600	12
Daniel Ricciardo	Red Bull	5	0:0:45.300	10
Valtteri Bottas	Williams	6	0:0:51.0	8
Max Verstappen	Red Bull	7	0:0:54.200	6
Sergio Perez	Force India	8	0:1:5.0	4
Felipe Massa	Williams	9	0:1:5.600	2
Nico Hulkenberg	Force India	10	0:1:18.700	1
Romain Grosjean	Haas F1 Team	11	No Time	
Jenson Button	McLaren	12	No Time	
Esteban Gutierrez	Haas F1 Team	13	No Time	
Fernando Alonso	McLaren	14	No Time	

The preceding screenshot shows how the existing Lightning record page has been extended with a new **Results** tab and how, on that tab, a custom Lightning component showing the race results can be added. In the next section, we will see how components can be used on new pages and tabs.

Using components on Lightning pages and tabs

Lightning pages (or FlexiPages) are essentially layouts created from a blank page with the **Lightning App Builder** tool. You or your customers can drop the preceding components and any others on them to create a new page. Unlike Visualforce pages, they do not have a URL for accessing them. The only way to display a Lightning page is to create a **Lightning tab** for it. This can be accessed under **Tabs** under the **Setup** menu. Lightning tabs work in Lightning Experience and Salesforce Mobile. This is how the Race Overview tab has been built.

Integrating with Lightning Flow

Lightning Flow is a tool that users can use to build interactive wizard-style user experiences. The tool, much like Lightning App Builder, is a drag and drop declarative tool that does not require coding skills. However, it has its limitations, as you can imagine, in terms of the sophistication of the user interface elements it supports.

In order to solve this problem, Salesforce has enhanced this tool to support using Lightning components. In the following screenshot, we can see how the **Race Results** component is being used as part of a Flow to capture **Race Feedback**. The Flow contains a variable containing the record ID that is passed to the component, as shown on the right:

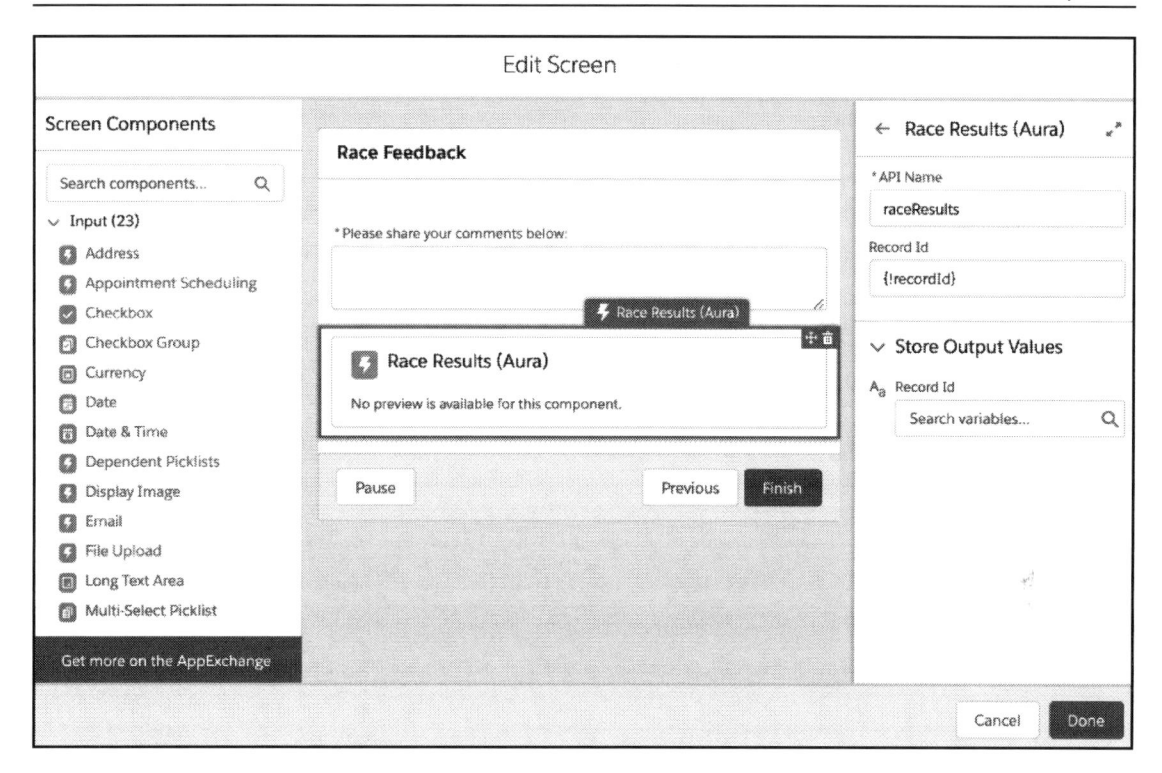

> **TIP:** At the time of writing, only Lightning Aura components are supported. Until Salesforce supports Lightning Web Components, you can use the wrapper pattern described earlier in this chapter in conjunction with the Race Setup Lightning Action.

The following screenshot shows the final Lightning Flow, which has been connected to a **Lightning Action** button on the **Race** object (the platform automatically passes in the record ID as a Flow variable). By exposing your packaged components accordingly, users can now easily create a brand new UI using this tool and your application. In this case, a UI to capture race feedback has been created easily by the user without the need to write any code:

Give Feedback

*Please share your comments below:

Results

DRIVER	TEAM	GRID	RACE TIME	POINTS
Nico Rosberg	Mercedes	1	1:17:28.89	25
Lewis Hamilton	Mercedes	2	0:0:15.100	18
Sebastian Vettel	Ferrari	3	0:0:21.0	15
Kimi Raikkonen	Ferrari	4	0:0:27.600	12
Daniel Ricciardo	Red Bull	5	0:0:45.300	10
Valtteri Bottas	Williams	6	0:0:51.0	8
Max Verstappen	Red Bull	7	0:0:54.200	6
Sergio Perez	Force India	8	0:1:5.0	4
Felipe Massa	Williams	9	0:1:5.600	2
Nico Hulkenberg	Force India	10	0:1:18.700	1
Romain Grosjean	Haas F1 Team	11	No Time	
Jenson Button	McLaren	12	No Time	
Esteban Gutierrez	Haas F1 Team	13	No Time	

Next

The preceding Flow has been included in the sample code for this chapter. It is quite simple in nature to illustrate this use case. Clicking the **Next** button will result in the comments entered being posted to the race chatter feed.

> **TIP**
> There is also the **Lightning Flow Lightning Component** provided by Salesforce, which will allow you to include customer-defined Flows within your own components at runtime. This is, in essence, a way of providing a very powerful extensibility feature to your own UIs without the customer having to write code for their own components. For example, your package could contain some Custom Metadata that the administrator uses to tell your component code which Flow to run, much in the same way that in an earlier chapter, we used a Custom Metadata type to provide a plugin feature for the service layer.

Integrating with Lightning Communities

Lightning Community is another container for your Lightning components that allows you or your customers to use components to build consumer-facing websites; as such, the components featured in this chapter are already close to being able to exist within it and the **Lightning Community Builder** tool. The same considerations for specifying a component metadata file as described in the previous section also apply so that the components appear correctly in the Lightning Community Builder tool, notably making sure that the component's targets include `lightningCommunity__Page`, as shown here:

```xml
<?xml version="1.0" encoding="UTF-8"?>
<LightningComponentBundle xmlns="http://soap.sforce.com/2006/04/metadata" fqn="raceCalendar">
    <apiVersion>45.0</apiVersion>
    <isExposed>true</isExposed>
    <masterLabel>Race Calendar</masterLabel>
    <targets>
        <target>lightning__RecordPage</target>
        <target>lightning__AppPage</target>
        <target>lightning__HomePage</target>
        <target>lightningCommunity__Page</target>
    </targets>
</LightningComponentBundle>
```

The following screenshot shows **Lightning Community Builder** containing the **Race Calendar** and **Race Results** components to build a basic fan site:

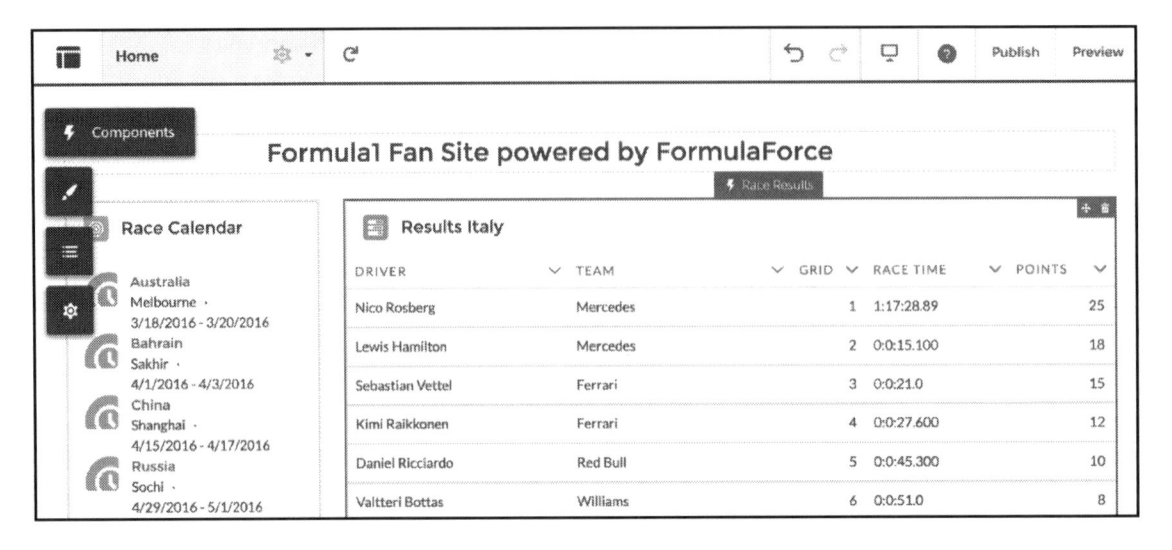

Exposing components with Lightning Out

Lightning Out is a JavaScript library that can be imported into regular HTML pages, such as Visualforce pages, and other websites or other containers, such as Google Apps. Once imported, it exposes an API that allows the page developer to instantiate a Lightning component and inject it into a given HTML element on that page. The host page must provide a Salesforce session or OAuth token to allow this to happen in a secure way.

> **TIP**: At the time of writing, Lightning Out does not support **Lightning Web Components**. In the meantime, you can wrap them in Aura-based components to work around this. Check the documentation for the latest on this here: https://developer.salesforce.com/docs/component-library/documentation/lwc/migrate_bundles.

The process of using **Lightning Out for Visualforce** pages is simplified through the use of the `apex:includeLightning` component on the page, which loads the JavaScript library and handles authentication. Call the `$Lightning.use` global method to begin the bootstrapping process to load the component into the page.

> **TIP**
> Using Lightning components on a Visualforce page does allow you to consider ways to develop new areas of your solution with Lightning while still delivering a Salesforce Classic user experience for customers that still require it. For more information on configuring Lightning Out, consult the applicable section in the *Lightning Developers Guide* (https://developer.salesforce.com/docs/atlas.en-us.lightning.meta/lightning/lightning_out.htm).

Updating the FormulaForce package

As in the previous chapters, feel free to update your package and try out an installation of the package in your test org.

Summary

In this chapter, you have learned about the high-level architecture of the Lightning Web Component framework, in terms of a standalone page as well as when it comes to integrating Lightning components within Lightning Experience, Lightning Community, Salesforce Mobile, and Lightning Flow.

Lightning Experience is now much more extensible than the original Salesforce Classic user interface. There are more options to consider before deciding whether your only option is to start building entirely new, from-the-ground-up, page-level experiences. Thinking about these integration capabilities as you consider your user experience requirements, along with aligning component thinking between developers and UX designers, is key to embracing this new way of building applications on Salesforce.

The need for separation of concerns and good coding practices is now as important at the client tier as it is at the backend. It is also more important to monitor your architecture for the encapsulation and containment of your business logic. This should still remain firmly at the backend, where different client types can access it.

Finally, it is pretty clear that Lightning is embracing the ongoing industry adoption of JavaScript, so if you need to brush up on your JavaScript skills, now is the time to start! With support for ECMAScript and other industry standards, such as web components, you can now also access a much wider range of resources to help you learn.

In the next chapter, we will be exploring platform features, tools, and best practices for providing integration opportunities to your application's customers and partners.

10
Providing Integration and Extensibility

Enterprise businesses have complex needs involving many human, device, and increasingly, machine interactions, often distributed across the globe. Allowing them to work together in an efficient and secure manner is no easy task, and as such, it is no great surprise that utilizing cloud-based software over the internet has become so popular. High-grade security, scalability, and availability is high on checklists when choosing a new application, often followed by API needs and the ability to customize.

By developing on the Lightning Platform, your application already has a good start. `http://trust.salesforce.com/` provides a wide selection of industry strength, compliance, and encryption standards that are equally applicable to your applications. With this comes a selection of standard APIs offered in the SOAP and REST forms, as well as the ability to create your own application APIs. We will also start to discuss platform events in this chapter, and with that comes a number of APIs and tools for data streaming. In my view, there is not a more integration-ready cloud platform available today than the Lightning Platform. This is further extended by Salesforce's general-purpose integration platform known as MuleSoft; something we will discuss in further detail in this chapter as well.

In this chapter, we will review the integration and extensibility options provided as standard on the platform and how your application can get the most from them, in addition to developing custom application APIs. Once again, the application enterprise patterns will come into play, supporting the need for APIs and UIs to have strong functionality parity through the use of the Domain and Service layers described in earlier chapters.

This chapter will cover the following topics:

- Reviewing integration and extensibility needs
- Understanding the Lightning Platform APIs for integration
- Understanding application-specific APIs
- Understanding the implications of the OpenAPI Specification and Swagger

- Alignment with the Lightning Platform's extensibility features
- Extending application logic with Apex interfaces
- Additional integration tools and products, such as MuleSoft

Reviewing your integration and extensibility needs

Before diving into the different ways in which you can provide APIs to those integrating or extending your application, let's review these needs through the eyes of *Developer X*. This is the name I give to a persona representing a consumer of your APIs and general integration and extensibility requirements. Much like its use in designing a user interface, we can use the persona concept to sense check the design and interpretation of an API.

Defining the Developer X persona

Asking a few people (internal and external to the project) to represent this persona is well worth doing, allow them to provide use cases and feedback on the features and functions of your application's API strategy. As it is too easy to design an API you think makes sense, but others with less knowledge of the application do not easily understand, a good way to develop a developer community around your API is to publish designs for feedback. Keep in mind the following when designing your API for *Developer X*:

- *Developer X* is skilled in many platforms and programming languages these days, which might not always be the Lightning Platform. Increasingly, *Developer X* is also creating mobile, JavaScript, and Heroku applications around your API.
- With **Internet of Things** (**IoT**) device integration, consumer devices such as watches, fridges, cars, and jet engines are but a few potential consumers of APIs. So, APIs that work well on-platform and off-platform are a must.
- *Developer X* might not have in-depth knowledge of the application domain (its functional concepts), thus it's important for them to be able to communicate with those that do, meaning that your API design and application functionality terminology has to be well aligned.

The upcoming sections outline general considerations and needs around providing both an integration API and the general extensibility of your application's functionality.

Understanding and managing versioning

As your product functionality grows, it is important to manage the impact this has on developers and partners who have already adopted your APIs in earlier releases of your application and not force them to make code changes unless needed. Where possible, maintain backward compatibility such that even after your application has been upgraded in a subscriber org, existing integrations and extensions continue to work without modification (multiple versions of your application code are not stored in a subscriber org).

> **TIP:** Consider adopting **Push Upgrades** (as discussed in Chapter 1, *Building and Publishing Your Application*) from the second release of your package and going forward to ensure that your customer base is always on the latest versions of your packages. Managing the released versions in your customer base helps manage your support and testing matrix costs. This chapter will talk about principles that help you avoid the usual concerns customers have when they are not in control of updates to your software. Note that, effectively, Salesforce products and platforms are all automatically upgraded as well.

Without backward compatibility you can inhibit upgrades to your application within your customer base, as the time spent by *Developer X* addressing API issues can delay upgrades and be expensive. Some subscribers might have utilized consulting services to deliver the original work or be dependent on one of your partners for add-on solution using your API.

Versioning falls into two categories: versioning the definition (or contract determined input and output of data) and the functionality (or behavior) each API represents.

Versioning the API definition

Once you have published a specific version of an API or Lightning Component (that has been declared as visible outside of your package), do not change its definition, for example, Custom Objects; Fields; Apex classes, methods, or members; equivalent REST or SOAP constructs; or component attributes. Even though the platform will help avoid certain changes, additions can be considered a breaking change, especially new required fields. Anything that changes the definition or signature of the API can be considered a potential breaking change.

Developer X should be able to modify and redeploy their existing integrations or extensions without having to recode or adjust their code using your API and without forcing them to upgrade to the latest version of your API, unless, of course, they want to access new functionality only accessible by completing new fields. Note that this is different from upgrading the package itself within the subscriber org, which must be allowed to happen.

The standard Salesforce APIs and platform help provide versioning when *Developer X* interacts with your Custom Objects and Application APIs. Versioning is implemented as follows:

- In an Apex code context, the platform retains the version of your package installed when the Apex code was first written by *Developer X*, and then only ensures that Apex classes, methods, members, Custom Objects, and fields visible in that packaged version are visible to the code. This feature is something that we will explore in further detail later in this chapter.
- In the case of the SOAP and REST APIs, by default, the latest version of your Custom Objects is visible. When using the SOAP API, header values can be passed in such calls to lock a particular package version if needed (search for `PackageVersionHeader` in *Apex Developer's Guide*). Alternatively, the packaged version used by these APIs can be set at an org-configuration level.

Versioning the API definition of the Salesforce APIs

Under the **Setup** menu, search for **API**. You will find a setup page that allows you to download the WSDLs for one of the many Salesforce SOAP APIs. In the next section, there are some versioning settings that determine which installed package version should be assumed during interactions with your packaged objects.

For example, when performing a `describeSObject` web service operation via the Salesforce Enterprise or Partner APIs, these APIs will return different Custom Fields depending on when new fields were added, as new versions of the package have been released over time. The default behavior will return all fields as the default is the current package version.

If this is important to *Developer X* or third-party solutions when using these Salesforce APIs, the subscriber administrator can specify an explicit previous version. If they do this, new fields available in future package versions will not be available unless this is changed. The following screenshot shows how these settings can be accessed on the API page under **Setup**:

> **Package Version Settings**
>
> **Enterprise Package Version Settings**
> These version settings are used if an API call doesn't include version information for an installed package. This ensures backwards compatibility.
>
> Configure Enterprise Package Version Settings
>
> **Partner Package Version Settings**
> These version settings are used if an API call doesn't include version information for an installed package.
>
> Configure Partner Package Version Settings

The preceding screen is only displayed if there is one or more managed package installed.

Versioning the API functionality

When offering new versions of your application to users through the UI, new features are accessed by the user—either by opting into the feature during configuration using a new page or button, or sometimes seamlessly, such as a new type of calculation, optimization, or improvement to existing behavior with added benefits.

As the API is just another way into your application's logic, you should think about enabling these new features through the API in, conceptually, the same way. If it is seamlessly available to users through the UI, it becomes so in the API regardless of the API version, and thus, solutions built around your application's API will also benefit automatically without changes to the integration or extension code. However, if a new field or button is needed in the UI, then a new API parameter or operation will be needed to enable the new feature. It is reasonable for this to be exposed in a new version of your API definition. Thus, *Developer X* will have to modify the existing code, test it, and deploy it before the solution can leverage it.

Trying to be sophisticated in your code by providing exactly the same behavior to older callers of your API will depend on the Service and Domain layers understanding the concept of API versus UI contexts and package versioning, which will rapidly become complex for you to develop, test, support, and document.

> Agree and communicate clearly to your customers and partners how many versions of your API you will support and give warnings about retirements. Always be sure to test your APIs on different versions to ensure the lack of fields that arrive later in your package, which are not provided by older callers, does not cause errors or unwanted behavior in these cases. Try to avoid adding new required fields to your applications without a way to default them.
>
> If, in your regression testing of older API versions, you notice a reduction in data volume throughput due to governors, it can be acceptable to condition newer logic (such as checks for newer fields). Again, be careful with how often you implant this type of conditional logic in your code base.

Translation and localization

As with the guidelines around the Service layer, which can be used as a means to form your application API later in this chapter, you should ensure that any error or status messages are translated according to your use of **Custom Labels**, as described in Chapter 2, *Leveraging Platform Features* (the Apex and Lightning Web Components runtimes will ensure that the user locale determines the translation used).

Some APIs expose error codes to provide a language-neutral way to recognize a certain error use case programmatically (parsing the message text is not reliable in a translated environment). As such, one approach is to use an Apex **enum** and a custom Apex **exception** class, which captures both the translated error message and the exception code. The following enum and exception types are defined in the Application class contained within the sample code for this chapter. Note the use of the global keyword in Apex; this will be discussed later in this chapter, in the *Providing Apex application APIs* section, in more detail:

```
global Application {
  global enum ExceptionCode {
    ComplianceFailure,
    UnableToVerifyCompliance
  }

  global virtual class ApplicationException extends Exception {

    global ExceptionCode ExceptionCode {get; private set;}

    public ApplicationException(
```

```
        ExceptionCode exceptionCode, String message) {
      this(message);
      this.exceptionCode = exceptionCode;
    }
  }
}
```

While the preceding `ApplicationException` class can be used as it is, the following `ComplianceService` class has its own custom exception that can then extend the `ApplicationException` class for more clarity:

```
global class ComplianceException
    extends Application.ApplicationException {

  global List<VerifyResult> failures {get; private set;}

  public ComplianceException(
     Application.ExceptionCode exceptionCode,
     String message, List<VerifyResult> failures) {
       super(exceptionCode, message);
       this.failures = failures;
  }
}
```

This code can then raise exceptions specifying the enum value related to the message, as follows:

```
throw new ComplianceException(
  Application.ExceptionCode.ComplianceFailure,
  Label.ComplianceFailuresFound,
  failedCompliances);

throw new ComplianceException(
  Application.ExceptionCode.UnableToVerifyCompliance,
  Label.UnableToVerifyCompliance,
  null);
```

As with the Service layer guidelines, the API should be client agnostic, and thus you cannot assume that the data values accepted or returned should be formatted or not. Thus, it is best to use the native Apex types for date, date/time, and number and allow the caller to decide whether or not to format the values. Returning formatted values is useful for UI callers, but for headless or automated solutions, it is not ideal.

Terminology and platform alignment

If you're following the guidelines of the Service layer when defining your classes, methods, parameters, and interfaces (as discussed later in this chapter), then any API based on this layer should already mirror the functional terms used in your application. Having a good alignment with your application terms makes your API easier to map to functional concepts in your application and thus for *Developer X* to navigate around, understand, and discuss with those that know the application in more functional depth.

In addition, like the Service layer, your API should support platform concerns such as bulkification and not prevent *Developer X* from calling your API in a bulkified way to make optimal use of the platform resources. This also includes *Developer X* utilizing Apex DML statements, and thus raises the importance of bulkified Domain layer logic as well as bulkified Service layer logic.

What are your integration use cases?

Typically, an integration use case arises from a controlling process or application that consumes the functionality of your application, effectively invoking the functionality within your application automatically on behalf of a user, or as part of an event or scheduled background process. Both the standard Salesforce APIs and any additional application APIs that you create can support this need. The following diagram shows a controlling system driving your application through either the standard Salesforce API and/or application APIs that you have provided as part of the managed package:

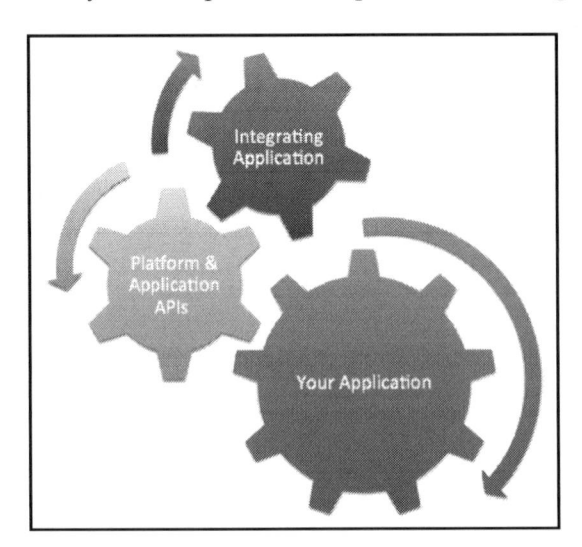

Although integrations are much easier when all applications are built based on the same platform, it is a good practice to have an API strategy that covers both on- and off-platform *Developer X* scenarios, ideally exposing the same functionality consistently.

Developer X calling your APIs on-platform

A Lightning Platform Apex developer can manipulate the data stored in your application through Apex DML statements. You can think of Apex DML as your free Apex API to your application data, as this approach avoids the need for you to build your own application APIs to purely manage record data, particularly for those Custom Objects that you are already exposing through the standard Salesforce UI.

> **TIP**: It can be a useful aid to these developers to browse your Custom Object schema through Salesforce Schema Builder, as highlighted earlier in this book. Try to avoid inconsistencies between your **field labels** and **field API** names (though the Schema Builder does permit toggling them), as this can make it harder for developers and those expressing the requirements to collaborate.

Just because Apex is being used does not mean that *Developer X* can bypass logic in your managed Apex Triggers. However, take note that they can also write Apex Triggers of their own, which can execute before yours (as the Apex Trigger order is nondeterministic). To prevent *Developer X* triggers making invalid changes to record data, ensure that you follow the best practice when you're writing the validation logic to place it in the after-phase of your application triggers. As discussed in the previous chapter, utilizing the Domain pattern will ensure this.

Later in this chapter, we will discuss application APIs that expose functionality that's not directly related to manipulating your Custom Object records, but functionality that is more business logic related, for example, exposing the `ComplianceService.verify` method. In this case, by making the Service class and methods `global` as opposed to `public`, you can make this same method available to *Developer X*. As an extension to your Apex API strategy, allow them to consume it in the same manner as you do within your application.

The motivation behind this approach, described later in this chapter, is to ensure that the maximum amount of your application functionality is available through your API as your application evolves. However, if you do not want to expose your full Service layer directly as your application API, you can elect to create separate Apex classes that define your API that delegate to the Service layer or selectively apply the `global` keyword to your Service methods.

Developer X calling your APIs off-platform

Developer X, using languages such as Java, .NET, Node.js, or Ruby, uses the HTTP protocol to connect between the two platforms. Salesforce provides APIs to log in and authorize access for you, as well as APIs to manipulate the data in your Custom Objects, much like using Apex DML. Salesforce currently chooses to expose both SOAP- and REST-based variants of its HTTP-based APIs. So, again, you need not develop your own APIs for this type of data integration.

> **TIP**: Many third-party Salesforce integration applications leverage platform APIs and, as such, will also work with your application data; this fact is a key platform benefit for you and *Developer X*.

When it comes to exposing application APIs, in order to support SOAP and REST, you will need to develop separate Apex classes in each case for each API that you want to expose. This is because the definition and design of these types are different, though the functionality you're exposing is the same. We will discuss this further later in this chapter.

SOAP versus REST

Whether you have been following the SOAP versus REST debate or just simply google it, you'll know that there is currently a general trend toward REST. As it's easier to code against and consume in mobile and JavaScript-based scenarios, most major cloud services such as Facebook and LinkedIn only provide REST versions of their APIs. For ease of use and the ability to be more self-describing, I prefer REST as well.

The OpenAPI Specification and Swagger

The need for standardization when expressing API functionality through either REST or XML endpoints in a platform-, transport-, and programming-language-agnostic way emerged as the **OpenAPI Specification** in 2015, with major organizations such as **Apple**, **IBM**, and **Google** contributing, lead by a company known as **SmartBear**. The formal website for this specification is `https://www.openapis.org/`. The specification states that APIs should be described via a file that contains either **YAML (Yet Another Markup Language)** or **JSON** that humans and tools can use to streamline the discovery and consumption of APIs.

At first, this standard was known as the **Swagger Specification**, though it was later renamed the OpenAPI Specification, or **OAS**. However, many still refer to the standard as Swagger. The Swagger website (`https://swagger.io/`) now focuses on tooling around the OpenAPI Specification, which includes ways to author an API specification and generate client- and server-side stubs to help developers consume the resulting API more easily. There is even support for generating Apex client stubs to call APIs described via OpenAPI specifications.

Salesforce has started to adopt this standard through its **MuleSoft** platform and also through Lightning Platform features such as **Lightning External Services**, which we will discuss in `Chapter 14`, *Integrating with External Services*, in more detail, along with a sample Swagger file.

> At the time of writing, there is no officially published OpenAPI specification for Salesforce APIs, nor an automatic way to generate one from your own Apex REST or XML-based APIs, as described in this chapter. However, you can use the tools on the Swagger website to create your own specification files and include them with your product documentation.

Developer X calling your APIs asynchronously through platform events

The previous sections highlighted traditional API patterns where Developer X writes code on- or off-platform that then calls a REST- or XML-based API to perform a specific operation against your application's objects or services. That API then returns a response immediately.

While this is an easy model to understand, it can have its downsides in terms of performance because the client is holding open connections and valuable resources while it waits for the API to return. Additionally, it also does not permit the backend to queue requests as needed. From a software design perspective, the tight coupling between Developer X's client code and a specific API code inhibits the ability to refine the overall architecture quickly as each point of integration needs to be modified, for example, if a totally new API needs to be introduced. This pattern is known as **point-to-point integration**. An alternative to this is known as **pub-sub** (publish and subscribe).

The pub-sub pattern can also be regarded as **loosely coupled API integration**. In this case, a message bus is required to keep track of messages that allow your application to declare messages that Developer X can respond to or send for your application to respond to. A message bus can support many different messages, known as message types. In this regard, the message type is an abstraction over the operation and allows for the handling of the operation to change without changing the client code, hence *loosely coupled*. The following diagram illustrates several clients sending events to the event bus to be received by one or more handlers, depending on the type of message:

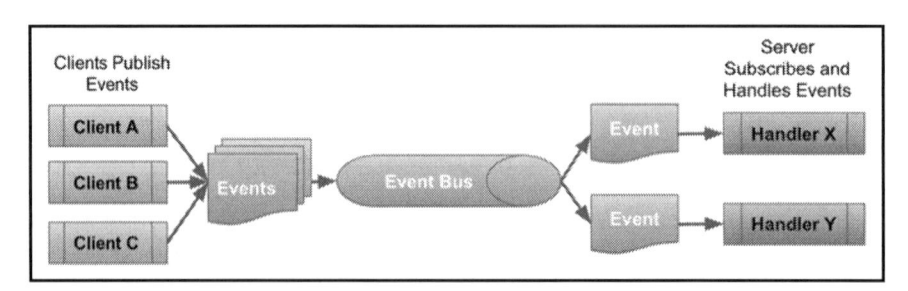

In the diagram, there are three clients, each sending (or publishing) events to the event bus. When the event bus receives these events, it dispatches them to handlers who have subscribed to each of the events. In this case, the client application code is unaware of how the events are eventually handled, hence the term **loosely coupled**.

In the Lightning Platform, the pub-sub concept is exposed through the **platform events** feature. Defining message types is achieved by creating a **platform event object**, much like you do with a Custom Object, where the fields defined describe the data to be contained in the message, as shown in the following screenshot:

Platform Events

Platform Event Definition Detail   [Edit] [Delete]

Singular Label	Race News Feed
Plural Label	Race News Feeds
Object Name	RaceNewsFeed
API Name	RaceNewsFeed__e
Event Type	High Volume
Publish Behavior	Publish Immediately
Created By	User User, 6/15/2019 2:23 PM
Description	Allow your race news reporters to get the very latest information when it happens!
Deployment Status	Deployed
Modified By	User User, 6/15/2019 2:23 PM

Standard Fields

Action	Field Label	Field Name	Data Type	Controlling Field	Indexed
	Created By	CreatedBy	Lookup(User)		
	Created Date	CreatedDate	Date/Time		
	Replay ID	ReplayId	External Lookup		

Custom Fields & Relationships   [New]

Action	Field Label	API Name	Data Type	Indexed	Controlling Field	Modified By
Edit | Del	Category	Category__c	Text(32)			User User, 6/15/2019 2:24 PM
Edit | Del	Content	Content__c	Long Text Area(32768)			User User, 6/15/2019 2:24 PM

While you can use platform events for your application's internal asynchronous processing needs (something that we will cover in the next chapter), you can also consider a platform event object as effectively **disclosing an asynchronous API for your application**. In this case, depending on the intent, Developer X would either send events (messages) to your application code or receive events from your application code asynchronously. The Lightning Platform provides a number of programmatic and declarative tool options for sending and receiving events via on-platform APIs, such as those in Apex and REST APIs for off-platform scenarios. In this chapter and the next, we will explore two examples highlighting this pattern further. Meanwhile, the **Platform Events Developers Guide** can be found at `https://developer.salesforce.com/docs/atlas.en-us.platform_events.meta/platform_events/platform_events_intro.htm`.

> **TIP**: Keep in mind that platform events are not excluded from the customer's maximum permitted object count like your Custom Objects are once your package has passed security review. You should not consider this pattern for every API in your application, only those that would attract potentially high concurrency or where the client would otherwise have to poll.

What are your application's extensibility use cases?

So far, we have been discussing providing facilities for *Developer X* to build custom solutions and applications around your application, which is one type of integration. Another form of integration is to consider providing ways to make extensions to its existing business logic. In an extensibility use case, *Developer X* or an administrator is happy for your users to consume your application's UI and functionality directly but wants to extend it in some way to add additional functionality or updates to other Custom Objects. Some examples of the type of extensions you might want to consider are as follows:

- Adding subscriber-created **Custom Fields** to your custom UIs using **field sets**.
- Providing alternatives to hardcoded **email messages** via **email templates**.
- Extending the application **business Apex logic** with the *Developer X* code.
- Extending the application UI JavaScript logic in **packaged Lightning Components** with *Developer X*-created Lightning Components that you dynamically create.

The last two options represent what I am calling callouts. The following diagram shows processes in your application's code that make use of this approach to execute **code** written by *Developer X*, the Application Extension. Later in this chapter, we will see an example of how can implement these through the use of Apex interfaces and Custom Metadata records.

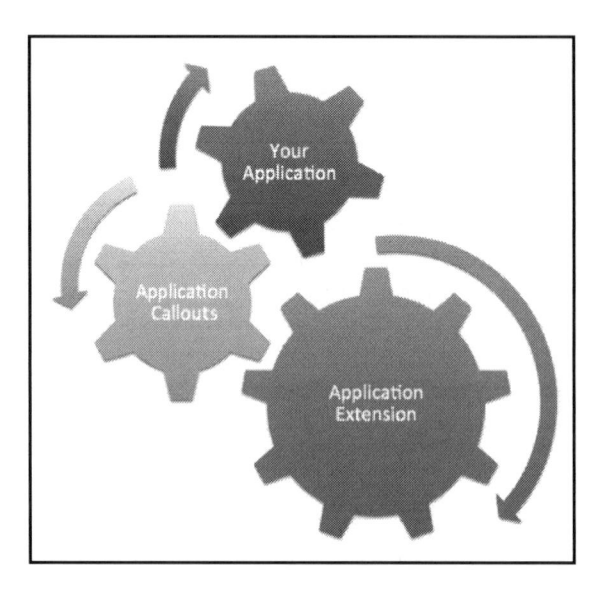

Tip: Although it is possible to dynamically create Lightning Components provided by *Developer X* and thus render them inside the UIs of your own custom Lightning Components, think carefully about this option. As discussed in previous chapters, there are many existing ways in which Lightning Platform tools provide this same functionality without code. It could be that in order to take advantage of these tools, you need to decompose a specific component and make the resulting components visible to these tools, and thus permit the administrator of your application the opportunity to recompose them, along with the *Developer X* components on the page.

Standard platform APIs for integration

Chapter 2, *Leveraging Platform Features*, provided a good overview of the many platform APIs that are available to those integrating with your application from outside of the Lightning Platform, from environments such as Java, .NET, PHP, and Ruby. It also covered best practices to ensure that your application and the developers using these APIs have the best experience.

As stated in that chapter, these APIs are mostly focused on record data manipulation and querying, often known as CRUD. Leveraging the Salesforce APIs means developers wishing to learn how to integrate with your application objects can leverage the standard Salesforce API documentation and websites such as https://developer.salesforce.com/.

Tip: Although the Enterprise API provides a strongly typed SOAP API, its larger size can be problematic to load into development environments (as it includes all Custom Objects and fields present in the org). As such, the more general Partner API is often a better recommendation to make to *Developer X*. Most developers are used to generic data access layers, such as JDBC or OData, and in essence, to them, the Partner API is similar and a lot smaller to embed in their applications. If, however, you are recommending an API for mobile or JavaScript integration, the Salesforce REST APIs are even lighter, though come at the added responsibility of the developer to parse and form the correct JSON responses and requests without the aid of generated class types provided via the WSDLs of the SOAP APIs. Typically, languages that prefer more strongly typed programming principles prefer the SOAP variants over the REST variant.

For Java developers, Salesforce provides an excellent **Web Service Connector (WSC)** framework, which offers an efficient way to consume the SOAP and REST APIs without the need for any other web service stacks. They provide compiled versions of their popular Partner and Metadata APIs, with plenty of examples online.

> "The Lightning Platform Web Service Connector (WSC) is a high performing web service client stack implemented using a streaming parser. WSC also makes it much easier to use the Lightning Platform API (Web Services/SOAP or Asynchronous/BULK API)."

The easiest way to download and start using this API is to use Apache Maven (`https://mvnrepository.com/artifact/com.force.api/force-wsc`). You can also download WSC from `https://github.com/forcedotcom/wsc`.

For .NET developers, Salesforce started an open source initiative, Lightning Platform Toolkits for .NET, to build precompiled assemblies providing access to their APIs, much in the same spirit as the WSC Java library described earlier.

> "The Lightning Platform Toolkits for .NET provides an easy way for .NET developers to interact with the Lightning Platform & Chatter REST APIs using native libraries."

You can download the toolkit for .NET from `https://github.com/developerforce/Lightning Platform-Toolkit-for-NET`. For Node.js developers, Salesforce also uses the popular `jsforce` library in their SFDX CLI tool.

> "Salesforce API Library for JavaScript applications (both on Node.js and web browser)"

You can download this toolkit for Node.js from `https://jsforce.github.io/`.

Apex Callable interface API

Later in this chapter, we will review a pattern whereby the FormulaForce package exposes a specific Apex interface for *Developer X* to implement to extend the business logic of the application. In doing so, however, the code written by *Developer X* becomes tightly coupled with the FormulaForce package since their code implements and thus references a specific interface contained in the package.

The `System.Callable` interface is included by Salesforce (so it doesn't need to be defined in your package) for situations where more loose coupling is more appropriate. The interface has only one method on it and is intentionally kept generic by design:

```
public Object call(String action, Map<String,Object> args)
```

The FormulaForce application is intentionally domain specific. It is only of interest to those working in the Formula 1 motor racing industry. However, if you were building a package that contains a tool or more generic application that would co-exist in a large ecosystem of different domains with other tools, you may want to consider supporting a more generally available interface such as this. In this case, *Developer X* would not have to explicitly depend on your package, and thus, this allows their code to be used by other packages that also support this interface, and they can also develop their code in isolation from your package without having to install it. You can read more about this interface at https://developer.salesforce.com/docs/atlas.en-us.apexcode.meta/apexcode/apex_interface_System_Callable.htm.

Application integration APIs

This section describes ways in which you can expose your application's business logic functionality that's encapsulated within your Service layer.

> In some cases, *Developer X* is able to achieve such functionality through the standard Salesforce APIs. However, depending on the requirement, it might be easier and safer to call an API that exposes existing business logic within the application. You can decide to do this for the same reason you would create a custom UI rather than expect the end users to solely utilize the standard UI (because using your objects directly requires them to understand the application's object schema in more detail).

Providing Apex application APIs

If your Service layer is developed and tested as robustly as possible, following the guidelines discussed in Chapter 5, *Application Service Layer*, it is worth considering exposing it to *Developer X* by simply updating the class, methods, members, properties, and any custom Apex types, such as global. This part of the chapter discusses the approach in more detail, though it can also be applied to dedicated Apex classes built specifically to expose an API that is delegating to your Service layer classes:

```
global class ComplianceService
{
   global static void verify(Set<Id> recordIds)
   {
```

Providing Integration and Extensibility

> **TIP**
> Make sure that you apply the global modifier carefully because it is not easy to deprecate it after your package has been released. Also, be sure to apply `global` to aspects of your Service layer only; avoid exposing Domain or Selector layer classes or types. If you need to expose behavior in these classes, write a Service layer method to do so. Also, note that the `ComplianceService.ICompliant` interface has not had the global modifier applied, as this is an internal aspect of the service.

As shown earlier in this chapter, we have also applied the `global` modifier to the Apex exception class defined within the `ComplianceService` class.

To try out this new application API, we will perform the following steps and execute some sample Apex test code in your test development org:

1. Download the sample code for this chapter.
2. Comment out the `ComplianceService.report` method (we will uncomment this shortly before performing another upload).
3. Create a package version from the sample code in this chapter. Remember to apply the namespace to `sfdx-project.json`, as described in Chapter 1, *Building and Publishing Your Application*. You do not need to worry about ancestry configuration if you are not already considering this.
4. Install the package in your test scratch org as per the instructions in Chapter 1, *Building and Publishing Your Application*.
5. Open the test scratch org and then open the **Developer Console** (from the menu under the user profile icon) and create an Apex class called `ApplicationAPITest`.

If you inspect the `ComplianceService` class in your test scratch org from the **Apex Classes** page under the **Setup** menu, you can see the new API methods and types you've just exposed are now visible (without the code). This provides a basic means for *Developer X* to learn about your API, in addition to any documentation you provide. A portion of what this looks like for `ComplianceService` is shown in the following screenshot.

You can also see a **Version** drop-down box, which allows *Developer X* to explore different versions of the API definition. Note that the version shown here might differ from yours, depending on how many uploads of the package you have done at this point in the book:

Apex Class Detail		Edit Security
Name	ComplianceService	
Namespace Prefix	fforce	
Last Modified By	Andy Admin, 09/05/2014 12:19	

Class Summary | Version Settings | Log Filters

Version: 1.8

global class ComplianceService
Available in Versions: 1.8 - Current

Constructors (1)

Signature
ComplianceService()

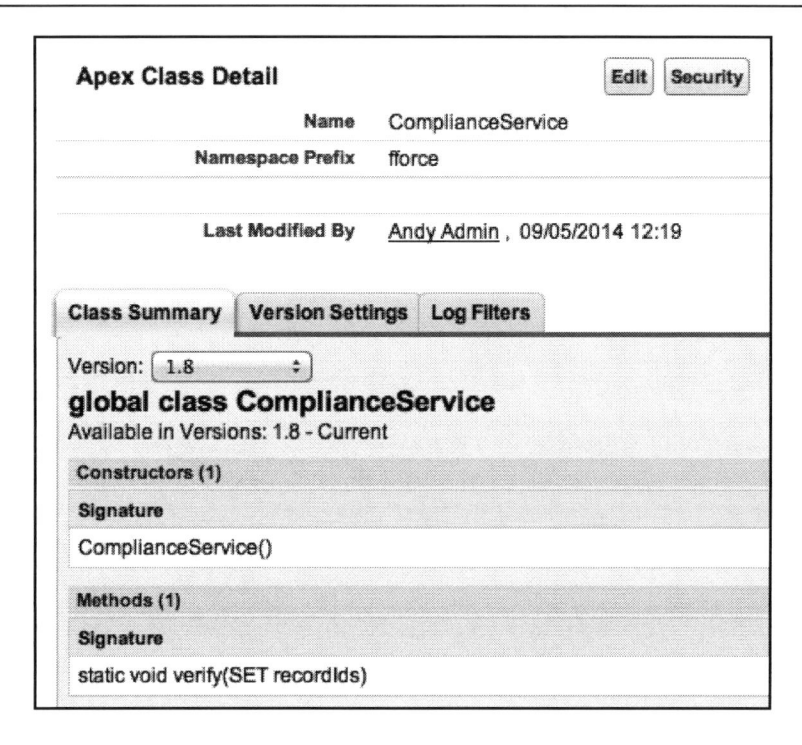

Methods (1)

Signature
static void verify(SET recordIds)

All `global` Apex classes will also show the **Security** link next to them in the list of classes in the subscriber org. This is so that the subscriber org administrator can control permissions around the execution of the APIs through Profiles. Note that this only applies to global controller methods custom or extension controller or Web Service calls by *Developer X*. You can also grant access through appropriate permission sets, as described in `Chapter 2`, *Leveraging Platform Features*. This means that if the user is assigned a permission set granting them access to a specific set of features in the application, accessing those features through APIs is included as well. If you want to control API permissions separately, create separate but functionality-scoped permission sets:

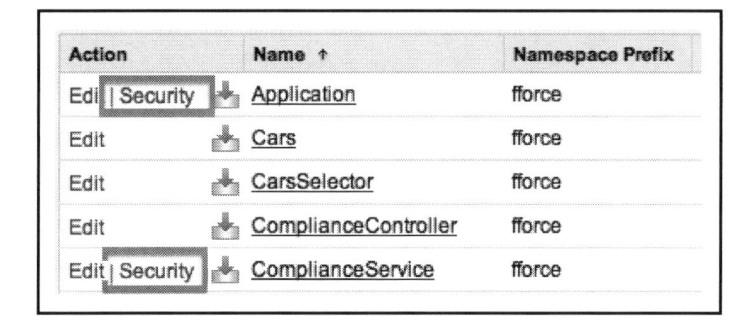

Action	Name ↑	Namespace Prefix
Edit | Security	Application	fforce
Edit	Cars	fforce
Edit	CarsSelector	fforce
Edit	ComplianceController	fforce
Edit | Security	ComplianceService	fforce

Calling an application API from Apex

The code used in this section uses Apex test methods (not included in the FormulaForce package) as an easy way to run the API code example in this chapter. We will be using an Apex test to illustrate the use of the Apex APIs included in the sample code in this chapter. The two test methods we will look at call the Compliance API after calling the season API to create some test data (which, of course, only exists on the database within the scope of the test execution).

In the following examples, the **Driver** records created by the `SeasonService.createTestSeason` API do not indicate that the drivers hold an **FIA Super License**. Thus, the expectation is that the `ComplianceService.verify` method will throw an exception reporting this problem. The following example test code asserts this behavior purely for illustration purposes in this chapter:

```
@IsTest
private class ApplicationAPITest {
    @IsTest
    private static void demoComplianceVerifyAPI() {


        // Create some test data via the SeasonService
        fforce.SeasonService.createTestSeason();
        // Query Drivers to test compliance against
        Map<Id, fforce__Driver__c> driversById =
            new Map<Id, fforce__Driver__c>(
                [select Id from fforce__Driver__c]);
        try {
            // Invoke the compliance engine for the drivers
            fforce.ComplianceService.verify(
                driversById.keySet());
            System.assert(false, 'Expected failures');
        }
        catch (fforce.ComplianceService.ComplianceException e) {
            // Check the results
            System.assertEquals(
                '4.1', e.failures[0].complianceCode);
            System.assertEquals(
                'Driver must have a FIA Super License.',
                e.failures[0].failureReason);
        }
    }
}
```

> The namespace used in this sample is `fforce`. Your namespace will differ. Replace the namespace to get the code sample to compile (you can also find this class in the sample code for this chapter).

Run the test to confirm whether the API is working as expected.

> **TIP**
> As you have used the same Service layer method that's used by the rest of the application, your existing unit and integration tests around this class should suffice in providing you confidence in the robustness of this as an API to your application. If not, improving your testing around your Service layer benefits both external and internal callers equally.

Notice that when you click on the **Show Dependencies** button in the `ApplicationAPITest` class, it shows the API and Custom Objects being referenced from the package:

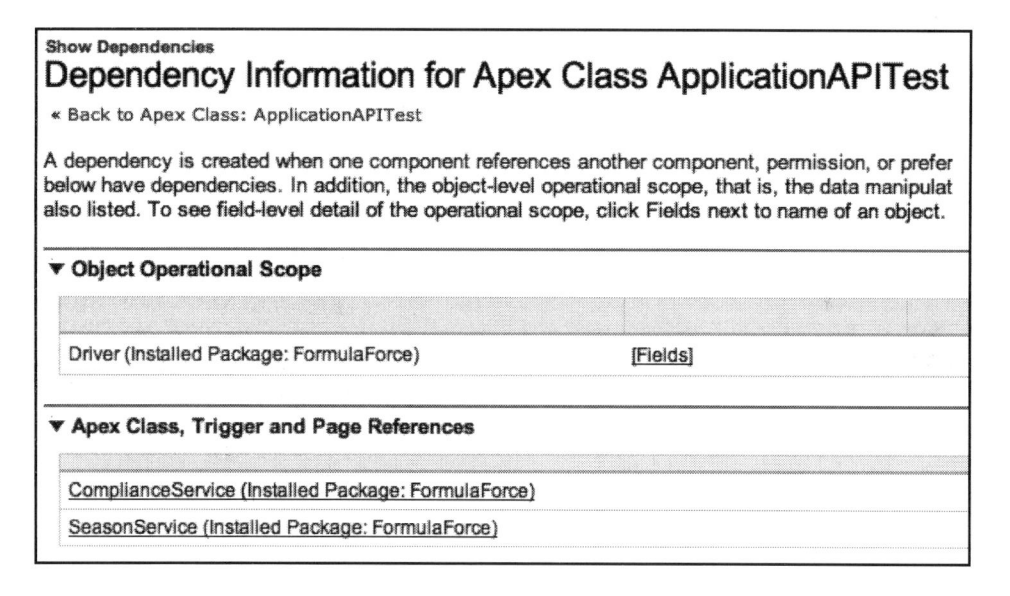

```
Show Dependencies
Dependency Information for Apex Class ApplicationAPITest
« Back to Apex Class: ApplicationAPITest

A dependency is created when one component references another component, permission, or prefer
below have dependencies. In addition, the object-level operational scope, that is, the data manipulat
also listed. To see field-level detail of the operational scope, click Fields next to name of an object.

▼ Object Operational Scope

    Driver (Installed Package: FormulaForce)              [Fields]

▼ Apex Class, Trigger and Page References

    ComplianceService (Installed Package: FormulaForce)
    SeasonService (Installed Package: FormulaForce)
```

Now that you understand how the platform exposes your APIs to your customers' developers, the next section goes into more detail about the implications and restrictions in modifying it.

Modifying and depreciating the application API

Once a `global` class method or member has been effectively published by including it in a released package, it cannot be removed or changed (this was discussed in Chapter 1, *Building and Publishing Your Application*, as part of the discussion on managing package ancestry). If you were to create a scratch org configured with your package ancestry, as described in Chapter 1, *Building and Publishing Your Application*, if you tried changing the `ComplianceService.verify` method by renaming it `verification` (for example), when you attempt to push the class to such a scratch org, you will receive the following error:

```
(ComplianceService) Global/WebService identifiers cannot be removed from
managed application: Method: void verify(SET<Id>)   (Line: 1)
```

> **TIP**
> If you want to perform some testing or distribute your package while reserving the ability to make changes to your new APIs, create your package as beta until you are happy with your API definition. Note that you can, of course, change the behavior of your API (determined by the Apex code behind it) at any time, though this has to be done with care.

The `@Deprecated` annotation can be used to effectively remove the visibility of the class, interface, method, or member that `global` has been applied to from the perspective of subsequent package version consumers. *Developer X* can still access the deprecated items by referencing an earlier version of the package through the class version settings shown via the **Version Settings** tab as described in more detail in the following sections.

> The `@Deprecated` annotation can only be used in scratch orgs configured with a package ancestry, as described in Chapter 1, *Building and Publishing Your Application*.

Versioning Apex API definitions

When saved, the `ApplicationAPITest` class, the **Version Settings** tab, and the **Dependencies** page reflect the fact that code within the class is referencing the `ComplianceService` and `SeasonService` classes from the FormulaForce package.

In the following screenshot, the version shown is v1.8, as this was the version of the package when the Apex class was first created (this might be different in your case, depending on how many times you have uploaded the package so far):

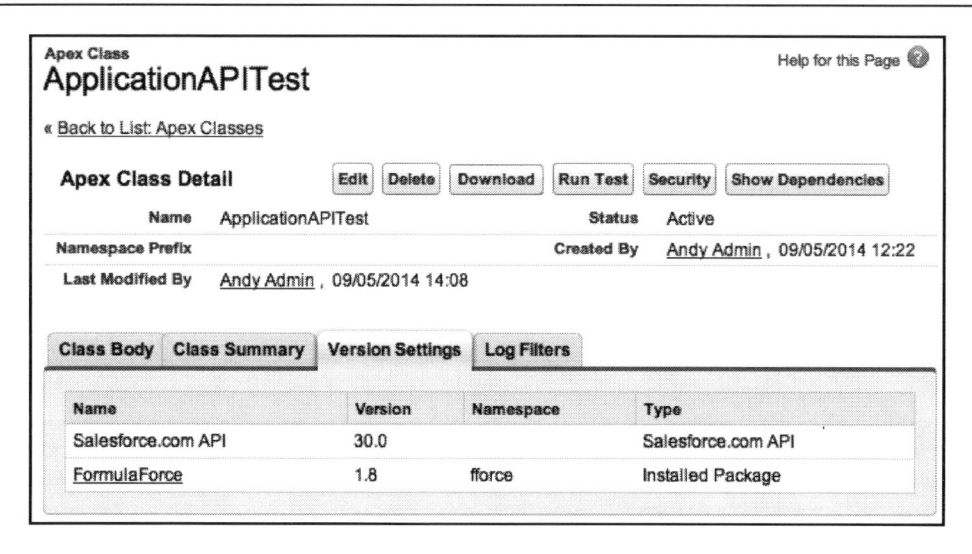

Apex Class Detail			
Name	ApplicationAPITest	Status	Active
Namespace Prefix		Created By	Andy Admin, 09/05/2014 12:22
Last Modified By	Andy Admin, 09/05/2014 14:08		

Name	Version	Namespace	Type
Salesforce.com API	30.0		Salesforce.com API
FormulaForce	1.8	fforce	Installed Package

In the following steps, we will release a new version of the package with a new compliance API to explore how the platform provides Apex API versioning:

1. In the scratch org, uncomment the `ComplianceService.report` method. This method works like the verify method but will not throw an exception; instead, it returns a full list of results, including compliance passes and failures.
2. Update the ancestry information as described in Chapter 1, *Building and Publishing Your Application*, to reflect the package version you last created.
3. Create a new release of the package and install it into the test scratch org you used earlier in this chapter. This performs a package upgrade.
4. In the test scratch org, open the Developer Console and open the `ApplicationAPITest` Apex class.

Attempt to add the following new test method and save the class:

```
@IsTest
private static void demoComplianceReportAPI() {

    // Create some test data via the SeasonService
    fforce.SeasonService.createTestSeason();
    // Query Drivers to test compliance against
    Map<Id, fforce__Driver__c> driversById =
        new Map<Id, fforce__Driver__c>(
            [select Id from fforce__Driver__c]);
    // Update the licenses for the drivers
    for(fforce__Driver__c driver : driversById.values())
```

```
            driver.fforce__FIASuperLicense__c = true;
        update driversById.values();
        // Invoke the compliance engine to verify the drivers
        List<fforce.ComplianceService.VerifyResult>
            reportResults =
                fforce.ComplianceService.report(
                    driversById.keySet());
        // Check the results
        System.assertEquals('4.1',
            reportResults[0].complianceCode);
        System.assertEquals(true, reportResults[0].passed);
        System.assertEquals(null,
            reportResults[0].failureReason);
    }
```

You should get an error indicating that the method does not exist:

```
Compile Error: Package Visibility: Method is not visible:
fforce.ComplianceService.report(SET<Id>) at line 21 column 13
```

This is due to the package version information in the Apex class metadata of the test class still referencing the release of the package installed at the time the code was originally written. Upgrading the package does not change this. Open the **Version Settings** tab and change to the release you have just installed to fix this compile problem:

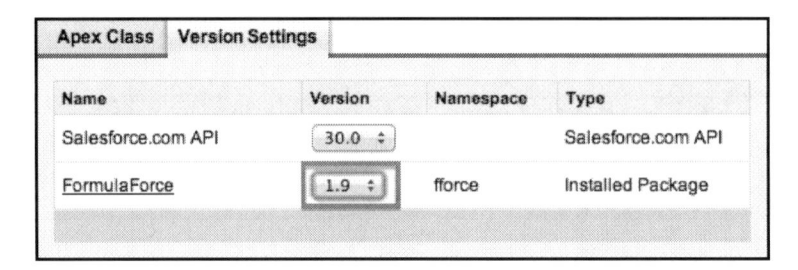

Apex Class	Version Settings		
Name	Version	Namespace	Type
Salesforce.com API	30.0		Salesforce.com API
FormulaForce	1.9	fforce	Installed Package

The preceding steps have illustrated how the Apex runtime manages the versioning of the Apex APIs you expose from your package. Thus, the requirement of versioning the API definition described earlier has been provided by the platform for you. There is no need to manage this yourself, though you do need to be aware of how it works.

Finally, revisit the `ComplianceService` Apex class page from within your test development org and notice that the available versions of this class now include the version that was just uploaded. Toggle between them; you can see the changes that the API definition has undergone between the last two package releases that we have just performed.

Select **All Versions** to get a full summary of which methods arrived with which package version. See the following screenshot:

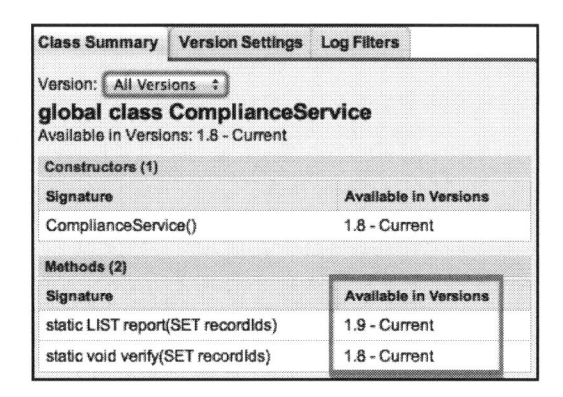

Class Summary	Version Settings	Log Filters

Version: [All Versions]
global class ComplianceService
Available in Versions: 1.8 - Current

Constructors (1)

Signature	Available in Versions
ComplianceService()	1.8 - Current

Methods (2)

Signature	Available in Versions
static LIST report(SET recordIds)	1.9 - Current
static void verify(SET recordIds)	1.8 - Current

Here, you can see that the `verify` method was first available in v1.8 and the `report` method in v1.9; again, your version numbers might differ.

Versioning Apex API behavior

The API definition is not the only aspect that can undergo changes between releases. Even if the definition stays the same, the code behind it can change the behavior of the API. The Apex runtime provides a means for the packaged code to determine which version the calling code written by *Developer X* is expecting. This can be obtained by calling the `System.requestVersion` method. With this information, your packaged code can modify its behavior according to the expectations of the calling code.

As you release more versions of your package and the functionality grows, the management of this type of code becomes more complex. Also note that this feature is only available in the code located within scratch orgs that have been configured with package ancestry (as discussed in `Chapter 1`, *Building and Publishing Your Application*). Otherwise, this method will throw a runtime exception.

Another way of versioning behavior is by considering whether changes in your application logic are something that *Developer X* would want to opt into or that should be immediately available to their existing code once the package has been upgraded. Changes to fix bugs or minor improvements in the way information is processed are probably things that you want to be available, regardless of the API version. However, other changes, such as the way values are calculated or the addition of significant new processing, may be something that justifies a new API method or a parameter for *Developer X* to modify their code so they can use it. Much like in the UI, you will choose to add a new tab, page, or button.

By considering when to version the API behavior, you put the choice of when to accept new API behaviors in the hands of *Developer X*. Critically, by considering backward compatibility you do not block upgrading to the latest version of your package due to integration failures. Spotting backward compatibility regressions caused by behavior changes will get harder the more versions you release and the more supported versions you have in your customer base. Therefore, making sure that you have a strong API-testing strategy becomes all the more critical.

Providing RESTful application APIs

So far, we have focused on *Developer X* being an on-platform Apex developer and the ways in which you can provide application APIs via Apex. However, it is also possible that *Developer X* is coding off-platform and needs to call your application APIs from Java, Microsoft .NET, or a mobile application. Perhaps they want to write a small dedicated mobile application to check compliance for teams, drivers, or cars.

This part of the chapter will focus on exposing a REST API of the preceding compliance API for use by off-platform developers writing integrations with your application. Don't forget, as with the on-platform scenario, Salesforce provides a number of standard Salesforce APIs via SOAP and REST, which, by coding off-platform, *Developer X* can use to create, read, update, and delete records held in your application's Custom Objects.

> Apex provides support to expose the application logic via web services (SOAP) through the use of the `webservice` keyword placed in your Apex classes. If you want to expose a SOAP API, the platform can generate the appropriate WSDLs once you have applied this keyword to methods on your Service classes. The design of the services designed in this book happens to align quite well with the general requirements of web services.
>
> Note that the aforementioned `@Deprecated` attribute cannot be used on Apex code exposed this way. One thing to consider though is that the WSDLs generated are not versioned; they are only generated based on the code for the installed version of your package. *Developer X* cannot generate historic versions of it from previous package versions. While Apex methods that use the `webservice` keyword fall under the same restrictions as `global`, you cannot exclude new methods or fields in your web services by version.

Apex also provides support for creating your own REST APIs, with some great reference documentation within the *Apex Developer's Guide*. However, what it doesn't cover are REST API design considerations, often referred to as RESTful.

Many mistakes are made when exposing REST APIs without first understanding what it means to be RESTful. Before we get into using your Service layer to deliver a REST API, let's learn more about being RESTful.

Key aspects of being RESTful

A full discussion and overview of RESTful API design could easily take up a full chapter. The following is a summary of the key RESTful design goals and how these apply to REST APIs delivered via Apex (some guidelines are handled for you by the platform). As we discuss this topic further, the use of the term *operation* represents the methods in the application's Service layer classes. This will be used to help expose the application's REST API but should not steer its design.

> There is no one list of guidelines, and some are open to interpretation. However, if you enter `Designing a RESTful API` in Google, you're sure to come up with some useful reading. I recommend that you focus on those articles that give insights into how some of the larger services, such as Facebook, LinkedIn, and Salesforce themselves, interpret RESTful, such as `http://www.apigee.com/`.

What are your application resources?

In the RESTful world, your operations are associated with a resource that is expressed via a **Uniform Resource Identifier** (**URI**). A resource can be a physical thing in your application, such as a Custom Object, or a conceptual thing. This is different from the Service layer design that drove the Apex API we looked at earlier, where operations are expressed by grouping them under functional areas of the application, which are then expressed by Apex Service classes and methods for each operation.

Providing Integration and Extensibility

The Salesforce REST API uses objects to define physical resources the REST URI uses, allowing you to build a URI and use the various HTTP methods to perform the create, read, update, and delete operations. For example, to retrieve a record, you can issue the following request via the Force.com REST API sObject Resources too (`https://developer.salesforce.com/docs/api-explorer`):

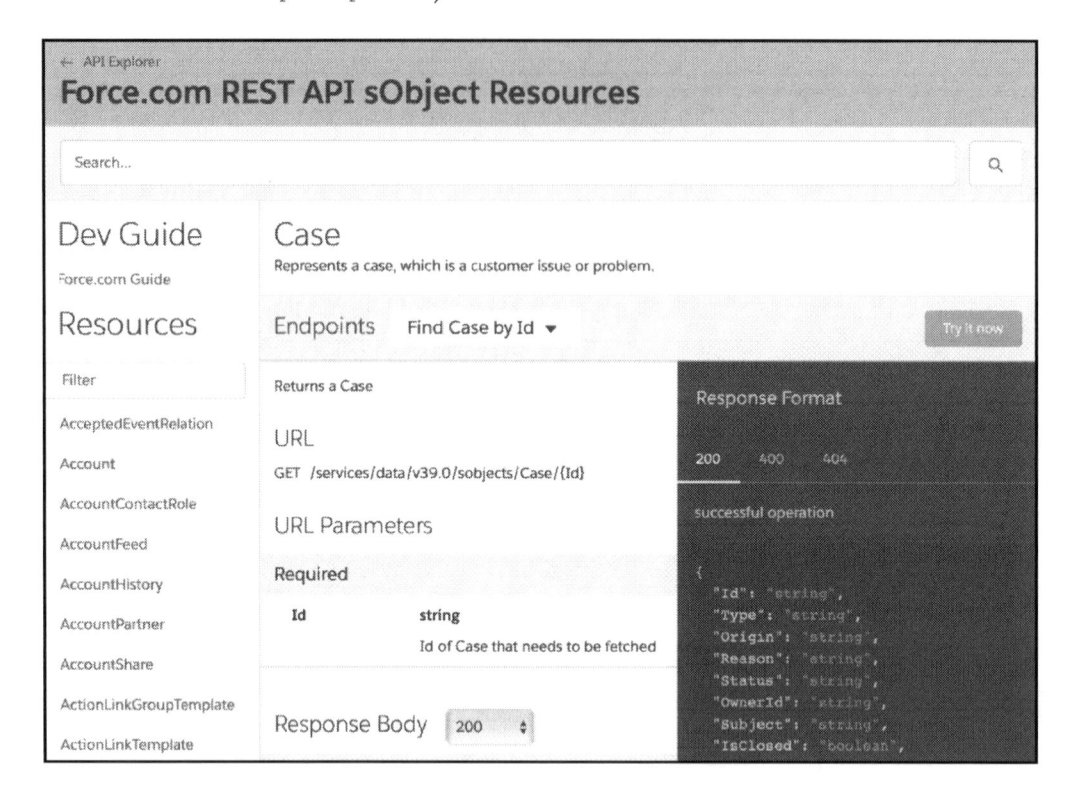

> **TIP**
>
> At the time of writing, the preceding tool is in developer preview, meaning that it is still being developed by Salesforce and is not yet ready for production use. As an older alternative, you can use the **Developer Workbench** tool. You will also need to use the `sfdx force:user:password:reset` command to generate a password for your scratch org user to log in to these tools. You can also use the `sfdx force:org:display` command to obtain the current scratch org's authentication token. This will allow you to use the `curl` command from the command line to invoke REST APIs. See the standard documentation for more information on this approach: `https://developer.salesforce.com/docs/atlas.en-us.api_rest.meta/api_rest/intro_curl.htm`.

In cases where you are exposing more business processes or task-orientated operations that are not data-centric, it can be difficult to decide what the resource name should actually be. So, it is worth taking the time to plan out and agree with the whole product team what the key REST resources are in the application and stick to them.

One operation that falls into this category in our FormulaForce package is the compliance report. This operates on a number of different Custom Object records to report compliance, such as the driver, car, and team. Should we define a URI that applies it to each of these physical resources individually, or create a new logical compliance resource?

I chose the latter in this chapter because it feels more extensible to do it this way, as it also leverages the compliance service in the application, which already supports adding new object types to the compliance checker. Thus, the REST API will support new object types without future changes to the API, as they are added to the compliance checker.

Salesforce dictates the initial parts of the URI used to define the resource and the developer gets to define the rest. For the compliance REST API, we will use this URI:

```
/services/apexrest/compliance
```

Once you package your Apex code implementing this REST API, you will find that the preceding URI needs to be qualified by your package namespace, so it will take on the format shown as follows from the point of view of *Developer X*, where `fforce` is my namespace. We will use this format of URI when we test the compliance REST API later in this chapter:

```
/services/apexrest/fforce/compliance
```

Mapping HTTP methods

Your application operations for a given resource URI should be mapped to one of the standard HTTP methods on which REST is based: `GET`, `POST`, `PUT`, `PATCH`, or `DELETE`. Choosing which to use and being consistent about its use throughout your REST API is vital. Again, there are many resources on the internet that discuss this topic in much more detail. Here is a brief summary of my interpretation of those readings:

- `GET`: This method is typically for operations that query the database and whose parameters are easily expressed in the URI structure and/or whose parameters fit well with this method.

- **PUT versus POST**: These methods are typically for operations that create, update, or query the database and where parameters are more complex, for example, lists or structures of information that cannot be reflected in URI parameters. There is also a consideration around the term **idempotent** (check out Wikipedia for a full definition of this), which relates to whether or not the request can be repeated over and over, resulting in the same state in the database. As you dig deeper into the RESTful design guidelines, this term typically drives the decision of whether to use PUT or POST.
- **PATCH**: This method is typically for operations that solely update existing information, such as a record or some other complex dataset spanning multiple records.
- **DELETE**: This method is, of course, to delete existing information expressed in the URI.

We will use the POST HTTP method with the `/services/apexrest/compliance` resource URI to implement our REST API for the compliance verify operation, passing the list of records to verify as a part of the HTTP request body using the JSON data format.

Providing Apex REST application APIs

The following Apex class follows the naming convention [ResourceName]Resource as the class name and then defines the appropriate methods (whose names are not as important in this case), mapping them accordingly to the HTTP method for the URL mapping. This is included in the sample code of this chapter:

```
@RestResource(urlMapping='/compliance')
global with sharing class ComplianceResource {
   @HttpPost
   global static List<ComplianceService.VerifyResult>
      report(List<Id> Ids) {
      return ComplianceService.report(new Set<Id>(Ids));
   }
}
```

The following are some things to note about the preceding example, and in general about wrapping Service layer methods in Apex REST methods to create REST APIs:

- The preceding example uses the `VerifyResult` class from `ComplianceService`. You may wish to create your own class scoped within the `ComplianceResource` class for further isolation.
- The methods in this class should delegate to one and only one applicable method in a Service class as per the general Service layer calling guidelines in order to maintain a transaction scope and also separation of concerns.
- It is not recommended to map your Apex resource classes only to a specific Service class as your earlier RESTful API design might not match your Service class design, though it should still delegate to it.
- Treat these classes like you would treat a UI controller, including only marshaling and error-handling logic as required.
- Typically, you don't need to catch exceptions from the Service layer (unlike Visualforce controller action method callers) as the Apex REST runtime catches the exception and returns the appropriate REST API error code and message. Avoid implementing your own REST API error handling.
- The `global` modifier is still required. Keep in mind that the same packaging restrictions regarding changes to these methods apply.
- It is possible for the *Developer X* Apex developer to call these methods from Apex, as they are `global`. However, this should be discouraged because these methods might reference the REST API context variables, which will not be initialized in a standard Apex context.
- The `Set` Apex data type is not supported by Apex REST methods. Unlike the standard, which has been established with the Service class methods, the `Set` Apex data type is not supported by Apex REST methods. Therefore, you will need to convert the `List<Id>` REST method parameters to the `Set<Id>` collections for your Service method calls.
- The `ComplianceService.verify` method throws an exception with additional information about the specific compliance failures. However, information in a custom Apex exception is not automatically serialized by the platform—only the error message is included. In this case, a custom response would be required to catch the exception and return the information.

Calling your Apex REST application APIs

The `curl` command can be used to call the preceding **Apex REST API**. Locate a **Driver** record without the **FIA Super License** field selected and note the record ID. First, run the following `sfdx` command to obtain an authorization token and install the URL for the current scratch org. Sample output is shown after the command to run:

`sfdx force:org:display`

```
Access Token 00D0m0000....MwwyTx
Alias lightningplatformenterprisearchitecturethirdedition
Client Id PlatformCLI
Created By afawcett@myhub.com
Created Date 2019-06-15T19:53:24.000+0000
Dev Hub Id afawcett@myhub.com
Edition Developer
Expiration Date 2019-06-22
Id 00D0m000000DXwNEAW
Instance Url https://dream-saas-9403-dev-ed.cs65.my.salesforce.com/
Org Name FormulaForce App Development
Status Active
Username test-6m0j7ozshuxe@example.com
```

The `Access Token` shown here has been shortened. Next, we will use the `curl` command to invoke the Apex REST API created here. You will also need to reference the `Instance Url` value.

Enter the following command all on one line in the command line, replacing `InstallURL` and `AccessToken` with the values output from the previous `sfdx` command:

```
curl InstallURL/apexrest/fforce/compliance
  -H 'Authorization: Bearer AccessToken'
  -H 'Content-Type: application/json'
  -d '{ "Ids" : [ "a020m000001piX7AAI" ]  }'
  -X POST
```

This command should output the following JSON response:

```
[{"recordId":"a020m000001piX7AAI","passed":false,"failureReason":"Driver must have a FIA Super License.","complianceCode":"4.1"}]
```

> **TIP**
>
> Note that the REST API URI shown in the preceding example contains the `fforce` namespace. To try this out, you need to replace this with your chosen namespace or remove `/fforce` from the URI if you are not using a namespace in your scratch org or do not have the package installed in your test scratch org.

If you are having problems getting the previous example `curl` command to work, consult the Salesforce documentation at https://developer.salesforce.com/docs/atlas.en-us.api_rest.meta/api_rest/quickstart.htm?search_text=curl.

Versioning Apex REST application APIs

The generally recognized way in which REST APIs are versioned is to include the version in the URI. Notice that `v30.0` (the Salesforce platform version) was included in the standard Salesforce REST API example shown earlier, but no version was included in the URI for the REST API exposing the compliance report operation. The platform does not provide a facility for versioning Apex REST APIs in the same way as its own APIs.

Behavior versioning

The Salesforce REST API, and any Apex REST APIs exposed, can receive from a new HTTP header, such as `x-sfdc-packageversion-fforce: 1.10`. With Apex REST APIs, this can be used to allow the packaged API code to implement behavior versioning. This can be used to set the version returned by `System.requestVersion`, as described earlier in this chapter.

This header is optional; without it, the current package version installed is assumed. My preceding recommendations around the utilization of behavior versioning also apply here. Because the header is optional, its usefulness is diluted.

Definition versioning

The preceding HTTP header does not affect the visibility of the API's definition in the same way that the platform does for Apex APIs, as illustrated earlier in the chapter. One way to address this is to map a versioned URI to a specific Apex resource class per version, for example, to support version v1.0 and v2.0 of the compliance REST API. This approach allows you to expose URIs with your version included:

```
/service/apexrest/fforce/v1.0/compliance
/service/apexrest/fforce/v2.0/compliance
```

Providing Integration and Extensibility

When versioning the API definition, you would need to also capture copies of the Apex data types used in the Service layer. This would isolate each REST API version from underlying changes of the Service layer as it evolves. The main coding overhead here is going to be marshaling between the Apex types defined in the Service layer (which are always the latest version) and those in the class implementing the REST API.

For example, to version the `report` API, we have to capture its types as inner Apex classes at the time the API class is created. The following example illustrates this for v1.0; you can see how the definition of the API can be encapsulated within the specific version of the Apex class denoted by the `v1_0` suffix:

```
@RestResource(urlMapping='/v1.0/compliance')
global with sharing class ComplianceResource_v1_0 {

  global class VerifyResult {
    global Id recordId;
    global String complianceCode;
    global Boolean passed;
    global String failureReason;
  }


  @HttpPost
  global static List<VerifyResult> report(List<Id> Ids) {

    List<VerifyResult> results = new List<VerifyResult>();
    for(ComplianceService.VerifyResult result :
      ComplianceService.report(new Set<Id>(Ids)))
    results.add(makeVerifyResult(result));
    return results;
  }

  private static VerifyResult
      makeVerifyResult(ComplianceService.VerifyResult verifyResult){
    VerifyResult restVerifyResult = new VerifyResult();
    restVerifyResult.recordId = verifyResult.recordId;
    restVerifyResult.complianceCode = verifyResult.complianceCode;
    restVerifyResult.passed = verifyResult.passed;
    restVerifyResult.failureReason = verifyResult.failureReason;
    return restVerifyResult;
  }
}
```

While the version number you use can be anything you like, you may want to consider following your package version numbering sequence.

Versioning Apex REST APIs this way is not ideal due to the manual way in which the definition has to be versioned by code and the overhead in managing that code for each release of your package. However, without this approach, it is always the latest definition of the Apex REST API in your package that is exposed.

This means that, after upgrades of your package, callers receive new fields in responses they do not expect. There is also no way to deprecate Apex REST APIs. However, due to the deletion restrictions on the `global` class members, there is some protection against developers accidentally removing fields that would break existing requests.

Exposing platform events

The sample code in this chapter contains a **Race News Feed** platform event object. As described earlier in this chapter, such objects can be used to define an asynchronous API for your application that applies the pub-sub communication pattern. In this use case, a mobile application (not included in this sample) is used by news reporters employed by the customers of your FormulaForce package. The goal is to ensure that whenever something not-worthy occurs in the application, they get real-time updates on their mobile devices.

The mobile application uses the **CometD** (https://cometd.org/) protocol in mobile applications' JavaScript to subscribe (listen) to the platform events from the **Race News Feed** object. Within the `RaceService.awardChampionshipPoints` method code shown here, the `RaceNewsFeed__e` object is registered with the Unit Of Work associated with the changes being made to the `Contestant_c` records resulting from the championship points calculation:

```
public void awardChampionshipPoints(Set<Id> raceIds) {
    fflib_ISObjectUnitOfWork uow =
        Application.UnitOfWork.newInstance();

    // Query Races and contestants
    List<Contestant__c> contestants = new List<Contestant__c>();
    for(Race__c race :
            new RacesSelector().selectByIdWithContestants(raceIds)) {
        contestants.addAll(race.Contestants__r);
    }
    // Delegate to Contestant Domain class
    new Contestants(contestants).awardChampionshipPoints(uow);

    // Send event notifying the press the results are published
    uow.registerNew(
        new RaceNewsFeed__e(
            Category__c = 'Race News',
```

```
            Content__c = 'Championship points calculated'));
    // Commit work
    uow.commitWork();
}
```

As an alternative implementation, the mobile application developer could have written code that queried the contestant records for updates based on a timer, or just made the new reporter manually refresh the display. By using platform events as the integration API, the mobile user experience and implementation were more optimal in both cases.

As an implementation note, it is important to know that the event is not sent if anything goes wrong with writing the **Contestants** object records. Thus, for this reason, the platform event has been configured to only send once the transaction is complete, as shown here:

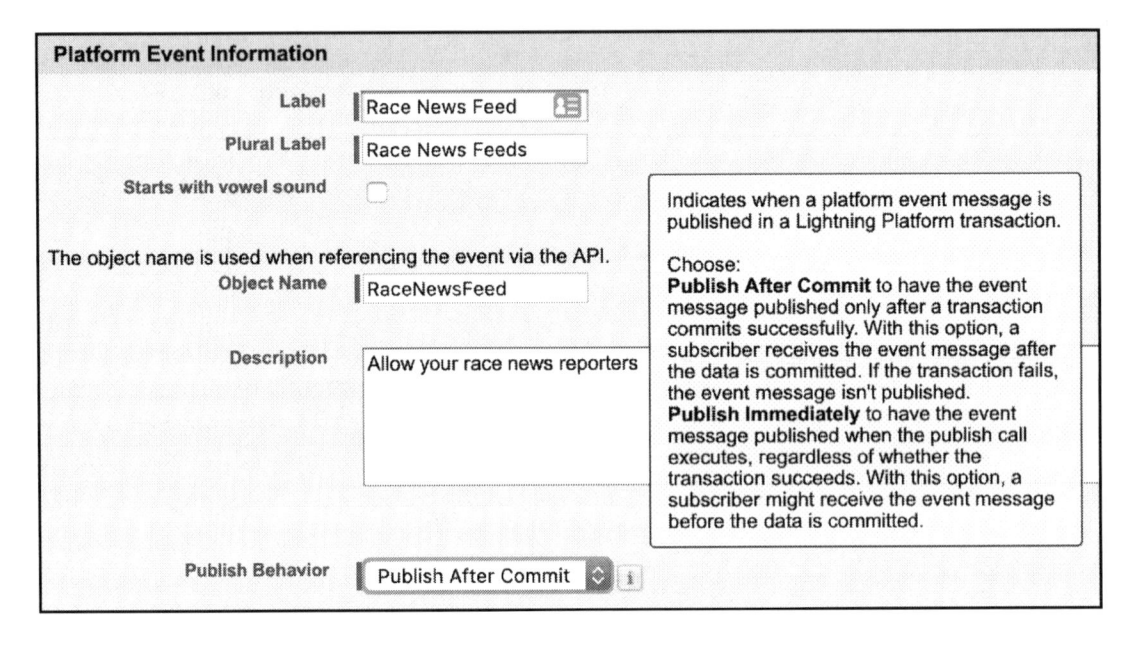

Platform Event Information

Label	Race News Feed
Plural Label	Race News Feeds
Starts with vowel sound	☐
Object Name	RaceNewsFeed
Description	Allow your race news reporters
Publish Behavior	Publish After Commit

The object name is used when referencing the event via the API.

Indicates when a platform event message is published in a Lightning Platform transaction.
Choose:
Publish After Commit to have the event message published only after a transaction commits successfully. With this option, a subscriber receives the event message after the data is committed. If the transaction fails, the event message isn't published.
Publish Immediately to have the event message published when the publish call executes, regardless of whether the transaction succeeds. With this option, a subscriber might receive the event message before the data is committed.

If the **Publish Immediately** behavior is selected, the event is sent regardless of whether the transaction commits successfully or not. With this setting, if for some reason there was an error updating the Contestant records (a custom Validation Rule or a customer-written Apex Trigger), then the event would still be sent and the news reporter could be provided with the wrong information.

In Chapter 11, *Asynchronous Processing and Big Data Volumes*, we will explore another use case for platform events, allowing external devices to send race data to the application by sending events off-platform to the **Race Telemetry** platform event object. In this use case, an external integration is triggering asynchronous processing at high scale within the FormulaForce application.

> **TIP**
> Salesforce also provides a platform-event-based feature known as **Salesforce Change Data Capture** (**CDC**). This feature results in events being sent each time record data changes on configured objects, such as updates or inserts to records. I would recommend against using such a feature to implement this scenario because it is harder for the *Developer X* code (the mobile app code in this case) to determine what the intent of the change to the record change was. The **Race News Feed** event conveys that intent and also is only fired when all **Contestant** records are updated at the end of a race.

Exposing Lightning Components

In the previous chapter, we looked at several components that are included in the FormulaForce package. These have all been exposed for use by tools and developers' code in the subscriber org through the `global` access level.

When developers consume these components inside their own component, there is a facility through the bundle metadata for them to express what package version they want the platform to assume when their code interacts with the packaged component. This allows the definition and behavior versioning of your components. If this information is not present, the currently installed package version is assumed.

`System.requestVersion`, `{!Version}`, and `cmp.getVersion()` are available to determine the version your component needs to honor in Apex or JavaScript.

> At the time of writing, this feature is not supported for **Lightning Web Components**, only **Lightning Aura Components**.

Extending Process Builder and Flow

The **Process Builder** and **Flow** tools allow users to create customized processes and wizard-like user experiences. Both tools offer a large selection of actions they can perform based on criteria defined by the user.

Available actions can be extended by packages installed in the org. This provides another way in which you can expose your functionality to build customized scenarios. This approach does not require the user to write any code.

The following code creates an **invocable method**, which is a `global` class and a single method with some specific annotations. These annotations are recognized by the tools to present a dynamic configuration UI to allow the user to pass information to and from the method you annotate:

```
global with sharing class UpdateStandingsAction {
    global class UpdateStandingsParameters {


        @InvocableVariable(
           Label='Season Id'
           Description='Season to update the standings for'
           Required=True)
        global Id seasonId;
        @InvocableVariable(
           Label='Issue News Letter'
            Description='Send the newsletter out
                         to the teams and drivers'
           Required=False)
        global Boolean issueNewsLetter;
        private SeasonService.UpdateStandings makeUpdateStandings(){
            SeasonService.UpdateStandings updateStandings =
                new SeasonService.UpdateStandings();
            updateStandings.seasonId = this.seasonId;
            updateStandings.issueNewsLetter = this.issueNewsLetter;
            return updateStandings;
        }
    }

    @InvocableMethod(
       Label='Update the leaderboard of the season'
       Description='Updates the standings and optionally
                    sends the newsletter.')    global static void
        updateStandings(
           List<UpdateStandingsParameters> parameters) {
```

```
        // Marshall parameters into service parameters
        List<SeasonService.UpdateStandings> updateStandings =
            new List<SeasonService.UpdateStandings>();
        for(UpdateStandingsParameters parameter : parameters) {
            updateStandings.add(parameter.makeUpdateStandings());
        }
        // Call the service
        SeasonService.updateStandings(updateStandings);
    }
}
```

> **TIP**: In order to isolate the parameters of this method from changes to the Service class methods, the `UpdateStandings` Apex class is used. This also allows the method to evolve in a different direction if necessary.

The following screenshot shows how the preceding invocable method appears in Process Builder:

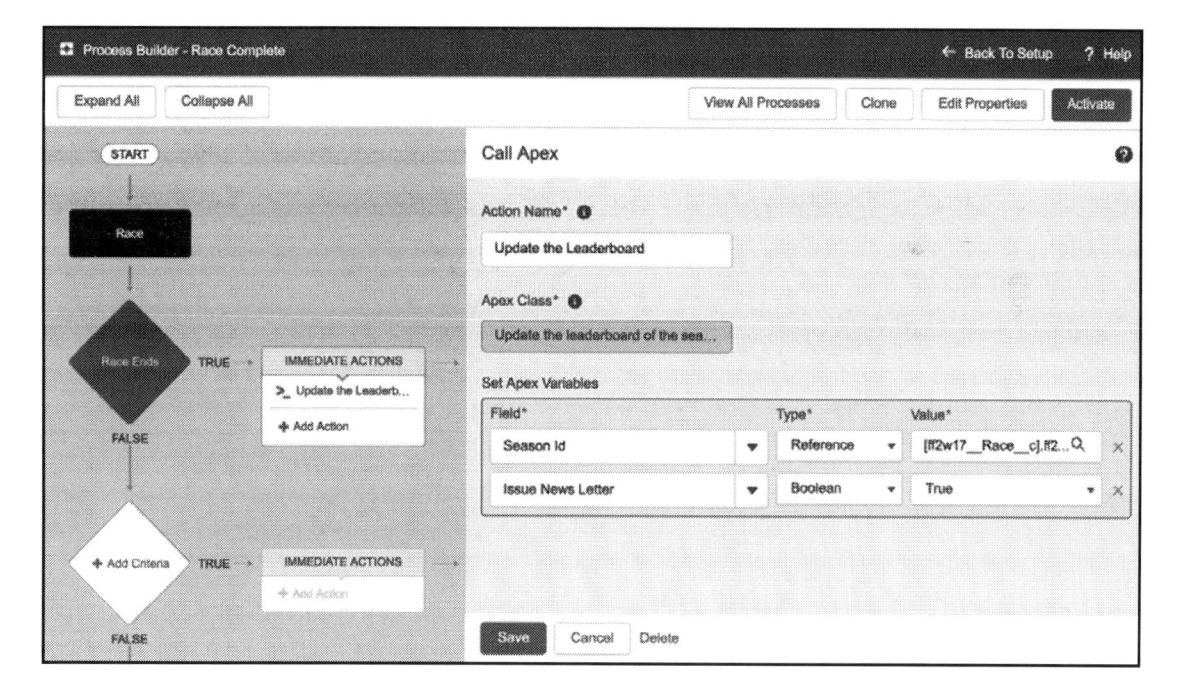

Providing Integration and Extensibility

The following screenshot shows how the preceding invocable method appears in Flow:

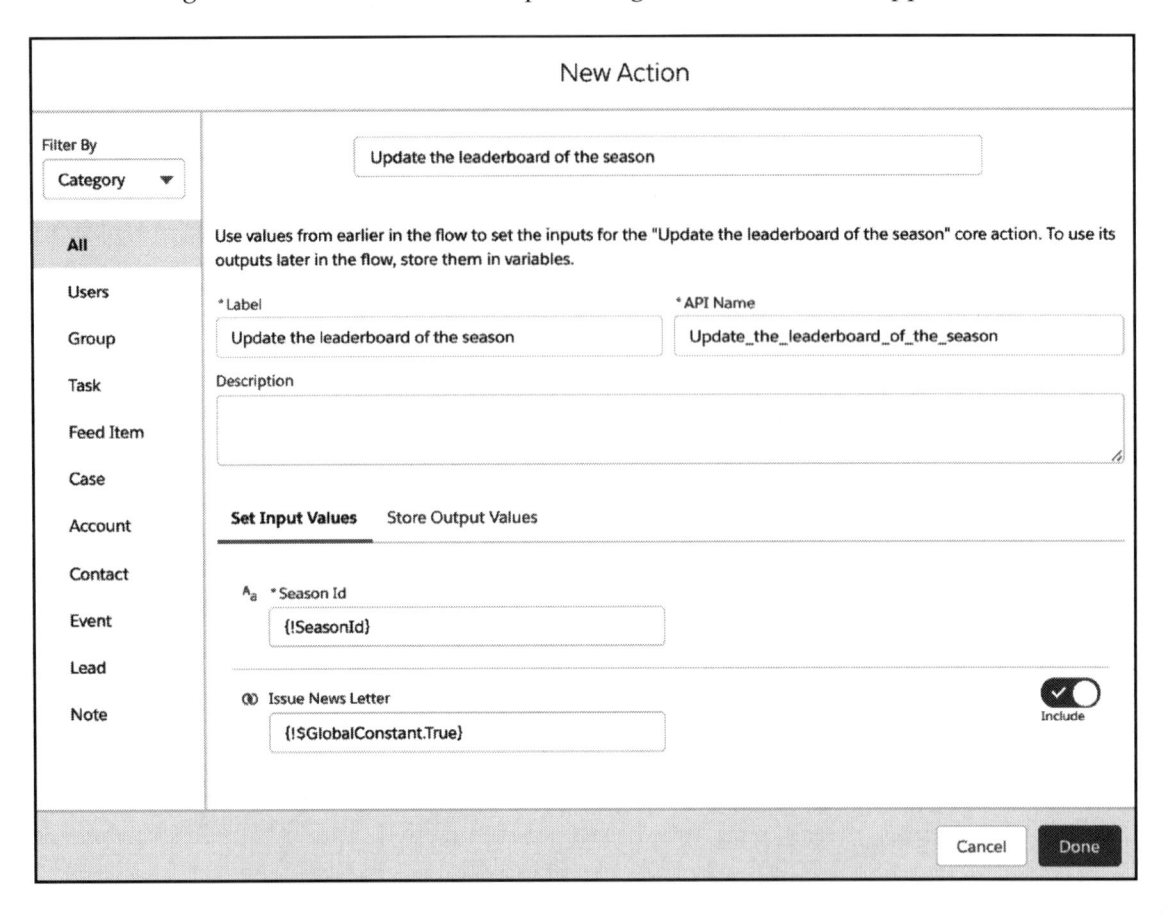

New Action

Filter By	Update the leaderboard of the season
Category ▼	
All	Use values from earlier in the flow to set the inputs for the "Update the leaderboard of the season" core action. To use its outputs later in the flow, store them in variables.
Users	*Label *API Name
Group	Update the leaderboard of the season Update_the_leaderboard_of_the_season
Task	Description
Feed Item	
Case	
Account	**Set Input Values** Store Output Values
Contact	
Event	*Season Id* {!SeasonId}
Lead	
Note	Issue News Letter Include {!$GlobalConstant.True}

                                                                                                    Cancel   **Done**

This method could, for example, be used as part of the preceding subscriber-defined Process Builder process when a race ends. While you could do this with an Apex Trigger, this might involve some additional conditions that are unique to the subscriber of your package. Thus, this is a good use case for Process Builder and exposing the `SeasonService.updateStandings` method via an invocable method.

> Check the Apex Developers' Guide (https://developer.salesforce.com/docs/atlas.en-us.apexcode.meta/apexcode/apex_dev_guide.htm) for more information on invocable methods and the preceding attributes. There are various restrictions on the types of parameters that can be passed. Such as parameters must be in list form. This fits well with the bulkified requirements of the Service layer.

Versioning invocable methods

Neither Process Builder or VisualFlow record the package version that was used when an invocable method is referenced. Thus, it is not possible to perform behavior versioning. `System.requestVersion` returns the currently installed package version. The definition of the invocable method is controlled by the constraints relating to the use of the `global` modifier, as we have already discussed in this chapter. As a best practice, avoid adding new required members (via `@InvocableVariable`) to your parameter classes.

Alignment with platform extensibility features

Here are some other platform features that can help ensure that your application's functionality is open to being extended by *Developer X* or subscriber org administrators:

- **Apex Triggers**: *Developer X* can write their own triggers against your application's managed Custom Objects. These will execute in addition to those packaged. This allows *Developer X* to implement the defaulting of fields or custom validations, for example. Salesforce does not guarantee that packaged triggers will execute before or after *Developer X* triggers in the subscriber org. To ensure that all changes are validated regardless of the trigger execution order, perform your validation logic in the after-phase of your packaged triggers. It is recommended that you advise *Developer X* to be considerate about how much code is written in triggers because the CPU that their code uses counts towards the overall CPU and can cause your application experience to run more slowly or hit limits. By using asynchronous coding patterns or **Async Apex Triggers**, you can avoid this problem. This is discussed in more detail in `Chapter 11`, *Asynchronous Processing and Big Data Volumes*.
- **Field Sets**: Field sets make it possible for your Lightning Components to show additional fields and tables that can be defined by administrators. They can also be used with JavaScript frameworks if you're developing a mobile UI. However, you should also ensure that you consider **Lightning Data Services**, record layout, and editing Lightning base components first, as described in `Chapter 9`, *User Interfaces with Lightning Framework*, since they leverage the standard record layout definitions for objects.

- **Email templates**: If you're writing code to emit emails, consider providing a means to allow the text to be customized using an email template. These templates can be referenced through their developer names using a custom setting. Field sets can also be leveraged here to provide an easy way to include additional Custom Fields added by the subscriber administrator.
- **Lightning Components**: Consider exposing Lightning Components used in your package for use with tools such as Lightning App Builder and Lightning Community Builder, as we explored in the previous chapter. This can provide administrators and developers with a great deal of flexibility to build and customize unique user experiences for their businesses.
- **Dynamic Apex type creation**: The `Type.forName` method can be used to create an instance of an Apex type, and from that, an instance of that type at runtime. This capability can be used to allow *Developer X* to write Apex code that your application code can dynamically call at a specified time. This approach is discussed in further detail in the upcoming section.

Extending application logic with Apex interfaces

An **Apex interface** can be used to describe a point in your application logic where custom code written by *Developer X* can be called. For example, in order to provide an alternative means to calculate championship points driven by *Developer X*, we might expose a global interface describing an application callout that looks like this:

```
global class ContestantService {
   global interface IAwardChampionshipPoints {
     void calculate(List<Contestant__c> contestants);
   }
}
```

By querying **Custom Metadata** records from the **Callouts** Custom Metadata type, which has been included in the source code for this chapter, code in the application can determine whether *Developer X* has provided an implementation of this interface to call instead of the standard calculation code.

Using Custom Metadata is an excellent use case for this sort of requirement because you can declare the callouts your package supports by packaging records. Then, by making certain fields subscriber editable, you can allow the subscriber (*Developer X*) to configure those callouts. This approach, in contrast with custom settings, avoids additional configuration and the risk of misconfiguration.

> **TIP**
> Partners extending your package can also package this configuration with their Apex class. Thus, administrators installing such partner extension packages have zero configuration to perform to activate the callout contained within.

This screenshot shows how the **Callouts** Custom Metadata Type is defined. Notice how the **Apex Class** and **Apex Class Namespace Prefix** fields are subscriber editable:

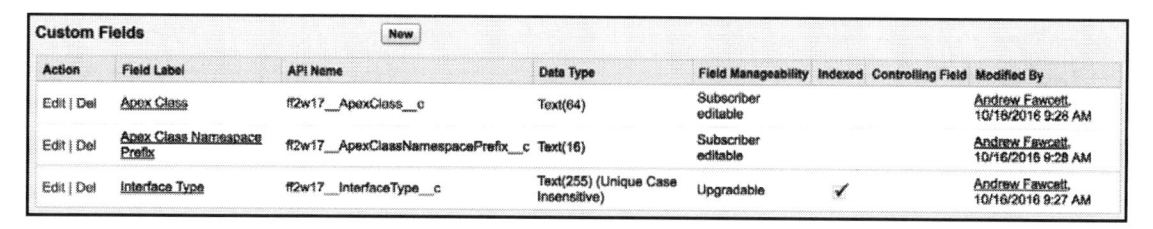

Custom Fields							
Action	Field Label	API Name	Data Type	Field Manageability	Indexed	Controlling Field	Modified By
Edit | Del	Apex Class	ff2w17__ApexClass__c	Text(64)	Subscriber editable			Andrew Fawcett, 10/16/2016 9:28 AM
Edit | Del	Apex Class Namespace Prefix	ff2w17__ApexClassNamespacePrefix__c	Text(16)	Subscriber editable			Andrew Fawcett, 10/16/2016 9:28 AM
Edit | Del	Interface Type	ff2w17__InterfaceType__c	Text(255) (Unique Case Insensitive)	Upgradable	✓		Andrew Fawcett, 10/16/2016 9:27 AM

The following record is defined by you, the packager developer, to effectively declare that the **Award Championship Points** callout exists and can be configured. This should also be included in your package:

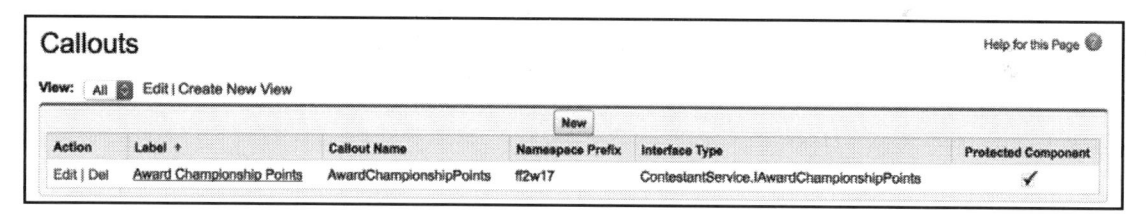

Callouts					
View: All Edit | Create New View					Help for this Page
			New		
Action	Label ↑	Callout Name	Namespace Prefix	Interface Type	Protected Component
Edit | Del	Award Championship Points	AwardChampionshipPoints	ff2w17	ContestantService.IAwardChampionshipPoints	✓

> **TIP**
> Notice how the Custom Metadata Type fields support *Developer X* providing a class name that is either fully qualified (perhaps from an extension package, for example, `fforceext.SimpleCalc`) or a local class (defined in the subscriber org), for example, `DeveloperXCustomCalc`.

The following code is a Selector method (see `CalloutsSelector`) class that reads the registered interface implementations. It uses the `Type.forName` method to construct applicable Apex types and returns a `Map` of Apex classes implementing each interface:

```
public Map<Type, Type> selectAllCallouts() {
    // Query custom metadata records for callouts
    Map<Type, Type> calloutsByInterfaceType =
        new Map<Type, Type>();
    for(Callout__mdt record :
          Database.query(newQueryFactory().toSOQL())) {
        if(Callout__mdt.ApexCLass__c!=null) {
            // Namespace of the interface is that
            //   of the custom metadata type
            Type interfaceType =
               Type.forName(
                  record.NamespacePrefix, record.InterfaceType__c);
            // Implementing class can optionally specify
            //   the namespace if needed
            Type implType =
                Type.forName(record.ApexCLassNamespacePrefix__c,
                             record.ApexCLass__c);
            calloutsByInterfaceType.put(interfaceType, implType);
        }
    }
    return calloutsByInterfaceType;
}
```

The following code uses a new `Application.Callout` class factory, which is not shown here but is included in the source code of this chapter. This is a simple class factory that uses the preceding Selector method and exposes the `newInstance` method to provide an easy way to instantiate the classes *Developer X* has registered. The following method in the `Contestants` Domain class now looks like this:

```
public void awardChampionshipPoints(fflib_ISObjectUnitOfWork uow)
{
    // Custom implementation configured by Developer X?
    Object registeredInterfaceImpl =
        Application.Callouts.newInstance(
          ContestantService.IAwardChampionshipPoints.class);
    if(registeredInterfaceImpl instanceof
      ContestantService.IAwardChampionshipPoints) {
      // Cast the interface to call the calculate method
      ContestantService.IAwardChampionshipPoints
          awardChampionshipPoints =
             (ContestantService.IAwardChampionshipPoints)
                registeredInterfaceImpl;
      // Invoke the custom method from Developer X
```

```
        awardChampionshipPoints.calculate(Records);
        // Mark dirty on behalf of Developer X
        for(Contestant__c contestant :
            (List<Contestant__c>) Records) {
           uow.registerDirty(contestant);
        }
        return;
     }
     // Continue with standard implementation...
```

In the subscriber org or the test development org, *Developer X* can then implement this interface as follows and configure the Apex Class field on the Callouts record corresponding to the **Award Championship Points** callout. The next time the award championship points service is called, this custom logic will be called instead:

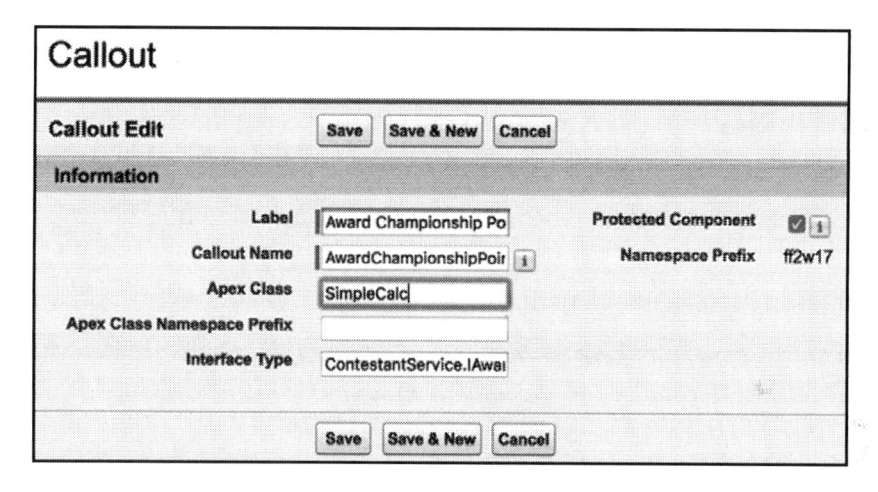

The following is a simple Application Callout implementation that assigns points according to the race position rather than using the default calculation:

```
public class SimpleCalc
   implements fforce.ContestantService.IAwardChampionshipPoints
{
   public void calculate(List<fforce__Contestant__c> contestants)
   {
      // Very simple, points equals race position
      for(fforce__Contestant__c contestant : contestants)
         contestant.fforce__ChampionshipPoints__c =
            contestant.fforce__RacePosition__c;
   }
}
```

Some aspects to consider when exposing global Apex interfaces are as follows:

- You cannot modify global interfaces once they are published by uploading them within a release-managed package.
- You can extend a global interface from another global interface, for example, `IAwardChampionshipPointsExt extends IAwardChampionshipPoints`.
- From a security perspective, consider carefully what you pass into an Application Callout via your Apex interface methods, especially if the parameters are objects whose values are later referenced by the application code. Be sure that you are happy for the Application Callout to make any changes to this object or data. If you're not comfortable with this, consider cloning the object before passing it as a parameter to the interface method.

The MuleSoft platform

The **MuleSoft** platform from Salesforce allows your customers to connect to a wide variety of APIs, not just those exposed via the Lightning Platform and your application, but ones from other platforms and products available throughout the industry. It contains many connectors so that it is easy for customers to integrate many different solutions together into one set of APIs. It also contains a strong orchestration engine that allows processes to be described with conditional logic and some level of programmatic transformation through its **DataWeave** scripting language. One of the most powerful features is composing new APIs from several APIs. These APIs can also be consumed from within Apex logic.

At the time of writing, there is no support for packaging MuleSoft configurations, so this is purely a customer-focused tool. However, you should take the time to understand its value and its various standard connectors in terms of your customers' broader needs regarding integrating your application with other services that already exist within their organization.

Summary

In this chapter, we have reviewed enterprise application integration and extensibility requirements through the eyes of a persona known as *Developer X*. By using this persona, much like your UI designs, you can ensure that your API tracks real use cases and requirements from the representative and, ideally, actual users of it.

When defining your API strategy, keep in mind the benefits of the standard Salesforce APIs, how to evangelize them, and the significant investment Salesforce puts into them in order to provide access to the information stored in your Custom Objects. We have also seen that platform tools such as Lightning App Builder, Lightning Process Builder, and Flow can be extended with embedded functionality from your package that can be accessed without the need for code. Platform events are also worth considering to provide an asynchronous loosely API to allow notifications to be sent from your application and data feeds into your application.

When needed, leverage your Service layer to create application APIs on- and/or off-platform using Apex and REST as delivery mechanisms. Keep in mind that REST requires additional design considerations to ensure that your REST API can be considered properly RESTful and thus familiar to *Developer X*, who has been using other REST APIs. Application callouts configured via Custom Metadata allow developers to extend the logic within your application.

Don't forget that while technologies such as Visualforce, Lightning, and Apex provide you with great flexibility as a developer and finely tuned functionality as a user, they can often lead to reduced opportunities for extensibility for the subscriber. By using Field Sets and Apex Application Extensions (leveraging `Type.forName`), you can readdress this balance. Also keep in mind that Field Sets provide a good extensibility tool beyond custom UI use cases. For example, they can be used to expose subscriber Custom Fields when building mobile UIs using JavaScript frameworks.

There is no need to upload a new version of the FormulaForce package in this chapter if you have been following along; if you haven't, take the latest code from the sample code provided with this chapter to update your packaging org and upload a new package.

In the next chapter, we will review approaches and features that help your application scale.

11
Asynchronous Processing and Big Data Volumes

This chapter covers two important aspects of developing an enterprise-level application on the Lightning Platform. While asynchronous processing and big data volumes are not necessarily linked, greater scalability and processing power of the platform can be achieved when embracing async programming patterns. However, making sure that your interactive user experience is still responsive when querying large volumes of data is also very important.

In this chapter, we will first review how to ensure SOQL queries are as performant as possible by understanding how to interpret query performance information returned by the platform and make use of the standard and custom indexes. This will benefit both interactive and batch (or async) processes in your application, in addition to how they are leveraged through native platform features such as reporting.

We will then take a look at the options, best practices, design, and usability considerations to move your application processing into the async mode and **event-driven architecture** (**EDA**) patterns, once again leveraging the **Service** layer as the shared backbone of your application. Finally, we will be exploring some thoughts and considerations when it comes to volume testing your application. We will cover the following topics in this chapter:

- Creating test data for volume testing
- Indexes, being selective, and query optimization
- Using big data storage to store and query millions to billions of records
- Asynchronous execution and event-driven architecture patterns for scale
- Volume testing

Creating a RaceData object with data

Throughout this chapter, we are going to use the `RaceData__c` **Custom Object**. We will be extending it with additional fields and running a script to populate it with some test volume data, before exploring the different ways of accessing it and processing the data held within it.

In the **Formula 1** racing world, a huge amount of data is captured from the drivers and the cars during the race. This information is used to perform real-time or post-race analysis in order to lead to further improvements or troubleshoot issues. Because of the huge volumes of data involved, the FormulaForce application considers ways to summarize this data such that it can be accessed quickly during races. It is also important to retain this data in the form of an archive for future analysis after races have completed. To do this, we will use a new type of object called a **big object**, and, later in this chapter, we will also discuss the `RaceLapHistory__b` object.

Meanwhile, with respect to the **Race Data** object, the following functionalities will be added to the FormulaForce application to process current race information and help demonstrate the Lightning Platform features described in this chapter:

- A Visualforce page able to perform some *What-If* analysis on the race data
- A Batch Apex process to validate and associate race data with contestants

The Apex and Visualforce code for this functionality are included in the code for this chapter.

> The Visualforce page used in this chapter uses the Lightning Design System so that it does not look out of place within the Lightning Experience user experience. Lightning Components are not used as they presently do not offer flexibility for querying in excess of the 50,000 records, which is something we will be exploring in this chapter. However, if you need to query less, you should consider Lightning Components before using this older UI technology from Salesforce.

The sample code for this chapter also contains updates to the **Race Data** object, as follows:

- The **Type** field represents the type of race data, for example, **Oil Pressure**, **Engine Temperature**, **Sector Time**, **Fuel Level**, and **Pit Stop Times**.
- The **Value** field is a numeric value dependent on the **Type** field.
- The **Lap** and **Sector** fields are numeric fields that represent the lap and sector number the data was captured on.

- The **Year**, **Race Name**, and **Driver Id** fields are text fields whose values, when later combined together, can be used to form a key to link each **Race Data** record with the appropriate **Contestant** record (which has its own relationships with the **Driver**, **Race**, and **Season** objects). In this use case, we assume that the electronic systems generating this raw data do not know or want to understand Salesforce IDs, so the FormulaForce application must correctly resolve the relationship with the **Contestant** record.
- The **Contestant** lookup field references the applicable **Contestant** record. As the incoming raw data does not contain Salesforce record IDs, this field is not initially populated. The FormulaForce applications logic will populate this later, as will be shown later in this chapter in the *Using external references in Apex DML* section.
- A new **Race Data ID** external ID field has been added to the **Contestant** object. The Apex code in the `Contestants` Domain class has been updated to ensure that this field is automatically populated as **Contestants** are added and that its value can be used during the processing of new **Race Data** to correctly associate **Race Data** records with **Contestant** records.

The **Race Data** object uses an **Auto Number** field type for its **Name** field. This ensures the insert order for the data is also retained.

> Note that we have added the **Race Data ID** field to an object already released in previous versions of the package, while the `Contestants` Domain class has been updated to populate this field for new records. The records already existing in subscriber orgs will not contain this value. Lightning Platform provides a means to execute the Apex code after installation (and uninstallation) of the package so that you can include the code to trigger a Batch Apex job to update this field value with the appropriate value on existing records. Refer to the `System.InstallHandler` interface in the *Apex Developers Guide*.

Using Apex to generate synthetic Race Data

Just like me, I doubt if you have a real Formula 1 race team or car to provide raw data input. We will be using an Apex code to generate synthetic test data in this section, though in reality, race data may be inserted through a CSV file import or through an IoT integration with the driver's car. Ingesting a live stream of race data via the Salesforce APIs using Platform Events is something we will be exploring later in this chapter in the *Asynchronous processing with Platform Events* section.

For now, the following Apex code will generate 10,000 rows, which is about enough to explore the **SOQL profiler**, which makes different choices dependent on row count. Due to the volumes of data being created, you must run each of the following Apex statements one by one to stay within the governors. Use the `sfdx force:apex:execute` command (without parameters) and paste in the following one at a time. Then, as indicated by the onscreen instructions, press the appropriate key to execute the code.

1. Run `TestData.resetTestSeason();`.
2. Run `TestData.purgeVolumeData(false);`.
3. Run `TestData.purgeVolumeData(true);`.
4. Run `TestData.createVolumeData('Spain', 52, 4);`.

> *Step 1* of the preceding steps will run a script that will clear down all other data from other FormulaForce objects in order to set up test **Season**, **Race**, and **Driver** data for the rest of the chapter. You can repeat *step 4* to generate a further 10,000 **Race Data** records for additional races—something we will do later in this chapter. This step might take a few seconds to complete.

Once the script has been executed, go to the **Race Data** tab and review the data. The values shown in the **Value** column are random values, so your results will differ:

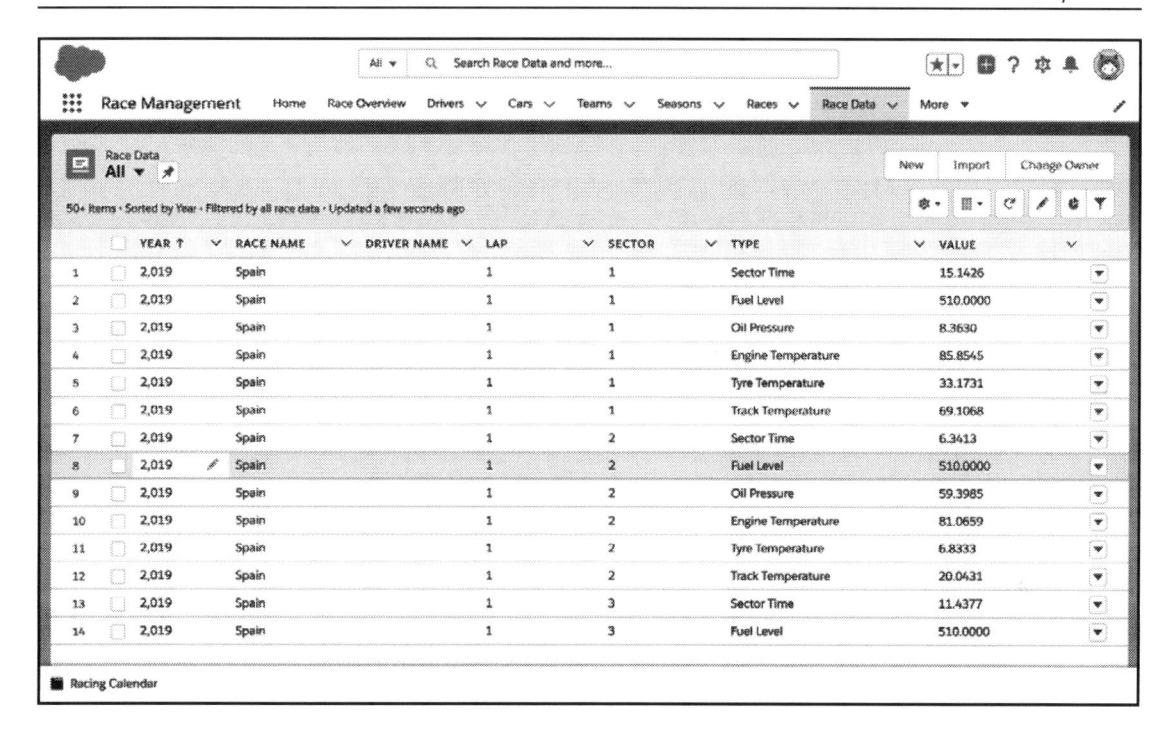

[Screenshot of Race Management app showing Race Data list with 14 rows of 2,019 Spain race data including Sector Time, Fuel Level, Oil Pressure, Engine Temperature, Tyre Temperature, and Track Temperature values across laps and sectors.]

You should also see the following row count if you review the **Storage Usage** page:

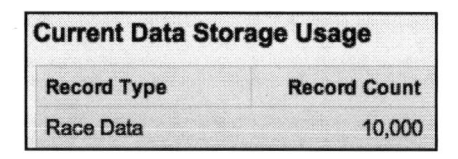

Current Data Storage Usage	
Record Type	Record Count
Race Data	10,000

Now that we have loaded some sample data through the preceding scripts, in the next section, we will review the effects of different queries on that data with respect to the presences of indexes.

Indexes, being selective, and query optimization

In this section, we will review when system and custom indexes maintained by the Lightning Platform are used to make queries more performant and, once larger query results are returned, the ways in which they can be most effectively consumed by your Apex logic.

Standard and custom indexes

As with other databases, Lightning Platform maintains database indexes as record data is manipulated to ensure that, when data is queried, such indexes can be used to improve query performance. Due to the Lightning Platform's multitenancy, it has its own database index implementation (instead of using the underlying Oracle database indexes) that considers the needs of each tenant. By default, it maintains standard indexes for the following fields:

- ID
- Name
- OwnerId
- CreateDate
- CreatedById
- LastModifiedDate
- LastModifiedById
- SystemModStamp
- RecordType
- Any Master Detail fields
- Any Lookup fields
- Any fields marked as Unique
- Any fields marked as External ID

Once your application is deployed into a subscriber org, you can also request Salesforce to consider creating additional custom indexes on fields not covered by the preceding list, such as fields used by your application logic to filter records, including custom formula fields and Custom Fields added to your objects by the subscriber as well.

> Formula fields can be indexed so long as the formula result is deterministic, which means that it does not use any dynamic data or time functions such as TODAY or NOW, or leverage-related fields via lookup fields or any other formula fields that are non-deterministic.

Since creating indexes and maintaining them consumes platform resources, custom indexes cannot be packaged, as the decision to enable them is determined by conditions only found in the subscriber org.

> Though objects can contain millions of records, standard indexes will only index up to 1 million records and custom indexes up to 333,333 records. These limits have a bearing on whether an index is used, depending on the query and filter criteria being used. This is discussed in more detail further in this chapter.

With respect to the **Race Data** object, some of its fields will be indexed by default by the platform. Only through contacting Salesforce support and by means of enabling in the subscriber org can additional custom indexes be created, for example, on the `Type__c` field. The following table shows the fields on the **Race Data** object that are indexed by default:

Field	Standard Index
CreatedBy	Yes (Lookup Field)
LastModifiedBy	Yes (Lookup Field)
Name	Yes
Owner	Yes
Contestant__c	Yes (Lookup Field)
Race__c	Yes (Lookup Field)
DriverId__c	No
Lap__c	No
RaceName__c	No
Sector__c	No
Type__c	No
Value__c	No
Year__c	No

> Under **Setup**, navigate to **Objects** and locate the **Race Data** object. When viewing fields listed in the **Standard Fields**, or **Custom Fields and Relationships**-related lists, observe the **Index** column. This is the easiest way to determine whether a field has a standard or custom index applied to it.

Thus, if a query filters by fields covered by a system or custom index, the index will be considered by the Lightning Platform query optimizer. This means that just because an index exists, it does not mean it will be used. The final decision is determined by how *selective* the query is. In the next section, we will explore how to determine whether your queries are selective.

By default, Salesforce does not include rows (that contain null values) within its indexes for the respective field. In this case, although the **Contestant** field is indexed by default, it initially contains a null value, and so initially, the index will be ineffective (this fact relates to why the use of nulls in filter criteria will deter the Lightning Platform query optimizer from using an index, as discussed in the next section). You can, however, get Salesforce Support to discuss enablement of the inclusion of nulls in indexes.

Ensuring queries leverage indexes

The process of selecting an appropriate index applies to queries made via SOQL through APIs and Apex, but also via **Reporting** and **List Views**. The use of an index is determined by the SOQL statement being selective or not. The following list provides definitions of being selective and being non-selective:

- Salesforce uses the term **selective** to describe queries filtering record data that are able to leverage indexes maintained behind the scenes by Salesforce, making such queries more efficient, and thus returning results more quickly.
- Conversely, the term **non-selective** implies a given query is not leveraging an index; thus, it will, in most cases, not perform as well. It will either time-out or, for objects containing more than 100,000 records, result in a runtime exception.

In a non-selective query situation, the platform will scan all the records in the object, applying the filtering to each; this is known as a **full table scan**. However, this is not necessarily the slowest option, depending on the number of records and the filter criteria.

The main goal of this part of the chapter is to explain what it takes for Salesforce to select an index for a given query. This depends on a number of factors, both when you build your application queries and the number of records in your objects within the subscriber org.

Factors affecting the use of indexes

There are two things that determine whether an index is used: Firstly, the **filter criteria** (or the `WHERE` clause in SOQL terms) of the query must comply with certain rules in terms of operators and conditions used; and secondly, the **total number of records** in the object versus the estimated number of records that will be returned by applying the filter criteria.

The filter criteria must, of course, reference a field that has either a standard or custom index defined for it. After this, unary, AND, OR, and LIKE operators can be used to filter records. However, other operators, such as negative operators, wild cards, and text comparison operators, as well as the use of null in the filter criteria, can easily disqualify the query from using an index. For example, a filter criteria that is more explicit in the rows it wants, Type__c = 'Sector Time', is more likely to leverage an index (assuming that this field has a custom index enabled), than say, for example, Type__c != 'Pit Stop Time', which will cause the platform to perform a full table scan, as the platform cannot leverage the internal statistics it maintains on the spread of data throughout the rows across this column.

The filtered record count must be below a certain percentage of the overall records in the object for an index to be used. You might well ask how Salesforce knows this information without actually performing the query in the first place? Though they do not give full details, they do describe what is known as a pre-query using statistical data that the platform captures as the standard or custom indexes are maintained. This statistical data helps to understand the spread of data based on the field values. For example, the percentage of rows loaded by the execution of the scripts to load sample data where the Type__c field contains the **PitStop Time** value is 0.16 percent, and thus, if a custom index was in place and the queries filter criteria were sufficiently selective (for example, Type__c = 'PitStop Time'), an index would be used.

A query for **Sector Time**, such as Type__c = 'Sector Time', will result in 1,664 records, which is 16.64 percent of the total rows being selected. So, while the filter criteria are selective, the filtered record count is above the threshold for custom index 10 percent or 333,333 records max. Thus, in this case, an index is not used. This might result in a timeout or runtime exception. So, in order to avoid this, the query must be made more selective, for example, by enabling a custom index and adding either Lap__c or Sector__c to the filter criteria.

Salesforce provides more detailed information on how to handle large data volumes, such as fully documenting the filter record count tolerances used to select indexes (note that they differ based on standard or custom indexes) and some insights as to how they store data within the Oracle database that help make more sense of things. These are a must-read in my view and can be found in various white papers and Wiki pages. Some of them are as follows:

- *Query and Search Optimization Cheat Sheet*: http://resources.docs.salesforce.com/rel1/doc/en-us/static/pdf/salesforce_query_search_optimization_developer_cheatsheet.pdf
- *Best Practices for Deployments with Large Data Volumes*: https://developer.salesforce.com/docs/atlas.en-us.salesforce_large_data_volumes_bp.meta/salesforce_large_data_volumes_bp/ldv_deployments_introduction.htm
- *Lightning Platform SOQL Best Practices: Nulls and Formula Fields*: https://developer.salesforce.com/blogs/engineering/2013/02/force-com-soql-best-practices-nulls-and-formula-fields.html
- *Developing Selective Lightning Platform Queries through the Query Resource Feedback Parameter Pilot*: https://developer.salesforce.com/blogs/engineering/2014/04/developing-selective-force-com-queries-query-resource-feedback-parameter-pilot.html

Profiling queries

As you can see, consideration for which indexes are needed and when they are used are very much determined by the rate of data growth in the subscriber org and also the spread of distinct groups of data values in that data. So, profiling is typically something that is only done in conjunction with your customers and Salesforce, within the subscriber org.

In some cases, disclosing the queries your application makes from Apex and Visualforce pages might help you and your subscribers plan ahead as to which indexes are going to be needed. You can also capture the SOQL queries made from your code through the debug logs, once you're logged in through the **Subscriber Support** feature.

Once you have a SOQL query you suspect is causing problems, you will profile it to determine which indexes are being used in order to determine what to do to resolve the issue, create a new index, and/or make the filter criteria select fewer records by adding more constraints. To do this, you can use a feature of the platform to ask it to explain its choices when considering which index (if any) to use for a given query. Again, it is important to use this in the subscriber org or the sandbox itself.

For the purposes of this chapter, the following example utilizes the `explain` parameter on the Salesforce REST API to execute a query within the packaging org we ran the preceding script in, so as to populate the **Race Data** object with 10,000 records.

> **Developer Console** includes **Query Planner Tool**, which can be enabled under the **Preferences** tab. When you run queries via **Query Editor**, a popup will appear with an explanation of the indexes considered. The information shown is basically the same as that described in this chapter via the `explain` parameter.

This section utilizes the `explain` parameter when running SOQL via the **Developer Workbench** tool (https://workbench.developerforce.com/login.php). Here, you can run the various queries in the explain mode and review the results. The results show a list of query plans that would have been used, had the query been actually executed. They are shown in order of preference by the platform. The following steps show how to log in to the Developer Workbench to obtain a query plan for a given query:

1. Use the `sfdx force:user:password:generate` command to generate a known password to your scratch org that you can use to log in to the Developer Workbench tool.
2. Use the `sfdx force:user:display` command to obtain the user and password.
3. Log in to **Developer Workbench**, selecting **Sandbox** as the **Environment** when prompted.
4. From the **Utilities** menu, select **REST Explorer**.
5. Enter `/services/data/v45.0/query?explain=` and then enter a **SOQL** statement of your choosing or use one of the ones shown in the following screenshot. You may also use whatever is the latest Salesforce API version in the URL.
6. Click on **Execute**.

First, let's try the following example without a custom index on the `Type__c` field:

```
select id from RaceData__c where Type__c = 'PitStop Time'
```

Note that no namespace prefix is used; if you have configured your scratch org with a namespace, simply prefix it to the object and field names, for example, `select id from fforce__RaceData__c where fforce__Type__c = 'PitStop Time'`.

The following screenshot shows the query plan result for this query:

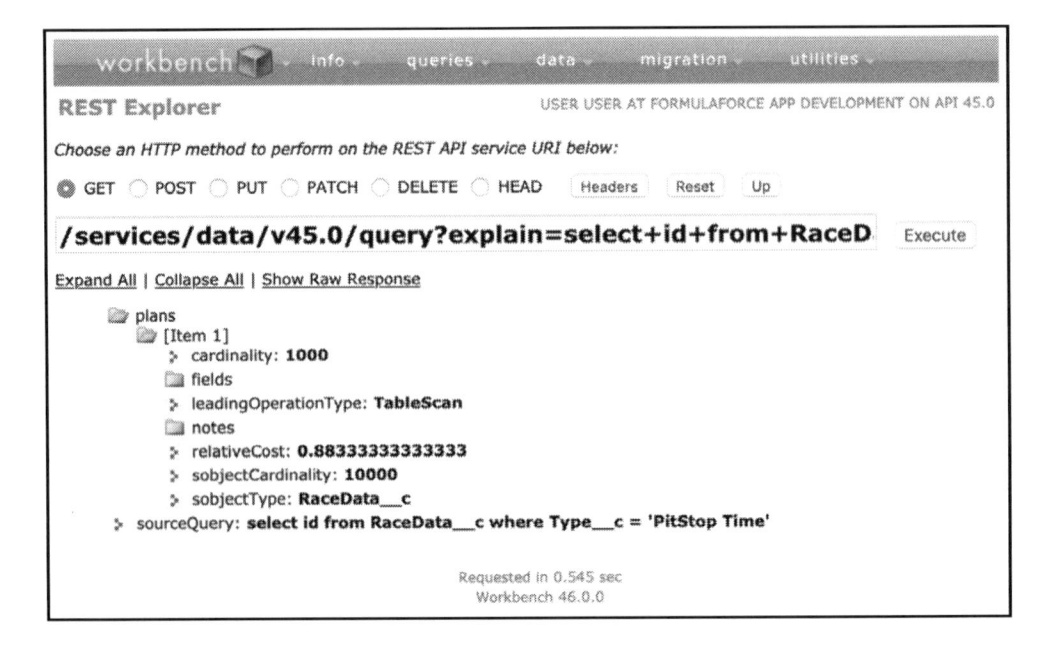

```
workbench — info — queries — data — migration — utilities
REST Explorer                    USER USER AT FORMULAFORCE APP DEVELOPMENT ON API 45.0
Choose an HTTP method to perform on the REST API service URI below:
● GET ○ POST ○ PUT ○ PATCH ○ DELETE ○ HEAD  Headers  Reset  Up
/services/data/v45.0/query?explain=select+id+from+RaceD   Execute

Expand All | Collapse All | Show Raw Response
  plans
    [Item 1]
      cardinality: 1000
      fields
      leadingOperationType: TableScan
      notes
      relativeCost: 0.88333333333333
      sobjectCardinality: 10000
      sobjectType: RaceData__c
  sourceQuery: select id from RaceData__c where Type__c = 'PitStop Time'

                    Requested in 0.545 sec
                    Workbench 46.0.0
```

You can see that, as expected, the result is **TableScan**, compared to the following query:

```
select id from RaceData__c where CreatedDate = TODAY
```

The following screenshot shows the query plan for this query:

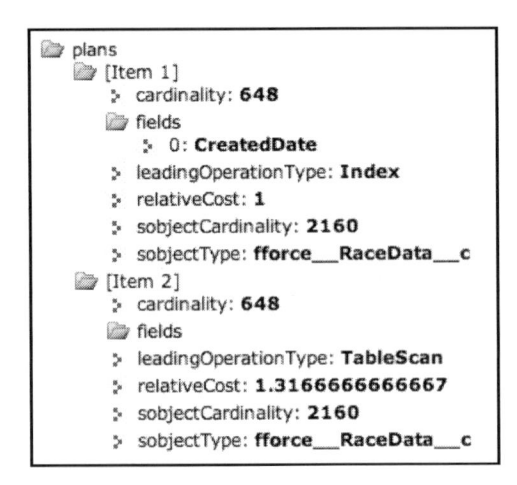

```
plans
  [Item 1]
    cardinality: 648
    fields
      0: CreatedDate
    leadingOperationType: Index
    relativeCost: 1
    sobjectCardinality: 2160
    sobjectType: fforce__RaceData__c
  [Item 2]
    cardinality: 648
    fields
    leadingOperationType: TableScan
    relativeCost: 1.3166666666667
    sobjectCardinality: 2160
    sobjectType: fforce__RaceData__c
```

This results in two plans; however, the standard **Index** was selected over **TableScan**.

The `cardinality` and `sobjectCardinality` fields are both estimates based on the aforementioned statistical information that Salesforce maintains internally relating to the spread of records (in this case, distinct records by `Type__c`). Thus, it gives the rows it thinks will be selected by the filter versus the total number of also estimated rows in the SObject.

> In this case, we can see that these are just estimates, as we know we have 10,000 records in the `RaceData__c` object; actually, 1,664 of those are **Sector Time** records. In general though, as long as these are broadly relative to the actual physical records, what the platform is doing is looking for the percentage of one from the other in order to decide whether an index will be worth using. It is actually the `relativeCost` field that is most important; basically, a value greater than 1 means that the query will not be executed using the associated plan.

Now that you have a general idea of how to obtain this information, let's review a few more samples, but this time with 100,000 `RaceData__c` records (10 races worth of data using the same distribution of records). In my org, I have also asked Salesforce Support to enable a custom index over the `Type__c`, `Lap__c`, and `Sector__c` Custom Fields. The namespace `fforce` prefix has been removed for clarity.

SOQL	Resulting plans
`select id from RaceData__c where Type__c = 'PitStop Time'` The number of records relating to **PitStop Time** is less than 10 percent of the overall record count, so an index was used.	```{
"plans" : [{
"cardinality" : 160,
"fields" : ["Type__c"],
"leadingOperationType" : "Index",
"relativeCost" : 0.016,
"sobjectCardinality" : 100000,
"sobjectType" : "RaceData__c"
}, {
"cardinality" : 160,
"fields" : [ ],
"leadingOperationType" : "TableScan",
"relativeCost" : 0.67013333333333334,
"sobjectCardinality" : 100000,
"sobjectType" : "RaceData__c"
}]
}```

SOQL	Resulting plans

`select id from RaceData__c where Type__c = 'Sector Time'`
A table scan plan was selected as the number of records relating to **Sector Times** was greater than 10 percent of the overall record count.
	``
	{
	    "plans" : [{
	        "cardinality" : 16640,
	        "fields" : [ ],
	        "leadingOperationType" : "TableScan",
	        "relativeCost" : 1.0272,
	        "sobjectCardinality" : 100000,
	        "sobjectType" : "RaceData__c"
	    }, {
	        "cardinality" : 16640,
	        "fields" : ["fforce__Type__c"],
	        "leadingOperationType" : "Index",
	        "relativeCost" : 1.664,
	        "sobjectCardinality" : 100000,
	        "sobjectType" : "RaceData__c"
	    }]
	}
	``

`select id from RaceData__c where Type__c = 'Sector Time' and RaceName__c = 'Spa'`
Again, a table scan was selected even though the query was made more selective by adding the race name. Adding a custom index over the race name would be advised here, as it is likely to be a common filter criterion.
	``
	{
	    "plans" : [{
	        "cardinality" : 1000,
	        "fields" : [ ],
	        "leadingOperationType" : "TableScan",
	        "relativeCost" : 0.6883333333333334,
	        "sobjectCardinality" : 100000,
	        "sobjectType" : "fforce__RaceData__c"
	    }, {
	        "cardinality" : 16640,
	        "fields" : ["fforce__Type__c"],
	        "leadingOperationType" : "Index",
	        "relativeCost" : 1.664,
	        "sobjectCardinality" : 100000,
	        "sobjectType" : "fforce__RaceData__c"
	    }]
	}
	``

`select id from RaceData__c where Type__c != 'PitStop Time'`
A table scan plan was selected, as a negative operator was used.
	``
	{
	    "plans" : [{
	        "cardinality" : 100000,
	        "fields" : [ ],
	        "leadingOperationType" : "TableScan",
	        "relativeCost" : 2.8333333333333335,
	        "sobjectCardinality" : 100000,
	        "sobjectType" : "RaceData__c"
	    }]
	}
	``

SOQL	Resulting plans

select id from RaceData__c where Type__c != 'PitStop' and Lap__c >=20 and Lap__c <=40
Even though a negative operator was used, by adding more selective criteria backed by a custom index, the platform chose to use the index over a table scan.
	``
	{
	    "plans" : [{
	        "cardinality" : 10000,
	        "fields" : ["Lap__c"],
	        "leadingOperationType" : "Index",
	        "relativeCost" : 1.0,
	        "sobjectCardinality" : 100000,
	        "sobjectType" : "RaceData__c"
	    }, {
	        "cardinality" : 40000,
	        "fields" : [ ],
	        "leadingOperationType" : "TableScan",
	        "relativeCost" : 1.5333333333333334,
	        "sobjectCardinality" : 100000,
	        "sobjectType" : "RaceData__c"
	    }]
	}
	``

Skinny tables

Internally, Salesforce stores Standard Object field data and Custom Field data for a given record in two separate physical Oracle tables. So, while you don't see it, when you execute a SOQL query to return a mixture of both standard and Custom Fields, this internally requires an Oracle SQL query, which requires an internal database join to be made.

If Salesforce Support determines that avoiding this join would speed up a given set of queries, they can create a skinny table. Such a table is not visible to the Lightning Platform developer and is kept in sync with your object records automatically by the platform, including any standard or custom indexes.

A skinny table can contain commonly used standard and Custom Fields that you, the subscriber, and Salesforce deem appropriate, all in the one Oracle table, and thus, it avoids the join (all at the internal cost of duplicating the record data). If a SOQL, Report, or List View query utilizes the fields or a subset, the platform will automatically use the skinny table instead of the join to improve performance. As an additional benefit, the record size needed internally is smaller, which means that the data bandwidth used to move chunks of records around the platform can be better utilized.

This is obviously quite an advanced feature of the platform, but worth considering as an additional means to improve query performance in a subscriber org.

> Skinny tables are not kept in sync if you change field types or add new fields to the corresponding object in the Lightning Platform world. Also, they are not replicated in sandbox environments. So, you or your subscriber will need to contact Salesforce Support again each time these types of changes occur. Also, note that skinny tables cannot be packaged; they are configurations only for subscriber orgs.

Handling large result sets

In most cases within Apex, it is only possible to read up to 50,000 records, regardless of whether they are read individually or as part of forming an aggregate query result. With the exception of the `COUNT` or `COUNT_DISTINCT` functions, these only count as one record. There is, however, a context parameter that can be applied that will allow an unlimited number of records to be read. However, this context does not permit any database updates. In this section, we will review the following three ways in which you can manage large datasets:

- Processing 50k maximum result sets in Apex
- Processing unlimited result sets in Apex
- Processing unlimited result sets via the Salesforce APIs

Processing 50k maximum result sets in Apex

One of the problems with reading 50,000 records is that you run the risk of hitting other governors, such as the **heap governor**, which, although increased in an async context, can still be hit depending on the processing being performed. Take a look at the following contrived example to generate attachments on each **Race Data** record:

```
List<Attachment> attachments = new List<Attachment>();
for(RaceData__c raceData :
    [select Id from RaceData__c limit 10000])
   attachments.add(
     new Attachment(
       Name = 'Some Attachment',
       ParentId = raceData.Id,
       Body = Blob.valueOf('Some Text'.repeat(1000))));
insert attachments;
```

If you try to execute the preceding code from an **Execute Anonymous** window, you will receive the following error, as the code quickly hits the **6 MB heap size limit**:

```
System.LimitException: Apex heap size too large: 6022466
```

The solution to this problem is to utilize what is known as **SOQL FOR LOOP** (as follows); this allows the record data to be returned to the Apex code in chunks of 200 records (a size set by the platform) so that not all the **Attachment** records will build up on the heap:

```
for(List<RaceData__c> raceDataChunk :
       [select Id from RaceData__c limit 10000]) {
  List<Attachment> attachments = new List<Attachment>();
  for(RaceData__c raceData : raceDataChunk)
    attachments.add(
      new Attachment(
        Name = 'Some Attachment',
        ParentId = raceData.Id,
        Body = Blob.valueOf('Some Text'.repeat(1000))));
  insert attachments;
}
```

Once this code completes, it will have generated over 80 MB of attachment data in one execution context! Note that in doing so, the preceding code does technically break a bulkification rule, in that there is a DML statement contained within the outer chunking loop. For 10,000 records split over 200 record chunks, this will result in 50 chunks, and thus, this will consume 50 out of the available 150 DML statements. In this case, the end justifies the means, so this is just something to be mindful of.

Processing unlimited result sets in Apex

In this section, a new **Race Analysis** page is created to allow the user to view the results of various calculations and simulations applied dynamically to selected race data. Ultimately, imagine that the page allows the user to input adjustments and other parameters to apply to the calculations and replay the race data to see how the race might have finished differently.

For the purposes of this section of the chapter, we are focusing on querying the **Race Data** object. With the standard row limit of 50,000 records, we can query approximately 5 races' worth of data within the standard Visualforce page execution context. The following changes have been made to the FormulaForce application to deliver this page and are present in the code samples associated with this chapter if you wish to deploy them:

- A new `analyzeData` method on the `RaceService` class has been added.
- The `RaceDataSelector` class has been created to encapsulate the query logic.
- `RaceAnalysisController` has been created for the Visualforce page.

- The `raceanalysis` Visualforce page has been created.
- A new **Race Analysis** list custom button has been added to the `Race__c` object. This button has been added to the list related to **Races** on the **Season** record page.

The user can now select one or more **Race** records from the related list to process as follows:

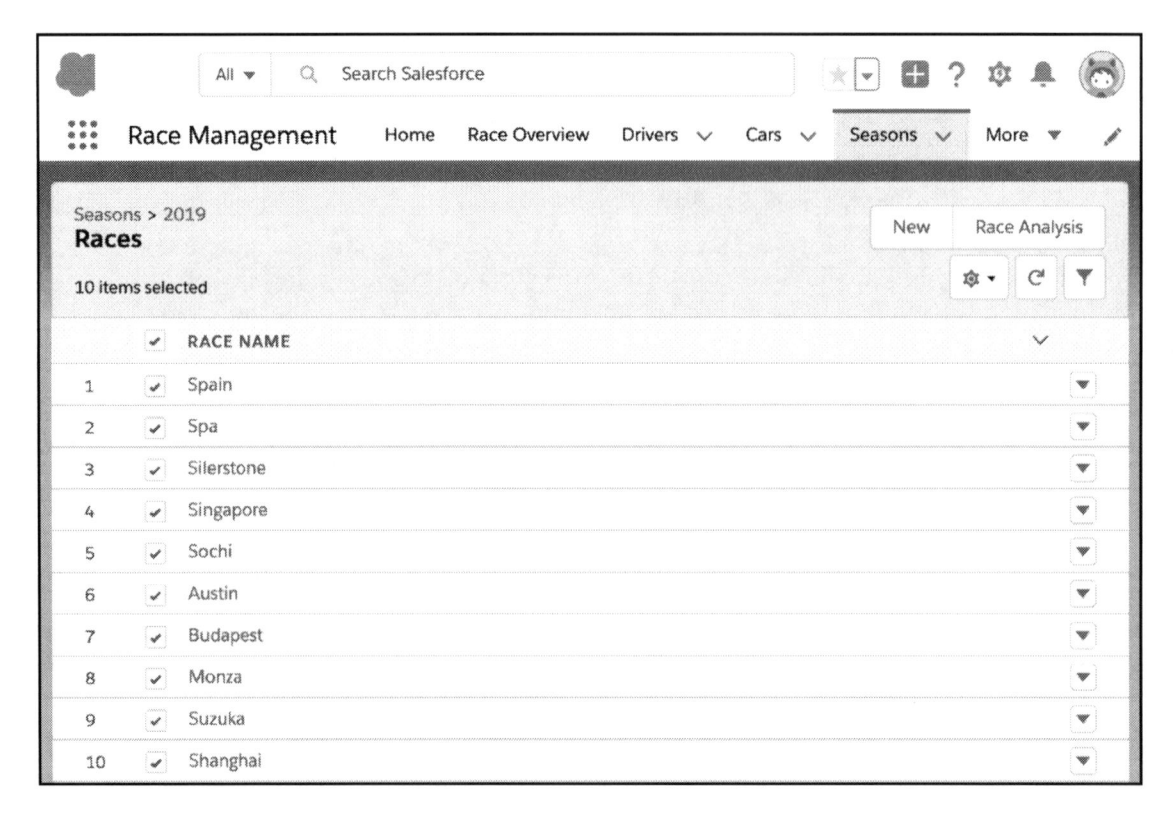

		RACE NAME	
1	✓	Spain	
2	✓	Spa	
3	✓	Silerstone	
4	✓	Singapore	
5	✓	Sochi	
6	✓	Austin	
7	✓	Budapest	
8	✓	Monza	
9	✓	Suzuka	
10	✓	Shanghai	

The next display provides a confirmation of the selected races before starting the calculations. This button invokes the `RaceService.analyzeData` method and attempts to query the applicable `RaceData__c` records:

Races to Analyize

RACE NAME
Budapest
Suzuka
Austin
Spa
Spain
Monza
Shanghai
Silerstone
Singapore
Sochi

[Start Analysis] [Cancel]

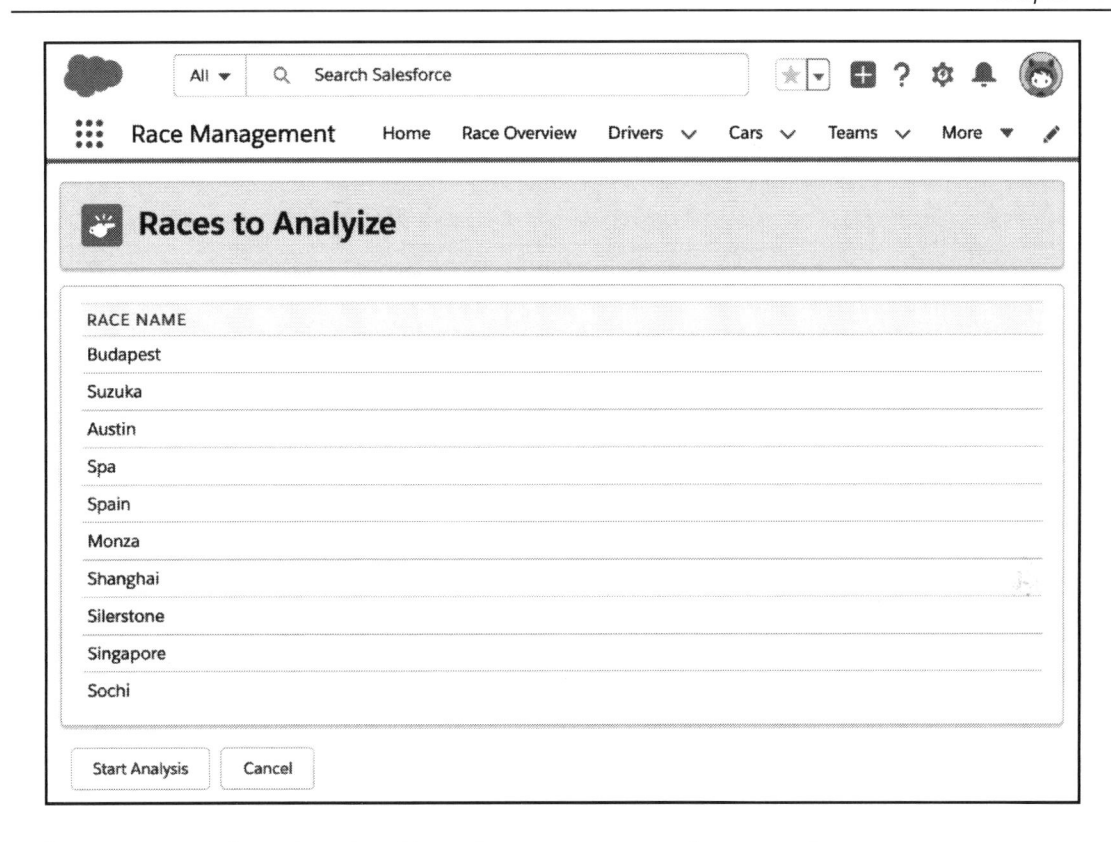

Before we can explore the Visualforce feature to process large result sets, we must create more than 50,000 records. The next section will walk through the steps to achieve this.

Generating more Race Data

To demonstrate how it is possible to read more than 50,000 records, we will need to generate some more **Race Data**. To do this, we can rerun a portion of the script we ran earlier in this chapter to generate up to 100,000 records.

Run the `sfdx force:apex:execute` command (without parameters) and paste in the following Apex code for each race; this should result in 100,000 records in the **Race Data** object (which you can verify through the **Data Storage** page under **Setup**):

```
TestData.createVolumeData(2017, 'Monza', 52, 4);
```

Run the preceding code again a further eight times, each time changing the name of the race to `Austin`, `Sochi`, `Singapore`, `Shanghai`, `Spa`, `Suzuka`, `Silverstone`, and `Budapest` (note that **Race Data** for `Spain` was generated earlier).

Asynchronous Processing and Big Data Volumes

> Note that in order to clear down the data for any reason, repeatedly call the following, then go to your **Recycle Bin** and delete all org data:
>
> `TestData.purgeVolumeData(false);`

Leveraging Visualforce and Apex read-only mode

The **Start Analysis** button calls the service to query the race data and analyze the data, and, for the purposes of this chapter, it outputs the total number of queried rows as follows:

```
ApexPages.addMessage(
  new ApexPages.Message(
    ApexPages.Severity.Info,
    'Just read ' + Limits.getQueryRows() +
      ' rows from RaceData__c'));
```

As per the previous screenshot, select all 10 races (click on the **Show 5 more** link to show more related list records). Click on the **Start Analysis** button to display a message, confirming the number of records processed is above the standard 50,000:

The reason this has been made possible is due to the Visualforce page enabling read-only mode via the `readOnly` attribute on the `apex:page` element, as follows:

```
<apex:page
   standardController="Race__c"
   extensions="RaceAnalysisController"
   recordSetVar="Races"
   readOnly="true">
```

This mode can also be enabled via the `@ReadOnly` Apex attribute on an Apex scheduled class or on an Apex Remote Action method. As the name suggests, the downside is that there can be no DML statements, so we have no means to update the database. For this use case, this restriction is not a problem. Note that, by using **JavaScript Remoting**, you can create a mix of methods with and without `@ReadOnly`. Currently, this attribute cannot be used in conjunction with `@AuraEnabled`.

> **TIP**: Note that in this mode, other governors are still active, such as heap and CPU timeout. You might also want to consider combining this mode with the SOQL FOR LOOP approach described earlier. Also, the SOQL aggregate queries will benefit from this (as these also count against the SOQL query rows governor).

Processing unlimited result sets using the Salesforce APIs

Salesforce does not limit the maximum number of rows that can be queried when using the Salesforce SOAP and REST APIs to retrieve record data, as in these contexts, the resources consuming and processing the resulting record data are off-platform.

One consideration to keep in mind, however, is the daily API limits—although you can read unlimited data, it is still chunked from the Salesforce servers and retrieving each chunk will consume an API call. Although less friendly, the Salesforce Bulk API is more efficient in retrieving more records while using fewer API calls to the Salesforce servers.

Handling billions of records with big objects

Lightning Platform inherits relational database design principles and values in a very explicit way and, when you create Custom Objects or when you add lookup or master-detail fields, you are defining a relationship. It is, of course, no secret that Salesforce themselves uses the Oracle **relational database management system** (**RDBMS**) under the hood to support this. Defining data in a relational way is a very powerful feature, allowing a rich set of domain-specific data to be expressed, as we have seen with **Seasons**, **Teams**, **Races**, and **Contestants** so far in this book. We have also seen how we can use access patterns such as SOQL and DML to access that data as a whole in one operation if needed through the use of query joins or transactions (unit of work) when updating data over several objects. This behavior is categorized by the acronym known as **Atomicity, Consistency, Isolation, Durability** (**ACID**).

When record volumes start to grow, the benefits of ACID come at a performance cost, mostly due to how relational databases in general physically store data on disk, but also its inherent commitment to maintaining integrity via the support for transactions. To improve access times, as we have seen earlier in this chapter, indexes are maintained to provide faster access routes that manage data pointers to the actual physical data on disk. From an update perspective, managing so many transactions while also avoiding locking issues becomes problematic to user response times, which will start to increase as the data volumes grow.

In short, when you are considering several millions and definitively billions of records and still require a consistent access time for your users, something has to change. Put another way, how the data is physically stored eventually influences the access patterns (for read and write) that are most optimal for accessing it. The rapid growth of the internet and business to consumer (B2C) websites has forced a rethink of how the industry thinks about accessing and storing data in situations when you will rapidly run into billions of records, yet consumers still require rapid and consistent access times to specific records (for example, your last Amazon order).

An alternative to RDBMS is today commonly known as **NoSQL**. NoSQL databases physically layout their data on disk to support a very specific set of access patterns, and they explicitly do not support transactions. The behaviors for such databases have been described by **Basically Available, Soft state, Eventual consistency (BASE)**. In researching this, I found that this is a less well-known acronym than ACID. It was defined by **Eric Brewer**, a professor at the University of California, Berkeley, and VP of Infrastructure at Google (at the time of writing). In short, it contrasts ACID by stating that it is okay to design a database where the client code may not always read the very latest data, but that the database will guarantee that it will eventually become consistent with past writes, or *"eventually consistent"* for short. This allows the database to scale across multiple physical disks and implement replication more easily. This compromise is key to read and write times remaining consistent even with billions of records!

Salesforce and NoSQL stores

Salesforce architects have publicly shared various insights over the years into how NoSQL technology has, in fact, been behind some of its own products that also need to store various event logs and audit information, for example, relating to field changes. Both of these can run into the high millions, and eventually billions, of records for its customers.

The `FieldHistoryArchive` object is one such object that is using a Salesforce managed instance of the open source **Apache HBase** database (https://hbase.apache.org/) as apposed to Oracle. As with Oracle-based standard and Custom Objects, this fact is, of course, totally abstracted away from its users. Salesforce still manages all the security, replication, and other hosting implications for you. As the name suggests, NoSQL databases have different access patterns. Notably, there is no traditional querying via SQL. So, how has Salesforce exposed objects to its Lightning Platform developers via its own query language, known as SOQL?

Lightning Platform **big objects** are an abstraction over Apache HBase and a sister technology known as **Apache Phoenix**. Apache Phoenix was initially created internally from within Salesforce by James Taylor and Mujtaba Chohan to provide a multitenant and SQL-based interface over NoSQL databases. It was later donated to the open source community (https://developer.salesforce.com/index.php?title=Apache_Phoenix:SFDC).

Salesforce is, as ever, the master at providing easy-to-use tools and APIs while retaining and passing on the values of such technologies to its developers and customers. In this case, these are technologies that are arguably very complex technologies to learn as a developer, let alone the cost of hosting them yourself. In the following sections, we will explore the declarative way in which you can create a big object, manage data within it, and, along the way, learn the key differences between these object types and Custom Objects.

> A full description of all the futures and implications of big objects is outside the scope of this book. Please be sure to reference the **Big Object Implementation Guide** (https://developer.salesforce.com/docs/atlas.en-us.bigobjects.meta/bigobjects) and the **Async SOQL** documentation (https://developer.salesforce.com/docs/atlas.en-us.bigobjects.meta/bigobjects/async_query_overview.htm) in addition to the information covered in the scenarios in this chapter.

Using a big object for race lap history

Formula 1 is a sport that has been running for many years and, as such, has likely gathered huge amounts of racing data captured from the various timing and telemetry devices around the racing circuits and, these days, within the cars themselves. The competing teams store and analyze that data to build better and faster cars to beat their opponents! In order to explore this on the Lightning Platform, we are going to create the **Race Lap History** object and import some publicly available historic lap timing data into it.

Asynchronous Processing and Big Data Volumes

The sample code included with this chapter includes this object. From the **Setup** menu, search for **Big Objects**. The following screenshot shows the **Race Lap History** object definition:

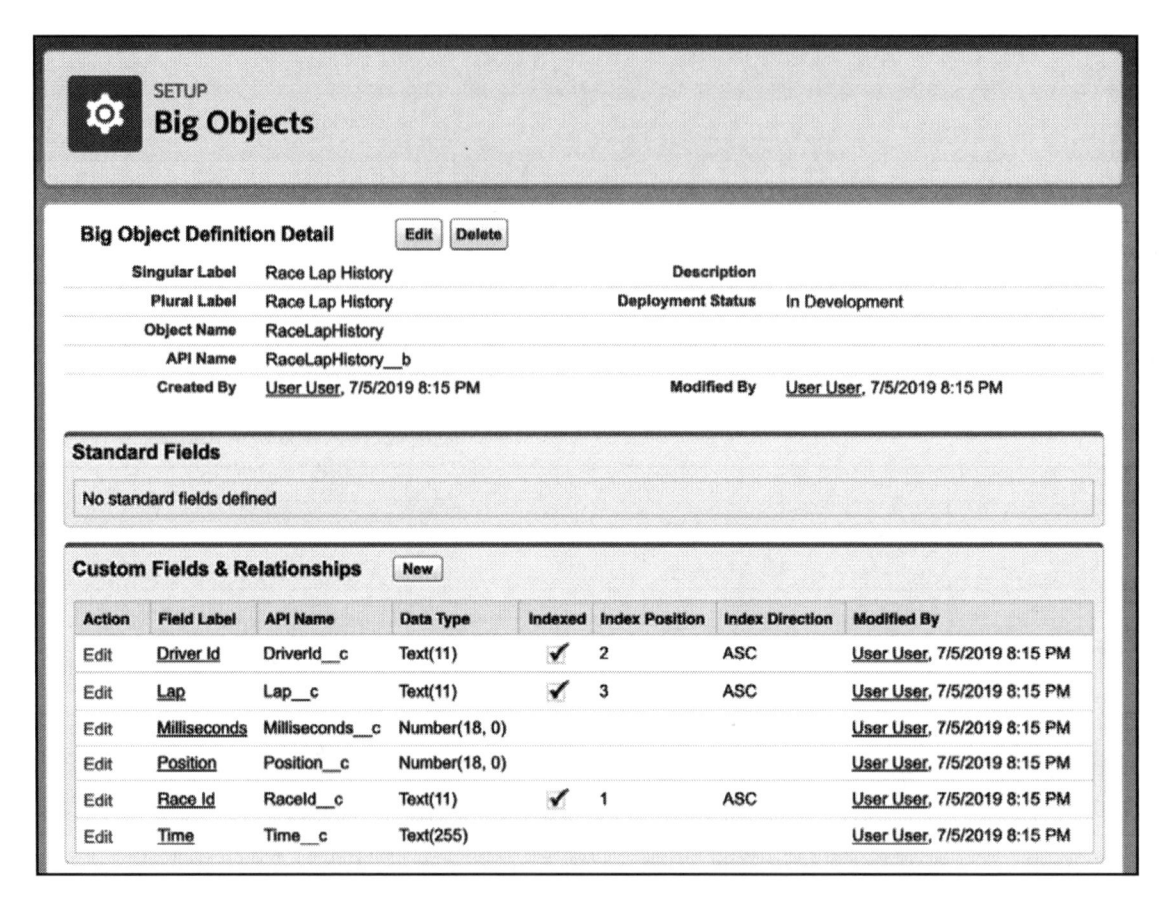

SETUP
Big Objects

Big Object Definition Detail [Edit] [Delete]

Singular Label	Race Lap History	Description	
Plural Label	Race Lap History	Deployment Status	In Development
Object Name	RaceLapHistory		
API Name	RaceLapHistory__b		
Created By	User User, 7/5/2019 8:15 PM	Modified By	User User, 7/5/2019 8:15 PM

Standard Fields

No standard fields defined

Custom Fields & Relationships [New]

Action	Field Label	API Name	Data Type	Indexed	Index Position	Index Direction	Modified By
Edit	Driver Id	DriverId__c	Text(11)	✓	2	ASC	User User, 7/5/2019 8:15 PM
Edit	Lap	Lap__c	Text(11)	✓	3	ASC	User User, 7/5/2019 8:15 PM
Edit	Milliseconds	Milliseconds__c	Number(18, 0)				User User, 7/5/2019 8:15 PM
Edit	Position	Position__c	Number(18, 0)				User User, 7/5/2019 8:15 PM
Edit	Race Id	RaceId__c	Text(11)	✓	1	ASC	User User, 7/5/2019 8:15 PM
Edit	Time	Time__c	Text(255)				User User, 7/5/2019 8:15 PM

Notice in the preceding screenshot that the object does not have the usual `Id` standard field. This represents the first main difference between big objects and Custom Objects. Keys to records in a big object are idempotent, they do not change, meaning that they must always be known before the record is inserted and that the record is always referenced by that known key forevermore. Sometimes, this is known as the "natural key" (because it's typically human-readable, such as an order number). This, in fact, bears some resemblance to the upsert semantics when using an external ID on a Custom Object. The use of natural keys to access records is an implication of the underlying NoSQL access patterns described earlier. Since there is no transaction support, you must be able to easily retry a failed operation without risking adding another record.

The implications of not having a standard Salesforce ID and the performance implications of displaying billions of records in real time does mean that big object record data cannot be accessed via the standard **Lightning Experience** and **Salesforce Mobile** user experiences, including **Salesforce Reports and Dashboards**. These are not designed at present to handle billions of records. However, it is possible to use **SOQL** and some `Database` class methods to build your own UIs that allow users to interact with big object data. Later in this chapter, you will see an Async SOQL example that exports a summarized fragment of big object data into a Custom Object that can then be used as normal in the standard UIs.

> **TIP**
> AppExchange is a great place to find applications and utilities. The **Big Object Utility package** (`https://appexchange.salesforce.com/appxListingDetail?listingId=a0N3A00000EcvSsUAJ`) is provided free of charge by a member of the community (not associated with Salesforce or myself) to help visualize the big object data in Lightning Experience. This utility uses the APIs discussed in this section.

For the **Race Lap History** object, the **Race Id**, **Driver Id**, and **Lap** fields are all used to form **a unique index** for the lap record data. This object and its fields have been designed to fit the dataset we will be leveraging in this chapter, which comes from a public-facing website known as **Ergast** (`https://ergast.com/mrd/`). The following screenshot shows the website's banner:

Ergast Developer API

The author of this website kindly provides Formula 1 racing data dating back from 1950 to the present day in both API form and as **downloadable CSV files**. In the next section, we are going to download the data and upload one of the files to the **Race Lap History** object. I want to give a special thanks to Chris, who runs the site, for his support in my using this data!

Importing big object data

Big objects support a subset of the standard **Salesforce REST API** (including **Salesforce Bulk API**) and **Apex** `Database` class methods, such as `insertImmediate`, in order to insert and delete data, as well as two subsets of the SOQL syntax for use with synchronous and asynchronous queries. These APIs allow for a variety of ways to ingest big data in bulk or in real time and then query that data synchronously or asynchronously, as needed. In the following sections, we will review these various read and write access patterns further.

Asynchronous Processing and Big Data Volumes

Using Data Loader to import data into a big object

For ease, and because the CSV file in the section is so large (nearly half a million records at the time of writing), we will use the **Salesforce Data Loader** tool. The process to import historical lap time data from the preceding website is as follows:

1. Search for **Data Loader** in the **Setup** menu and select the applicable link to download the tool to your computer and follow the install instructions.
2. Navigate to the **Database images** section of the site (https://ergast.com/mrd/db/) and download the f1db_csv.zip file and unzip it.
3. Edit the lap_times.csv file to insert the following column headers as the first row: RaceId__c, DriverId__c, Lap__c, Position__c, Time__c, and Milliseconds__c.
4. Run the **Data Loader** tool from your installed location and click the **Insert** button.
5. When prompted, log in to your scratch org by selecting **OAuth** and **Sandbox** from the **Environment** drop-down prompt and click **Login**. Refer to the SFDX commands used earlier in this chapter to obtain the username and password if needed.
6. Select the **Race Lap History** object as shown in the following screenshot and click **Next**:

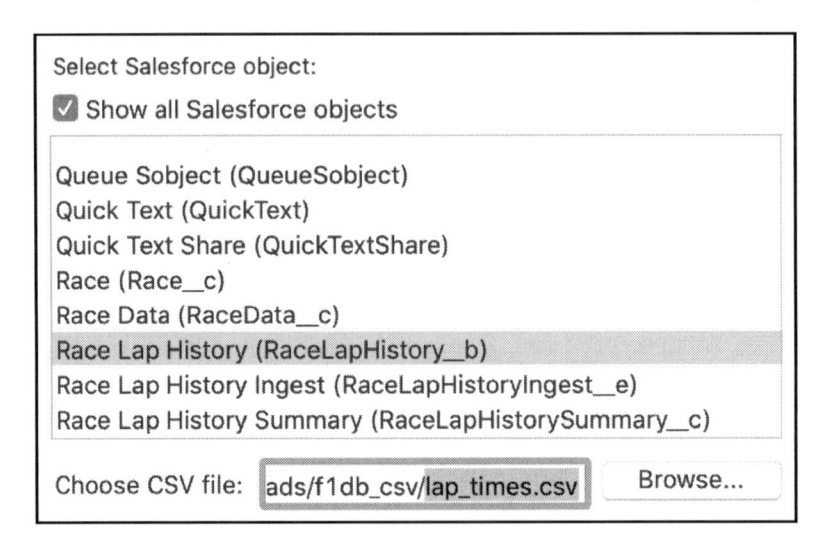

```
Select Salesforce object:
☑ Show all Salesforce objects

Queue Sobject (QueueSobject)
Quick Text (QuickText)
Quick Text Share (QuickTextShare)
Race (Race__c)
Race Data (RaceData__c)
Race Lap History (RaceLapHistory__b)
Race Lap History Ingest (RaceLapHistoryIngest__e)
Race Lap History Summary (RaceLapHistorySummary__c)

Choose CSV file:  ads/f1db_csv/lap_times.csv    Browse...
```

7. Click on **Ok** to confirm the number of records.

8. In **Step 3: Mapping**, click **Create or Edit Map** and then **Auto-Match Fields to Columns**, click **Ok** to accept the defaults, and then click **Next**. If you do not see the field names, ensure you have completed step 3 and then retry this step.
9. In **Step 4: Finish**, confirm the output directory for success and error files will be written and then click **Finish**.
10. Click **Yes** when prompted to start the import and monitor the progress:

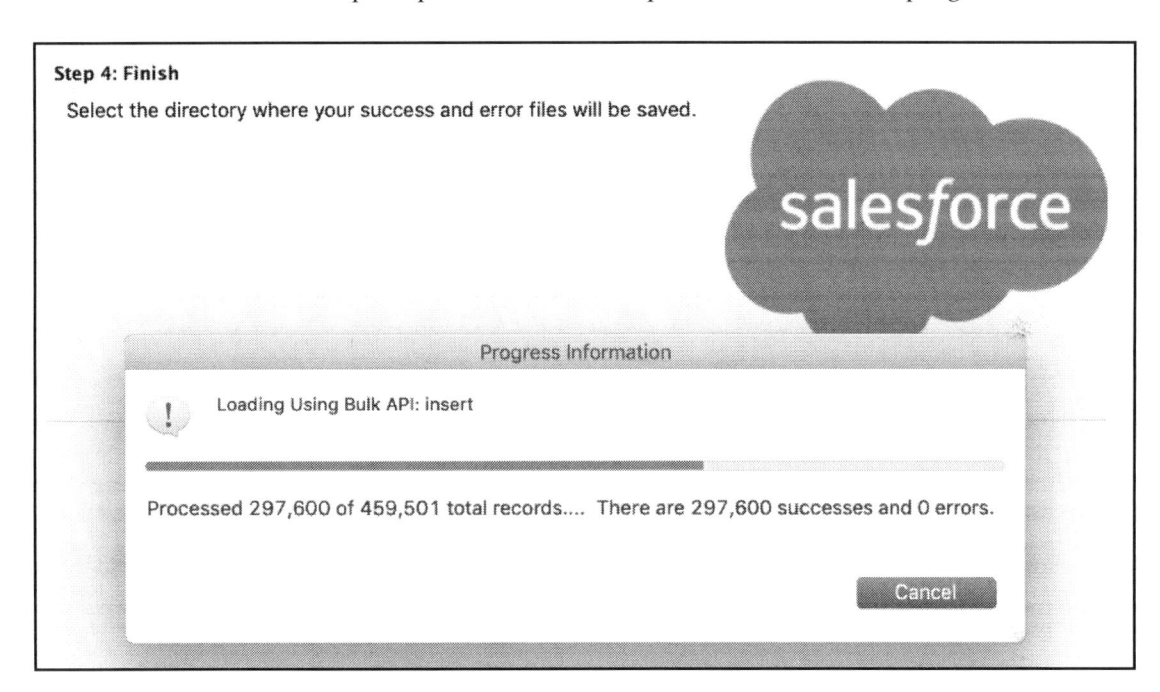

Step 4: Finish

Select the directory where your success and error files will be saved.

Progress Information

Loading Using Bulk API: insert

Processed 297,600 of 459,501 total records.... There are 297,600 successes and 0 errors.

Cancel

> **TIP**
> Since inserting data into a big object is equivalent to an upsert operation, it's possible to retry failed uploads over and over without risking duplicate data for those records that have been inserted. This behavior is by design since big objects do not support transactions; this is the recovery path when errors occur.

After the process completes, the **Storage Usage** page (under **Setup**) will update in the next few hours to show the number of records present in big objects. Salesforce **sells Big Object storage** by the number of records, in **50 million chunks**, regardless of the size of the records. Each org gets 1 million records for free, including the scratch orgs used in this chapter!

Options to query big object data

Despite the NoSQL nature of the underlying data store, Salesforce has leveraged its investment in creating the Apache Phoenix technology and made it possible to deliver the ability to use a subset of the well-known **SOQL** syntax to query big objects. In this section, we will review some key differences with regular standard and custom big objects.

There are also two ways in which you can perform SOQL queries: **synchronously** and **asynchronously**. The available SOQL feature set varies depending on which path you take. Developers can leverage the **Salesforce REST API** or **Apex SOQL APIs** to perform synchronous queries, while only the Salesforce REST API has support for running asynchronous queries.

Synchronous big object SOQL queries

Using synchronous SOQL performed via Apex or the Salesforce REST API, you can only filter records based on the index fields defined when you created the big object. In other words, it is not possible to filter by the `Time__c`, `Position__c`, or `Milliseconds__c` fields. Records are returned in the order defined by the index fields, defining an `ORDER BY` clause that does not match the index fields sequence and sorting is not supported.

The order in which you defined the index fields is very important as it determines the constraints of your filter criteria. It will help in the following examples to think about the index fields as being defined from **left to right**, where the **left-most** field is `RaceId__c`, and the **right-most** field is `Lap__c`. The following screenshot shows how the fields are defined:

Custom Indexes Fields

Field Label	API Name	Sort Direction
Race Id	RaceId__c	Ascending
Driver Id	DriverId__c	Ascending
Lap	Lap__c	Ascending

> **TIP**: Note that these fields cannot be modified once you have created a big object. In order to change the index fields, you would need to create a new big object with the desired index fields and then migrate the data from the old object.

For ease, try out the following examples using the SFDX CLI to perform the query from the command line, though these could equally be performed from Apex code as well. This first example shows the full command line, a query, and a sample of the output:

```
sfdx force:data:soql:query -q "select RaceId__c, DriverId__c, Lap__c,
Time__c from RaceLapHistory__b where RaceId__c = '904'"
...
904 828 7 1:35.692
904 828 8 1:35.768
904 828 9 1:35.603
Total number of records retrieved: 1361.
```

You can add further index fields to the `where` clause to further reduce the result set returned. The next example focuses on lap data for race `904` (Spain) as before, but this time only for driver `1` (Lewis Hamilton). Remember to keep in mind the index field order defined on the object when reviewing the following examples; it was from left to right defined as follows, `RaceId_c`, `DriverId__c`, and then `Lap__c`. The following is a valid query:

```
select RaceId__c, DriverId__c, Lap__c, Time__c
  from RaceLapHistory__b
  where RaceId__c = '904' and DriverId__c = '1'
```

This next example shows an invalid query:

```
select RaceId__c, DriverId__c, Lap__c, Time__c
  from RaceLapHistory__b
  where RaceId__c = '904' and Lap__c ='20'"
```

The preceding query gives the following error:

ERROR: Filters may not have any gaps within the composite key

This is because the record data is stored physically on disc based on all the index field values and their sequence. Thus, it is not possible to perform a query that effectively omits (or skips) the `DriverId__c` index field value, since without this information, the database simply does not know where to go on the disk to start reading the record data from.

The previous examples are illustrating a specific syntax rule, which states you can only define your filter criteria from left to right and that you may only omit (or skip) index fields to the far right. This is why the preceding first and second examples were valid, as they used the first and then the first and second index fields.

Now that we understand a key rule with respect to specifying filter criteria using the left-most index fields, let's consider how other range operators can be used. This rule states that range operators such as <, >, <=, >=, or IN can only be used on the **last right-most index** in the criteria. The following is a valid query example:

```
select RaceId__c, DriverId__c, Lap__c, Time__c
  from RaceLapHistory__b
  where RaceId__c = '904' and DriverId__c = '1' and Lap__c >='20'
```

The following is an invalid query example:

```
select RaceId__c, DriverId__c, Lap__c, Time__c
  from RaceLapHistory__b
  where RaceId__c = '904' and DriverId__c > '1' and Lap__c >='20'"
```

The preceding query gives the following error:

`ERROR: Range filter columns must be last in filter in relation to the composite key columns`

The following example shows invalid queries since you cannot include any non-index fields in your criteria nor use any aggregate SOQL functions such as SUM or AVG:

```
select RaceId__c, DriverId__c, Lap__c, Time__c
  from RaceLapHistory__b
  where RaceId__c = '904' and DriverId__c = '1'
    and Milliseconds__c < 20000"
```

The preceding query gives the following error:

`ERROR: field 'Milliseconds__c' can not be filtered in a query call`

The following is another example of an invalid query:

```
select Count(RaceId__c)
  from RaceLapHistory__b
  where RaceId__c = '904'
```

The preceding query gives the following error:

`ERROR: Count function is not supported`

To perform aggregate- or non-aggregate-based queries based on non-index fields, you need to move to asynchronous SOQL, which is capable of performing the compute required to navigate larger volumes of records and filter them in memory.

Finally, it is possible via the Salesforce REST API to run an unbounded query (one without the `where` clause) in order to download all the records in the object:

```
select RaceId__c, DriverId__c, Lap__c, Time__c
  from RaceLapHistory__b
```

> You can read more about the SOQL constraints from the formal Salesforce documentation at https://developer.salesforce.com/docs/atlas.en-us.bigobjects.meta/bigobjects/big_object_querying.htm.

Asynchronous big object SOQL queries

Synchronous queries described in the previous section are generally only suitable for when you know specifically what the user is looking for and are confident you can reduce the query results to a level that can be handled in real time and within the synchronous Apex limits. The key features of Async SOQL are as follows:

- **Asynchronous** queries bypass query limits because they run in the background. They are focused on allowing you to **perform aggregations** to learn more information from the full dataset of billions of records, or a smaller subset of the data.
- You can also use them to **extract a filtered subset of the raw data** and place it into a Custom Object for further reporting and querying using the full SOQL query language, standard UIs, and platform reporting tools.
- Asynchronous queries also offer more flexibility within the filter criteria, allowing you to reference non-index fields, for example, the **Milliseconds** field.
- SOQL functions such as `MIN`, `MAX`, and `AVG` can also be used.

> For more information on the support SOQL syntax for asynchronous queries, refer to the Salesforce documentation at https://developer.salesforce.com/docs/atlas.en-us.bigobjects.meta/bigobjects/async_query_reference.htm. Also note that the Async SOQL API is **not presently enabled in all org types**. Meanwhile, you can use the screenshots to continue to learn until you can gain access to it, or until Salesforce enables more org types.

In this section, we will focus on an aggregation use case. To determine **the fastest lap for each race**, we will use the `MIN` SOQL aggregation function and group by the `RaceId__c` field. This will query over half a million records in one query!

Asynchronous Processing and Big Data Volumes

Async SOQL queries do not return results to the calling code, as the results could take some time to calculate and could be too large for the client context to manage. Instead, the results are returned into a **target Custom Object** of your choosing. In this case, the sample code in this chapter contains a **Race Lap History Summaries** Custom Object for the target object. The following steps perform an Async SOQL query to find the fastest lap time for every race:

1. **Race Lap History Summaries** are related to their respective **Race** record using an **External ID** field on the **Race** object. Edit the **Spain** race record and enter `904` in the **Race Id** field in order to associate the correct aggregate query result record. Note that the Async SOQL API does not have the ability to form this relationship itself when writing to target objects, so this is accomplished by an Apex Trigger; see `RaceLapHistorySummaries.cls`.

2. The **Async SOQL API** is a **Salesforce REST API**, so we must log in to the **Developer Workbench** tool (`https://workbench.developerforce.com/login.php`) to invoke it. Use the username and password of your scratch org and remember to select Sandbox for the environment. Use the `sfdx force:user:password:reset` command to obtain the password if you have not done so already.

3. From the **queries** menu, select **Async SOQL Query.**

4. Complete the query fields as shown in the following screenshot:

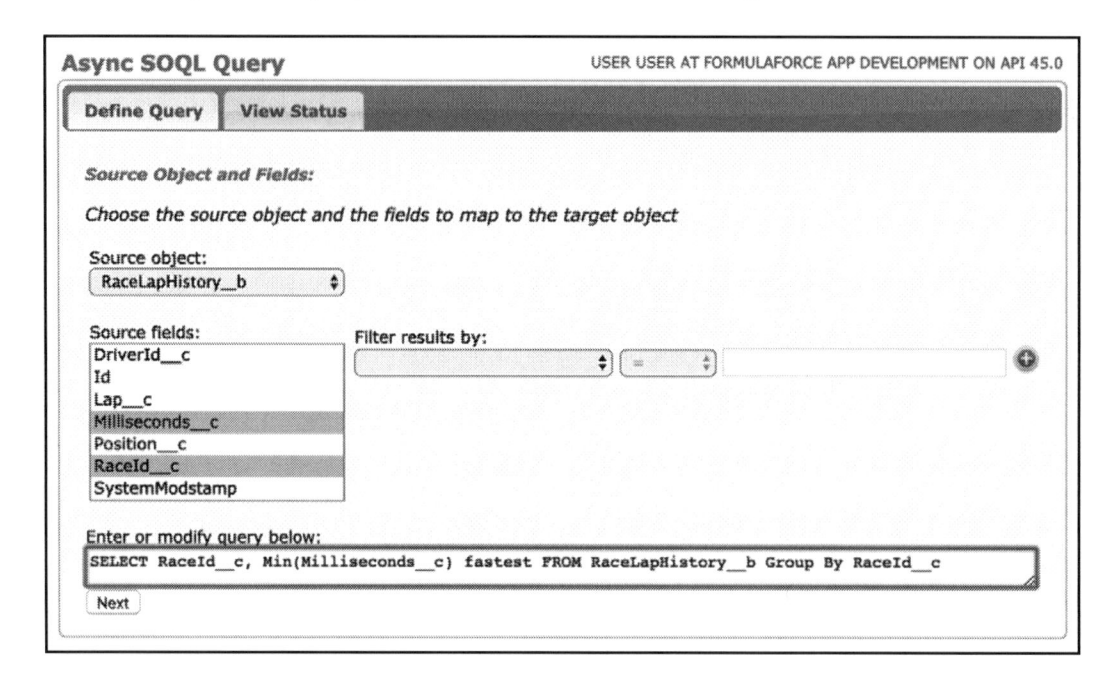

5. Click **Next** and complete the fields as shown in the following screenshot:

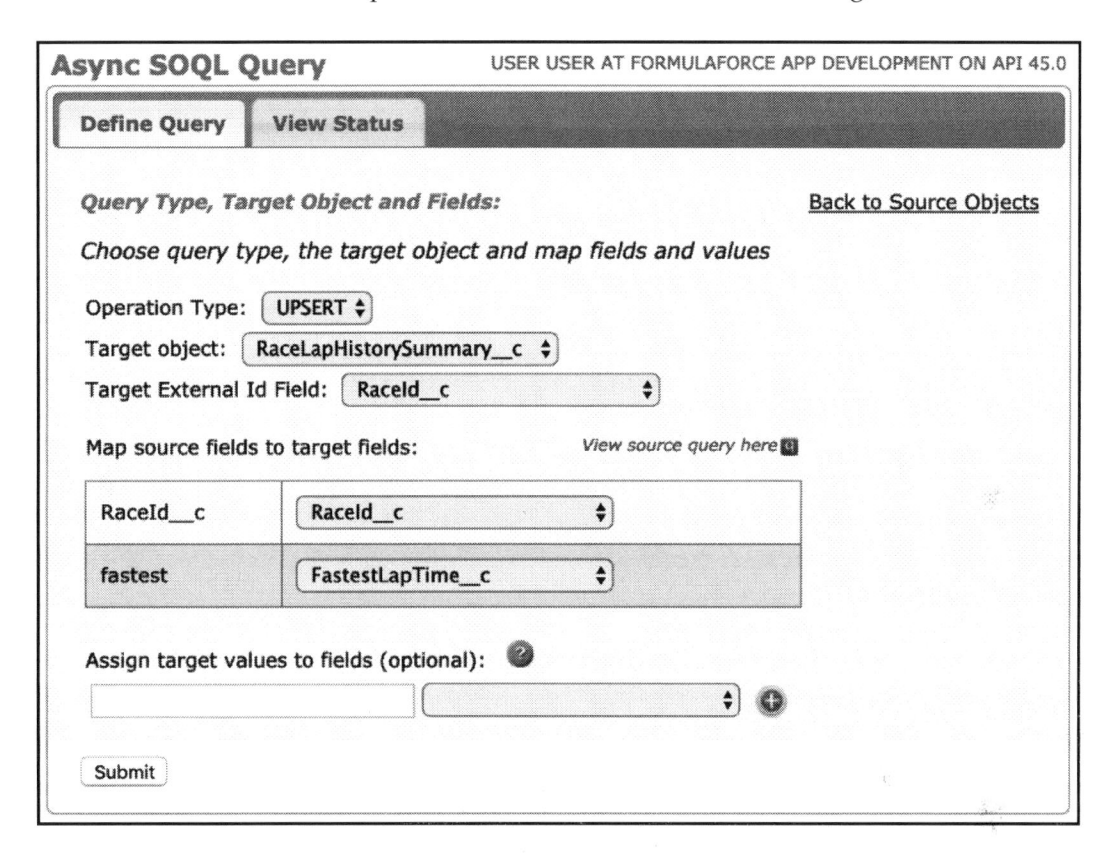

Async SOQL Query USER USER AT FORMULAFORCE APP DEVELOPMENT ON API 45.0

Define Query | **View Status**

Query Type, Target Object and Fields: Back to Source Objects
Choose query type, the target object and map fields and values

Operation Type: [UPSERT]
Target object: [RaceLapHistorySummary__c]
Target External Id Field: [RaceId__c]

Map source fields to target fields: View source query here

| RaceId__c | RaceId__c |
| fastest | FastestLapTime__c |

Assign target values to fields (optional):

[Submit]

6. Click **Submit** to start the query process and monitor it until completion using the **View Status** tab and by clicking on the active job.

> **TIP**
> The UPSERT operation is used to populate the target **Race Lap Histories Summary** object using the RaceId__c external ID field. This ensures that even if the query is run again (after more data has been loaded for example), it updates any pre-existing result records rather than creating new ones.

Once the Async SOQL job completes, follow these steps to navigate to the results:

1. Click on the **Race Lap Histories Summaries** tab.
2. Click on the **Race** column to sort by records associated with known races.

Have a look at the following screenshot:

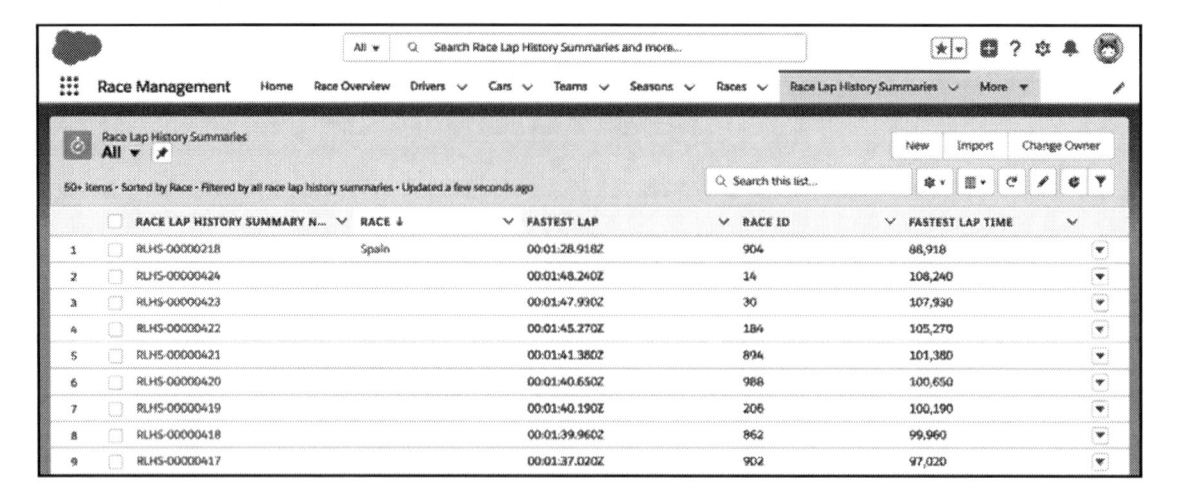

	RACE LAP HISTORY SUMMARY N...	RACE ↓	FASTEST LAP	RACE ID	FASTEST LAP TIME	
1	RLHS-00000218	Spain	00:01:28.918Z	904	88,918	▼
2	RLHS-00000424		00:01:48.240Z	14	108,240	▼
3	RLHS-00000423		00:01:47.930Z	30	107,930	▼
4	RLHS-00000422		00:01:45.270Z	184	105,270	▼
5	RLHS-00000421		00:01:41.380Z	894	101,380	▼
6	RLHS-00000420		00:01:40.650Z	988	100,650	▼
7	RLHS-00000419		00:01:40.190Z	208	100,190	▼
8	RLHS-00000418		00:01:39.960Z	862	99,960	▼
9	RLHS-00000417		00:01:37.020Z	902	97,020	▼

It shows the resulting Async SOQL calculated record.

Asynchronous processing

Salesforce is committed to ensuring that the interactive user experience (browser or mobile response times) of your applications and that of its own is as optimal as possible. In a multitenant environment, it uses the governors as one way to manage this. The other approach is to provide a means for you to move the processing of code from the foreground (interactive) into the background (async mode). This section of the chapter discusses the design considerations, implementation options, and benefits available in this context.

As the code running in the background is, by definition, not holding up the response times of the pages the users are using, Salesforce can and does throttle when and how often async processes execute, depending on the load on the servers at the time. For this reason, it currently does not provide an **SLA** on exactly when an async piece of code will run or guarantee exactly when the Apex Scheduler code will run at the allotted time. This aspect of the platform can, at times, be a source of frustration for end users, waiting for critical business processes to complete. However, there are some design, implementation, user interface, and messaging considerations that can make a big difference in terms of managing their expectations.

The good news is that the platform rewards you for running your code in async by giving you increased governors in areas such as heap, SOQL queries, and CPU governor. You can find the full details in their documentation (attempting to document them in a book is a nonstarter as they are constantly being improved and removed in some cases).

> For more information on Understanding Execution Governors and Limits, visit `http://www.salesforce.com/us/developer/docs/apexcode/Content/apex_gov_limits.htm`.

Asynchronous user experience design considerations

The platform provides some straightforward ways in which you can execute code asynchronously. What is often overlooked though is error handling and general user experience considerations. This section presents some points to consider functionally when moving a task or process into async, or the background, to use a more end user-facing term:

- **Type of background work**: I categorize work performed in the background in two ways, application and end user:
    - **Application** is something that the application requires to support future end user tasks, such as periodic recalculation, major data manipulation, or onboarding of data from an external service, for example.
    - **End user** is something that is related (typically initiated) to an end user activity that just happens to require more platform resources than are available in the interactive (or foreground) context. Background work can be much harder to accept for business analysts and end users, who are constantly demanding real-time response times. If you do find that this is your only route, focus hard on the user interaction and messaging aspects.

- **User experience**: A well-crafted user experience around the execution of background work can make all the difference when the platform is choosing to queue or slow the processing of work. Here are some considerations to keep in mind:
    - **Starting the background work**: Decide how the user starts the background process; is it explicit via a button or indirect via a scheduled job or a side effect of performing another task? Starting the background work explicitly from a user interface button gives you the opportunity to set expectations. A critical one is whether the work is queued or whether it has actually started; if they didn't know this, they might be inclined to attempt to start the work again, thus resulting in potentially two jobs processing in parallel! If you decide to start the process indirectly, make sure that you focus on error handling and recovery to ensure that the user has a way of being notified of any important failures at a later point in time.
    - **Progress bar indicators**: These can be used to allow the user to monitor the progress of the job from start to finish. Providing messages during the progress of the work can also help the user understand what is going on.
    - **Monitoring**: Ensuring that the user can continue to monitor the progress between sessions or other tasks can also be important. Often, users might close tabs or get logged out, and so consider providing a means to revisit the place where they started the job and have the user interface recognize that the job is still being processed, allowing the user to resume monitoring of the job.
- **Messaging and Logging**: Think about the ways in which your background process communicates and notifies the end user of the work it has done and any errors that occurred. While emails can be the default choice, consider yourself how such emails can get lost easily, and look for alternative notification and logging approaches that are more aligned with the platform and the application environment. Here are some considerations to keep in mind:
    - **Logging**: Ideally, persist log information within the application through an associated log (such as a logging Custom Object) with other Custom Objects that are associated with records being processed by the job so that the end users can leverage related lists to see log entries contextually. You might also consider emitting platform events that your UI code can subscribe to that allows users to follow progress visually.

- **Unhandled exceptions**: They are caught by the platform and displayed on the **Apex Jobs** page. The problem with this page is that it's not very user-friendly and also lacks the context as to what the job was actually doing with which records (the Apex class name might not be enough to determine this alone). Try to handle exceptions by routing them via your end user-facing messaging. Some Apex exceptions cannot be handled and will still require admins or support consultants to check for these. Your interactive monitoring solutions can also query `AsyncApexJob` for such messages. More recently, the platform now provides a standard platform event called `BatchApexErrorEvent` that you or admins can subscribe to in order to receive further information about all the exceptions produced.
- **Notifications**: Notifications that a job has completed or failed with an error can be sent via an email; however, also consider creating a child record as part of the logging alternative. A user-related task or a chatter post can also work quite well. The benefit of options that leverage information stored in the org is that these can also be a place to display custom buttons to restart the process.

- **Concurrency**: Consider what would happen if two or more users attempted to run your jobs at the same time, or if the data being processed overlaps between two jobs. Note that this scenario can also occur when scheduled jobs execute. You might want to store the Apex job ID during the processing of the job against an appropriate record to effectively lock it from being processed by other jobs until it is cleared. We will also discuss using platform events as a means to orchestrate background work later in this chapter. This platform feature explicitly processes events in sequence.
- **Error recovery**: Consider whether the user needs to rerun the job processing that has only failed records, or if the job can simply be designed in a way that is re-entrant, which means that it checks whether executions of a previous job might have already been made over the same data and cleans up or resets as it goes along. Platform events provide a built-in error retry mechanism, which we will be reviewing later in this chapter in more detail.

Asynchronous processing with workers and jobs

There are four ways to implement asynchronous code with the Lightning Platform; apart from platform events, which we will discuss later, the three approaches discussed in this section all run with the same extended governors compared to the interactive execution context. The following lists the four ways to implement asynchronous code on Lightning Platform:

- Apex `@future` annotation
- Queueables
- Batch Apex
- Platform events

Each of these asynchronous processes is started through additional code implementing your users' user experience, such as Apex controllers for Lightning Components or from within Apex Triggers. They are essentially **workers** or **jobs** for functionality that needs additional resources and is not needed in real time. Workers are similar to threads, which you might have encountered on other platforms. Jobs are longer, running over a given dataset that can be millions of rows in size.

As stated previously, there is no guarantee when asynchronous code will be executed by the platform. Salesforce monitors the frequency and length of each execution, adjusting an internal queue that takes into consideration the performance over the entire instance and not just the subscriber org where your application is running. It also caps the number of async jobs over a rolling 24-hour period. See the *Understanding execution governors and limits* section for more details. Salesforce also provides a detailed resource describing the queuing, called **Asynchronous Processing in Lightning Platform**, that is available at https://trailhead.salesforce.com/content/learn/modules/asynchronous_apex.

> **TIP:** Apex Scheduler can be used to execute code in an async context via its `execute` method. This also provides enhanced governors. Depending on the processing involved, you might choose to start a Batch Apex job from the `execute` method. Otherwise, if you want a one-off, scheduled execution, you can use the `Database.scheduleBatch` method.

Implementing a worker with @future

Adding the `@future` annotation to a **static method** indicates that you want that method's code to execute asynchronously. It is the easiest way to implement a worker, but has some restrictions that have been addressed with subsequently available alternatives.

> **TIP**: I would recommend **Queueables** over `@future` since they have additional flexibility in terms of the type of information that can be passed to them and they are more easily tracked once submitted.

Consider the following implementation guidelines when utilizing the `@future` workers:

- Avoid flooding the async queue with many `@future` jobs (consider Batch Apex).
- Methods must execute quickly or risk platform throttling, which will delay the execution.
- It is easier to implement as they require only a method annotation to be added.
- Typically, the time taken to dequeue and execute the work is less than Batch Apex.
- You can express, via a method annotation, an increase in a specific governor to customize the governor limits to your needs.
- Parameter types are limited to simple types and lists.
- Be careful while passing in list parameters by ensuring that you volume test with large lists.
- There is no way to track execution as the **Apex Job ID** is not returned.
- Executing from an Apex Trigger should be considered carefully; `@future` methods should be bulkified, and if there is a possibility of bulk data loading, there is a greater chance of hitting the daily per-user limit for `@future` jobs.
- You cannot start another `@future`, Batch Apex, or Queueables job. This is particularly an issue if your packaged code can be invoked by code (such as that written by developer X) in a subscriber org. If they have their own `@future` methods indirectly invoking your use of this feature, an exception will occur. As such, try to avoid using these features from a packaged Apex Trigger context.

Implementing a worker with Queueables

A Queueable worker closely resembles a thread from Java, though it lacks some of the finer-grained controls such as a join and sleep. Using an ID for each worker, you can develop tracking code to manage sophisticated serial and parallel execution strategies. Consider the following implementation guidelines when utilizing `Queueables` workers:

- Implement the `Queueables` interface and the `execute` method. Then, use the `System.enqueueJob` method to start your job.

- You must execute quickly or risk platform throttling, which will delay the execution.
- Avoid flooding the async queue with many jobs (consider Batch Apex).
- The member various of the class implementing `Queueables` can contain serializable state that represents the work to be undertaken. This can be complex lists, maps, or your own Apex types.
- Typically, the time taken to de-queue and execute the work is less than Batch Apex.
- Be careful while processing lists, ensuring that you volume test with large volumes of lists to ensure that the job can complex with maximum data.
- You can track execution as the **Apex Job ID** is returned.
- Executing from an Apex Trigger should be considered carefully. Use of Queueables should be bulkified, and if there is a possibility of bulk data loading, there is a greater chance of hitting the daily per-user limit for `@future` jobs.
- You can start up to 50 queueable jobs in a sync context.
- You can start only one queueable job within an existing queueable job; this is known as chaining. The depth of the chain is unlimited, though the platform will narrow the gaps between jobs as the depth grows. Also, Developer Edition orgs are limited to a depth of 5.
- If code attempts to issue more than 1 queueable job within an existing queueable context, an error occurs. This can particularly be an issue if your packaged code can be invoked by code (such as that written by Developer X) in a subscriber org. If they have their own async methods indirectly invoking your use of this feature, an exception will occur. As such, try to avoid using these features from a packaged Apex Trigger context.
- It is possible to run more queueable jobs concurrently than Batch Apex, which can be used to improve the throughput of your processing by leveraging parallel execution. The exact limit is not documented. However, be sure to avoid flooding the system by putting logic in place that controls how chaining and concurrency are used.

Implementing a job with Batch Apex

With the **Batch Apex** framework, you can implement a chain of workers that form a job that iterates over a large set of data that you need to process. The platform takes care of sequencing the workers and allows you to maintain optionally some state between each if desired. In this section, we will review a job that processes **Race Data** records in bulk.

So far, the **Race Data** records created using the Apex code you ran earlier are not, by default, associated with the applicable **Contestant** records (this was intentional to emulate an external data load that would not be aware of the corresponding **Contestant** record IDs). In order to make use of the **Race Data** records in the rest of the application, this relationship needs to be resolved for every record. As noted earlier, the **Contestant** record has a **Race Data Id** field, which contains an Apex-calculated unique value made up from the **Year**, **Race Name**, and **Driver Id** fields concatenated together. This is a good use case for a Batch Apex job!

The following Batch Apex job is designed to process all the **Race Data** records, calculate the compound **Contestant Race Data Id** field, and update the records with the associated **Contestant** record relationship. The following example highlights a number of other things in terms of the Selector and Service layer patterns usage within this context:

- The `RaceDataSelector` class is used to provide the `QueryLocator` method needed, keeping the SOQL logic (albeit simple in this case) encapsulated in the Selector layer.
- The `RaceService.processData` method (added to support this job) is passed in the IDs of the records rather than the records passed to the `execute` method in the `scope` parameter. This general approach avoids any concern over the record data being old, as Batch Apex serialized all record data at the start of the job.
- As per the standard practice, the Service layer does not handle exceptions; these are thrown to the caller and it handles them appropriately. In this case, a new `LogService` class is used to capture exceptions thrown and log them to a Custom Object, utilizing the Apex job ID as a means to differentiate log entries from other jobs. Note that the use of `LogService` is for illustration only; it is not implemented in the sample code for this chapter.
- In the `finish` method, new `NotificationService` encapsulates logic, which is able to notify end users (perhaps via email, tasks, or Chatter as considered earlier) of the result of the job, passing on the Apex job ID, such that it can leverage the information stored in the log Custom Object and/or `ApexAsyncJob` to form an appropriate message to the user. Again, this is for illustration purposes only.

The following code shows the implementation of the Batch Apex job to process the race data records returned through `QueryLocator` created by `RaceDataSelector`:

```
public class ProcessRaceDataJob
    implements Database.Batchable<SObject>,
               Database.RaisesPlatformEvents {

    public Database.QueryLocator
```

```
    start(Database.BatchableContext ctx) {
      return
         RaceDataSelector.newInstance().selectAllQueryLocator();
    }

    public void execute(
       Database.BatchableContext ctx, List<RaceData__c> scope) {
      try {
        Set<Id> raceDataIds =
           new Map<Id, SObject>(scope).keySet();
        RaceService.processData(raceDataIds);
      }
      catch (Exception e) {
        LogService.log(ctx.getJobId(), e);
      }
    }

    public void finish(Database.BatchableContext ctx) {
      NotificationService.notify(
         ctx.getJobId(), 'Process Race Data');
    }
}
```

The code to start the preceding job is implemented in the `RaceService.runProcessDataJob` method; this allows for certain pre-checks for concurrency and configuration to be encapsulated. To start this job, run the `sfdx force:apex:execute` command (without parameters) from the command line and paste the following Apex code. Then, follow the onscreen instructions to press the applicable keyboard shortcut to run it:

```
Id jobId = RaceService.runProcessDataJob();
```

You can monitor the execution of the job on the **Apex Jobs** page under **Setup**. It may take a minute or more to complete, with several thousand rows to process. The following screenshot shows the completed **Driver Name** column on the **Race Data** list view:

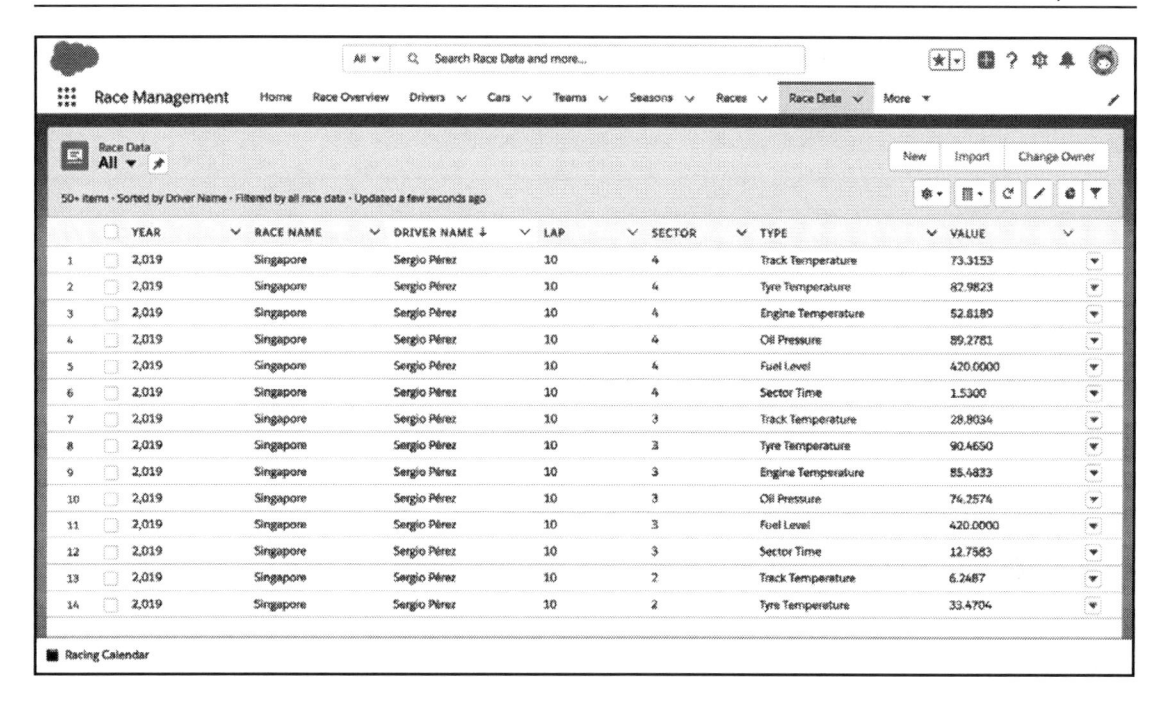

	YEAR	RACE NAME	DRIVER NAME ↓	LAP	SECTOR	TYPE	VALUE	
1	2,019	Singapore	Sergio Pérez	10	4	Track Temperature	73.3153	▼
2	2,019	Singapore	Sergio Pérez	10	4	Tyre Temperature	82.9823	▼
3	2,019	Singapore	Sergio Pérez	10	4	Engine Temperature	52.8189	▼
4	2,019	Singapore	Sergio Pérez	10	4	Oil Pressure	89.2781	▼
5	2,019	Singapore	Sergio Pérez	10	4	Fuel Level	420.0000	▼
6	2,019	Singapore	Sergio Pérez	10	4	Sector Time	1.5300	▼
7	2,019	Singapore	Sergio Pérez	10	3	Track Temperature	28.8034	▼
8	2,019	Singapore	Sergio Pérez	10	3	Tyre Temperature	90.4650	▼
9	2,019	Singapore	Sergio Pérez	10	3	Engine Temperature	85.4833	▼
10	2,019	Singapore	Sergio Pérez	10	3	Oil Pressure	74.2574	▼
11	2,019	Singapore	Sergio Pérez	10	3	Fuel Level	420.0000	▼
12	2,019	Singapore	Sergio Pérez	10	3	Sector Time	12.7583	▼
13	2,019	Singapore	Sergio Pérez	10	2	Track Temperature	6.2487	▼
14	2,019	Singapore	Sergio Pérez	10	2	Tyre Temperature	33.4704	▼

Consider the following implementation guidelines when utilizing Batch Apex:

- A maximum of five active Apex Jobs can run in the org.
- **Apex Flex Queue** (available under **Setup**) can queue up to 100 jobs. The platform automatically removes items from this queue when jobs complete. You can also reorder items in the queue through the UI or via an API. Jobs in the queue have a special holding status.
- An exception is thrown if 100 jobs in an org are already enqueued or executing.
- It is more complex to implement Batch Apex, which requires three methods.
- Typically, the time taken to de-queue and execute can be several minutes or hours.
- Typically, the time taken to execute (depending on the number of items) can be hours.
- Up to 50 million database records or 50 thousand iterator items can be processed.

- Records or iterator items returned from the `start` method are cached by the platform and passed back via the `execute` method, as opposed to being the latest records at that time from the database. Depending on how long the job takes to execute, such information might have changed on the database in the meantime.
- Consider re-reading record data in each execute method for the latest record state.
- You can track Batch Apex progress via its Apex job ID.
- Executing from an Apex Trigger is not advised from a bulkification perspective, especially if you are expecting users to utilize bulk data load tools.
- You can start another Batch Apex job from another (from the finish method).
- Calibrate the default scope size (the number of records passed by the platform to each `execute` method call) to the optimum use of governors and throughput.
- Provide a subscriber org configuration (through a protected custom setting or Custom Metadata) to change the default scope size of 200.
- Implement the `Database.RaisesPlatformEvents` interface to ensure that the platform will send `BatchApexErrorEvent` platform events relating to exceptions not handled by your code (including unhandled limit exceptions). In this case, you may want to consider exclusively logging errors through this event instead of using the `try/catch` pattern shown in the preceding example. Note that administrators can also implement monitoring and logging solutions using Process Builder this way (https://developer.salesforce.com/docs/atlas.en-us.platform_events.meta/platform_events/platform_events_subscribe.htm).

> **TIP**
> Note that the ability to start a Batch Apex job from the `finish` method of another can be a very powerful feature in terms of processing large amounts of data through various stages or implementing a clean-up process. This is often referred to as **Batch Apex chaining**. However, keep in mind that there is no guarantee the second job will start successfully, so ensure you have considered error handling and recovery situations carefully.

Performance of Batch Apex jobs

As stated previously, the platform ultimately controls when and how long your job can take. However, there are a few tips that you can use to improve things:

- **Getting off to a quick start**: Ensure that your `start` method returns as quickly as possible by leveraging indexes. Avoid using sub-queries in your SOQL as this results in a less optimal internal processing strategy for your batch job. In general, I recommend only selecting the ID field and querying again within the `execute` method.
- **Calibrating**: Calibrate the scope size of the records passed to the `execute` method. This will be a balance between the maximum number of records that can be passed to each `execute` (which is currently 2,000) and the governors required to process the records. The preceding example uses 2,000 as the operation is fairly inexpensive. This means that only 50 chunks are required to execute the job (given the test volume data created in this chapter), which, in general, allows the job to execute faster as each burst of activity gets more done at a time. Utilize the `Limits` class with some debug statements when volume testing to determine how much of the governors your code is using, and, if you can afford to do so, increase the scope size applied. Note that if you get this wrong (as in the data complexity in the subscriber's orgs is more than you calibrated for your test data), it can be adjusted further in the subscriber org via a protected custom setting.
- **Frequency of Batch Apex jobs**: If the use of your application results in the submission of more Batch Apex jobs more frequently, perhaps because they are executed from an Apex Trigger (not recommended) or a UI feature used by many users, your application will quickly flood the org's Batch Apex queue and hit the concurrent limit of 5, leaving no room for your Batch Apex jobs or those from other applications. Consider carefully how often you need to submit a job and whether you can queue work up within your application to be consumed by a batch Apex scheduled job at a later time. The **Batch Apex Flex Queue** is a feature provided by the platform that will queue up to 100 jobs automatically. After this your code will receive an error when it attempts to submit the job. Administrators and developers can also adjust the priority of jobs in the Batch Apex Flex Queue.

Using external references in Apex DML

The `RaceService.processData` service method demonstrates a great use of external ID fields when performing DML to associate records. Note that in the following code, it has not been necessary to query the `Contestant__c` records to determine the applicable record ID to place in the `RaceData__c.Contestants__c` field. Instead, the `Contestants__r` relationship field is used to store an instance of the `Contestant__c` object, with only the external ID field populated, as it is also unique, and it can be used in this way instead of the ID:

```
public void processData(Set<Id> raceDataIds)
{
  fflib_SObjectUnitOfWork uow =
     Application.UnitOfWork.newInstance();
  for(RaceData__c raceData :
        (List<RaceData__c>)
          Application.Selector.selectById(raceDataIds))
  {
    raceData.Contestant__r =
      new Contestant__c(
        RaceDataId__c =
          Contestants.makeRaceDataId(
            raceData.Year__c,
            raceData.RaceName__c,
            raceData.DriverId__c));
    uow.registerDirty(raceData);
  }
  uow.commitWork();
}
```

If the lookup by external ID fails during the DML update (performed by the **Unit Of Work** in the preceding case), a DML exception is thrown, for example:

```
Foreign key external ID: 2014-suzuka-98 not found for field RaceDataId__c
in entity Contestant__c
```

This approach of relating records without using or looking up the Salesforce ID explicitly is also available in the Salesforce SOAP and REST APIs as well as through the various **Data Loader** tools. However, in a data loader scenario, the season, race, and driver ID values will have to be pre-concatenated within the CSV file.

Asynchronous processing with platform events

Platform events and the **Event Bus** offer an opportunity to execute background processing continuously in real time rather than being based on ad hoc workers or jobs that are triggered based on a schedule or user action. This means that there is less chance of processing hitting limits or being queued due to the interim build-up of unprocessed data or other jobs.

Earlier in this chapter, you ran the `TestData.createVolumeData` script that created some synthetic race data and inserted it in bulk into the `RaceData__c` object. Later, you ran a **Batch Apex job** to post-process that data to associate it with the `Contestant_c` records. Recall that Batch Apex jobs have limits around the number of concurrent jobs that might place them in a queue if the customer is running other jobs, further delaying the post-processing of the data and its usefulness to the rest of the application and the users.

I am using a sequence diagram to show how the race data flows in real time from the driver's car into the system and results in updates to race statistics, such as fastest sector times. By using platform events, all this happens continuously within a few seconds. Salesforce Event Bus is engineering to handle high levels of ingestion and has built-in retry and recovery features.

> **What is a race sector?** A lap is broken into three sections and timings are taken between each as each car passes between the sector markers. During the race, fans and the teams monitor who completes the fastest sector.

The following sequence diagram shows how the `RaceService.ingestTelemetry` and `RaceService.processTelemetry` services are connected to two platform events. The first event occurs when the driver's car sends data to the `RaceTelemetry__e` event, and the second event occurs when the `RaceData__c` records are inserted into the system through a feature called **Change Data Capture**:

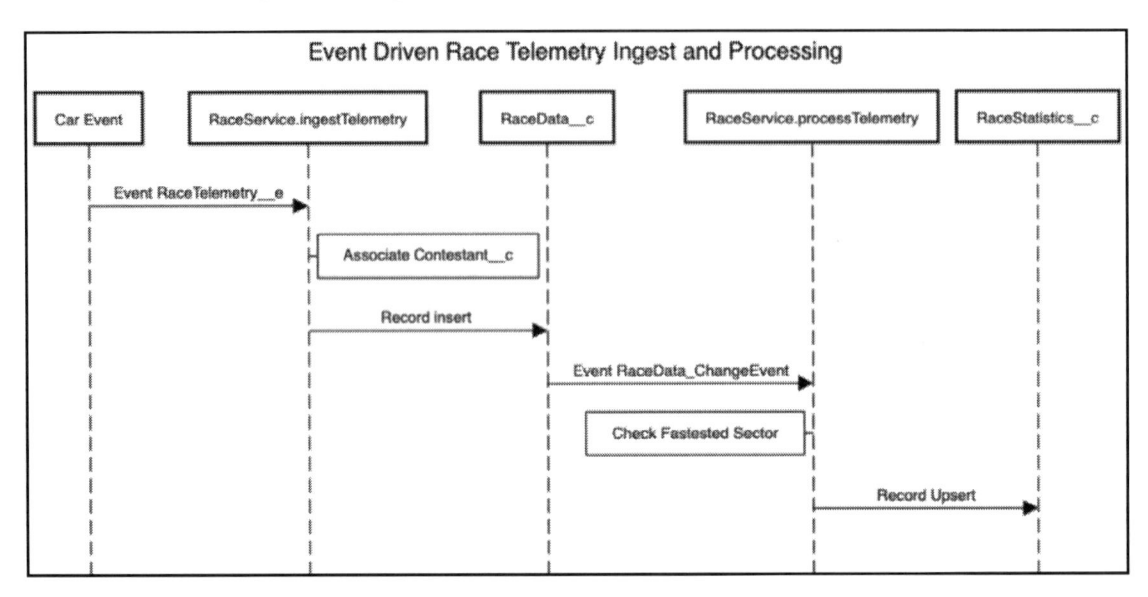

Event Driven Race Telemetry Ingest and Processing

Using the **publish and subscribe model** to decompose processing and separation of concerns manages future extensibility and helps to manage resources and associated limits. This is due to each batch of events being handled within its own execution context. This is an example of applying **event-driven architecture** programming patterns to achieve scale and to improve responsiveness. The following sections further elaborate on how this has been implemented through the sample code included with this chapter.

Chapter 11

Using high-scale platform events to stream data ingestion

The following screenshot shows the `RaceTelemetry_e` event definition:

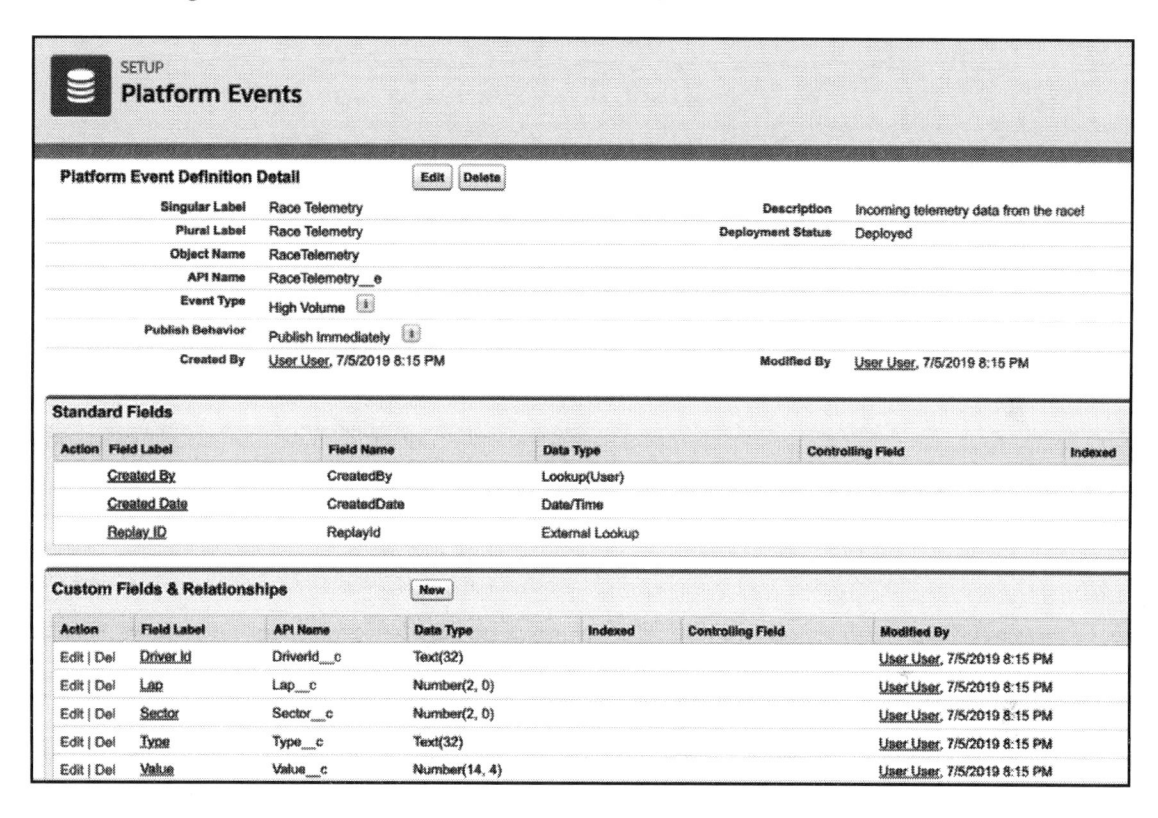

SETUP
Platform Events

Platform Event Definition Detail [Edit] [Delete]

Singular Label	Race Telemetry
Plural Label	Race Telemetry
Object Name	RaceTelemetry
API Name	RaceTelemetry__e
Event Type	High Volume
Publish Behavior	Publish Immediately
Created By	User User, 7/5/2019 8:15 PM

Description	Incoming telemetry data from the race!
Deployment Status	Deployed
Modified By	User User, 7/5/2019 8:15 PM

Standard Fields

Action	Field Label	Field Name	Data Type	Controlling Field	Indexed
	Created By	CreatedBy	Lookup(User)		
	Created Date	CreatedDate	Date/Time		
	Replay ID	ReplayId	External Lookup		

Custom Fields & Relationships [New]

Action	Field Label	API Name	Data Type	Indexed	Controlling Field	Modified By
Edit | Del	Driver Id	DriverId__c	Text(32)			User User, 7/5/2019 8:15 PM
Edit | Del	Lap	Lap__c	Number(2, 0)			User User, 7/5/2019 8:15 PM
Edit | Del	Sector	Sector__c	Number(2, 0)			User User, 7/5/2019 8:15 PM
Edit | Del	Type	Type__c	Text(32)			User User, 7/5/2019 8:15 PM
Edit | Del	Value	Value__c	Number(14, 4)			User User, 7/5/2019 8:15 PM

Since this event object is designed to be used off-platform, its fields are kept simple and map to external ID values defined on other objects, since the control module within a Formula 1 racing car that is sending events to this object is unlikely to know about Salesforce IDs. It will, however, know about its **current lap**, the **driver's ID**, and the **type of telemetry** it is capturing, such as the last racing **sector completion time**. The code to send the event from the car's control module is not relevant, but let's just assume it is using the Salesforce REST API.

[469]

Asynchronous Processing and Big Data Volumes

The following Apex Trigger code is used to receive and process the events sent by the car. Note that while the Apex Trigger syntax is used here, this does not warrant the use of the Domain pattern. While it looks like a regular Apex Trigger, the similarities are only on the surface. Only the after event is supported, and thus there is no `Trigger.old` concept. It is really acting more like a controller class with its own concerns in terms of managing the events and handling errors. As such, it maps the incoming state to a service method:

```
trigger RaceTelemetry on RaceTelemetry__e (after insert) {
    List<RaceService.Telemetry> incomingTelemetry =
        new List<RaceService.Telemetry>();
    for(RaceTelemetry__e event : Trigger.New) {
        RaceService.Telemetry telemetry =
            new RaceService.Telemetry();
        telemetry.DriverId = event.DriverId__c;
        telemetry.Lap = Integer.valueOf(event.Lap__c);
        telemetry.Sector = Integer.valueOf(event.Sector__c);
        telemetry.Type = event.Type__c;
        telemetry.Value = event.Value__c;
        incomingTelemetry.add(telemetry);
    }
    RaceService.ingestTelemetry(incomingTelemetry);
}
```

Though not shown in the example, Apex event handlers can leverage APIs that allow it to **control how many events are processed** and if errors occur that may be transient in cause, such as a timeout or database write error, the code can signal that the event bus should **resend the events again after a short pause (retry)**. Consult the Salesforce documentation relating to
the `EventBus.TriggerContext.currentContext().setResumeCheckpoint` method and the `EventBus.RetryableException` exception: https://developer.salesforce.com/docs/atlas.en-us.platform_events.meta/platform_events/platform_events_subscribe_apex.htm.

The `RaceService.ingestTelemetry` code can be seen by browsing the sample code included in this chapter. Its main role is to associate the correct `Contestant_c` record with the `RaceData__c` record before inserting it into the database.

Using Change Data Capture platform events to compute data

Change Data Capture is a feature that, when enabled (under **Setup**), emits platform events when records in standard or Custom Objects are created, updated, deleted, or undeleted. You do not have to create the platform events because they are defined by the platform. Enabling CDC for your application's objects cannot be packaged, so it is currently something you will need to ask your customers to enable as a post-install task. The setup page looks like this:

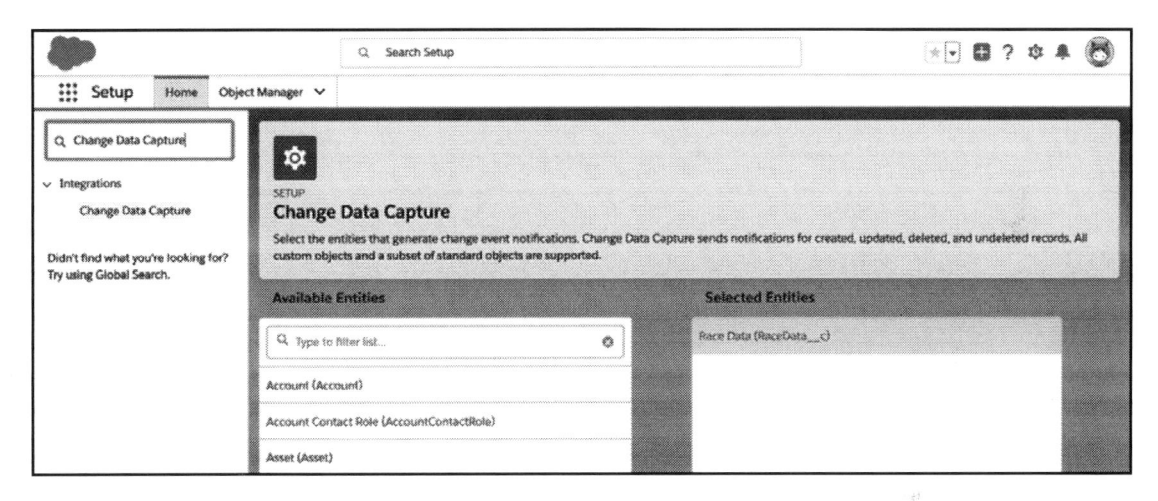

The `RaceData__ChangeEvent` event is defined by the platform and can be subscribed to by implementing an Apex Trigger, much like the example in the previous section. Notice, though, that there is some further specialized handling to determine the nature of the record change through the `EventBus.ChangeEventHeader` type. Again, it is best that this logic is not conflated with the Domain pattern and is dealt with as a concern within the trigger:

```
trigger RaceDataChangeEvent on RaceData__ChangeEvent (after insert) {
    List<RaceService.ContestantResolvedTelemetry>
      resovledTelemetry =
        new List<RaceService.ContestantResolvedTelemetry>();
    for(RaceData__ChangeEvent event : Trigger.New) {
        EventBus.ChangeEventHeader header =
            event.ChangeEventHeader;
        if (header.changetype == 'CREATE' &&
            event.Contestant__c != null) {
            RaceService.ContestantResolvedTelemetry telemetry =
                new RaceService.ContestantResolvedTelemetry();
```

```
            telemetry.ContestantId = event.Contestant__c;
            telemetry.DriverId = event.DriverId__c;
            telemetry.Lap = Integer.valueOf(event.Lap__c);
            telemetry.Sector = Integer.valueOf(event.Sector__c);
            telemetry.Type = event.Type__c;
            telemetry.Value = event.Value__c;
            resovledTelemetry.add(telemetry);
        }
    }
    RaceService.processTelemetry(resovledTelemetry);
}
```

The `RaceService.processTelemetry` code can be seen by browsing the sample code included in this chapter. Its role is to process race data that has been associated with a contestant and determine whether the sector times received are faster than those previously recorded. If that is the case, it will update the `RaceStatistics_c` record to allow fans and race team members to see who is currently the fastest per sector.

Sending race data telemetry events through the Salesforce DX CLI

Since we don't have an actual Formula 1 racing car to generate real telemetry from, we will have to make do with using Salesforce DX commands. The following command can be used to send events to the `RaceTelemetry_e` event to simulate different drivers registering competing sector times. You can then use the **Race Data** and **Race Statistics** tabs to review the results.

Execute the following command from the command line to simulate sending a **20 second sector time** from **Lewis Hamilton** (driver ID 44) for **lap 1 during sector 1**:

```
sfdx force:data:record:create -s RaceTelemetry__e -v "DriverId__c='44'
Lap__c=1 Sector__c=1 Type__c='Sector Time' Value__c=20000"
```

Try executing different commands while varying `DriverId_c` between `44` and `14` (Fernando Alonso) while also changing `Value__c` up or down to simulate each driver recording different times. Observe the **Race Statistics** changing accordingly, remembering that only the fastest driver for a given sector should be displayed on the **Race Statistics** record page. All race telemetry will be recorded in the **Race Data** object regardless.

> **TIP**
> It may be easier to see new records if you clear down the **Race Data** object, especially if you have used the scripts earlier in this chapter. So you can see data generated from the preceding commands. To do this quickly, you can enable the **Truncate** button on the **Race Data Custom Object Definition Detail** page under **Setup** (Salesforce Classic UI only). Search for **User Interface** in the **Setup** menu and tick the **Enable Custom Object Truncate** checkbox, and then click the **Save** button.

The following screenshot shows a series of **Race Data** records that have been received:

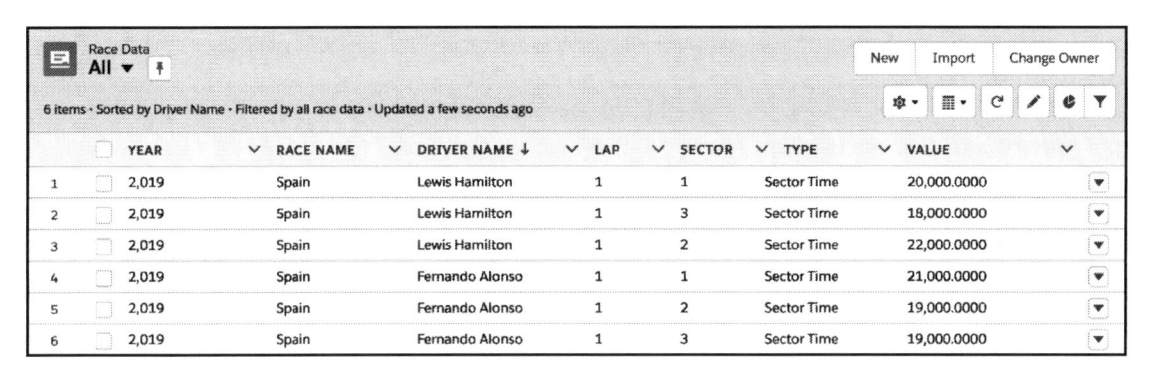

	YEAR	RACE NAME	DRIVER NAME ↓	LAP	SECTOR	TYPE	VALUE	
1	2,019	Spain	Lewis Hamilton	1	1	Sector Time	20,000.0000	
2	2,019	Spain	Lewis Hamilton	1	3	Sector Time	18,000.0000	
3	2,019	Spain	Lewis Hamilton	1	2	Sector Time	22,000.0000	
4	2,019	Spain	Fernando Alonso	1	1	Sector Time	21,000.0000	
5	2,019	Spain	Fernando Alonso	1	2	Sector Time	19,000.0000	
6	2,019	Spain	Fernando Alonso	1	3	Sector Time	19,000.0000	

The following screenshot shows how the **Race Statistics** have been updated:

	RACE ↑	SECTOR 1 DRIVER...	SECTOR 1 TIME	SECTOR 2 DRIVER ...	SECTOR 2 TIME	SECTOR 3 DRIVER...	SECTOR 3 TIME	
1	Spain	Lewis Hamilton	00:00:20.000Z	Fernando Alonso	00:00:19.000Z	Lewis Hamilton	00:00:18.000Z	

If you do not see any records in the **Race Statistics** tab, make sure that you have enabled **Change Data Capture** under the **Setup** menu for the **Race Data** object.

Volume testing

In this chapter, we have used Apex code to generate additional data to explore how the platform applies indexes and the use of Batch Apex. It is important to always perform some volume testing, even if it is just with 200 records to ensure that your triggers are bulkified. Testing with more than this gives you a better idea of other limitations in your software search, such as query performance and any Visualforce scalability issues.

One of the biggest pitfalls with volume testing is the quality of the test data. It is not often that easy to get hold of actual customer data, so we must emulate the spread of information by varying field values among the records to properly simulate how the software will not only behave under load with more records, but under load with a different dispersion of values. This will tease out further bugs that might only manifest if the data values change within a batch of records. For example, the Apex script used in this chapter could be updated to apply a different pit stop strategy to the drivers, varying those types of records per race per driver.

The second challenge is to understand how long a process will take, for example, a Batch Apex job. As it is a multitenant environment, this can vary a lot. This does not mean to say that you should not try a few times during different times of the day and get a rough guide on how long jobs take with different data volumes. You should also experiment with your Batch Apex scope size during your volume testing. The higher the scope size, the fewer chunks of work to perform and, typically, the jobs need to execute for a reduced elapsed time.

As we have seen in this chapter, it only takes 100,000 records to load a scratch org near to its capacity of 250 MB. The Partner Portal test orgs offer an increase to 1 GB so that you can push the volume testing further. You should also encourage relationships with your larger customers to utilize Beta package versions of your application in their sandboxes.

Finally, consider other ways to generate volume data; bulk loading CSV files can work, but can lead to less varied data because CSV files are typically static and are not very easy to edit. It can be well worth investing in some off-platform code that either generates dynamic CSV files or directly invokes the Salesforce API or Bulk API to push data into an org directly. Also, remember that while you're doing this, you're also testing your Apex Trigger code.

Summary

In this chapter, we have learned that understanding not just the volume of records, but also how the data within them is dispersed, can affect the need for indexes to ensure that queries perform without having to resort to expensive table scans or, in the case of Apex Trigger, runtime exceptions. Ensuring that you and your customers understand the best way to apply indexes is critical to both interactive and batch performance. Big objects provide a means to access the benefits of NoSQL databases to manage billions of records using specialized Salesforce APIs and Apex programming patterns using platform events to ingest data.

Chapter 11

Asynchronous execution contexts and platform events open up extended and flexible control over the governors available in the interactive context, but need to be designed from the beginning with careful consideration for the user experience, so that the user is always aware of what is, and what is not, going on in the background. Messaging is the key when there is no immediate user interface to relay errors and resolve them. Don't depend on the **Apex Jobs** screen; instead, try to contextualize error information through custom log objects related to key records in your application that drive background processes, allowing related lists to help relay information in context about the state and result of jobs.

The execution of background processes is not scoped to your application, but affects the whole subscriber org, so the frequency at which your application submits processes to the background needs to be carefully considered. Understand the difference between application and end user jobs; the latter are more likely to flood an org and cause delays or, worse, result in end users having to retry requests. Consider leveraging Apex Scheduler to implement your own application queue to stage different work items for later processing. Salesforce allows up to 100 Batch Apex jobs to queue, allowing the subscriber to control priority. Queueable Apex offers more flexibility than `@future` and is thus recommended. Queueable Apex supports more concurrent jobs and dequeues faster, though it is less elastic in terms of volumes of variables than Batch Apex. Platform events provide a means to perform computation as new data arrives into the application as opposed to in bulk, which can help you manage resources and limits better than attempting to process larger chunks of data at once.

In the next chapter, we will be moving out of the packaging org as the primary development environment and moving into a place that supports multiple developers and an application development life cycle backed by source control and continuous integration to ensure that you have a real-time view of test execution and auditability over your application's source code.

12
Unit Testing

Unit testing is a key technique used by developers to maintain a healthy and robust code base. This approach allows developers to write smaller tests that invoke more varied permutations of a given method or a unit of code. Treating each method as a distinct testable piece of code means that not only is the current usage of that method safe from regression, but that future usage is protected as well. This frees the developer to focus on other permutations, such as error scenarios and parameter values beyond those currently in use.

Unit testing is different from **integration testing**, where many method invocations are tested as a part of an overall business process. Both have a place on the Lightning Platform. In this chapter, we will explore when to use one over the other.

To understand how to adopt unit testing, we first need to understand **dependency injection**. This is the ability to dynamically substitute the behavior of a dependency, such as a class method or component, for a test or stub version. Using a so-called **mock** implementation of a dependency creates a clear testing focus, which allows the developer to build more expressive test conditions when they are free from the overheads of setting up the test contexts that dependent code requires, such as database records. We will explore the ways in which dependency injection can be implemented, including the use of the **Apex Stub API** available through **Apex**, and how this is achieved when writing **Lightning Web Components** unit tests in **JavaScript**.

This chapter shows how unit testing can be applied to the **Apex Enterprise Patterns** introduced earlier in this book. Using the popular open source **ApexMocks framework** with the Apex Stub API, developers can write unit tests for Controller, Service, Domain and Selector classes. Finally, using the **Jest open source framework**, developers can write Lightning Web Components unit tests that mock components and server communications, including Apex Controller logic.

This chapter will cover the following aspects of unit testing:

- Exploring the difference between unit and system testing
- Understanding dependency injection and how to implement it
- Leveraging the Apex Stub API
- Applying the ApexMocks mocking framework to FormulaForce
- Applying the Jest mocking framework to FormulaForce Lightning Web Components

Comparing unit testing and integration testing

Much of the difference between **unit** and **integration testing** relates to the scope of the code being tested and the goals of the test. Chances are you have been mixing a combination of the two on the Lightning Platform without realizing it. Before we go deeper into these differences, let's consider some characteristics of integration testing:

- Integration tests test your key application features and related code paths under different scenarios, which can span multiple classes, including frontend code. Thus, the term "integration" refers to **all code executing end to end** together for a given set of inputs (including database rows) to assert a given output at the end.
- This type of testing occurs after **unit testing**, but also eventually forms a key part of what is sometimes referred to as your **regression (or system) test suite**.
- **Regression tests** are simply a type of integration test that can be even more broad, involving several modules representing key end-to-end critical scenarios in your application, which, if failed, would cause business standstill for your customers. You should regularly review and update regression test coverage as features are added.

For **Apex** code, most of the published guidance on writing Apex tests falls into this integration testing category. Indeed, the only way to cover Apex Trigger code is to physically write to the database. There is also the need to test declarative aspects of your solution (a unit test only tests code) and how they affect broader application processes. In respect of your application's **user experience**, you may also have been using tools such as **Selenium** (https://www.seleniumhq.org/) or **Puppeteer** (https://dev.to/endtest/puppeteer-vs-selenium-1938).

Chapter 12

When I think about the preceding description, it described the Apex tests I had been writing before discovering how to write true unit tests on this platform (more on this in the *Introducing unit testing* section later). Visually, my tests used to look like the following:

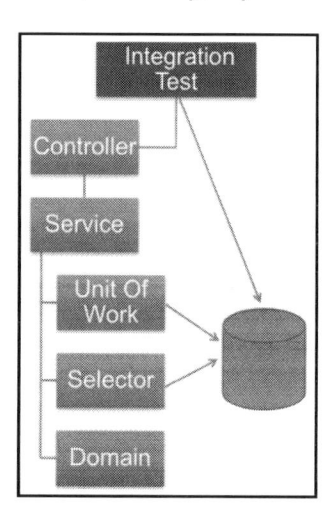

Historically, I would write Apex test code to set up my records or execute my controller code or service layer code (to test the API). This code would update or query the database accordingly. Then, I would write test code to query the result records to ascertain that the behavior was what I was expecting. This approach, as per the preceding diagram, would ensure that all the classes involved in the functionality, such as Service, Domain, Unit Of Work, and Selector, got executed. It also ensured that they did just what they needed to in the scenario I was testing to result in the overall goal of completing the end user or API process being tested. Essentially, I had been writing integration tests and that, of course, is better than nothing!

Integration tests are still necessary to test your key processes, and, in the case of Apex, to obtain code coverage on the Apex Triggers required to package your solution. However, regardless of its Apex code or your user experience code, integration tests do have some downsides:

- **Execution time**: Since each test method needs to set up, update, and query the database executing it, all or individual test methods can start to take increasingly longer to execute, slowing the developer's productivity.
- **Scenario coverage**: Introducing more varied scenarios can become less practical due to the preceding performance concern. This discourages developers from doing thorough testing (we hate waiting!). This, in turn, reduces code coverage and the value of the tests. And this ultimately increases the risk of bugs being left undiscovered by the developer.

- **Code coverage challenges**: Obtaining 100% code coverage is the desirable goal, but it can be impossible to achieve in certain scenarios. For example, error handling for some system events cannot be emulated in an integration test.
- **Ensuring future-proofing and reliability for other developers**: Methodologies such as Scrum teach us to write code incrementally and just in time for market needs. However, developers are often aware of future needs and wish to build frameworks, engines, or libraries to support both current and future needs. It may not be possible to write integration tests that ensure that, when that time comes, such code is robust and reliable for other developers.

As client development is now more component-driven, when considering testing the **user experience** directly through **browser automation tools** such as Selenium, the preceding considerations are equally valid. This means that it is also important to think about integration versus unit testing at the client tier, specifically, **unit testing Lightning Web Components**.

The testing pyramid on the Lightning Platform

A pyramid metaphor is often used to express the functional granularity or scope of tests since it nicely illustrates, as it gets wider toward the bottom, the number of tests – and thus investment – you should undertake when thinking about your testing strategy. The following diagram shows what this looks like on the Lightning Platform and helps visualize the two unit testing focus areas for this chapter in respect of **Apex** and **Lightning Web Components**:

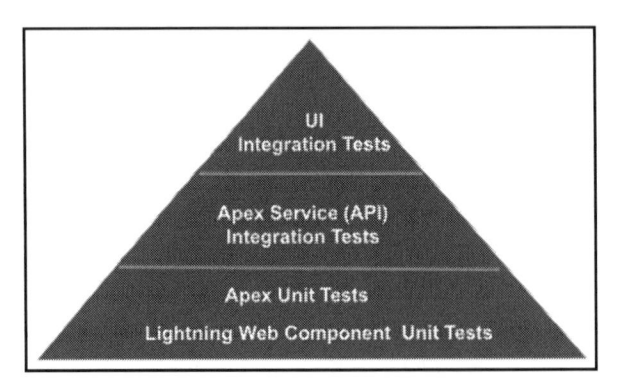

In the following section, we will start at the bottom of this pyramid to better understand what unit testing is and how it can be applied to the Lightning Platform.

Introducing unit testing

As we will discover throughout this chapter, unit testing helps to address the preceding challenges. When used in combination with integration tests, the resulting test suite creates a much stronger and more efficient set of Apex tests for your application.

Learning about and writing unit tests can often seem difficult because it requires you to learn other concepts, some of which determine how you write your application code. Things such as **separation of concerns** (**SOC**), dependency injection, mocking, and test-driven development are concepts you will come across when googling about unit tests. We will be looking into these throughout this chapter. Of course, you are already, by now, quite familiar with SOC and how it is applied to Apex Enterprise Patterns. As a reminder, in Chapter 6, *Application Domain Layer*, we briefly described unit testing as having the following characteristics:

- The term "**unit**" refers to a small portion of application code that has inputs and outputs (including exceptions) you want to focus on ensuring quality for as a developer. In object-orientated programming languages such as Apex, this could be an interface, or public methods on a class, or just a specific method.
- The unit "**test code**" for such a method focuses on invoking the method or interface in as many different combinations of inputs and expected outputs (including exceptions) as possible.
- It's **good practice** to write test code that uses as many inputs as possible and not just those you imagine the current callers might use. This ensures the unit of code being tested is robust enough for future scenarios. This can be quite important for Domain-class code testing, as this class of code protects the integrity of customers' data.

The biggest difference between unit and integration testing is evident through this definition. Unit tests can cover methods on potentially any class in your code base, not just the outer controller classes or service classes. Furthermore, the goal is to test the execution and behavior of only the code in the chosen method and nothing else.

The hard part can be preventing the execution of other methods that the method being unit tested calls. This is done by substituting parts of the real production code (within the test context only) for stubbed code, or what is referred to as *mocked code*, which emulates the behavior of those methods. Then, the method you're unit testing can still execute. Ideally, the method should be unaware of this substitution, or *injection* as it's known.

Unit Testing

For example, a unit test for an Apex Controller method should test the behavior of that method only, such as interaction with the view state or the handling of UI requests and responses with the service layer calls. What the service layer method does is not of interest. Developers should not have to consider any requirements of dependent methods like this (for example, database setup) in the unit test code. Likewise, when testing the Apex service layer logic, its use of the Unit Of Work, Selector, and Domain classes are not of interest or concern. However, these dependencies need to be resolved. The next section discusses how to inject dependencies.

The following diagram shows a series of **unit tests focusing on Apex classes** using mock alternatives of the dependent class to avoid having to be concerned with their needs:

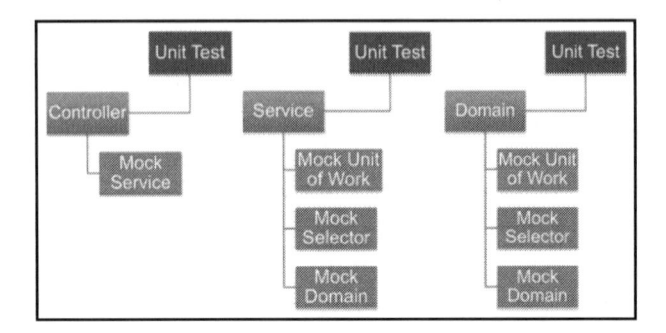

In contrast, the following diagram shows a series of **unit tests focusing on Lightning Web Components** and uses mock alternatives for the dependent components and services:

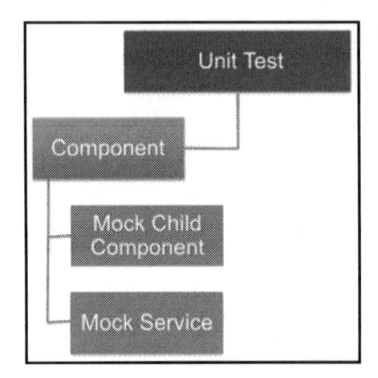

A mock version of a dependent class, component, or service should emulate the expectations of the calling code (the code the unit test is focusing on) by returning a value or throwing an exception, for example. Configuring mocking is a key setup aspect of unit testing you need to master. It can allow you to write some very sophisticated and varied tests. We will go into more detail on mocking later in the chapter.

Chapter 12

The more developers invest in unit tests, the less likely integration tests and your end users are to find defects. Keep in mind, however, that proving that methods work in isolation does not prove your application works as designed. Integration tests are still a critical tool in testing your application.

Introduction to unit testing with Apex

At this stage, you're probably wondering just how it is technically possible, using code, to substitute or *inject* (to use the correct term) different compiled code during test execution. To illustrate the various options for dependency injection, let's start with a simple code example. We will explore how unit testing can be applied to Apex Enterprise Patterns later in this chapter.

The following diagram shows the **Unified Modeling Language** (**UML**) for a `Car` class model, which has been designed with SOC in mind. Responsibilities such as the engine, dashboard, and the digital readout display have been separated. This is a pure Apex code example to illustrate how dependencies between classes can be managed with **dependency injection** (**DI**):

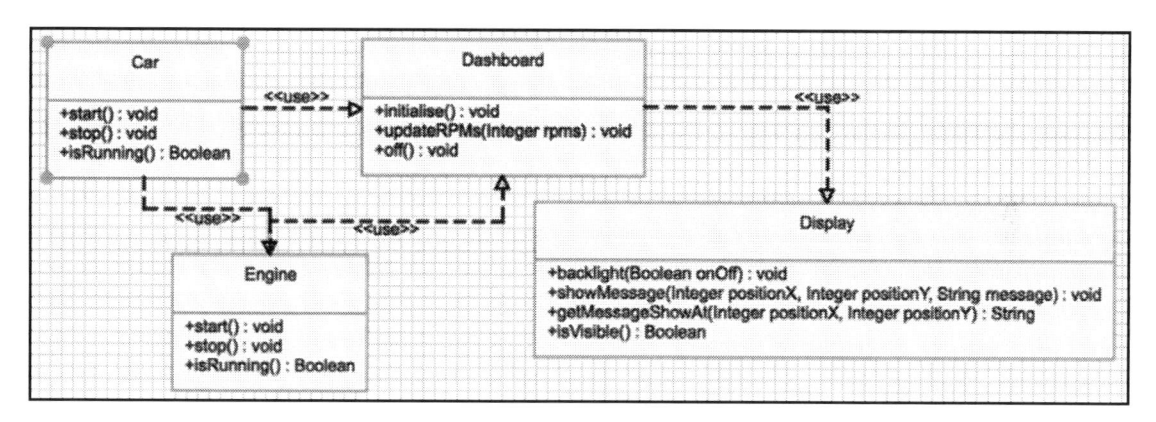

The following code is for the `Car` class. It has a dependency on methods from the `Dashboard` and `Engine` classes. The caller must set up and provide instances of these classes for the methods to function correctly:

```
public class Car {
    private Engine engine;
    private Dashboard dashboard;
    private Boolean isRunning;
    public Car(Engine engine, Dashboard dashboard) {
        this.dashboard = dashboard;
```

Unit Testing

```
        this.engine = engine;
    }
    public void start() {
        dashboard.initialise();
        engine.start();
    }
    public void stop() {
        engine.stop();
        dashboard.off();
    }
    public Boolean isRunning() {
        return engine.isRunning();
    }
}
```

The `start` and `stop` methods contain functionality that ensures that the dashboard and engine are initialized accordingly. The following code for the `Dashboard` class requires an instance of the `Display` class, which handles the display of information:

```
public class Dashboard {
    private Display display;
    public Dashboard(Display display) {
        this.display = display;
    }
    public void initialise() {
        display.backlight(true);
        display.showMessage(10, 20, 'Hello Driver!');
    }
    public void updateRPMs(Integer rpms) {
        display.showMessage(10,10, 'RPM:' + rpms);
    }
    public void off() {
        display.backlight(false);
    }
}
```

The methods on the `Dashboard` class integrate with the `Display` class to show messages on the digital display of the car at various locations. The `Display` class has no dependencies, so, for simplicity, is not shown here. (If you want to view its code, you can refer to the sample code for this chapter.) Finally, the `Engine` class is shown as follows:

```
public class Engine {

    private Dashboard dashboard;
    private Boolean isRunning;

    public Engine(Dashboard dashboard) {
```

```
            this.dashboard = dashboard;
        }
        public void start() {
            dashboard.updateRPMs(1000);
            isRunning = true;
        }
        public void stop() {
            dashboard.updateRPMs(0);
            isRunning = false;
        }
        public Boolean isRunning() {
            return isRunning;
        }
    }
```

The methods in the `Engine` class call methods on the `Dashboard` class to update the driver on the **revolutions per minute (RPM)** of the engine.

> This is sample code. Real code would likely include classes representing various hardware sensors.

First, let's take a look at what an integration test looks like for `Car`:

```
@IsTest
private class CarTest {
    @IsTest
    private static void integrationTestStartCar() {
        // Given
        Display display = new Display();
        Dashboard dashboard = new Dashboard(display);
        Engine engine = new Engine(dashboard);

        // When
        Car car = new Car(engine, dashboard);
        car.start();
        // Then
        System.assertEquals(true, car.isRunning());
        System.assertEquals(true, engine.isRunning());
        System.assertEquals(true, display.isVisible());
        System.assertEquals('Hello Driver!',
            display.getMessageShowAt(10,20));
                System.assertEquals('RPM:1000',
            display.getMessageShowAt(10,10));
    }
}
```

Unit Testing

The setup for this test looks simple, but imagine if each of the classes constructed required other configuration and data to be created—the setup logic could grow quickly. This integration test is perfectly valid and useful in its own right. However, as I mentioned earlier, you cannot assume just because you have fully unit tested methods that everything still works when you put it all together!

The preceding test code is split into three main sections: *Given*, *When*, and *Then*. This type of approach and thinking originates from another practice, known as **behavior-driven development** (BDD). You can read more about this on Martin Fowler's website at `https://martinfowler.com/bliki/GivenWhenThen.html`.

Deciding what to test for and what not to test for in a unit test

In this section, let's review what type of unit tests we would want to write and what these tests should assert for some of the methods in the preceding example.

Let's consider what we would assert in writing a unit test that just tested the following logic in the `Car.start` method. (Remember, we are not interested in testing the `dashboard.initialise` or `engine.start` methods yet):

```
public void start() {
    dashboard.initialise();
    engine.start();
}
```

For this method, we would assert that the `dashboard.initialise` and `engine.start` methods actually get called. So, in a unit test for this method, we are testing the behavior of the `start` method only. In separate unit tests, we would also test the `dashboard.initialise` and `engine.start` methods themselves.

> Solely testing the behavior or implementation of a method (for example, what methods it called) might seem odd, compared to asserting values. But sometimes, asserting that certain methods are called (and how many times they get called) and any parameters that may exist are passed to them is a key validation that the code is working as expected. Asserting values returned from methods, as a means of testing correct behavior, is also valid in a unit test.

In the case of the `engine.start` method, shown again in the following code, we want to assert that the `dashboard.updateRPMs` method was called with the correct idle RPM value and that the state of the engine was correctly set up as running:

```
public void start() {
    dashboard.updateRPMs(1000); // Idle speed
    isRunning = true;
}
```

We are not interested in testing whether the method updated the display; that's the concern of another unit test, which tests the `Dashboard.updateRPMs` method directly.

Here is the `Dashboard.updateRPMs` method code again. When writing a unit test for this method, we should validate that any value passed to the `rpms` parameter was correctly passed to the `Display.showMessage` method:

```
public void updateRPMs(Integer rpms) {
    display.showMessage(10,10, 'RPM:' + rpms);
}
```

In order to write unit tests for these methods and these methods alone, we need the `dashboard`, `display`, and `engine` variables to reference something the compiler will recognize as having the required methods. But this kind of testing also needs to allow us to substitute the real implementation of these methods with special test-only versions so that we can record when the methods are called in order to assert behavior. What we need is mock implementations of the `Dashboard`, `Engine`, and `Display` classes.

Constructor dependency injection

The preceding code makes explicit hardcoded dependencies between classes. To work around this, CDI can be applied. This has been used in other languages, such as Java. In the following examples, **Apex interfaces** are utilized to express the dependencies between various units of code that you want to test in isolation.

> It is not required to apply this to all method-to-method calling dependencies; only those that you want to apply unit testing to. Apex Enterprise Patterns focus mainly on the Services, Domain, Selector, and Unit Of Work classes.

Unit Testing

By leveraging the ability to have multiple implementations of a given interface, we can vary which implementation gets executed. We can execute the real implementation of a method (this is provided by the preceding classes) or test only the mock behavior of it, typically defined in the test itself. Thus, depending on the type of test being written – an integration test or a unit test – you then pass the appropriate implementation of the Car class.

To support this type of injection, the following three things must be changed:

1. Firstly, interfaces are created to reflect the methods on the Engine, Dashboard, and Display classes. The following code shows how these interfaces are defined:

   ```
   public interface IEngine {
       void start();
       void stop();
       Boolean isRunning();
   }
   public interface IDashboard {
       void initialise();
       void updateRPMs(Integer rpms);
       void off();
   }
   public interface IDisplay {
       void backlight(Boolean onOff);
       void showMessage(
           Integer positionX, Integer positionY, String message);
       String getMessageShowAt(
           Integer positionX, Integer positionY);
       Boolean isVisible();
   }
   ```

2. Secondly, the real implementation of the classes must implement the interfaces, since the interfaces are based on their methods. This typically just requires stating that the class implements the interface:

   ```
   public class Engine implements IEngine {

   public class Dashboard implements IDashboard {

   public class Display implements IDisplay {
   ```

3. Finally, references to the interface types, and not the concrete classes, must be made throughout the code base. For example, the `Car` constructor now takes the interface types, as do the `engine` and `dashboard` member types, used to call the methods:

```
public class Car {
    private IEngine engine;
    private IDashboard dashboard;
    private Boolean isRunning;
    public Car(IEngine engine, IDashboard dashboard) {
        this.dashboard = dashboard;
        this.engine = engine;
    }
```

> Notice that the integration test shown earlier in this chapter for the `Car` class still works without modification, since the real implementation it uses implements the interfaces.

Implementing unit tests with CDI and mocking

The mock implementations of the interfaces can now also be implemented. These mock classes can be as simple or as complex as you desire, depending on what behavior you need to emulate and what it is you're asserting. Note that you do not have to fully implement all methods; stubs are fine. Implement what is needed for your test scenarios:

```
private class MockDashboard implements IDashboard {
    public Boolean initialiseCalled = false;
    public Boolean updateRPMsCalled = false;
    public Integer updateRPMsCalledWith = null;
    public void initialise() { initialiseCalled = true; }
    public void updateRPMs(Integer rpms) {
        updateRPMsCalled = true;
        updateRPMsCalledWith = rpms;
    }
    public void off() { }
}

private class MockEngine implements IEngine {
    public Boolean startCalled = false;
    public void start() { startCalled = true; }
    public void stop() { }
    public Boolean isRunning() { return true; }
}
```

Unit Testing

```
private class MockDisplay implements IDisplay {
    public Boolean showMessageCalled = false;
    public String showMessageCalledWithMessage = null;
    public void backlight(Boolean onOff) { }
    public void showMessage(
        Integer positionX, Integer positionY, String message) {
        showMessageCalled = true;
        showMessageCalledWithMessage = message;
    }
    public String getMessageShowAt(
        Integer positionX, Integer positionY) { return null; }
    public Boolean isVisible() { return false; }
}
```

> **TIP** You can keep the implementation of these mock classes contained and scoped within your Apex test classes or use inner classes within a single class, if needed. Additionally, the Salesforce DX folder structure is flexible and allows you to create sub-folders under the /classes folder, for example,/classes/tests/mocks.

After making the preceding changes and the introduction of the mocking classes, the implementation of the Car class object model now supports unit testing through CDI.

Each of the following unit tests resides in the corresponding test class within the sample code for this chapter, for example, CarTest, EngingeTest, and DashboardTest.

The following is a unit test for the Car.start method:

```
@IsTest
private static void
  whenCarStartCalledDashboardAndEngineInitialised () {
    // Given
    MockDashboard mockDashboard = new MockDashboard();
    MockEngine mockEngine = new MockEngine();
    // When
    Car car = new Car(mockEngine, mockDashboard);
    car.start();
    // Then
    System.assert(car.isRunning());
    System.assert(mockDashboard.initialiseCalled);
    System.assert(mockEngine.startCalled);
}
```

> **TIP**
>
> Notice the method naming approach used by the test method. This is deliberate, as unit testing often results in the creation of many small unit test methods. Having a naming convention such as the examples shown in this section helps make it clearer at a glance what the test is covering. Once again, this convention is borrowed from the BDD principles referenced earlier in this chapter.

Notice that the test did not need any setup to fulfill the setup requirements of the engine and dashboard dependencies, such as constructing an instance of the `Display` class.

Mock classes can also record the values passed as parameters for assertion later. The following is a unit test for the `engine.start` method:

```
@IsTest
private static void whenStartCalledDashboardUpdated() {
    // Given
    MockDashboard mockDashboard = new MockDashboard();
    // When
    Engine engine = new Engine(mockDashboard);
    engine.start();
    // Then
    System.assert(engine.isRunning());
    System.assert(mockDashboard.updateRPMsCalled);
    System.assertEquals(1000,
        mockDashboard.updateRPMsCalledWith);
}
```

It uses the mock implementation of the dashboard to confirm that the `Dashboard.updateRPMs` method was correctly passed the corresponding value. The following unit test is for the `Dashboard.updateRPMs` method:

```
@IsTest
private static void whenUpdateRPMsCalledMessageIsDisplayed() {
    // Given
    MockDisplay mockDisplay = new MockDisplay();
    // When
    Dashboard dashboard = new Dashboard(mockDisplay);
    dashboard.updateRPMs(5000);
    // Then
    System.assert(mockDisplay.showMessageCalled);
    System.assertEquals('RPM:5000',
        mockDisplay.showMessageCalledWithMessage);
}
```

The preceding code uses a mock implementation of the `Display` class to test the correct interaction between the `Dashboard` and the `Display` class. The interaction being tested here is that the display text is correctly calculated and passed to the `Display` class when the `updateRPMs` method is called on the `Dashboard` class.

Using interfaces to achieve dependency injection has an overhead in the development and use of interfaces in the production code. This is something Salesforce has improved on with the introduction of the Apex Stub API, described later in this chapter. As the Stub API is still quite new, you may still see the DI accomplished with interfaces. The **Apex Enterprise Patterns** library utilized it prior to the arrival of the Stub API. Also keep in mind, as we have seen in previous sections of this book, that Apex interfaces also have many other uses in providing flexibility in your architecture's evolution and reducing coupling between clearly defined boundaries, such as those in this book and those your logic can also define.

Other dependency injection approaches

A variation on the constructor pattern is to use **setter methods** to inject references into the instance of a class being unit tested. These should use the `@TestVisible` annotation so that these methods do not get used to override the instance setup to point to the real instances of dependent classes, which might be set up in the constructor.

The **factory pattern** discussed earlier in this book can also be used to inject alternative implementations of the mock implementations. The factory approach does not require constructors to be declared with a list of dependencies for each class. Instead, instances of the interfaces are obtained by calling factory methods.

> The use of factory dependency injection over CDI can be a matter of preference regarding whether the dependencies need to be declared upfront. The Apex Enterprise Patterns library uses a factory pattern for injection over CDI since layers such as Service, Domain, and Selector are well defined and consistently applied throughout an application's code base.

The `Application` class factories used in the preceding chapters of this book allow you to implement the runtime injection of Services, Domain, or Selector implementations by calling the respective methods on each of the corresponding factories.

The following `Application` class factory methods allow you to obtain an instance of an object implementing the specified service, Unit Of Work, Domain, or Selector class. These are the same methods that have been used in earlier chapters to implement various dynamic configuration behaviors' runtime:

You must cast the result to the applicable Apex class or interface:

```
Application.Service.newInstance
Application.Domain.newInstance
Application.Selector.newInstance
Application.UnitOfWOrk.newInstance
```

The following methods can be used to register an alternative implementation during the test setup of a given Service, Domain, or Selector class:

```
Application.Service.setMock
Application.Domain.setMock
Application.Selector.setMock
Application.UnitOfWork.setMock
```

The preceding `newInstance` methods will then return these in preference to instances of the real classes you configured in the `Application` class.

`RaceService` uses an interface called `IRaceService`. The following unit test for the `RaceController` class leverages this interface and the `Application.Service.setMock` method to register a mock implementation of the `IRaceService` interface with the factory. In order to implement a unit test that validates the controllers, a record `Id` is correctly passed to the called service method:

```
@IsTest
private static void whenAwardPointsCalledIdPassedToService() {
    // Given
    MockRaceService mockService = new MockRaceService();
    Application.Service.setMock(IRaceService.class, mockService);
    // When
    Id raceId = fflib_IDGenerator.generate(Race__c.SObjectType);
    RaceController raceController =
        new RaceController(
            new ApexPages.StandardController(
                new Race__c(Id = raceId)));
    raceController.awardPoints();
    // Then
    System.assert(mockService.awardChampionshipPointsCalled);
    System.assertEquals(new Set<Id> { raceId },
        mockService.awardChampionshipPointsCalledWithRaceIds);
}
```

`MockRaceService` is not shown here for brevity, but it follows the same pattern as the other mock classes shown so far in this chapter. Refer to it within the `RaceControllerTestMockingDemo` class included in the sample code of this chapter. Also, recall that the `RaceService.service` method utilizes the `Application` service factory to create an instance of the service to execute.

Benefits of dependency injection frameworks

So far, we have discussed ways in which you can achieve dependency injection by using factories or constructors and implementing Apex interfaces to inject alternative mock implementations of classes you wish to mock. DI frameworks offer ways for developers to access certain underlying language runtime features that can provide more direct ways to implement these aspects.

Thus, DI frameworks tend to help developers gain easier access to the benefits of DI with much less boilerplate coding, such as utilizing interfaces, especially in older code bases. However, the developer may still have to write mock implementations such as those we have seen above and manage dependencies between classes carefully via SOC.

Java, for example, leverages its reflection API to allow injection at runtime without the need for interfaces. The Spring Framework for Java extends this feature by allowing configuration via XML files to allow for different runtime configurations. Some frameworks will also intercept the use of the native `new` operator. This avoids the need to implement the factory- or constructor-based injection approaches outlined in the preceding code.

In Apex, at the time of writing, the developer still needs to implement an injection approach such as those described earlier. However, it does make it easier to adopt mocking in legacy code bases (where interfaces have not been applied). The rest of this chapter will continue to explore this API in more detail and frameworks will be built on top of it.

> **TIP**
> I have had the pleasure of developing an open source DI library for the Lightning Platform with fellow members of the Salesforce community, **John Daniels** and **Doug Ayers**. This is known as **Force DI**. In part, it is a more formalized version of the Custom Metadata factory-based injection approaches used in this book, delivered in a more general form to allow the dynamic injection of Apex, Flow, Visualforce, and Lightning Components. You can read more about it at http://github.com/afawcett/force-di.

Writing unit tests with the Apex Stub API

The **Apex Stub** API applies only within an Apex test context, so it cannot be used to implement DI outside of tests. To do that, you still need to leverage Apex interfaces. Utilizing Apex Stub APIs requires an understanding of the following:

- **Implementing the Stub Provider interface**: The `System.StubProvider` system-provided Apex interface is effectively a callback style interface. It allows your mocking code to be informed when method calls are against classes you are mocking in your test. You can implement this interface multiple times, once per class you're mocking, or a single implementation for building sophisticated generalized mocking frameworks. The Apex Mocks open source framework from FinancialForce.com is one such framework that we will be reviewing later.
- **Dynamic creation of stubs for mocking**: The platform automatically creates instances of classes you wish to mock through the `Test.createStub` method. You do not need to create Apex interfaces to perform DI when using the Stub API. The only requirement is that you provide the platform with an implementation of the `Test.StubProvider` interface to call back on when methods on the created stub instance are called during test execution.

In the following sub-sections, we will dig a little deeper into the preceding bullets with some simple sample code that is intended to help illustrate the key concepts.

Implementing mock classes using Test.StubProvider

Implementing mock handling code with `System.StubProvider` requires only one method to be implemented as opposed to each of the methods being mocked individually. This is because this interface is a generic interface for all possible method signatures.

As you can see from the following implementation of the `MockDashboard` class, the `handleMethodCall` method on this interface passes all the information your mocking code needs in order to identify which method on which object has been called:

```
private class MockDashboard implements System.StubProvider {
    public Boolean initialiseCalled = false;
    public Object handleMethodCall(
        Object stubbedObject,
        String stubbedMethodName,
        Type returnType,
        List<Type> listOfParamTypes,
```

Unit Testing

```
        List<String> listOfParamNames,
        List<Object> listOfArgs) {

    // Record method call
    if(stubbedMethodName == 'initialise') {
        initialiseCalled = true;
    }
    return null;
    }
}
```

Once again, this mock implementation is implementing only the minimum needed to satisfy the mocking requirements of the test being performed. It simply validates the fact that the `initialise` method was called.

> Salesforce provides a rich set of parameters to allow more generic implementations of this method to occur. We will review these later in this chapter, through the Apex Mocks framework.

Creating dynamic stubs for mocking classes

Having implemented the `System.StubProvider` interface, it is still not possible to pass an instance of the `MockDashboard` class to the `Car` class since it cannot be cast to an instance of `Dashboard`. To make this possible, the platform-provided `Test.createStub` method must be called. This internally creates an instance of the `Dashboard` class, but routes method calls to the provided stub provider instead of the real code.

A convention I decided to follow in these samples is to wrap the call to this method through a `createStub` method of my own on the mocking class:

```
    private class MockDashboard implements System.StubProvider {
        public Boolean initialiseCalled = false;
        public Object handleMethodCall( ... ) {
            ...
        }
        public Dashboard createStub() {
            return (Dashboard) Test.createStub(Dashboard.class, this);
        }
    }
```

As we can see, this reduces the amount of repetition when calling it (boilerplate code) and makes it easier to use when writing the unit testing code, as you will see in the next section.

Mocking examples with the Apex Stub API

After implementing the `MockDashboard` class, we can use it in a unit test. The resulting unit test is similar to those illustrated using Apex interfaces:

```
@IsTest
private static void
    whenCarStartCalledDashboardAndEngineInitialised() {
    // Given
    MockDashboard mockDashboard = new MockDashboard();
    MockEngine mockEngine = new MockEngine();
    // When
    Car car = new Car(
        mockEngine.createStub(),
        mockDashboard.createStub());
    car.start();
    // Then
    System.assert(car.isRunning());
    System.assert(mockDashboard.initialiseCalled);
    System.assert(mockEngine.startCalled);
}
```

> The sample unit test code and mocks used for this unit test are implemented in the `CarTestApexStubAPIDemo` class.

The main difference from the Apex interface approach is the creation of the stub instances of the classes being mocked using the applicable `createStub` methods.

The following code shows the `handleMethodCall` method in the `MockEngine` class used in the preceding unit test. It illustrates how a mock response can be returned for the `Engine.isRunning` method:

```
public Object handleMethodCall(
    Object stubbedObject,
    String stubbedMethodName,
    Type returnType,
    List<Type> listOfParamTypes,
    List<String> listOfParamNames,
    List<Object> listOfArgs) {

    // Record method call
    if(stubbedMethodName == 'isRunning') {
        isRunningCalled = true;
        return true;
    } else if(stubbedMethodName == 'start') {
```

Unit Testing

```
            startCalled = true;
        }
        return null;
    }
```

The following code shows the `handleMethodCall` method from the `MockDisplay` class (see the `DashboardTestApexStubAPIDemo` class for the full code) and the use of the `listOfArgs` parameter:

```
public Object handleMethodCall(
    Object stubbedObject,
    String stubbedMethodName,
    Type returnType,
    List<Type> listOfParamTypes,
    List<String> listOfParamNames,
    List<Object> listOfArgs) {

    // Record method call and parameter values
    if(stubbedMethodName == 'showMessage') {
        showMessageCalled = true;
        showMessageCalledWithMessage = (String) listOfArgs[2];
    }
    return null;
}
```

The preceding mock handler code monitors the `showMessage` method being called by the `Dashboard` `updateRPMs` method. It then stores the parameter values for assertion later, in addition to the fact that the method itself was called.

The following unit test code leverages this to test that the correct information is passed to the display when the `updateRPMs` method is called:

```
@IsTest
private static void whenUpdateRPMsCalledMessageIsDisplayed() {
    // Given
    MockDisplay mockDisplay = new MockDisplay();
    // When
    Dashboard dashboard = new Dashboard(mockDisplay.createStub());
    dashboard.updateRPMs(5000);
    // Then
    System.assert(mockDisplay.showMessageCalled);
    System.assertEquals('RPM:5000',
        mockDisplay.showMessageCalledWithMessage);
}
```

Now that you have seen some specific examples of how to use the Apex Stub API, the next section provides some more general notes and considerations to keep mind.

Considerations when using the Apex Stub API

The following are some general notes and considerations for the Apex Stub API:

- The Apex `new` operator still creates an instance of the type referenced when used in your application code. Therefore, you still need to leverage a dependency injection convention, such as one of those described in this chapter, to inject the alternative implementation of any dependent class you wish to mock in your unit tests.
- Explicitly defined interfaces between the dependency boundaries of your classes are not strictly required, but might be a useful means of further enforcing SOC boundaries or for further configuration of your application.
- Not all methods and classes can be stubbed using the `Test.createStub` method. Examples include inner classes, get/set accessors, and methods returning `Iterator`. For a full list, consult the *Apex Developers Guide*.
- Static methods are also not able to be stubbed – this is by design since these methods are not open to dependency injection. Although the service layer design convention utilizes static methods, the actual implementation of those methods goes through the service factory to access the actual service implementation via instance methods. This can be seen in `RaceService` included in the sample code.
- Other restrictions on what can be mocked, such as private methods and constructors, might seem like an omission. However, in principle, you should only be testing the public behavior of your classes in your unit test in any case. Once you mock an object method, the constructor used to instantiate the object is not significant, as your mocking code determines what each method returns.
- Keep in mind that changes to method signatures can break the late-bound references to parameters and return types made in your mock implementations. In this respect, explicit interface-based mock implementations have an advantage, as a compilation error will occur if you make breaking changes. Mocking frameworks can help to mitigate this risk, as we will discuss in the next section.

Using the Apex Stub API with mocking frameworks

Implementing mock classes for small code bases, or as an aid to get a better understanding of the concept of unit testing, as we have done in this chapter, is fine. However, it can quickly become onerous and a maintenance overhead for larger code bases. The Apex Stub API was designed to handle any class shape for a reason.

The `stubbedObject` parameter can be used to determine to what type the method being called belongs. This allows for the creation of a single `System.StubProvider` implementation that can implement more advanced services that can be leveraged by unit tests without the need to write their own mock classes over and over. The playback of preconfigured responses to mocked methods and the recording of each method call it receives for later assertion is an example of this.

The concept of a **mocking framework** is not new. There are many well-established frameworks, such as the popular **Mockito** framework for Java or **Jasmine** for JavaScript/Node.js applications. However, mocking is a relatively new concept and capability in Apex, so there is an opportunity for building Apex-based mocking frameworks.

FinancialForce.com has published an open source mocking framework known as **ApexMocks**. While it predates the arrival of the Apex Stub API, it has been updated to work with this API. The advantage is that the code generator used to create the mock classes for use with Apex Mocks is no longer required, nor is the explicit use of Apex interfaces.

In the remainder of this chapter, we will review the benefits of a mocking framework through the use of the ApexMocks framework (now included in the sample code of this chapter). We'll apply it first to our sample `Car` class model and then to unit test scenarios from the FormulaForce application. A full walk-through is worthy of an entire book in my view. You can read more about ApexMocks through the various blog and documentation links on its README file: `https://github.com/financialforcedev/fflib-apex-mocks/blob/master/README.md`.

> Credit should be given to Paul Hardaker for the original conception and creation of ApexMocks. As an experienced Java developer coming to the platform and used to using Mockito, he was quickly driven to find out whether a similar unit testing facility could be created on the platform. Thus, ApexMocks inherits much of its API design from Mockito. Since then, the framework has gone from strength to strength and received several other submissions and support from the community, including presentations at Dreamforce. Much of what I know about the area of unit testing is also due to Paul's tutoring. Thank you!

Understanding how ApexMocks works

The `whenCarStartCalledDashboardAndEngineInitialised` unit test method in the `CarTestApexMocksDemo` test class uses the ApexMocks library. The structure of this unit test is similar to those we have looked at so far in this chapter. It creates the mocks, runs the method to test, and asserts the results.

The big difference is that you do not need to write any code for classes you wish to mock. Instead, you use the ApexMocks framework to configure your mock responses and to assert what methods were recorded. Then, through its integration with the Apex Stub API, it creates a stub that wraps itself around any class you wish to mock.

The main class within the ApexMocks framework is `fflib_ApexMocks`. This class implements the `System.StubProvider` interface for you. It automatically echoes any mock responses to mocked methods called and records that they got called and with what parameters. This applies to all public methods on the classes you ask it to mock for you.

Much of the skill in using ApexMocks is knowing how to configure the mocked responses it gives when mocked methods are called, and how to write matching logic to assert not only when a method was called, but how many times and with what parameters. This latter facility is incredibly powerful and opens up some sophisticated options for verifying the behavior of your code.

The following code initializes the ApexMocks framework (every test method needs this):

```
@IsTest
private static void
    whenCarStartCalledDashboardAndEngineInitialised() {
    fflib_ApexMocks mocks = new fflib_ApexMocks();
```

Next, create the mock implementations that you need:

```
// Given
Dashboard mockDashboard =
    (Dashboard) mocks.factory(Dashboard.class);   Engine mockEngine =
    (Engine) mocks.factory(Engine.class);
```

The following code replaces the need for you to write mock methods that return test values during the execution of the code being tested. In ApexMock terms, this configuration code is known as **stubbing** code. You must surround stubbing code with `startStubbing` and `stopStubbing` method calls, as shown here:

```
mocks.startStubbing();
mocks.when(mockEngine.isRunning()).thenReturn(true);
mocks.stopStubbing();
```

Unit Testing

> **TIP:** The syntax gets a little tricky to understand at this stage, but you will get used to it, I promise! As I stated earlier, much of the inspiration for the ApexMocks API was taken from the Java Mockito library. So much so that articles and documentation around the internet should also aid you in learning the API, as well as the documentation provided in the GitHub repo.

Your eyes are not deceiving you; the preceding code is calling the method you're attempting to mock a response for. First of all, this is a compile-time reference, so it is much safer than a late-bound string reference, as we used when using the Apex Stub API raw.

Secondly, because `mockEngine` points to a dynamically generated stub, it is not calling the real implementation of this method. Instead, it is registering in the framework that the next method call, `thenReturn`, should store the given value as a response to this method. This will be given back at a later point in the test when that mocked method is called again, this time in the test case context. In this case, when the `Car.isRunning` method calls `engine.isRunning` (refer to the `Car` code if you need to refresh your memory as to what the implementation does), it returns the value `true`.

The next part of the unit test, the actual code being tested, is more familiar:

```
// When
Car car = new Car(mockEngine, mockDashboard);
car.start();
```

Ensuring that the `dashboard.initialise` and `engine.start` methods have been called, as well as that the value returned by `Car.isRunning` is as expected, is also a little different from when calling the handwritten mock class methods:

```
// Then
System.assertEquals(true, car.isRunning());
((Dashboard) mocks.verify(mockDashboard, 1)).initialise();
((Engine) mocks.verify(mockEngine, 1)).start();
}
```

> Due to the explicit casting requirements of Apex, the last two lines do not quite match what you would see in an equivalent Java Mockito example. This can make the syntax harder to read. In Java Mockito, it would look as follows:
>
> ```
> mocks.verify(mockDashboard, 1).initialise();
> mocks.verify(mockEngine, 1).start();
> ```

[502]

The assertion code is a mixture of traditional `System.assert` and calls to the `fflib_ApexMocks.verify` method, followed by a call to the methods being mocked. Once again, this compiler-checked reference is preferable to late-bound string references.

The `verify` method takes an instance of the mocked object and number. This number allows you to assert that the method was called once, and only once. Once the `verify` method exits and the mocked method is called, the expected result passed to the `verify` method is checked. If it is not met, either because the method was not called, or it was called more than once, the framework actually has the mocked method use `System.assert` to halt the test with an exception message describing why.

Another example is the `whenUpdateRPMsCalledMessageIsDisplayed` test method in the `DashboardTestApexMocksDemo` class. This utilizes a more advanced form of asserting that the desired mocked method was called. This approach not only validates that it was called, but with specific parameter values:

```
@IsTest
private static void whenUpdateRPMsCalledMessageIsDisplayed() {
    fflib_ApexMocks mocks = new fflib_ApexMocks();
    // Given
    Display mockDisplay = (Display) mocks.factory(Display.class);
    // When
    Dashboard dashboard = new Dashboard(mockDisplay);
    dashboard.updateRPMs(5000);
    // Then
    ((Display) mocks.verify(mockDisplay, 1)).
        showMessage(10, 10, 'RPM:5000');
}
```

The preceding use of the `verify` method is no different from the previous test. However, the following mocked method call illustrates a very cool feature of the ApexMocks verification logic. The parameters passed in the call to the mocked method are used by the framework to compare with those recorded during the prior execution of the method during the preceding test. If any differences are detected, an assertion is thrown and the test is stopped.

> Some of the preceding examples include a `System.assert` method call inline. Other unit tests you write may not require the use of this statement as they solely assert that the correct dependent methods have been called through the `verify` method. This can lead to a false positive in the **Salesforce Security Review** scanner since the `verify` method is not recognized as a method verifying quality. If this happens, you can add a comment neutral assert to pacify the scanner, or record the reason why in the false-positive document you attach to the review.

ApexMocks Matchers

As you can see, there are two key parts to using ApexMocks—setting up the mocked responses through stubbing, and asserting the behavior through verification. Both these facilities support the ability to customize what mocked values are returned or what parameters are matched during the verification phase of the test.

For example, if the code you're unit testing calls a mocked method several times with different parameters, you can vary the mocked value returned using a convention known as a matcher during the stubbing phase of your test code.

> It is also possible to configure the framework's throwing of exceptions when mocked methods are called, if that is the desired test case you want to cover.

When asserting behavior, if you wish to check that a mocked method is called twice – once with a certain set of parameter values and a second time with a different set of parameters – then Matchers can be used to express this desired outcome. Matchers is an advanced feature, but well worth further investment in terms of the time it takes to learn.

ApexMocks and Apex Enterprise Patterns

As we saw earlier, the supporting library, or **Apex Enterprise Patterns**, provides methods that provide a dependency injection facility through the factories in the `Application` class. This facility is also compatible with the use of ApexMocks and the Apex Stub API. The following sections contain examples of the use of ApexMocks to unit test the layers within the application architecture introduced in earlier chapters.

Unit testing a controller method

The following test can be found in the `RaceControllerTest` class and demonstrates how to mock a service layer class:

```
@IsTest
private static void whenAwardPointsCalledIdPassedToService() {
    fflib_ApexMocks mocks = new fflib_ApexMocks();

  // Given
  RaceServiceImpl mockService =
       (RaceServiceImpl) mocks.factory(RaceServiceImpl.class);
  Application.Service.setMock(RaceService.class, mockService);
  // When
  Id raceId = fflib_IDGenerator.generate(Race__c.SObjectType);
  RaceController raceController =
     new RaceController(
        new ApexPages.StandardController(
           new Race__c(Id = raceId)));
raceController.awardPoints();
// Then
((RaceServiceImpl) mocks.verify(mockService, 1)).
       awardChampionshipPoints(new Set<Id> { raceId });
}
```

Consider the following notable aspects of the preceding test code:

- Controllers, in general, use only Service or Selector classes. It could be considered a code review discussion point if other classes are used. Perhaps the separation of concerns within the controller needs further review?
- This test simply creates a mock instance of the Service class and confirms the method was called with the correct parameter value from the controller. There is no mock response required. However, the ApexMocks framework does permit exceptions to be mocked. Thus, another test could be written to confirm that the error handling in the controller is working.

Unit testing a Service method

The following test method can be found in the `RaceServiceTest` class and demonstrates how to mock classes implementing the Unit Of Work, Domain, and Selector layers:

```
@isTest
private static void
    whenAwardChampionshipPointsCallsDomainAndCommits() {
```

Unit Testing

```
    fflib_ApexMocks mocks = new fflib_ApexMocks();
    // Given - Create mocks
    fflib_SObjectUnitOfWork mockUow = (fflib_SObjectUnitOfWork)
        mocks.factory(fflib_SObjectUnitOfWork.class);
    RacesSelector mockSelector = (RacesSelector)
        mocks.factory(RacesSelector.class);
    Contestants mockDomain = (Contestants)
        mocks.factory(Contestants.class);

    // Given - Configure mock responses
    Id testRaceId =
        fflib_IDGenerator.generate(Race__c.SObjectType);
    Id testContestantId =
        fflib_IDGenerator.generate(Contestant__c.SObjectType);
    List<Race__c> testRacesAndContestants = (List<Race__c>)
        fflib_ApexMocksUtils.makeRelationship(
            List<Race__c>.class,
            new List<Race__c> { new Race__c ( Id = testRaceId) },
            Contestant__c.Race__c,
            new List<List<Contestant__c>> {
                new List<Contestant__c> {
                    new Contestant__c (Id = testContestantId) } });
    mocks.startStubbing();
    mocks.when(mockSelector.SObjectType()).
        thenReturn(Race__c.SObjectType);
    mocks.when(mockSelector.selectByIdWithContestants(
        new Set<Id> { testRaceId })).
            thenReturn(testRacesAndContestants);
    mocks.when(mockDomain.SObjectType()).
        thenReturn(Contestant__c.SObjectType);
    mocks.stopStubbing();

    // Given - Inject mocks
    Application.UnitOfWork.setMock(mockUow);
    Application.Selector.setMock(mockSelector);
    Application.Domain.setMock(mockDomain);
    // When
    RaceService.awardChampionshipPoints(
        new Set<Id> { testRaceId });
    // Then
 ((RacesSelector) mocks.verify(mockSelector, 1)).
        selectByIdWithContestants(new Set<Id> { testRaceId }); ((Contestants)
mocks.verify(mockDomain, 1)).
        awardChampionshipPoints(mockUow);         ((fflib_SObjectUnitOfWork)
mocks.verify(mockUow, 1)).
        commitWork();
}
```

Consider the following notable aspects of the preceding test code:

- The `fflib_ApexMocksUtils.makeRelationship` method is used to construct in memory a list of records containing child records. This utility method (part of ApexMocks) works around a platform limitation in mocking this data construct. This method is very useful for returning more complex record sets returned from the Selector methods your tests are mocking.
- Prior to calling the `Application.Selector.setMock` and `Application.Domain.setMock` methods to inject the mock implementations of the `RacesSelector` and `Contestants` Domain classes, the mocking framework is used to mock responses to the `SObjectType` methods for the mocked instances of these classes, which is called by the `setMock` methods. Mocking this method ensures that the mocked Selector instance gets correctly registered with the Selector factory.
- The `fflib_IDGenerator.generate` method (part of ApexMocks) is used to generate an in-memory ID that is used to populate the mock records returned from the mock Selector. These same IDs are used to confirm that what was passed into the Selector is the same IDs that were passed to the Service method.
- The `Contestants` Domain class gained a default constructor, as required by the `Test.createStub` method, used by the `fflib_ApexMocks.factory` method.

Unit testing a Domain method

The following test method can be found in the `ContestantsTest` class and demonstrates mocking Selector method responses to return database rows created in memory. It tests that the same records are subsequently passed to a mocked Unit Of Work:

```
@IsTest
private static void whenAwardChampionshipPointsUowRegisterDirty() {
    fflib_ApexMocks mocks = new fflib_ApexMocks();
    // Given
    fflib_SObjectUnitOfWork mockUow = (fflib_SObjectUnitOfWork)
        mocks.factory(fflib_SObjectUnitOfWork.class);
    Application.UnitOfWork.setMock(mockUow);
    Id testContestantId =
        fflib_IDGenerator.generate(Contestant__c.SObjectType);
    List<Contestant__c> testContestants =
        new List<Contestant__c> {
            new Contestant__c (
                Id = testContestantId,
                RacePosition__c = 1 )};
```

```
    // When
      Contestants contestants = new Contestants(testContestants);
      contestants.awardChampionshipPoints(mockUow);
    // Then
      ((fflib_SObjectUnitOfWork)
          mocks.verify(mockUow, 1)).registerDirty(
            fflib_Match.sObjectWith(
              new Map<SObjectField, Object>{
                Contestant__c.Id => testContestantId,
                Contestant__c.RacePosition__c => 1,
                Contestant__c.ChampionshipPoints__c => 25} ));
}
```

Consider the following notable aspects of the preceding test code:

- An in-memory list of records is created in the test code and passed to the Domain classes constructor. The `awardChampionshipPoins` method being unit tested is then called to determine whether it correctly interacts with the Unit Of Work.
- A custom ApexMocks matcher is used to check that the `SObject` passed to the mocked `fflib_SObjectUnitOfWork.registerDirty` method is the expected method. The matcher also helps the test code confirm that the correct championship points have been calculated.
- As this test uses a mocked Unit Of Work, no DML is performed.

Unit testing a Selector method

The main logic to be tested by Selector methods is that of constructing SOQL strings dynamically. Ideally, it would be good if it were possible to mock the `Database.query` method and, thus, unit tests could be written around complex Selector methods to assert the SOQL strings generated. As this is currently not possible, there is little benefit in mocking Selector classes. Your Selector classes can instead obtain coverage and validation through their executions as part of your integration tests.

Unit testing with Lightning Web Components

In this section, we are going to build a unit test for the **Race Setup Lightning Web Component**. This component has a number of dependencies that need to be mocked in order to build a successful unit test that covers the component's HTML and JavaScript code. Here is a reminder of what the component looks like:

When the user selects drivers and clicks **Add Drivers**, a confirmation toast message is shown:

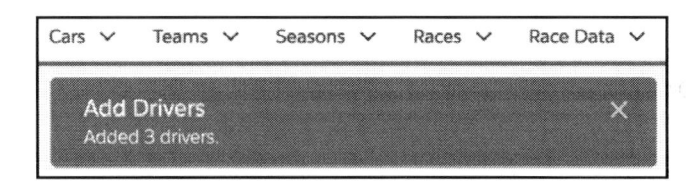

The **Race Setup** component uses a `lightning-table` child component defined in its HTML and methods from an Apex Controller `RaceSetupComponentController` class defined in its JavaScript controller. Lightning Web Components unit tests focus solely on the logic directly in the Race Setup component code (`raceSetup.html` and `raceSetup.js`) and no other concerns, thus, we will focus on testing the following behaviors:

- When the component has loaded, the list of drivers is correctly bound to the table.
- When **Add Drivers** is clicked, the correct drivers are passed to the Apex Controller.
- The correct toast and custom events are sent.
- When there are errors from the Apex Controller, the correct events are sent.

Unit Testing

In the following sections, we will learn the basics of setting up unit tests for Lightning Web Components within a Salesforce DX project and the layout of the test code. We will then look at mocking approaches to emulate the preceding dependencies to test the desired behaviors.

Introduction to unit testing with Lightning Web Components

Salesforce has fully embraced industry standards with Lightning Web Components and this has enabled the ability to leverage existing testing tools. Much like **Mockito** and **ApexMocks**, the **Jest** open source framework (https://jestjs.io/) for testing JavaScript code aims to make creating and configuring mocks as simple as possible, so your test code remains simple to read and, hence, easy to maintain. Salesforce has embraced this framework and extended it with some useful utilities and built-in mock implementations for its own components.

> The sample code for this chapter includes required Jest configurations and unit test code for the **Race Setup** component. Salesforce provides excellent documentation that describes how to set up your DX project to enable its use here (https://developer.salesforce.com/docs/component-library/documentation/lwc/lwc.testing). You should also take the time to review the excellent Jest documentation (https://jestjs.io/docs/en/api) as many of the methods used in this chapter are supplied by that framework.

You can run Jest-based tests from the following command line:

```
npm run test:unit
```

The test included in this chapter should output the following:

```
PASS  force-app/main/default/lwc/raceSetup/__tests__/raceSetup.test.js
 c-raceSetup
   ✓ displays drivers (47ms)
   ✓ add drivers success (186ms)
   ✓ add drivers fail (131ms)

Test Suites: 1 passed, 1 total
Tests:       3 passed, 3 total
Snapshots:   0 total
Time:        5.671s
Ran all test suites.
```

Chapter 12

As we did in the previous section, I always like to take a few moments away from the keyboard to think about the things I want to test and then plan out (often, in my head) the specific tests I will actually write. Each of the preceding three tests covers the behaviors listed, which we set out to cover in this Race Setup unit test.

As with Apex tests, the Jest tool automatically discovers your test code. The following code shows a cut-down version of the full test included in this chapter in order to illustrate the general structure of a test file, which is stored in the __tests__ sub-folder of the component code itself. You can name your test files anything you want, but it is best to follow a convention. Salesforce recommends suffixing the component name with .test.js:

```js
// raceSetup.test.js
import { createElement } from 'lwc';
import RaceSetup from 'c/raceSetup';

describe('c-raceSetup', () => {

    // Test: displays drivers
    it('displays drivers', () => {
        // Given
        // Then
        // When
    });
    // Test: add drivers success
    it('add drivers success', () => {
        // Given
        // Then
        // When
    });

    // Test: add drivers fail
    it('add drivers fail', () => {
        // Given
        // Then
        // When
    });
});
```

Unit Testing

In the following sections, we will go into more detail about each of the three preceding tests.

> In order to focus on the unique aspects of writing Lightning Web Components unit tests, **common boilerplate code is not referenced in this chapter**, but is included in the full sample code within `raceSetup.test.js`. Such code handles teardown after each class and some helper functions that encapsulate code that pauses the test code while asynchronous processing completes. These methods are described in full detail within the Salesforce documentation previously referenced.

Validating that the driver list is correctly bound to the table

In this test, we are focusing on validating the fact that a mocked list of drivers is correctly linked (bound) to the table child component. As a reminder, you will recall that this is actually achieved mostly through HTML code and some annotations in the JavaScript controller, as shown:

Here's a fragment from the `raceSetup.html` file:

```
<lightning-datatable
    key-field="RecordId"
    data={drivers.data}
    columns={columns}>
</lightning-datatable>
```

Here's a fragment from the `raceSetup.js` file:

```
import getDriverList from
    '@salesforce/apex/RaceSetupComponentController.getDriverList';

...

@wire(getDriverList)
drivers;
```

This might seem like a basic thing to write test code for, given that this component is quite simple, but imagine if you had more bindings and, thus, greater potential for the binding references and/or imports in the controller code to fall out of sync.

In order to write a unit test for the preceding, we need to use DI APIs to inject an alternative code path to actually go to the server and instead respond with a sample set of data. The first step is to define the sample (or mock data) and then inject it. The getDriversList.json file is stored in the data folder within the __test__ folder and looks like this:

```
[
    {
        "RecordId": "a015800000AmuwHAAR",
        "Name": "Lewis Hamilton",
        "Selected": false
    },
    {
        "RecordId": "a015800000AmuwMAAR",
        "Name": "Jenson Button",
        "Selected": false
    },
    {
        "RecordId": "a015800000AmuwRAAR",
        "Name": "Sergio Pérez",
        "Selected": false
    }
]
```

The preceding JSON must match the output from the Apex Controller method, `RaceSetupComponentController.getDriverList`. The JSON data reflects the structure of the `RaceSetupComponentController.DriverSelection` inner class.

When the Lightning framework observes the `@wire` annotation on the `drivers` property, it looks to see whether a response from the server has been injected by the test code. The following highlights the key steps to injecting a mock response from an Apex Controller:

```
// Step 1: the Apex Controller method is imported to the test code
import getDriverList from
    '@salesforce/apex/RaceSetupComponentController.getDriverList';

// Step 2: The sample data is read into the test code
const mockGetDriverList = require('./data/getDriverList.json');

// Step 3: The Salesforce registerApexTestWireAdapter method is
//    used to get a reference to a mock LWC write adapter
const getDriverListAdapter =
    registerApexTestWireAdapter(getDriverList);

// Step 4: Test code emits the mock response (emulating the server)
getDriverListAdapter.emit(mockGetDriverList);
```

Steps 1, 2, and 3 are defined outside of the specific test at the top of the test file. Step 4 is executed at the appropriate point in the test code itself. The following code shows the full test code and uses the Salesforce-provided `createElement` method (imported at the top of the test file) to create an instance of the component to test. This is appended into a test instance of the page managed by the Jest framework:

```
// Test: displays drivers
it('displays drivers', () => {

    // Given
    const element = createElement('c-raceSetup', {
        is: RaceSetup
    });

    // Then
    document.body.appendChild(element);
    getDriverListAdapter.emit(mockGetDriverList);

    // When
    return Promise.resolve().then(() => {
        const tableEl =
            element.shadowRoot.querySelector('lightning-datatable');
        expect(tableEl.data.length).toBe(mockGetDriverList.length);
    });
});
```

The industry standard `querySelector` method is used to obtain a reference to the mocked `lightning-datatable` instance, which is automatically set up for you. Finally, the `expect` method (provided by Jest at https://jestjs.io/docs/en/expect#expectvalue) is used to ensure that the number of records defined in the mock data shown above matches the number of table items as a result of the binding being tested. Notice that you did not have to mock the `lightning-datatable` component; this is handled for you by Salesforce.

Validating that the selected drivers are sent to the server

In this test, we are focused on validating the fact that whatever the user selected from the data table is processed correctly and results in an expected JSON request to the Apex Controller. Of course, the real Apex Controller code is not actually invoked; its mock is!

In this case, the code uses the ability of the **Jest framework** to record interactions with the mock object it creates and later allows test code to assert that expected parameters were passed. We will also be asserting that toast and custom events got sent by the code.

As a reminder, here is a shortened version of the **Race Setup** controller code this test will be testing. For the full version, review the `raceSetup.js` file in this chapter's sample code:

```
handleAddDrivers() {
    // Construct list of selected drivers
    var selectedRows = this.template.querySelector(
        'lightning-datatable').getSelectedRows();
    var selectedDrivers = [];
    selectedRows.forEach(element => {
        selectedDrivers.push(element.RecordId);
    });
    // Call Apex controller methods to add drivers
    addDrivers(
            { raceId : this.raceId,
              driversToAdd : selectedDrivers })
        .then(result => {
            // Send toast confirmation to user
            this.dispatchEvent(
                new ShowToastEvent({
                    title: 'Add Drivers',
                    message: 'Add ' + result + ' drivers.',
                    variant: 'success',
                }));
            // Send custom event
            this.dispatchEvent(
                new CustomEvent('added', { detail: result }));
        })
        .catch(error => {
            // Send toast confirmation to user
            this.dispatchEvent( ...
        });
}
```

There are two key dependencies in the preceding code that need to be mocked. The first is the `lightning-datatable` component and return value from the `getSelectedRows` method. The second is the call to the `addDrivers` Apex Controller method.

Unit Testing

Finally, we want to assert that the events resulting from the `dispatchEvent` method were fired with the expected arguments. Jest and Salesforce inject mocks for these dependencies for us; all we have to do is configure them and use the `expect` function to check the results. The following highlights the key steps to this process:

```
// Step 1: The Apex Controller method is imported to the test code
import addDrivers from
    '@salesforce/apex/RaceSetupComponentController.addDriversLwc';

// Step 2: Mock above the Apex Controller method adapter module
jest.mock(
    '@salesforce/apex/RaceSetupComponentController.addDriversLwc',
    () => {
        return {
            default: jest.fn()
        };
    },
    { virtual: true }
);

// Step 3: Setup a mock Apex response the test code expects
addDrivers.mockResolvedValue(MOCK_APEX_RESPONSE);

// Step 4: Setup mocked functions for event listeners
const showToastHandler = jest.fn();
const addedHandler = jest.fn();
element.addEventListener(ShowToastEventName, showToastHandler);
element.addEventListener('added', addedHandler);

// Step 5: Define a mock response for getSelectedRows
tableEl.getSelectedRows = jest.fn().mockReturnValue(SELECTED_ROWS);
```

Much of the **standard Jest API** is used in the preceding sample. The `jest.mock` method shown in step 2 mocks an `import` statement and is documented at https://jestjs.io/docs/en/jest-object#jestmockmodulename-factory-options. The `jest.fn` method is used to create a **JavaScript function** pointer that records all of the calls made to it for later reference by the test code using the `expect` method. `jest.fn` is documented at https://jestjs.io/docs/en/jest-object#jestfnimplementation.

Steps 1 and 2 are executed outside of the specific test code at the top of the test file. Steps 3, 4, and 5, as you can see here, are executed at the appropriate point in the test code itself. As before, the following code uses the Salesforce-provided createElement method to create an instance of the component to test, followed by mock configuration code and code to invoke the handler to simulate the user pressing the **Add Drivers** button:

```
// Test: add drivers success
it('add drivers success', () => {
    // Given
    const MOCK_APEX_RESPONSE = 2;
    const RACE_ID = 'a02580000050sJmAAI';
    const DRIVER1_ID = 'a015800000AmuwHAAR';
    const DRIVER2_ID = 'a015800000AmuwRAAR';
    const SELECTED_ROWS =
        [
            {
                "RecordId": DRIVER1_ID,
                "Name": "Lewis Hamilton",
                "Selected": true
            },
            {
                "RecordId": DRIVER2_ID,
                "Name": "Sergio Pérez",
                "Selected": true
            }
        ];
    const EXPECTED_APEX_PARAMETERS =
        {
            "raceId" : RACE_ID,
            "driversToAdd" : [DRIVER1_ID, DRIVER2_ID]
        };
    const showToastHandler = jest.fn();
    const addedHandler = jest.fn();
    const element = createElement('c-raceSetup', {
        is: RaceSetup
    });
    element.raceId = RACE_ID;
    element.addEventListener(ShowToastEventName, showToastHandler);
    element.addEventListener('added', addedHandler);
    addDrivers.mockResolvedValue(MOCK_APEX_RESPONSE);

    // Then
    document.body.appendChild(element);
    const tableEl =
        element.shadowRoot.querySelector('lightning-datatable');
    tableEl.getSelectedRows =
```

Unit Testing

```
            jest.fn().mockReturnValue(SELECTED_ROWS);
// When
const buttonEl =
    element.shadowRoot.querySelectorAll('lightning-button')[1];
buttonEl.click();
return flushPromises().then(() => {
    expect(addDrivers.mock.calls[0][0])
        .toEqual(EXPECTED_APEX_PARAMETERS);
    expect(addedHandler).toHaveBeenCalled();
    expect(showToastHandler).toHaveBeenCalled();
    expect(showToastHandler.mock.calls[0][0].detail.message)
        .toBe('Add ' + MOCK_APEX_RESPONSE + ' drivers.');
    });
});
```

The following are some key aspects of the preceding code to consider:

- Variables are used to clearly define test data that is used to both build mock responses and, later, to validate the fact that the mocked methods subsequently called received the same values. In other words, the logic correctly passed the inputs and outputs between the test and dependencies, such as the Apex Controller method calls.
- The standard `querySelectorAll` method is used to locate the mocked `lightning-button` component for the **Add Drivers** button. This is also automatically mocked by the framework, such that when the test code calls the `click` method, the `handleAddDrivers` method from the `raceSetup.js` file is invoked to start the test.
- The `expect` method leverages the Jest framework's ability to record interaction with mocked functions. For example, by using `.showToastEventHandler.mock.calls`, it checks the first invocation and the first parameter of the mock handler associated with the `ShowToastEvent` sent by the controller code. This confirms that the expected message contains the expected number of drivers. You can read more about the `.mocks.calls` property here: https://jestjs.io/docs/en/mock-function-api#mockfnmockcalls.
- The `flushPromise` method is a boilerplate method defined in the full version of this test, included in the sample code for this chapter. As noted previously, such boilerplate methods are described in more detail in the Salesforce documentation (https://developer.salesforce.com/docs/component-library/documentation/lwc/testing).

Summary

In this chapter, you learned that integration testing focuses on the scope of UIs or APIs exposed via your services to test the full stack of your code. It requires setting up the database, executing the code to be tested, and querying the database. These tests are critical to ensuring that all the components of your application deliver the expected behavior.

This chapter also introduced unit testing. Here, you learned that in order to make individual code components, classes, and methods as robust and future-proof as possible, developers can test each method in isolation without incurring the overhead of setting up the database or updating it. As such, unit tests run more quickly. Unit tests can increase coverage, as more corner-case testing scenarios can be emulated using the mocking of scenarios that would otherwise be impossible or difficult to set up on the database.

One key lesson of this chapter was that unit testing requires an understanding of some other patterns, such as dependency injection and mocking. Dependency injection can be implemented in a number of ways, using constructors, factories, and setter methods. The approach you use for dependency injection will depend on your personal preference and/or the preference of the libraries you're using. Multiple approaches to dependency injection can be combined if needed.

In this chapter, we learned that one way of implementing dependency injection is to use Apex interfaces. Utilizing multiple implementations of interfaces that represent the boundaries between the dependencies of your code base allows you to implement the real code and the test code separately. Mocking is most effective when the code being tested is not aware of which implementation is being used. We then looked at examples using the **Apex Stub API** and **Jest API** methods, which allow the creation of dynamic mocks for classes without using interfaces. The summary we arrived at was that the Apex Stub API is good for existing code bases or scenarios where using interfaces doesn't make sense or adds overhead.

This chapter also introduced **ApexMocks,** a mocking framework library that reduces the work involved in building mock objects, removing the need to physically code them. Based on Mockito, it offers advanced facilities to configure mocked method responses or throw exceptions to help test error handling. This framework also records the mock methods invoked and provides a sophisticated matching syntax to assert which methods were called. The Apex Commons open source library used in this book utilizes the factory pattern to provide built-in methods for injecting mock implementations of the Service, Unit Of Work, Domain, and Selector layers. Additionally, this chapter introduced **Jest,** which is a mocking framework library for **JavaScript** and has been embraced by Salesforce to aid in writing **Lightning Web Components** unit tests. Unit testing client components, in addition to traditional browser automation testing, has become important as richer user experiences have become common, which has necessitated more component-based thinking.

In summary, my advice is to appreciate that, in the end, unit testing and its associated prerequisites make it a difficult concept to master and requires a lot of work upfront. Start with a few simple examples at first and continue leveraging your existing testing approaches until you're ready to expand. Once you have mastered the APIs and best practice principles, it becomes second nature and can help open up access to other development coding practices, such as test-driven development.

In the next chapter of this book, we will take a step back and look at how to scale your development around multiple developers and set up the continuous and automated execution of your tests whenever changes are made.

13
Source Control and Continuous Integration

So far, we have been making changes in a scratch org for the **FormulaForce** application. This has worked well enough, as you're the sole developer in this case. However, when you add more developers and teams, other considerations come into play—mainly, the traceability of code changes and the monitoring of code quality as multiple streams of changes are merged together.

This chapter also sees packaging take on more of a prominent role. As discussed in Chapter 1, *Building and Publishing Your Application*, there is a need to create a beta or release package for your own internal testing and, of course, for the eventual release to your customers. Careful management of your release process is important to you and your customers if they want you to demonstrate compliance and auditability with respect to controls for your software development process and life cycle.

As the code base grows and the number of contributions to it (at any given time) increases, it's important to monitor the quality of the code more frequently. Finding out that your **Apex** or **Lightning Web Components** tests are failing prior to creating a package version is frustrating and costly when you're trying to release the software to your customers. **Continuous Integration** works with a **Source Control** system to validate the integrity and quality (through your tests) of your application on an automated basis, often triggered by developers committing changes to source control.

In this chapter, you will learn about the following topics:

- Developer workflow
- Developing with source control
- Hooking up to continuous integration
- Releasing from source control
- Automated regression testing

This chapter and, in fact, the entire book tries to avoid being biased toward a particular operating system and only includes tools that run on most popular systems. However, at times, certain keyboard references or CLIs are used that may assume macOS is being used.

Development workflow and infrastructure

A development workflow describes the day-to-day activities of a developer in order to obtain the latest build, make changes, and submit them back to a repository that maintains the current overall state of the source code. Having a solid, well-defined developer workflow, supporting tools, and infrastructure is critical to the efficiency of any development team.

The first thing a developer will want to know is where the source code is; basically, a source control system, such as **Git**. The next will be how to get it into a form that they can start executing, and then, of course, make changes to implement whatever feature they are working on.

Throughout this book, we have been using the **Salesforce DX CLI**; however, in this chapter, we will compose a number of commands together to automate some aspects you have been performing manually, such as checking code deploys and that all tests are passing. Such scripts are also used by continuous integration build servers described later in this chapter, in the *Hooking up continuous integration* section.

The Salesforce DX CLI also provides a means to extract from Salesforce org source files, which have all the components needed to represent your application in source form; not just Apex and Lightning Components source files, but XML files describing Custom Objects, fields, tabs, and practically any other component that can be packaged.

We will use the source code of this chapter to initially populate a Git repository with all the component files needed to manage further changes to the source code through your own source control system repository.

A big part of the development workflow is managing development environments. In the next section, we will revisit scratch orgs and what we have learned thus far about them.

Creating and preparing your scratch orgs

Salesforce DX allows you to tailor the scratch org configuration to ensure that the resulting org is of a specific org type (for example, Professional or Enterprise), as well as having various features enabled (for example, Chatter or Multi-Currency). This is intended to allow developers to develop and test an application in an environment as close as possible to that of the target customer.

Here is a reminder of what this might look like in a scratch org configuration file:

```
{
    "orgName": "FormulaForce App Testing with Multi Currency",
    "edition": "Enterprise",
    "features": ["MultiCurrency"]
}
```

In addition to the configuration of the org type and features, there are two other considerations that impact how the code runs once it is in its packaged form. These are the **namespace** and **ancestry** configurations. Configuring these is critical to ensuring you avoid namespace-related bugs or changes that could break your API contract from previous package versions. Finding these at this stage avoids delays later in the development cycle, or even customer issues once the application reaches your customers' orgs.

As a reminder, the namespace configuration goes into the `sfdx-project.json` file and uses the `namespace` configuration. It mainly ensures that, if you are writing code that dynamically instantiates classes or components, it is namespace-aware. You can see an example of this in the following code:

```
{
    "packageDirectories": [
        {
            "path": "force-app",
            "default": true
        }
    ],
    "namespace": "fforce",
    "sfdcLoginUrl": "https://login.salesforce.com",
    "sourceApiVersion": "45.0"
}
```

Careful use of the `ancestryId` setting ensures that, if you are making changes in a scratch org, the platform has the ability to inform you of changes that would break the backward compatibility of your next release; for example, deleting a field or object or changing the method signature of an Apex class method marked as global. Finding this out during development is much less stressful than doing so further down the road! The following sample shows how the `ancestorId` setting can be used:

```json
{
    "packageDirectories": [
        {
            "path": "force-app",
            "package": "FormulaForce App",
            "versionName": "ver 0.1",
            "versionNumber": "0.1.0.NEXT",
            "ancestorId": "05i6A000000XZLyQAO",
            "default": true
        }
    ],
    "namespace": "fforce",
    "sfdcLoginUrl": "https://login.salesforce.com",
    "sourceApiVersion": "45.0",
    "packageAliases": {
        "FormulaForce App": "0Ho6A000000CaVxSAK",
        "FormulaForce App@0.1.0-1": "04t6A0000038K3GQAU"
    }
}
```

The preceding JSON configuration shows how the `ancestorId` configuration can be used.

> **TIP**
> You do not have to test your application by creating a package in all cases, and if you did, this might result in a lot of test package versions in the system. By using the preceding configurations, you can effectively deploy your code in such a way that it behaves as if it had been deployed via a package.
>
> That being said, it can be worth considering the creation of a beta package from a stable build of your code at various intervals throughout your release development cycles. This grants you additional sanity and smoke testing ahead of your final upload process. The uploading and installation of packages can be automated via the Tooling and Metadata APIs.

In this chapter, we are going to create a Git-based source control repository using a free GitHub service. This chapter's sample code will be uploaded into that so we can explore working with source control to allow the tracking and audibility of changes in a more robust way than is permitted by simply storing your source files on your disk. We will then use this repository to populate new scratch orgs, make some changes, and commit those changes back to the repository. This is known as the **developer workflow**.

Understanding the developer workflow

There are many options when it comes to choosing an appropriate source control system in which to store your application code. In this book, we will use GitHub as a remote source control store and a local source control repository. The aim here is not to prescribe which tools to use, but to give a general walk-through of a Lightning Platform developer flow that you can adapt and explore different options within later. The following diagram illustrates the developer workflow that we will be walking through in this chapter:

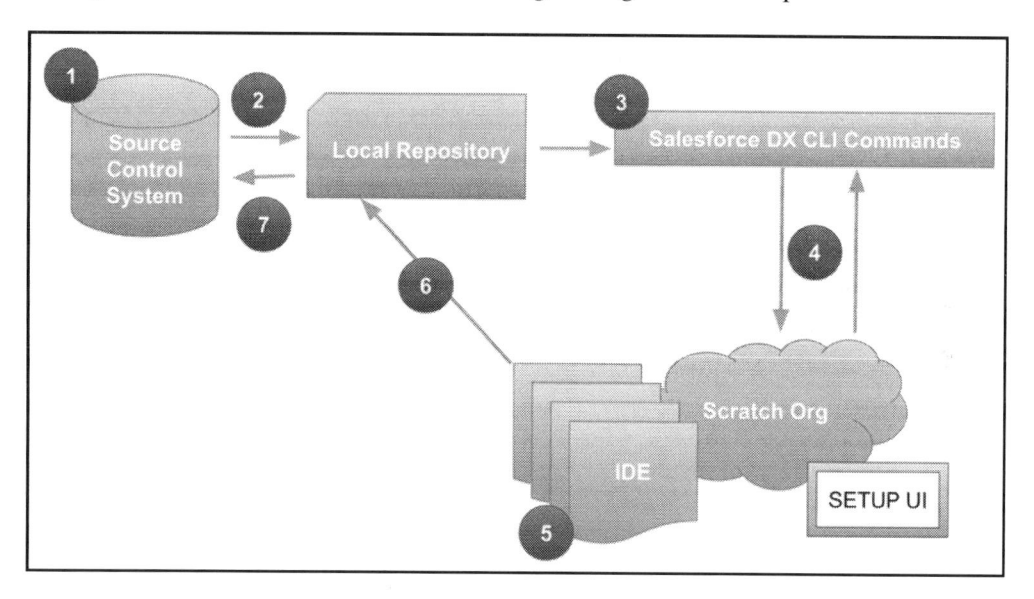

The following points relate to the preceding diagram:

1. Choosing a source control product and server is an important decision, for which you should consider security, accessibility, and durability. The source code of your application needs to be securely managed for only authorized personnel, ideally managed through clear processes in your business when employees arrive and leave. Where you choose to run your source control server also adds further importance to this; whether, for accessibility reasons, you choose to use one of the many cloud-based source control hosting services or indeed manage your own, for example via **Amazon EC2**. Perform durability tests from each location, ensuring that the server operates efficiently (developers hate waiting!). Finally, make sure that you have a backup and recovery process that is defined and tested, focusing on minimizing the downtime of your developers should the worst happen. The next section in this chapter will walk through populating a GitHub repository from the contents of our packaging org.

2. Populating a local repository with files stored in your source control server is the initial activity that most developers will perform. As described previously, this should be as efficient as possible. If you are using a cloud-based server, the amount of bandwidth needed to synchronize the remote and local repository is important. Some source control products offer more efficient implementations in this regard than others. Git is especially tailored for this kind of scenario, providing the ability to clone the whole or specific branches of the repository locally, complete with file history, followed by incrementally updating it as desired. Most common source control products offer excellent choices for the GUI as well as the standard command line interfaces.

> **TIP**
> In this chapter, we will use GitHub's Desktop GUI to clone the repository to a local folder ready for the next step in the developer flow.

3. The **Salesforce DX CLI** tool offers a good platform-neutral solution to making a standard build (deploy) script and other custom development tools you might want to build through its custom plugin technology known as **Oclif** (https://oclif.io/).

4. In its most basic form, the Salesforce DX CLI command—`sfdx force:source:push`—is used to deploy the content of the local repository to the default or given scratch. However, as we will discuss in the *Hooking up continuous integration* section, it also forms a part of your continuous integration solution. Typically, you would also run other commands to assign permission sets and load sample data. Some developers wrap these up in a shell script to save typing.
5. Once deployed to a scratch org, the tools used to develop on the Lightning Platform range from using combinations of the **Setup** menu, **Schema Builder** (often overlooked), **Developer Console**, and **VisualStudio Code with Salesforce Extensions** to other third-party IDEs that have emerged, such as **IlluminatedCloud**: `http://www.illuminatedcloud.com/`.
6. The key requirement is that once the developer is ready to submit to source control, there is the ability to synchronize the component files stored locally with the content of the scratch org. Most desktop-based IDEs provide a means to do this, though you can also leverage a Salesforce DX CLI command—`sfdx force:source:pull`—to do this manually.
7. Once files have been synchronized from the scratch org, the developer can use standard source control commit processes to review their changes and commit changes to the source control server (Git requires developers to commit to their local repository first). We will use the GitHub GUI for this. Later, in the *Hooking up continuous integration* section, we will see how this action can be used to automatically trigger a build that confirms that the integration of the developer's changes with the current state of the source control has not broken anything by automatically executing all Apex and Lightning Web Components unit tests.

> **TIP**
> More advanced developer flows can also utilize continuous integration to pre-validate commits before ultimately allowing developer changes (made to so-called feature branches) to be propagated or merged with the main branch. One such advanced flow is known as **GitFlow**, describing staged processing for code flowing from developer/feature branches to release branches. It was invented by **Vincent Driessen**. See his website for more information: `https://nvie.com/posts/a-successful-git-branching-model/`.

Note that it is only after *step 4* that a developer can actually start being productive, so it's worth ensuring that you check regularly with your developers that this part of the developer flow is working well for them. Likewise, step 5 is where most of their time is spent. Try to allow as much freedom for developers as possible to choose the tools that make each of them the most efficient but still work within the boundaries of your agreed development flow.

Debugging within SalesforceDX and Visual Studio code has been dramatically improved over the previous tooling. The standard debugging experience within Visual Studio Code has been adopted and can be used to debug live requests (a paid feature) or debug after a request has completed by leveraging debug logs to effectively replay the execution (a free feature).

Apex Replay Debugger is very easy to enable through the Command Palette by pressing *Shift + Cmd + P (Ctrl + Shift + P* on Windows) and searching for **Replay**. This will show the command to enable and disable it. Set breakpoints in the usual way by clicking in the Visual Studio Code gutter bar in the code editor. Perform whatever operation or test you want to debug and then use the Command Palette to search for the **Get Apex Debug Logs** command.

Once you have found the debug log (usually the first one), right-click on the log and click **SFDX: Launch Apex Replay Debugger with Current File**. You can then step through or click play until your breakpoint is hit. Use the debug view to inspect variables as you step through the code.

In this section, we focused on retrieving the code from source control, pushing it to a scratch org, synchronizing with the project on the developer's local disc and using some additional tools to aid in debugging it. Of course, the next step is to share their work back into a source control system so it can be further tested and, of course, integrated into the rest of the product to be shipped to customers. In the next section, we'll focus more on the source control workflow.

Developing with source control

Now that we understand the general developer flow a bit more, let's take a deeper dive into using some of the tools and approaches that you can use to share changes in source control. In this case, we will be using some specific tools to populate and manage the content of our chosen source control repository—**Git**. To provide an easy means to explore the benefits of a more distributed solution, we will use **GitHub** as a hosted instance of Git (others are available, including broader developer flow features). The following is a list of the tools that we will be using in this chapter:

- **GitHub**: Ensure that you have a GitHub account. Public accounts are free, but you can also use a private account for the purposes of this chapter. Download the excellent GitHub GUI for either: `https://desktop.github.com/`. This chapter will use the Mac edition, though not to the level that it will not be possible to find and perform equivalent operations in the Windows edition; both clients are really easy to use.

- **The Salesforce DX CLI**: If you have been following from the start of this book, you will have this already installed. Otherwise, download it at `https://developer.salesforce.com/platform/dx`.
- **Visual Studio Code with Salesforce extensions**: You can download this IDE at `https://code.visualstudio.com/download`. Once installed, search for the **Salesforce Extension Pack** extension and install it.

Now that we have established our tools, the following sections will walk through further details on using them and how they fit into the process of interacting with source control.

Populating your source control repository

A key decision when populating your source control repository is the folder structure. Often, this reflects what is optimal for your preferred IDE and related tools. The following table shows one folder structure that you might want to consider:

Folder	Purpose
`/`	Keep the content of the root as clean as possible. Some key files in the root will be the `sfdx-project.json` and `package.json` (if you have Lightning Web Components) files. You might also have a `README.md` file, which is a common Git convention to provide important usage and documentation links. This is a simple text file that uses a simple notation syntax (known as **MarkDown**) to represent sections, bold, italics, and so on. Later in this chapter, in the *Hooking up continuous integration* section, we will introduce `Jenkinsfile`, which configures the CI build system.
`/data`	This folder contains sample data files, in either CSV or JSON format. Developers can then use the various Salesforce DX CLI data commands to insert test or development data into the scratch org.
`/force-app`	This folder contains the standard Salesforce DX source format structure. Its initial structure is fixed, but you have the flexibility to move files around to group them according to feature or purpose. For example, the `/force-app/main/default/classes` folder uses a subfolder called `/libs` for the various open source frameworks used by this book's application. The `/force-app` folder can actually be renamed to anything you like so long as you update the `sfdx-project.json` file when you do so. You can also have multiple top-level source folders if desired, representing different packages in your solution.

Source Control and Continuous Integration

Folder	Purpose
/force-app /main /default /classes /lib	While SFDX provides a default folder structure, you can also customize it to place files in different folders to group them logically by function or a specific library that you are using. In this book, the /lib folder contains some open source libraries, for example. This is an easy practice for large packages. If you have multiple packages, you can use the packageDirectories configuration in the sfdx-project.json file to define multiple source folders, each representing its own package.
/config	As discussed in the previous section, you can set up and configure your scratch orgs to represent different environments using scratch org configuration files, which typically reside in this folder. You can name them anything you wish.

> If you want to follow through the steps in this chapter, follow the source code contained in the Chapter13 branch.

Perform the following steps to create the new repository and clone it in order to create a local repository on your computer to populate with initial content:

1. Log in to your GitHub account from your web browser and select the option from the dropdown from the + button to create a new repository:

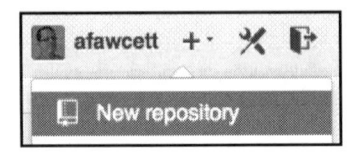

Also, select the option to create a default README file.

> **TIP**
> If you plan to try out the continuous integration steps later in this chapter, the easiest option with respect to the configuration at this point is to create a **public repository**. An in-depth walk-through on how to configure Jenkins authentication with GitHub is outside the scope of this chapter.

2. From the web browser project page for the new repository, locate the **Setup in Desktop** button on the right-hand side of the toolbar to open the GitHub desktop client and begin cloning the repository, or open the GitHub desktop client manually and select the **Clone to Computer** option.

3. The preceding clone process should have prompted you for a location on your hard drive in which the local repository is to be stored. Make a note of this location, as we will be populating this location in the following steps.

4. Copy the following files and folders from the sample code for this chapter into the repository folder:

   ```
   .forceignore
   .gitignore
   .prettierignore
   .prettiersrc
   config
   data
   force-app
   Jenkinsfile
   jest.config.js
   LICENSE
   package-lock.json
   package.json
   README.md
   sfdx-project.json
   ```

   You should see something like the following screenshot in your local repository folder:

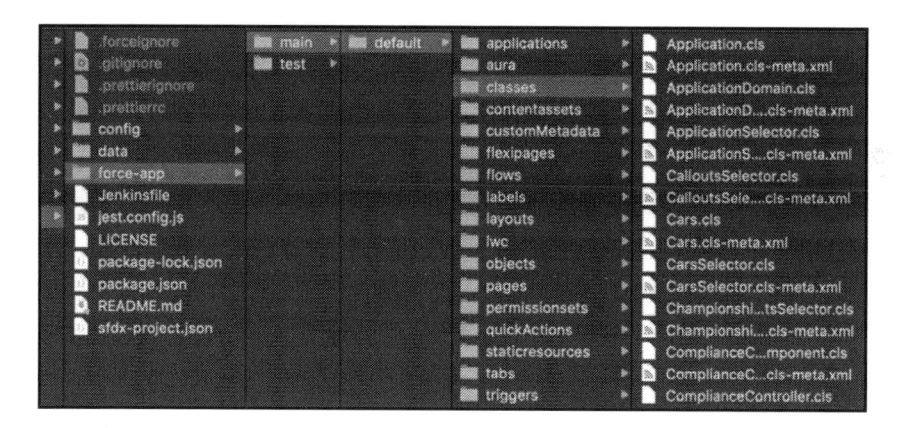

5. Finally, commit and sync the preceding changes to your local repository using the GitHub UI tool and push (to use the correct Git term). If you run the tool, you should see that it is already reporting that new files have been detected in the repository folder on your hard disk, as shown in the following screenshot of the Mac version of the tool.

Source Control and Continuous Integration

6. Now, simply enter a summary and description and click on **Commit to master**. This has committed changes to a local copy of the repository only. To share the files to the central repository, click the **Publish branch** button located at the top right of the screen, as shown in the following screenshot:

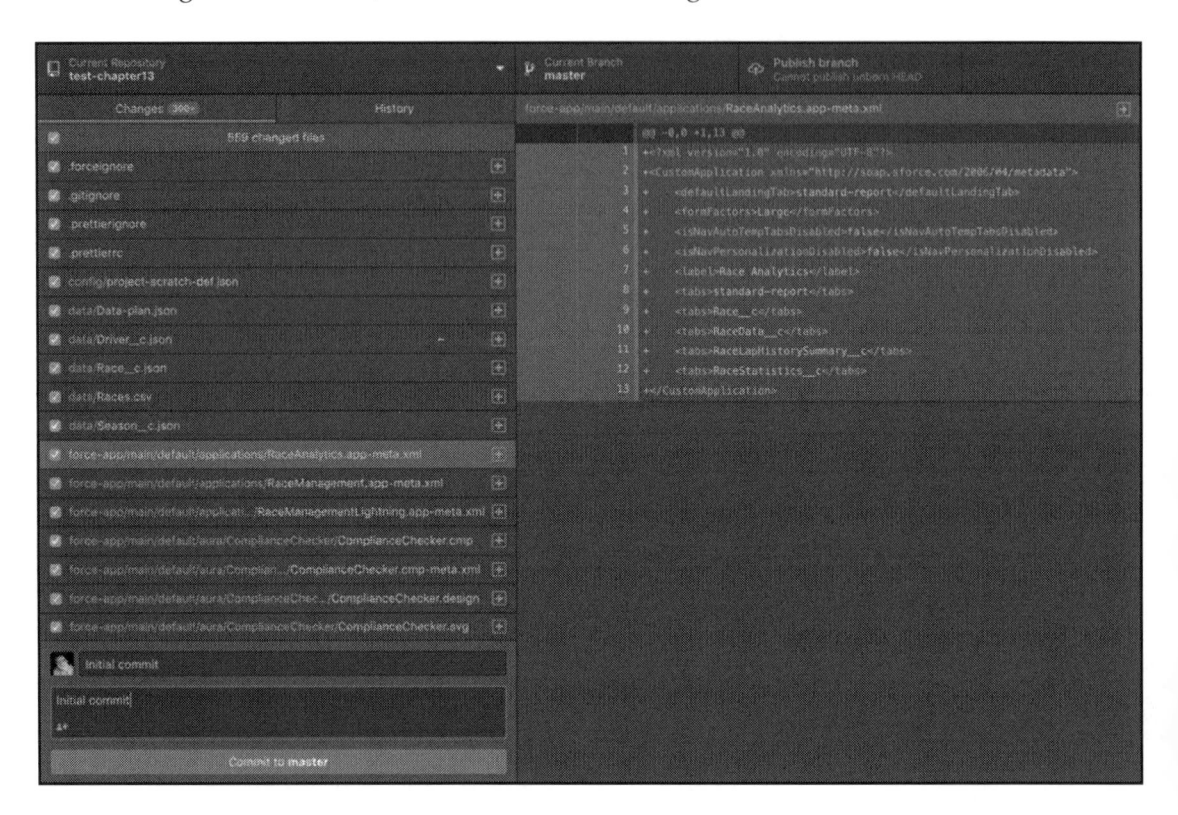

Note that what you just did was commit your changes to the local repository and push to the remote repository. Typically, developers work on a set of changes and commit them locally in increments, before deciding to push all changes as one operation to the remote repository. Developers can also use the local repository to roll back changes if desired.

If you're not familiar with Git, this might seem a bit confusing, as you have already physically copied or updated files in the repository folder. However, in order to push to the remote Git repository stored on the GitHub servers, you must first update a local copy of the state of the repository held in the `.git` folder, which is a hidden folder in the root of your repository folder. You should never edit or view this folder as it is entirely managed by Git.

Having safely stored your code in source control, in the next section, we will walk through the process of a new developer checking out (downloading) the application code for the first time and becoming productive in making changes as soon as possible.

Deploying the code from source control

Now that we have our initial source control content for the application created, you could safely delete your source code from your local machine and re-download it at any time by selecting the **Clone or Download** button in the GitHub browser UI.

Let's imagine you have just done that! How do you go from having nothing in Salesforce to something you can start developing with? If you have been following along since Chapter 1, *Building and Publishing Your Application*, then you will have used the following commands already. The following is a reminder of them all together (enter them all as one line if you want to try them out):

```
sfdx force:org:create
   --definitionfile config/project-scratch-def.json --setalias dev
   --durationdays 7 --setdefaultusername --json

sfdx force:source:push

sfdx force:user:permset:assign
   --permsetname FormulaForceRaceManagement

sfdx force:data:tree:import --plan ./data/Data-plan.json

sfdx force:org:open
```

The preceding commands can get repetitive, so you may want to write a **shell script** or **Batch File** if you are using Windows to automate them for your developers. Typically, this is called `setup.sh`, or `setup.bat` for Windows.

Congratulations—you have now taken the first step in utilizing source control! This also means that you can now allow other developers to start working independently on your code base by following the same developer flow using their own developer orgs.

Salesforce does not automatically grant access to applications, tabs, pages, objects, and fields deployed using the `sfdx force:source:push` command. So, you will find that before you can see these components, you need to assign your Permission Sets to your developer org user. Doing this is a good way to ensure that these are kept up to date with new components and are valid.

In general, testing as a **system administrator** is not a reliable confirmation of your application working in an end user scenario. This is why Salesforce has adopted this policy, to make the developer think about which permissions need to be applied, even in a developer org.

Developing in scratch orgs with a namespace

As previously mentioned, it's a good idea to avoid hardcoding the namespace in your code, so that you can move the code between packages or reuse it in non-packaged situations. When making explicit references, the Apex compiler avoids the need for this and infers the namespace reference required.

However, Apex that utilizes Dynamic Apex to create and populate SObject instances and fields through the `SObject.get` and `SObject.put` methods will need to dynamically apply the namespace prefix. The following code snippet is a good way to determine whether the code is running in a namespace context. You can place this in a test utility class, as shown here:

```
DescribeSObjectResult seasonDescribe =
    Season__c.SObjectType.getDescribe();
String namespace =
    seasonDescribe.getName().
    removeEnd(seasonDescribe.getLocalName()).
    removeEnd('__');
```

Apex tests that utilize `Type.forName` to create instances of Apex classes (for example, a test written for an application plugin feature) will also need to dynamically apply the namespace prefix to the class name given to the plugin configuration (such as the Custom Metadata type featured in `Chapter 10`, *Providing Integration and Extensibility*).

Leveraging the Salesforce REST APIs from the SFDX CLI and custom plugins

Under the hood, the Salesforce DX CLI code uses the Metadata and Tooling APIs. While most of what these APIs have to offer is exposed through the Salesforce CLI commands for easier access, there are times when you want to automate other tasks using features of these APIs and others. This section provides an overview of two approaches to building your own tools.

Firstly, you may want to simply consider writing **Shell** (Unix/Mac) or **Batch File** (Windows) scripts. The following commands are useful when writing such scripts:

- `force:data:soql:query`: Use this command to query records from standard and Custom Objects. You can also use `--toolingapi` to query objects exposed via the Tooling API.
- `force:apex:execute`: Use this command to run some Apex code.
- `force:schema:sobject:list`: Use this command to list Custom Object details such as fields.
- `force:schema:sobject:describe`: Use this command to list all object information.

All of the preceding commands support the `--json` parameter, which enables your scripts to parse the output of the commands more easily. A key utility for doing this is `jq`, a lightweight command line JSON parser (https://stedolan.github.io/jq/). The following shell script uses the `jq` command to obtain the results from a SOQL query:

```
accountName=$(sfdx force:data:soql:query -q "select Name from Account" --json | jq .result.records[0].Name -r)
echo ${accountName}
```

Sometimes, you need a more flexible and sophisticated programming language than shell scripts. While you can use the Metadata and Tooling APIs from programming languages such as **Node.js** or **Java**, you will have to write some boilerplate code to authenticate with the scratch org and also parse the command line parameters, not to mention giving a good usage summary.

The **Salesforce DX Plugin** architecture enables you to write your own commands easily. Using this architecture, Salesforce has saved you the trouble of writing boilerplate code by open sourcing the same framework they use to build their own CLIs—it is called **Oclif** (https://oclif.io/).

By using the Oclif framework, you can get straight to defining your parameters and then using them to directly access the desired APIs via a provided authentication context established by the framework for you. This will generate usage output for your command and even supports popular command line autocomplete integrations. It is really a great accelerator for writing your own custom CLIs for Salesforce.

Source Control and Continuous Integration

To get started, you run the following command with the name of your new plugin:

```
sfdx plugins:generate awesomeplugin
```

> **TIP**: If you receive the `Please install yarn with npm install -g yarn and try again` error, then run the command included in the error message and retry the preceding command.

This outputs the following files:

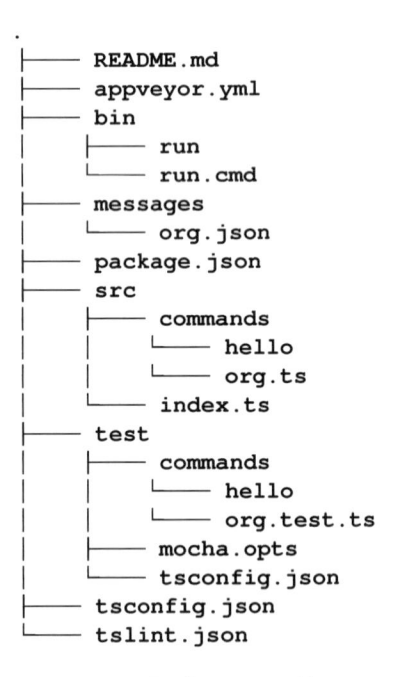

```
.
├── README.md
├── appveyor.yml
├── bin
│   ├── run
│   └── run.cmd
├── messages
│   └── org.json
├── package.json
├── src
│   ├── commands
│   │   └── hello
│   │       └── org.ts
│   └── index.ts
├── test
│   ├── commands
│   │   └── hello
│   │       └── org.test.ts
│   ├── mocha.opts
│   └── tsconfig.json
├── tsconfig.json
└── tslint.json
```

As you can see in the preceding output source files, the framework uses **TypeScript**, a type-safe version of the **JavaScript/ECMAScript** programming language. The folder structure helps define the command names, and the default generated command is `hello:org`.

The `org.ts` file contains a definition of the parameters, as shown:

```
name: flags.string({char: 'n', description: 'Name parameter'}),
force: flags.boolean({char: 'f', description: 'Force parameter})
```

Later in the `org.ts` file, you can see that it makes a query using the `conn` variable:

```
const conn = this.org.getConnection();
const query = 'Select Name, TrialExpirationDate from Organization';
const result = await conn.query<Organization>(query);
```

A full walk-through of Salesforce DX plugins is outside the scope of this book, though there is a wealth of information and examples to be found from making reference to the *Getting Started* guide at `https://oclif.io/docs/introduction`. You should also make reference to the *Salesforce CLI Plug-In Developer Guide* at `https://developer.salesforce.com/docs/atlas.en-us.sfdx_cli_plugins.meta/sfdx_cli_plugins/cli_plugins.htm`. In the next section, we will discuss how file changes are submitted back to source control.

Updating your source control repository

At this stage, you have a source control repository and you can deploy its contents to a scratch org. As you locally edit source files such as Apex classes using the Visual Studio Code editor window and save those changes, they become candidates to submit to source control. Visual Studio automatically tracks such changes, as does the GitHub desktop client. In this section, we will take a brief look at how this works.

Keep in mind when developing on the Lightning Platform that you can also use the **Setup** menu in your scratch org to make changes, such as creating objects or fields or editing layouts. In this case, those changes will not be visible to source control until you perform `sfdx force:source:pull`. Browser-based tools, such as the **Setup** menu and **Schema Builder**, provide an easier way of editing **Custom Objects**, **Fields**, **Layouts**, and **Permission Sets** than their XML-based formats. However, for other aspects of development, the browser-based developer console is not to everyone's liking when it comes to editing Apex and Visualforce code. I personally prefer a desktop tool such as Visual Studio Code to edit these types of files.

In the next section, we will discuss how to control what files are updated or created when you pull changes made by using the **Setup** menu in your scratch org.

Controlling what gets pulled down locally from your org

Once the `sfdx force:source:pull` command completes, you can use the Git tools to review changed files, accepting, ignoring, or discarding (reverting back to the last committed version) accordingly. These are some use cases you might encounter with this approach and ways to handle them:

- **Additional files downloaded**: Sometimes, you are not interested in certain **Setup** menu-driven changes being reflected on your local filesystem. For example, if you have embraced Permission Sets, you want to explicitly ignore Profile metadata. To enable this, you should use the `.forceIgnore` file. The one used in this chapter's sample code has the following entry in it: `**/profiles/**`.

- **Differences in file content order or additional elements**: Sometimes, file changes are flagged up by the Git tools when you have not directly made modifications to the corresponding component in the browser tools. This can be the case after a platform upgrade when new features arise or an org-wide configuration change is made (such as switching on Multi-Currency support), or on occasions when the order of the XML elements has changed, but the overall effect on the object is the same. If you experience these changes often and they result in a change that you're happy to accept, it can be tempting to initially accept them, such that fewer false differences appear in the future. However, don't let such browser-based development differences go unexplained; the root cause could be quite important! The use of different org types or org templates between developers can also result in this type of issue. Ensure that all developers are sourcing their developer orgs from the same sign-up page and are of the same org type.

Now that you understand what you do and do not want to share, the next step is committing your changes to source control. There are a number of ways to do this that are offered by Git and related desktop applications referenced earlier.

Managing local files and committing to source control

One of the key benefits of desktop-based tools and source control is that they allow you to edit the Lightning Platform source files while synchronizing with both source control and an attached scratch org. By default, you must use the **push** or **pull** commands to perform this manually based on changes you make either locally or in the org via the **Setup** menu. There are also many other benefits, such as code completion and the Apex Replay Debugger.

Chapter 13

In the **Visual Studio Code IDE**, the default is not to automatically push to the attached scratch org each time a file, such as an Apex class, is saved. To change this, go to **Code | Preferences | Settings**, search for push-or-deploy-on-save, and tick the box to enable the push on save feature. So long as you are editing files from the local repository folder location, file edits are automatically seen by the source control system, which, in our case, is Git.

The **Visual Studio Code IDE** and **GitHub** desktop applications automatically recognize changes to your files and offer a convenient way to commit your changes without having to understand the Git command line interface. The following shows how file changes appear in Visual Studio Code, along with the ability to enter a commit message and commit the changes (the tick icon):

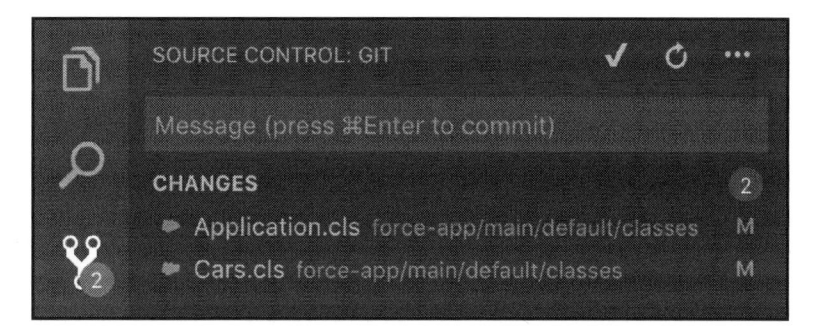

SOURCE CONTROL: GIT   ✓ ⟳ •••

Message (press ⌘Enter to commit)

CHANGES   2
  ● Application.cls force-app/main/default/classes   M
  ● Cars.cls force-app/main/default/classes   M

The preceding screenshot shows two files that need to be committed to source control.

> Visual Studio Code Salesforce Extensions creates two folders to store temporary files. These are /.sfdx and /.vscode. You can use the .gitignore facility to omit these from source control visibility.

As an alternative to making changes under **Setup** and performing `sfdx force:source:pull`, you are also able to edit files that represent Custom Objects and fields, but if you do, make sure to push your changes through the SFDX CLI `sfdx force:source:push` command or the Command Palette shortcut. The XML representation of the **Driver** Custom Object is shown in the following screenshot:

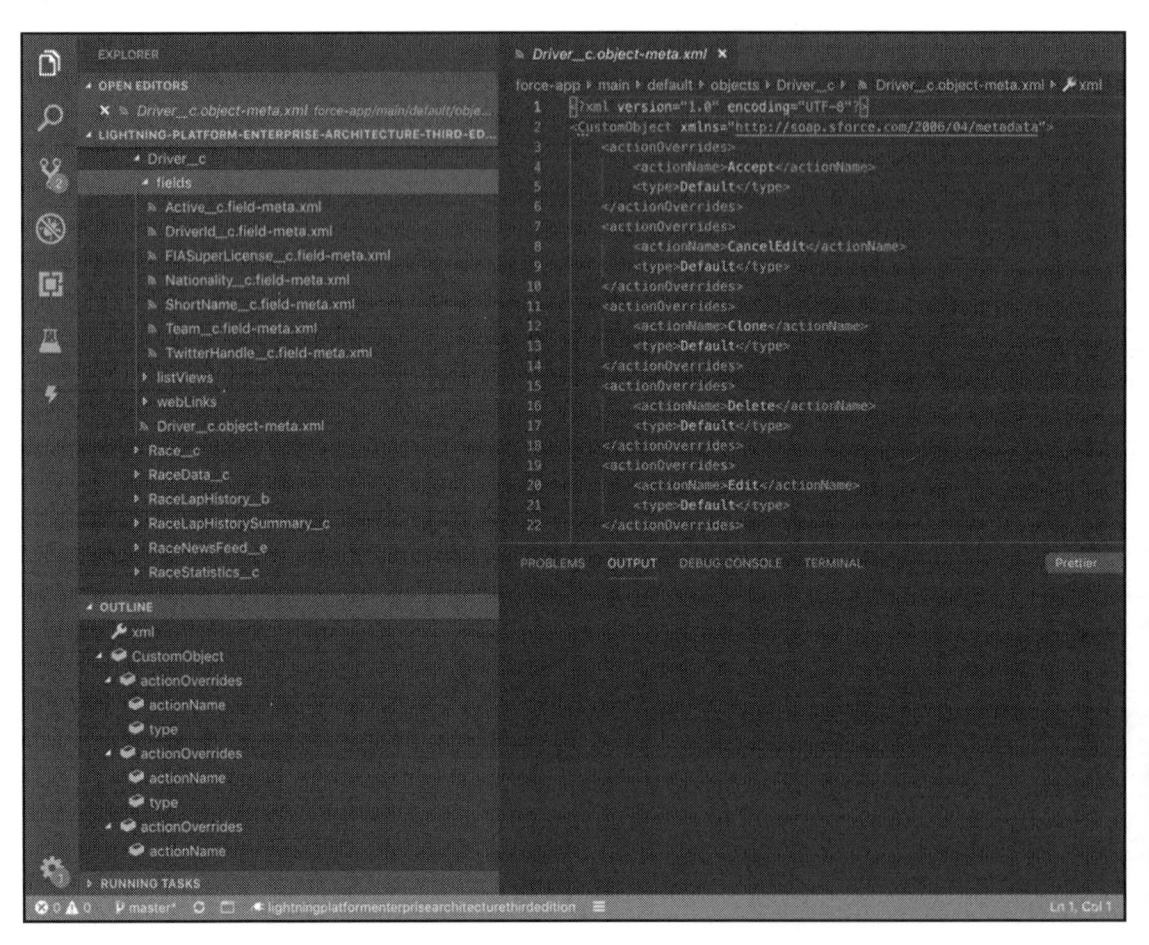

Finally, do keep in mind that you need to be a good developer and run your tests before committing your changes. Developing and running tests for Apex and Lightning Web Components was discussed in `Chapter 12`, *Unit Testing*.

In the next section, we will see how we can automate the deployment process, including the running of tests as developers contribute their changes. Despite running tests locally, this may have been on an older version of the code base, hence, running tests on the latest version of the code is critical.

Hooking up continuous integration

So far, we have been depending on the developer to ensure that the changes they push to the GitHub remote repository do not cause regressions elsewhere in the application. However, this is not always a fully reliable means of determining the quality of the code, as the main code base will likely have moved on due to other developers also pushing their changes. When integrated together, they might cause tests or even code to fail to compile.

Continuous integration monitors changes to the source control repository and automatically starts its own build on the fully integrated source code base. Failures are reported back to the developers who last pushed code to the repository.

In this part of the chapter, we are going to explore this process using the popular Jenkins Continuous Integration server, which uses a script that is also stored in source control to perform the build and test steps. Before we get into setting this up, let's take a moment to review the Continuous Integration (CI) process that we are going to use.

Using continuous integration to maintain code health

The following diagram shows the CI process that we will be setting up over the course of the next few sections. Once you have a basic CI setup like this, you can start to add other features, such as code documentation generation, static code analysis, a security code scanner, and automated regression testing (something we will discuss briefly later on):

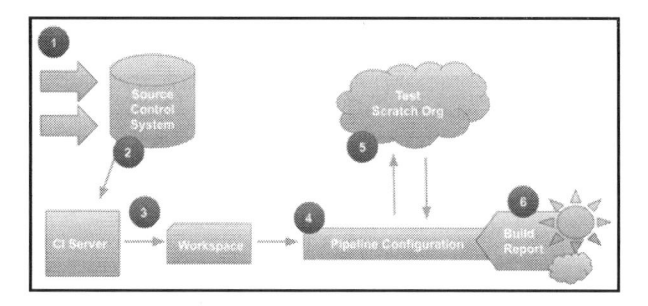

The following is the CI process:

1. Developers make multiple contributions to source control, just as we did earlier in this chapter, via the GitHub UI desktop client.
2. The CI server is able to poll, when configured to do so, the source control server (in our case, the GitHub remote repository) for changes.

3. Once changes are detected, it downloads the latest source code into a local workspace folder.
4. A part of the configuration of the CI server is to inform it of the location of the `Jenkinsfile` script to execute after the workspace is set up. This file is included in the sample code for this chapter and will be discussed in more detail later in this chapter.
5. A scratch org is dynamically created and set aside solely for the use of the CI process job. It is important to also explicitly delete these scratch orgs as part of this process since there is, by default, a limited number of active scratch orgs allowed by Salesforce. This limit includes those used by developers as well.
6. Finally, the CI server will record the log and results of the build for analysis, and the number of successful versus failed builds, and provide reports and notifications on the overall health of the source code in source control. If there are failures, there are options to email certain team members as well as specific targets (those who made the most recent changes). Making sure a team stops what they are doing and attends to a broken build is very important. The longer broken builds exist, the harder they are to solve, especially when further changes occur.

The preceding process is a high-level overview of continuous integration. In the next section, we will walk through this in more detail, using a Jenkins CI server.

Introducing the Jenkinsfile for CI

The term "pipeline" is used in a CI server to describe the steps used to process the source code, from building it and testing it, to eventually deploying it to production. In the case of a packaged application such as this one, you may want to manage the deployment to production separately, though it is technically feasible to use the Package Push API to automate your package releases to your customers.

For this section, we will focus on the build and testing part of the pipeline, using a script file known as `Jenkinsfile`. This uses the **Groovy programming language** (http://groovy-lang.org/syntax.html) to define the stages in the pipeline to perform and how they interact with the **Salesforce DX CLI**. It is common for CI servers to provide visualizations of such pipelines. The following screenshot shows the pipeline we will be focusing on in this section:

Chapter 13

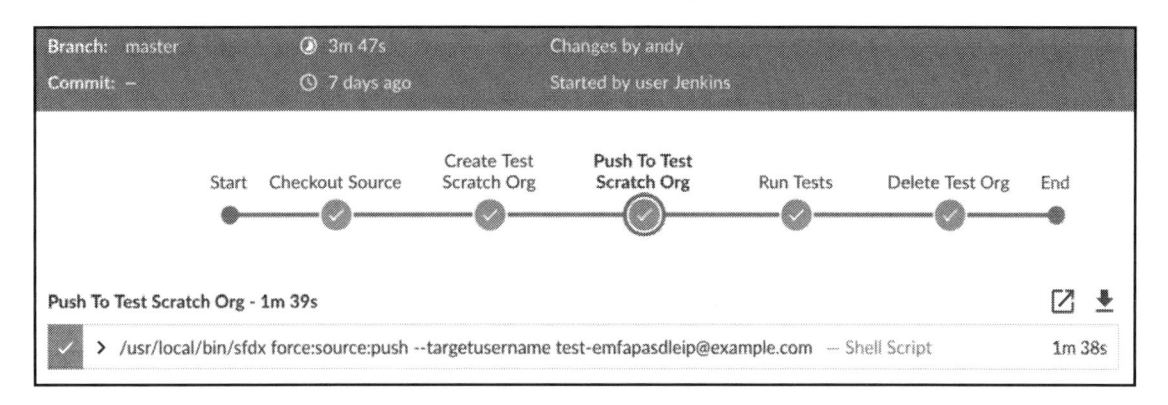

![Jenkins pipeline screenshot showing stages: Start, Checkout Source, Create Test Scratch Org, Push To Test Scratch Org (currently running), Run Tests, Delete Test Org, End. Push To Test Scratch Org - 1m 39s, running /usr/local/bin/sfdx force:source:push --targetusername test-emfapasdleip@example.com]

The preceding screenshot shows that the **Push to Test Scratch Org** step is currently running.

> **Source-driven configuration.** If you have used CI servers in the past, you might be familiar with configuring the preceding pipeline manually through the setup screens your CI server provides. Due to the ever-growing complexities of managing cloud-based configurations, it has become popular to store configuration in the form of source code. This allows a UI to generate the source code driving the pipeline and also provides the same benefits in terms of revision control and reuse experienced when developing the application code itself.

In the following code snippet, the Jenkins file included in the root of the sample code folder for this chapter is shown. The preceding stages and the Salesforce DX commands embedded within it are shown in bold:

```
#!groovy
import groovy.json.JsonSlurperClassic
node {

    // Test Scratch Org Username
    def SFDC_USERNAME

    // Path to SFDX CLI (configured via Custom Tools)
    def toolbelt = tool 'toolbelt'

    stage('Checkout Source') {
        checkout scm
    }

    withCredentials([file(
        credentialsId: env.JWT_CRED_ID_DH,
        variable: 'jwt_key_file')]) {
```

[543]

Source Control and Continuous Integration

```
stage('Create Test Scratch Org') {

    // Authorizate with DevHub via JWT grant
    rc = sh returnStatus: true,
        script: "${toolbelt}/sfdx force:auth:jwt:grant
            --clientid ${env.CONNECTED_APP_CONSUMER_KEY_DH}
            --username ${env.HUB_ORG_DH}
            --jwtkeyfile ${jwt_key_file}
            --instanceurl ${env.SFDC_HOST_DH}"
    if (rc != 0)
        { error 'hub org authorization failed' }

    // Create Scratch Org and determine login username
    rmsg = sh returnStdout: true,
        script: "${toolbelt}/sfdx force:org:create
            --targetdevhubusername ${env.HUB_ORG_DH}
            --definitionfile config/project-scratch-def.json
            --json"
    def robj = new JsonSlurperClassic().parseText(rmsg)
    if (robj.status != 0)
        { error 'org creation failed: ' + robj.message }
    SFDC_USERNAME=robj.result.username
}

stage('Push To Test Scratch Org') {

    // Push code via sfdx force:source:push
    rc = sh returnStatus: true,
        script: "${toolbelt}/sfdx force:source:push
            --targetusername ${SFDC_USERNAME}"
    if (rc != 0) {
        error 'push failed'
    }
}

stage('Run Tests') {

    // Create test output directory, run tests
    sh "mkdir -p tests/${env.BUILD_NUMBER}"

    // Run Apex Tests
    rc = sh returnStatus: true,
      script: "${toolbelt}/sfdx force:apex:test:run
         --testlevel RunLocalTests
         --outputdir tests/${env.BUILD_NUMBER}
         --resultformat junit
         --targetusername ${SFDC_USERNAME}"
```

```
            // Run Lightning Web Component Tests
            env.NODEJS_HOME = "${tool 'node'}"
            env.PATH="${env.NODEJS_HOME}/bin:${env.PATH}"
            sh 'npm install'
            rc = sh returnStatus: true, script: 'npm run test:unit'
            // Have Jenkins capture the test results
            junit keepLongStdio: true,
                testResults: 'tests/**/*-junit.xml'
            junit keepLongStdio: true,
                testResults: 'junit.xml'
        }

        stage('Delete Test Org') {

            // Delete Test Scratch Org
            rc = sh returnStatus: true,
                script: "${toolbelt}/sfdx force:org:delete
                    --targetusername ${SFDC_USERNAME}"
            if (rc != 0) {
                error 'org delete failed'
            }
        }
    }
}
```

A full walk-through of the **Jenkinsfile** syntax is outside the scope of this chapter. Extensive documentation can be found online (https://jenkins.io/doc/book/pipeline/syntax/). The following are some key aspects to consider from the preceding pipeline configuration in respect of Salesforce DX integration:

- When you first started using Salesforce DX in Chapter 1, *Building and Publishing Your Application*, you had to manually **authorize with your Salesforce DX Dev Hub** org by responding to the usual login page from Salesforce with your username and password. In this case, the authorization is automated via the JWT authorization process and the sfdx force:auth:jwt:grant command. This command does not require the CI server to know a username and password for the Dev Hub (a good security practice). Instead, it uses a **private certificate** to identify itself. The configuration of this will be discussed further in the next section.
- Commands are run via the sh command. The sh command returns the numeric value of 0 for success; all other values represent a failure of some kind.

Source Control and Continuous Integration

- Salesforce DX commands can return **JSON-formatted responses** through the use of the `--json` parameter. The `sh` command returns this into a variable for the Groovy code to parse and extract details such as the username of the scratch org. This username is used later in the pipeline to deploy the code and run tests.
- Both the **Apex and Lightning Web Components test executions** are configured to output test results in **JUnit XML format**. The built-in `junit` command is then used to channel this information into a single test results page, shown as follows.
- Finally, the scratch org is explicitly deleted.

The following screenshot shows how the test results have been integrated into the Jenkins CI UI. We will see later in this chapter how test failures are presented:

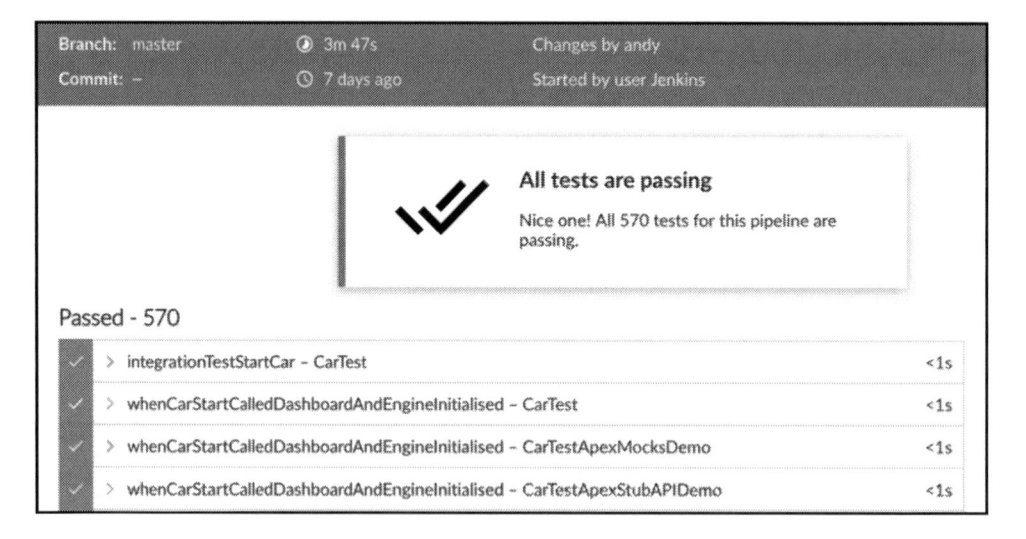

| Branch: | master | 3m 47s | Changes by andy |
| Commit: | – | 7 days ago | Started by user Jenkins |

All tests are passing
Nice one! All 570 tests for this pipeline are passing.

Passed - 570

> integrationTestStartCar – CarTest		<1s
> whenCarStartCalledDashboardAndEngineInitialised – CarTest		<1s
> whenCarStartCalledDashboardAndEngineInitialised – CarTestApexMocksDemo		<1s
> whenCarStartCalledDashboardAndEngineInitialised – CarTestApexStubAPIDemo		<1s

In the next section, we will go through the steps to set up the GitHub repository you created earlier in this chapter with the preceding pipeline configuration.

Installing, configuring, and testing a Jenkins CI server

Setting up a Jenkins server is a broad topic beyond the scope of this chapter. A good way, however, to get started on your local computer is to go to `http://jenkins-ci.org/` and download one of the prebuilt installations for your operating system.

In this case, I used the Mac `pkg` file download. Select the most common plugins during the installation process, as this includes the Pipeline feature and Groovy programming language integration previously described. After installation, I was able to navigate to `http://localhost:8080` to find Jenkins waiting for me, as shown here:

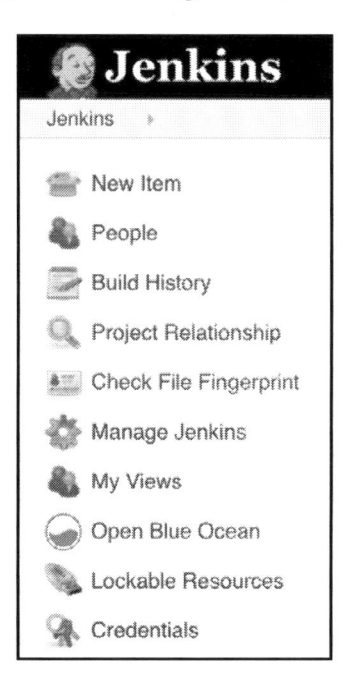

Jenkins has a plugin system that permits many custom extensions to its base functionality, by clicking on **Manage Jenkins** and then **Manage Plugins.** Install the following plugins:

- **Blue Ocean** provides the pipeline UI shown in the previous section.
- **Custom Tool** allows you to integrate the Salesforce DX CLI.
- **Node.js** allows you to run `npm` and other commands from Jenkinsfiles.

Since you already have a Jenkinsfile in the repository you created earlier, the process to actually create a working pipeline is quite straightforward as Jenkins will auto detect the file and create the necessary jobs to run your pipeline.

Source Control and Continuous Integration

> Even though much of the configuration is encapsulated in the Jenkinsfile, there is still some **further configuration to be performed that is not covered in this book**. This configuration is done at a server level so that it is shared by other pipelines. It includes ensuring that Jenkins knows where the SFDX CLI is installed and how to authenticate with it through a private certificate. You can review detailed documentation about Jenkins and other CI servers here: https://developer.salesforce.com/docs/atlas.en-us.sfdx_dev.meta/sfdx_dev/sfdx_dev_ci.htm. You must perform this setup before following the steps that follow. Or, if you prefer, just follow along!

The following steps cover the overall process of adding an existing repository to Jenkins through the **Blue Ocean user interface**. This is an optional user interface for setting up pipelines, but is much easier to use than the traditional Jenkins management UI:

1. Click **Open Blue Ocean** on the sidebar (as shown in the preceding screenshot).
2. Click **Create a new Pipeline** (this will only display if there are no existing pipelines).
3. Click the **GitHub** tile when prompted for your desired source control server.
4. Authenticate with GitHub if needed and select your GitHub Organization if prompted.
5. When prompted, enter the name of the GitHub repository you created earlier.
6. Click **Create Pipeline**.

Once the pipeline is created, Jenkins will automatically start to execute it for the first time:

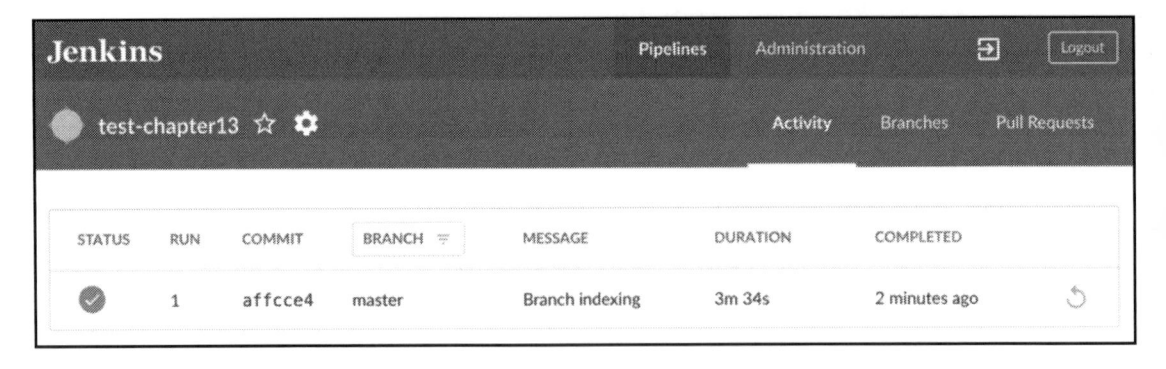

STATUS	RUN	COMMIT	BRANCH	MESSAGE	DURATION	COMPLETED	
✓	1	affcce4	master	Branch indexing	3m 34s	2 minutes ago	↻

The preceding screenshot shows Jenkins automatically running a pipeline.

If you see errors, carefully review the documentation linked previously to make sure you have not missed any server setup steps. In addition to the documented steps, I found that I did need to ensure that I had the `SFDX_USE_GENERIC_UNIX_KEYCHAIN` environment variable defined under **Manage Jenkins** | **Configure System** | **Environment Variables**. Do not forget to **configure the Node.js plugin** once installed. You may also see some security approvals to accept. These can be viewed on the **Manage Jenkins** page.

If you click on the row of the build itself as it is running, you can monitor the output of the commands in real time, just as if you had run them manually:

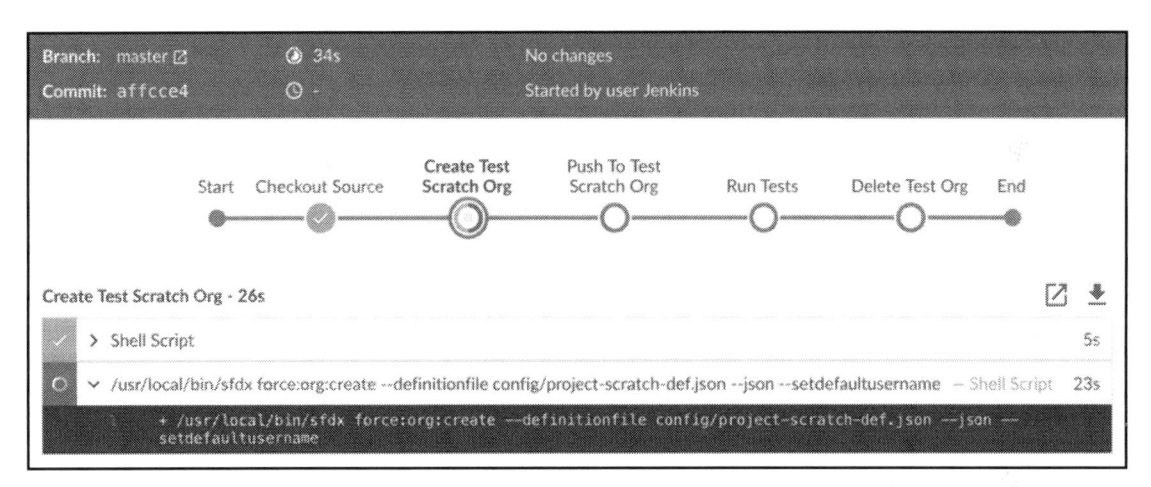

![Jenkins build pipeline screenshot showing stages: Start, Checkout Source, Create Test Scratch Org, Push To Test Scratch Org, Run Tests, Delete Test Org, End. Create Test Scratch Org - 26s, Shell Script 5s, /usr/local/bin/sfdx force:org:create --definitionfile config/project-scratch-def.json --json --setdefaultusername - Shell Script 23s]

Jenkins has many ways to detect whether future builds are required by monitoring for changes in the associated source control system. These can be found by navigating to the build configuration. From the main Jenkins home page, find your repository in the dashboard view and hover your mouse pointer over it to access the drop-down menu and select the **Configure** page. In the **Scan Repository Triggers** section of the configuration page, set the interval to **1 minute**. Not that you would not normally do this in practice; this is just to explore further in the next section.

Exploring Jenkins and CI further

This section has just scratched the surface of what is possible with Jenkins and `Jenkinsfile`. You can continue to extend your `Jenkinsfile` to perform additional stages, such as static code analysis and/or even custom DX CLI plugins to write statistics back to your own Salesforce production environment. You can read more about the commands and features of `Jenkinsfile` here: https://jenkins.io/doc/book/pipeline/syntax/.

Continue to explore this process a bit further by making changes to the repository to see how the Jenkins pipeline responds. Let's deliberately break some tests and commit the changes straight away! This, of course, would normally be bad practice, but the point of this is to see how pipelines defend the overall quality of the code base, even if mistakes happen:

1. Edit the `ContestantsTest.testAddContestantNoneScheduled` method Apex test as shown here:

   Line 12:
   ```
   Race__c race = new Race__c(Name = 'Spa', Status__c = 'Scheduled', Season__c = season.Id);
   ```

2. Edit the `raceSetup.test.js` Lightning Web Components test as shown here:

   Line 69:
   ```
   const SELECTED_ROWS =
       [
           {
               "RecordId": DRIVER2_ID,
               "Name": "Sergio Pérez",
               "Selected": true
           }
       ];
   ```

3. Use the Visual Studio Code source control integration (highlighted earlier in this chapter) to commit and publish your changes to the GitHub repository. Note that, normally, you would do this via a pull request; committing directly to the master branch is typically not good practice.

4. After a minute, you will see that the Jenkins pipeline has observed that a change has occurred and started a build. The following screenshot shows that the build has failed due to test failures:

Chapter 13

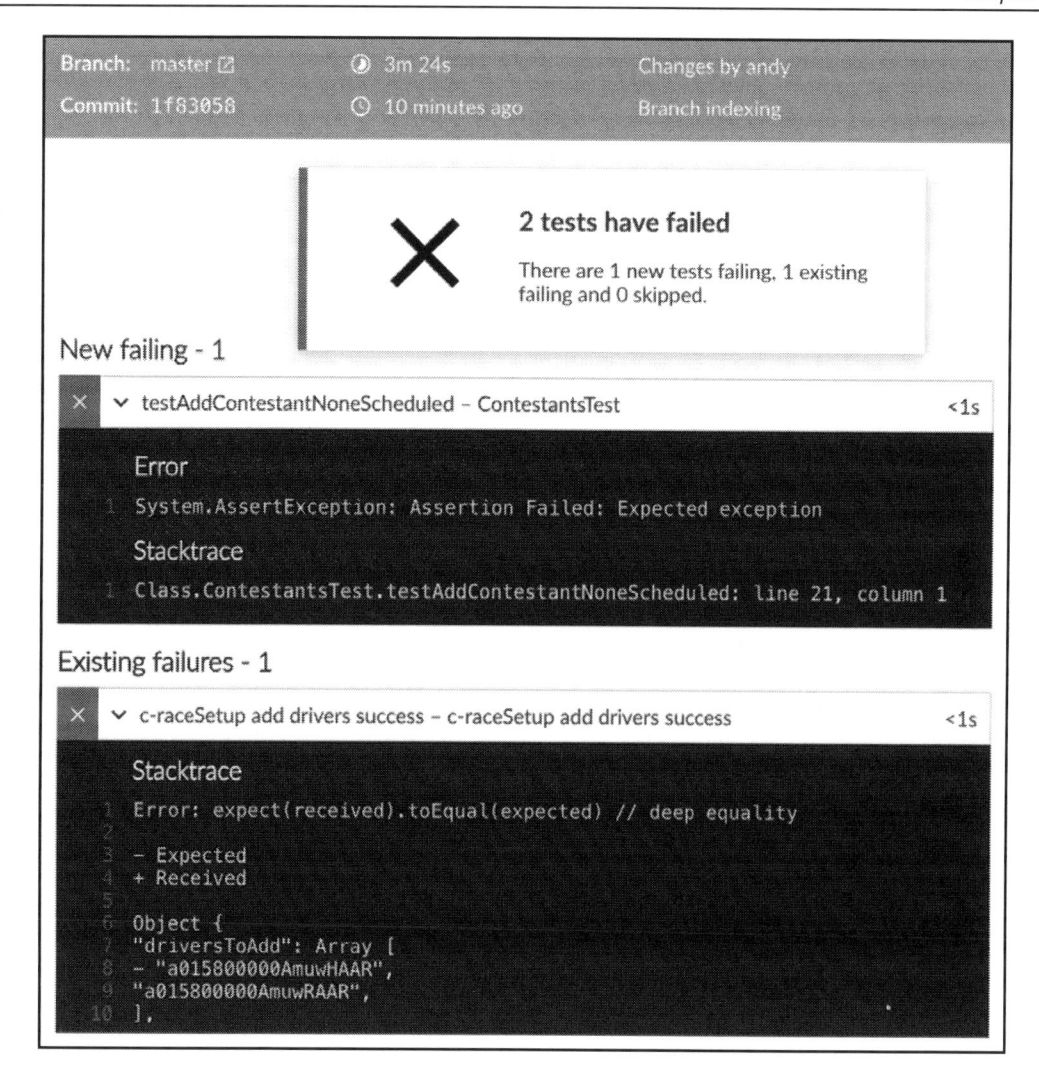

```
Branch:  master                3m 24s              Changes by andy
Commit:  1f83058               10 minutes ago      Branch indexing
```

2 tests have failed

There are 1 new tests failing, 1 existing failing and 0 skipped.

New failing - 1

× testAddContestantNoneScheduled – ContestantsTest   <1s

Error
```
System.AssertException: Assertion Failed: Expected exception
```

Stacktrace
```
Class.ContestantsTest.testAddContestantNoneScheduled: line 21, column 1
```

Existing failures - 1

× c-raceSetup add drivers success – c-raceSetup add drivers success   <1s

Stacktrace
```
Error: expect(received).toEqual(expected) // deep equality

- Expected
+ Received

Object {
  "driversToAdd": Array [
-   "a015800000AmuwHAAR",
+   "a015800000AmuwRAAR",
  ],
```

If you revert the preceding changes and commit then push those changes, you will see that the build will recover and reward you with a nice sunshine icon! Next, let's see how to release from source control.

Releasing from source control

Throughout this book, we have been creating packages using the Salesforce DX CLI manually. When you are starting out with a new package, creating packages is arguably a less frequent operation, and you can certainly continue to issue these commands manually, using the preceding pipeline to simply confirm that your code base is stable enough to create a test package (I would recommend you use Git tags for each package version). However, once your number of releases and their frequency grows, you may want to start to add some more automation.

It is possible to automate the Salesforce DX CLI commands related to **packaging** through the `Jenkinsfile`. To consider this, though, you must first think about your use of **branches** within source control and, from that, determine what changes in source control warrant a new package version to be created, and, more importantly, when to promote a package version to release status so that it can be shared with your customers.

GitFlow is a well-established industry blueprint for how to use branches to implement a set of best practices around managing a release development process with multiple developers and teams. It was invented by **Vincent Driessen** and has been widely adopted on many platforms. The author makes available a great article describing how to implement GitFlow available on the internet (`https://nvie.com/posts/a-successful-git-branching-model/`). It will take a few read-throughs to understand and to get a good understanding of Git.

We can consider the following packaging needs mapping to GitFlow as follows:

- **Commits** to **Feature branches** can create packages to allow customer testing to take place with the resulting beta package. Use the `--branch` parameter to associate the branch name with the package. Such packages are purely for testing and cannot be promoted for release. At the time of writing, it is not possible to delete such packages once the feature branch is deleted, though Salesforce have stated that this capability is a priority.
- **Commits** to **Release branches** can also create packages and should leverage the `ancestoryId` of the previously released package on which the release branch is based. You should use the `--tag` parameter to record the release version.
- **Tags** on the **Release branches** can be used to promote (mark as a release package) the most recent package version created on that branch. Jenkins can be used to monitor for tags as well, so long as you install the **Basic Branch Build Strategies** plugin and configure it for your pipeline.

Chapter 13

Even if you do not embrace the automation of packaging and choose to continue to manage it manually for now, hopefully, this chapter has allowed you to get going with a basic pipeline that you can go on to extend as your team and requirements grow.

Automated regression testing

While Apex and Lightning Web Components tests are very much key tools for monitoring regressions in your application, the limitations and scope of the functionality such tests can cover is small by design, since they are unit tests, not integration tests. Thus, they are not particularly suited to performing large data volume or full end-to-end user interface testing.

> **TIP**
> The preceding pipeline configuration creates only one scratch org with a given configuration. You can, of course, create scratch orgs of different types to perform different kinds of testing. At the time of writing, the **Scratch Org Template** feature is in Pilot. This allows you to customize your scratch orgs to pre-install other packages, test configurations, and data. This is ideal for creating a suite of test org templates, for example.

Here are some considerations for implementing further testing approaches:

- It is possible to execute the Apex code from shell scripts using the approach described earlier in this chapter, when we populated the developer org with sample data by calling the `SeasonService.createTestSeason` method. You can extend this approach by using loop constructs within shell scripts to create volume data or start more Batch Apex jobs (Apex tests only permit a single chunk of 200 records to be processed), pause for completion, and assert the results.
- The Salesforce Data Loader tool is actually a Java program with a command line interface. Thus, you could consider using it to load data into a build org to test against different datasets, used in combination with the preceding Apex code, executed to clean records between tests.
- Once you have the data loaded into the build org, you can execute tests using a number of Salesforce testing tools. For example, the **Selenium WebDriver** tool is an excellent choice, as it provides a headless mode (no need for a physical screen) and can be run on multiple operating systems. This tool allows you to test Visualforce pages with large amounts of JavaScript (http://docs.seleniumhq.org/projects/webdriver/).

Having considered the regression testing approaches that you can explore, let's summarize what has been covered in this chapter.

Summary

In this chapter, we have seen how to scale developer resources for the development of your enterprise application using industry-strength source control tools, development processes, and servers such as Jenkins.

Some of the steps described in this chapter might initially seem excessive and overly complex compared to developing in a more manual way. Ultimately, more time is lost resolving conflicts manually, not to mention the increased risk of losing changes.

Certainly, if your business is aiming to be audited for its development processes, adopting a more controlled approach with tighter controls over who has the ability to package the source code, and also your mechanism to release it, is a must.

Opening up the Lightning Platform development process to tools such as Git and GitFlow, for example, allows for a much better developer interaction for aspects such as code reviews and carefully staging features in development to release. Such tools also give a greater insight into statistics regarding your development process, which allows you to optimize your development standards and productivity further over time.

In the next chapter, we will explore ways for you and your customers to easily and safely integrate features and services that exist outside of the Lightning Platform, and conversely, for external developers to integrate with the platform.

14
Integrating with External Services

In today's world, the internet provides your customers with a wide variety of services to help them run their business efficiently. Once your application is released, your customers will want to integrate many of these services into your application's services as well. While there are significant application management optimizations and data security benefits to customers choosing multiple applications based on the same platform, the reality is that other services and platforms exist and may already be a part of your customer's infrastructure, which is why we need to use External Services.

Fortunately, Salesforce understands this and embraces the integration of external services in a variety of ways, regardless of whether it is an external process calling one of your application services and/or existing platform services (**inbound**) or the need to invoke an external service within the Lightning Platform (**outbound**). The platform allows you to package such external integrations and/or your customers to access easy-to-use tools and products that fast-track the process, leveraging the fact that your application is built on a platform; those tools are easier to use as they inherently understand your application's data and code and how to expose it.

In this chapter, we will explore working with external services that represent external processes, as well as external data to be integrated. We will cover the following topics:

- Understanding inbound and outbound integrations
- Managing inbound integrations with Connected Apps
- Options for outbound integrations
- Managing outbound integrations with Named Credentials
- Invoking outbound integrations
- Accessing external services via External Services
- Accessing external data seamlessly via External Objects

To help with this process, we will use a variety of existing services and some sample services hosted using the Salesforce Heroku platform. Let's start with the first topic: inbound and outbound integrations.

Understanding inbound and outbound integrations

How you approach configuring integrations depends on the direction of the integration. This chapter uses the terms **inbound** and **outbound** to distinguish between those directions. The following outlines the definitions used in this book for both of these terms:

- An **inbound connection** is an *external system calling Salesforce APIs* or those APIs you have created via Apex. While managing these types of connections, you can use features and APIs such as Connect Apps, OAuth, Certificates, and Permission Sets.
- An **outbound connection** is when *Salesforce calls out to external system APIs*. While managing these types of connections, you can use features such as Remote Sites and Named Credentials.

> It is worth pointing out that making HTTP callouts is very commonplace in most languages today, and therefore it can initially seem quite simple to implement integrations. However, as complexity grows, dangers arise, especially when it comes to storing the credentials (username/password) or private certificates for such connections securely, as well as providing administrators with visibility and control over them. Implementing these integrations often require more investment on behalf of the developer to code, configure, and own.
>
> The Lightning Platform features covered in this chapter are aimed at minimizing or, in some cases, totally removing the need for that investment, allowing the developer to focus entirely on the business requirement behind the integration need.

The Salesforce REST APIs and your own Apex REST-based APIs (covered in `Chapter 10`, *Providing Integration and Extensibility*) are essentially providing inbound endpoints (URLs that point to the APIs) that expose access to your application's data and features. You can call these APIs from program code running on devices or other clouds in a variety of different ways.

This is due to the underlying HTTP, JSON, XML, and OAuth protocols being so widely supported throughout the industry. The OAuth standard provides a secure means to authenticate and access APIs. In this chapter, we will cover the use of **Connected Apps** and other related features to enable such connections to be made securely and in such a way that an administrator can monitor and manage them directly without the aid of a developer.

For making outbound connections, we will explore the **External Services** and **Salesforce Connect** features offered by Lightning Platform. These offer more tailored options for making outbound integrations depending on the nature of the integration.

Salesforce also provides a feature known as **Outbound Messaging,** which is an action supported by the Workflow engine. This is the oldest integration feature that is still available on the platform today. You can configure it in the **Setup** menu and then create Workflow rules associated with objects and user actions, such as updating a record based on certain Workflow criteria.

Salesforce then generates a **Web Service Definition Language (WSDL)** specification for your external platform developer to implement. Notice that WSDL is an XML/SOAP-based definition, so there is no support for JSON. When the Workflow conditions are met, that endpoint is called by the platform, where there is no coding on the platform required.

External Services, when combined with Process Builder, offers a more flexible and less prescriptive means to accomplish this goal today. With that said, Outbound Messaging does work in the background and has some retry capabilities, while External Services on its own does not. Though, arguably, Platform Events in conjunction with External Services should also be considered if this is an important requirement.

> Outbound Messaging is covered in more detail by Salesforce in its official documentation here: `https://developer.salesforce.com/docs/atlas.en-us.api.meta/api/sforce_api_om_outboundmessaging.htm`.

The next sections will give you a detailed discussion of these features along with some examples.

Managing inbound integrations

While setting up user access to applications and objects stored in Salesforce, an administrator will grant access to applicable applications, tabs, and related objects via a Profile or Permission Set. By default, a user will log into the org through the standard Salesforce login page by entering their username and password. Salesforce provides standard user experiences for your users to access your objects, and, in doing so, fully tests that they honor security configurations. As such, they can be considered trusted experiences.

> **TIP:** In fact, all standard Salesforce REST and SOAP APIs that are also used by the Lightning UIs honor the security configuration for a given user. This follows a best practice when building any type of API, which is to never trust the caller of the API.

Now, consider if you or another developer wanted to integrate Salesforce into another website or mobile experience. This experience could provide its own simple UI page to capture the user's name and password, and then use the Salesforce Login API to obtain a session token to perform operations on behalf of the user through a website or mobile app UI.

There are, however, several problems with the preceding approach:

- **Username and password exposure:** This is the most important problem, the fact that external integrating code will become aware of the user's name and password, which is very bad for security. Even if you trust the developer, what if their code was compromised or logging inadvertently captured the credentials to a log stored on a disc? This can create a problem.
- **Full user permissions:** The external integrating code has the full scope (that is, all the user's accessible objects) of what the user can perform even though it may only need a subset of objects in reality to perform its task. It is a good practice to reduce the scope (that is, what APIs and objects it can access) of any external integration to what it specifically needs, just in case the session token is leaked or even a bug in the application causes its code to do more than intended.

- **Lack of login UI features:** Also, remember that the login UI from Salesforce offers quite a rich user experience, including things such as password reset, network challenges, and single sign-on facilities. Although it is possible to access some of these features through the Salesforce APIs, I would not recommend it as you will continually be updating the external applications UI to be updated with the new features.

> I am not a security expert, but the preceding points are just a few good reasons why you should try to avoid capturing the user logins. You should always consult the official documentation if you have any doubts: `https://developer.salesforce.com/docs/atlas.en-us.integration_patterns_and_practices.meta/integration_patterns_and_practices/integ_pat_intro_overview.htm`.

Thankfully, Salesforce provides a much safer way for external integrations to obtain a session token – one that leverages the industry standard known as **OAuth** (`https://oauth.net/2/`). The following section goes through a worked example of using a **Connected App**.

Introducing Salesforce Connected Apps

In this section, we are going to create a special type of application using **App Manager**, which you first used in `Chapter 1`, *Building and Publishing Your Application*. The **Connected App** type represents an application that is external to the Lightning Platform and, as such, does not have any tabs or objects associated with it. However, administrators can still control and monitor its access.

Integrating with External Services

In this part of the chapter, using a simple **Node.js** application, we will use a **Connected App** to make an inbound call to the Salesforce org while authenticating the user through the standard **Salesforce Login** page:

1. The first step in this process is to create a **Connected App** via **App Manager** under the **Setup** menu. The name you give to the application is not important, but be sure to complete the **API (Enable OAuth Settings)** part of the page, as shown in the following screenshot:

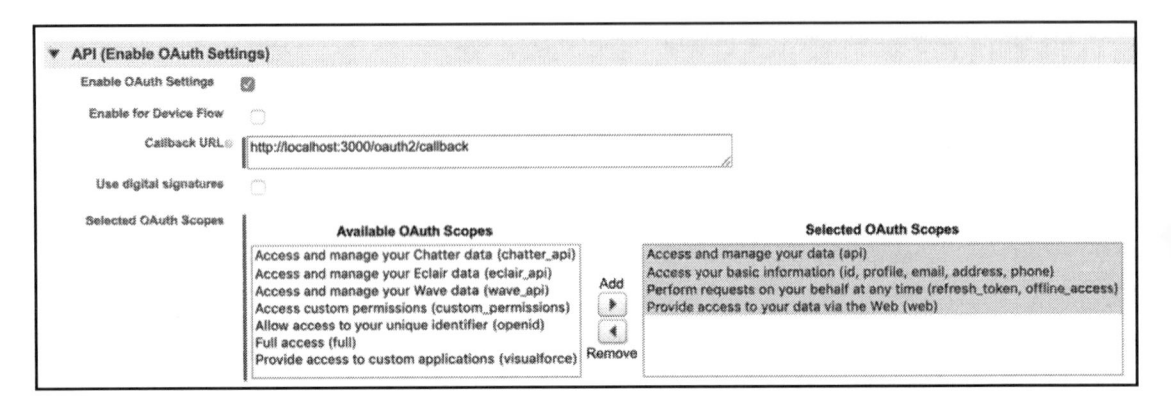

```
▼ API (Enable OAuth Settings)
    Enable OAuth Settings          ☑
    Enable for Device Flow         ☐
    Callback URL                   http://localhost:3000/oauth2/callback
    Use digital signatures         ☐
    Selected OAuth Scopes
                                   Available OAuth Scopes                                    Selected OAuth Scopes
                                   Access and manage your Chatter data (chatter_api)         Access and manage your data (api)
                                   Access and manage your Eclair data (eclair_api)           Access your basic information (id, profile, email, address, phone)
                                   Access and manage your Wave data (wave_api)        Add   Perform requests on your behalf at any time (refresh_token, offline_access)
                                   Access custom permissions (custom_permissions)      ▶    Provide access to your data via the Web (web)
                                   Allow access to your unique identifier (openid)     ◀
                                   Full access (full)
                                   Provide access to custom applications (visualforce) Remove
```

The preceding configuration enables the OAuth authentication scheme. There are many authentication approaches supported by **Connected App** that are outside the scope of this chapter, such as **JWT** authentication mode (although, if you complete the steps to configure your Jenkins server for Salesforce DX, you will have performed these steps).

Notice that, here, we only permitted external applications using this **Connected App** to have certain levels of access on the user's behalf—these are known as the *scopes* and will be referenced later. Once you click on **Save**, you will see a warning message informing you that your app will not be usable for several minutes while Salesforce completes the necessary setup in the backend. Meanwhile, expand the **API (Enable OAuth Settings)** section once again and take note of the **Consumer Id** and **Consumer Secret** field values.

> The sample code included in this chapter contains the /node-app folder, which contains a small **Node.js web server application** that you can run on your local computer (providing you have Node.js installed). As per the best practices mentioned previously, this Node.js application does not have any login code or UI within it—it simply delegates these requirements fully to Salesforce via the OAuth protocol. Only once the user login is complete, Salesforce redirects back to the integrating application to continue processing.
>
> In this case, it will perform a very simple SOQL query to display the org name.

2. Before we attempt to run the application, we need to configure it with the **Consumer Id** and **Consumer Secret** values you obtained earlier. In this case, we are just going to edit the app.js file directly. The best practice is to not hardcode this information within plain sight in your code, but instead, read it from an environment variable (where you can also vary it between test values and production values) and retrieve the values dynamically at runtime. For now, edit the following variable values to reflect the **Consumer Id** and **Consumer Secret** values on the **Connected App** details page:

   ```
   //
   // OAuth2 client information can be shared with multiple
   connections.
   //
   var oauth2 = new jsforce.OAuth2({
     loginUrl : 'https://test.salesforce.com',
     clientId : 'Paste Consumer Id here',
     clientSecret : 'Paste Consumer Secret here',
     redirectUri : 'http://localhost:3000/oauth2/callback'
   });
   ```

3. By default, scratch orgs do not expose their password: you will need this to test the integration. Run the following command to generate a password for your scratch org user:

   ```
   sfdx force:user:password:generate
   ```

4. Then, in order to build and run the Node.js application, perform the following commands:

   ```
   cd node-app
   npm install
   node app.js
   ```

Integrating with External Services

5. Navigate to `http://localhost:3000` in your browser. The application detects that there is no current user login and begins the OAuth UI Flow to request that the user logs in first.
6. Complete the standard **Salesforce Login** page with the username and password obtained previously. You will then be presented with a confirmation page that allows users of the external application to better understand what type of access they will be given if they continue. An example confirmation page is shown here:

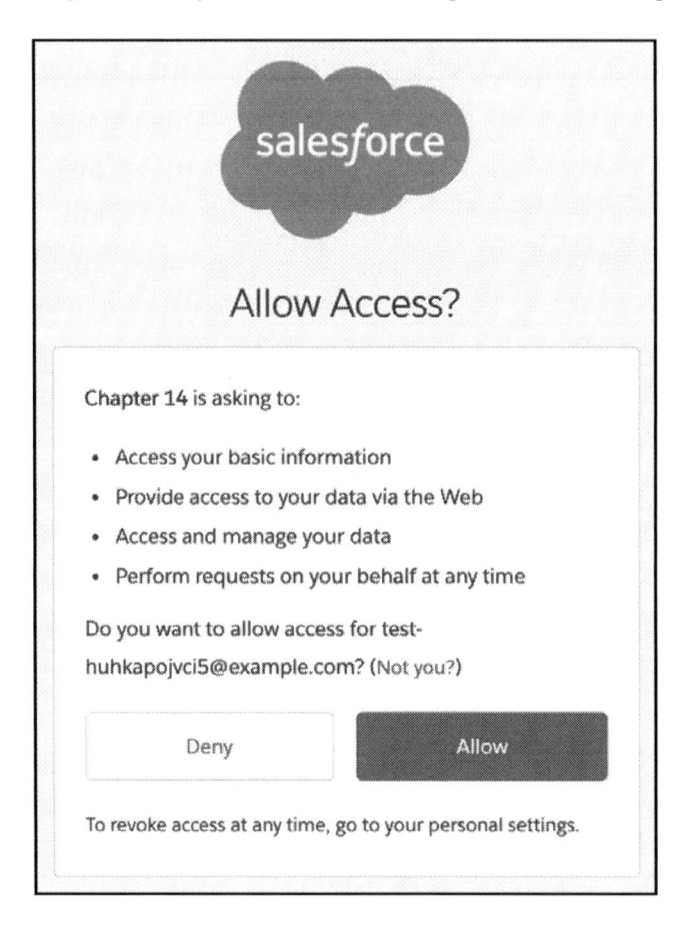

Allow Access?

Chapter 14 is asking to:

- Access your basic information
- Provide access to your data via the Web
- Access and manage your data
- Perform requests on your behalf at any time

Do you want to allow access for test-huhkapojvci5@example.com? (Not you?)

Deny | Allow

To revoke access at any time, go to your personal settings.

The preceding screenshot shows a Connected App access confirmation page.

> **TIP:** Think carefully when defining your **Connected App** for real, and make sure you only request the level of access required for the external application. If you request too much, users may be discouraged from using the external application.

7. Once you click on **Allow**, the control is returned back to your Node.js application through the **Callback Url** you entered when setting up the preceding **Connected App**. The code in the Node.js applications stores the Session ID for later use and redirects you to a page to perform a SOQL query:

Org Name is "FormulaForce App Development"

8. Now, log in to your scratch org and click on the user avatar in the top-right corner of the page to select the user's **My Personal Information** menu. From this menu, you can view application connections and revoke them if needed:

Connections

OAuth Connected Apps

Action	Created Date	Last Used	Application	Use Count
Revoke	8/24/2019 4:50:59 PM PDT	8/24/2019 4:51:00 PM PDT	Chapter 14	1
Revoke	8/24/2019 4:46:16 PM PDT	8/24/2019 4:46:16 PM PDT	Chapter 14	1
Revoke	8/24/2019 3:19:25 PM PDT	8/24/2019 3:19:30 PM PDT	Salesforce CLI	1

Third-Party Account Links

This account is not authorized for access from any third-party accounts

Integrating with External Services

In addition, you can also view the connection history on the **Security Central** page:

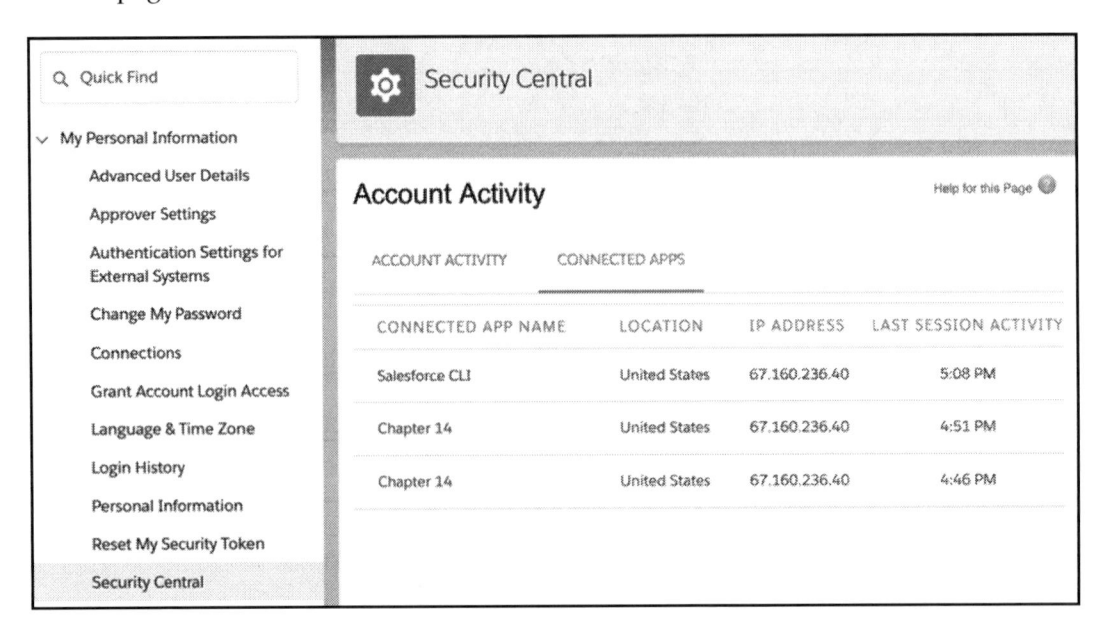

CONNECTED APP NAME	LOCATION	IP ADDRESS	LAST SESSION ACTIVITY
Salesforce CLI	United States	67.160.236.40	5:08 PM
Chapter 14	United States	67.160.236.40	4:51 PM
Chapter 14	United States	67.160.236.40	4:46 PM

Finally, administrators can access two **Setup** pages to control which users can utilize the Connected App or revoke access for all users. There are also other settings that determine how long the external application can remain connected in the background, or if the desired behavior is to revoke access when the user logs out of the Lightning UIs.

The following screenshot shows the **Connected Apps OAuth Usage** page:

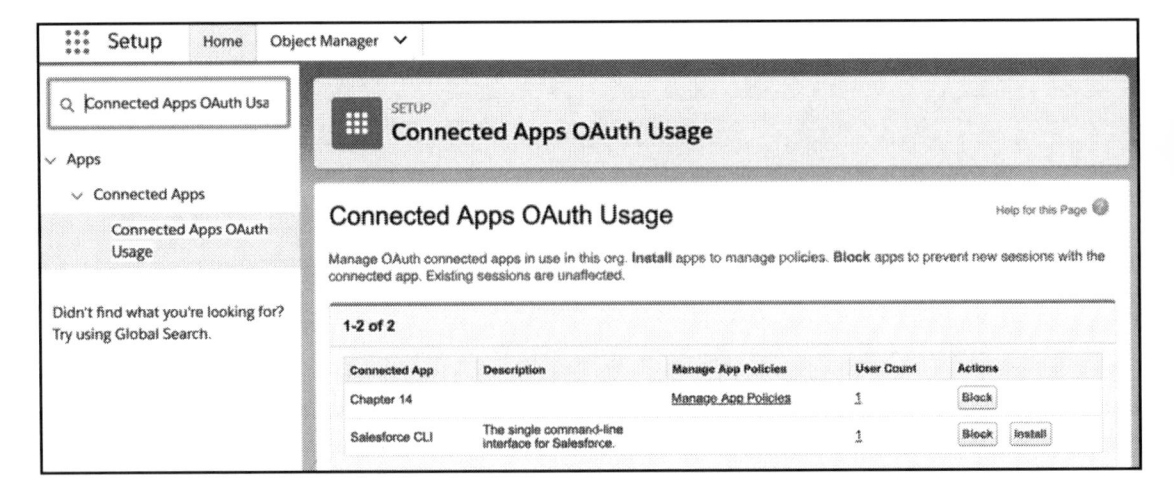

Connected Apps OAuth Usage

Manage OAuth connected apps in use in this org. **Install** apps to manage policies. **Block** apps to prevent new sessions with the connected app. Existing sessions are unaffected.

1-2 of 2

Connected App	Description	Manage App Policies	User Count	Actions
Chapter 14		Manage App Policies	1	Block
Salesforce CLI	The single command-line interface for Salesforce.		1	Block Install

[564]

The following screenshot shows the **Manage Connected Apps** page and the settings that the administrator can use to control who has access to a given Connected App, as well as the policies for refreshing access tokens:

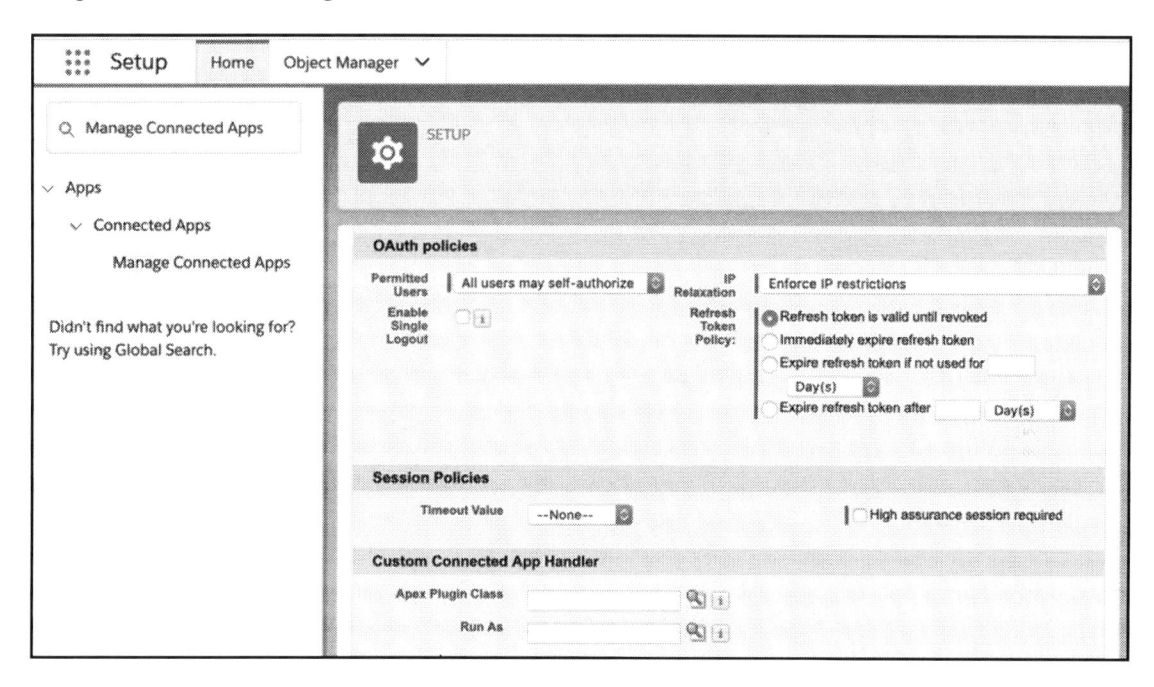

![Manage Connected Apps screenshot showing OAuth policies, Session Policies, and Custom Connected App Handler sections]

As you can see, using **Connected Apps** gives the external developer the ability to focus on building the required integration without having to reimplement a login user experience or risk security implications associated with storing user credentials. From an administrator perspective, they gain more visibility and control as opposed to external developers using API-based logins.

In the next section, we will review a sample external application that uses this Connected App and the OAuth protocol to implement a secure login for an external application.

Node.js application using a Connected App

Node.js is an increasingly popular language for building applications and is also used by Lightning Web Components development, although any language that supports HTTP callouts can be used for integration needs.

Integrating with External Services

The following sample code illustrates how Node.js can be used to leverage the preceding Connected App definition:

```
var jsforce = require('jsforce');
const express = require('express')
const session = require('express-session');
const app = express()
const port = 3000

//
// Configure express-session to store Session Id and Instance URL
//
app.use(session(
  { secret: 'keyboard cat',
     resave: true, saveUninitialized: true}))

//
// OAuth2 client information can be shared
//
var oauth2 = new jsforce.OAuth2({
  loginUrl : 'https://test.salesforce.com',
  clientId : 'Paste Consumer Id here',
  clientSecret : 'Paste Consumer Secret here',
  redirectUri : 'http://localhost:3000/oauth2/callback'
});

//
// Get authorization url and redirect to it.
//
app.get('/oauth2/auth', function(req, res) {
  res.redirect(oauth2.getAuthorizationUrl(
      { scope : 'api id web refresh_token' }));
});

//
// Handle oAuth callback and extract and store session token
//
app.get('/oauth2/callback', function(req, res) {
    var conn = new jsforce.Connection({ oauth2 : oauth2 });
    var code = req.param('code');
    conn.authorize(code, function(err, userInfo) {
      if (err) { return console.error(err); }
      req.session.accessToken = conn.accessToken;
      req.session.instanceUrl = conn.instanceUrl;
      // Redirect to main page
      res.redirect('/');
    });
});
```

```
//
// Run a simple SOQL query and outputs the Org Name
//
app.get('/', function(req, res) {
    // Previously saved session token?
    if (!req.session.accessToken || !req.session.instanceUrl) {
        res.redirect('/oauth2/auth');
        return;
    }
    // Connect and output query results
    var conn = new jsforce.Connection(
        {accessToken: req.session.accessToken,
         instanceUrl: req.session.instanceUrl });
    conn.query('select Name from Organization',
      function(err, result) {
        if (err) {
            console.error(err);
            res.send('Error');
        } else {
            res.send(
              'Org Name is "' + result.records[0].Name + '"');
        }
      });
});

// Start the web server up!
app.listen(port, () => console.log(`Listening on port ${port}!`))
```

The following points are notable from the preceding code:

- Three Node.js open source libraries are used: jsforce, express, and express-session. Express (https://expressjs.com/) provides a web server stack for Node.js, along with the ability to manage session information without storing it via local cookies in **Express Session** (https://www.npmjs.com/package/express-session). Finally, the jsforce library (https://jsforce.github.io/) is a very popular Node.js library for accessing Salesforce REST APIs from Node.js and also includes code that implements the OAuth protocol for you.
- The /oauth2/auth path is associated with the required code to start the authentication process with Salesforce and must reference the scopes configured when the **Connected App** was created. In this case, api id web refresh_token is specified (space-delimited).

> **TIP**
> These values appear in the brackets next to the scope descriptions on the **Connected App** definition page.

- The `/oauth2/callback` path is associated with the required code to receive the Session ID and instance URL information, which is later used to perform the query. This code uses the `express-session` library to securely store this information on the server side, to avoid it being stored in client-side cookies. Finally, notice that this path is the **Callback URL** given when the Connected App was created previously. This is a critical part of the configuration as it ensures that this Connected App can only be used with the external website domain intended. In practice, you will have multiple Connected Apps, including test and production Connected Apps with different callback URLs.
- The `/` path is associated with the required code to check whether the user has logged in or not, and, if so, perform the SOQL query. If the user is not logged in, the code redirects to the `/oauth2/auth` page and logic described previously.

So far, we have covered inbound integrations into the platform and your application services. However, if you or your customers want to keep the user engaged within the Salesforce user experience, there are also a number of options for calling out to services from the platform without the user leaving the system. In the next section, we will review outbound integrations.

Understanding options for outbound integrations

In the following sections, I am categorizing outbound integrations accordingly:

- **Data integrations:** When there is a need to access external databases or data stored in a relational form, this is called **data integration**. A new type of object known as an **External Object** is used to reflect external data in the Lightning Platform.
- **Service integrations:** When there is a need to access External Services that perform some form of compute or complex task, this is called **service integration**. Providing such services are expressed using an Open API (also known as Swagger) specification. The **External Services** feature can be used to import such services for usage by Lightning Process Builder, Flow, and Apex.

With the exception of External Objects, outbound connections leverage the **Named Credentials** feature to manage authentication on behalf of the tool or Apex code invoking the integration. Let's first understand how to configure Named Credentials.

Managing outbound connections with Named Credentials

Named Credentials offer a secure means of managing credentials that are needed to access external endpoints when making outbound calls. This separation of concerns allows the calling logic to focus on the integration and not on how to store credentials and, thus, protected username/password or tokens for multiple users and/or external services. This also gives administrators more control and consistency in how all outbound connections are managed regardless of their usage.

> If you do not define a **Named Credential** or a **Remote Site** setting for a given endpoint, Salesforce will block callouts and throw a runtime exception. This is by design and means that the administrator is ultimately in control of data leaving the org via outbound connections.
>
> Named Credentials and Remote Sites can be packaged. During package installation, the administrator is prompted to accept a list of outbound connections a package will make. Remote Site settings are an older means of declaring callouts, but do not support managing credentials.

For this example, I am going to revisit an integration I wrote about 10 years prior to writing this book! **Basecamp** is a friendly, easy-to-use project management service. When I first wrote an integration to Basecamp APIs, I needed to set up the authentication information in my Apex code and figure out a safe place to store the API key the service needed at the time. Fast forward, and Basecamp API v3 supports OAuth and is a perfect way to explore Named Credentials. Check the following steps to set up a secure Basecamp API connection:

1. Basecamp offers free accounts; you can head over to `https://basecamp.com` to create one.
2. Navigate to `https://launchpad.37signals.com/integrations` to set up a **Basecamp Application**, and complete the required fields.

> *TIP*
> I used `Chapter 14 Demo` as the application name, but you can use whatever name you like.

3. When prompted for the **Redirect URI**, enter `https://example.com/auth` for now – we will come back to this later.
4. Click on **Save** and then click on the **Connected App** you just created. Take note of the **Client ID** and **Client Secret** field values.

> **TIP**: If the preceding feels familiar, it's because you just effectively created the equivalent of a Connected App on the Basecamp platform. You will find this a familiar pattern when connecting between services using OAuth. Google is a little more complex, but it is basically the same process.

Back in your scratch org, you need to now *set up an Auth Provider* to describe the various URLs that Basecamp exposes to support OAuth authentication. Once this is set up, it can be used to configure a **Name Credential**. The following are the steps to set up an **Auth Provider**:

1. Under **Setup**, search for **Auth. Providers** and click on **New**.
2. Enter `Basecamp` in the **Name** and **URL Suffice** fields.
3. In the **Consumer Key** field, enter the **Client ID** you captured previously.
4. In the **Consumer Secret** field, enter the **Client Secret** you captured previously.
5. For the **Authorize Endpoint URL**, enter `https://launchpad.37signals.com/authorization/new?type=web_server`.
6. For the **Token Endpoint URL**, enter `https://launchpad.37signals.com/authorization/token?type=web_server`.
7. Click on **Save**.
8. From the **Auth. Providers** page, click on the **Basecamp** entry you just created and copy and paste the **Callback URL** field value shown at the bottom of the details page. This is a calculated value that is unique to the org as it includes the org's unique domain.
9. Navigate back to `https://launchpad.37signals.com/integrations` and edit the **Basecamp Application** you created earlier.
10. Update the **Redirect URI** field with the **Callback URL** value captured in the previous step and click on **Save changes**.

> **TIP**: The **Authorize Endpoint URL** and **Token Endpoint URL** information for other services should be provided by each service in their developer documentation. For example, Basecamp documented it here: `https://github.com/basecamp/bc3-api#authentication`.

Finally, we set up the Named Credential and authenticated it with Basecamp. In this case, we are using a **Named Principle** for the connection, which essentially means every callout will use the same Basecamp user login; we will be exploring the per-user alternative to this in the next section. The following steps will create the `Basecamp` Named Credential:

1. Under **Setup**, search for **Named Credentials** and click on **New**.
2. Enter `Basecamp` in the **Label** and **Name** fields.
3. Enter `https://3.basecampapi.com` in the **URL** field.
4. For **Identity Type**, select **Named Principle**.
5. For **Authentication Protocol**, select **OAuth 2.0**.
6. For **Authentication Provider**, select the **Basecamp** provider created previously.
7. Check the **Start Authentication Flow on Save** checkbox and click on **Save**.

If you have configured everything correctly, you should see the following prompt once you have logged into your Basecamp account:

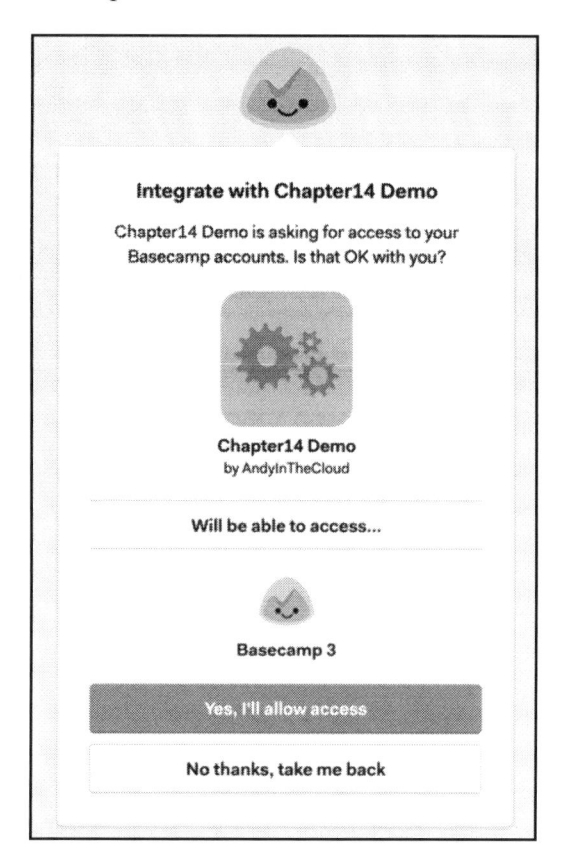

Once you complete the login process, the details page should look like the following:

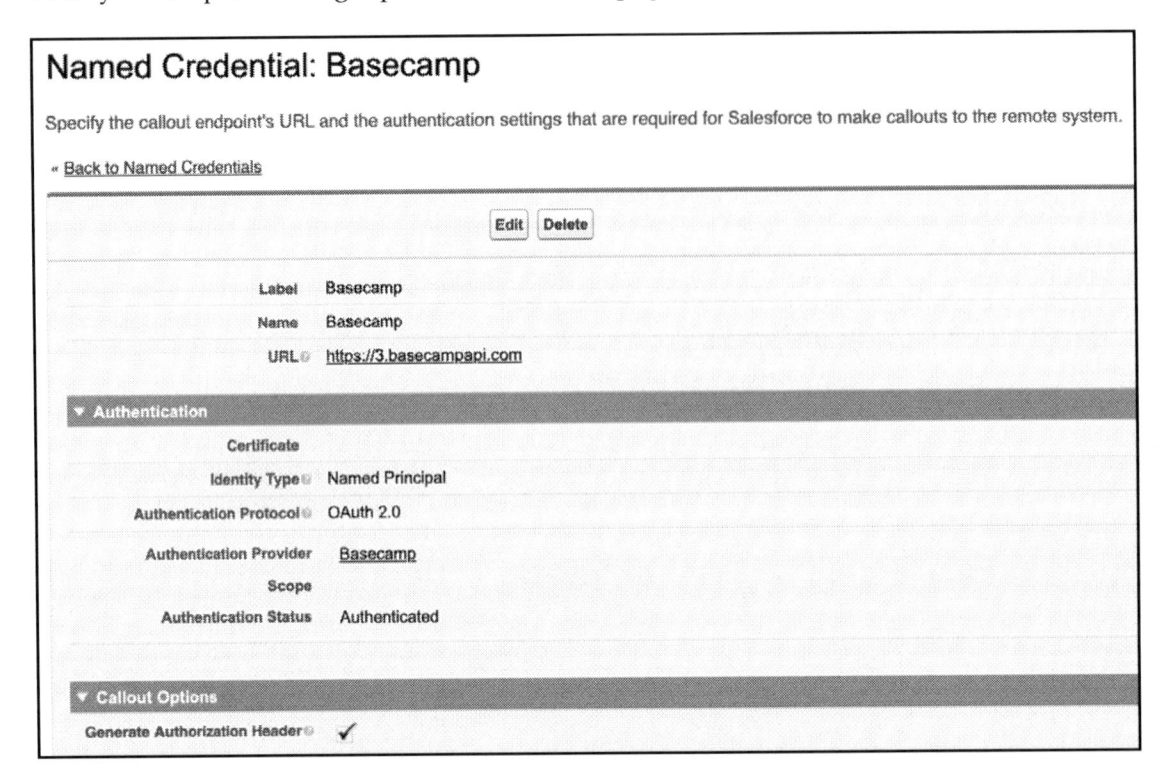

Named Credential: Basecamp

Specify the callout endpoint's URL and the authentication settings that are required for Salesforce to make callouts to the remote system.

« Back to Named Credentials

[Edit] [Delete]

- Label: Basecamp
- Name: Basecamp
- URL: https://3.basecampapi.com

Authentication
- Certificate:
- Identity Type: Named Principal
- Authentication Protocol: OAuth 2.0
- Authentication Provider: Basecamp
- Scope:
- Authentication Status: Authenticated

Callout Options
- Generate Authorization Header: ✓

Salesforce will now securely store the authentication tokens required to access the Basecamp API for you. It will also refresh the tokens as needed. As you will see in the next section, you simply need to reference the name `Basecamp` in your code and Salesforce will automatically generate and inject the standard HTTP Authorization header when needed.

> **TIP**
>
> You may want to disable the **Generate Authorization Header** feature shown in the preceding screenshot if the authorization approach for a given service does not fit into the standard OAuth protocol.
>
> For example, if you are using password authentication as the **Authentication Protocol**, this information can still be stored by Salesforce and you can use merge fields in your code to have Salesforce inject it into a place your code determines. You can read more about this here: `https://developer.salesforce.com/docs/atlas.en-us.apexcode.meta/apexcode/apex_callouts_named_credentials_merge_fields.htm`.

Now that we have securely defined the connection with the Basecamp service, we are ready to focus on making the callout and letting the platform inject the required authentication. In the next section, we will review how this is achieved in Apex.

Calling outbound connections from Apex

When referencing a **Name Credential** in Apex, you do so through the URL format, using `callout` as the **protocol** and the **Name Credential** name as the **domain**; for example, `callout:Basecamp`. The platform then expands this at runtime to the **URL** that you defined previously. Your code can add any other URL path information to address a specific API. The following example creates a Basecamp project using the Named Credential created previously:

1. Copy and paste the following Apex code into a text editor and edit the `999999` value to reflect your own Basecamp account number (this is present in the browser URL when logged into Basecamp).
2. Run the `sfdx force:apex:execute` command and then paste in the edited Apex fragment.
3. Then, press the key combination shown on your screen to execute:

   ```
   HttpRequest req = new HttpRequest();
   req.setEndpoint('callout:Basecamp/999999/projects.json');
   req.setHeader('Content-Type', 'application/json');
   req.setHeader('User-Agent', 'MyApp (yourname@example.com)');
   req.setMethod('POST');
   req.setBody('{ "name": "My new project!" }');
   Http http = new Http();
   HTTPResponse res = http.send(req);
   System.debug(res.getBody());
   ```

Notice that the usual `Authorization: Bearer` HTTP header is not set in the preceding code. This is calculated and injected automatically by using a Named Credential.

Integrating with External Services

The following screenshot shows the resulting project in Basecamp:

Basecamp is a collaboration tool and, as such, it would be confusing for users to see all the changes made by a single user or a **Named Principle** (as was configured previously). In the next section, we can see how it is possible to map Salesforce users to Basecamp users so that the user's identity travels between Salesforce and the external system, which, in this case, is Basecamp.

Using per-user Named Credentials

The preceding configuration assumed that the same Basecamp login would be used for all users in the org. This may be acceptable for some integrations; however, given that Basecamp is a project management solution, it's best to ensure that any updates are made by distinct users.

To ensure this is the case, each user must have a user in the Salesforce org as well as in Basecamp. By setting the **Identity Type** to **Per User** rather than **Named Principle**, Salesforce exposes the ability for administrators and/or each user to authenticate themselves with their own Basecamp account through the **My Personal Setting** menu accessed from the user's avatar. The following screenshot shows a Salesforce user being associated with a Named Credential:

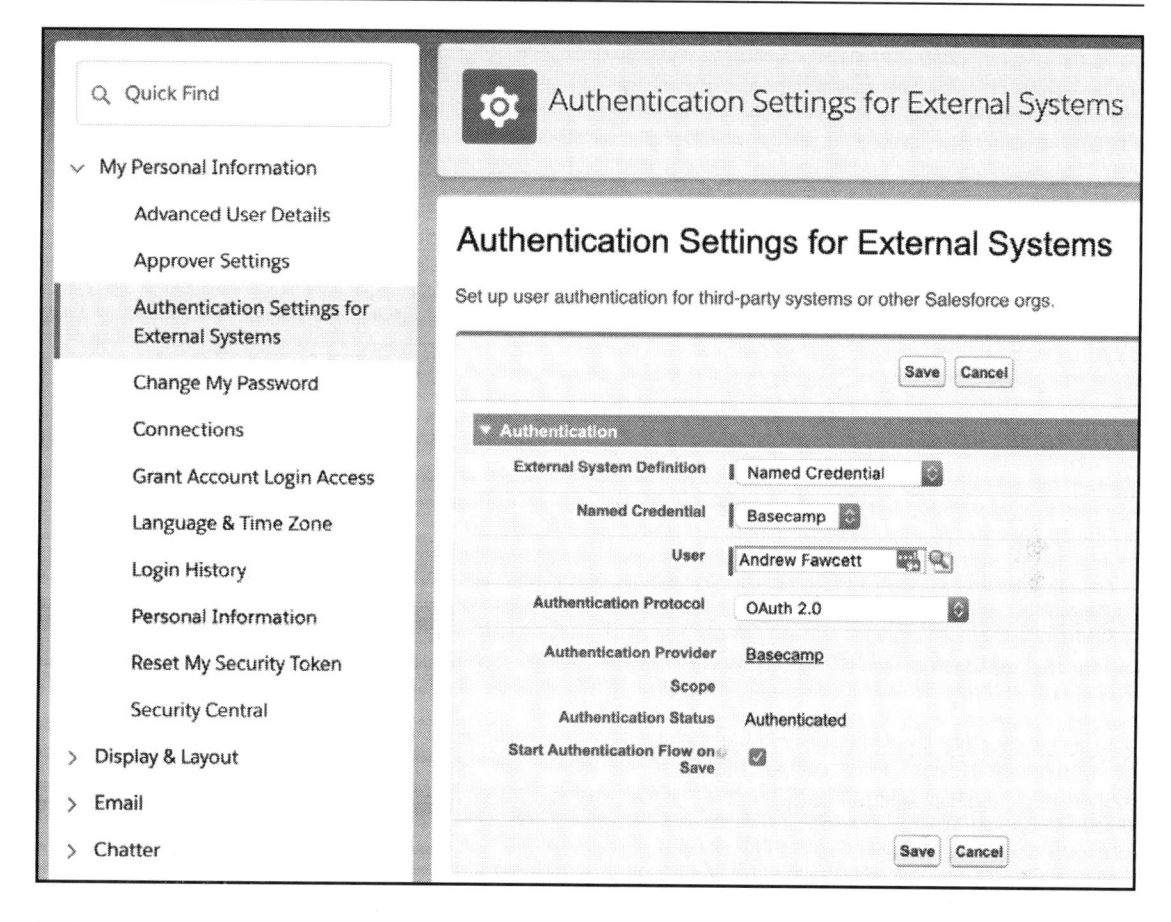

So far, we have configured an external service via Named Credentials and made an external callout via Apex. In the next section, we will review the ability to do this without code, so long as the service has been described according to a specific industry standard.

Accessing external services via External Services

In this section, we will begin to look at options for making outbound calls to allow us to **consume off-platform services** from within the Lightning Platform. We will be focusing on services that represent calculations or actions to be performed. For ease, we will be using an existing publicly hosted service running on **Salesforce Heroku**, which is written in **Node.js**. Its purpose is to generate a QR code representation of a given input string. The source code for this service has also been included in the `/node-service` directory in the sample code for this chapter.

Integrating with External Services

> This chapter does not cover how to deploy the service code to **Heroku**, since there is already a publicly running version of it that can be referenced for you to use. However, if the sample service is down, or if you just prefer to know more about deploying Heroku Node.js applications, then copy the contents of the /node-service folder to a new folder and follow the steps here: https://www.heroku.com/nodejs.

External Services empowers the administrator or non-coders to consume external services through other tools such as **Lightning Flow** and **Lightning Process Builder**, without writing any code at all. In order to allow this to happen, the developer that authored the service must have exposed a description of the service in a certain format known as **Open API** (or **Swagger**). You may recall this since it was covered in Chapter 13, *Source Control and Continuous Integration*. A portion of the swagger.yaml file in the /node-service/api/swagger folder is shown here:

```yaml
swagger: "2.0"
# ... see swagger.yaml file for full code ...
paths:
  /qrcode:
    # binds app logic to a route
    x-swagger-router-controller: qrcode
    post:
      description: Returns QRCode to the caller
      # used as the method name of the controller
      operationId: qrcode
      consumes:
        - application/json
      parameters:
        - in: body
          name: body
          description: Message to convert to a QR Code
          schema:
            type: object
            required:
              - message
            properties:
              message:
                type: string
      responses:
        "200":
          description: Success
          schema:
            # a pointer to a definition
            $ref: "#/definitions/QRCodeResponse"
  /schema:
    x-swagger-pipe: swagger_raw
```

```
# complex objects have schema definitions
definitions:
  QRCodeResponse:
    required:
      - qrcode
    properties:
      qrcode:
        type: string
```

A full walk-through of the preceding format is outside the scope of this chapter; however, here are a few key aspects to highlight and keep in mind as this definition is consumed by External Services:

- The `paths:` element defines the URL for each operation exposed by the service; in this case, there is only one, `/qrcode`. Below that you can see `post:`. This determines that an **HTTP POST method** should be used to invoke the operation.
- The `x-swagger-router-controller:` element indicates the **Node.js** code file that implements the service being described, which, in this case, is `qrcode.js`.
- The `parameters:` and `response:` elements contain a description of the inputs and outputs supported; in this case, it is a simple string input and output.

> **TIP**
> When using the External Services tool, you can either paste a definition given to you by a developer or point the tool to a URL where the definition already exists. It is best practice to provide the definition with the service so that the two are maintained together. The preceding definition is co-located with the external service on the internet here: https://createqrcode.herokuapp.com/schema/.

Before you can import this definition into the Lightning Platform with External Services, as with the Basecamp service, you must first create a Named Credential, although, in this case, there are no authentication requirements, so an Auth Provider is not required. In the following steps, we will create a simple Named Credential for an existing service:

1. Under **Setup**, search for **Named Credentials** and click on **New**.
2. Enter QRCode in the **Label** and **Name** fields.
3. Enter https://createqrcode.herokuapp.com in the **URL** field.
4. Click on **Save**.

Integrating with External Services

The **External Services** tool can be found under the **Setup** menu:

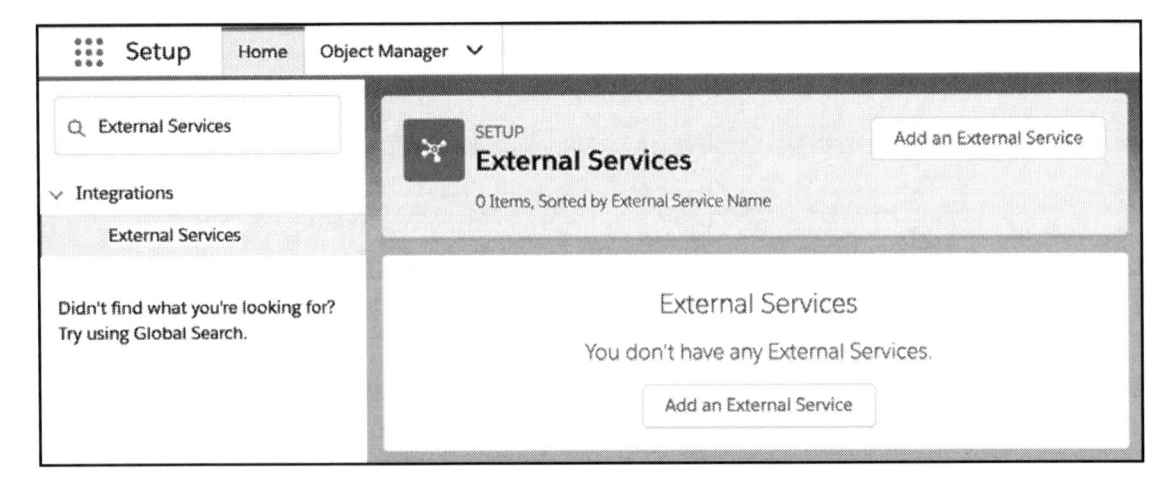

The following steps import the AsciiArt service as an External Service:

1. Click on **Add an External Service** to start the wizard.
2. Enter QRCode in the **External Service Name** field.
3. Select **QRCode** from the **Select a Named Credential** drop-down field.
4. Enter /schema in the **Service Schema Relative URL** field.
5. Click on **Next** and then **Done** to complete the wizard.
6. From the **External Services** page, click on the entry you just created:

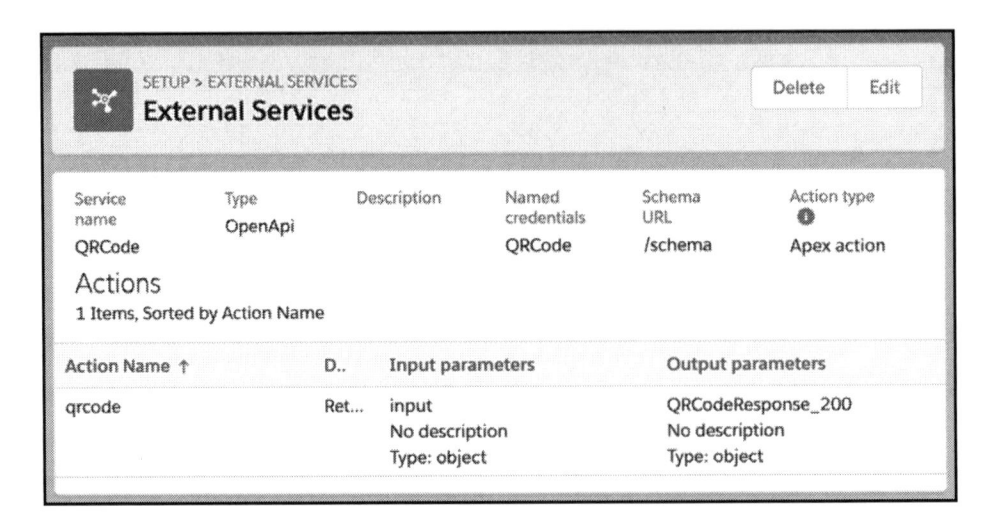

Chapter 14

The preceding screenshot shows the QRCode service configured through an External Service.

> At the time of publishing, there is an **Enhanced External Services Pilot** that adds the ability to support more complex inputs and outputs than just the basic data types used in the preceding example.

Now that the service has been created, it can be referenced from tools such as **Lightning Process Builder** and **Lightning Flow**. In the simple Lightning Flow shown in the following screenshot, the **Call QRCode Service** action was automatically added to the steps available to the user when defining the Flow by completing the preceding External Services wizard. The following Flow simply asks the user for an input message, calls the service, and then shows the resulting output in the last step of the Flow:

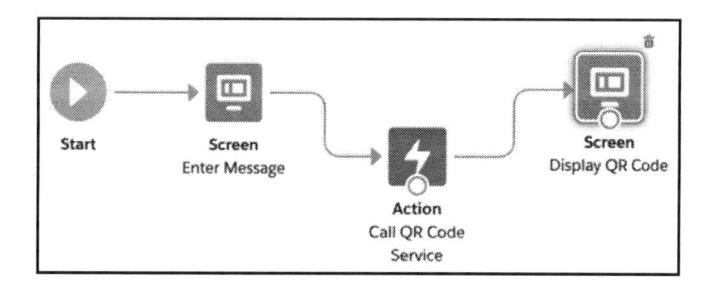

As you can see in the following screenshot, the **Lightning Flow Designer** allows you to map the inputs and outputs of the QR code service (as per the preceding definition) to **Flow variables**:

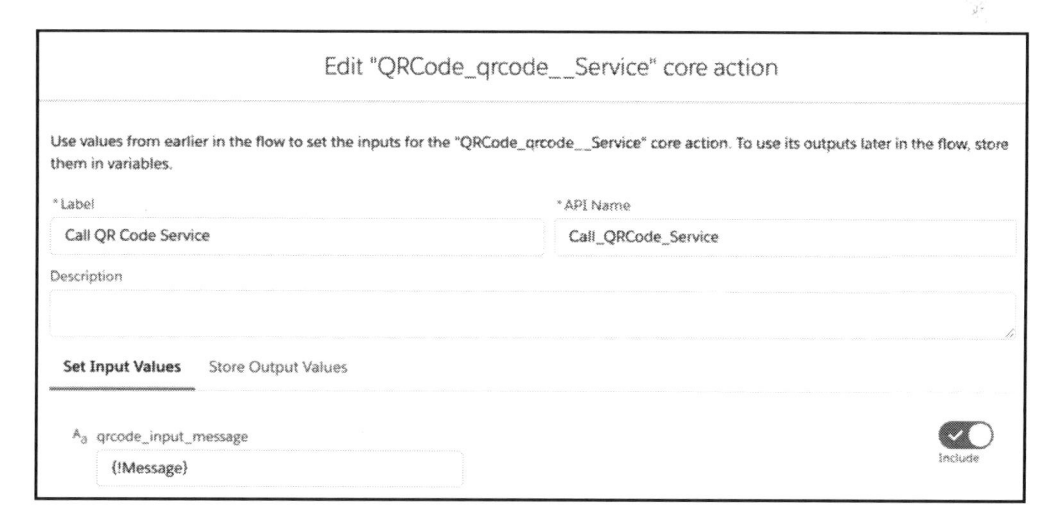

Once the Flow is saved, it can be run from the Flow Designer. The following screenshot shows the step requesting the message to be passed to the service:

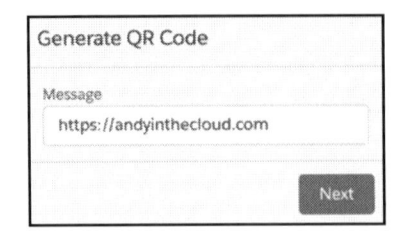

Finally, the output is displayed in the last step:

In this section, we have used Named Credentials and External Services to import an external service into the platform so that the user can invoke it from tools such as Lightning Flow and Process Builder. If the integration is more of a relational data integration that you wish to combine with existing data in your application objects and/or Salesforce objects, you can leverage External Objects, as described in the following section.

Accessing external data seamlessly via External Objects

As you have discovered throughout this book, Lightning Platform provides many rich user experiences for **Standard** and **Custom Objects**, which are managed by the platform. When you create a Custom Object, you automatically get the ability through the various **Lightning UI** containers to access the record data without having to build a new UI each time. Through the **standard Salesforce APIs**, you also get API access to your Custom Objects.

With **External Objects**, you can get a subset of these features for data stored off-platform as well. Furthermore, the data can also be edited through the Lightning UIs and APIs, allowing users to stay within the same Lightning platform, thereby avoiding them having to move between different application experiences. External Object data is never stored within Salesforce, so there are none of the typical synchronization challenges with data becoming out of date or stale. You can think of External Objects as "editable views" to externally accessible data.

Much like the proceeding example, in order to make this possible, external services need to comply with a specific standard. This standard is OData (https://www.odata.org/); it was originally introduced by Microsoft and is now additionally backed by IBM, SAP, and others.

> **TIP**
> It is possible to use **Apex** to wrap other external services that do not support OData, using **Apex Connectors**. For more information on this, you can refer to the documentation here: https://developer.salesforce.com/docs/atlas.en-us.apexcode.meta/apexcode/apex_connector_start.htm. There are also a number of examples for **Google**, **GitHub**, and **StackOverflow**.

The **OData website** (https://www.odata.org/odata-services/) includes a number of publicly available sample data stores for testing purposes. The following steps utilize the **Northwind sample database** that became popular during the era of the Microsoft Access product. Click on https://services.odata.org/V2/Northwind/Northwind.svc/Employees to see the raw record data for the Employee table through the OData API.

To create an **External Object** for the Employee table, first create an **External Data Source**:

1. Under **Setup**, search for **External Data Sources** and click on **New External Data Source**.
2. Enter Northwind in the **External Data Source** and **Name** fields.
3. Select **Salesforce Connect: OData 2.0** from the **Type** drop-down field.
4. Enter https://services.odata.org/V2/Northwind/Northwind.svc/ in the **URL** field.
5. Click on **Save**.

> As the **Northwind database** external service is a publicly available sample, it has no authentication enabled and, therefore, an **Auth Provider** was not required in the preceding steps. External data sources reference **Auth Providers**, including the **URL** to the service and other OData related configurations, and, therefore, do not require the use of **Named Credentials**.

Now that an **External Data Source** has been created, it's time to create the **External Objects**. Part of the OData specification includes the ability to describe the exposed database tables. Salesforce leverages this capability to provide a tool to automatically create External Objects:

1. Open the **Northwind** data source via the **External Data Sources** page under **Setup**.
2. Click on the **Validate and Sync** button, select the **Employee** table, and then click on the **Sync** button.
3. After a few moments, the details page is shown; locate the **Employee** object in the **External Objects** related list.
4. Delete the **Notes** and **Photo** fields as, at the time of publishing, these cause problems with Lightning Experience.
5. Create a new tab for the **Employee** object and assign it to the **Administrator** profile.
6. Optionally, create an **Application** via the **Setup** menu and add the **Employee** tab to it.

You can now locate the **Employees** tab in the application launcher in Lightning Experience. In the following screenshot, I have customized the List View columns to show additional fields:

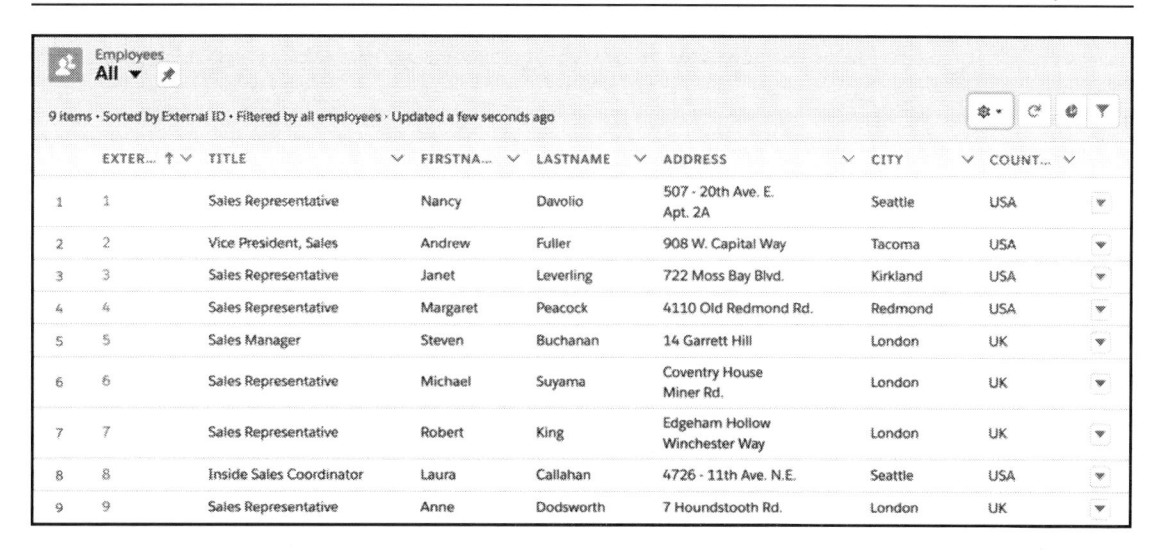

	EXTER... ↑ ∨	TITLE	∨	FIRSTNA... ∨	LASTNAME ∨	ADDRESS	∨	CITY	∨	COUNT... ∨	
1	1	Sales Representative		Nancy	Davolio	507 - 20th Ave. E. Apt. 2A		Seattle		USA	▾
2	2	Vice President, Sales		Andrew	Fuller	908 W. Capital Way		Tacoma		USA	▾
3	3	Sales Representative		Janet	Leverling	722 Moss Bay Blvd.		Kirkland		USA	▾
4	4	Sales Representative		Margaret	Peacock	4110 Old Redmond Rd.		Redmond		USA	▾
5	5	Sales Manager		Steven	Buchanan	14 Garrett Hill		London		UK	▾
6	6	Sales Representative		Michael	Suyama	Coventry House Miner Rd.		London		UK	▾
7	7	Sales Representative		Robert	King	Edgeham Hollow Winchester Way		London		UK	▾
8	8	Inside Sales Coordinator		Laura	Callahan	4726 - 11th Ave. N.E.		Seattle		USA	▾
9	9	Sales Representative		Anne	Dodsworth	7 Houndstooth Rd.		London		UK	▾

You can click on the records as normal and open a **Details** view, as shown here:

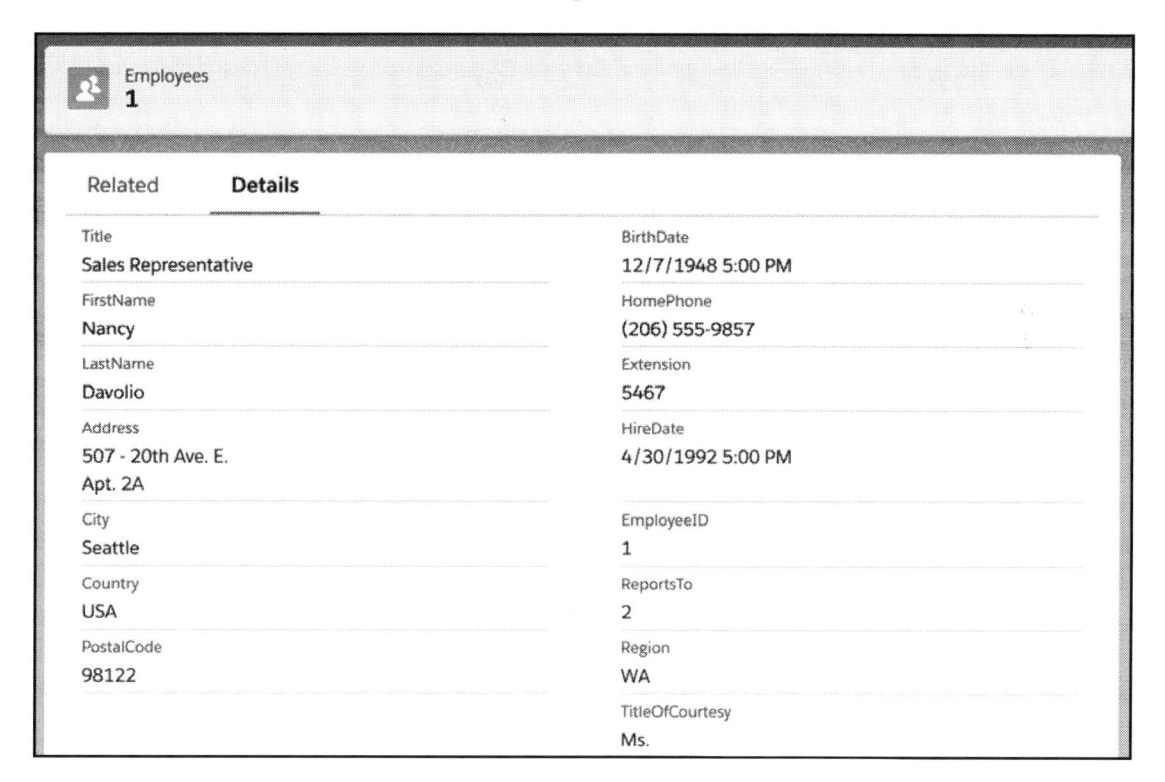

Employees
1

Related   **Details**

Title
Sales Representative

FirstName
Nancy

LastName
Davolio

Address
507 - 20th Ave. E.
Apt. 2A

City
Seattle

Country
USA

PostalCode
98122

BirthDate
12/7/1948 5:00 PM

HomePhone
(206) 555-9857

Extension
5467

HireDate
4/30/1992 5:00 PM

EmployeeID
1

ReportsTo
2

Region
WA

TitleOfCourtesy
Ms.

[583]

Integrating with External Services

The preceding screenshots demonstrate a record from the **Employees** External Object.

> External Objects also support **relationships** between one another, and thus **Related Lists** are also supported in the user experience. **Layouts** can also be used to customize the fields displayed. Finally, you can also enable (if supported by the external service) the **ability to edit records**. For more information relating to External Objects, review the Salesforce Connect guide here: https://help.salesforce.com/articleView?id=platform_connect_about.htmtype=5.

To try out the API support for External Objects, run the following command:

```
sfdx force:data:soql:query -q 'select FirstName__c, LastName__c from Employees__x'
```

```
FIRSTNAME__C  LASTNAME__C
─────────────────────────
Nancy         Davolio
Andrew        Fuller
Janet         Leverling
Margaret      Peacock
Steven        Buchanan
Michael       Suyama
Robert        King
Laura         Callahan
Anne          Dodsworth
Total number of records retrieved: 9.
```

This concludes our brief walk-through of External Objects. External data sources can be imported into Salesforce and integrated into an existing UI through tabs and programmatic experiences, as shown in the preceding example.

You can also relate External Object data to custom or standard object data. Most importantly, it keeps your users within a single experience and environment, avoiding them having to switch between environments to look up information, thus saving them time.

Summary

In this chapter, you saw how integrations are the lifeblood of the internet and are key to a business making the most out of the efficiencies offered by combining services from multiple vendors into a single process or experience for its employees and customers.

You learned that managing integrations can become complex and costly; however, this is something Salesforce has made easier by providing features that not only reduce the coding involved through External Services, but also improves security by taking this responsibility away from the developer and consolidating it as a set of features such as Connected Apps (inbound) and Auth Providers (outbound).

You also learned that administrators can audit and monitor external solutions, accessing precious data as well as controlling the flow of data potentially leaving the org through such features. Keep in mind that, depending on the integration needs, user identity can flow between integrations as needed using Named Credentials configured with Per User authentication.

On an additional note, Salesforce also owns the popular Mulesoft integration platform, which is worthy of further consideration, as it provides additional features that help compose brand new APIs from smaller APIs and create orchestrations between APIs that form long-running processes.

In the next chapter, you will see how you and your customers can use the capabilities of Salesforce Einstein to add AI and machine learning features to your application.

15
Adding AI with Einstein

Artificial Intelligence (**AI**) has become very much the norm in our personal and business lives. The reason for this is the ongoing democratization of cloud-based services that make it increasingly easy to access sophisticated AI algorithms, not just as a consumer via various AIs such as Siri, Alexa, and Google, but also as a developer. You no longer need to be a data scientist or understand the complexities of creating and executing complex models that drive such AI experiences; what you need is accurate data and a clear idea of the kind of problems—or rather AI-driven predictions—you want to discover. This is harder than you might think. Hence, the real key to AI is not the algorithms; it is the amount and quality of data!

In this chapter, you will gain an appreciation of how Salesforce has democratized these complex new innovations and technologies, helping you to easily extend your application with AI. In the case of the objects in your application, these can be enabled with AI and machine learning capabilities, which brings AI value to your customer's data. AI, or **Einstein** as Salesforce refers to it, represents a vast array of services that help empower you and your customers to leverage AI.

This is indeed a huge topic, and not something that can be covered in detail in a single chapter. Instead, we will cover the following areas in summary, so that you have a good understanding of what products and services you and your customers can leverage:

- Understanding Salesforce Einstein services and products
- Adding intelligence with the Einstein Prediction Builder tool
- Discovering insights with Einstein Discovery through Einstein Analytics
- Adding sentiment and vision recognition with code using Einstein Platform Services

By the end of this chapter, you will have an overview of the features, specifically in terms of packaging and who configures them (you and/or your customers). This information will not only allow you to consider approaches to directly embedding AI in your application, but it will also allow you to reflect on what fields or new objects you might want to add in order to make it easier for your customers to adopt these Salesforce features in your application.

Understanding Salesforce Einstein services and products

Salesforce provides a number of services and features, both general and specific, related to AI so as to suit different types of users, use cases, and product features. Regardless of whether you are a developer, an admin, or an end user of one of the specific clouds (such as Sales Cloud), there is likely something for you. As you would expect, the options open to developers or admins help fill in any specific gaps where Salesforce has not delivered a specific prediction need. In this section, and those that follow, we will explore these services in detail.

For **administrators** and **data analysts**, these are the options:

- **Einstein Prediction Builder**: This works with the data stored in custom or standard objects to look for ways to predict a given outcome, such as the likelihood of a given customer paying on time or using historical race data to predict a race winner! The prediction is calculated in the background and the result is stored as a Custom Field that you can define further. You can configure predictions by completing a short wizard-based UI under the **Setup** menu.
- **Einstein Discovery**: This is part of **Einstein Analytics**. It scans datasets that you define to discover patterns to drive information about business events (insights) or needs so that you can be proactive in resolving issues or making improvements. One insight might be a particular region that is not performing well in terms of sales, maybe due to certain products not being well promoted, consulting teams failing due to being overworked, or staffing issues due to market demand increases. Datasets can be from Salesforce (your Standard or Custom Objects) or from externally available data. For example, in Formula 1, you might use it to compare data from your competitors against your own. It also allows you to perform *what-if* analysis to determine whether changing certain aspects of your business would have the desired effect. Finally, as an advanced feature, it is possible to have your developers create Lightning Components that display insights directly while viewing specific records.

- **Einstein Next Best Action**: This integrates with your user experience to provide contextual actions, depending on the field values of the record they have open. For example, you could automatically display the **Give Feedback** action defined earlier in this book as a recommended action, once the race completes. You can also use fields populated by Einstein Prediction Builder to display actions based on predictions; for example, creating a task for the pit stop team if it appears that your team is predicted to lose an upcoming race given the current time it takes them to change tires. Finally, it is also possible to use insights returned from Einstein Discovery to determine actions displayed to the end user.

For **developers**, these are the options:

- **Einstein Vision REST API**: This helps you integrate image recognition into your applications, allowing you to not only recognize (or classify) a single item in a given picture, but also detect multiple items, for example, cars and people. Salesforce provides some standard models that they have built with images they have obtained, though you also have the option to provide your own.
- **Einstein Language REST API**: This helps you to integrate different ways to recognize free-format text in your application. This allows you to determine whether a phrase is reflecting a good or a bad sentiment from the user, or even pick out specific aspects of a sentence, such as a place or product being referenced. Using this API, you can discover the intent of such a message from the user, for example, as a desire to book travel to a specific place or reset a password.

Finally, there is an array of ever-expanding features built into Salesforce products, such as **Einstein Lead and Opportunity Scoring**, **Einstein Opportunity and Account Scoring and Insights**, **and Einstein Forecasting**. You can learn more about **Sales Cloud** and **Einstein** here: https://www.salesforce.com/products/sales-cloud/features/sales-cloud-einstein/.

As you can see, there are a number of powerful features and services to choose from for you or your users to enable AI capabilities that enhance your application. In the following sections, we will explore each of them in more detail. Let's start with Einstein Prediction Builder.

Understanding Einstein Prediction Builder

For each prediction you set up with Prediction Builder, it scans a subset of records within a given Standard or Custom Object that you define. For each of those records, it reads a set of values from specific fields you provide (**predictors**). It then observes any correlations with the value of another field, which is known as the **prediction** field, also of your choosing.

After it has scanned the records, and when future records are created, it reviews the predictor field values and, using AI algorithms, outputs a prediction into a **prediction result field**. You can then use the predicted result field with an existing platform UI or reporting tools to display the prediction to the user (Process Builder rules or Apex Triggers are not supported). There are many AI algorithms available to perform this task, such as **Random Forest** and **Logistic Regression**, but you don't have to be an expert or even be aware of them; it compares the results of each for you and picks the one that's most accurate.

You can predict the value of a checkbox field or a numeric field (in Beta at the time of publishing). When you first process the records, the value of the prediction field must be accurate, and the fields it is related to (predictors) must also contain valid values.

Accuracy of this data is very important; the AI algorithms are good, but they are only as good as the data they learn from. You should also periodically rerun the builder, so that it continues to learn from fresh valid data. The recommended amount of records for optimum processing is 400 records.

> You can read more about Prediction Builder at `https://help.salesforce.com/articleView?id=custom_ai_prediction_builder.htm`, and more about the prediction result field here: `https://help.salesforce.com/articleView?id=custom_field_set_prediction_ai.htm`.

Sometimes, you or your users don't know what predictions or insights you are looking for and need a little help discovering them. In this next section, we will understand how **Einstein Discovery** (part of Einstein Analytics) helps solve this problem.

Understanding Einstein Discovery

Einstein Discovery uses AI algorithms to make observations (or **insights**) about the datasets loaded into Einstein Analytics. To get started, you define a story that begins by asking a simple question—*What is it you want to maximize or minimize?*—because there can be many ways to achieve this goal. Einstein Discovery is different from Einstein Prediction Builder, which only gives one prediction and does not explain why it has reached its conclusion.

As with Einstein Prediction Builder, you start by choosing a single field that is the sole focus of your goal; this is known as the **outcome measure field**. This has to be a numeric field, for example, the **Amount** field on the **Opportunity** object. The question behind your goal would then be—*How do I increase the size of my opportunities?* Next, you select **influencer fields**, basically, field values that can influence in the real world the value of your outcome measure field. For example, the region and salesperson fields effect the outcome (value) of the amount field. You can also use date fields as influencers, although in this case, you would convert them into a number of days from a given moment in time, such as when the opportunity was created. The data loading tools provided with Einstein Discovery provide many options to help with this.

The high-level process to get started with this tool involves the following:

- **Create a dataset** from various sources, such as Salesforce objects, CSV files, or externally supported data sources. This dataset can consist of multiple smaller datasets all related to each other. As mentioned before, clean data is key. Here, there are also options to help clean the data using other AI algorithms.
- **Create a story from a dataset** that defines what you want to maximize or minimize in your business goal. This will result in a **number of insights** that describe how the values of the influencer fields affect the outcome; for example, how the impact of combinations of the region and salesperson affects the opportunity amount.
- **Share and integrate calculated insights** with business users through an interactive point and click experience, generating a Salesforce Quip Document or Lightning Components you can place on record detail pages.

> **TIP**: You can integrate insights from stories into Process Builder and other websites using the **Einstein Discovery Managed Package**, which exposes an API to Apex. For more information, refer to `https://help.salesforce.com/articleView?id=bi_integrate_bring_data_into_analytics.htm`. With Process Builder, you can implement near real-time updates to insights and predictions to store in Custom Fields or process programmatically.

Adding AI with Einstein

Einstein Analytics is a powerful report and analytics tool on its own, but it is only as powerful as the information you think you need to know in order to run your business. When combined with Einstein Discovery, you can discover things you don't even know you needed to know! For more information, see here: https://help.salesforce.com/articleView?id=analytics_landing_page.htm.

Discovering insights from Formula 1 race results

In this section, we will be making use of historic race results from Formula 1. You can download this data through a publicly available ZIP file containing multiple CSV files representing drivers, races, and the results of each race since 1950. We will be loading CSV files into Einstein Analytics and using Einstein Discovery to explore insights and predictions in relation to the data.

> **TIP**: The steps in this section do not provide click-by-click steps for using the Einstein Analytics and Discovery user interfaces and tools. If you plan to try out the Formula 1 motor racing scenario described in this part of the chapter, then make sure you have completed the **Einstein Discovery Trail**: https://trailhead.salesforce.com/content/learn/modules/wave_exploration_smart_data_discovery_basics.

In the following steps, we are going to upload several CSV files and then create a combined dataset from which we can then create predictions and insights:

1. Obtain a **Salesforce Analytics trial org** through this website: https://developer.salesforce.com/promotions/orgs/analytics-de. We will not be using Salesforce DX for this chapter.
2. Navigate to https://ergast.com/mrd/db/, download the f1db_csv.zip file, and unzip it into a folder of your choice.
3. We will be using the following CSV files: results.csv, status.csv, races.csv, driver.csv, constructors.csv, and circuits.csv.
4. Open each of these files in your favorite text editor and perform the following steps:
    1. Observe the **column names** described on http://ergast.com/schemas/f1db_schema.txt and then add them as a comma-delimited list at the top of each file. For example, for the results.csv file, add the following:

       resultId,raceId,driverId,constructorId,number,grid,position,positionText,positionOrder,poi.

[592]

2. Einstein Discovery does not support the CSV \N null escape character. Find and replace all references to \N with an empty string.
3. Save the preceding changes to the file.

5. Launch **Analytics Studio** from the **App Launcher** in your Salesforce Analytics trial org created earlier. Click **Create** and select **Dataset**, followed by **CSV** as the data source:
    1. Repeat the preceding process to upload each of the 6 CSV files listed in *step 3*. The order is not important.
    2. When prompted for the **Data Schema File**, select the applicable .json file from the /analytics folder in the sample code for this chapter.
    3. For example, when uploading results.csv, ensure that you also select results.json for the **Data Schema File**. This JSON file ensures that columns in the CSV file are correctly identified by Einstein Discovery as being influencer fields or outcome fields.
    4. The following shows the datasets representing the CSV files uploaded:

Analytics Studio		
ANALYTICS **Recent** 11 items		
ANALYTICS	ALL APPS DASHBOARDS STORIES LENSES DATASETS	
Recent	circuits	My Private App
Created by Me	constructors	My Private App
Shared with Me	driver	My Private App
Pinned Apps	races	My Private App
Notifications	results	My Private App
LEARN	status	My Private App

Adding AI with Einstein

6. Each of the six datasets that have been created are all related through IDs and must be joined into a brand new dataset that will be used to build insights and predictions. Once again, launch **Analytics Studio** from the **App Launcher** in your Salesforce Analytics trial org, and then click **Create** and select **Data Set**, followed by **Your Dataset**:
    1. You create **recipes to join datasets together**. When prompted for **Select the base data for your recipe**, click on **Results**.
    2. When prompted, enter `resultsfull` for the **Recipe Name** and click **Next**.
    3. Click the **Add Data** button to add the `status`, `races`, `driver`, `constructors`, and `circuits` datasets you created in *step 5*:
        1. When adding the `status` dataset, enter the **Lookup Keys** as `results.status` and `status.statusid`. Select the `status` column.
        2. When adding the `races` dataset, enter the **Lookup Keys** as `results.raceId` and `races.raceId`. Select the columns `year`, `name`, `circuitId`, and `round`.
        3. When adding the `driver` dataset, enter the **Lookup Keys** as `results.driverid` and `driver.driverId`. Select the `forename`, `surname`, and `nationality` columns.
        4. When adding the `constructors` dataset, enter the **Lookup Keys** as `results.constructorId` and `constructors.constructorId`. Select the `nationality` and `name` columns.
        5. When adding the `circuits` dataset, enter the **Lookup Keys** as `results.circuitId` and `circuits.circuitId`. Select the `country`, `name`, and `location` columns.
    4. Click **Create Dataset** to create the new dataset. This may take a few moments to process and you will be notified on screen when it is complete.

> If you want to know more about adding data to recipes, you can review the **Add More Data in a Recipe** Salesforce help topic here: `https://help.salesforce.com/articleView?id=bi_integrate_data_prep_recipe_add_data.htmtype=5`.

[594]

The following screenshot shows what the `resultsfull` dataset should look like:

	nationality	surname	status
	Spanish	Alonso	Finished
	Finnish	Kovalainen	Finished
	Japanese	Nakajima	+1 Lap
	French	Bourdais	Engine
	Finnish	Räikkönen	Engine
	Polish	Kubica	Collision
	German	Glock	Accident
	Japanese	Sato	Transmission
	Brazilian	Piquet Jr.	Clutch
	Brazilian	Massa	Engine
	British	Coulthard	Collision
	Italian	Trulli	Electrical
	German	Sutil	Hydraulics
	Australian	Webber	Collision
	British	Button	Collision
	British	Davidson	Collision

Data Manager — resultsfull

DATASET RECIPE: resultsfull

1. **LOOKUP** — Look up 3 fields from 'driver'. Merge keys: 'driverId' and 'driverId'
2. **LOOKUP** — Look up 2 fields from 'status'. Merge keys: 'status' and 'statusId'
3. **LOOKUP** — Look up 4 fields from 'races'. Merge keys: 'resultId' and 'raceId'
4. **LOOKUP** — Look up 3 fields from 'circuits'. Merge keys: 'circuitId' and 'circuitId'
5. **LOOKUP** — Look up 3 fields from 'constructors'. Merge keys: 'constructorId' and 'constructorId'

Einstein Suggestions — Lowercase Uppercase Substring Bucket By Clusters

Adding AI with Einstein

You will now see the `resultsfull` dataset in the list of datasets, along with the six you uploaded from the CSV files in the earlier steps. In the following steps, we will create a **Story**, which is the term used to define a collection of observations and predictions in relation to the data:

1. Locate the `resultsfull` dataset and select **Create Story** from its action drop-down menu. The following screenshot shows the default assumption that you want to ask Einstein Discovery how best to maximize the points your drivers earn in races:

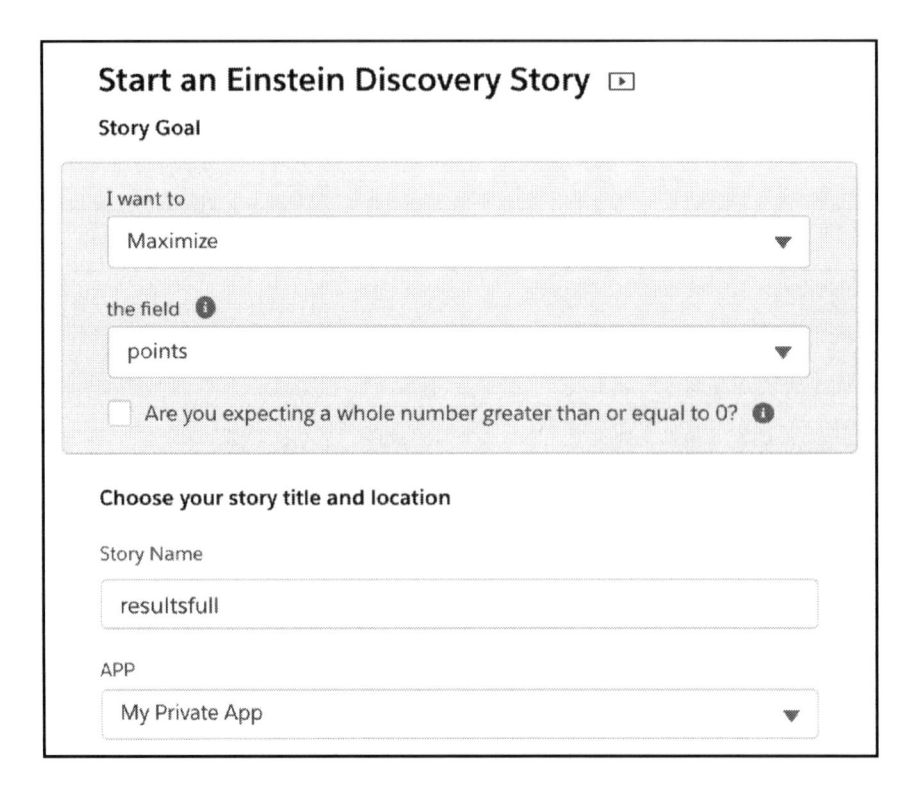

Start an Einstein Discovery Story

Story Goal

I want to

> Maximize

the field

> points

☐ Are you expecting a whole number greater than or equal to 0?

Choose your story title and location

Story Name

> resultsfull

APP

> My Private App

2. Click **Data Options** and select `surname`, `constru.name`, `circuit.name`, `status`, and `races.name` as the fields to drive your story. Einstein will use these fields to determine reasons why points vary; for example, how combinations of the driver, circuit, or team make a difference.
3. Click **Create Story** to begin processing the data.

Chapter 15

4. Once the story completes, you will see that Einstein has some recommendations on how to improve the accuracy of the story. Click the **Recommended Updates** button. You will see that Einstein is saying that **position explains 40.4% of the variation in point**, select **Ignore position (Recommended)**. It is recommended that this is ignored because the final position a driver ends up completing the race in is a well-known influencer on total points they obtain, and thus should be ignored to allow less known influencers, such as the team, driver, and location, to be considered.
5. Click **Create New Story** to restart the process after following the preceding recommendation. Note that Einstein always keeps your past stories.

The following screenshot shows one of the first observations discovered from the story:

POINTS BY SURNAME

surname explains 35.3% of the variation in points.

■ Significant ■ Insignificant

Here are some cases where points was better than average:

- Hamilton is 9.785 above average. This result may have been improved by name is Mercedes.
- Vettel is 9.074 above average. This result may have been improved by name is Red Bull.
- Verstappen is 5.397 above average. This result may have been improved by name is Red Bull.
- Bottas is 5.263 above average. This result may have been worsened by name is Williams.
- Ricciardo is 4.227 above average. This result may have been improved by name is Red Bull.

Here are some cases where points was worse than average:

- Panis is 4.201 below average. This result may have been worsened by name is Other

Adding AI with Einstein

Racing drivers **Hamilton**, **Vettel**, and **Verstappen** are among the top drivers in the sport at the time of publication of this book. Einstein Discovery has correctly recognized that they have thrived in scoring the most points when driving in the **Mercedes** and **Red Bull** racing teams. As a fan of the sport, I can confirm that this deduction is correct!

The following screenshot shows comparative observations that can be made:

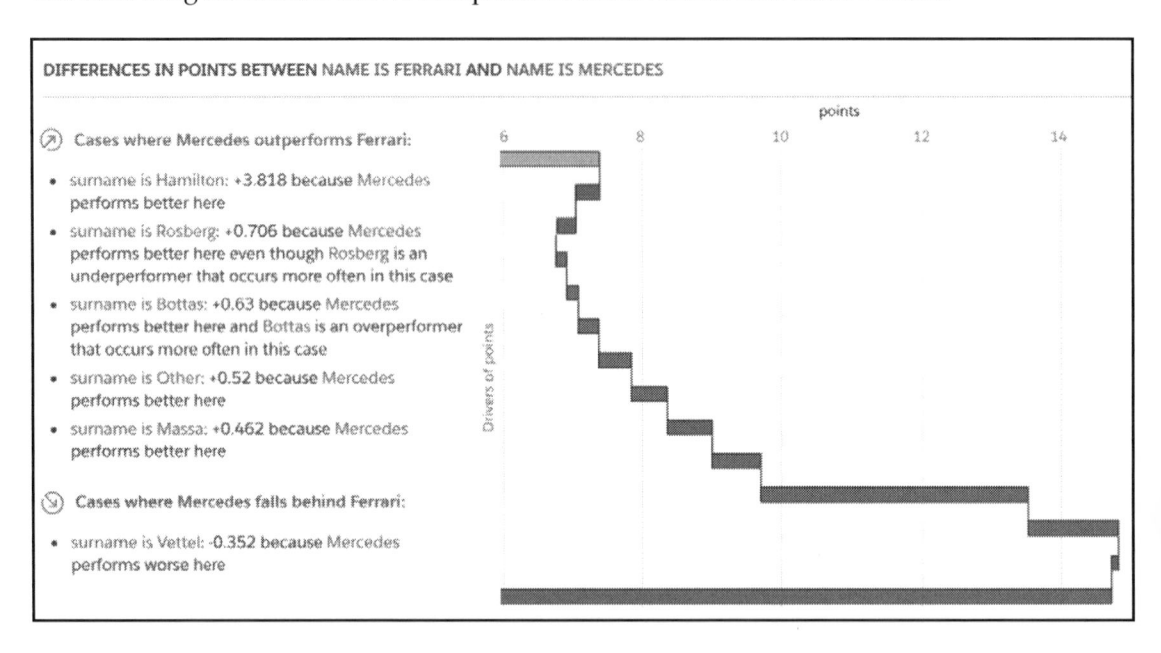

```
DIFFERENCES IN POINTS BETWEEN NAME IS FERRARI AND NAME IS MERCEDES
                                                              points
                                        6           8        10         12         14
  ⊘  Cases where Mercedes outperforms Ferrari:

     • surname is Hamilton: +3.818 because Mercedes
       performs better here
     • surname is Rosberg: +0.706 because Mercedes
       performs better here even though Rosberg is an
       underperformer that occurs more often in this case
     • surname is Bottas: +0.63 because Mercedes
       performs better here and Bottas is an overperformer
       that occurs more often in this case
     • surname is Other: +0.52 because Mercedes
       performs better here
     • surname is Massa: +0.462 because Mercedes
       performs better here

  ⊘  Cases where Mercedes falls behind Ferrari:

     • surname is Vettel: -0.352 because Mercedes
       performs worse here
```

The preceding observation is also very accurate as it indeed confirms the fact that **Mercedes** has been outperforming **Ferrari** for the last several years (at the time of publication), since **Hamilton**, **Roseberg**, and **Bottas** have been driving in the **Mercedes** team.

Both Einstein Prediction Builder and Einstein Discovery products are powerful tools for customers wishing to apply AI to your application data using their historic data. However, there are times when you need to add more AI to specific user experiences, or simply just have more control over the data that is used to drive the AI algorithms, especially when your customers have very little of their own initially. The programmatic APIs of **Einstein Platform Services** help provide a more custom AI experience packaged into your application through your Apex code calling specific APIs, which we will see in the next section.

Understanding Einstein Platform Services

You can access Einstein Platform Services through **REST APIs** using either **Apex** or other languages of your choosing. Regardless of whether you are using these services for **image detection** or **text sentiment analysis**, the following high-level process is followed:

- **Define labels** that represent how you want to categorize information, such as **dogs**, **cats**, **cars**, **vans**, **positive**, and **negative**.
- **Create datasets** using the APIs to upload examples for each of the labels you define. You should aim to obtain around 200–500 examples per label for Einstein Language services, and at least 1,000 images per label for Einstein Vision services (for example, 1,000 images of **dogs**). Once again, the quality of the data you provide directly affects the accuracy of the predictions these APIs provide to your application.
- **Create a model** by invoking the training process for a given dataset. This process results in a model ID that is later used when your application requires predictions. You also have the option to retrain portions of your model; for example, if you have new example data to improve the accuracy of predictions or even corrections to previously incorrectly classified (labeled) example data.
- **Obtain predictions** by calling the applicable language or vision API with your model ID. The results provide information on the level of confidence. You can also provide means for your users to contest the result and, if it is wrong, make suggestions for you to consider retraining the model with classification corrections.

> **TIP**
> If you do not have the example text or images to train your own models, Salesforce does provide a standard model for language sentiment trained from community forum posts that determines negative, positive, and neutral. For image recognition, they provide predefined data models food, general images, and various scenes. You can read more about them at https://metamind.readme.io/docs/use-pre-built-models and https://metamind.readme.io/docs/use-pre-built-models.

Calling these REST APIs from Apex may not be as straightforward as native Apex features, and also requires some additional authentication over and above the standard Salesforce user authentication your Apex code runs as. Salesforce has provided a great set of sample code to get you started. You can read more about this here: https://metamind.readme.io/docs/code-samples-and-learning-resources. You can include references to these services in your managed package, though you must also include the required **Named Credentials** or **Remote Site** settings as well.

Summary

Salesforce has done a great job of providing a varied range of features and services to suit different needs, both for your customers directly and/or you as a package developer.

In general, **Einstein Prediction Builder** and **Einstein Discovery** (part of Einstein Analytics) are intended for your customers to implement with the data contained in your packaged Custom Objects that is accumulated during the use of your application over time. However, through this chapter, and as a result of exploring these features further, it allows you to consider what packaged fields you can add to your objects to better facilitate configuring each of these features and tools. This will reduce the effort required for customers to AI-enable your application.

If you want to deliver more AI capabilities without the customer performing configuration, you can also choose to embed AI directly into your application code and user experiences via the **Einstein Platform Service APIs.** Additionally, keep in mind that **Einstein Discovery** also has an API available, so you can also consider packaging tighter integration with this product to further reduce the configuration time for this product.

You are also now aware of all the options in respect to embedding AI features directly into your application package, or at least consider it when designing your object model for use with tools used post-installation. In the end, by understanding all the options, you can advise your customers during the implementation phase of your product more effectively, thereby enabling them to get the best value for their investment in the platform and your product.

> At the time of publishing, Salesforce announced **Einstein Voice**, `https://www.salesforce.com/products/einstein/einstein-voice/`, as a way to introduce voice recognition into your applications and Salesforce features.

Further reading

This chapter concludes the book, but it is not the end of your learning journey. Use the links listed here to continue to learn about new releases and gain experience through Salesforce's training platform, Trailhead:

- **Salesforce Release Notes** (`https://releasenotes.docs.salesforce.com`)
- **Salesforce Developer** (`https://developer.salesforce.com/`)
- **Salesforce Trailhead** (`https://trailhead.salesforce.com/`)

I hope you have enjoyed reading this book and that you go on to create the next great application that drives you and your customers to new levels of success!

Other Books You May Enjoy

If you enjoyed this book, you may be interested in these other books by Packt:

Salesforce Platform Developer I Certification Guide
Jan Vandevelde, Gunther Roskams

ISBN: 978-1-78980-207-8

- Solve sample questions and mock tests and work with exam patterns
- Gain an understanding of declarative Salesforce tools such as Process Builder, flows, and many more
- Code in Salesforce using the Developer Console and IDEs
- Grasp the basics of object-oriented programming
- Write Apex classes, Visualforce pages, and Apex test classes with easy-to-follow steps
- Explore the different deployment tools that you can use to push metadata to different environments
- Build custom declarative apps and programs on Force.com platforms

Salesforce CRM - The Definitive Admin Handbook - Fifth Edition
Paul Goodey

ISBN: 978-1-78961-978-2

- Configure a variety of user interface features in Salesforce CRM
- Understand the capabilities of the Salesforce CRM sharing model
- Explore Einstein Analytics - Salesforce's new wave of advanced reporting
- Get to grips with the Lightning Process Builder workflow
- Set up user profiles, security, and login access mechanisms
- Find out how Apex and Visualforce coding can be used in Salesforce CRM
- Manage the transition from Salesforce Classic to Lightning Experience
- Implement data manipulation features to apply best practices in data management

Leave a review - let other readers know what you think

Please share your thoughts on this book with others by leaving a review on the site that you bought it from. If you purchased the book from Amazon, please leave us an honest review on this book's Amazon page. This is vital so that other potential readers can see and use your unbiased opinion to make purchasing decisions, we can understand what our customers think about our products, and our authors can see your feedback on the title that they have worked with Packt to create. It will only take a few minutes of your time, but is valuable to other potential customers, our authors, and Packt. Thank you!

Index

1
1st Generation Packaging (1GP) 13

2
2nd Generation Packaging (2GP) 13

@
@future annotation
  used, for implementing worker 458, 459

A
Advanced Encryption Standard (AES) 58
aggregate SOQL queries 264
Alexa 270
Amazon EC2 526
ancestry 523
AngularJS 308
Apache HBase database
  reference link 443
Apache Phoenix
  reference link 443
Apex API behavior
  versioning 397, 398
Apex API definitions
  versioning 394, 395, 397
Apex application APIs
  providing 389, 390, 391
Apex Callable interface API 388, 389
Apex classes 199, 240
Apex code evolution 145
Apex compiler 201
Apex Connectors
  reference link 581
Apex controller 328
Apex controller method 329
Apex data types
  combining, with SObject types 263
Apex Describe 344
Apex Developer Guide
  reference link 455
Apex Enterprise Patterns 477, 492, 504
Apex governors 135
Apex inheritance 201
Apex inner class 261
Apex Interface example
  about 215
  Domain class Factory pattern 218, 219
  Domain class interface, implementing 217, 218
  generic service, defining 216, 217
  generic service, implementing 219, 220
  generic service, using from generic controller 221
Apex interfaces
  about 414, 487
  application logic, extending with 414, 416
Apex property 169
Apex read-only mode
  leveraging 440
Apex Replay Debugger 528
Apex REST application APIs
  behavior versioning 405
  calling 404
  definition versioning 405, 406
  providing 402, 403
  versioning 405
Apex Scheduler 195
Apex Stub API
  mocking examples with 497, 498
  using, considerations 499
  using, with mocking frameworks 499, 500
Apex Trigger 200
Apex Trigger event handling
  about 210

field values, defaulting on insert 211
validation on insert 211, 212
validation on update 212, 213
Apex Trigger methods
  testing, DML used 230
  testing, SOQL used 230
Apex Triggers 413
Apex
  50k maximum results, processing 436, 437
  about 477, 521
  application API, calling from 392, 393
  outbound connections, calling from 573, 574
  Race Data, generating 439
  Separation of Concerns (SoC) 145, 146
  unlimited result sets, processing 437, 438, 439
  used, for generating synthetic Race Data 424, 425
  using 140, 141, 142, 143, 144
ApexMocks framework 477
ApexMocks Matchers 504
ApexMocks works 501, 503
ApexMocks
  about 500, 504, 510
  controller method, unit testing 505
  Domain method, unit testing 507, 508
  reference link 500
  Selector method, unit testing 508
  Service method, unit testing 505, 507
API definition
  versioning 375
  versioning, of Salesforce APIs 376
API functionality
  versioning 377
AppExchange 34, 35
Apple 382
application API
  calling, from Apex 392, 393
  depreciating 394
  modifying 394
application events 338
application integration APIs 389
application logic
  extending, with Apex interfaces 414, 416, 417
  versus execution context 149, 150
applications

extensibility use cases 386
Async Apex Triggers 199, 413
Async SOQL documentation
  reference link 443
asynchronous big object SOQL queries 451, 452, 453
Asynchronous JavaScript and XML (AJAX) 319
Asynchronous Processing in Lightning Platform 458
asynchronous processing
  about 454
  with jobs 458
  with platform events 467, 468
  with workers 458
asynchronous user experience design
  considerations 455, 456, 457
Atomicity, Consistency, Isolation, Durability (ACID) 441
Aura 273, 340
Aura, versus Lightning Web Components
  reference link 342
Auto Number Display Format
  customizing 113
automated regression testing
  about 553
  approaches 553
automating package
  installing 38, 39

B

base Lightning components 317, 340
Basecamp
  about 569
  URL 569
Basically Available, Soft state, Eventual consistency (BASE) 442
Batch Apex chaining
  reference link 464
Batch Apex jobs
  performance 465
Batch Apex layers 266
Batch Apex
  about 150, 240
  used, for implementing job 460, 462, 463, 464
Batch File 533

behavior, expressing
    about 334
    child component events 336, 337
    inter-component events 338, 339
    methods 335
    visibility keywords, used for access control 334, 335
behavior-driven development (BDD) 486
beta packages 24, 25
Big Object data
    importing 445
    querying, options 448
Big Object Implementation Guide
    reference link 443
Big Object Utility package
    reference link 445
Big Objects
    about 96
    data, importing with Data Loader 446, 447
    storage 108
    used, for handling records 441, 442
    using, for race lap history 443, 444, 445
Blue Ocean user interface 548
branches 552
browser automation tools 480

C

Call Apex Methods
    reference link 348
CDI
    unit testing, implementing with 489, 490, 491, 492
chaining 460
Change Data Capture
    about 468
    using, to compare data 471, 472
Chatter 86, 88, 90, 91, 276
CheckMarx
    reference link 31
Chris Peterson 256
client response size 245
client-server communication
    about 286
    API governors 288
    availability 288

client calls 289
database transaction scope 289
for Lightning Aura Components 286
for Lightning Web Components 286
for Visualforce 286
offline support 290
options 286, 288
code samples
    reference link 599
code
    packaging 156, 157
CometD
    URL 407
Command-Line Interface (CLI) 8
common Apex Interface 264
communities
    creating 309
compliance application framework
    creating 214
Compliance Checker component 226
compliance framework implementation
    summarizing 225
component controller (.js) 328
component CSS (.css) 329
component documentation (.auradoc) 331
component management 320
component markup (.html)
    XHTML markup 327, 328
component metadata (.js-meta.xml) 330
component SVG (.svg) files 330
component tests (test subfolder) 332
components, packable attributes
    custom fields, picklist values 53
    global picklists 54
    upgrade tasks, automating with Metadata API 54, 56
components
    customizing 359, 360, 361
    packaging 52, 53
    upgradable components 52, 53
Connected Apps
    using 557
considerations, client-side logic
    Apex Enum types 306
    remoting client bias, avoiding 305

single service method per remoting method 305
considerations, for JavaScript libraries
  developer flow 308
  frameworks, testing 308
  security 308
consume off-platform services 575
Content Security Policy (CSP) 333
Continuous Integration (CI)
  about 31, 38, 521
  exploring 550, 551
  hooking up 541
  Jenkinsfile 542, 545
  using, to maintain code health 541, 542
Contract-Driven Development 186, 187, 189, 190, 192
Controllers layers 266
custom Apex data type 260
custom Domain logic
  implementing 213
custom elements
  using, reference link 318
custom field features
  about 56
  default field values 56, 58
  encrypted fields 58
  filters 60, 62, 65
  layouts 60, 62, 65
  lookup options 60, 62, 65
  rollup summaries 66, 68
  Salesforce limits 66, 68
custom indexes 426, 428
custom labels
  about 378
  reference link 358
Custom Metadata Type storage 103, 104, 105, 106, 107
Custom Metadata Types
  reference link 120
custom Publisher Actions 308
custom query language
  aggregate SOQL queries 264
  Salesforce Object Search Language (SOSL) 264
custom query logic
  custom Selector method 256
  custom Selector method, with custom dataset 260, 261, 262
  custom Selector method, with related fields 258, 259
  custom Selector method, with sub-select 256, 257
  implementing 255
custom reporting 310
custom Selector method
  about 256
  with custom dataset 260, 261, 262
  with related fields 258, 259
  with sub-select 256, 257
Custom Settings storage 107
custom UIs
  embedding, in standard UI 277, 279
  leveraging 270, 272
customer licenses
  managing 42
customer metrics 48
customizable user interfaces
  building 82
  layouts 83

D

Data Import Wizard 120, 122
data integrations 568
Data Loader
  using, to import data into big object 446, 447
Data Mapper layer
  about 240
  reference link 155, 240
data security
  about 74, 76
  code, and security review considerations 77
data storage
  about 98
  columns, versus rows 98, 99
  configuration data, considerations 101, 103
  object model, visualizing 99
Data Transformation Objects (DTO) 155
data, adding in recipe
  reference link 594
Data, Analyzing
  reference link 592
data

exporting 116
importing 116
replicating, options 122, 123
using, for creating RaceData object 422, 423
database access
  using 304
DataWeave 418
Debugging 528
default field values 56, 58
dependency injection (DI)
  about 483
  benefits 494
design guidelines
  bulkification 165
  checklist 172
  compound services 171, 172
  data, defining 168, 169
  data, passing 168, 169
  implementing 161
  naming conventions 162, 163, 164, 165
  rules enforcement, sharing 166, 167
  transaction management 170
deterministic governors 138
Developer Workbench tool
  about 400
  reference link 431
developer workflow 525
Developer X persona
  developing 374
Developer X
  APIs, calling asynchronously through platform events 383
  APIs, calling off-platform 382
  APIs, calling on-platform 381
development infrastructure 522
development workflow
  about 522, 525, 527, 528
  scratch orgs, creating 523, 524
  scratch orgs, preparing 523, 524
devices
  targeting 270
DML
  Apex Trigger methods, testing 230
  handling, with Unit Of Work 177, 179, 180
  handling, with Unit Of Work pattern 173, 174, 175
  handling, without Unit Of Work 176
Domain class methods
  testing 231, 233
  trigger events, routing to 207, 208
Domain class template 205, 206
Domain classes, in Apex
  comparing, to other platforms 200, 201
Domain factory 264
Domain layer interactions 235, 237
Domain layer pattern, design guidelines
  bulkification 204
  data, defining 204
  data, passing 204
  implementing 201
  naming conventions 202, 203
  transaction management 204
Domain layer pattern
  about 198
  object's behavior, encapsulating in code 198
Domain layer
  about 266
  calling 233
  interpreting 199, 200
  reference link 198
  testing 229
  unit testing 229
domain model layer
  reference link 154
Domain Trigger logic
  implementing 207
  object security, enforcing 209
downloadable content
  generating 282, 283
dummy implementation 187
Dynamic Apex 240, 254
Dynamic Apex type creation 414
Dynamic SOQL 240
dynamic stubs
  creating, for mocking classes 496

E

ECMAScript classes
  reference link 344
ECMAScript programming language 536

ECMAScript
  about 343
  reference link 318
Einstein Analytics 588, 592
Einstein Discovery 588, 590, 591
Einstein Discovery Managed Package 591
Einstein Discovery Trail
  about 592
  reference link 592
Einstein Language REST API 589
Einstein Next Best Action 589
Einstein Platform Services 598, 599
Einstein Prediction Builder
  about 588, 590
  reference link 590
Einstein Vision REST API 589
email customization
  with email templates 84
email templates
  about 414
  using, for email customization 84
encapsulation
  JavaScript Code, sharing between components 332
  behavior, expressing 334
  component controller (.js) 328
  component CSS (.css) 329
  component documentation (.auradoc) 331
  component markup (.html) 327
  component metadata (.js-meta.xml) 330
  component SVG (.svg) files 330
  component tests (test subfolder) 332
  during development 326
  enforcing 333
encrypted fields, Platform Encryption
  about 58
  considerations 59, 60
encrypted fields
  about 58
  Classic Encryption 58
end user storage requirements
  mapping 96
Entity Relationship Diagram (ERD) 99
enum 378
Ergast
  reference link 445
Eric Brewer 442
ES6 modules 332
events
  managing, reference link 337
exception class 378
execution context, security types
  about 134
  CRUD security 134
  FLS security 134
  sharing security 134
execution context
  about 130
  state 130
  transaction management 135
  versus application logic 149, 150
execution contexts
  about 128
  exploring 128, 129, 130
Express Session
  reference link 567
extensibility needs
  reviewing 374
extension packages 13, 21, 23
external data seamlessly
  accessing, via external objects 580, 582, 583, 584
external data sources 123
external objects
  about 568
  external data seamlessly, accessing via 580, 582, 583, 584
external references, in Apex DML
  using 466
external services
  accessing, via External Services 575, 577, 578, 579, 580
External Services
  external services, accessing via 575, 577, 578, 579, 580

F

factory pattern
  about 492
  reference link 218

Feature Management Application (FMA) 31, 43
Feature Management feature 21
Feature Parameters 21
Feature Parameters tab 43
features
    managing 43
Federation Internationale de l'Automobile (FIA) 184
fflib_SObjectSelector class
    about 246
    method 248
FIA Super License 214
field API 381
field labels 381
field sets 413
field-level read security 250
field-level security (FLS) 74, 134
file storage 109
filters 60, 62, 65
FinancialForce Apex Enterprise Pattern library 177
FinancialForce.com Apex Commons library 155
FinancialForce.com Enterprise Apex Patterns 246
Flow
    extending 410, 412
fluent design model 255
Fluent interface
    reference link 255
folder structure
    overview 529
Force DI 494
Force.com platform 340
Force.com Sites 309
FormulaForce application 11, 12, 13, 521
FormulaForce Lightning components
    about 344
    Race Calendar accessibility 345
    Race Feedback Survey 345
    Race Overview 345
    Race Results overview 345
    Race Setup assistance 345
    RaceCalendar component 349, 350
    RaceResults component 351, 352, 354
    RaceSetup component 354, 358
    RaceStandings component 346, 347, 348
FormulaForce package version
    creating 124, 125, 126
FormulaForce package
    updating 196, 237, 238, 267, 311, 371
full table scan 428
functional security
    about 69, 70, 73
    code, and security review considerations 73, 74

G

Generic Compliance Verification UI
    with Lightning Component 221, 222, 223
    with Visualforce 224, 225
Git 528
Git branching model
    reference link 527
Git tools
    use cases 538
GitFlow
    about 527, 552
    commits, to feature branches 552
    commits, to release branches 552
    tags, on release branches 552
GitHub 528, 539
GitHub GUI
    download link 528
Google 382
governor scope 136, 137, 138
Groovy programming language
    about 542
    reference link 542

H

heap 130
heap governor 436
Heroku Connect
    reference link 123
high-scale platform events
    using, to stream data ingestion 469, 470
HTTP methods
    DELETE 402
    GET 401
    mapping 401
    PATCH 402
    POST 402
    PUT 402

I

IBM 382
IlluminatedCloud
  reference link 527
image detection 599
inbound connection 556
inbound integrations
  about 556, 557
  managing 558, 559
incremental code reuse
  improving 151, 152, 153
Independent Software Vendor (ISV) 29
indexes optimization 425
indexes
  affecting factors 428, 430
influencer fields 591
inheritance 343
insights
  discovering, from Formula 1 race results 592, 594, 596, 597, 598
integration needs
  reviewing 374
integration testing
  about 477
  downsides 479
  versus unit testing 478, 479, 480
integration use cases 380, 381
internal view state 303
Internet of Things (IoT) 108, 374
invocable methods
  about 410
  versioning 413
ISVforce Guide
  reference link 289

J

Jasmine 500
Java 535
Java Server Pages (JSP) 319
JavaScript classes
  reference link 329
JavaScript Code
  sharing, between components 332
JavaScript function
  reference link 516
JavaScript libraries
  using, considerations 307
JavaScript programming language 536
JavaScript Remote Objects 306
JavaScript Remoting 440
JavaScript
  class definitions 329
  used, for database access 306
Jenkins CI server
  configuring 546, 547, 549
  installing 546, 547, 549
  reference link 547
  testing 546, 547, 549
Jenkins
  exploring 550, 551
  URL 546
Jenkinsfile syntax
  about 545
  reference link 545
Jenkinsfile, commands and features
  reference link 550
Jenkinsfile
  for Continuous Integration (CI) 542, 545
Jest
  URL 332, 510
  using 477
jobs
  implementing, with batch Apex 460, 462, 463, 464
  used, for asynchronous processing 458
jq command
  reference link 535
JSON 382
JUnit XML format 546

K

key governors
  for Apex package developers 139

L

large component trees
  managing, considerations 303
large result sets
  handling 436

layouts 60, 62, 65
Least Recently Used (LRU) 133
License Management Application (LMA) 31, 71
Licenses tab 42
lightning 313
Lightning Action Component 184
Lightning App Builder
  about 84, 335
  using 365
Lightning application 314
Lightning architecture
  about 320
  base components 342
  components 325
  containers 320, 321
  field-level security 344
  Lightning Data Service 342
  object-level security 344
  object-oriented programming 343
  platform namespaces 340, 341
Lightning Aura Components
  about 146, 338, 409
  Separation of Concerns (SoC) 148
Lightning Aura Developers Guide
  reference link 355
Lightning Communities
  integrating with 369
Lightning Community Builder 309
Lightning component actions 345
Lightning Component Apex Controllers 193
Lightning Component technology 270
Lightning Components
  about 84, 414
  customizing 84
  exposing 409
  programming frameworks 273
  Separation of Concerns (SoC) 146
Lightning Data Service
  about 306
  benefits 343
  reference link 306
Lightning Design System (LDS)
  about 313, 316, 319
  comparing, with other UI frameworks 319
  Lightning Web Component, building 317, 318

reference link 316
Lightning Experience (LEX)
  about 271, 272, 322
  and Salesforce Mobile 323, 324, 325
  integrating with 362, 364, 365
Lightning Experience utility bar 345
Lightning External Services 383
Lightning Flow Lightning Component 368
Lightning Flow tool
  about 85, 86
  integrating with 366
Lightning Flow
  integrating with 368
Lightning Inspector 300
Lightning Locker
  about 333
  reference link 333
Lightning Out for Visualforce 370
Lightning Out
  about 313
  reference link 370
  used, for exposing components 370
Lightning Pages
  about 274
  components, using 366
Lightning Platform
  pyramid, testing on 480
Lightning Process Builder 85, 86
Lightning tab
  components, using 366
Lightning Tools
  used, for monitoring locker service performance 302
  used, for monitoring response times 300
  used, for monitoring size 300
Lightning UI
  building 314, 315
Lightning Web Component Developers Guide
  reference link 302
Lightning Web Components (LWC)
  about 146, 273, 314, 343, 409, 508
  enforcing 292, 294
  reference link 370
  Separation of Concerns (SoC) 147
limits

[615]

     managing 290
listings 34, 35
localization 80, 81, 378
Logistic Regression 590
lookup filters 61
lookup options 60, 62, 65
loosely coupled API integration 384
low heap 245

M

managed packages
    about 14
    assigning, to namespace 18
    benefits 14, 15
    components, adding 19, 20, 21
    creating 15, 18
    features 14, 15
    namespace, registering 16, 17
    namespace, setting 16, 17
MarkDown 529
Metadata API 54
Metadata API Developers Guide
    reference link 327
Metadata Coverage Report
    reference link 55
Microsoft Visual Studio Code (VSCode) 8
mobile application strategy 309
Mobile Publisher
    reference link 310
mock 477
mocking
    about 193, 267, 500
    unit testing, implementing with 489, 490, 491, 492
Mockito 500, 510
Model View Controller (MVC) 146, 308
MuleSoft platform 383, 418
Multi-Currency 254

N

Named Credentials
    about 569
    outbound connections, managing with 569, 570, 571, 572
namespaces 135, 523

namespaces scope 136, 137, 138
naming conventions
    about 242, 243
    class name 242
    method name 242
    method signatures 243
natural key 444
new package version
    creating 92, 93
    testing 92, 93
Node.js application
    Salesforce Connected Apps, using 565, 567, 568
Node.js web server application 560
Node.js
    about 535
    URL 388
NodeJS plugin
    configuring 549
non-deterministic governors 138
Northwind sample database
    reference link 581
NoSQL 442

O

OAuth
    URL 559
object and field security
    default behavior 250
    default behavior, overriding 250, 252
    enforcing 250
object read security 250
Object Relational Mapping (ORM) 198
object security, Domain Trigger logic
    default behavior 209
    default behavior, overriding 210
object- and field-level security
    about 291
    security, enforcing in LWC 292, 293, 294
    security, enforcing in Visualforce 295, 299
object-oriented programming (OOP) 145, 214, 343
Oclif
    about 526, 535
    URL 526, 535

OData website
  URL 581
OData
  URL 581
Open API 576
open source framework 340
OpenAPI Specification
  URL 382
outbound connections
  about 556
  calling, from Apex 573, 574
  managing, with Named Credentials 569, 570, 571, 572
outbound integrations
  about 556
  data integrations 568
  options 568
  service integrations 568
Outbound Messaging
  about 557
  reference link 557
outcome measure field 591

P

package ancestry
  managing 26, 28
package dependencies
  about 23, 24, 25
  dynamic bindings 25
  extension packages 26
package upgradability
  supporting 26
package version 267
packages, types
  about 13
  managed packages 14
  unlocked packages 14
packages
  benefits 13
  installing 36, 37, 38
  licensing 40, 41, 42
  support, providing 46, 47
  testing 36, 37, 38
packaging 52, 53, 552
Packaging Guide 15

Partner Account Manager 289
Partner Black Tab 45
Partner Business Org 30
patterns of enterprise application architecture
  about 153
  Data Mapper (selector) layer 155
  domain model layer 154
  reference link 153
  Service layer 154
per-user Named Credentials
  using 574, 575
performance
  managing 300
personas 96
Plain Old Java Object (POJO) 155, 240
platform alignment 380
platform APIs
  about 77, 78, 79
  considerations 79, 80
  for integration 387
Platform Cache 131, 133
platform event object 384
Platform Event Subscriptions 199
Platform Events Developers Guide
  URL 385
platform events
  about 384
  exposing 407, 408, 409
point-to-point integration 383
prebuilt models
  reference link 599
prediction field 590
prediction result field 590
primitive obsession
  URL 168
printable content
  generating 284, 285
  page language, overriding 285
private certificate 545
Process Builder
  extending 410, 411
production implementation 187
pub-sub 383
public repository 530
pull command 538

[617]

Puppeteer
  URL 478
push command 538
Push Upgrade feature 21
Push Upgrades 375
pyramid
  testing, on Lightning Platform 480

Q

queries leverage indexes
  ensuring 428
queries
  profiling 430, 431, 432, 433, 434
query optimization 425
querying fields consistently 244, 245
Queueables
  used, for implementing worker 459, 460

R

race data telemetry events
  sending, through Salesforce DX CLI 472, 473
race lap history
  big object, using for 443, 444, 445
Race Record page 345
race sector 467
RaceCalendar component 349, 350, 351
RaceData object
  creating, with data 422, 423
RaceResults component 351, 352, 354
RaceSetup component 354, 355, 356, 358
RaceStandings component 346, 348
Racing Overview Lightning app 322, 323
Random Forest 590
record auto numbering 109
record identification 109
record order consistency 243
record relationships 113, 115
record uniqueness 109
records
  Auto Number fields 110, 112
  external ID fields 110
  handling, with Big Objects 441, 442
  unique ID fields 110
relational database management system (RDBMS) 441

release packages 24, 25
Report Designer 310
response times
  managing 300
  monitoring, with Lightning tools 300
REST APIs 599
REST
  versus SOAP 382
RESTful application APIs
  providing 398
RESTful
  about 399
  application resources 399
  HTTP methods, mapping 401
revolutions per minute (RPM) 485
rollup summaries 66, 68

S

Sales Cloud and Einstein
  reference link 589
Salesforce Analytics API 310
Salesforce Analytics trial org
  reference link 592
Salesforce APIs
  API definition, versioning of 376
  used, for processing unlimited result sets 441
Salesforce Change Data Capture (CDC) 409
Salesforce Classic 227, 228, 271
Salesforce Connected Apps
  about 559, 560, 561, 563, 564, 565
  distributing 49
  using, for Node.js application 565, 567, 568
Salesforce developer
  reference link 9
Salesforce documentation
  reference link 332, 518
Salesforce DX 8
Salesforce DX CLI Data
  exporting 116, 119, 120
  importing 116, 119, 120
Salesforce DX CLI
  about 522, 526, 542
  download link 529
  race data telemetry events, sending 472, 473
Salesforce DX Plugin 535

Salesforce Einstein products 588
Salesforce Einstein services 588
Salesforce Heroku
  about 575
  reference link 576
Salesforce limits 66, 68
Salesforce Metadata Coverage 15
Salesforce Mobile application 271
Salesforce Mobile
  about 323, 324, 325
  URL 310
Salesforce Object Search Language (SOSL) 60, 264
Salesforce organizations 9, 10
Salesforce Partner Community 32, 33
Salesforce Partner Program
  advantages 29, 30
  benefits 30, 32
  demo orgs, creating via Environment Hub 34
  security review 30, 32
  test, creating via Environment Hub 34
Salesforce Security Review 503
Salesforce standard UI actions
  overriding 275, 276
Salesforce standard UIs and tools
  leveraging 274, 275
Salesforce standard UIs
  areas, accepting Lightning Components 281
  areas, accepting Visualforce pages 281, 282
  extending 281
Salesforce
  about 442
  help topic, reference link 339
Schema Builder 99
Scratch Org Snapshots feature 22
Scratch Org Template 553
scratch orgs, containing ancestry information
  developing 28
Scratch Orgs
  about 8, 11, 315
  creating 523, 525
  preparing 523, 525
security features
  about 68
  data security 74, 76

functional security 69, 70, 73
security review 30
security
  enforcing, at runtime 333
Selector base class
  Field Sets 253
  Multi-Currency 254, 255
  object and field security, enforcing 250
  ordering 252
  standard features 249
Selector class method
  tests, writing 266
Selector class template 246, 247, 248
Selector factory
  about 264, 265
  methods 265
Selector layer pattern 240, 241
Selector layer pattern, design guidelines
  bulkification 243
  implementing 241
  naming conventions 242, 243
  querying fields consistently 244, 245
  record order consistency 243
  sharing conventions 241
Selector pattern 183
Selenium WebDriver tool 553
Selenium
  URL 478
Separation of Concerns (SoC)
  about 144, 305, 325, 481
  in Apex 145, 146
  in Lightning Aura Component 148
  in Lightning Components 146
  in LWC 147
server-side rendering 272
service integrations 568
service layer interactions 234
Service layer pattern
  about 160, 161
  reference link 160
Service layer
  about 266
  calling 193
  calling, from Apex Scheduler 195
  calling, from Lightning Component Apex

Controllers 193
  calling, from Visualforce Apex Controllers 194,
    195
  calling, from Visualforce JavaScript Remoting
    305
  FormulaForce package, updating 196
  mocking 192
  reference link 154
  testing 192
  use cases 193
  using 304
Service methods
  implementing 182, 184, 185, 186
setter methods 492
shadow DOM
  reference link 318, 326
sharing conventions 241
Shell Script 533
Single-Page Application (SPA) 319
Sites.com 309
skinny tables 435
SmartBear 382
SOAP
  versus REST 382
SObject field expressions 295
SObject types
  used, for combining Apex data types 263
SObject, using in Service layer interface
  considerations 170
SObjects 240, 340
SOQL FOR LOOP 437
SOQL-injection vulnerabilities 256
SOQL
  Apex Trigger methods, testing 230
source control
  code, deploying 533
  committing 538, 540
  developing 528
  Git tools, using 538
  local files, managing 538, 540
  releasing 552
  repository, populating 529, 530, 532
  repository, updating 537
  Salesforce REST APIs, leveraging from custom
    plugins 534, 536

Salesforce REST APIs, leveraging from SFDX
  CLI 534, 536
  scratch orgs, developing with namespace 534
Source-driven configuration 543
Standalone Lightning App
  reference link 315
standard indexes 426, 428
standard Jest API
  using 516
Standard Objects
  reusing 115, 116
standard query logic
  implementing 248
  Selector base class, standard features 249
standard UIs
  combining, with custom UIs 277
  embedding, in custom UI 280
  leveraging 270, 272
state management 131
storage types
  about 96, 97
  data storage 98
  file storage 109
  record auto numbering 109
  record identification 109
  record relationships 113, 115
  record uniqueness 109
Stub 187
stubbing code 501
sub-select 256
subscriber org
  about 14
  licensing 46
Subscriber Overview page 45
Subscribers tab 44
Swagger Specification 383
Swagger
  URL 383
synchronous big object SOQL queries 448, 449,
  450
synthetic Race Data
  generating, with Apex 424, 425
system administrator 534
system testing
  versus unit testing 155, 156

T

Technical Account Manager (TAM) 74
template method pattern
  reference link 208
templates and slots
  using, reference link 318
terminology 380
Test Drive 48, 49
test-driven development (TDD) 156
Test.StubProvider
  used, for implementing mock classes 495, 496
text sentiment analysis 599
token 330
toolkit, for .NET
  URL 388
Trailforce Source Org (TSO) 34
translation 80, 81, 82, 378
Trialforce 48, 49
trigger events
  routing, to Domain class methods 207, 208
TypeScript 536

U

Unified Modeling Language (UML) 483
Uniform Resource Identifier (URI) 399
unit 229
Unit Of Work pattern
  about 135, 159, 214
  considerations 181, 182
  DML, handling with 173, 174, 175
  reference link 173
  scope 180
  used, for handling DML 177, 179, 180
unit testing Lightning Web Components 480
unit testing, with Apex
  about 483, 484, 485, 486
  constructor dependency injection 487, 488
  deciding, types of test 486, 487
  dependency injection approaches 492, 493, 494
  dependency injection frameworks, benefits 494
unit testing, with Lightning Web Components
  about 508, 509, 510, 511, 512
  driver list, validating that is correctly bound to table 512, 513, 514
  selected drivers, validating that are sent to server 514, 515, 517, 518
unit testing
  about 477, 481, 482, 483
  implementing, with CDI 489, 490, 491, 492
  implementing, with mocking 489, 490, 491, 492
  versus integration testing 478, 479, 480
  versus system testing 155, 156
unit tests, writing with Apex Stub API
  about 495
  dynamic stubs, creating for mocking classes 496
  mock classes, implementing with Test.StubProvider 495, 496
  mocking examples, with Apex Stub API 497, 498
unlocked packages 14
upgradable components 52, 53
Usage Metrics Visualization 48
user experiences (UXs) 313
utility bar 362

V

versioning
  managing 375
Vincent Driessen 527, 552
Visual Studio Code IDE 539
  with Salesforce extensions 529
Visualforce Apex Controllers 194, 195
Visualforce Developer Guide
  reference link 306
Visualforce pages
  customizing 84
Visualforce
  about 224, 271
  leveraging 440
  reference link 303
  security, enforcing 295, 298
  versus Lightning Framework 273
  view state size 303
volume testing 473, 474

W

W3C Web Components
  reference link 273
web components

[621]

reference link 318
Web Service Connector (WSC)
  about 388
  download link 388
Web Service Definition Language (WSDL) 123, 557
websites
  creating 309
workers
implementing, with @future annotation 458, 459
implementing, with Queueables 459, 460
used, for asynchronous processing 458
Workflow 85, 86
wrapper class approach 201

Y

Yet Another Markup Language (YAML) 382

Made in the USA
Coppell, TX
10 September 2020